Constantinople

Constantinople

City of the World's Desire

1453–1924

PHILIP MANSEL

John Murray
50 Albemarle Street, London

To Istanbul friends

© Philip Mansel 1995

First published in 1995
by John Murray (Publishers) Ltd.,
50 Albemarle Street, London W1X 4BD

Reprinted in 1995, 1996

A catalogue record for this book is available from the British Library

ISBN 0-7195-5076 9

Maps by Venture Graphics, Chislehurst, Kent

Typeset in Monotype Garamond
by Servis Filmsetting Ltd, Manchester

Printed and bound in Great Britain by
The University Press, Cambridge

Contents

Illustrations

The author and publishers would like to thank the following for permission to reproduce illustrations:

Plate 1, 38, Coll. Elia, Athens; 2, National Gallery, London; 3, 16, 19, 22, 23, 25, 27, 29, 30, 33, 37, 44, 45, 48, 52, 56, Private collection; 4, 21, Photo Fine Arts Society; 5, 32, 42, 49, 57, Photo Deutsche Archaeologisches Institut, Istanbul; 6, Photo Roberto Falchi; 7, 9, The Trustees of the Chester Beatty Library, Dublin; 8, 15, 50, Bibliothèque Nationale, Paris; 10, 12, 17, 26, Rijksmuseum, Amsterdam; 11, Nationalmuseum, Stockholm; 13, 35, Topkapi Palace Museum, Istanbul, photo Ara Guler; 14, Photo Philip Mansel; 18, 31, Osterreichisches Nationalbibliothek; 20, Musée de Versailles; 24, Photo Hervé Poulain-Rémy Le Fur Commissaires-Priseurs; 28, Coll. John Murray; 34, 46, 47, Photo Sotheby's, London; 36, The Royal Collection, © H.M. The Queen; 39, 40, 41, 51, 54, Author's collection; 43, Photo Turkish Touring Club; 53, Z. Duckett Ferriman, *Turkey and the Turks*, 1911; 55, Private collection; 58, Coll. Mrs N. Yashar; 59, photo National Maritime Museum, Greenwich; 60, Photo Coll. Shirin Devrim

Acknowledgements

The author would like to express his profound gratitude to the staffs of the British Library, the London Library and the Istanbul Library. He would also like to thank all those who have shared with him their time and knowledge: among others, Nicolaos Adjemoglou, Khaldun al-Husri, Nigar Alemdar, Tulay Artan, Munevver Ayasli, Safiya Ayla, Cuneyt Ayral, Murat and Taciser Belge, Kemal Beydilli, Toby Buchan, Fredrik E. von Celsing, Alkis Courcoulas, Johan Danielsson, Basri Danishmend, Shirin Devrim, Selim Dringil, Selim Dirvana, Nestorin Dirvana, Ayla Erduran, Osman Erk, Selcuk Esenbel, Roberto Falchi, Andrew Finkel, Sarah Fox-Pitt, John Freely, David Gilmour, Nilufer Gokay, Sevgi Gonul, Eric Grunberg, Manos Haritatis, Frederic Hitzel, Fevzi Katircioglu, Alexander Kedros, Orhan Kologlu, Sinan Kuneralp, Orhan Koprulu, Wolf-Dieter Lemke, Geoffrey Lewis, Nina Lobanov, Bertul Mardin, Ronnie Margulies, George Mavrogordato, Achilles Melas, Aysegul Nadir, André Nieuwaszny, Tarquin and Zelfa Olivier, Ismet Ozbek, Lady Katherine Page, Kevork Pamukyan, Jacques Perot, Frank G. Perry, Yanni Petsopoulos, Baruh Pinto, Julian Raby, Alan de Lacy Rush, Necdet Sakaoglu, Prince Sami, John Scott, Sherifa Sfyne, Costas Stamatopoulos, Metin Tanriverdi, E. F. de Testa, Berin Torolsan, Taha Toros, Baroness Elena Tornow, Monsieur and Madame de Tugny, Monsieur and Madame de Tugny-Vergennes, Geoffrey Whittall, Michael Whittall, Prince Alexander Wolkonsky, Necla Yashar, Signora Mafalda Zonaro Meneguzzer. Particular thanks are due to Douglas Matthews for his index, to Ali Acikalin for his translations and to those

Acknowledgements

who read and commented on the manuscript: Iakovos Akstoglou, Howard Davies, Caroline Finkel, Roger Hudson, Caroline Knox, Fouad Nahas. The author is above all grateful for the hospitality and encouragement of Metin Munir and Augusta Rieber.

Foreword

Constantinople is the story of a city and a family. It is written in the belief that dynasties have been as decisive in shaping cities as nationality, climate and geography. Between the fifteenth and nineteenth centuries dynastic capitals such as Paris, Vienna, Berlin eclipsed cities that owed their prominence to geography or economics: Lyons, Frankfurt, Nuremberg. *Constantinople* is the story of what was, for a long time, the greatest dynastic city of all. For the interaction of the Ottoman dynasty and Constantinople produced the only capital to function on every level: political, military, naval, religious (both Muslim and Christian), economic, cultural and gastronomic.

Constantinople is the name of the city used in this book: it was frequently used on Ottoman documents and coins, and was the name most often used in other languages. (When other names appear in quotations, they are not altered.) Few people consistently used one name for the city. Other names, epithets and abbreviations included: Istanbul, Islambol, Stambul, Estambol, Kushta, Cons/ple, Gosdantnubolis, Tsarigrad, Rumiyya al-kubra, New Rome, New Jerusalem, the City of Pilgrimage, the City of Saints, the House of the Caliphate, the Throne of the Sultanate, the House of State, the Gate of Happiness, the Eye of the World, the Refuge of the Universe, Polis, the City.

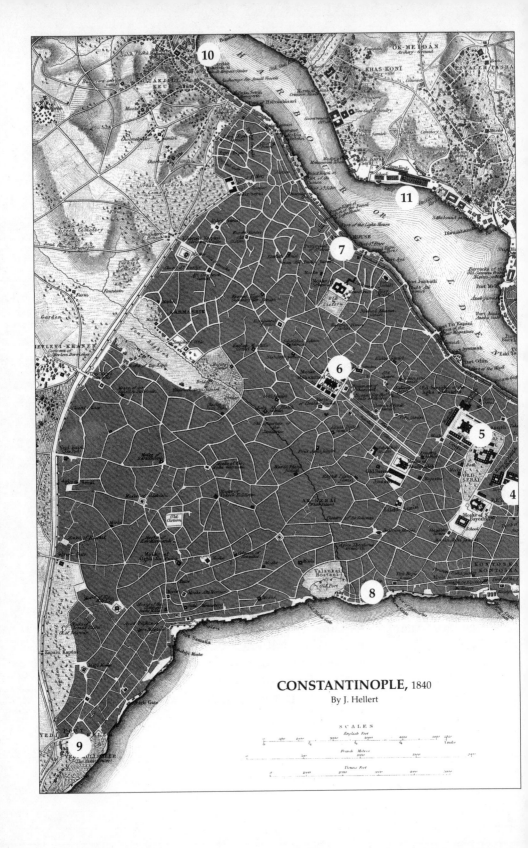

CONSTANTINOPLE, 1840

By J. Hellert

SCALES

English Feet

French Metres

Vienna Feet

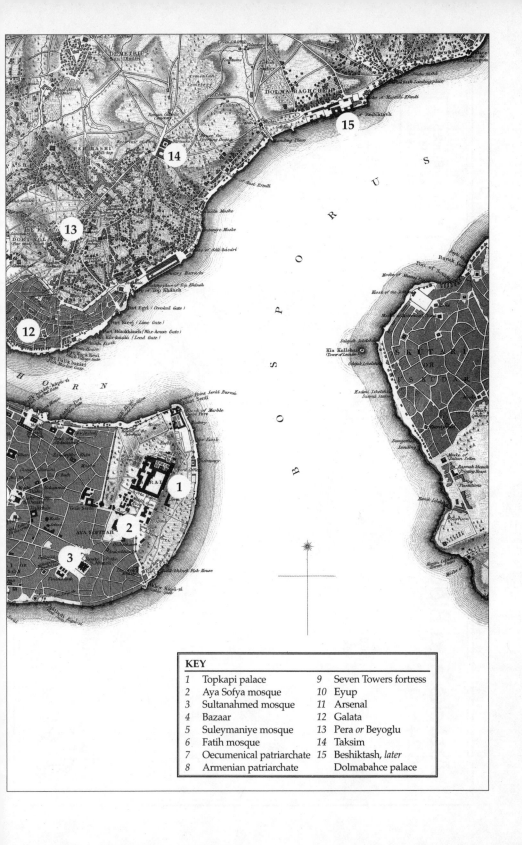

KEY

1	Topkapi palace	9	Seven Towers fortress
2	Aya Sofya mosque	10	Eyup
3	Sultanahmed mosque	11	Arsenal
4	Bazaar	12	Galata
5	Suleymaniye mosque	13	Pera *or* Beyoglu
6	Fatih mosque	14	Taksim
7	Oecumenical patriarchate	15	Beshiktash, *later*
8	Armenian patriarchate		Dolmabahce palace

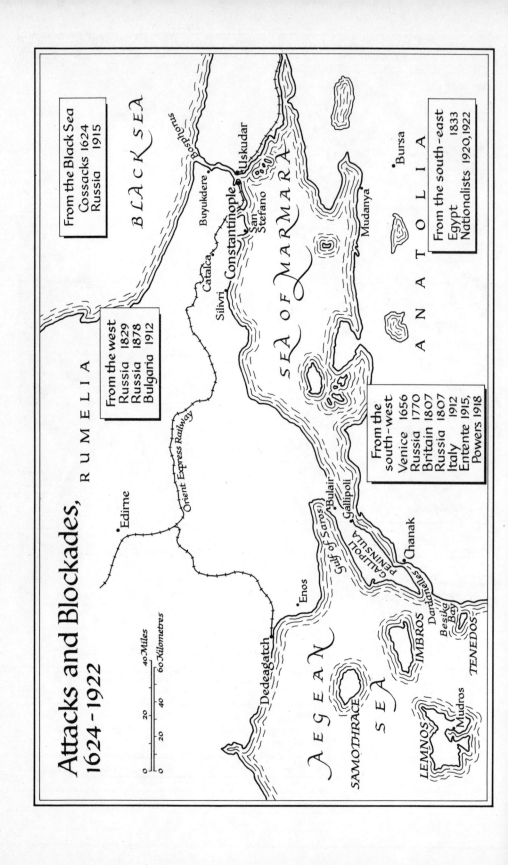

Attacks and Blockades, 1624–1922

From the Black Sea
Cossacks 1624
Russia 1915

BLACK SEA

From the west
Russia 1829
Russia 1878
Bulgaria 1912

RUMELIA

Bosphorus

Buyukdere

Catalca

Silivri

Constantinople

Uskudar

San Stefano

SEA OF MARMARA

Mudanya

ANATOLIA

Bursa

From the south-east
Egypt 1833
Nationalists 1920,1922

Edirne

Orient Express Railway

From the south-west
Venice 1656
Russia 1770
Britain 1807
Russia 1807
Italy 1912
Entente 1915,
Powers 1918

Bulair

Gallipoli

GALLIPOLI PENINSULA

Gulf of Saros

Chanak

Dardanelles

Enos

Dedeagatch

AEGEAN SEA

SAMOTHRACE

IMBROS

Besika Bay

TENEDOS

LEMNOS

Mudros

40 Miles
60 Kilometres
0   20   40
0   20   40

Constantinople! Constantinople! . . . C'est l'empire du monde!
Napoleon I, 1807

I

The Conqueror

The seat of the Roman Empire is Constantinople . . . Therefore you are the legitimate Emperor of the Romans . . . And he who is and remains Emperor of the Romans is also Emperor of the whole earth.

George Trapezuntios to Mehmed the Conqueror, 1466

ON THE AFTERNOON of 29 May 1453 the Sultan entered the long-desired city. Riding a white horse, he advanced down an avenue of death. The city of Constantinople was being put to the sack by the triumphant Ottoman army. According to an observer from Venice, blood flowed through the streets like rainwater after a sudden storm; corpses floated out to sea like melons along a canal.[1] An Ottoman official, Tursun Beg, wrote that the troops 'took silver and gold vessels, precious stones, and all sorts of valuable goods and fabrics from the imperial palace and the houses of the rich. In this fashion many people were delivered from poverty and made rich. Every tent was filled with handsome boys and beautiful girls.' On rode the Sultan, until he reached the mother church of Eastern Christendom and seat of the Oecumenical Patriarch, the cathedral of the Holy Wisdom built 900 years earlier by the Emperor Justinian with the largest dome in Europe. He dismounted and bent down to pick up a handful of earth, which he poured over his turban as an act of humility before God.

Inside the shrine which Greeks considered 'the earthly heaven, throne of God's glory, the vehicle of the cherubim', a Turk proclaimed: 'There is no God but Allah: Muhammad is his Prophet.' The cathedral of Haghia Sophia had become the mosque of Aya Sofya. As the Sultan entered, hundreds of Greeks who had taken refuge in the cathedral hoping to be saved by a miracle, were being herded out by their captors. He stopped one of his soldiers hacking at the marble floor, saying, with a conqueror's pride: 'Be satisfied with the booty and the captives; the buildings of the city belong to me.' Below golden mosaics of Jesus Christ and the Virgin Mary, Orthodox saints and Byzantine emperors, he prayed to Allah. After receiving the congratulations of his retinue, he replied: 'May the house of Osman there forever continue! May success on the stone of its seal be graven!'[2]

Mehmed II, Sultan of the Ottoman Empire, known in Turkish as *Fatih*, the Conqueror, was only 20 in 1453. Born in Edirne, the Ottoman capital 200 miles north-west of Constantinople, he had, according to a chronicle which he himself commissioned, been possessed since his childhood with the idea of conquering Constantinople, and constantly insisted on the necessity of taking the city without delay. The opportunity to realize his ambition came after he inherited the throne in 1451 on the death of his father Murad II.

Constantinople was a natural object of desire, for it appeared to have been designed by geography and history to be capital of a great empire. Situated at the end of a triangular peninsula, it was surrounded by water on three sides. To the north lay a harbour a kilometre wide and six kilometres long, called the Golden Horn, probably because it turns golden in the rays of the setting sun; to the east the Bosphorus, a narrow waterway separating Europe and Asia; to the south, the Sea of Marmara, a small inland sea connecting the Aegean to the Black Sea. The city was both a natural fortress and a matchless deep-water port, enjoying easy access by sea to Africa, the Mediterranean and the Black Sea. In addition it was situated on the crossroads of the mainland routes between Europe and Asia, the Danube and the Euphrates. Its site seemed to have been expressly created to receive the wealth of the four corners of the earth.

Founded as a Greek colony, allegedly in the seventh century BC, Byzantium had been re-founded in 324 AD by Constantine the Great as New Rome, a new capital in a better strategic position than the old Rome on the Tiber. For over a thousand years thereafter, it had been capital of the Roman Empire in the East. In the sixth century the Emperor Justinian, the builder of Haghia Sophia, had ruled in Constantinople over an empire which stretched from the Euphrates to the Straits of Gibraltar. To the grandeur of Rome, the city added the magic of time: ninety-two emperors had reigned in the 'Queen of Cities'. No other city in the world has such a continuous imperial history. Moreover, for much of its thousand years of empire it had been the largest and most sophisticated city in Europe, a treasure-house of the statues and manuscripts of the classical past, and the nerve-centre of Eastern Christendom. Its wealth had led one medieval traveller, Benjamin of Tudela, to write: 'The Greek inhabitants are very rich in gold and precious stones and they go clothed in garments of silk with gold embroidery, and they ride horses and look like princes . . . Wealth like that of Constantinople is not to be found in the whole world.' A crusading knight, the Sieur de Villehardouin, wrote that in 1203 his fellow Crusaders looked with wonder at Constantinople 'when they saw these high walls and these rich towers by which it was completely enclosed and those rich palaces and those lofty churches of which there were so many that no one could believe it unless he had seen it with his own eyes'.

For Constantinople was surrounded by the most majestic city walls in Europe, built between 412 and 422 AD. Moated, battlemented, interspersed by 192 towers, and of treble thickness throughout, the walls marched a distance of six kilometres from the Golden Horn to the Sea of Marmara, rising and descending with the inequalities of the ground. They also extended along the Sea of Marmara and the Golden Horn, completely enclosing the city. By the nineteenth century the moat had been covered in gardens and graveyards. Crumbling, choked in ivy, the walls were patrolled by more goats than guards. Yet Byron wrote: 'I have seen the ruins of Athens, of Ephesus and Delphi: I have traversed the great part of Turkey and many other parts of Europe, and some of Asia; but I never beheld a work of nature or art which yielded an impression like the prospect on each side from the Seven Towers to the end of the Golden Horn.'[3]

The walls had been built because Constantinople was, as one Byzantine had written, 'the city of the world's desire'. No city has endured more attacks and sieges: by Slavs (540, 559, 581), Persians and Avars (626), Arabs (669–79 and 717–18), Bulgarians (813, 913 and 924) and Russians (four times between 860 and 1043). It had never recovered from its sack by a Western crusade in 1204, organized by its commercial rival Venice. After the city reverted to the Byzantines in 1261, repeated defeats of the Byzantine Empire by Muslim enemies, and civil wars between rival emperors, had reduced the city's population from a peak of 400,000 inhabitants to about 50,000 Greeks – or 'Romans', as they were still proud to call themselves.* By 1400 it had shrunk to a collection of small towns, separated by farms and orchards.

---

*Today the Turkish state still calls its Orthodox citizens Rum Ortodoks.

In 1453 the last Emperor, Constantine XI, ruled over no more than the city, a few islands and coastal districts and the Peloponnese. Commerce had passed into the hands of Venetians and Genoese. The classical statues had been sold or stolen. The lead on the roof of the imperial palace had been used to mint coins. From the roof of Aya Sofya, surveying the ruined palace, the Sultan thought of other fallen empires, and emperors, and uttered the following lines:

> The spider serves as gatekeeper in the halls of Chosroes.
> The owl calls the watches in the palace of Afrasyab.[4]

If history and geography made Constantinople an incomparable imperial capital, the Ottomans considered themselves destined to rule a great empire. While still nomads in central Asia, many Turks had regarded themselves as 'a chosen people of God'. Demons in war and angels in peace, equally heroic and humane, they were destined to rule the world. The Ottoman dynasty were originally members of the Kayi tribe of the Oghuz clan of Turks, which had arrived in Anatolia from central Asia, with thousands of other Turks, in the twelfth century. They were pastoral nomads attracted by the climate and the power vacuum caused by the decay both of the Byzantine Empire and the Seljuk sultanate, a once-powerful Turkish state based on Konya in western Anatolia. In the early fourteenth century Osman, the first Ottoman Sultan, carved out an independent principality in north-west Anatolia on the edge of the Byzantine Empire, around Bursa, the first Ottoman capital.

Owing to a succession of remarkable sultans, the creation of an invincible élite force known as Janissaries (from the Turkish *yeni ceri*, or new troops), and the weakness and disunity of neighbouring states, the Ottomans had enjoyed a lightning ascent to world power. They exploited the Muslims' eagerness to fight as *gazis*, or warriors in a holy war against Christians – a war which guaranteed opportunities for loot. Yet the rise of the Ottomans also cut across divisions between Muslims and Christians. Turks fought for Greeks and vice versa: indeed Ottoman Turks were first ferried across to Europe, in 1352, as mercenaries for the Emperor John Cantacuzenus in a Byzantine civil war. On five separate occasions Ottoman princes married Greek or Slav princesses (although the Conqueror, whose mother was a slave of either Christian or Jewish origin, had no imperial Byzantine blood in his veins). At first mercenaries of the Byzantine Emperor, the Ottomans soon became his rivals, helped by an alliance with the rich trading republic of Genoa. By 1366 the Ottoman capital had moved from Bursa in Asia to Edirne in Europe. In the next thirty years the Ottomans defeated the two great Orthodox monarchies of Bulgaria and Serbia, both of which had had ambitions to win Constantinople.

Expansion was briefly checked by the rise of a rival Turkish conqueror, Tamburlane, in central Asia. In 1402 he defeated and captured the Ottoman Sultan Bayezid I – who did not always deserve his name *Yildirim* or thunderbolt. After Tamburlane's death, however, the Ottoman bid for world power resumed. Most of Anatolia and the Balkans were conquered. Constantinople became a Greek island in an Ottoman sea. Bayezid I and the Conqueror's own father Murad II both besieged it. It was a miracle that it had not already been taken.

After its fall, in accordance with Islamic law governing treatment of a city which had refused to surrender, the Sultan's troops were allowed to enslave and deport about 30,000 Christian inhabitants. Thousands more became 'food for the sword'. The last Emperor Constantine XI died fighting, with the Roman Empire as his winding-sheet. His chief minister, Lucas Notaras, was executed, either from fear that he would work for the Sultan's Western enemies, Venice and the Papacy, or because he refused to yield his son to the Sultan's pleasure. Most of the Greek and Venetian nobles remaining in the city shared his fate.

Constantinople had been taken by the sword; and until the end of the Ottoman Empire 469 years later force remained the Ottomans' principal means of control, as it did for other dynasties. Already in 1452, in preparation for the siege, the Sultan had designed and built the great fortress of Rumeli Hisari on the Bosphorus. 'In all haste', between 1453 and 1455 the massive seven-towered citadel of Yedi Kule ('Turkish for 'seven towers') was built in the west of the city, where the land walls meet the Sea of Marmara. Its present abandoned condition gives no indication that once the Seven Towers was more feared than the Bastille or the Tower of London. It was a citadel where treasure was stored, enemy ambassadors imprisoned, the Sultan's enemies – and on occasion the Sultan – executed. It received its baptism of blood on 1 November 1463, when David Comnenus, last Greek Emperor of Trebizond on the Black Sea, suspected of correspondence with the Sultan's enemies, was murdered – together with six sons, a brother and a nephew – in front of his wife, the Empress Helena. Their corpses were then flung outside, where they were gnawed by local dogs. The Empress was fined for attempting to bury them.[5]

No poet or traveller has been as intoxicated by Constantinople as the Conqueror. The Ottoman sultans already used *Khan*, Turkish for 'emperor', in their title – as well as the Persian titles *Padishah* (Great King) and *Shahinshah* (King of Kings), and the Arabic *Sultan* (ruler). From 1453 Mehmed II, like his successors, also saw himself as heir to the Roman Empire and the only true Emperor in Europe. A few days after the siege, a Genoese living in the city wrote: 'In sum he has become so insolent after the capture of Constantinople that he sees himself soon becoming master of the whole world and swears publicly that before two years have passed he intends to reach Rome.' Europe and Rome interested the Ottomans, as a field of expansion, more than Turkish-speaking territory in central Asia or the Caucasus. The Turkish metaphor for worldly dominion was the Red Apple. Before 1453 the Red Apple was believed to be the globe held in the right hand of a giant statue of the Emperor Justinian in front of Haghia Sophia. After the statue's destruction in 1453, the apple moved west and came to symbolize the Ottomans' next goal: the city of Rome. 'To Rome! To Rome!' was the constant cry of Mehmed II's great-grandson Suleyman the Magnificent. For later sultans the Red Apple was Vienna, capital of the Habsburg Holy Roman emperors.[6] Ottoman ambition had no rival. In comparison, the Shah of Persia was restrained, the King of France modest, and the Holy Roman Emperor provincial.

The Ottomans were also inspired by a desire to equal the glory of Alexander the Great. Mehmed II identified himself so strongly with Alexander that he commissioned a biography of himself in Greek, from a minor Greek official, Michael Kritovoulos, on the same paper and in the same format as the copy of Arrian's life of Alexander in his library, which was read to him 'daily'. A Venetian envoy wrote that Mehmed II 'declares that he will advance from East to West, as in former times the Westerners advanced into the Orient. There must, he says, be only one Empire, one faith and one sovereignty in the world. No place was more deserving than Constantinople for the creation of this unity in the world.'[7]

The empire ruled from Constantinople by Mehmed II and his descendants was a dynastic state. Trapped in the prison of their own nationalism, Europeans often called the Sultan the 'Grand Turk', and the Ottoman Empire 'Turkey', as if it were a national state. Its official name conveys its dynastic essence: it was the 'divinely protected' or 'exalted' 'domain of the House of Osman', or for short 'the Exalted', or 'the Sublime State'. The governing élite of soldiers, officials and judges, and from the mid-nineteenth century all citizens, were called Ottomans, after the dynasty. Until the end of the nineteenth century, 'Turk' was a pejorative term applied to Anatolian peasants.

As the Habsburg dynasty created Vienna, so was Constantinople a creation of the Ottomans. They required a world city, worthy of their empire. Mehmed II and his successors called themselves 'world-conqueror', 'the King of the World'. One of the favourite epithets, both of the sultans and their city, soon became *alem penah*, 'refuge of the world'. It appeared appropriate to create a multinational capital for an empire which, it was later calculated, contained seventy-two and a half nationalities.*

Multinationalism became the essence of Constantinople. A common literary device of Ottoman writers would be to compare the merits and looks of the many nationalities in the empire and its capital. In the fifteenth century national differences, based on history and geography more than race, could be acutely felt: Gennadios, first Oecumenical Patriarch under the Ottomans, called Greeks 'a race than which there has been none finer on earth'. A medieval Polish proverb stated: 'As long as the world is the world, the Pole will not be the German's brother.' Mustafa Ali, a prominent sixteenth-century historian, extolled as a source of strength the number of nationalities in the empire – Turks, Greeks, Franks, Kurds, Serbs, Arabs and others. In the nine-teenth century a minister of the Sultan, Cevdet Pasha, called the Ottoman Empire a great society 'because its people spoke many lan-guages and because it selected the best talents, customs and manners from among its various nations'.[8] The variety of nationalities in Constantinople was proudly advertised in drawings, photographs and the composition of the Sultan's bodyguard; in the twentieth, in political processions and the deputation sent to depose a Sultan.

Realpolitik, however, was the principal reason for Constantinople's variety of nationalities. In his new capital the Conqueror needed a large and prosperous population to service the palace and the state machine. Yet there were not enough Muslim Turks for Constantinople to be a wholly Turkish city. The majority of the empire's population, at this stage, was Christian. Turks were needed throughout the empire, to

---

*Gypsies were considered half a nationality.

people Balkan cities and the Anatolian countryside. Accordingly, so the historian Kritovoulos wrote, after 1453 the Sultan gathered people in Constantinople 'from all parts of Asia and Europe, and he transferred them with all possible care and speed, people of all nations, but more especially of Christians. So profound was the passion that came into his soul for the city and its peopling, and for bringing it back to its former prosperity.' In the new capital each *mahalle* or quarter (the basic living unit of the city, with its own places of worship, shops, fountains and night-watchmen) kept, with the name of its inhabitants' city of origin, its special customs, language and style of architecture.[9]

Turks were the first and largest group whom the Sultan brought to Constantinople. In the years following its capture in 1453 the city remained a ruin devastated by plague. The Sultan had to use an Ottoman technique known as *surgun*, or forced transfer of populations, to move Turks to his new capital. The chronicler Ashikpashazade wrote that the Sultan

> sent officers to all his lands to announce that whoever wished should come and take possession in Constantinople, as freehold, of houses and orchards and gardens . . . Despite this measure, the city was not repopulated; so then the Sultan commanded that from every land families, poor and rich alike, should be brought in by force. And they sent officers with firmans to the kadis and prefects of every land . . . and now the city began to become populous.

Mehmed II personally went to Bursa to force artisans and merchants of this rich trading city to move to the capital. Laments still exist for the fate of the artists and craftsmen brutally transported from the comforts of the old Seljuk capital of Konya in Anatolia to the blood-stained city on the Bosphorus. At moments the Conqueror himself had qualms about his new prize, and withdrew to the former capital Edirne. Edirne had the treble attraction of tranquillity, proximity to hunting grounds and geography: it was the natural mobilization centre for Ottoman campaigns in Europe.[10] However, the Sultan's doubts did not last.

Like Constantine the Great eleven hundred years earlier, when he summoned senators from Rome to Constantinople, and Peter the Great two hundred and fifty years later, in St Petersburg, the Sultan ordered 'the pillars of the empire' to move to his new capital. He told them 'to build grand houses in the city wherever each chose to build. He also commanded them to build baths and inns and market-places and very many and very beautiful workshops, to erect places of worship.'

Mahmud Pasha, the ablest statesman of his reign, was one of the first to build his own mosque, now embedded in the warren of *hans* (inns) and alleys beside the Grand Bazaar.[11]

The Conqueror also imported Greeks. Some areas of the city had never lost their Greek population. Psamatya, present-day Koca Mustafa Pasha, in the south-west of the city near the walls, had surrendered separately. It was therefore spared pillage – which explains the large number of churches there today. In the centre of the city, its second largest church, the church of the Holy Apostles, burial place of Byzantine emperors and model for St Mark's in Venice, by the Sultan's express wish remained undamaged. Mehmed II was at war with neighbouring rulers, both Christian and Muslim, in Anatolia and the Balkans for most of his reign. He conquered Trebizond, the Crimea, Serbia, Euboea, and the rival Turkish state of Karaman in Anatolia. As his empire expanded, more Greeks were taken by force to Constantinople. Greek slave peasants (freed in the next century) were settled in villages outside the city in order to ensure its food supplies.[12]

There was no religious barrier to Greeks and Turks living together. Christians are 'people of the Book': their religion has been superseded by, but is not wholly alien to, the final revelation of Islam. Abraham and Mary are revered by Muslims; 'Jesus on whom salvation be poured', as one Ottoman decree described him, is one of Islam's greatest prophets. According to Islamic law, as set out in the Koran, in return for paying a poll and other taxes, Christians received the status of *zimmi*, or protected persons, with the right to worship in freedom and to live by their own laws.

Mehmed II went further. Owing to disputes between supporters and opponents of reconciliation with the Pope, there was no Patriarch in Constantinople in 1453; the Sultan could have left the see vacant and let it disappear, as many Orthodox bishoprics in Ottoman Anatolia already had. But the Conqueror was the most open-minded monarch of his age. His originality was to revive the Oecumenical Patriarchate which had presided over the Orthodox Church from Constantinople since the fourth century.

One of the most learned and admired Orthodox churchmen was a Constantinople-born monk, George-Gennadios Scholarius. About 50 years of age, he had been leader of the Orthodox faithful opposed to union with Rome. Enslaved during the sack of Constantinople, he was treated with honour by his Turkish captors in a village near Edirne. There, in the words of Kritovoulos, confirmed by modern scholarship, the Conqueror sought him out, and gave him freedom and gifts: 'In the end he made him Patriarch and High Priest of the Christians, and gave him among many other rights and privileges the rule of the Church, and all its power and authority no less than that enjoyed previously under the emperors.' He was consecrated and enthroned on 5 January 1454 in the church of the Holy Apostles.

The document of appointment has not survived, and later Greeks exaggerated the privileges bestowed on Gennadios: in an anteroom of the patriarchate in Istanbul today hangs an improbable picture of Mehmed II and Gennadios, embracing as equals. Nevertheless the Patriarch was henceforward a servant of the Ottoman Empire. On payment of a large fee, the new Patriarch received confirmation in person from the Sultan, who addressed him with the formula: 'Be Patriarch with good fortune and be assured of our friendship, keeping all the privileges that the Patriarchs before you enjoyed.'

There was a bargain. The Sultan protected the Patriarch from rival Slav Orthodox churches, and Muslim fanatics. In return the Patriarch helped raise taxes for the Sultan and, in theory, guaranteed the loyalty of the Greeks and prevented them aiding the empire's Catholic enemies, Venice and the Papacy, both of whom had assisted in the city's defence in 1453, and were trying to reconquer it. As head of the Orthodox community, the Patriarch administered a separate Orthodox legal system, based on Justinian's code, with the power to fine, imprison and exile. Although weaker and poorer than its Western equivalent the Vatican, the Patriarchate of Constantinople was more important for its flock. It was the symbol and institution which kept faith and hope alive: after the conquest of Constantinople, the rate of conversion to Islam in Ottoman domains diminished.[13]

Mehmed II, who in all these measures took the initiative, appreciated Greek culture, as well as the prosperity Greeks could bring to his capital. Constantinople did, on occasion, serve as a door in the wall between Islam and Christianity. In either 1455 or 1456 the Sultan, with the dignitaries of his court, went to the Patriarch's residence and asked Gennadios to write an explanation of Christianity, which was translated from Greek into Turkish for the Sultan's benefit. Entitled *A Short Outline of the Christian Faith*, it is long and complex. It is hard for even a Christian to understand such remarks as 'We believe that the Word of God and the man, which the Word of God put on, is the Christ; and whereas the life of Christ in his flesh was the life of a very holy man, the power of his wisdom and works was the power of God.' The Sultan nevertheless retained an interest in Christianity: among his collection of Christian relics were the cradle 'in which Christ was born', which he told a Venetian envoy he would not sell for five hundred thousand ducats, and the armbone and skull of St John the Baptist.[14]

Some of his followers were less broad-minded. A few months after his consecration, Gennadios found a dead Turk in the courtyard of the church of the Holy Apostles. Even the Sultan himself might not be able to protect the Patriarch from an angry Muslim crowd ready to think the worst of Christians. Gennadios moved the patriarchate, its relics and treasures to the twelfth-century brick church of the Theotokos Pammacaristos, the Joyful Mother of God, in the district of the Phanar along the shore of the Golden Horn. Since the Sultan had settled many Greek captives there, it was solidly Greek.

Armenians were another Christian element brought to Constantinople by the Sultan. They were a distinct nationality which had lived since at least the sixth century BC in eastern Anatolia and the Caucasus. Since the Ecclesiastical Council held at Chalcedon – modern Kadikoy – opposite Constantinople in 451, both Orthodox and Catholics have held the belief that Jesus Christ is of two distinct natures, human and divine. Armenians, however, are Monophysites who believe that Jesus Christ has one nature, at once human and divine. Their use of the Armenian language and alphabet maintained their distinct identity, despite the disappearance of the last Armenian kingdom in southern Anatolia in the fourteenth century. They were prominent in the eastern Mediterranean as jewellers, craftsmen (especially builders) and traders – skills which naturally appealed to the Conqueror. Kritovoulos writes that Mehmed II 'transported to the city those of the Armenians under his rule who were outstanding in point of property, wealth, technical knowledge and other qualifications and in addition those who were of the merchant class'. This is the Sultan's smooth official version. An Armenian merchant called Nerses, writing in 1480, blamed the Sultan for raising 'an immense storm upon the Christians and upon his own people by transporting them from place to place . . . I composed this in times of bitterness, for they brought us from Amasya to Konstandnupolis by force and against our will; and I copied this tearfully with much lamentation.'

Armenian tradition, reflected in an inscription on the façade of the present Armenian patriarchate in the Kumkapi district of Istanbul, asserts that Mehmed II appointed an Armenian Patriarch in Constantinople in 1461. In reality the Armenian Patriarch remained in

Sis in Cilicia or Echmiadzin in the Caucasus, where he still is. Such historical myths are a tribute to the Armenians' desire to raise their position in the Ottoman Empire, and to Mehmed II's reputation as a supranational hero like Alexander the Great, whom different nationalities could invoke as a protector. Nevertheless as the Armenians grew in wealth and influence, the status of their bishop rose. By the seventeenth century he was recognized as an honorary Patriarch, or 'prelate called Patriarch', and administered his own law-courts and prison like the Oecumenical Patriarch.[15]

North of the Golden Horn, in every sense opposite to Constantinople itself, lay the wealthy district of Galata. Since the thirteenth century it had been controlled and inhabited by Genoese. It had become the Shanghai of the Levant: a semi-independent colony taking control of regional commerce from the dying Byzantine Empire, as Shanghai would do from the dying Chinese empire four hundred years later. In contrast to Constantinople proper, Galata (also known as Pera, from the Greek word for 'beyond') resembled a small Italian city, with Catholic churches, straight streets, well-built stone houses, and a piazzetta. Its tallest building, which still dominates the skyline today, was the pointed Tower of Galata, a Gothic monument strayed to the banks of the Bosphorus. In 1453 Galata was more prosperous and densely populated than the Byzantine city south of the Golden Horn.

Genoa and the Ottoman Empire had long been allies. Nevertheless, many Galata Genoese had fought against the Ottomans; the Sultan said they had prevented him taking the city on the first day of the siege. Yet he was more interested in prosperity than revenge. A privilege he granted on 1 June 1453 in Greek* to 'the people of Galata and their noblemen' survives in the British Library. In return for submission, and payment of the poll tax, they would be protected subjects of the empire. They were allowed to keep their possessions, and 'to follow their own customs and rites', except for 'ringing their church bells and rattle' – a particular phobia of the Ottomans, who tolerated no competition to the call to prayer from the minaret. The citizens' weapons were confiscated, and part of the city wall was destroyed – all that survives today is a fragment near the Golden Horn, bearing the arms of the great Genoese house of Doria. Otherwise Galata was not pun-

---

*Until the early sixteenth century, the Ottoman sultans employed some Greek secretaries and issued documents in Greek as well as Turkish.

ished. According to a letter written a few days later by the former *podestà*, or mayor, to his brother in Genoa: 'He has also had lists made of all the property belonging to the merchants and citizens who have left here, saying "If they return, they shall have them back, and if not it will all belong to me."'[16] Most returned.

The Sultan liked to have Franks (that is, western Europeans) at his court. For many years he used a wealthy alum merchant of Genoese origin, Francesco Draperio, as an unofficial diplomat (his family is commemorated today in the church of St Maria Draperis, on Istiklal Caddesi). So fond was the Sultan of Galata's Latin ambience that he once entered a Franciscan church and watched a mass.

As the Sultan's conquests extended, more Italians were brought to the city, in 1460 from Genoese colonies on the Aegean, and in 1475 from the Crimea. Italians, like Greeks, were useful to the Sultan. In the Adriatic and the Aegean he faced Venice, one of the great powers of the age, with a better navy than the Ottoman. Florence was the principal Italian rival of Venice. The Sultan therefore encouraged Florentines to move to Galata, granting them the houses of expelled Venetians; he even consulted the Florentine consul over his decision to declare war on Venice in 1463. That year the Florentines of Galata decorated their houses to celebrate the Ottoman conquest of the independent kingdom of Bosnia (which rapidly became an Ottoman bulwark, known as 'the lion that guards the gates of Stamboul'). In 1465 the Sultan was the Florentines' guest at dinner in their chief trading depot, where he received *'galanterie con tutte splendidezza e magnificenza'*. By 1469 fifty Florentine firms were operating in the Ottoman Empire. They imported silk, velvet, paper – most Ottoman documents were written on Italian paper – glass and fox pelts. Their main problems in 'keeping the market moving' – a common phrase – came from plague and the Venetians, not the Ottomans.[17]

The example of Galata shows that, in Constantinople, East and West could live together. The Ottoman Empire was never, as Braudel claims, 'an anti-Europe, a counter-Christendom'. Galata's merchant dynasties – the Testa, Draperis, Fornetti – were the longest established families in the city. Turks called them 'sweet water Franks', in contrast to 'salt water Franks' from Europe. A body of twelve counsellors, the *Magnifica Communità di Pera*, managed the churches of the Catholic community. Merchants met twice a day to discuss business in the equivalent of the Exchange in London, the loggia of the Palazzo del Commune, a Gothic building modelled on the Palazzo San Giorgio in

13

Genoa.* When the empire was at peace with Venice, the Bailo (bailiff) of Venice ran a law-court for civil cases concerning Venetian subjects (and other Europeans), whose decisions were enforced by the Ottoman authorities. He also organized a postal service which left twice a month, by land through the Balkans, to Cattaro on the Dalmatian coast, and then by sea to Venice. Letters between the two cities generally took about a month to arrive.

Galata was a centre for pleasure as well as business. Every Lent there was a carnival: 'One would think one was in a town in Italy,' wrote Marcantonio Pignafetta. Alvise Gritti was one of the many western Europeans who made his fortune on the banks of the Bosphorus. Born in Constantinople, where his father served as Venetian Bailo, debarred by illegitimate birth from a career in Venice, he lived in state in Galata (whose Turkish name Beyoglu, 'son of the Bey', is said to come from the fact that his father was a Doge of Venice). A diplomatic agent of the Grand Vizier, and dealer in jewels, he was said to live as a Turk among the Turks and as a Christian among the Christians. In 1524, soon after his father became Doge in Venice, he gave a banquet in Constantinople for 300 guests, including Turks. They dined off deer, partridge and peacock. They were then entertained by women of Galata dancing with 'such lascivious movements that they could make marbles melt', followed by a comedy, *Psyche and Cupid*, a tournament and a representation of the Portuguese occupation of Ceylon. A Turkish writer of the seventeenth century said of Galata, 'Who says Galata says taverns – may God forgive us!': the beer was iced, in summer, by snow brought from mountains above Bursa. Magnificently dressed, wearing all their wealth in jewels, the women kept the reputation, into the twentieth century, of the ability *di fare di un santo un diavolo*.[18†]

Thus from 1453 Constantinople was capital, not only of the Ottoman Empire and the Orthodox Church, but also of that commercial subculture, native to the ports of the eastern Mediterranean, known

---

*Shorn of its Genoese coats of arms and Gothic windows, it is now a workshop known as the Bereket Hani, on the corner of Galatakulesi and Bankalar Caddesi. It is probably the oldest civilian building in the city. See *Studia Turcologica memoriae Alexii Bombacii Dicata*, Naples, 1982, 166–79.

†According to a later proverb:

Che vuol' fare sua rovina
Prende moglie levantina.

as the Levant. Until the early nineteenth century Italian, language of commerce and the sea, was its second language, spoken by all Franks, most Greeks and Armenians, and some Turks. Numerous Italian nautical terms, such as *caravel* and *bombarda*, for types of ship, or *iskele*, from the Italian *scala*, for landing-place, entered the Turkish language. (In another reflection of the dominance of Italian, before 1830 English merchants referred to the ports of the eastern Mediterranean as 'the scales of the Levant'.) A form of pidgin Italian, including French, Greek, Spanish, Arabic and Turkish words and known as *Lingua Franca*, was also common. Until the early twentieth century cries such as *'Guarda! Guarda!'* to avert collision, or *'Monsu, arrivar!'* to indicate arrival, could still be heard in the city.[19] Under Mehmed II Galata was a subservient suburb. In years to come, it would exercise a powerful, finally an overpowering, influence on trade, culture and diplomacy in Constantinople.

Like other world cities – Amsterdam in the seventeenth century, Vienna in the nineteenth, New York in the twentieth – Constantinople also attracted Jews. The Jews of Constantinople had suffered like its other inhabitants from the conquest. Hebrew poems survive, lamenting their enslavement and deportation, and the cruelty of the Ottomans. To replace them most of the Jews in the Ottoman Empire were brought to Constantinople against their will, by *surgun*. Forbidden to leave without official permission, they regarded themselves as 'ensnared in the net of captivity'. Until the nineteenth century, the *surgunlu* remained distinct in ritual and tax payments from the *kendi gelen*, those who came voluntarily.[20]

For after 1453 Jews were encouraged to immigrate from Europe. A letter from one rabbi to his persecuted brethren in Europe burns with the fervour of a Zionist immigration prospectus, urging settlement in the Promised Land:

Here in the land of the Turks we have nothing to complain of. We possess great fortunes; much gold and silver are in our hands. We are not oppressed with heavy taxes and our commerce is free and unhindered. Rich are the fruits of the earth. Everything is cheap and every one of us lives in peace and freedom. Here the Jew is not compelled to wear a yellow star as a badge of shame as is the case in Germany where even wealth and great fortune are a curse for a Jew because he therewith arouses jealousy among the Christians and they devise all kind of slander against him to rob him of his gold. Arise my brethren, gird up your loins, collect all your forces and come to us.

In 'the refuge of the world', in contrast to western Europe, there were no restrictions on freedom of trade and few limits on the construction of synagogues. Jews soon flourished as perfumers, blacksmiths, carpenters and, in exceptional cases, tax farmers, bankers and doctors. With their new-found wealth they were able to outbid Christian and Muslim consortiums for the lease of Constantinople's customs. After the first decades, their history is that rarity in Jewish history, a happy story. In Constantinople the words pogrom, ghetto, inquisition had no meaning.

From the late fifteenth century to within living memory the centres of Jewish life in Constantinople were the districts of Balat and Haskoy on either side of the Golden Horn, which had contained Jewish populations before the conquest. It was said that 'the lads of Balat are real strong youths, those of Haskoy are just dried raisins.' The synagogues dominated Jewish lives. They maintained the customs and rituals of the locality from which the worshippers came, ran local schools and benevolent societies and arranged the payment of taxes to the government. Rabbis acted as judges in the Jewish courts, which enjoyed remarkable independence and had the power to legislate for Jews.[21]

The most successful Jew in Constantinople was a doctor, Giacomo di Gaeta, who had left the intolerance of Renaissance Italy for the haven of the Ottoman Empire. Physician to the Sultan, Yakup Pasha, as he was called after his conversion to Islam, won a privilege of tax exemption for himself and his descendants, whether Jewish or Muslim. Constantinople was a city of double identities. Like Gennadios, Alvise Gritti, and the Sultan himself, Yakup Pasha moved with ease between different worlds. He frequented not only the Sultan's palace, but also the house of the Venetian Bailo in Galata. There, probably on the Sultan's orders, he relayed disinformation to confuse Venetian policymakers, such as the claim, in 1465, that the Sultan had turned Christian.[22]

Greeks, Armenians, Italians and Jews were brought to the city mainly for economic reasons. The dynastic state itself imported a fifth racial element. The Ottoman government was called the Gate, from the part of the ruler's palace most visibly associated with power: Ottoman government was seen as the administration of the state and of justice in front of the Sultan's gate by his extended household and administrators. The main body of the Sultan's officials and soldiers were slaves known as *kapi kulu*, or 'slaves of the Gate'. Their composition reflected Ottoman faith in racial variety. They were youths between the ages of 8

and 16, conscripted according to need from the rural Christian population of the Balkans and, less frequently, Anatolia, by the process known
as *devshirme* or 'gathering'. They could not be Turkish. After the conquest of Bosnia in 1463, although the Koran forbade the enslavement
of Muslims, Muslim Slavs could be 'gathered'. Muslims of Turkish
origin could not.

The youths' date of birth and details of parentage were recorded.
They were then taken to Constantinople, circumcised and converted to
Islam. The best looking and best born were educated in the palace
school or a Pasha's household, and eventually entered government
service. The others were 'given to the Turk' – sent to farms in Anatolia
to learn Turkish. They then worked as gardeners in the imperial palace,
sailors in the imperial navy, or on building sites in the city. Eventually
they joined the Janissaries. A force numbering some fifteen to twenty
thousand, the Janissaries were the spearhead of the Ottoman army and
the principal military and police force in Constantinople itself. They
patrolled the walls, garrisoned the Seven Towers, enforced law and
order, guarded the Patriarch and the Sultan himself.

Some Christian families were heart-broken to see their children
'gathered'. There was a song:

> Be damned, O Emperor, be thrice damned
> For the evil you have done and the evil you do.
> You catch and shackle the old and the archpriests
> In order to take the children as Janissaries.
> Their parents weep and their sisters and brothers too
> And I cry until it pains me;
> As long as I live I shall cry,
> For last year it was my son and this year my brother.

More worldly families were delighted to see their children secure a
footing on the Ottoman career ladder. Slavery was less degrading in the
Islamic than in the Christian world. *Devshirme* youths educated in the
Sultan's or viziers' households had the chance to occupy the highest
posts in the empire – and look after their relations. 'Slaves of the Gate'
were free from many of the legal restraints imposed on other slaves in
matters of marriage and property. It was the Bosnian Slavs themselves
who demanded to remain eligible for 'gathering', despite their conversion
from Christianity to Islam. A Venetian Bailo wrote that the Janissaries
'take great pleasure in being able to say "I am a slave of the Grand
Signior", since they know that this is a lordship or republic of slaves

where it is theirs to command'. A hundred years ago, might not selected Irish Catholic youths have felt a similar pride, if they had been converted to Protestantism, sent to Eton and then told to govern the British Empire as servants of the Queen Empress?[23]

A specifically Ottoman practice, *devshirme* was particularly favoured by Mehmed II. An Italian wrote: 'In this he shows a remarkable tenacity of purpose, as if by his own efforts he wished to produce a new people.' The process removed potential rebels and transformed them into loyal Ottomans. Moreover traditional Islamic 'mirrors for princes', which were read by Ottoman bureaucrats, taught the advantages of racial variety. According to the *Book of Government or Rules for Kings*, if the Sultan employed different races, 'all races endeavoured to surpass one another . . . When troops are all of one race dangers arise; they lack zeal and are apt to be disorderly.'

Distrust of Turks was, however, the main reason for 'gathering'. One inmate of the palace wrote: 'There are few native-speaking Turks in the palace because the Sultan finds himself more faithfully served by Christian converts who have neither hearth nor home nor parents nor friends. They conceive such an affection for his service that if it were in their power they would voluntarily expose a thousand lives for the life of his person and the increase of his empire.' Many of the Turkish Muslim élite, on the other hand, pre-dated and envied the Ottomans: there had been ancient Turkish states in Anatolia, like Rum and Danishmend, when the Ottomans were new arrivals. Mehmed II had experienced the dangers of a powerful Muslim élite: after a first reign of two years, he had been deposed in 1446. Probably at the instigation of the Grand Vizier Candarli Halil, a cousin and member of a family which had supplied three grand viziers, his father Murad II had then returned to the throne for two years. Out of fear of Western reaction, the Grand Vizier had continued to oppose Mehmed II's decision to attack Constantinople: he called it the 'follies of an intoxicated youth'. Soon after the siege, Mehmed II had him executed. Henceforth most grand viziers, and pashas, were 'slaves of the Gate': only five of the first forty-eight grand viziers after 1453 were native-born Turks. In disgust some Turks called the Sultan's council, or *divan*, 'the slave market'.[24]

The presence of the Janissaries meant that many of the soldiers – and the great mosque builders and viziers – in Constantinople were Slavs. In 1542, according to a French traveller, in the palace 'Sclavonian' (Serbo-Croat) was the language 'most used and understood of all . . . all the more since it is common to the Janissaries'. Contrary to what historians used to believe, slaves of the Gate were also able to straddle two worlds, maintaining contact from the capital with their family in the provinces. The Grand Vizier Mahmud Pasha, for example, conducted negotiations with Serbia in 1457. If they led to a favourable peace and a higher tribute for the Ottoman Empire, it was no doubt because the highest official in the Serbian court, the Grand Voivode Michael Angelovic, was his brother.[25]

Some slaves of the Gate formed a Serb lobby in the capital, often in conflict with the Greek-dominated Patriarchate. The most prominent Constantinople Serb, and one of the most prominent figures of Ottoman history, was born Bajica Sokolovic in 1505, fifty years after the conquest, in the small town of Visegrad on the Serbian-Bosnian frontier. A man of imposing presence, with a black beard and a hawk nose, he rose swiftly through the ranks of the *devshirme*, occupying successively the posts of falconer, Grand Admiral, vizier, Viceroy of Europe. Finally, from 1564 to 1579, Sokollu Mehmed Pasha, as he had become, was Grand Vizier. Courteous, prudent, avaricious, he was a statesman with a world view. From his palaces in Constantinople he planned canals between the Don and the Volga and the Red Sea and the Mediterranean, in order to help Muslim states against Russia and Portugal respectively, sent munitions to Sumatra, helped select a new king for Poland, ordered pictures and clocks from Venice and arranged a successful peace with Spain, Venice and the Papacy, despite the Ottoman naval defeat at Lepanto, in 1573.

Yet he kept links with his Serb roots. He placed relations in the Ottoman central government and in 1557, at his insistence, the Serbian archbishopric of Pecs was revived, against the wishes of the Patriarchate: his brother was the first Archbishop. Himself destined for the priesthood when 'gathered' for the Sultan, he is said, on occasion, to have accompanied his nephews to church, on their visits to Constantinople.

Architecture perpetuates the links between the two worlds of Sokollu Mehmed Pasha. In Constantinople his wife Ismihan Sultan, daughter of Sultan Selim II, built him a masterpiece from the golden age of Ottoman architecture, the Sokollu Mehmed Pasha mosque by the old Roman hippodrome. Near his birthplace in Bosnia, the Grand Vizier himself commissioned an eleven-arched bridge over the River Drina, 'one of the noblest spans you are likely to see'. Damaged in both world wars, twice rebuilt, it was finally destroyed by Croatian bombs in 1994.[26]

Twenty-four years after the conquest, in 1477, a census was taken by the city judge of Constantinople, for the personal information of the Sultan. There were, in Constantinople and Galata: 9,486 houses inhabited by Muslims; 3,743 houses inhabited by Greeks; 1,647 houses inhabited by Jews; 434 houses inhabited by Armenians; 384 houses inhabited by Karamanians of Armenian appearance; 332 houses inhabited by Franks (all in Galata); 267 houses inhabited by Christians from the Crimea, and 31 houses inhabited by gypsies. In all there were perhaps 80,000 inhabitants (excluding the slaves of the Gate). Constantinople was a city which defied nationalism, in whose streets Greek, Armenian, Italian, Lingua Franca, Albanian, Bulgarian* and Serbian, as well as Turkish, Persian and Arabic, were spoken.

The only multinational capital in Europe, Constantinople received names in more languages than any other city. Serbs, Bulgarians and Russians admired *Tsarigrad* – the city of Emperors. Armenians lived in *Gosdantnubolis* – the city of Constantine. In everyday language Greeks called it – as some still do – *polis*, the city: there is no other. Its official Greek name had been *Constantinoupolis Nea Roma*, after which Ottomans called it, on coins and most official documents, *Kostantiniyye* (which is also its name in Arabic). In literary Ottoman it was called *Der-i Sa'adet*, 'the House of Good Fortune', since it had the good fortune to be the Sultan's residence, or *Asithane*, Persian for 'house of state'. However its name, in everyday spoken Turkish, even before the conquest, was a corruption of the Greek phrase for 'into the city', *eis teen polin*: Istanbul.

Heads and feet, as well as names, demonstrated the city's multinational character. The inhabitants of Constantinople, whatever their religion, generally wore simple robes or tunics, like those of Gulf Arabs today, but of darker colours. Over the tunic they wore a dolman of satin or linen, padded with cotton in winter, and a sash. They laughed at western Europeans who spoiled their clothes with trimmings, pleats and slashes.

Until the nineteenth century, in order both to demonstrate Muslim superiority and to foster national rivalries, the Ottoman government enforced distinctions of dress between the different communities. Only

---

*Another Slav contingent in Constantinople, until the early twentieth century, were the *voynuks*, or Bulgarian grooms, and falconers, who worked in the imperial stables. They supplemented their income by dancing in the streets to the sound of bagpipes. See Nicolas de Nicolay, *Dans l'Empire de Soliman le Magnifique*, 1989, 183.

Muslims could wear white or green turbans and yellow slippers. Greeks, Armenians and Jews were distinguished respectively by sky blue, dark blue (later red) and yellow hats, and by black, violet and blue slippers. The rules governing the costume of religious minorities were regularly reasserted. In 1580, for example, 'considering that their attitude from the point of view of the *sheriat* [Muslim holy law] and of logic should be humility and abjection', Jews and Christians were formally forbidden 'to dress like Muslims', to wear silk, fur, or red shoes, and instead were enjoined to wear dark colours or blue. They were also repeatedly forbidden to live near mosques, to build tall houses or to buy slaves.[27]

Such reiterations show that the rules were often flouted: the status of Muslims was so attractive that the minorities' desire to resemble them was irrepressible. Individuals could also buy exemption from dress regulations. However, for most people most of the time, the clothes they wore reinforced their sense of belonging to a specific community. Contrasts of feature could reinforce those of dress.

Most inhabitants of Constantinople still claim that they can tell by sight whether a neighbour is Turkish, Greek, Jewish or Armenian. In the nineteenth century, after the end of the dress laws, a travel-writer, Edmondo de Amicis, wrote that a Turk and Greek sitting beside each other, even if they were dressed in the same style, could at once be distinguished by the silent immobility of the former and the latter's 'thousand changing expressions of life and eye' as he tossed his head 'with the movement of a spirited horse'. In the first century of the empire, faces and gestures made plain the multinationalism of Constantinople.[28]

In 1477, the year of the census, the creator of this multinational microcosm, Mehmed II, was 47. To a page at his court, Gian Maria Angiolello, he appeared 'of medium height, fat and fleshy; he had a wide forehead, large eyes with thick lashes, an aquiline nose, a small mouth with a round copious reddish-tinged beard, a short thick neck, a sallow complexion, rather high shoulders and a loud voice'.[29] After a reign of conquest he now had time to relax in his capital.

Like the city itself, he was a collection of contrasts: cruel and gentle, ruthless and tolerant, pious and pederast. He built schools and markets as enthusiastically as he ordered tortures and massacres. Regarding himself both as the supreme *gazi*, or warrior for Islam, and the new Alexander, he read, or listened to, the Koran, expositions of the Gospels, Persian poets, chronicles of emperors, popes and the kings of France, Arrian's life of Alexander, Homer, Herodotus, Livy and

Xenophon.[30] He treated language as an instrument of communication, not domination. Although not comparable to the great enemy of the Ottoman Empire, the Emperor Charles V, who was said to speak Spanish to God, French to gentlemen, Italian to ladies, and German to his horse, Mehmed II spoke Turkish, Persian, Arabic, and almost certainly had some knowledge of Greek and Serbo-Croat. In his poems he called himself not *Fatih*, the conqueror, but *Avni*, the helper. He was author of a typical Ottoman couplet:

> Footman, pour me some wine, for one day the tulip garden will be
> destroyed;
> Autumn will come soon and the spring season will be no more!

Although he wrote and governed in Turkish, he revered Persian culture, which enjoyed some of the prestige, in the Muslim world, of French culture in eighteenth-century Europe. A further language was added to the polyphony of the city. Among the Persian scholars he attracted to Constantinople was the last great medieval Islamic astronomer, Ali Kuscu of Samarkand, who taught at the school attached to Aya Sofya. When Mehmed II discovered that another poet, although Persian-educated, was in fact Turkish in origin, the Sultan took away the ruined Greek church which had been given to him as a sign of favour.[31]

Persian culture was so influential that Ottoman, the language of the palace and the governing élite, although Turkish in structure, was partly Persian – and Arabic – in vocabulary: in the 1920s only 37 per cent of words in the dictionary were of Turkish origin. The complexities of its vocabulary and sentence structure made the Ottoman language one of the principal barriers to the spread of literacy and of contact with the outside world. To heighten the contrast with the simple Turkish of the street, 'gilded' expressions were deliberately employed. When a famous calligrapher died, for example, it was said that 'the dots of his script became transformed into moles on the cheeks of the houris of Paradise'. There were few rebels. A sixteenth-century poet, Yahya Bey, refused to be 'the dragoman of the Persians' or 'to eat the food of dead Persians', and wrote in vigorous Turkish. Yet he was not Turkish but a Janissary, proud of his Albanian birth.[32]

Mehmed II patronized Muslim scholars and theologians, often paying surprise visits to the college he founded beside his mosque, to listen to lectures and test teachers and pupils. Yet he was also a student of Greek philosophy, the greatest single patron of the Italian

Renaissance medal, and the first Muslim ruler to appreciate Italian artists. Among the artists he invited to and employed in Constantinople were Matteo de' Pasti from Rimini, Maestro Paoli from Dubrovnik, and the medallist Costanzo da Ferrara.[33]

In the last years of his reign Constantinople was diplomatically, commercially and culturally part of Europe. In 1479, after sixteen years of war, Mehmed II made peace with Venice. That September, in answer to his request for 'a good painter', the Doge's official artist, Gentile Bellini, came to Constantinople and was presented to the Sultan by the Bailo of Venice. Having spent the previous five years repainting the Hall of the Great Council in the Doge's Palace, for the next year and a quarter he painted portraits of Mehmed II and his court and erotic frescos (*cose di lussúria*) for the 'inner chambers' of the palace the Sultan was building on the easternmost point of Constantinople.

By 1481, though only 48, the Sultan was emaciated and debilitated. Not even his viziers knew what country he was planning to conquer, when he died that year from blocked intestines, leading his army east from Constantinople into Asia. Certain circumstances attending his death make it likely that he was poisoned – possibly with the help of his Persian physician al-Lari, acting for his son Bayezid II.[34]

His death left his capital at a crossroads. It was a city like a chemical experiment, containing disparate elements that could either combine or combust. In theory a multinational dynastic capital, in practice it attracted conflicts between nationalism and empire, ambition and realism, love of the city and the desire to transform or leave it.

With its Greek population and Byzantine past, Constantinople was a controversial choice as Ottoman capital. While Kritovoulos sang the Conqueror's praises, some Turks, especially those with a connection with the previous capital Edirne, were enraged by the Conqueror's repopulation policies. Despite the Sultan's original promises of properties in freehold for immigrants, Turks sometimes had to pay rent to the Sultan, or even to original Greek owners. They were furious: 'You forced us to leave our old homes, which we owned. Did you bring us here that we should pay rent for these houses of the infidels?' Some left their families and fled the city. Criticism was directed at the Sultan and his Greek-born Grand Vizier, Mehmed Pasha:

> If the Sultan is capricious in the decrees he makes
> Then his territory always suffers harm.

> And if his vizier should be an infidel,
> He always seeks to cause damage to the true faith.

In the end protest was so fierce that Mehmed II gave certificates adorned with his *tughra* (the Sultan's monogram) freeing Turks from paying rent.

The cosmopolitanism of the Conqueror's court was another source of horror. A poet wrote:

> If you wish to stand in high honour on the Sultan's threshold,
> You must be either a Jew, a Persian or a Frank.

For anonymous historians, writing in the simple Turkish of the people, Constantinople was 'the island of torments and distress, the reunion of calamities, the source of failures and annihilation'. The accursed city should be left in ruins until the day of the Apocalypse. The capital should return to Edirne.[35]

As well as Turkish malcontents, the Ottoman state itself could threaten the capital's future. In the absence of representative assemblies, or a powerful hereditary nobility, power lay with the slaves of the Gate. Yet, as Tacitus said of another imperial guard, the Praetorians of the Roman Empire: *quis custodiet ipsos custodes?* The Sultan might call his Janissaries, to their face, 'my sweet lambs'. He knew better than anyone that they were ravenous wolves. In 1451, intoxicated by their own power, they had shouted at him, 'This was our Sultan's first campaign and he should reward us with the customary bonus.'[36] They frequently murmured against his policies. What was there to prevent this incomparable military machine from disposing of the throne as it pleased; or even taking power from the dynasty, as other slave guards in Muslim countries had done, in Baghdad and Cairo?

Turks were not the only people to resent Ottoman Constantinople. The Sultan's pro-Greek policy was based on a gamble: that the might of the Ottoman Empire and the profits to be made in its stable and expanding trade area would keep Christians content to be, in the Ottoman language, *re'aya*, 'the flock', sheared by the Ottoman shepherd.

Historians, contaminated by the plague of nationalism that has raged since 1830, have exaggerated its scope and power. Just as the Ottoman dynasty combined Islamic, Turkish and European aspects, so many of its subjects combined several identities. It was possible to feel Greek (or Arab, Jewish or Serb) and Ottoman. Some Greeks remained more anti-Western than anti-Ottoman, believing 'Better the Sultan's turban than the Cardinal's hat'. Manuel Palaeologus, for example, a nephew of the last Emperor, returned to Constantinople from Italy in 1477 and was given an estate. One of his sons converted to Islam; another remained Greek. A century later it was said by a German visitor that the Greeks 'do not want anyone else but the Turks to dominate them, not even a Christian'.[37] Yet other Greeks regarded the Ottoman Empire as alien and oppressive. The Patriarch Gennadios was grateful to the Conqueror and admitted that some Ottomans were more sympathetic to his policies than his own clergy. Yet in private he called Turks 'the bloody dogs of Hagar' and 'the outsiders'. His relationship with the Sultan was based not on loyalty but on necessity.

If the Sultan's personal appointee felt such hate, it is not hard to imagine the feelings of less favoured Greeks. In church services in Constantinople Turks were regularly anathematized as 'infidel' and 'damned'. Among the kinder epithets bestowed on Mehmed II by the chronicler Ducas, from the safety of Corfu, were 'the wild beast . . . the forerunner of Antichrist'. So great was the trauma of the capture of Constantinople that, until recently, Greeks regarded Tuesday – the day it fell – as unlucky. Many Greeks believed in the resurrection of the Byzantine Empire almost as fervently as they believed in that of Jesus Christ.[38]

From the day the Ottomans conquered the city, there were prophecies of their expulsion. A priest had been interrupted saying mass in Haghia Sophia by the arrival of the 'Turkish dogs'. He had disappeared into a pillar, where he was awaiting the Greek return. He would then emerge from his hiding-place, with a radiant face and chalice in hand, mount the steps of the high altar, and resume the service. The last Emperor was not dead; he had been turned into marble and was sleeping in a subterranean cave beneath the Golden Gate, the traditional point of entry for victorious emperors, which Michael Palaeologus had used in 1261. One day he would hear a call from heaven: 'an angel will give him a sword, restore him to life and let him drive the Turks as far as the Red Apple on the Persian frontier' – in alliance with a fair-haired people from the North. To Turks the Red Apple was a symbol of Turkish power, to Greeks a portent of Turkish defeat.

Constantinople was a city with an exceptionally long historical memory. Until this century, such legends, familiar to every Greek, helped to inspire Greek dreams of empire. In the presence of Turks, in the mosque of Aya Sofya itself, Greek guides told the legend of the interrupted mass to appreciative foreign visitors. The Ottomans, who had many superstitions of their own about a possible Christian invasion or rising, walled up the Golden Gate.[39]

Ottoman Constantinople had external as well as internal foes. In Florence, Venice and Rome (where the Pope appointed the leading pro-Western Greek, Cardinal Bessarion, Patriarch of Constantinople in 1463), Greek exiles from 'the city' urged Western powers to launch a crusade against the Ottomans, assuring them of Greek support. Janus Lascaris, for example, born in Constantinople around 1445, spent much of his career as a Greek teacher in Florence and Venice urging Christian monarchs, the Pope, the Holy Roman Emperor and the King of France, to lead a crusade against the Ottoman Empire.[40] Many Venetians and Genoese hoped to recapture the city, as they had during the Fourth Crusade in 1204. What nineteenth-century statesmen referred to as the 'Eastern Question' – the design of the European powers to conquer Ottoman territory – began in 1453.

The Sultan was alarmed by the powerful and determined foes – Hungary, Austria, Venice – that surrounded his empire. A Serbian soldier in the Sultan's service remembered that, at a time when there was talk of the Pope leading a European crusade, 'the Emperor [Mehmed II] was afraid that all the Christian lands which he had conquered would oppose him'. The Pope's attempts produced no result. However, the threat from the King of Hungary so alarmed the Sultan that in 1473, while campaigning in the East, he employed 10,000 workmen to strengthen the walls of the capital.[41]

Western Europe had a potential fifth column in Constantinople in the European colony, and European diplomats, in Galata. It was a source not only of information and profit to, but also of intrigues against, the Exalted State. Within days of the entry of the Sultan, the former Genoese *podestà* wrote from Galata to Genoa that he hoped 'Constantinople will be the beginning of his ruin.' Venice made fourteen attempts to poison the Sultan.[42]

Thus from the moment it became capital of the Ottoman Empire, Constantinople was a contested city. This microcosm of empire had no exclusive hold over the loyalties of its Turkish, Greek, Armenian, Jewish and Italian inhabitants. The Conqueror's capital could be either their meeting-place or their battleground.

2

City of God

True art is to create a glorious city. And to fill the people's hearts with felicity.
Mehmed II, prelude to the foundation deed of the Fatih mosque

ISLAM ITSELF PRESENTED one potential challenge to the Ottoman capital. Islam is a religion with revolutionary implications. Rulers are considered legitimate only if they enforce the *sheriat*, the holy law of Islam based on the teaching of the Koran. The *sheriat* was considered above, rather than a product of, the state. The French maxim, *Si veut le roi, si veut la loi*, would have been unthinkable in the Ottoman Empire. Conflict between dynastic power and Islam emerged throughout the history of the city.

The Sultan's army besieging the city had included Christian Serbs and Hungarians. Nevertheless many of the Sultan's soldiers had seen themselves as *gazis*, holy warriors eager for victory or 'the honey of martyrdom'. In retrospect the fall of Constantinople was perceived as a Muslim miracle. The saints in white robes, led by the supreme Muslim saint Hizir, 'the green man', the Muslim Elijah, had fought in the Sultan's armies. Overwhelmed by the truth of Islam, Greek priests had surged out of the city to join them.[1]

Some Muslim dervishes later challenged Mehmed II, saying that the conquest of the city was not his victory but theirs. As in modern Algeria or Egypt, in Constantinople social and political discontent could be expressed through Islam. The sixteenth-century Ottoman philosopher and political writer Mustafa Ali denounced preachers who 'gathering around them a crowd of brainless rabble . . . boldly attack with various nonsense now the conduct and words of God's Caliph, the order of the world, now the behaviour and acts of the imperial statesmen'.

27

Moreover the Ottomans owed their authority to military success. Unlike other Muslim dynasties such as the Sherifs, the senior descendants of the Prophet who had ruled in Mecca and Medina since the tenth century, they could not claim long-established right or the blood of the Qureish, the Prophet's tribe. This 'legitimacy deficit' created conflict, even in the mind of a sixteenth-century Grand Vizier like Lutfi Pasha.[2] Could the Ottoman Sultan be, as he frequently proclaimed, 'Shadow of God'?

The Ottoman solution was to multiply connections between Islam and the dynasty. The Ottoman Sultans were pious Muslims who tried to advance the law of God. They were also dynasts who, like the Habsburg emperors and the tsars of Russia, used religion as an instrument of control over their subjects. Mehmed II's fervently Muslim speech to his troops before the conquest was also unashamedly dynastic: 'The *gaza* [holy war] is our basic duty as it was in the case of our fathers. Constantinople, situated as it is in the middle of our dominions, protects the enemies of our state [including a Muslim, his uncle Orhan] and incites them against us. The conquest of this city is therefore essential to the future and the safety of the Ottoman state.'

Architecture revealed the dynasty's reverence for Islam. One of Mehmed II's most famous buildings was a mosque begun around 1459, at the top of the Golden Horn. It was on the site where the Sultan's revered spiritual guide, Akshemseddin, claimed to have found the grave of a companion of the Prophet Muhammad called Abu Ayyub al-Ansari, who had died fighting in the Arab army besieging Constantinople in 669. This convenient discovery provided a charismatic link between the new capital and the Prophet himself.

Pilgrims came to revere the grave in the courtyard, surrounded by a silver grating, gilded candlesticks and open Korans. A Moroccan ambassador wrote, after a visit to Constantinople in 1591:

> Crowds of visitors press unceasingly around the tomb. The grandees of the empire compete for the burial places available near him. They acquire plots there at the highest price. All good men even of modest condition also do all they can to obtain their place beside this tomb. We paid a visit to this holy person and we profited from his aura. Through his mediation – let God accept it! – we addressed our prayers to God.[3]

Abu Ayyub became the patron of Ottoman Constantinople. Non-Muslims were not permitted to open shops in such a sacred district. Today the district around his tomb, known as Eyup, is the most revered

Muslim site in Turkey. Particularly during the holy month of Ramadan, it is palpably different from the rest of the city. Surrounded by grave-yards and streets of marble mausoleums, the mosque remains open to a sea of believers until late into the night.

Through the sanctification of Eyup, Constantinople became a holy city of Islam. A Muslim name for the city was coined, possibly by Mehmed II himself: *Islambol*, 'where Islam abounds'.[4] The Conqueror built another mosque between 1463 and 1470, in the middle of Constantinople, on the site of, and using materials from, the church of the Holy Apostles. Called Fatih, 'the Conqueror', after the Sultan himself, it expresses his vision of his capital no les than the stronghold of the Seven Towers. The mosques the Ottomans had built in Bursa and Edirne are relatively modest and, in their decoration, show strong Seljuk and Persian influence. The new capital demanded a bolder, more monumental style: the Fatih mosque was the most ambitious architec-tural project yet undertaken by the Ottomans and its architect, known as 'Old Sinan' (later executed on his master's orders), may have been of Christian origin. Like Aya Sofya, which it was intended to rival, the Fatih mosque is crowned by a series of lead-covered domes rising to one enormous dome – the largest the Ottomans had yet built. Rebuilt on the original plan, after an earthquake in 1766, it creates a space which imposes a feeling of physical, as well as religious, humility on the faith-ful below. The Conqueror's historian and contemporary Tursun Beg compared the mosque interior to 'the miracle of the burning bush'. The great seventeenth-century writer Evliya Celebi, whose accounts of Constantinople and the empire have become classics, thought it resembled 'the vault of heaven'.

The eight-gated square courtyard, as large as the mosque itself, is lined with a colonnade, with a fountain in the middle. On a white marble tablet inside the main entrance of the mosque, a *hadith*, or saying, attributed to the Prophet himself, is inscribed in golden letters. Quoted by the Conqueror to his troops before the final assault on the city, it shows that the fame of Constantinople had enthralled the Prophet himself: 'They will conquer Kostantiniyye. Truly their com-mander will be an excellent one! Truly that army will be an excellent one!'

In another courtyard beside the mosque is an octagonal domed mau-soleum containing the Conqueror's simple stone tomb, covered in green cloth, with a white turban at one end. Guarded night and day by religious elders, it at once became a place of pilgrimage. The people of

Constantinople believed that the Conqueror's intercession would add power to the prayers they offered as they pressed against the windows of the mausoleum. New sultans hoped to acquire his courage and vigour by visiting his tomb.[5]

The mosque was central to the life of the city. The main function of the Fatih mosque, like other of the city's mosques, was to be a clean and austere place of worship. At the appointed times for communal prayer, having washed face, hands, arms and feet in a fountain outside, and removed their slippers, lines of men filled the mosques, rising and falling, praying and crying '*Allah!*', or listening to a sermon. At other times mosques were packed with individuals praying or reciting the Koran.[6] In the West churches combined the roles of theatre, club and market, and could be filthy. St Paul's Cathedral in London, for example, swarmed with prostitutes, merchants and workmen for hire. In Constantinople, wrote an astonished Christian, 'No one lounges or walks about a church [mosque], no one chatters with one another, and nothing else is heard but fervent prayer.'[7]

Mosques were used for education as well as prayer. On either side of the Fatih mosque, two groups of eight many-domed *medreses*, or colleges, one or two storeys high, named after the Black Sea and the White Sea (the Mediterranean) respectively, provided board, lodging and instruction for about a thousand students. The senior Muslim academic institution in the empire, the nursery of generations of future judges and *ulema* (the learned men who ran mosques and the legal system), the Fatih *medrese* is regarded today as an ancestor of Istanbul University; some former *medrese* buildings are used for student accommodation. Endowed with a library of 1,770 books, of which 839 had been donated by the Conqueror himself, it provided a traditional Muslim education, based on the ten sciences: grammar, syntax, logic, scholastic philosophy, humanity, signification, exposition, euphuism, geometry and astronomy. Successful students could become *imams*, or teachers, at a mosque. If they pursued higher studies of jurisprudence, rhetoric, tradition, dogma and exegesis, they could become *kadis* (judges), either in Constantinople or in other cities of the empire.

Around the Fatih mosque the Sultan also built more domed complexes, as orderly as an army on parade. There was a hospice for dervishes; a *han*, or inn, for travellers; a hospital which provided patients with two meals a day (partridge and pheasant were often on the menu), and music to soothe the sick and insane; an *imaret*, or soup-kitchen, where food was distributed to the poor; and a *hamam*, or bath-house.

Over a thousand persons received two meals a day at Fatih. The Fatih complex was copied in Constantinople and beyond, for the Ottoman Empire was a system of social welfare as well as a dynastic state. In the words of a Greek from the city, Theodore Cantacuzenos, a contemporary of Mehmed II and his son Bayezid II: 'Generally the Turkish lords, of every rank, only think of building churches [*sic*] and hospitals and to endow them and make hostelries for travellers, cutting roads, building bridges, drains and several other charities which they perform, with the result that I esteem beyond all comparison Turkish lords far more generous than our Christian lords.'

The mosques of Constantinople were also part of the city's economic fabric. They were funded by the revenues of foundations, or *vakifs*, which owned houses, water systems or bazaars in the city. The *vakif* which Mehmed II created for the Fatih mosque was endowed with properties such as a nearby leather or saddle market containing 110 shops. Of the revenue of the *vakif* – 1.5 million *akces* or 30,000 Venetian gold ducats – 869,280 *akces* were spent on personnel, 461,417 on food for the hospice, 72,000 on the hospital itself, and 18,522 in repairs. The total staff, in the entire complex, was 383.[8]

Every mosque had a large staff of *ulema*, or learned men. Unlike the Sultan's servants and the Janissaries, they were born Muslims. This was the career which absorbed much of the energy and ambition of the Turks of Constantinople. *Sheikhs* delivered sermons; *imams* led prayers; *muezzins* chanted the call to prayer, or recited verses from the Koran, as one Italian traveller wrote, 'in a soprano's voice, full of unction, clear and graceful. To hear them without seeing them one would think they were little children.' Mosques also employed door-keepers, lesson readers, supervisors of ablutions, all enumerated and salaried, with the Ottoman obsession for lists and regulations, in the foundation deed of a *vakif*. The proportion of the *vakif* revenues devoted to their salaries helps explain why so many Turks wanted to found, or work in, mosques. Until this century, the founders' descendants could inherit the right to administer, and receive salaries from, the *vakifs*. Like properties assigned to tax-avoiding family trusts in post-war Britain, the *vakif* provided a house and income secure from the grasp of the state.

The life of a famous writer like 'the Sultan of poets' Baqi (1520–99), the favourite poet of Suleyman the Magnificent, began and ended at the mosque of Fatih. Son of one of the mosque's muezzin, after an interval as a saddler's apprentice he turned to the law, and rose to be a teacher at another mosque in the city. In an early poem he celebrated a particular obsession of the Ottomans: the replacement of church towers and their 'jangled bells' by minarets and the sound of the muezzin's call to prayer. The right move in the capital could win high office, and property, in a distant provincial city. Baqi became Kadi first of Mecca then of Constantinople itself, and subsequently rose to be the supreme legal official (*kadiasker*) of the European provinces of the empire. The Mufti of Constantinople himself conducted Baqi's funeral service before an immense assembly in the Fatih mosque.[9]

Constantinople became more Muslim after Mehmed II's death. His son Bayezid II was a pious and pacific ruler known as *Veli*, the Saint. He believed that his father 'by the counsel of mischiefmakers and hypocrites' had 'infringed the Law of the Prophet'. Most of the Conqueror's Italian pictures and sculptures were sold in disgust. The erotic frescos in the palace were painted over. Mehmed II's frequent use of *urf*, the Sultan's executive authority, and of *kanun* or state law, as a basis for government regulations, was condemned as contrary to the holy law of Islam.*

At the head of the *ulema* was the Mufti of Constantinople, a post created by Mehmed II. By the late fifteenth century, the Mufti, also called *Seyhulislam*, was the third man in the state after the Sultan and Grand Vizier. On occasion Bayezid II stood to receive him and gave him a seat higher than his own. The Mufti issued *fetvas* (or fatwas), religious rulings guaranteeing that the Sultan's acts were in accordance with the *sheriat*. Despite all the Sultan's military power, this legitimizing role was considered so important that one Mufti remembered: 'Sultan Mehmed was very insistent with me to the end that I should give *fetvas*.' By the late seventeenth century it could be said of the Mufti: 'He is possessed of absolute power in matters of religion. Affairs of state derive from religion; religion is the root, the state the branch. The only chief of religion is the *Seyhulislam*, the only chief of the state the Grand Vizier, but the chief of them both is the Sultan.'

By then the *ulema* had become a cultivated, semi-hereditary *noblesse de robe*, distinct from the power élite based on the Bab-i Aali, the High or Exalted Gate, known in the West as the Sublime Porte, but with a considerable influence on the manners and customs of the city itself. In the eighteenth century twenty-four muftis of Constantinople were sons of

---

*However state law remained important. In 1508, referring to the use of *urf*, one of Bayezid's sons, Korkud, asked not to be Sultan since, in a land like Rum (the Ottoman Empire), it was impossible to be both a good ruler and a good Muslim.

former muftis of the city; they were called 'cradle *ulema*'. The Durrizade family, for example, produced six muftis for ten terms of office, between 1734 and 1920. The *ulema* often saw the Sultan at Friday prayers and in diplomatic despatches were referred to as 'the old nobility'.[10]

Bayezid II was a relatively peaceful monarch, in part because of the threat from his brother, Fatih's favourite son Cem – a popular prince who might have continued his father's open-minded policies. Cem had fled to Europe, where he became a pawn in the great game between the Ottoman Empire and its enemies. He was the only Ottoman who realized the dynastic dream of reaching Rome – although not as a conquering general. In return for a subsidy from Bayezid II, negotiated through a Genoese merchant of Galata, the Pope kept Cem in the Vatican as an 'honoured guest' – that is, a prisoner. He died, perhaps poisoned, in Naples in 1495. In 1512 Bayezid II was succeeded by his son Selim, known as *Yavuz Selim*, Selim the Resolute.

Like his grandfather the Conqueror, Selim I regarded himself as a new Alexander the Great, ordered by God to conquer the world from the East to the West. In 1517 he defeated his principal Muslim rival, the Mameluke Sultan of Egypt, who was hanged from one of the gates of Cairo. For the next four centuries, Egypt, Syria, and the part of Arabia containing the two holy cities of Mecca and Medina were provinces of the Ottoman Empire. The Ottoman Sultan ruled over half the Middle East and almost all the Balkans. He was the most powerful Muslim ruler, the supreme Imam, guardian of the pilgrimage routes to Medina and Mecca. One of his proudest titles was henceforth 'Servant of the Two Holy Places'. The Ottoman Sultan's power, piety and prestige left him with no rival, except in distant Morocco and India, for his title of 'Caliph of God on earth'. The last shadow Abbasid Caliph, a descendant of the Abbasid caliphs of Baghdad, who had become a paid official of the Mameluke Sultan in Cairo, died there forgotten in 1543.[11] After 1517, in a way it had not been before, Constantinople was capital of Islam. In official lists of cities of the Ottoman Empire, it was followed by the former dynastic capitals, Edirne and Bursa. They preceded the holy cities of Mecca, Medina and Jerusalem. The former Muslim capitals – Damascus 'which exhales the balm of Paradise', Baghdad 'the house of salvation' and Cairo 'the incomparable' – ranked seventh, eighth and ninth.

The Prophet's senior descendant, the Emir and Sherif of Mecca, sent

Selim I the keys of the Ka'ba, the sacred black rock in the middle of the great mosque at Mecca. Ottoman power, more than Muslim solidarity, induced him to submit to the Sultan without a shot being fired. The Sherif of Mecca needed Egyptian wheat to feed the Hejaz, and Ottoman protection against Portuguese plans to control the Red Sea and conquer Mecca from Portugal's power-base in India. In return the prestige of the Sherifs so impressed the Ottomans that they received greater privileges and pensions than they had enjoyed under the sultans of Egypt.[12]

With the return of prosperity and the expansion of the empire, the population of Constantinople rose rapidly. From some 80,000 in the last years of Fatih's reign, it reached approximately 400,000 in 1530. Mosque construction matched the growth in population. Whatever their date, Constantinople's mosques were built in the same severe Ottoman imperial style, using the grey stone quarried on the southern shores of the Sea of Marmara. As Godfrey Goodwin says, tradition was 'the most prominent Ottoman architect at all periods'. Officials, princesses, above all the sultans themselves, paid for the mosques. Aya Sofya was the supreme imperial mosque of the city with the largest *vakif*, supported by revenues from the city's customs, the main bazaar, and houses erected outside the city walls. Fatih's son Bayezid built a mosque (1500–6) at the entrance to the main bazaar. In order to make Islam as visible as possible, his grandson Selim I and his great-grandson Suleyman built mosques on hills overlooking the Golden Horn: the Selimiye (1518–22), the Shehzade (1542–8) and the Suleymaniye (1548–57).

The Suleymaniye was surrounded by a phalanx of colleges, libraries, shops and hospitals larger than those around Fatih: the library and the hospital, which had the reputation of curing the sick 'within three days', still function today. The Shehzade and Suleymaniye mosques were the work of Sinan, head of the *Hassa Mimarlar Ocagi* (Imperial Architects Organization) from 1538 until his death fifty years later, aged about 90. Probably born an Armenian in central Anatolia, after being 'gathered' into the *devshirme*, Sinan had first served as a Janissary and an engineer. He built or restored 477 buildings (of which 159 were mosques), 319 of them in Constantinople, often producing architects' models for the Sultan's inspection before construction began. The stream of orders Sinan sent out, about the opening of new windows in an old mosque, the construction of drains, or the shortage of skilled carpenters, show his grasp of detail. His surviving buildings prove him the greatest and most prolific architect in Ottoman history.[13]

The imperial mosques were not only places of worship but also assertions in stone of the dynasty's orthodoxy, justice, charity and generosity. Like the art galleries commissioned by modern millionaires, or the mosques built by Gulf sheikhs, the sultans' mosques at once advertised and absolved their wealth. According to one eighteenth-century estimate, they fed 30,000 people a day in the capital – thereby helping to ensure that hunger never reached the danger level of Paris in 1789. Western visitors agreed that – except in the Greek districts – there were fewer beggars in Constantinople than in any other city in Europe.[14]

Ottoman mosques were also assertions of power, proclaiming the Sultan's right to rule as 'God's shadow on earth', and the permanence and glory of his empire. A dome was a symbol of imperial unity. The sultans' mosques had larger domes than others, and two or four minarets; other mosques never had more than one. To challenge the achievements of King Solomon, Alexander the Great and Justinian, Suleyman the Magnificent, in operations of enormous complexity and expense, had granite columns transported from Baalbek,* Alexandria and within Constantinople, to be incorporated in the majestic interior of the Suleymaniye mosque. The mosque itself, started after the Emperor Charles V had agreed to pay him tribute in 1547, may have been a celebration of his supremacy in Europe.[15]

In 1609 the empire was exhausted by long and unsuccessful wars with Austria and Persia. The economy was in ruins. Both the Grand Vizier and the Mufti begged Sultan Ahmed I not to construct a new mosque. Yet he insisted – and helped dig the foundations himself. The poet Ca'fer revealed the purpose of the new mosque, the largest in the city, visible to all ships sailing in from the south:

> As the world revealed itself with beautiful images,
> The mosque of the Ruler of the World proclaimed his aspect . . .
> No one [but Sultan Ahmed] could build a mosque like this,
> For there is not another dignified ruler of the people his equal.
> The victorious shah and sovereign ruler Ahmed Han
> What works he created in that most crafted Ka'aba![16]

The Sultanahmed mosque is the only mosque outside Medina with six minarets. By the second half of the seventeenth century there were

*From the Temple of the Sun, which had also supplied columns a thousand years earlier for Haghia Sophia.

485 mosques and 4,492 *mesjids* (oratories not used for Friday noon prayers) in Constantinople.* Constantinople was not the most Muslim city in the world, but no city had more mosques. The question is frequently asked – where did the wealth of the Ottoman Empire go? One answer is: on mosque construction.[17]

The domes and minarets of the imperial mosques create the incomparable skyline of modern Istanbul. In the past their flat rectangular spaces, clean straight lines and soaring grey or white stone structures stood out against a mass of red-roofed houses. Since there was so much space within the city walls, most people in the city were able to live in the privacy of small two- to four-roomed houses rather than, as in Venice or Cairo, in large communal blocks. Melchior Lorichs's drawing of around 1560 shows houses continuously lining the Golden Horn from the palace to the city walls. Western travellers were generally contemptuous, calling them badly built and 'less than mediocre'.

The houses' wooden walls, projecting upper storeys, and latticed windows – to prevent men in the street from seeing the women within – gave the streets of Constantinople 'a singular aspect of mystery and gloom'. Moreover the Imperial Architects Organization was obliged to respect the privacy demanded by Islam. Private houses were built as casually as Muslim tombstones were scattered in the graveyards. In some districts the streets were so crooked and narrow, without regularity or order, that houses on either side almost touched each other. To heighten privacy, many streets were *cikmaz*, culs de sac. The largest street, the *divan yolu* ('way to the palace') which proceeded through the middle of the city to the walls, was based on the principal Byzantine thoroughfare, the *mese*. Constantinople did not possess the officially planned streets which had already appeared in Rome, Florence and Venice, and would be built in Paris after 1600. There was no equivalent to the succession of concentric rectangles in which Peking, the new imperial capital of China, was being laid out after 1421.

The confusion was accentuated by the presence of five separate hills south of the Golden Horn, and the great hill of Galata on the other side. Streets climbed over hills and valleys in every direction, making the city a mass of crooked lanes, wooden houses, walls, gardens, graveyards. The atmosphere of the disorderly Ottoman city remains in a few resid-

---

*In comparison there were about 100 churches in the city of London in the sixteenth century, and 162 churches and chapels in Paris in the eighteenth century.

ential quarters, such as the area of winding streets and wooden houses between Sultanahmed and the sea. It is evoked by the great Italian travel writer Edmondo de Amicis, who visited Constantinople in 1874 when the appearance of most quarters had hardly changed from previous centuries:

> The streets, bent into infinite angles, wind about among small hills, are raised on terraces, skirt ravines; pass under aqueducts, break into alleys, run down steps, through bushes, rocks, ruins, sand, hills. Here and there the great city takes as it were a breathing time in the country, and then begins again thicker, livelier, more highly coloured . . .[18]

In this chaotic wooden city, the mosque complexes were the only element of urban order.

Orthodox Islam is relatively austere. There is little ceremonial and no music. However, Constantinople also attracted a more dramatic form of Islam: the dervish *tekke*, or lodge. Dervishes practised Sufism, the drive for mystic ecstasy and loss of self by union with God. This personal search for God most often took the form of *zikir*, the ceremony of the recollection and repetition of His name.

The dervishes were organized into brotherhoods, under a particular guide or *sheikh*, devoted to the memory of 'friends of God', who were, for some Muslims, equivalents of Christian saints. Dervish lodges were usually constructed beside the tomb of a 'friend of God', with an open window looking on to the street, through which passers-by could pay their respects. These 'friends of God', like Abu Ayyub or Fatih himself, were believed to exist beside their tombs in 'the infinite world'. There they had the power to protect and bestow favours on their followers in 'the finite world'.

Muslims paid frequent visits to their tombs to ask for cures for ailments, to pray for success in a birth, a circumcision, or a marriage – or simply to imbibe the saint's 'spiritual aura'. As in Christian countries, music was played, incense burnt, offerings made: meat, money, a shawl. A lamp burnt with sweet oil in a niche in the wall. Coloured rags were tied to the window grating or the tomb, to remind the saint of the expected blessings. A stone beside the tomb of a 'friend of God' at Merdivenkoy, opposite Constantinople in Asia, was believed to grant the wish of any person standing on it. In the nineteenth century, according to an English resident, Lucy Garnett, 'A Turkish lady of my acquaintance, the late Besma Sultan, attributed her elevation to the high and exceptional position of legal wife of Sultan Abdul Medjid to the wish she mentally expressed when standing on this stone, after of course depositing her devotional offering on the neighbouring shrine.'

The larger *tekkes* included separate living quarters for families, bachelors and the sheikh, a prayer hall (*semahane*) where the *zikir* took place, a library, a dining hall and a large kitchen building. Food was sacred in dervish eyes. At the end of a meal's ritual preparation, the sheikh would chant:

> We are the Sufis on the path; we are those who dine at the table of
>   the King.
> Make eternal, O Lord, this bowl and this feast.[19]

The most fashionable dervish order in Constantinople was the Mevlevi. Its main lodge was at the end of what is now Istiklal Caddesi in Galata (Beyoglu). In some ways the dervish lodges were the equivalent of Christian monasteries, and the Galata *mevlevihanesi* was founded by Mehmed II on the site of a Byzantine monastery – perhaps in order to assert the superiority of Islam over Christianity. There the Mevlevis, wearing a special turban and long woollen skirt, performed (on occasion still perform) a slow ritual dance. With arms outstretched, eyes closed, and heads inclined on the left shoulder, they whirled in a circle, their robes flaring around them, 'to the music of flute and tambourine, accompanied by a monotonous chant on the unity of God and the nullity of earthly existence'. So intense was their rapture that they could whirl for fifteen minutes at a time, without giddiness or fatigue.[20]

Another order, the Rufai, or Howling Dervishes, discovered the pleasure of pain. In their main lodge at Uskudar in Asia, they performed the *zikir*, shouting and sobbing '*Ya Allah! Ya Hu!*' (Oh God! Oh Him!) with sepulchral howls, rising and falling like a field of wheat in a wind. Once they had achieved delirium, metal instruments, with points in their bulbous ends, were taken down from the walls. They were heated in a brazier, and held red-hot against the dervish's skin, inserted in his mouth, or pressed upon his eyeballs. 'Others seize daggers from their resting place on the walls or hot coals from the brazier with which they cut or burn their flesh. Some fall, overcome by their excitement, into the arms of their brethren; and all finally succumb, exhausted and unconscious [and blood-stained], on the floor.' The breath of their sheikh, the holy words he uttered, were believed to heal all wounds.

In the nineteenth century the Rufai lodge, lined with 'atrocious instruments,' reminded Théophile Gautier of a torture chamber of the Inquisition. But he was seeing through ironic Parisian eyes. To the dervishes their pain symbolized renunciation of individual will and the material world. Their scars were 'roses', leading them to closer communion with 'the rose-bush' – Allah himself.[21]

Dervish rites and fervour, their 'horrid howls and yells' could arouse disapproval from the *ulema* of the mosques. They could be suspected of innovation, or abominable practices. Many of their beliefs were linked to the detested heresy of Shi'ism, a rival form of Islam doubly hated after its adoption in 1506 as the state religion of Persia, the principal enemy of the empire. One dervish, Ismail Mashuki, known as 'the boy sheikh', attracted congregations of thousands in Aya Sofya. Alarmed at his ecstatic mysticism, the Mufti ordered him executed in 1529 at the age of 21. The sites where his head and trunk were buried became centres of pilgrimage.

For their part, the dervishes were proud of their secret communion with God, and often mocked what they regarded as the ignorance and hypocrisy of the *ulema*. One dervish wrote: 'O orthodox teacher, to me the mosque and the tavern are one. The voice of the pious and the cry of the drunken are one.' Sufism, rather than the mosque, satisfied many Muslims' yearning for union with God. Bayezid II himself was a sufi, who brought the Halveti order to Constantinople and settled it on the site of a former Orthodox monastery. Halvetis specialized in solitary silent retreats in windowless cells, with as little food and sleep as possible: they would leave only to go to mosque, along a corridor shielding them from human contact.

By the nineteenth century there were, in Constantinople, 300 lodges and thirty-seven active brotherhoods, to one of which most Muslim men were affiliated. A *tekke* could combine the excitements of a modern opera-house, commune and aerobics class. One dervish praised the skills of his 'guide' in lines which convey the power of Sufism:

> My teacher and my master is Zakiri.
> In all the arts his match is hard to find.
> His name is Hasan and his nature is like Husayn.
> God beautified him with spiritual insight.
> The fame of his *zikir* reaches the horizons.
> His tune is the food of the spirit of lovers.
> He passes the five times of prayer as Imam.

> He is the joy of those who know rhythm.
> He spends months and years in prayer.
> He is the truth of those who know Union.[22]

The prime religious duties of Muslims were pilgrimage to Mecca, alms-giving, fasting during Ramadan, proclamation of belief in Allah, and above all to pray five times a day – before dawn, at midday, three hours later in the middle of the afternoon, in the evening before sunset, and about an hour after sunset. The faithful were called to prayer by the muezzin, as he walked around the open terraces on the minarets, built specifically to ensure that the call could be heard in every direction:

> God is most great. I testify that there is no god but Allah. I testify that Muhammad is the Prophet of Allah. Come to prayer! Come to salvation! There is no god but Allah.

In a quiet street near a mosque, he can still deafen today. Before the nineteenth century there were few carriages and horses. The streets were 'so silent that people's voices were heard as in a room' according to a British traveller, Dr Meryon, in 1810; the muezzin's call to prayer was one of the loudest sounds in the city.

Time itself was Muslim. For Muslims and Jews the hours of the day were measured, not from midnight but from sunset. For them 12 a.m. was therefore at a changing time in the evening rather than a fixed time at night. Muezzins were human clocks: the sound of their call to prayer was the standard means of checking the time. Despite the presence of a colony of foreign clock and watch makers in Galata (including, in the early eighteenth century, the father of Jean-Jacques Rousseau), and frequent imports from abroad, only the richest Muslims had mechanical clocks, and they often broke down.

Until the fall of the empire, Islam not only measured but occupied the hours. Although the Koran was in Arabic, a language of which few Turkish-speakers understood more than a few words, many Muslims learnt it by heart. Evliya Celebi, for example, could recite it quickly in seven hours, without hurrying in eight: as a reward he became a *musahib*, or chamberlain, in the palace. Recitation of the Koran was the principal entertainment of the Muslim city. A new Koran reciter aroused as much joy, and critical appraisal, in Constantinople, as a new opera singer in Milan. Muslims stopped whatever they were doing when they heard the call to prayer. Mouradgea d'Ohsson, a

Constantinople-born Armenian and one of the city's greatest historians, wrote:

> Unless you have seen this nation on its own ground, you will never have anything but an imperfect idea of its constant and scrupulous attention, men and women, high and low, rich and poor, priests and laymen to satisfy this desire of the five *namaz* [prayers]. One would say that this immense population is nothing but one religious order.

During the nights of Ramadan, when the mosques were packed with believers, and their domes and minarets were outlined by candles, the city glowed with Islam. (The effect cannot be compared to modern Ramadan illuminations, which compete with advertising and street lighting.) The night of 27 Ramadan was 'the night of power', better than a thousand months. Aya Sofya, overflowing with faithful, was lit so brightly that it flashed in the night like a meteor. In this city of faith, there was no place for sceptics. Lutfi Tokadi, one of the first librarians at the Fatih library, a protégé of the Conqueror and outstanding mathematician, mocked superstition. He was executed in 1494, on the orders of Bayezid II, in front of large crowds in the Hippodrome, on the grounds of 'indifference'.[23]

Islam also gave the Ottoman dynasty a nimbus of sanctity. Inside the mosques the *hutbe*, or sermon after prayers, was read in the Sultan's name. From the early seventeenth century until the end of the empire, part of the Sultan's inauguration ritual was to be girded with the dragon-handled sword of Osman, founder of the dynasty. The ceremony, performed by a leading sheikh, generally the Grand Master of the Mevlevis, took place on a platform in the main courtyard of the most sacred mosque in the city, at Eyup.

The greatest annual ceremony in Constantinople, the departure of the pilgrim caravan to Mecca on 12 Redjeb,* was associated with the Ottoman dynasty. The caravan was led by a special official, the *Surre Emini*. Every year until the First World War the Sultan sent a piece of black cloth covered in gold embroidery, the *mahmal*, to cover the Ka'ba in Mecca, and for the Emir of Mecca gold, a letter enclosed in four silk bags, and a cloak of cloth of gold lined with ermine. His gifts were handed over in the palace by the chief black eunuch to the Surre Emini. A richly caparisoned camel, said to be descended from those used by

---

*Since the Muslim calendar is a lunar calendar, this date is a movable feast.

the Prophet, carried the *mahmal* out of the palace, followed by another camel bearing a replica of the Prophet's saddle, and seven sacred mules with more presents. A procession escorted by officials, guards, Arab dancers, dervishes, perfume-sprinklers, tambourine players, and half the Muslim population of the city, paraded from the palace through the streets as far as Beshiktash, near where the first motorway bridge now crosses the Bosphorus. Pilgrims joined along the route. While the sacred camel returned to the palace until the following year, the pilgrims crossed over to Uskudar in Asia, where, with many displays of affection, they took leave of their relations before starting the long, hard road to Mecca.[24]

One of the principal sources of self-esteem and popular respect for the Ottoman dynasty, after 1517, was its protection of the pilgrim route to the Hejaz through an expensive system of inns, armed escorts and well-bribed bedouin tribes. A special treasury in Constantinople collected revenues from a variety of sources, including *vakifs*, and sent them every year for the mosques and the poor in the Hejaz. By the eighteenth century the pilgrimage cost more than the upkeep of the imperial palace, absorbing between 10 and 17 per cent of government revenue.[25]

The Sultan and his palace were further sanctified by the arrival of relics of the Prophet from Cairo and Mecca after 1517. They included the Prophet's cloak, seal and swords, one of his teeth, and hairs from his beard. His banner, of black wool, arrived from Damascus in 1593. These relics were not exposed in a mosque for public reverence but, like the Holy Shroud of Turin, remained secluded in the ruler's palace, as a private dynastic treasure – although the banner of the Prophet, as we shall see, was paraded through the streets of Constantinople at moments of supreme tension. The special Pavilion of the Holy Mantle, faced with marble panels taken from Cairo, was built for them in the third court of the imperial palace near the Sultan's bedroom. The Koran was recited there continously, day and night, by relays of readers. Once a year on 15 Ramadan, the Holy Mantle was washed in rose water by the pages of the privy chamber. Members of the imperial family (men and women) and the government were then admitted, by order of precedence, to revere it. Each individual was given a bottle containing water in which the mantle had been washed, and a piece of paper engraved with the seal of the Prophet. They then soaked the latter in the former, and swallowed it.[26]

The Sultan's Friday prayers, a ceremony later known as the *selamlik*, demonstrated both his piety and his power to the city. Except on solemn festivals, Western monarchs worshipped God in the chapels of their palaces, visible only to their courts and a restricted number of the public. In Constantinople, however, most sultans went in state to a public mosque, usually Fatih or the Suleymaniye, every Friday. Luigi Bassano, a former page, described Suleyman the Magnificent's procession as he went to mosque:

> The order of his cavalcade is as follows: First go thirty *chiaous* or Mace-bearers, crying '*Ottea, ottea, ste chinachera gellar*', which is to say: 'here comes Our Lord the Sultan' and dealing furious blows. They are followed by perhaps two thousand Janissaries on foot, with swords, axes at their girdles and guns with barrels five palms long at their backs; and by about the same number of *spahis* [cavalry] and Solacks [the Sultan's guards] on horseback with swords, bows and arrows and maces at their saddle bows. All march in silence nothing being heard but the sound of their feet and the trampling of the horses. Then come fifteen or twenty led horses all with rich head-trappings adorned with carbuncles, diamonds, sapphires, turquoises and great pearls, the saddles not being seen becasue they are covered with scarlet velvet. Near the Grand Turk himself no one rides but four grooms walking on either side of him about a pike's length off to keep off the people, unless he should call one of the pashas or other officers to talk with him. Before him always go three pages, one carrying his bow and arrows, another his sabre and the third a golden bottle of scented water to wash with at the door of the great mosque, wherein having entered he goes to a place raised about four cubits, surrounded with blinds called jalousies for his especial use. Here he prays alone unless one of his sons be with him. The people who attend him, generally about four thousand, are in the body of the mosque below. This he does every Friday for the satisfaction of his people or as some say and as I believe, because it is his duty to do so. He remains in the Mosque about two hours and then returns always by the way he came [usually the Divan Yolu] ever looking at the populace with a benignant countenance and returning the salutations of everybody, whether Christian, Turk or Jew, man or woman, moving his head a little, now to the right, now to the left, in sign of recognition of those who throng the way. These do not remove their head-gear [as they would have done in the West] which is held to be improper but only bow their heads. So any Friday may the Grand Turk be seen, in spite of the liars who say he never shows himself at all.

The *selamlik* continued, in different forms, until 27 February 1924. In 1573 a French diplomat, Philippe du Fresne Canaye, was particularly impressed by the silence surrounding Selim II. The Sultan appeared to have the power to turn men to stone. His horse had been deprived of food and sleep the night before, to ensure that it walked with 'the slow and heavy step suitable to the majesty of such a great king'. For Thomas Watkins two hundred years later, the *selamlik* was

> the most magnificent and interesting [procession] I ever beheld. The rich and various costumes, the beauty and furniture of the Arabian horses, the comely appearance of the janizaries and *bostangis* or corps of royal gardeners (whose singularly formed caps of scarlet cloth are particularly remarkable) in a word the splendour, the novelty, the silence and solemnity of this spectacle cannot I think but make a most powerful impression upon every foreign spectator.[27]

One Sultan was killed by his *selamlik*. On 13 December 1754, although close to death, Mahmud I was determined to go to Friday prayers. On the way back from the mosque, in the first courtyard of the palace, he died, literally 'in the saddle'.[28]

The Islamicization of Constantinople had two principal results. After the death of Mehmed II, there are few references to an 'impious' Sultan or 'accursed city'. There could be no Muslim backlash against this city of mosques and saints. The Ottoman Sultan, at first a relatively secular figure compared to the Abbasid Caliph or the Byzantine Emperor, acquired an aura of holiness. His subjects prayed for his life and prosperity in the mosque, in the market-place, after a meal. The sultans' tombs, built throughout the city from Eyup to Aya Sofya, were visited during Ramadan and the seven holy nights as if they were shrines. The Ottomans were regarded as a blessed dynasty to whom eternity was promised. The late sixteenth-century writer Mustafa Ali, who by no means lacked critical spirit, wrote: 'Their religious convictions being immaculate, and their character like a shining mirror, it has never happened that a single member of that noble family ever swerved from the road of orthodoxy.'[29]

The Islamicization of the city also contributed to the closing of the Ottoman mind. It was sodden by a surfeit of religion, as the modern mind is sodden by a surfeit of television. Muslim Constantinople lacked the intellectual originality, and spirit of enquiry, of Baghdad or Cordoba. It produced few literary masterpieces. With his taste for Persian culture, Mehmed II had brought a famous philosopher, Nasiruddin Tusi, from Iran to debate an old Islamic controversy: whether religion and philosophy could be reconciled, and whether human logic was necessary to comprehend God. The Ottoman *ulema*, rejecting the Persian viewpoint, concluded that the application of reason to religion could only lead to error, and concentrated on an ever-narrowing scholastic approach.

After 1454 printing changed the face of Europe. By 1500 every major city from Oxford to Naples had a printing press, and publishing was one of the largest industries in western Europe. Printed books spread literacy, knowledge and, through the substitution of duplication for copying, a spirit of precision. However, in 1515 a decree of Selim I threatened with death anyone occupying himself with the science of printing. Possibly the government wished to restrict the use of books to an élite. The *ulema* may have opposed printing on the grounds of its danger to public order and their own interpretation of Islam. The lightning spread of Protestantism in Catholic Europe, for example, would have been impossible without the 300,000 copies of Luther's works which were printed between 1517 and 1520.[30]

A further reason for opposition to printing was the mystical bond between Islam and calligraphy, the art of fine writing. Because the Koran is the literal word of God, eternal and divine, the physical act of writing it is especially meritorious; its reproduction by machine could appear blasphemous. The Prophet himself is believed to have said: 'Good writing makes the truth stand out.' No Muslim dynasty valued calligraphy as highly as the Ottomans: many sultans were calligraphers themselves. The greatest of Ottoman calligraphers, Hamdullah al-Amasi (1429–1520), who wrote out forty-seven Korans, was working in Constantinople at the time western Europe was embracing print. He had a workshop in the palace; his pupil Bayezid II felt honoured to hold the master's ink-pot. The style he created, known as the 'Seyh Hamdullah style', flourished for the next three centuries.

There is a saying: 'The Koran was revealed in Mecca, recited in Egypt and written in Istanbul.' Pen and ink (often scented, coloured or gilded) were as revered in Constantinople as, in other cultures, swords or boomerangs. A 'victorious army' of calligraphic inscriptions covers the surfaces of the mosques and palaces of the city. The calligraphers were one of the city's main trade guilds and could provide copies cheaply and quickly. They worked in styles which could differ as much as Dürer and Clouet. Other craftsmen framed pieces of calligraphy, surrounded them with marbled paper, gilded them or decorated them with flowers. They were then hung on the wall, in mosques or houses, in the same fashion as pictures in the West. For all these reasons, dynastic, ideological, commercial, aesthetic, there was no printing revolution in Constantinople. A sixteenth-century ambassador of the Holy Roman

Emperor, the Baron de Busbecq, a perceptive observer of the city, wrote:

> No nation has shown less reluctance to adopt the useful inventions of others: for example they have appropriated to their own use large and small cannons and many other of our discoveries. They have, however, never been able to bring themselves to print books and set up public clocks. They hold that their scriptures, that is their sacred books, would no longer be scriptures if they were printed; and if they established public clocks they think that the authority of their muezzins and their ancient rites would suffer diminution.[31]

The distaste for printing was not shared by non-Muslims. In 1493 a code of Jewish law in Hebrew, *The Four Columns*, was printed by David and Samuel Nahmias, as they wrote, 'here in the great Constantinople, under Muslim rule of the great King Sultan Bayezid, may he live for ever, may the Lord be his help and his rule be exalted!' It was the first book printed in the Ottoman Empire, and was followed by other works of Jewish law and religious commentary.

In 1567 the first Armenian press was established, by an Armenian educated in Venice, in St Nicholas church near Yenikapi. It only lasted three years, but, after another false start in 1677–9, from 1698 Constantinople always contained a functioning Armenian press – although it did not rival the other world cities of Venice and Amsterdam as a centre of Armenian printing until the nineteenth century. Not until 1627 was a Greek press started with the help of the English ambassador, beside his embassy in Galata. Most of its early publications were anti-Catholic or anti-Jewish tracts. It had lasted for less than a year when, following representations from the French ambassador, protector of the Catholic Church in the Ottoman Empire, it was destroyed by Janissaries. However, there was no restriction on the import of books. Through books printed abroad, generally in Venice, the minorities in Constantinople henceforth had quicker access than the Ottoman ruling class to printed information and the latest discoveries. The supremacy of the Ottoman élite was being undermined.

Distaste for print was not the only example of the *ulema*'s resistance to the spread of knowledge. In 1580 the Mufti incited a mob to destroy a large, ultra-modern observatory completed three years before in Galata for Sultan Murad III: the Mufti considered it a bad omen and a source of calamity for the empire. The next Ottoman observatory did not open until 1868. In 1605 the mechanical organ sent by Elizabeth I to Mehmed III was destroyed, since its location within the sacred precincts of Topkapi palace was considered unsuitable. In 1716 the Mufti prevented donation to a public library of books on history, astronomy and philosophy from the library of a former Grand Vizier. Having created a Muslim city, the Ottoman dynasty, perhaps without fully realizing, had become its prisoner.[32]

Constantinople was, and remains, a city of antitheses. It had become a holy city for Muslims. At the same time it remained a holy city for Orthodox Christians. Had not the last Byzantine Emperor called it, in a speech to his troops, 'this city which thrice blessed Constantine the Great [a saint in the Orthodox calendar] founded and dedicated to the all holy, most chaste Mother of God, our Lady Mary, the eternal virgin'? The city had been blessed by a profusion of holy relics. It had contained the robe of the Mother of God and 'the Purple Cloak, the Spear, the Sponge and the Reed [proffered to Christ during the Crucifixion], which allowed us when we venerated them to believe that we saw Him raised upon the Cross'. Lesser relics included the table from the Last Supper, the doors of Noah's Ark, the body of the Apostle Andrew. Most relics had disappeared in the sacks of 1204 and 1453. The aura of holiness remained.[33]

After 1453 most Europeans believed that a state could flourish only if it imposed religious uniformity. In the sixteenth century 'heretics' were burnt alive in London and Berlin, massacred in Paris, expelled from Vienna. In 1685 Louis XIV expelled all Huguenots from France; until 1700 appreciative crowds, led by kings and queens of Spain, watched heretics burn alive in the Plaza Mayor of Madrid. The Ottoman Empire, however, gave religious freedom to Christians and Jews. George of Hungary wrote in the fifteenth century: 'The Turks do not compel anyone to renounce his faith, do not try hard to persuade anyone and do not have a great opinion of renegades.' In the seventeenth, in the view of the traveller and writer Monsieur de La Motraye: 'There is no country on earth where the exercise of all sorts of Religions is more free and less subject to being troubled, than in Turkey.' He knew what he was writing about, since he himself was a Huguenot forced to leave France after 1685.[34]

A moment of truth occurred in the sixteenth century. In 1521, and again in 1537, at a time of war with Christian powers, Suleyman the Magnificent, son of Yavuz Selim, considered converting all the churches into mosques, even in 1521 killing all Christians who did not accept Islam. The 'Law-Giver', as he was subsequently known in Turkish, could not understand why, since Constantinople had refused to surrender, it had, contrary to the holy law of Islam, kept its churches. On both occasions the city's establishment intervened to protect the *status quo*. In 1521 the Patriarch was forewarned by the Mufti and the Grand Vizier. A lawyer found him three aged Janissaries who swore that they had seen Greek notables surrendering the keys of their districts to the Conqueror on a golden bowl.

On the second occasion, the area between the palace and Aya Sofya was crowded with Muslims, Christians and Jews awaiting the decision. The Patriarch was drenched in sweat like Christ on the Cross. However the Grand Vizier supported him. The Mufti, as the highest Muslim legal authority, pronounced: 'As far as was known Constantinople was taken by force; but the fact that the churches were untouched must mean that the city surrendered by capitulation.' The Sultan accepted the decision.[35]

For much of Ottoman history, the population of Constantinople remained about 58 per cent Muslim and 42 per cent Christian and Jewish, probably as a result of deliberate government policy (the same proportions are noticeable in other Ottoman cities). There was no attempt by the government to convert non-Muslims by force; Christians paid higher taxes than Muslims, and the Ottoman government was more interested in raising revenue than saving souls. In 1547 there were sixty-seven churches operating in Constantinople and ten (the majority Catholic) in Galata. By 1640 the Franciscans, the Dominicans, the Jesuits and the Capucins, the pillars of the Counter-Reformation, each had a church in Galata. Catholic street processions, including public flagellations, took place at Christmas and on the feast of Corpus Christi.

The Orthodox Church played a more prominent part in the life of the city. Every Epiphany (6 January), before an excited crowd at Arnavutkoy, Tarabya or another predominantly Orthodox village, a bishop blessed the waters of the Bosphorus. A Greek cross was then hurled into the sea with all his force by a priest. Semi-naked men plunged after it, accompanied by cheers and shouts, watched by crowds of Greeks in boats. The swimmer who found the cross, and kept it from his rivals, subsequently earned large sums carrying it from house to house, and was considered lucky for the rest of the year. For three days every Easter, like schoolboys let out of school, Greeks were allowed to dance in the streets of the predominantly Greek districts of the Phanar and Pera. According to the chronicler Dapontes, the Grand Vizier himself sometimes came to watch the dancing 'and there was in Constantinople one sole rejoicing and one sole festival those three days'.

The election of a new Patriarch, by a council of metropolitans and notables, was a regular, if expensive event (the Ottoman authorities demanding constantly higher fees). There were so many candidates eager to reign that between 1595 and 1695 there were sixty-one changes of Patriarch, although only thirty-one individual patriarchs.[36]

Multiple identity was the essence of Constantinople; and it received visual expression in the return of a new Patriarch from the Sultan's palace after he had received his *berat* of appointment. Escorted by Orthodox priests on horseback and Ottoman Janissaries, he wore a bright Ottoman kaftan over his black Orthodox vestments. In front of the patriarchal church one of the Grand Vizier's secretaries read out the order of appointment and then led him up the nave to the patriarchal throne (of wood inlaid with mother-of-pearl and ivory, it is as Ottoman as a kaftan). After a service of mass, he was complimented by former patriarchs and metropolitans. The faithful who packed the church kissed the Patriarch's hand, received his blessing and lit candles in honour of the occasion.

Heir to part of the mystique of the Byzantine emperors, the Patriarch was served by a satellite court and administration. The Grand Economus supervised the finances and extensive estates of the Great Church; the Grand Logothete was keeper of the seals; the Grand Referendius carried the Patriarch's communications, in Greek, to the Ottoman authorities. While such senior officials were generally wealthy laymen, the Patriarch's household was served by monks. Simplicity was its keynote. About fifteen priests and monks sat at table with 'His All-Holiness'. He generally wore a monastic robe and a felt hat, and was addressed by his staff without timidity.[37] His household was financed by fees from weddings, baptisms and ordinations, a small levy on Christian households and the sale of sees.

The Oecumenical Patriarch's sway stretched further than the Sultan's, into the independent Orthodox states of Georgia and Muscovy. If one pilgrim route led Muslims out of Constantinople to Mecca and Medina, another brought Christians into Constantinople from 'Holy Russia'. They came not only because it was on the way to Jerusalem, but also to revere the remaining Orthodox shrines and relics. The city was also the scene of regular councils of the Orthodox Church, often attended by

49

the subordinate patriarchs of Alexandria, Antioch and Jerusalem. They frequently resided in Constantinople. On Easter Day 1704, for example, all four patriarchs celebrated mass in the city.

Dynastic links with Russia reaffirmed Constantinople's Orthodox destiny. The niece of the last Byzantine Emperor, Zoe Palaeologina, educated by the Pope, married Ivan III, Grand Prince of Moscow in 1472. Russia's claim, as the last Orthodox great power, to be the 'third Rome' and heir to the Byzantine Empire was strengthened. In 1498 the Grand Prince was crowned, for the first time, as Tsar or Caesar, using a version of the Byzantine coronation ceremonial. The double-headed eagle of the Byzantine Empire now stretched its wings on the Tsar's coat of arms. In 1516 the Oecumenical Patriarch Theoleptus I hinted to the Tsar that a Russo-Byzantine empire might be created.[38]

One Oecumenical Patriarch, Jeremiah II 'the Great', was allowed to travel in search of funds. In Moscow in 1588, he told the Tsar: 'Since the first Rome fell through the Apollinarian heresy and the second Rome, which is Constantinople, is held by the infidel Turks, so then thy great Russian Tsardom, pious Tsar, which is more pious than previous kingdoms, is the third Rome . . . and thou alone under heaven art now called Christian Emperor for all Christians in the whole world.' Clearly the Patriarch had no objection to 'the Christian Emperor for all Christians' expelling 'the infidel Turks'. In the sixteenth and seventeenth centuries the Ottoman Empire was too strong for the tsars to be able to expand on its territory; moreover the tsars were concentrating on recovering land lost to Poland–Lithuania in the west. However, the stage had been set for one of the dramas of nineteenth- and early twentieth-century European history: the Russian drive south to the Black Sea, the Balkans and the ultimate prize, 'Russia's baptismal font' – Tsarigrad, the city of emperors. The Patriarch of Constantinople was one of the authors of the drama.

Jeremiah II also revived Greek education, deciding, in 1593, to establish schools 'for the divine and esoteric scriptures, for the benefit of those who want to teach and learn'. The best school open to Greeks, attended by many of their religious and intellectual leaders, was the Patriarchal Academy, a direct continuation of the pre-1453 university of Constantinople.[39]

Links between Constantinople and Russia led to one of the four deaths of an Oecumenical Patriarch under the Ottoman Empire. Tsar Alexis, father of Peter the Great, was one of the strongest tsars since Ivan the Terrible, and there was a revival of Orthodox hopes in

Constantinople. In the 1650s prayers were being offered for him and his wife in the patriarchal church, and he promised 'to the last drop' of his blood to deliver the Greeks. On 21 March 1657, on the orders of the Grand Vizier, Patriarch Parthenius III was hanged from a city gate for writing to the Prince of Wallachia saying that the era of Islam was approaching its end, and that soon 'the lords of the cross and the bells will be the lords of the empire'. Thenceforth, as a sign of disgrace, the Patriarch received his investiture from the Grand Vizier not the Sultan.[40]

Tension, as well as toleration, marked religious life in Constantinople. Muslims frequently expressed contempt and distrust for Christians. Hoca Sa'deddin, tutor of Murad III and Mehmed III, boasted that 'churches which were within the city were emptied of their vile idols and cleansed from the filthy and idolatrous impurities and by the defacement of their images and the erection of the Islamic prayer niches and pulpits many monasteries and chapels became the envy of the gardens of Paradise.' Repeated Ottoman confiscations of churches asserted the supremacy of Islam. They led to the plastering-over of Christian mosaics and frescos, the expulsion of icons and the insertion of an oval prayer niche facing south-east to Mecca to the right of the former high altar facing south to Jerusalem. In the 1490s the late Byzantine church of St Saviour in Chora, with its incomparable mosaics of the life of Christ, became the Kariye Cami. In Galata in 1545 the cathedral of St Michael was torn down and replaced by the han of Rustem Pasha. In 1586 the seat of the Patriarch himself, the resplendent church of the Pammacaristos, was taken, on the excuse that, when Mehmed II had visited the Patriarch Gennadios, he had prayed there.[41] It was renamed Fethiye Cami, the Mosque of Victory, since the empire had just conquered Azerbaijan.*

After further peregrinations, in 1601 the Patriarchate installed itself beside the church of St George in the Phanar, where it remains. According to one account the Sultan sent the architects used on the mosque of Sultanahmed to restore and reconstruct the church. The Patriarch's residence is a three-storey wooden building, well hidden behind an outer courtyard wall. Low, and without a visible dome, the

---

*Further churches were transformed into mosques in 1627, 1640, 1695. The only church to have remained a church without a break since 1453 is the small church of St Mary of the Mongols, above the Phanar, which still displays its imperial firman of protection on a wall.

mother church of Orthodox Christianity is smaller than most English parish churches. Its principal decoration is the carved wooden iconostasis inside and the double-headed eagle of Byzantium without. The contrast with the glory of the sultans' mosques in Constantinople and of the Catholic counterpart, St Peter's in Rome, is remarkable.

In theory, according to Islamic law, no new churches could be built in a Muslim city. Nor could a church be rebuilt, unless local Muslim elders certified that one had already existed on the site, and an official architect checked that it was not rebuilt on a bigger scale. In reality, Greek money and determination frequently overcame Ottoman regulations. As old churches were lost, new ones were built. Without towers or visible domes, they had to be discreet: even today those built before 1800 are hidden behind walls and invisible from the street. Church bells were forbidden: the faithful were summoned by clappers on bars of wood or iron, or criers in the street. By the eighteenth century there were forty Orthodox churches, of which only three had been built before the conquest.* From 1453 to the present day fifty-five new Armenian churches have been built in Constantinople, some as early as the sixteenth century.[42]

Tension between Muslims and Christians could lead to individual martyrdoms. The reason was generally not their original faith but a neighbour's accusation that they had turned Muslim and since reverted to Christianity. Abjuration of Islam is, according to the Koran, punishable by death. The Ottoman authorities were often reluctant to act, and encouraged the Christian to feign Islam; but few Christians consented. The following incident, recorded by a Habsburg diplomat Baron Wratislaw in 1599, is an example of Christian steadfastness under Muslim pressure.

A Greek boy and girl fell in love. He left Constantinople to buy the best sweet wine in Crete for the wedding. One day, while she was going to the bath unveiled – in the street Muslim women were 'entirely shrouded' – she was seen by an elderly Turk. Exclaiming 'O the most beautiful and lovely maiden!' he fell in love. Since he was a wealthy messenger in the Sultan's court, he was able to have her family imprisoned and marry her. While remaining Christian at heart, she became a Muslim.

When her beloved returned, they began to meet secretly in a tent in her husband's garden. She gave him money. The husband eventually

---

*In the entire history of the Byzantine city, there had been about 450 churches.

found out, 'as everything can be obtained there for money' (a remark made by most foreign observers of Ottoman Constantinople). The enraged husband had them condemned to death for adultery. On his way to his execution the young man looked so handsome that the chief imperial messenger offered to save his life if he became Muslim. 'But the young man did not allow himself to be moved, but answered that he was sprung from Christian parents, had been baptized and brought up a Christian and would also die as a Christian.' Since his refusal was also sealing her fate, his beloved urged him to convert 'with the most earnest entreaty possible'. His firmness drove her to insults: 'Dog! Traitor! Pagan! Jew! Die since thou deservest to die.' Finally she cursed the day she had met him. The Muslim crowd, sympathizing with the young lovers, also urged him to embrace Islam. He resisted. He suffered three days 'hanging on the hook' until someone took pity on him and shot him dead. She was taken to sea, pushed out of the boat and held under water until she drowned – by no means the only woman in Constantinople for whom the Bosphorus was a watery grave.[43]

There were many such tragedies. In the late seventeenth century a Greek boy was heard imitating the muezzin's call to prayer. Having thereby inadvertently made a profession of Islam, he was asked by Turkish passers-by to live as a Muslim. When he refused, he was put in prison, and finally executed – hailed by Greeks as another martyr.

The sight of the mosques and the sound of the muezzin made Islam visible and audible throughout Constantinople. Beneath the surface of triumphant Islam, however, was a hidden, Christian world of water. The concept of holy water or holy springs stems from the primeval association of water with life and purification. It is not restricted to Orthodoxy: there are Catholic holy springs in Ireland and France. Pilgrims to Eyup believed diseases could be cured by drinking water from a cistern beside Abu Ayyub's tomb. However no city contained as many holy springs as Constantinople. Usually established by laymen, they bore witness to Christian fervour – and to the fact that Ottoman building regulations did not extend below the earth's surface.

The holy water, like the aura at the tombs of Muslim 'friends of God', was considered to bring luck and to effect cures. On the feast day of the saint after whom the spring (*ayazma*) was named, pilgrims would arrive and pray. They would then drink the holy water, wash their faces and hair in it, pour it over their clothes. Later they would eat, dance or wrestle. Until this century new springs were found throughout the city, under private houses, near mosques, even beside the Sultan's palace. A

Greek historian from the city, Nikolaos Adjemoglou, President of the Constantinopolitan Society in Athens, has counted 514.[44]

The most famous *ayazma* was outside the city walls, in the courtyard of the revered Orthodox church of Our Lady of the Fish at Balikli, founded in the fifth century. In 1453 a monk was frying fish there when he was told that the city had fallen to the Ottomans. He refused to believe the news unless the half-fried fish came back to life and leapt out of the frying pan into the well. They did so, and the half-blackened fish, miraculously preserved, have been shown to visitors, in a well at the bottom of a long flight of steps, until this century. Many believed that when the fish were fully fried, the city would become Christian again.*

Families came to beg Our Lady of the Fish for a child. If one arrived, they paid the monastery a small annual tribute for seven years. In search of a cure, diseased pilgrims came barefoot once a week. Silver eyes, teeth or arms were on sale in the courtyard, to be fixed to the appropriate member. If pilgrims saw a fish in the well, they shouted for joy. Priests poured pitchers of water on them, in return for a fee. An icon of Our Lady of the Fish was regularly transported around the city, bringing comfort to the bedsides of the sick, and benediction to newly constructed houses.

Constantinople was not only a city of antitheses. The palace, especially in the cosmopolitan reign of Mehmed II, was one source of synthesis between East and West. Folk religion was another. Constantinople is one of the few cities where Muslims and Christians have lived together, over several centuries, in nearly equal proportions. It is not surprising that the two religions influenced each other. Balikli, for example, was revered by Muslims as well as Christians. In 1638 Sultan Murad IV is said to have asked the monks to pray for his victory over the Persians. The day they prayed, he took Baghdad.

The feast day of Our Lady of the Fish took place on the first Friday after Easter. After a procession around the monastery, according to one disarmingly snobbish nineteenth-century account, 'everyone sits in the open air indulging in the innocent pleasures beloved of the people' – food, drink and dance. The crowd, drawn from rich and poor, Muslim and Christian, Bulgarian, Armenian and Catholic, was sometimes so great that the whole city seemed to be present.[45]

---

*On a visit one Sunday in April 1992, to a shrine bereft of worshippers, no fish could be seen in the well. Have they finally died?

Other shrines also attracted people of different faiths – particularly women. From a well beneath the Kiosk of Pearls inside the palace, water was channelled to the fountain of Christ the Saviour, between the palace walls and the sea. On the Feast of the Transfiguration every 6 August Christians came by boat to immerse themselves in the fountain; they then danced to the sound of horns and drums, and swam in the sea. From behind the kiosk's latticed windows the Sultan, who enjoyed the carnival atmosphere, threw coins to his Christian subjects. Other holy springs, such as that of St John the Baptist by Aya Sofya, were controlled by a Muslim official who lived off the proceeds of selling holy water to the Christians.

Although there is no written proof, certain Muslim ceremonies appeared to reflect Christian influence. The formalization in 1588 of the ceremony of the *Mevlud* or birthday of the Prophet, which nearly always took place in the mosque of Sultanahmed, may reflect a desire to rival Christian celebrations of Christmas. Dervish veneration of saints, reprehended by many orthodox Muslims, showed clear traces of Christian and pre-Christian practice. The Bektashi order, to whom most Janissaries were affiliated, associated Allah, Muhammad and his son-in-law Ali in a holy trinity. Calling themselves 'moths in the divine fire', they drank wine. In total contrast to ceremonies in mosques, their rites included women and in some cases were reserved for male-female couples.[46]

For their part, whereas Western visitors generally found it possible to visit mosques, the Christians of Constantinople, probably from choice, rarely entered them. However, although hamams and imarets were built beside mosques for Muslim charitable purposes, Christians and Jews were permitted to use them.

Christian, Jewish and Muslim women went to the tomb of Helvaci Baba in the Shehzade mosque near Fatih. They took crippled children there in search of a cure, young girls or widows in pursuit of a husband, a friend in need of a place to live. Depending on the object of their desires, they gave the muezzin a child's bonnet, a white handkerchief or the key of a house. While holding the object entrusted to him, he then issued the call to prayer from the top of the minaret. Even today Christian women will sacrifice a cock to a Muslim 'friend of God', Sunbul Sinan, at Koca Mustafa Pasha. Muslims go to Armenian churches, Surp Hireshdagabet or Surp Kevork (St George) at Balat, and even spend the night there, to cure epileptic children or consult a medium.[47]

Members of different religions used each other's law-courts as well as each other's saints. Christians frequently used Muslim, rather than Christian, courts for cases of marriage and inheritance. By the early nineteenth century they were also sometimes using Jewish courts, while some Muslims were using the patriarchal courts. Jews frequently used Muslim courts to escape the strictness of rabbinical courts, despite the rabbis' protests that such acts denied the validity of Jewish law.[48] The everyday lives and needs of ordinary people softened barriers between religions in Constantinople. The collective memory and state of mind of the city acquired an instinctive tolerance, or acceptance, of other religions. The Conqueror's calculation, that it was possible to run a multi-confessional capital, proved correct. Hatred might be expressed in words; it rarely exploded in acts.

3

The Palace

The Grand Sinyore . . . satt in great estate, yeat the sighte of him was nothinge in Comparrison of the traine that stood behinde him, the sight wheareof did make me almoste to thinke that I was in another worlde.

                                                            Thomas Dallam, 1599

ONSTANTINOPLE WAS SYNONYMOUS with imperial splendour. Its source lay in the palace built on the eastern end of the peninsula, where the Bosphorus, the Golden Horn and the Sea of Marmara meet. Set on the edge of Europe, the palace has a commanding view into Asia. It was a site suitable for the 'World Conqueror'.

On land and sea, the palace was enclosed by a high battlemented wall. Most of the sea wall has been destroyed. However, the land wall still climbs from the Sea of Marmara, across one of the hills on which Constantinople is built, down to the Golden Horn. In the middle of the wall, a towering portal of grey marble, the Imperial Gate, leads the visitor out of the tumult of the city into the peace of a tree-lined courtyard. It is the first of three courts around which the palace is built.

Like so much in Constantinople, Topkapi palace, as it is now called (from one of its gates, the *top kapi* or cannon gate), owes its existence to Mehmed the Conqueror. Begun in 1459, the palace was finished in 1478. Since he had already built one palace in the middle of the city, its official name was the New Imperial Palace.

Until the departure of the Sultan and his household in the nineteenth century, the first courtyard contained the outer offices of the household: a weapons depot, housed in the ancient Byzantine church of St Irene, dedicated to peace; stables for 4,000 horses; the mint; a hospital; a kiosk for scribes receiving petitions and dispensing the

Sultan's decrees or firmans. Like palace precincts in Western capitals, the first courtyard was open to all, even foreigners. From across the Golden Horn, the palace appeared as a peninsula of pavilions, surrounded by trees and gardens cascading down to the sea: the windows were compared to imperial eyes watching the world outside. Inside this courtyard, however, the palace looked like a medley of buildings, which most visitors considered unworthy of the Sultan. The sole visible elements of splendour were the size of the courtyard and the presence of large numbers of richly clad soldiers – and exotic animals, including the occasional leopard or elephant.[1]

Only the Sultan was permitted to ride a horse through the next gate, the Gate of Salutation, into the second courtyard. Filled with fountains and cypresses, it is both courtyard and garden and is so spacious that people on one side are inaudible on the other. The visitor is surrounded by a series of low, arcaded, wide-eaved buildings. Reflecting the Ottoman obsession with rules and boundaries, each building was conceived separately for a specific function, like a series of tents. They contained living quarters for different groups of household servants, for example the 'tressed halberdiers', who wore their hair in long ringlets to prevent them from glimpsing the women when they delivered firewood to the harem. The buildings are on a human and domestic, rather than palatial, scale, in contrast to architectural unities built to impress like the Louvre, the Doge's Palace in Venice, or the imperial mosques.

Like most monarchs' palaces until the eighteenth century, the same complex housed both government offices and the monarch's household. On the left of the second courtyard was one of the power-centres of Europe, the Imperial Divan, the chamber where the Grand Vizier and other viziers debated policy and decided law-suits, after morning prayers, four times a week. In theory every Ottoman subject, whatever their sex, race, rank or religion, had access to the Divan to present grievances. Here, for example, the Patriarch had come in 1521 and 1537 to save the churches of the city. With the brisk simplicity of much Ottoman government, the plaintiff acted as his own lawyer: cases were decided on the spot. Ottoman bureaucracy might be slow; its legal system was not. On the other side of the courtyard were the high chimneys of the palace kitchens – so efficient that they could feed 12,000 people at a time.

At the end of the second court was the gate called the Bab-i Aali or the High Gate, often referred to by western Europeans as the Sublime

Porte.* It is a colonnaded structure with the wide projecting roof characteristic of Turkish architecture, below which the Sultan's throne was installed during receptions to mark the great Muslim festivals of Bayram at the end of Ramadan. Beyond was the Sultan's throne room.

Here at the epicentre of the palace, it is necessary to define the ethos which drove its inhabitants, from the Sultan to the lowest of his servants, to devote themselves to the power and splendour of the Ottoman dynasty. Before 1453, in Bursa and Edirne, the Ottoman court had been relatively casual. A Christian captive, Brother George of Muhlenbach, wrote: 'There is no sign of vanity or superfluity . . . The great lords and princes display such simplicity in everything that they cannot possibly be singled out from the crowd.' The Sultan attended mosque with two pages, and prayed on a carpet on the floor beside other Muslims. Constantinople, however, imposed different standards. Mehmed II may have been influenced by his Greek-born scribes and pashas and their memories of the awestruck ceremonial surrounding the semi-divine figure of the emperor, the 'thirteenth apostle' (two of Mehmed II's pashas, relations of the last Byzantine Emperor, had converted to Islam). Refugee princes certainly told the Sultan of the pomp of Persian courts. Above all Mehmed II wanted to express through his palace his vision of himself as Padishah, Caesar, Khan.[2]

The dynastic law code, or *kanunname*, of Mehmed II (probably written in 1477–81) abolished such customs as the Sultan's appearance for fifteen minutes every dawn to eat a ceremonial meal in the presence of his troops: 'It is my command that no one dine with my noble self except members of my family. My great ancestors are said to have dined with their viziers; I have abolished this practice.'

At first the Sultan had sat in the Divan with his viziers. However, on one occasion during Mehmed II's reign a petitioner is said to have burst in and asked: 'Which of you is the fortunate sovereign?' Humiliated, the Sultan thenceforth usually attended the Divan 'behind the curtain' – sitting in an alcove which still overlooks the council room. It was covered by a green silk curtain, so that the viziers were not sure when the Sultan was listening.[3]

In addition to the Sultan's aloofness, the majesty of death reinforced the dynasty's power. There was an Ottoman saying: 'The neck of a

---

*It was later renamed the Bab-i Sa'adet, or Gate of Felicity, while the name Bab-i Aali was transferred to the Grand Vizier's residence outside the palace. As a result, the Sublime Porte became a synonym for the Ottoman government.

servant of the Sultan is thinner than a hair's breadth.' For the Sultan frequently used his power of life and death over his slaves and his family. The opening by the Sultan of a latticed window in the Tower of Justice, above the Divan chamber in the second courtyard, or the stamping of his foot during an audience in the throne room, were signals for execution, by strangulation, axe or dagger.[4] Grand viziers were killed, on occasion by the Sultan himself. One Ottoman curse was: 'May you be a vizier of Selim' – referring to the number of viziers executed by Selim I. In 1606 Grand Vizier Dervish Pasha was strangled by imperial gardeners. Shortly after, wrote the great seventeenth-century chronicler Naima, 'a movement being perceived in his feet, the emperor drew his dagger and cut his throat'. Of seventeen grand viziers between 1644 and 1656, only two died natural deaths.* Most Ottomans, however, regarded the execution of officials as evidence of the Sultan's vigilance and justice and a means to keep the people obedient. The sanction of the Mufti was generally, but not always, sought. Huseyin Hezarfenn wrote in 1669: 'Let them not abolish discretionary bodily punishment altogether, for punishment is a condition of kingship.'[5]

Moreover the victims' sense of obedience to the Sultan was so overpowering that few protested at their fate. If Ottomans went to war as to a wedding, they went to execution as to their Friday prayers. An order of the Padishah had to be obeyed; his power came from God. A Grand Vizier once asked a dervish sheikh whom he held to be the biggest fool: 'You, O mighty vizier. For you have done everything in your power to gain your office, although you rode past the bleeding head of your predecessor, which lay in the same spot as his predecessor.'[6]

Whereas in London rebels' heads were generally exhibited on a bridge or a gate of the city, the heads of viziers and pashas were exhibited on white marble pillars in the first courtyard of the palace, with the writ of accusation attached, and in some cases signed by themselves. The heads of lesser offenders were exposed in niches to the right and left of the outer façade of the Imperial Gate: in cases of congestion, piles of smaller organs (noses, ears, tongues) were heaped on the ground in front of the gate. The stuffing of a head reflected the rank of the deceased: cotton for viziers, straw for lesser officials. The public of Constantinople liked a display of heads, since it confirmed their belief that the executed had been vampires gorging on the state. Female offenders were despatched more discreetly. They were taken in sacks,

---

*In all, before 1839, 32 of 178 grand viziers (18 per cent) died a violent death.

laden with stones, and dropped in the Bosphorus: yet another of Constantinople's geographical advantages was the current flowing through the Bosphorus, which removed corpses quickly. When a palace favourite in the sixteenth century, a Jewish businesswoman called Esperanza Malchi, was torn to pieces in the streets of the city by Janissaries who accused her of debasing the coinage in which they were paid, the mother of Sultan Mehmed III scolded him: 'If it was determined that the Jewish woman had to be punished with death, did it have to be in such an obscene fashion? Why couldn't she have been thrown in the sea?'[7]

The splendour of the palace, like the power of the empire, reached its peak under the most impressive of all sultans, the Conqueror's great-grandson Suleyman the Magnificent. His reign completed the transformation of Constantinople into a synonym for grandeur, as the reign of his father Selim I had completed its transformation into a holy city of Islam. Less than a month after Suleyman's accession in 1520, a Venetian wrote:

> He is twenty-five years of age, tall but wiry, and of a delicate complexion. His neck is a little too long, his face thin and his nose aquiline. He has a shadow of a moustache and a small beard; nevertheless he has a pleasant mien, though his skin tends to pallor. He is said to be a wise Lord, fond of study, and all men hope for good from his rule.[8]

By 1523, Suleyman had conquered two Christian bastions which had resisted the Conqueror himself, the city of Belgrade and the island of Rhodes. At the battle of Mohacs in 1526 he annihilated the Hungarian nobility: the last independent King of Hungary was killed fleeing the battlefield. By 1540 Buda had become an Ottoman city and the Ottoman frontier was within a hundred miles of Vienna. From Algeria to India, Ottoman fleets ruled the waves. On land, Suleyman boasted: 'Day and night our horse is saddled and our sabre is girt.' He could inflict the same hammer-blows on 'the accursed red-heads' (the Ottoman name for Persians, from the red headgear they wore) in the East, as on the Hungarians in the West. In his reign the epithet 'asylum of the universe' became reality: from Crimea and Hungary, Morocco and Persia, princes took refuge at his court. The King of France implored his help; the Habsburgs paid him tribute.

The increase in the Sultan's empire was reflected in his title. In the gilt inscription in Arabic above the imperial gate in the outer wall of the palace, Mehmed II had called himself the Sultan of the Two Continents and the Emperor of the Two Seas, the Shadow of God in this world and the next, the favourite of God on the Two Horizons [East and West], the Monarch of the Terraqueous Orb, the Conqueror of the Castle of Constantinople, the Father of Conquest Sultan Mehmed Khan, son of Sultan Murad Khan, son of Sultan Mehmed Khan, may God make eternal his empire and exalt his residence above the brightest stars of the firmament!

Suleyman I's letters, from 'the place of the residence of the sublime Sultanate, Constantinople the well-guarded, the protected', began with a formula of cosmic grandeur:

I who am the Sultan of Sultans, the Sovereign of Sovereigns, the distributor of crowns to the monarchs of the globe, the Shadow of God upon Earth, the Sultan and Padishah of the White Sea, the Black Sea, Rumelia, Anatolia, Karamania, Rum, Dulkadir, Diyarbekir, Kurdistan, Azerbayjan, Persia, Damascus, Aleppo, Cairo, Mekka, Medina, Jerusalem, all Arabia, Yemen and those other countries which my noble ancestors – may God brighten their tombs! – conquered and my august majesty has likewise conquered with my flaming sword, Sultan Suleyman Khan, son of Sultan Selim, son of Sultan Bayezid.

In the Ottoman world view, other monarchs owed their crowns, not to their swords or their ancestors, but to their overlord the Sultan. Only he was Emperor. The Habsburg Holy Roman Emperor in the West, his enemy Charles V, whom he tried to outshine in ceremonial grandeur as well as military might, was 'King of the land of Spain and the places which depend on it'. His successors as Holy Roman Emperor were called 'King of Vienna'. In 1531 the Venetian ambassador reported that 'Sultan Suleyman . . . detests the Emperor for his title of Caesar, he, the Turk, causing himself to be called Caesar.' Ottoman poets were beginning to call the Sultan 'the World Emperor and Messiah of the Last Age'. He may have believed them.[9]

His sense of triumph was expressed within the palace. The wall of the Divan was redecorated with gold and jewels. In 1527, after a six years' absence, a Venetian ambassador wrote: 'I found the Porte excellent in order, differing from the other time I came here as ambassador . . . there is a great difference between this and the other time.' Suleyman, the first Sultan to sit majestically on a throne in the European manner, rather than cross-legged on a carpet, built a new throne room in 1533. An ambassador from Charles V found the Sultan seated on a slightly elevated throne completely covered with gold cloth, replete and strewn with numerous precious stones and there were on all sides many cushions of inestimable value; the walls of the chamber were covered with mosaic works spangled with azure and gold. The exterior of the fire-place of this chamber was of solid silver and covered with gold and at one side of the chamber a fountain gushed forth from a wall.

In peace or war, victory or defeat, the throne room continued to dazzle like a jewel-box. Seventeenth-century palace inventories show that the throne itself was decorated with five cushions, six 'skirts' and fifteen bolsters, sewn with emeralds, rubies and pearls and, like the mats on the floor, drenched in gold thread.[10] In 1799, when the wife of Lord Elgin, the British ambassador, slipped into the throne room disguised as a member of her husband's retinue, she wrote:

> It was a small room and dark, but of all the magnificent places in the world I suppose it was the first. His throne was like a good honest English bed, the counterpane on which the Monster [her term for Sultan Selim III] sat was embroidered all over with immense large pearls. By him was an inkstand of one mass of large Diamonds, on his other side lay his saber studded all over with thumping Brilliants.
>
> In his turban he wore the famous Aigrette, his robe was of yellow satin with black sable and in a window there were two turbans covered with dia-monds. You can conceive nothing in *The Arabian Nights* equal to that room.

In addition to the Sultan's power of life and death, his remoteness and the splendour of his throne room, three codes – of manners, silence and costume – gave the Sultan an aura of majesty unknown in other palaces. Both East and West of Constantinople, other courts were, at this stage, relatively informal (with the partial exception of Vienna and Madrid). Neither the Shah of Persia nor the Mogul Emperor demanded as much deference as the Ottoman Sultan. English ambassador first to the Mogul Emperor, then to the Ottoman Sultan, in the 1620s, Sir Thomas Roe preferred the informality of Delhi, where he 'treated familiarly with an affable and courteous prince', to the rigidity of Constantinople where, gripped under each elbow by a chief footman, he 'spake to a dumb image'.

The grace and gravity of Ottoman manners created a chain of defer-ence linking the Sultan in his throne room to the humblest Janissary in the courtyard beyond. At the Tudor and Valois courts, courtiers did no more than bow to the monarch and kiss hands. Viziers and ambassadors honoured by admission into the imperial throne room prostrated themselves three times to the ground – although mention of such abasement was often omitted from diplomats' despatches. Depending on their rank or favour, the Sultan then permitted them to kiss either his hand, held rigidly on his knee, the hem of his kaftan or the tip of his hanging sleeve. All left walking backwards. A Moroccan ambassador wrote of the viziers:

> Never must any of them behave as an equal towards his superior, either by marching in the same rank, or by wearing a turban or other clothes of the same quality, or by sitting on a similar seat. I have never seen men more scrupulous in their observance of precedence. In the presence of the Sultan none can sit down either before him or within his sight. All stand respectfully with their hands clasped as they do at prayers.[11]

In an age when manners were taught like riding or Greek, and were a standard of judgement almost as important as rank, wealth or dress, the manners of the Ottoman élite were a means to impress, and control, inferiors and foreigners. In 1749 Lord Charlemont wrote of the viziers:

> Their manner was dignified in the highest degree and yet as pleasing as possible. They seemed to possess, unknown to themselves, an air of superiority which they did not in the least appear to assume and which commanded respect without their seeming to demand it. How different from the petulance of France where every coxcomb assumes a superior air which turns his very civility into rudeness and insult! But that which most struck me and seemed to surpass anything of the kind I had yet seen was their action in speaking, their manner of moving the head and arms. Every gesture was a mixture of ease, grace and dignity . . . the very sight of their speaking, if I may be allowed the phrase, was highly pleasing to me.

Deference was expressed most compellingly in silence. In the second and third courtyards, the silence was so deep that it created a sense of imminent drama. After the reign of Suleyman the Magnificent, the Sultan himself received ambassadors in silence, rarely condescending to say more than '*Peki*' – 'It is well.' If he tried to speak, the viziers, *plus royalistes que le roi*, reminded him that it was not fitting. In the third courtyard, in his presence, no vizier spoke except on official business; the pages of the privy chamber, his personal attendants, maintained 'a complete silence at all times in his presence' and walked on the tips of their toes. They communicated in sign language, introduced by Suleyman the Magnificent in order to heighten the respect surrounding the Sultan. By the seventeenth century it was taught by mute experts who 'know the significance of everything by sign', and had replaced Serbo-Croat as the second language of the palace.[12]

The Ottoman Sultan projected silence in his palace as well as on his way to Friday prayers. To impress foreign ambassadors, the date of their audience was chosen to coincide with the Janissaries' pay-day. Two to six thousand Janissaries and other troops were drawn up in the second courtyard. They stood still for hours like statues, hardly daring to spit or cough. As Baron Wratislaw reported in 1591:

> Although there were some thousands of people there, nevertheless there was no shouting, no conversation, no moving hither and thither, but all stood so quietly that we could not help wondering; nay even the Janissaries, although furious and licentious people in war, here observed greater obedience towards their commander than boys toward their preceptor, standing as quiet as if they had been hewn out of marble.

In 1657 the Swedish ambassador was feasted by the Grand Vizier in the Divan: 'There was such a silence during dinner that not one word was spoke, nor the least noise perceived': the Sultan was known to be watching from his alcove.[13]

At certain moments of the day, however, the silence was broken by the music of the imperial band, consisting of fifes, trumpets, drums and cymbals. Its extremely loud music saluted the Sultan one hour before dawn and an hour and a half after sunset. It also accompanied him on parades and, to their dismay, serenaded foreign ambassadors, in their embassies, after their audience with the Sultan.[14]

Costume was another code conveying the grandeur of the Ottoman sultanate. There was a saying of the Prophet: 'Do not drink in vessels of gold or silver and do not dress in silks or brocade, for they belong to the infidel in this world and to you in the next.' In the palace, however, the lure of the kaftan was more compelling than the words of the Prophet. Kaftans were single robes, cut straight from the neck to the feet, often with a flare at the waist. They were made of velvet, satin or brocaded silk. Costume was one of Constantinople's principal industries. By 1577 there were 268 looms in the city, of which 88 were 'attached to the palace': only they were allowed to make 'cloth of gold'. At times the mint threatened to run out of gold and silver since so much went in the making of gold and silver thread. In vain the Sultan issued edicts forbidding their use in clothes: his orders were rarely obeyed.[15]

A collection of 1,000 kaftans survives in Topkapi palace, owing to the Ottoman custom of putting a dead Sultan's belongings in wrappers, sealing them with his name and storing them either in his mausoleum or the palace treasury. Most of the kaftans are monochrome and unpatterned (like the black silk kaftan often worn by Suleyman the Magnificent). However some are decorated with flowers and trees in vibrant colours, tulips falling in undulating crimson streams, and golden leaves swirling in an unseen wind. Other kaftans are more original. A kaftan of gold spots and stripes on scarlet satin, made for a seventeenth-century Sultan, another with a pattern of white triangles on deep crimson satin, possibly of the eighteenth century, seem to leap-frog time. Like Coptic textiles or Biedermeier silver, they look as if they could have been designed for Paris in the 1920s.

As with the number of minarets permitted on a mosque, costume was governed by dynastic priorities. Whereas his predecessors had worn camelot or mohair, Suleyman wore cloth of gold. Although in theory it was reserved for the Sultan alone, as a special favour he permitted his beloved Grand Vizier, Ibrahim Pasha, to wear 'gold brocade and on campaign a suit of cloth of gold'. The Sultan and his viziers would sometimes wear three kaftans, so that the contrasting fabrics and colours, peeping out under sleeves, could be admired. Three centuries before uniforms began to appear in Western courts, the colours of officials' turbans and robes on ceremonial occasions were regulated by law. The *ulema* wore purple, viziers green, chamberlains scarlet. In such costumes, Ottoman writers noted with pride, the Sultan's servants resembled a parterre of tulips.[16]

Worn mainly on ceremonial occasions, kaftans were as important to the Ottoman honours system as knighthoods to the British. Ambassadors judged their standing in Constantinople by the number and quality of the kaftans they received when they paid their respects in the imperial palace. In the seventeenth century the French ambassador generally received 24, the British 16, the Venetian and Dutch 12. By 1775, however, the Ottoman Empire was so weakened that the Russian ambassador received one hundred. Ambassadors refused to proceed from the Grand Vizier's divan to the Sultan's throne room until they had sent servants to an adjoining vestibule, to check that a suitable number of kaftans awaited them. Kaftans were then put on, over European dress, as a sign of respect for the Sultan.[17]

Fur was a second language of splendour for the palace. Winds from the north can make the city bitterly cold. Furs were useful as well as sumptuous and their purchase in Russia by the Ottoman treasury became an affair of state. Sultans alone wore black fox. Other furs were worn by the Sultan and his officials in a special timed sequence: ermine in autumn, followed by an interval of squirrel, and sable in winter. The day the Sultan changed fur, the Grand Vizier and the pashas followed suit.[18]

The palace combined colour, deference, silence and majesty. Ottoman historians recorded that foreign ambassadors or princes were 'astonished, bewildered, stupefied and completely enraptured' by the sight of the Sultan and his train. The Imperial ambassador Baron de Busbecq wrote: 'Everywhere the brilliance of gold, silver, purple, silk and satin . . . No mere words could give an adequate idea of the novelty of the sight. A more beautiful spectacle was never presented to my gaze.' Two hundred years later, seeing the ministers and Janissary officers in the second courtyard, each wearing his ceremonial turban and accompanied by a retinue of servants, a Florentine scholar Domenico Sestini wrote: 'It is in this very circumstance that one sees all the majesty, all the splendour and the pride of the Ottomans.' From the sixteenth to the nineteenth centuries, western Europeans called the Ottoman Sultan 'the Grand Signor' [or 'the G.S.'], as if there was only one.[19]

Art was yet another means by which the palace projected a message of imperial grandeur. During the five hundred years of the Ottoman Empire many works of art were given away by the Sultan to his sisters and daughters, to the mosques of Constantinople, Mecca and Medina, or to foreign monarchs. Other works of art were melted down, at times of crisis, to pay the troops. However some of the 600 items in the Topkapi Palace Museum have never left the palace. The palace was the setting for which they were made, by the Sultan's own craftsmen, often from precious materials (gold, jade, amber, ivory, shark's tooth) stored in the Sultan's treasury. Four domed and arcaded rooms, built by Mehmed II in the third courtyard, for 350 years housed the private treasury of the sultans (as opposed to the state treasury beside the Divan in the second courtyard): today the same rooms act as the treasury of the Topkapi Palace Museum. This element of continuity makes Topkapi one of the great dynastic treasure-houses of the world, comparable to the Kremlin or the Hofburg. Since no other Muslim capital has sheltered one dynasty and its collection for so long, it is also the only collection in the Islamic world which has been continuously growing since the fifteenth century. Until it was opened to the public in the twentieth century, the palace treasury was one of the invisible attractions of Constantinople, often imagined, frequently exaggerated, never visited.

The treasury contained an abundance of 'palace objects', incomprehensible in any other context. One Koran is bound in gold and jade. A gold turban ornament is set with rubies, emeralds, pearls and diamonds and crowned with peacock feathers. A bejewelled gold flask once contained Suleyman the Magnificent's drinking water. Horse-trappings are inlaid with diamonds, rubies and emeralds. The throne used for Bayram receptions is faced with plaques of solid gold. These treasures were stored in chests under the authority of the Inspector of the Privy Purse and subordinate officials such as the Keepers of the Turban Ornaments and the Gala Robes. In the third hall one chest contained nothing but jewels. Diamonds were stored in one drawer, rubies in another, emeralds in a third. Near this building was the Sultan's secret treasury containing bags of gold coins, sealed in red wax stamped with the Sultan's personal seal from his gold ring.[20]

Many items in the palace treasury were booty from the sultans' conquests, particularly from former capitals like Tabriz, Cairo and Buda. They were so carefully stored that books from the library of King Matthias Corvinus of Hungary, taken after 1526, could be returned to Buda in 1877, when the Ottoman Empire wanted Hungarian support during a war with Russia. Other objects had belonged to pashas and been taken by the Sultan on their death. However most were made by a corporation of craftsmen on retainer called the *ehl-i hiref*, or 'artisans'. Among them were painters, bookbinders, furriers, goldsmiths, and makers of decorative globes to hang above the Sultan's throne. Abraham the Jew, for example, was employed solely to back jewels with gold or silver foil, in order to give them more sparkle.[21] The craftsmen were often visited by the sultans, who themselves generally learnt a trade. Suleyman was a goldsmith: later sultans practised embroidery, carpentry or painting muslin handkerchiefs.

Numbering 360 under Bayezid II around 1500, and 598 in 1526, the tally of craftsmen rose to 636 in 1566, but thereafter declined. The organization was haphazard and inefficient. Most craftsmen worked for private clients as well as the Sultan, in buildings near the palace; some workshops were in the first courtyard of the palace 'just as in front of the palace at Prague', according to Baron Wratislaw. The jewellers had shops in the middle of the bazaar, where there are still jewellers' shops today. The imperial weaving factory was near the Bayezid mosque.[22]

Craftsmen were imported from as far as Tabriz, Cairo and Bosnia. They worked with fabrics from Venice, and copied designs from China. However, in Constantinople their style soon became as Ottoman as the sultans' mosques. In different mediums, craftsmen repeated similar patterns, using arabesques, calligraphy, above all flowers. Such repetition may have been the instinctive use of traditional symbols: in Middle Eastern tradition, roses symbolized sacred love, cypresses the soul's ascension to heaven. On the other hand, after the reign of Mehmed II, when the city had been open to many different styles, there may have been a deliberate effort to create an Ottoman imperial style, using vibrantly contrasting colours with an immediate visual impact.

Whatever the reason, Constantinople had as wide an artistic empire as Paris or Venice. Merchants built houses in Plovdiv or Damascus, pashas erected mosques in Salonica or Cairo, priests commissioned churches in Jerusalem and Mount Athos, which are unmistakable visual tributes to the Ottoman capital. As far away as Sweden, Poland and Venice, in part through the Sultan's diplomatic presents of tents and kaftans, there were fashions for Ottoman fabrics, uniforms, jewels and interior decoration. The national dress of Hungarian and Polish kings and nobles, after 1550, and of military units like hussars and uhlans, was Ottoman in inspiration. Ottoman grandeur and prowess were the attraction: the richer the noble, the more he tried to dress like the Sultan.[23]

Unrivalled for hardness and range of colour, Ottoman ceramics are one of the high points in the technical history of their art. Tiles, bowls and jugs were made in the nearby town of Iznik but used above all in the mosques and palaces of Constantinople. Like many forms of Ottoman splendour, they reached their peak under Suleyman, particularly after the introduction around 1550 of a brownish red often known as Armenian red. Until the seventeenth century Iznik tiles were used throughout the palace. They line the 'Golden Path' from the Sultan's living quarters to the Harem, so called because the Sultan threw gold coins to the ladies of the harem as he walked down it on festival days, and the walls of the Baghdad Pavilion in the fourth courtyard. The walls of the great mosques, such as the Suleymaniye and Sultanahmed, are ceramic gardens, evoking the gardens of paradise promised to the righteous in the Koran. Leaves and flowers, trees and bushes, form tile pictures in blue, white and red, 'a miracle of subtlety and softness of texture and technical proficiency to which no reproduction can do justice'.[24] Their impact is heightened by the contrast of their dense and forceful colours with the grey walls of the mosques.

Iznik plates are, today, considered masterpieces. Yet they were not good enough for the Sultan. Called 'pottery', they were used in the palace kitchens, where they were regularly destroyed in fires and earthquakes. The imperial family and senior officials used pieces from China, many of which had been taken as booty during wars in Syria and Iran. Called 'porcelain', they were kept in well-protected palace cellars. Hence the 10,600 pieces of porcelain still in the Topkapi Palace Museum, which make it the third collection in the world after those of Peking and Dresden. The Sultan himself ate off silver or gold, or green celadon, which was thought both to detect and neutralize poison.

One of the most important palace workshops was the studio outside the walls, the *nakkashane*. It was used by a guild of officially regulated, well-paid painters, gilders, bookbinders and scribes, some of whom followed the Sultan on campaign to record his victories. Under Bayezid II and Selim I they had created conventional illuminated manuscripts of Persian poets like Sa'di and Hafiz, and indeed Selim I himself, who was an accomplished Persian poet, for the imperial library. Again it was under Suleyman I that the artists turned from Persian themes, and a specifically Ottoman style emerged.

Realism, accuracy of detail and interest in historical events and people distinguish the miniature painters of Constantinople from other Muslim painters. For although there was a popular prejudice against representation of the human figure, there was no formal Koranic injunction. The representation of faces and bodies in Ottoman painting, although stiff, is less formulaic than in other Islamic painting, except in the art of the Mogul Empire. There is an obsessive concentration on the achievements of the dynasty. The Sultan goes to mosque, receives ambassadors, wins victories. Lavish use of gold, silver, scarlet, lilac and a peculiar yellow green, creates an even greater boldness of colour than in Iznik tiles.

Palace miniaturists also produced geographical views, such as the representation of Constantinople by Matrakci Nasuh in 1537. Landmarks such as Galata Tower, Seven Towers, Aya Sofya and the mosque of Mehmed II are depicted both frontally and from the air, with the force of naïve art. The numbers employed in the *nakkashane* declined from 124 in 1596 to about sixty in the mid-seventeenth century, and thereafter to about ten. A decline in quality, noticeable at the same time in Ottoman textiles, matched the decline in quantity. By then the Ottoman capital was thinking of survival, not glory.[25]

In the second courtyard a separate corps of scribes produced documents in a variety of scripts such as *Siyakat* for financial records (a special script with barely differentiated letters to render the falsification of amounts more difficult), and *divani*, the standard formal script used in the Sultan's letters and decrees (called *firman*, Persian for 'command'). Firmans dealt with everything from army supplies to market regulations. It has been calculated that in Suleyman's reign alone 150,000 such documents were produced.

A firman was headed by an art form peculiar to Constantinople: the Sultan's *tughra*, or monogram. Also appearing on coins, and some buildings, it was the Ottoman dynastic equivalent of the ubiquitous royal portrait or effigy in Western monarchies. It consisted of loops of script, in gold, blue and black, sometimes surrounded by clouds and spirals of flowers and arabesques. Guaranteeing the legality of the document it prefaced, the *tughra* recorded a formula which varied little over six centuries. Under Suleyman the Magnificent, for example, it read 'Suleyman the Emperor, son of Selim the Emperor, ever victorious Khan'. The *tughra* can be over 100 or even 200 centimetres high, even on occasion of greater than human height. The ultimate assertion, in script, of imperial grandeur, it helps explain why Ottomans sultans did not rush to print.[26]

The palace was not only a machine for splendour but also the residence of the Sultan and his household. Numbering 726 before 1481, in the surge of grandeur under Suleyman the personnel of the palace rose to around 5,000. The household consisted of servants devoted to the Sultan's personal well-being – turban-folders, coffee-makers, messengers, door-keepers – and an outer galaxy of staff manning schools, workshops, hospitals, mosques (at least thirteen within the palace walls) and bakeries.

Of these departments one of the most important was the palace school, reorganized by Mehmed II to contain between three and four hundred youths, the cream of the *devshirme*, and was housed in buildings on the right of the third courtyard. Now destroyed by fire, they included dormitories, class-rooms, teachers' offices, a music conservatory and the school's own mosque and hamam. According to Giovantonio Menavino, himself a page at the 'court of world refuge' from 1505 to 1514, each inmate was educated by tutors and eunuchs, for a period of fourteen years, to be 'the warrior statesman and loyal Muslim who at the same time should be a man of letters and polished speech, profound courtesy and honest morals'. The curriculum, markedly more secular than in the mosque schools, included court etiquette, sports, and the classic Ottoman trio of Turkish, Persian and Arabic, the languages of government, literature and religion. Pages trained their bodies with wooden weights, and their minds with the Koran, or the *Thousand and One Nights.*[27]

One of the many intermediaries between Constantinople and the Western world, who contributed both to Constantinople's modernization and to the West's knowledge of the Ottoman Empire, was Ali Bey, as he became known. Formerly a young Pole by the name of Albert Bobowski, he had been enslaved by the Tartars of the Crimea, sold in Constantinople, and educated in the palace in the early seventeenth century. Becoming one of the Sultan's translators, he was also the first to record the words and notes of Turkish songs and music. He noted the differences between Ottoman military music; the soft, melancholy and complex palace music, based on a small violin, a three-stringed guitar, pan-pipes and Persian horn; and popular songs 'whose tunes are practically imprinted in the ears of everyone. They are called *Turku* and deal for the most part with the country's wars, victories, loves, suffering, absences etc. The learned and civilized do not appreciate them.'

After Bobowski had been dismissed for drunkenness in about 1657, he wrote a treatise on the palace, possibly for the Pera embassies. Even when the Janissaries had long been infiltrated by native Turks, he recorded that 'though one encounters all nations in the palace nevertheless the greater percentage of the pages comes from the Christian subjects of the Ottoman Empire.' Like two other dynastic foundations, Eton and the Imperial Lycée at Tsarskoe Seloe, the Topkapi palace school was considered the best school in the empire, and a nursery of chief ministers. Of a group of sixty grand viziers, forty-eight had been trained there, including Sokollu Mehmed Pasha, Koprulu Mehmed, founder of the great seventeenth-century dynasty of grand viziers, and some nineteenth-century reformers.[28]

The palace was a world of its own and a page's admission was marked by a drastic purification ceremony. For three days the new page was left alone, with no one to speak to, until the leading eunuch told him that henceforth he had joined the ranks of the Sultan's slaves. Their hair was divided into tresses near their ears, 'as a reminder that they must be eternal slaves of the Sultan, the same as Joseph who was the page of the

Pharaoh in Egypt and wore similar tresses'. Thereafter they were kept like dogs on a leash. If they infringed a rule, beating was so severe that the Sultan himself, hearing their cries, sometimes told a servant to shout for mercy. While they were at prayers, the eunuchs searched their trunks for groceries and love letters.

In the belief that no good mind could inhabit a weak or unpleasing body, the forty ablest and best-looking pages were selected for service in the Sultan's privy chamber. Each page had a separate domain. One looked after the Sultan's sword, another his parrots. A third shaved the Sultan, a fourth clipped his finger and toe nails. Until the Sultan's withdrawal into the harem in the 1570s, they also set and served at his table, looked after his wardrobe, and cleaned and guarded the royal bedchamber, whose walls scintillated 'with an abundance of gold and silver'. At night the pages' beds were placed in the four corners of the room. The Sultan's double bed, covered in Persian silk rugs, Bursa quilts and leopardskins, and surrounded by silver candelabra, was in the middle.[29] Two pages accompanied the Sultan in his excursions into the world beyond the third courtyard. In Ottoman miniatures they look inappropriately young and innocent, in robes of red and gold, beside the Sultan and his stern-faced viziers.

The recruitment of viziers and pages from the ranks of slaves is evidence of one of the distinguishing features of the Ottoman palace, and of Constantinople itself: freedom from class. There was no hierarchy of disdain, no obsession with family which, in the West (and among some Arab tribes), clouded so many minds and decided so many careers. As late as the nineteenth century people considered in the West 'persons base and vile' could become leading officials in the palace. In 1830 Mahmud II noticed a face in the Egyptian bazaar: 'What is your name?' 'Riza.' 'Well then, follow me, Riza Bey.' In the twinkling of an eye, a shop assistant had become a *bey*, or lord. Subsequently he rose to be, in turn, page, equerry, chamberlain, Grand Marshal of the Palace, Minister of War, favourite of the Sultan's mother, the Valide Sultan. In 1843 he was called 'the most powerful and influential man in the empire'. When he died in 1877, he was said to be the richest pasha in Constantinople.[30]

Another difference between the Ottoman and Western courts was the absence of a court society. The social companions of the Sultan and his family, and of the leading viziers, were generally chosen from within their households. Wealthy families prominent in the provinces, some of whom pre-dated the Ottomans, rarely resided in Constantinople. There were no court entertainments to attract and domesticate them, like those of Versailles and Vienna. The palace was not an instrument for exercising control and distributing patronage. Relations with the central government were conducted through the provincial governor, not the monarch.

Exceptions to this rule were two families brought to the capital by the Sultan as both hostages and honoured guests, in an attempt to secure their loyalty. After 1532 one or two members of the ruling family of Crimea, the Giray Khans, resided in Constantinople and on their nearby property at Catalca, where the hunting was good. Enjoying the prestige of descent from Genghis Khan, they were the first to present their respects to the Sultan at Bayram, and were considered to have a right to the throne if the Ottoman dynasty died out. They lost the Crimea to Russia in 1783, but members of the family continued to reside in Constantinople, as some still do today.

Members of the Hashemite dynasty of Mecca, which had accepted Ottoman suzerainty in 1517, had first visited the capital to pay homage to Suleyman the Magnificent in 1539. They came again in 1589 and 1677 and some were obliged to settle there – although, at this stage, they would have preferred to live in the Arab-speaking city of Cairo. Relations between the two dynasties, the Hashemites and the Ottomans, remained an ambiguous combination of fear and respect, loyalty and bribery, rivalry and mutual need. There was a feud between the Hashemites and the Ottoman governor of the Hejaz for control of the revenue from pilgrims and customs. Some Hashemites resented subjection to 'the son of a slave' – the Sultan. The Sultan therefore wanted members of this dangerous dynasty under his eye in Constantinople. It was the start of the alternation between Constantinople and Mecca which was to control the pattern of the Hashemites' lives until the end of the empire.[31]

The splendour of the Sultan and his household were used to impress the city. Most Fridays the Sultan went in state to the mosque. Excursions on the Bosphorus, to visit the palaces at Beshiktash and Beylerbey built in the early seventeenth century, or across into Asia to hunt, allowed further displays of grandeur. In Constantinople men and boats, not horses and carriages, were the principal means of transport. The elegant, narrow *kayik*, with its long pointed prow, was as symbolic of the city as the gondola of Venice. The Sultan's kayiks were rowed by members of the corps of *Bostancis*. The Bostancis were not only imperial gardeners but also a distinct naval and military unit seven or eight thousand strong, separate from the Janissaries, which guarded the Sultan and controlled the Bosphorus and Golden Horn and their shores. By night they patrolled the port of Constantinople in launches, to arrest trouble-makers, and by day the outskirts of the city, to prevent traders evading customs dues.

The oars of the imperial kayiks, which were between thirty and forty metres long, were manned by twenty-six Bostancis, wearing red skull-caps with blue tassels, and loose white muslin breeches and shirts exposing their chests and arms. At one end lay the Sultan, shielded from sun and wind, propped on cushions in a kiosk of gilded wood inlaid with ivory, tortoiseshell and jewels. The Bostancis rowed with such vigour that his kayik shot through the water like an arrow from a bow: in the nineteenth century, it could outpace a steamboat. The Sultan's kayik was generally preceded by six subordinate kayiks carrying his attendants.

On the water, as on land, a special sound barrier enveloped the Sultan: his embarcation and disembarcation, and the passage of his kayik, were saluted by volleys of cannon fired from the shore – and from warships anchored in the Bosphorus. As the clouds of gunsmoke dispersed, the Bostancis began to 'barke like doggs', in order not to overhear the conversation between the Sultan and their commander the Bostanci Pasha, who had the honour of steering the tiller.[32]

Imperial grandeur flooded the streets of Constantinople during celebrations for the circumcision of the Sultan's sons or the marriage of his daughters. Like the *selamlik*, the celebrations were more public than in Western monarchies. On 27 June 1530 Suleyman the Magnificent, at the height of his power and glory, started the celebrations for the cir-cumcision of his sons Mustafa, Mehmed and Selim. Tents were erected in the largest open space in the city, the old Roman hippodrome. Protected from rain by a green covering, with interiors sewn with tulips, roses and carnations embroidered in silver and gold, and held upright by gold-plated poles, the Sultan's tents were palaces of silk and canvas. His throne was placed under an awning of cloth of gold. The 32-year-old Sultan was surrounded by the dignitaries of the empire, headed by the Grand Vizier Ibrahim Pasha, and attended by captive princes.

Where the future Empress Theodora had exposed herself to cheer-ing Byzantine crowds, jugglers and buffoons entertained the more decorous subjects of the Ottoman Sultan. Where teams of Blues and Greens had competed in chariot races, soldiers fought sailors in simu-lated combat. Tightrope walkers walked along cords strung between the

Obelisk of Thutmose III (1549–1503 BC), brought from Egypt and erected under Theodosius I in 390, and a stone pillar from the same reign. Presents of crystal, Chinese porcelain, Syrian damask, Indian muslin, and slaves from Ethiopia and Hungary, given to the Sultan by his viziers, Kurdish beys and foreign ambassadors, were displayed to the public. Poets recited works composed in honour of the occasion.

The claims of Islam were not forgotten. During contests of Koranic scholarship between *ulema*, one professor died of vexation at not being able to find the right words. On the eighteenth day, the Sultan's sons were fetched from the old palace in the centre of the city: their circumcisions were performed in the palace which the Grand Vizier Ibrahim had built overlooking the Hippodrome (the present Museum of Turkish and Islamic Art). In celebration the Sultan gave kaftans to viziers and *ulema*. The public was fed on roast oxen, out of which rushed live foxes, jackals and wolves in order to impress the crowd.[33]

In 1582 the circumcision of Prince Mehmed, son of Murad III, was an affair of state, planned a year in advance. Senior officials were given special festive functions. The commander-in-chief of Anatolia, for example, was appointed superintendent of sherbets. Some 1,500 copper plates and trays were made for the banquets. The palaces around the Hippodrome were restored to provide better seating, and viewing, for ambassadors from Samarkand, Persia, Georgia, Morocco, Venice, Poland and the Holy Roman Empire, as well as for the ladies of the palace behind a grilled stand.

On 1 June the Sultan's arrival opened the celebrations. Two innovations show the emergence of an urban ethos. All the guilds of Constantinople processed past the Sultan on his golden throne, at the rate of two or three a day. On horse-drawn floats they displayed their skill at a particular trade. One float showed a tiled hamam with men in black skirts performing ablutions and massage. Cooks went by showing sheep's and bulls' heads and feet, crying 'Take it my dear, all greasy, all hot, all vinegared and garlicked!' Tar makers threw pitch and tar into the crowd and played 'a thousand merry tricks of that kind'. Keepers of lunatic asylums led laughing and weeping madmen in gold and silver chains. A contingent of 150 boys covered in bits of glass flashed reflections of the summer sun back to spectators, to display the mirror-makers' skill. Fireworks representing cities, churches and unicorns were prepared with the help of a captured English engineer called Edward Webbe. The Sultan offered a series of banquets, one evening to the pashas, the next to the *ulema*, the third to his troops. A thousand plates of rice and twenty roast ox were prepared every evening for the people of Constantinople.

In a humble way, Jews and Christians joined in the celebrations. Both Greek and Armenian Patriarchs, as well as the Mufti and dervishes, made obeisance to the Sultan, blessing him with the words: 'May God maintain Sultan Murad in long happiness!' A mock battle in the Hippodrome pitted Muslims against Christians. Naturally the first won, and captured the Christians' castle, out of which emerged four pigs – a contemptuous reference to Christians' consumption of pork. The populace was regaled with Jewish comedies and dances. One hundred Greeks from Galata, in red jackets and Phrygian caps, with bells attached to their legs, performed lascivious dances from Alexandria. Some Christians (but not Jews) were so overcome by the occasion – or, according to a Christian source, by offers of money – that they held up their thumbs as a sign of readiness to convert to Islam. They were at once carried off to the palace to be circumcised.

The prince, the future Mehmed III, dressed in scarlet satin and white brocade, with heron plumes in his turban and a red ruby in his right ear, was circumcised on 7 July. The foreskin was despatched on a golden plate to the prince's mother: his grandmother was sent the knife with which it was severed. The cutter was rewarded with 3,000 gold coins, a golden bowl and ewer, thirty lengths of cloth, robes of honour and, subsequently, marriage to one of the Sultan's daughters. Finally the Sultan returned to the palace on 22 July. The celebrations had lasted so long – fifty-five days – that the start of the campaigning season was delayed.[34] Constantinople might have been another Capua, the city whose pleasures diverted Hannibal's army from the attack on Rome.

An unusual ornament displayed at city festivals was the traditional Turkish *nahil*, an artificial palm tree made of wire and wax. Decorated with precious stones, fruit, flowers and mirrors, they were regarded as symbols of virility and fertility, and could be as high as twenty-two metres. For a week before the circumcisions in 1582, five large and 360 small and medium *nahils* were carried in processions around the city. In particularly narrow streets, houses had to be demolished to let them through: imperial splendour took precedence over urban fabric.[35]

The display of grandeur, at the wedding of a Sultan's daughter, could be more important than the wedding itself. In 1709 at the wedding of the 5-year-old Princess Fatma, the groom's presents – cases of jewels, Korans, pearl-studded shoes, two silver *nahils*, fifteen purses of gold, one hundred and twenty trays of sweetmeats – were carried in state through the city to the palace. Inside the palace the trousseau was displayed to the viziers, who responded with further gifts. Fifty-five mules then carried the entire trousseau through cheering crowds, escorted by most of the imperial household in ceremonial dress, to the princess's new palace at Eyup. The bride herself was taken there in a procession of thirty-one coaches.

On successive days fireworks, jugglers, wrestling competitions, and mock battles featuring a warship which had been dragged through the streets, entertained the city. The Sultan's glory could be demonstrated on the streets of Constantinople, if not on the battlefields of Europe (his armies had suffered repeated defeats by Austrian forces since the failure of the siege of Vienna in 1683). The marriage, however, was never consummated. Before his bride had reached the age of puberty, the groom was killed in yet another Ottoman defeat.[36]

In 1720 four of the Sultan's sons were circumcised and two of his nieces married at the same time. Four nine-metre high *nahils* and forty small *nahils* were made for each prince. The celebrations on the Okmeydan, outside the city walls near Galata, lasted fifteen days and nights: five thousand other boys were circumcised at the same time. There was a procession of guilds past the Sultan, sitting in the Alay (Ceremonial) Kiosk built on the palace wall specifically to enable him to observe what was happening outside. Carriages were driven on tightropes between the masts of ships anchored in the Bosphorus.[37]

Grandiose celebrations also marked the birth of a child to the Sultan. From the sea walls of the palace cannon fired seven rounds for a boy, three for a girl, five times in twenty-four hours. Firmans announced the news to the rest of the empire. Processions escorted a jewelled cradle and cradle-cover through the streets of the city to the imperial palace. In the palace the bedroom of the mother was crowded with the wives of the most senior officials of the empire, who rose in respect when the cradle arrived.

The night sky also reflected the Sultan's splendour. To mark dynastic weddings and circumcisions, and religious festivals such as the Prophet's birthday, ships, mosques and palaces were illuminated by small lamps. Illuminated messages, strung between the minarets, spelt out: 'My sovereign, may you live a thousand years!' Boats with red, blue or green paper lanterns, looking like fireflies, turned the Bosphorus and the Golden Horn into a sea of fire. Witnessing the illuminations for the Prophet's birthday in 1841, Hans Christian Andersen felt that he had entered one of his own tales: 'Everything looked as if it were outlined with flame . . . Everything was enveloped in a magic light.'[38]

Embassies allowed both the Sultan and foreign monarchs to display their power and wealth to the people of Constantinople. The city was one of the diplomatic capitals of the world and an ambassador to Constantinople was obliged to bring with him a princely household. As the Bailo of Venice wrote in 1583: '*È certo che se nelle altre corti de' principi è necessario splendore, in Constantinopoli è necessarissimo*' ('It is certain that if in the other courts of princes splendour is necessary, in Constantinople it is most necessary'). Such splendour pleased, and was noticed by, the people as well as the Sultan. In 1573 Philippe du Fresne Canaye, in the suite of the French ambassador going to Topkapi palace, wrote: 'The bank was full of so many people and the walls and the neighbouring houses packed to the roofs with so many spectators that I have never seen so many people at the same time in my life.' Herr von Kuefstein arrived from Vienna as Imperial ambassador in 1628. He wrote: 'I was splendidly escorted into the town where all the windows and streets were extraordinarily crowded with spectators.' Any innovation in the number or dress of the accompanying officials would be noted by the keen-eyed crowd.[39]

The Sultan's departure to and return from Edirne, or a campaign, provided further opportunities for display. Evliya Celebi saw delirious crowds welcome Murad IV in 1638, when he returned from the reconquest of Baghdad. Packing roofs and windows, they cried: 'The blessing of God be upon thee, O Conqueror! Welcome, Murad! May thy victory be fortunate!' So many ships fired salutes that the sea seemed to be on fire. Wearing a Persian turban to symbolize his victory over Persian armies, and followed by chiefs in chains 'like a lion who has seized his prey', he proceeded in triumph to the palace. There he received the congratulations of his court, seated on a golden throne on which had been inscribed the following verse:

> You are the pole to which the world turns.
> The world trembles before you like the needle in the compass.
> It does not tremble from fear of annihilation,
> But from desire to offer itself as a sacrifice before your throne of
> power.

Seven days of celebration ended when the Sultan went to pray at Eyup.

In 1671 the French ambassador, the Marquis de Nointel, was writing a description of the Sultan Mehmed IV's departure through Constantinople to Edirne, escorted by guards and viziers gleaming with jewels, velvet and brocade. In the middle of his despatch he remembers that he is ambassador of Louis XIV, and that the Sun King does not care for rivals. He embarks on the *mea culpa* of a French courtier: 'If this ceremony has some splendour, one must take guard not to be overwhelmed by it . . . The true remedy to avoid being prejudiced is to think of the grandeur of the King's Household . . . His Majesty wanting to make an entry, can efface without difficulty the finest spectacles in these regions and in the rest of the Levant.' Does the ambassador protest too much?

This routine of imperial weddings, circumcisions, illuminations, embassies, *selamliks*, brought greater show, more often, to Constantinople than to other capitals. In combination with the hidden majesty of the Seraglio, and the visible beauty of the city's setting and skyline, such processions made imperial splendour part of Constantinople's image in the outside world.

Processions also helped to create in the city the love of pomp and splendour which was to be one of its hallmarks until the twentieth century. Like Viennese before 1918, and Londoners before 1960, the people of Constantinople were instinctive imperialists. Consciousness of empire conditioned their minds as much as realities of empire conditioned their material lives. Did not travellers who had visited all the cities in the world say that they had found no city like it? Did not writers call it 'the envy of the kings of the world'? Was it not destined to flourish 'until the end of time'? In the early eighteenth century the Ottoman poet Nedim wrote in praise of it:

> O city of Istanbul, priceless and peerless!
> I would sacrifice all Persia for one of your stones!

Even in the nineteenth century, after the Ottoman Empire had suffered repeated defeats, since China had not 'come to Constantinople' – that is, had sent no embassy – Ottomans could not believe that China was truly an empire.[40] The Viennese might think that their city was the only true *kaiserstadt*, and deserved to be capital of Europe. The people of Isfahan – capital of Persia – might claim that their city was 'half the world'. Citizens of Constantinople knew that theirs was the centre of the universe.

4

Harems and Hamams

By God and again by God, I burn day and night in the fire of separation from you.
Hurrem to her husband Suleyman the Magnificent, *c.* 1535

Really pasha! White beards and black beards are not the issue. Good policy comes not from age but from intelligence.
Turhan, mother of Mehmed IV, to a pasha boasting of his age and wisdom, *c.* 1655

FOR CENTURIES IN the Caucasus, mothers sang a lullaby over their daughters' cradles, beginning 'Live among diamonds and splendour as the wife of the Sultan'. In their eagerness to follow such advice, some girls offered themselves, for nothing, to visiting slave-dealers.[1] Their goal was the imperial harem in Constantinople. *Harem* means 'sanctuary', thence, by derivation, female quarters. The imperial harem was a sanctuary of women and eunuchs, which affected the public life of Constantinople as well as the private life of the Sultan.

The harem existed in order to channel the Sultan's sexuality, and reproductive faculties, in the interests of the dynasty. The wars of the Spanish and Austrian successions show the catastrophic results, for a dynasty, of lack of a male heir. How could a dynasty guarantee its biological survival in the male line? Early sultans had sometimes followed standard dynastic practice and married princesses from neighbouring Christian or Muslim dynasties. However these marriages had been made for political not biological reasons, to strengthen an alliance rather than to produce an heir. The Sultan may never have slept with such wives, in order to avoid having children by them. After 1500, moreover, the Sultan was so powerful that, unlike lesser monarchs, he did not need dynastic alliances (although suitable candidates from the Giray dynasty of the Crimea and the Sherifs of Mecca were available). Bayezid II (1481–1512) was the last Sultan to make a dynastic match, with a princess of the Turkish dynasty of Dulkadir in Anatolia.

More than any other dynasty, the Ottoman dynasty chose to reproduce itself by serial concubinage with slaves. The principal reason was the same desire for control which led it to employ slave Janissaries as guards. Neither group had ambitious or greedy relations in the capital. They were, in theory, completely dependent on the Sultan. Slave concubines within the palace could be more easily manipulated in the interests of the dynasty than free Muslim women with legal rights prescribed by the *sheriat*. Fertilized concubines were restricted to one son each, after which sexual congress with the Sultan usually ceased. Thereby each son was provided with the support of a single devoted mother.

Desire was another reason for the size of the harem. Most sultans were likely to desire a variety of sexual partners. Royal mistresses in France and, down to the present day, England provide examples of the embarrassments caused by dynastic amours within the ruling élite. Slave concubines, chosen for health and beauty rather than birth, would gratify the Sultan's desires without damaging consequences.

Biology was the third reason for the harem system. Concubines' sons – unlike those of married mistresses – enlarged the dynastic reserve. The number of concubines fertilized ensured that there was always a male heir. Like a prize stallion, the Sultan was constantly encouraged to move on and 'cover' more mates, in order to breed more stock. There was no war of the Ottoman succession, as there might have been if the dynasty had married for rank rather than reproduction. For all these reasons, half conscious, half embedded in the dynastic metastructure, the Sultan was sexually restricted to slaves within the harem walls.[2]

The greatest Sultan, however, defied the palace rules. At the beginning of his reign Suleyman the Magnificent, 'very lustful', had frequently visited 'the palace of the women', the first palace built by Mehmed II in the centre of Constantinople, and there 'done justice'. By 1524, however, contrary to precedent, he had chosen monogamy with a woman called Hurrem. The Sultan was frequently away from the city at the head of his armies, and so wrote and received letters and poems. They reveal that this paradigm of imperial power, the terror of his neighbours, was pious, gentle and faithful to his wife.

The harem was a forbidden city. Facts about inmates' careers before they entered are hard to establish. Once in the palace, like footmen in a grand English country-house, women were given new names, to mark the break with their old identity. The names were generally Persian –

Mihrimah, Mahpeyker, Shevkiyar: in order to be remembered, the names were pinned to the new arrival's breasts. Hurrem was probably born Alexandra Lisowska, daughter of an Orthodox priest of Ukrainian extraction living near Lvov in Poland. She had been captured in a slave raid from the neighbouring Tartar khanate of the Crimea. *Hurrem* means 'the laughing one'. She quickly annihilated her main rival.

Soon after Suleyman had begun to notice Hurrem, Mahidevran, the Circassian mother of the Sultan's eldest son Mustafa, picked a quarrel, and scratched her face, calling her 'traitor' and 'soiled meat'. The next time Suleyman summoned Hurrem, she refused to come, repeating that she was 'soiled meat', unworthy of the Sultan's favour. Finally the Sultan asked Mahidevran if the story of their quarrel was true. According to a Venetian report, 'she replied that it was and that she had done less to her [Hurrem] than she deserved. She believed that all the women should yield to her and recognize her as mistress since she had been in the service of his majesty first.' Mahidevran was dismissed, and died forgotten in Bursa in 1581.[3]

Hurrem, on the other hand, became a power in the palace. Years later the Venetian Bailo wrote: 'There has never been in the history of the Ottoman house a woman who enjoyed greater authority. It is said that she is agreeable, modest and that she knows the wishes of the Sultan very well.' Around 1534, perhaps by threatening to withhold her favours, she persuaded the Sultan to grant her the unthinkable honour of marriage.

As at the court of Henry VIII or Louis XIV, possession of the right apartment was an essential means to retain, and advertise, the monarch's favour. After a fire in the Old Palace, Hurrem moved into the New Imperial Palace itself, near her husband. A former page in the palace described her quarters:

> The Seraglio of the Sultana is in the same [complex] as the Grand Turk's and one can go through secret rooms from one to the other. No one enters the palace of the Sultana except the Grand Turk, the eunuchs and another person called the procurator [*Kethuda* – her man of affairs] of the Sultana who always comes and goes whenever he wishes . . . the rooms of the Sultana are equally exquisite, with prayer halls, baths, gardens and other comforts.[4]

It was the nucleus of what would become one of the most powerful institutions in the city, the imperial harem.

The love between Suleyman and Hurrem is one of the few relationships between man and wife in Constantinople which is recorded in their own words. The Ottoman dynasty had a tradition of poetry: Bayezid and Cem, while competing for the throne, had corresponded in verse. Suleyman wrote under the name *Muhibbi*, 'the Friendly One'. The principal foreign historian of Ottoman poetry, Edward Gibb, writes: 'The chief feature of his poems is not, as with so many of his contemporaries, mere verbal elegance; it is their evident sincerity of feeling which strikes us most as we read those verses with their undertone of calm humility.' He writes of the the vanity of worldly power, the pleasures of poverty, or wine (possibly a metaphor for love of God). Constant ill-health, which turned his face 'a very bad colour' (so bad that, to deceive foreign ambassadors, he sometimes wore rouge), humbled the Sultan. His most famous verse is:

> The people think of wealth and power as the greatest fate,
> But in this world a spell of health is the best state.
> What men call sovereignty is worldly strife and constant war;
> Worship of God is the highest throne, the happiest estate.

Many of his poems are addressed to Hurrem. He desired neither wealth nor thrones, since he had the infinite happiness of being a slave in her palace. 'Sometimes you treat me with kindness, sometimes you torment me. My love, whatever your mood, I will always adapt to it.' He is the Sultan of love – a favourite phrase. The tears pouring down both sides of his face were his troops. To express his love, the Sultan ransacked nature and his own empire for metaphors. Hurrem was:

> The green of my garden, my sweet sugar, my treasure, my love who
>   cares for nothing in this world.
> My master of Egypt, my Joseph, my everything, the queen of my
>   heart's realm.
> My Stanbul, my Karaman, my land of the Roman Caesars,
> My Badahshan, my Kipcak, my Baghdad and Khorasan.
> O my love of black hair with bow-like eyebrows, with languorous
>   perfidious eyes.
> If I die you are my killer, O merciless, infidel woman.[5]

Hurrem's letters are equally passionate – although they may have been composed, in part, by a harem official writing under her direction. she calls him 'heart-stealing radiance', 'horizon of prosperity', 'my hope in the two worlds': 'May one of your days be a thousand [days]!' A hair of his moustache is worth more than 5,000 or even 1,000,000 florins.

She asks for 'pity for my feeling of loneliness and separation from the Lord of the Worlds . . . If the seas were to become ink and these trees pens, when could they write an account of this parting?' She regrets a quarrel: 'I supplicate that the words separating you from me may be destroyed.' One letter begins: 'After trailing this ugly face of mine in the noble dust of your blessed feet', and ends: 'For the rest, may felicity in the two worlds be certain. Your poor and humble handmaid Hurrem.'

She tells him news of the city: 'For the moment there is disease but not as it was before. May it be that my Sultan comes. The Lord will show grace and it will pass away. Our great ones reply that when autumn sheds its leaves, it will pass.' This priest's daughter had become passionately Ottoman:

> News of your victory has arrived. When I heard it, God knows, my Padishah, my Sultan, I had died but this gave me life again. A thousand thousand thanks to the Almighty. All the world has emerged from darkness and everyone is overwhelmed by the light of divine mercy. I hope you will wage war and level the enemy with the earth and you will take kingdoms and conquer the seven climes.

Through their children she gave the Sultan a degree of family life unusual in the history of the Ottoman dynasty. She tells him constantly how much he is missed:

> When your noble letters are read, it made your servant and son Mir Mehmed and your slave and daughter Mihrimah weep and wail from missing you. Their weeping has made me mad, it is as if we were in mourning. My Sultan, your son Mir Mehmed and your daughter Mihrimah and Selim Khan and Abdullah send you many greetings and rub their faces in the dust at your feet.[6]

Love was not the only bond between Hurrem and the Sultan. The wife of the most powerful monarch in Europe could not avoid politics. Unlike her contemporary Anne Boleyn, Hurrem did not enjoy a public coronation at which the entire capital celebrated her elevation. Nor did she obtain a public rank at court and a household of several hundred men and women at her orders. However, from behind the harem walls, she exercised greater influence than the Queen of England. Although Suleyman and Henry VIII used a similar language of love and submission to their 'mistress', the Sultan was more sincere. Above all Hurrem had the treasure which Anne Boleyn lacked: sons.

The Sultan consulted her over politics at least as much as Henry VIII did Anne Boleyn. She had not entirely lost contact with her previous identity. To promote peace she corresponded with the King of Poland and sent him handkerchiefs embroidered by her own hands. The Sultan advertised her role – possibly in order to demonstrate his concern for his female subjects – by building in her name a vast mosque complex, called *Hasseki* (Imperial), in the west of the city. Attached to it were a soup-kitchen, a hospital and a school. It is the only such complex built for a Sultan's wife or concubine in his lifetime: and other foundations, more numerous than any commissioned by a Queen Consort of England, were built on Hurrem's orders in Edirne, Jerusalem, Medina and Mecca.

By his fidelity to Hurrem, Suleyman the Magnificent outraged the palace and the city. Like Anne Boleyn, she was accused of having 'bewitched' her husband: 'but because he loves her no one dares to protest.'[7] Hurrem also acted as an independent political operator. Her principal motive was to save her sons' lives. Before 1607 the Ottoman Empire had no fixed rule of succession. The throne belonged to whichever prince first reached Constantinople and the imperial treasury. His success meant that he had God's blessing and was the legitimate Sultan. Other princes might foment the civil wars which had plagued the Ottoman dynasty in the early fifteenth century, or be the instruments of palace or Janissary factions; the new Sultan therefore usually had them killed. Princes were as expendable as viziers. With that disabused realism which was no less characteristic of Ottoman official style than imperial grandiloquence, Mehmed II had written: 'Whichever of my sons inherits the Sultan's throne, it behoves him to kill his brothers in the interest of the world order [the Ottoman Empire]. Most of the jurists have approved this procedure. Let action be taken accordingly.' Like the physical separation of *devshirme* youths from their families, such a policy ignored the family ties celebrated in the Koran. The imperial palace, however, was governed by the requirements of the dynasty, not the law of Islam. Mehmed II executed two brothers; Selim I two brothers, three sons and four nephews. He may also have ordered his father poisoned. In the entire history of the dynasty about eighty princes were killed, generally through strangulation with a bow-string, to avoid spilling the Ottomans' sacred blood.[8]

Execution as a means of dynastic control was not an Ottoman invention. Thirty of eighty-eight Byzantine emperors had died by strangulation, poison or torture in Constantinople itself. Edward V and his brother were murdered in the Tower of London, almost certainly on the orders of their uncle Richard III: the Maréchal d'Ancre in the palace of the Louvre on those of Louis XIII in 1616. The annals of the Mogul emperors in Delhi are stained with blood. However, in other dynasties bloodshed was, in theory, exceptional. Only the Ottoman dynasty made fratricide (and the execution of ministers) into a rule.

In the glittering jungle of the Ottoman palace, attack was the best means of defence. Hurrem first achieved the destruction of her husband's closest friend, the Grand Vizier Ibrahim Pasha. Ibrahim was a Greek from Parga on the Ionian Sea, born about 1493. Captured by pirates, he was sold to a widow living in the provincial capital of Manisa, but subsequently entered the palace school. Short, swarthy, intelligent and well-read, Ibrahim knew Persian, Greek, Serbo-Croat and Italian, and played the lute. When he entered the household of Suleyman, the young prince was captivated.

As in other courts, personal service to the monarch could lead to the highest offices of state. After Suleyman's accession, Ibrahim rose rapidly through the intimate court offices of falconer and head of the privy chamber until in 1523, despite the claims of older viziers, he became Grand Vizier. Contrary to imperial etiquette, Suleyman and Ibrahim dined together. Their beds were side by side. Alone in Ottoman history Ibrahim had the honour of having six horse-tails – the ancient Turkish symbol of rank – one less than the Sultan himself, erected beside his tent.[9] Ottoman government had become a partnership.

Ibrahim Pasha was an able general and vizier, compared by an Ottoman contemporary to 'the sun which sheds its rays upon the universe'. In 1535, his treatment of the captured city of Tabriz was more merciful than Charles V's, the same year, of Tunis. His conversation, reported in the despatches of foreign ambassadors, expressed the Bismarckian arrogance of the Ottoman capital:

How foolish are they who say that kings are kings because of their crowns. Not gold nor gems command but iron – the sword – by which obedience is assured.

Though I am the Sultan's slave, whatsoever I do is done. I can at a stroke make a pasha out of a stable-boy. I can give kingdoms and provinces to whomsoever I choose and my lord will say nothing against it. Even if he has ordered a thing himself, if I do not want it, it is not done. And if I order a thing to be done and he has ordered to the contrary, what I wish and not what he wishes is done.[10]

Ibrahim Pasha was a man of double identity, in the cosmopolitan tradition of Mehmed II. He summoned artists from Brussels and Venice to Constantinople, and was said to do 'much good to the Christians'. To the disgust of some Muslims, he placed statues of Hercules, Apollo and Diana, taken from the royal palace of Buda, in front of the stone palace which the Sultan had built for him overlooking the Hippodrome. Owing to Muslim prejudice against representations of humans, they were the only statues erected in public in Constantinople between 1453 and 1924. A poet sneered that, whereas the Patriarch Abraham had destroyed idols, Ibrahim erected them: the poet was paraded through the city on an ass and hanged.

In his personal life, although he had a male favourite, the influential merchant diplomat Alvise Gritti, he also loved his wife, the Sultan's sister Hatice, to whom he wrote: 'Night and day I am busy praying for you. God knows I love you still with all my heart.' In his years of glory his own family was not forgotten. His mother and two brothers were installed in his palace; his old father, however, was '*homme de riens et inutile, tavernier, yvrogne et couchant par les rues comme les bestes*'.[11]

For most of his career, Ibrahim had the support of the Sultan's mother, his own mother-in-law, Hafsa, a forceful woman who rarely left her son's side. After Hafsa's death in 1534, Hurrem moved in for the kill – abetted by the Grand Vizier's own arrogance and extravagance. Partisans of the Finance Minister Iskender Celebi spread calumnies, such as Ibrahim's supposed ambition to share the sultanate. In one letter Suleyman questioned Hurrem about her displeasure with 'the pasha'. Too shrewd to denounce him when absent from the Sultan, she replied, in the elliptical language of the court: 'And now you enquire about why I am not with Ibrahim Pasha. You will hear about it when, God willing, my meeting with you will be granted to me. For the moment tell the Pasha our greetings. We hope they [the Pasha] accept them.'[12]

On 15 March 1536 Ibrahim dined with the Sultan as usual, and spent the night in an adjoining chamber. Next morning his strangled body was found outside the palace. Scars showed that he had put up a good fight. Ibrahim's alleged blood stains were displayed as a warning for the next hundred years. Years later Hurrem and her daughter Mihrimah suggested that Mihrimah's husband, the Grand Vizier Rustem, should enter the third courtyard and dine with the Sultan. He retorted that one mistake of that sort was enough.[13] After Ibrahim's death the taste for luxury and cosmopolitanism in the palace declined.

Ibrahim's elimination was not Hurrem's only triumph. In the 1540s she formed a triumvirate with Mihrimah and her son-in-law Rustem Pasha, against the popular prince Mustafa, son of her former rival Mahidevran. The Sultan's daughter Mihrimah wrote to her father, calling Mustafa 'that howling dog'. The Sultan was persuaded that Mustafa was plotting his downfall. In later letters this forceful princess, who also corresponded with the King of Poland, used the imperative to her own father: 'My Sultan, write with some gentleness too, and at the end write somewhat strongly.' In 1553 Mustafa was strangled in his father's tent by three mutes.[14] Mustafa's hunchbacked half-brother Cihangir died of grief two months later: the elaborate Shehzade mosque was built on a hill above the Golden Horn to house his remains.

The Janissaries overturned their pilav cauldrons in anger at news of Mustafa's death and demanded that Rustem Pasha be whipped. Busbecq, the Imperial ambassador, wrote: 'First they inveighed against Suleyman as a crazy old lunatic; then they railed against the treachery and cruelty of the young man's stepmother and the wickedness of Rustem who together had extinguished the brightest star of the house of Osman.' An elegy by the Albanian Yahya Bey also expressed the horror felt in the capital. When blamed by Rustem Pasha, the poet replied: 'We indeed condemned him with the Padishah but we bewailed him with the people.'

In order to appease the people, Suleyman dismissed Rustem Pasha. Hurrem wrote to Suleyman in protest: 'Rustem Pasha is your slave. Do not withhold your noble face from him, my fortune-favoured. Do not listen to what anyone says. Just this once, let it be for the sake of your slave Mihrimah, my fortune-favoured, my emperor, for your own sake, and my sake too, my prosperous Sultan.'[15] 'Just this once' has a nagging edge. Hurrem died in 1558. She had been much blamed for her husband's policies, but after her death, like Saturn, he continued to devour his own children. In 1561 another son, Bayezid, who had fought Prince Selim for the succession, was strangled, with four infant sons, on the Sultan's orders. Suleyman died in 1566, his end hastened by the decision, despite his ill health, to undertake yet another Hungarian campaign. He was succeeded by Selim.

The new Sultan loved, and may have married, a woman called Nurbanu (Princess Light), tall with dark hair and eyes, and delicate features, who bore him the future Murad III. The screen of secrecy protecting the harem was so effective that, until recently, she was thought to have been a Venetian, Cecilia Venier Baffo, taken prisoner on the island of Paros in the Aegean in 1537, during a war between Venice and the Ottoman Empire. However, it is more likely that she was a wealthy Greek noblewoman called Kale Kastanos, captured on Corfu during the same war. She may have used rumours of her Venetian origin to extract better presents from the Venetian government.

Selim II died from a fall in 1574, when inspecting, possibly drunk, new buildings in the harem bath-house. Nurbanu kept Selim II's corpse in an icebox until her son Murad III had reached the capital from Manisa in Anatolia, where he had been acting as provincial governor. After he was proclaimed Sultan, in accordance with the fratricide law, five of his half-brothers were executed and buried with their father.[16]

Murad III, small, fat and proud, had 'large pale eyes, an aquiline nose, good skin colour and a big blond beard'. On his accession in 1574, in a step of symbolic importance, he moved his bedroom and privy chamber from the male world of the third courtyard to the female world of the harem, to the left of the third and fourth courtyards. So pressing was his need for a new bedroom that no other tiles could be made at Iznik until those for the Sultan's new apartments had been finished. His room is a sumptuous domed hall, covered with red, blue and green Iznik tiles. Koranic inscriptions on a band of blue and white tiles run round the walls; the window shutters are inlaid with mother-of-pearl. His routine was to sleep in the harem. After a late breakfast, he would return to the male world of the second and third courtyards. There he gave audiences to the Grand Vizier, the Aga (commander) of the Janissaries, pashas and beylerbeys (senior generals), and received ambassadors. He always had dinner in the harem, for the conversation there, according to a Venetian diplomat, amused him 'extremely'.[17]

Murad III was the epitome of the new, sedentary style of Sultan. Insatiable for sex not victory, he rarely left Constantinople. Constantinople and, within the city the palace itself, were beginning to overshadow the rest of the empire. Though loving his concubine Safiye, he finally yielded to the temptations placed in his way by his sister Ismihan, wife of the Grand Vizier Sokollu Mehmed Pasha, and by his mother Nurbanu. By supplying beauties for the Sultan, the Sultan's mother, the Valide Sultan, and the princesses were performing their dynastic duty to increase the number of princes. The seventeenth-century palace official Bobowski wrote of a later Valide: 'She always searches for beautiful girls to be presented to him.' Attractive newcomers poured the Sultan's coffee when he came to visit his mother. If he noticed one, she was called *gozde*, 'in the eye'. If he wanted her in his bed, he told the chief black eunuch. (The story of his choosing a partner by dropping a handkerchief in front of her is a myth.) The other women congratulated the new favourite. They accompanied her to the bath, washed, perfumed and dressed her. Finally they led her, with music and song, to the Sultan's bedroom. After he had slept with her, she was called an *ikbal*, or favourite. By the end of his reign Murad III had lost all restraint and was said to 'do justice' to two or three women a night, and to have fathered 102 children. After each act of intercourse, to conform with Muslim injunctions on post-coital washing, he took a bath. He began to have epileptic fits.[18]

Under Murad III in the 1570s, there was a rise in the physical size, political importance and numbers of the harem. The harem consisted of a labyrinth of rooms, passages and courtyards – courtyards of the Women, of the Eunuchs, of the Valide, of the Favourites and of the Hospital. The Valide enjoyed a majestic suite of bathroom, prayer room, dining room, throne hall and bedroom. Centrally located, it enjoyed easy access to all quarters of the harem – and to the harem prison directly below.

The other 300 or so rooms were surprisingly small, possibly to make them easier to heat. They were decorated with marble doors, gilded arabesque ceilings, and Iznik tiles. Some window recesses contained taps, so that private conversations were protected by the sound of running water. Inscriptions on the tiles broadcast the city's obsessive message of imperial grandeur. Above the main entrance to the harem beside the Divan, the inscription from the reign of Murad III states that it is the entrance to the harem of heaven, the charms of which would astonish paradise itself. On tiles inside were such sentences as: 'God save Sultan Osman . . . and may this always be the door to the Emperor's victory!' 'Seated in purity may you ever be the Emperor of the World!' 'His Excellency Sultan Ahmed, a second Alexander, built the palace, having designed it himself. It perfumes the brain. Each breath and breeze is the purest musk and amber of love.'[19]

From 1574 until her death in 1583, Murad III's mother Nurbanu was the first of the great Valide Sultans or Queen Mothers. Even though she lived in a separate palace outside the city walls, Nurbanu controlled the harem and the Sultan: 'all good and all evil,' it was said, 'come from the Queen Mother.' Through her *kira* or Jewish intermediary, Esther, she kept contact with the outside world and frequently wrote to the Venetian Bailo in Pera, asking for gifts of silk, brocade and cushions.

Since she helped to keep peace between Venice and the Ottoman Empire, and arranged ransoms for prisoners of war, he hastened to oblige. Nurbanu also corresponded, as 'the Sultan Queen Mother of the Grand Seigneur', with 'the Queen Mother of the King', Catherine de Medici, about treaty relations between France and the Ottoman Empire. The following note from her, in 1583, shows the imperious tone of the harem, and the importance its inhabitants attached to material objects, or animals: 'Thus let it be known to the Baliyus [the Bailo of Venice]! You have sent two lap-dogs. Now lap-dogs like that are not required, and they are big, also long-haired. Thus shall you know! let them be white and let them be little!'

Brought up an Orthodox Christian, in 1582 Nurbanu commissioned from the chief imperial architect Sinan a mosque radiant with the joy of religion, the Atik Valide Cami, on a hill above Uskudar. Attached to it were a hospital, a hamam, inns and a soup-kitchen for 'the poor and the wretched'. Whether Nurbanu's principal motive was piety or vanity can be judged from the wording of the foundation deed of the mosque *vakif*:

> To achieve her desire of acquiring merit in Allah's sight, the Valide Sultan allotted from her unencumbered possessions and properties those parts that will be mentioned in detail in this deed of trust. In genuine and sincere determination, devoid of hypocrisy and deceit, with only the purest of intentions, she ordered the erection of many great and magnificent edifices of charity.

Three schools, for learning and reciting the Koran and studying the Hadith, were built beside the mosque 'because she gives much value and importance to education and in order to elevate and ennoble scholarship among the people'.[20]

The people of Constantinople and the Ottoman government accepted the Valide's authority. At times it was no less than that of the queen mothers Catherine de Medici, Marie de Medici and Anne of Austria in Paris. In their different situations all commanded men, and helped preserve their son's authority. As a mother, a Valide was a symbol of stability and hierarchy. After 1574, by the chance of dynastic biology, the sultans were younger and less able than their predecessors. The Valide, as much as the Sultan, came to represent the prestige and munificence of the dynasty and, on occasion, its last remnant of common sense. An Ottoman Valide could be called 'the crown of the veiled coronet of the modest', or 'the mother of all believers'.

By the seventeenth century the revenues of certain crown lands were set aside for the Sultan's mother. She received the highest stipend in the empire, higher than the Grand Vizier's: 3,000 *akces* a day, frequently augmented by gifts from ambassadors, pashas and her son the Sultan. Her power was regularly advertised in the city. When one Valide returned from a visit to Edirne in 1668, she made her entry into Constantinople surrounded by at least 5,000 troops, footmen, court gardeners, masters of ceremonies, eunuchs, members of the *ulema*, and the Sultan's favourite dressed in red brocade. The procession took three hours to pass by. When a new Sultan ascended the throne, his mother was taken in public procession from the old palace in the middle of the city to the new palace on Seraglio Point. Surrounded by courtiers and footmen, halberdiers and Janissaries, a visible symbol of matriarchy, the Valide advanced in a six-horse carriage, followed by a smaller carriage from which coins were scattered to cheering crowds. Presents were given to every guard-house of Janissaries along the route. In the outer courtyard of the palace, she was met by her son who performed the *temenna*, or salute of respect, and kissed his mother's hand through the window.[21]

A hole in a wall symbolizes harem power: at an unknown date in the late sixteenth century, a round hole was made in the Golden Path in the harem, overlooking the Council Hall. Thereby the latest political information reached the harem, literally through the window, before all but the most senior government officials.[22]

The precise mode of operation, and purpose, of harem influence is difficult to establish. However, the reign of Murad III was seen at the time, by both Ottoman and foreign observers, as a turning-point in the fortunes of the Ottoman Empire – and of the harem. The historian Mustafa Selaniki wrote at the end of the sixteenth century: 'The ostentation of the state is excessive and the imperial pomp is increasing; wastage and excessive expenditure have reached such a peak that the public treasury can no longer suffice . . . Nobody cares any longer to go on campaign for the sake of God. People do not desire the bliss of martyrdom.' The waste in food and drink in the palace, according to another Ottoman intellectual, Mustafa Ali, was 'beyond description . . . The corrupt breed of cooks, bread-bakers and pantry stewards has found protection with the agas of the Honourable Harem . . . Secretly or openly a flowing ocean invades the continent of the Porte. A copious flood of expensive beverages begins to move crock by crock from the Imperial Pantry to the apartment of the Palace Guards.' Some 168 kilos of almonds and 224 kilos of musk-scented rose water were consumed in the palace every day. If a vizier tried to check waste, the courtiers went to the Sultan crying, 'They have cut the food that is assigned to us!' The order was rescinded.[23]

The Venetian ambassador was more specific: 'The women and eunuchs are always around him [Murad III] and can usually put in the last word . . . There is no worthwhile person for him to talk with . . . he trusts no one and is wise not to, for he knows that all the people who serve him can easily be bribed.' In the early sixteenth century pashas already had the reputation of being more eager for money 'than devils for souls'. Under Murad III bribery began to devour the edifice of empire. Semsi Pasha, a poet popular with three sultans, and enemy of the Grand Vizier Sokollu Mehmed, was the last of a dynasty which had ruled near the Black Sea before the rise of the Ottomans. He helped Murad III answer the petitions addressed to him on the way to Friday prayers. One day he was seen smiling as he left the palace. When he was asked the reason, his reply confirmed that some of the Ottomans' worst enemies were their Muslim subjects: 'At last I have avenged the dynasty of the Kizil Ahmedoglu on that of the Ottomans; for if they caused our ruin, then I have just prepared theirs.' Asked how, he replied: 'By determining the Sultan to sell his own favours . . . from today the Sultan will himself give the example of corruption and corruption will dissolve the empire.'[24] However, the Pasha underestimated the empire's resilience.

In both the old and the new palaces the numbers of women rapidly rose, from 167 in 1552, to 230 in 1574, 373 in 1600, 642 in 1622 and 967 in 1652. As well as a sixfold growth in numbers there was a fourteen-fold growth in expenditure. In the eighteenth century the number of women in the harem varied between four and eight hundred, but rose again to 809 in 1870.

The eunuchs in the harem were almost as important as the women themselves. By 1603 there were 111.[25] Sold or captured in the Sudan, black boys would be taken to Asyut on the Nile. There, to increase market value, they would be castrated by a Copt, since castration was forbidden in the Koran, and Muslims were ashamed to perform the deed. They were then shipped to Constantinople and bought for the harem in the slave market, which was situated beside the bazaar in the centre of the city. They were given pet-names, perhaps in deliberate contrast to their appearance: tulip, saffron, goldfinch or emerald. In miniatures of the funeral of a Valide Sultan or the circumcision of a prince, their black faces form a startling contrast to the white turbans on their heads, and the white Ottoman faces around them. For three hundred and thirty years, from 1574 until 1908, one of the most power-ful men in the empire, the chief black eunuch, was an African. Almost equal in influence to the Grand Vizier and the Mufti, he controlled the finances of the harem and, by the seventeenth century, those of the imperial mosques in Constantinople as well.

He also controlled entrance to and discipline in the harem, and access to the Sultan himself. Bobowski wrote: 'This officer . . . has easier access to the prince and has more occasion to approach him at any hour even when he has retired with his mistresses'; he 'has a thou-sand ways of making the Sultan do what they wish'. Like many palace officials, his authority stretched far beyond the city. He controlled the finances of the shrines of Mecca and Medina and from 1645 to 1760 the town of Athens. One chief black eunuch became so rich that he built a new port at the mouth of the Danube.[26]

According to one aggrieved courtier, eunuchs were able to make love to women: usually the testicles, but not the penis, were cut off. An eighteenth-century historian, Ali Seydi Bey, wrote:

> I am a witness to the fact that these black infidels are so traitorous that they may fall in love with one or two of the odalisques and spend all that they earn on them. At every opportunity they meet secretly and make love . . . You might ask, do the odalisques who establish relations with these black eunuchs find pleasure in them? It is notorious in Istanbul that the odalisques find such pleasure. Two halberdiers of our unit who married odalisques from the imperial palace divorced them within a week when the odalisques told their husbands: 'We do not enjoy relations with you as we did with the black eunuchs.'[27]

One of the eunuchs' main duties was to supervise the imperial princes. The fratricide law of Mehmed II had continued throughout the sixteenth century. At the accession of Mehmed III in 1597, nineteen of the new Sultan's brothers were taken out of the harem. They kissed the Sultan's hand, were circumcised, then strangled with a silken handker-chief. One young prince said: 'Let me eat my chestnuts and strangle me afterwards.' Another, according to the great seventeenth-century chronicler Evliya Celebi, was torn from his mother's breast and put to death, emitting at the same time his mother's milk by his nose and his soul by his mouth. Nineteen coffins, poignantly small, followed that of the dead Sultan out of the palace. The wives and daughters of the dead Sultan were then taken to the old palace in the middle of the city, known with good reason as 'the palace of tears'. Both processions were watched by the people of the city. Evliya wrote: 'The angels in heaven heard the sighs and lamentations of the people of Istanbul.'* For among the populace, unlike its rulers, family ties were, according to a later inhabitant of the city, intensely felt and faithfully maintained.[28]

After 1607 fear of dynastic extinction led to a change in policy (although the reasons for this, as for many Ottoman government decisions, were not recorded). Fratricide was replaced by a policy of immuring princes in suites in the imperial harem, in effect luxury prisons. Under the guard and instruction of eunuchs they received a formal Ottoman education and learnt crafts – such as making ivory rings, or embroidery. A harem of sterile women consoled them for their exclusion, not only from the throne, but also from the outside world. A Sultan was henceforth succeeded not by the first son who seized Constantinople, but by the eldest male in the dynasty.

In addition to eunuchs, the harem was inhabited by mutes and dwarfs whose physical disabilities, in the eyes of the Sultan, made them excellent servants or jesters. Once, in the seventeenth century, the Sultan was presented with a unique phenomenon: a dwarf mute eunuch. The imperial harem became his paradise. Favourite of both the Sultan and the Valide, he could go where he liked, was 'dressed in precious vests', and 'lacked for nothing'.[29]

The harem was a machine to perpetuate the dynasty, even against the Sultan's will. It was also a school which, like its model the pages' school, bred an élite of talent and loyalty. Pupils learnt deportment, sewing, music, how to read and write – not always, from the evidence of surviving letters, very well – and the art of pleasing. If they failed to catch the Sultan's eye, they helped run the harem. Its senior officials were called *usta* or *kalfa* – the same words as those used, in a guild, for masters of a craft. Wearing a fur-lined robe, a train, a large bejewelled head-dress and high stilted clogs, with a ceremonial staff of office in her hand, a *kalfa* looked, and was, a very powerful official. Below the *kalfa* was a staff of

---

*Hence the accession speech of Henry V to his brothers in *2 Henry IV*, V.2:

> Brothers, you mix your sadness with some fear.
> This is the English, not the Turkish court.

However the wars over succession to the crown, described in Shakespeare's history plays, are precisely what the fratricide law was designed to prevent. Moreover, as the plays show, the houses of Lancaster, York and Tudor subsequently achieved almost Ottoman execution rates.

cariyes, or servants, who ran the apartments, the laundry, pantry, boiler-room and infirmary, and organized the births and upbringing of the Sultan's children.[30]

Thanks to an English mechanic called Thomas Dallam we can look through the keyhole and see the ladies of the harem. Dallam arrived in Constantinople in 1599, sent by Elizabeth I, with the present of an organ for the Sultan. He was told to install it in the fourth courtyard of the palace. There his Janissary escort showed him a grating in the wall through which he could see the ladies of the harem. They were playing with a ball:

> At the first sight of them I thought they had been young men, but when I saw the hair of their heads hang down on their backs plaited together with a tassel of small pearls hanging in the end of it and other plain tokens, I did know them to be women and very pretty ones indeed. They wore upon their heads nothing but a little cap of cloth of gold which did but cover the crown of her head; no bands about the necks nor anything but fair chains of pearl and a jewel hanging on their breast and jewels in their ears; their coats were like a soldier's mankilion [jacket], some of red satin and some of blue and some of other colours and girded like a lace of contrary colour; they wore breeches of scamatie [a fine cloth made of cotton wool], as white as snow and as fine as lawn; for I could discern the skin of their thighs through it.

Finally the Janissary dragged him away, 'the which I was very loth to do for that sight did please me wondrous well'.

After nine years' service, if they formally requested, women whom the Sultan had not 'noticed' could leave the palace and marry. Their education and connections made them popular brides. At the end of the empire one teacher wrote: 'When I saw their exquisite manners and civility, I understood why pashas always preferred to marry women who had served at the palace.'[31]

The most powerful woman to rule the harem was neither Hurrem nor Nurbanu, but the magnetic and ambitious Valide Kosem (her name means either 'hairless' or 'leader' – because one morning she was the first girl in line waiting for the Sultan). Born around 1589, possibly the daughter of a Greek priest on the island of Tinos, she was a consort of Ahmed I, who built the Sultanahmed mosque. Despite the temptations on offer, and pressure from their mothers, several sultans did succeed in enjoying genuine love affairs. In Ahmed's lifetime it was said 'she [Kosem] can do what she likes with the king and possesses his heart absolutely, nor is anything ever denied to her'. Banished to the Old

Palace on his death in 1617, she returned to the New Palace as Valide, when her young son Murad IV ascended the throne in 1623.

From her power-base in the harem, in charge of a boy Sultan, Kosem helped stabilize the government by melting down much of the palace gold and silver to pay the troops. The interests of the Sultan sometimes threatened those of his dynasty. When Murad IV reached manhood, he reverted to the tradition of fratricide and, in order to remove two rivals, had two brothers killed. His mother prevented him from murdering the sole surviving brother, Ibrahim, by arguing that he was too mad to be a threat. Often, however, the Valide found both the Sultan and the empire hard to control. She wrote to a Grand Vizier: 'Something absolutely must be done about Yemen – it's the gate to Mecca. You must do what you can . . . My son leaves in the morning and comes back at night. I never see him. He won't stay out of the cold, he's going to get sick again. I tell you, this grieving over the child is destroying me. Talk to him when you get a chance.' When he insisted on going to the Hippodrome, to practise the favourite Ottoman sport of *jirid*, or throwing the javelin while mounted on horseback: 'What can I do?' she complained. 'My words are bitter to him now. Just let him stay alive, he is vital to all of us. I have so many troubles I cannot begin to write them all.' After a brutal but successful reign, Murad IV died in 1640.[32]

At first his successor Ibrahim was too frightened to leave his apartment in the harem. Until Kosem had ordered his brother's corpse to be displayed before him, he was convinced he faced strangulation, not inauguration. During his sultanate the harem achieved new levels of luxury in perfumes, textiles and jewellery. Ibrahim's love of women and furs led him to have a room entirely lined with lynx and sable, in which to 'do justice'. Kosem helped to provide him with the virgins, and fat women, for whom he craved. When vigour flagged, he restricted himself to a new woman every Friday. Outraging the traditions of the dynasty, Ibrahim married a concubine at a formal ceremony: the chief black eunuch acted as her proxy, the Grand Vizier as the Sultan's. He was an eccentric who threatened to stuff a Grand Vizier with straw unless he recovered presents made by previous sultans to the shrine at Medina, and who drank amber-flavoured coffee to calm his nerves.[33] The government slid into chaos. Janissaries, enraged by arrears of pay, and emboldened by government weakness, cut up the body of an ex-Grand Vizier and sold it in the street.

The Valide Sultan had to act. Draped from head to foot in black silk, while a black eunuch waved a large fan beside her, Kosem attended a conference with leading viziers at the entrance to the harem. The Aga of the Janissaries addressed her: 'Gracious mistress, the folly and madness of the Padishah have put the world in danger; the infidels have taken forty castles on the frontiers of Bosnia and are blockading the Dardanelles with eighty ships while the Padishah thinks only of pleasure, debauch and selling offices. The pipes and trumpets and flutes from the palace are drowning the sound of the call to prayer from the minarets of Aya Sofya' – the recurrent phobia of Ottoman Constantinople.[34]

Finally Kosem agreed to her son's deposition. She had little reason to regret him for he had tried to exile her to Rhodes (like Cyprus and Egypt a habitual place of exile from the Ottoman capital), and had forced the princesses her daughters to serve his favourite concubine with soap and water. According to one account, Kosem presented the Sultan's 7-year-old son Mehmed to the council with the words: 'Here he is! See what you can do with him!' With the backing of a fatwa from the Mufti of Constantinople, Ibrahim was deposed, and later strangled. As the executioner approached, Ibrahim's last words were: 'Is there no one among those who have eaten my bread who will take pity on me and protect me? These cruel men have come to kill me. Mercy! Mercy!'

Such was her force of character that Kosem remained Valide, in place of Turhan, mother of the new Sultan Mehmed IV. Known now as Buyuk Valide or Queen Grandmother, Kosem, in her moment of glory in 1651, in keeping with her practical nature, built not a mosque but the grandest of all *hans* or inns in the city, the many-domed Buyuk Valide Han, near the great bazaar. Built around three courtyards, three storeys high, it was so large that it could accommodate 3,000 travellers.

Kosem won the love of the city for her many charitable works. She freed her slaves after two or three years' service and provided them with dowries, and furnished lodgings, to enable them to marry. In the month of Rejeb she would leave the palace in disguise and personally arrange the release of imprisoned debtors and payment of their debts.[35] If the Sultan's presence was required at council meetings, Kosem sat beside him hidden by a curtain. Her frankness outweighed her prudence. In abrasive, Thatcheresque tones, she criticized the viziers to their faces. 'Have I made you vizier to spend your time in gardens and vineyards? Devote yourself to the affairs of the empire and let me hear no more of your deportments!'[36]

In the end, as in Westminster in 1990, the men turned on their tormentor. They had an ally within the harem in the person of the Sultan's mother Turhan – a woman discovered and presented to Ibrahim by Kosem herself. Kosem may have planned to consolidate her power by deposing Turhan's son Mehmed and enthroning his younger brother Suleyman, whose mother she considered more tractable than Turhan. One of Kosem's slaves informed Turhan. A rumour was started, possibly by the chief black eunuch, that Kosem wanted to strangle the Padishah. On 2 September 1651 outraged eunuchs and pages hunted her down in the harem. A loyal slave tried to save her mistress, saying 'I am the Valide!' They were not deceived. Kosem is said to have hidden in a cupboard in the wall of a staircase in the Valide's apartment. A piece of dress protruding under the door betrayed her to a halberdier, who strangled her with a curtain. She struggled so much that blood spurted out of her ears and nose and soiled the murderer's clothes. 'The massacred Valide', as she became known, left 2,700 shawls, twenty chests of gold and a lasting reputation in the city for piety and generosity. When news of her death was known, the people of Constantinople spontaneously observed three days of mourning.[37]

No subsequent Valide was as powerful as Kosem or Nurbanu. However, a lasting symbol of the period known as 'the sultanate of women', when the Valide was almost as important as the Sultan, is the large and graceful Valide Sultan mosque by the Golden Horn. It is not at the edge of the city, like previous mosques commissioned by female members of the dynasty, but in its commercial heart, between the port and the bazaar. It was founded by Safiye Sultan, Valide from 1595 to 1603, who was said to sell the office of Grand Vizier as she wished. Begun in 1597, it was halted in 1603 on Safiye's death and was only finished by Turhan in 1660. No one moving between Galata and Istanbul can miss it.

Few letters, poems or memoirs by Istanbul women living outside the imperial harem have been published. Their life is hard to evoke. Only in the nineteenth century do many individual voices begin to be heard. Marriage was the overriding goal. And marriage began – and in some cases ended – in the hamam. According to the Koran, cleanliness was not next to, but an essential part of, godliness. Every district of the city had a communal hamam, consisting of a series of domed marble rooms with hot and cold baths and fountains, reserved for women on certain days of the week: Hurrem, characteristically, built a splendid double hamam, between Aya Sofya and the mosque of Sultanahmed, where men and women could be received at the same time in two separate, but almost equal, sections. In all there were about 150 hamams in the city.

These marble temples produced a social life of bathing, massage and conversation, comparable to the beach culture of California. As in Western spas, company was as important a motive as health for visiting the baths. Even if she had a hamam in her own house, a wealthy woman went to the communal hamam at least once a week. She would arrive, attended by servants with towels, brushes, henna, kohl, a bar of Cretan soap and a pair of bath clogs inlaid with mother-of-pearl. Hamam visits became parties to which food and pets could be brought, friends and musicians invited. After the bath and a massage, wearing nothing but linen shifts, women plucked their eyebrows, hennaed their hair – and sometimes their feet and hands. The Hanafi branch of Islam, to which Sunni Turks belonged, enjoins removal of hair from all parts of the body: ears, nostrils, legs, armpits. Women used special depilatory pastes made of sugar syrup, or lime and arsenic.[38]

A vivid description of the world of the hamam – so different from the city outside – comes from Lady Mary Wortley Montagu, wife of the British ambassador in 1717–18, at a time when the empire was turning from war to pleasure.

> The first sofas were covered with cushions and rich carpets, on which sat the ladies and on the second their slaves behind them but without any distinction of rank by their dress, all being in the state of nature, that is in plain English stark naked without any beauty or defect concealed. Yet there was not the least wanton smile or immodest gesture among them . . . so many fine women naked, in different postures, some in conversation, some working [sewing], others drinking coffee or sherbet, while their slaves (generally pretty girls of seventeen or eighteen) were employed in braiding their hair in several pretty fancies. In short it is the women's coffee-house, where all the news of the world is told, scandal invented, etc. They generally take this diversion once a week and stay at least four or five hours.[39]

Relaxing in the hamam, a mother was able to enquire among her friends about, or to choose for herself, a suitable bride for her son (although some mothers relied on professional matchmakers going from house to house). A ritual of visits to the girl's family followed, in order to test her beauty and skill at embroidery, jam-making and the other necessities of life. If the mother was impressed, she told her son. If the match was agreed, the young man sent a present to the bride: a shawl, an embroidery, a diamond. Acceptance was the equivalent of engagement.

Two or three days before the marriage, a hamam was rented for the day by the bride's family. Friends were entertained by dancing girls, music, ribald stories. The day before the wedding – generally a Wednesday – to mark her passage from the unmarried to the married state, the bride had a henna party at home, to which guests wore their best silk and velvet dresses. Coins were scattered over the bride's head as a symbol of abundance. Holding lighted candles set on trays of henna, weaving in and out of the house and garden, the bride's friends sang songs about the coming wedding night:

> The panes of the new room, My Night
> Burn candles fancy with gold and silver, My Night
> I had not hoped for this from you, My Night . . .
> May the wish of the night come true, My Night.

The mother-in-law then applied henna to the bride's hands and gypsies performed a dance described in the 1870s by Lady Blunt, wife of a British merchant in the Ottoman capital, as 'of the most unrestrained and immodest nature'.

On Thursday morning the bride, dressed in her finery and covered in jewels, received from her father the girdle which symbolized her new status as a married woman. The bride's head-dress, of jewels and flowers, was prepared days in advance by a woman called a *bashlikci*: one *bashlikci*, known from the size of her house as 'half Constantinople', was murdered for the sake of her jewels.

On the day of the wedding the bridegroom's friends and relations assembled at his house. Firing guns in the air, they then proceeded to the bride's house leading a donkey. Completely veiled, the bride was put on the donkey and escorted back to the bridegroom's house, in yet another procession, formed by jesters, and others bearing her trousseau and a wedding-palm. Members of her family might have been working on the trousseau since the day she was born: it might contain a prayer rug, a silver mirror, a pair of bath clogs, walnut boxes. The trousseau was then placed on display in the new house.

Wealthy families tried to rival the splendour of an imperial trousseau. One pasha determined to give his daughter a trousseau that would defy criticism. Its crowning glory was a brazier of solid gold. He hid himself nearby to catch the compliments, but heard one old woman say: 'All show! All show!' When he dashed out to ask what she meant, she replied: 'You forgot the tongs!'

More music, dancing girls and refreshments entertained both the *haremlik* (women's quarters) and *selamlik* (men's quarters) in the bride-groom's house. At about nine in the evening the imam, in a passage between the two, pronounced the couple man and wife. 'Soon the bride is conducted alone to the bridal chamber where she is left alone. Eventually the bridegroom arrives and begs permission to remove her veil and feast his eyes on her beauty. She refuses repeatedly but eventually yields. He begins to kiss.' She enters a new world.[40]

Did happiness await her? Most women appear to have identified joy-fully with the closed world of the household, bound by the demands of cleaning, cooking and child-rearing – in part because a woman had more status if married. When there were opportunities to work outside the home, for example in domestic service, they were not taken. Private harems were far smaller than the imperial harem, since private individuals lacked both the Sultan's wealth and the dynastic need to manipulate biology and ensure the succession. No doubt private houses in Constantinople contained many women as beloved as Hurrem, as domineering as Nurbanu and Kosem.

For a rich heterosexual male with a taste for variety, however, Constantinople could be paradise. Some changed wives frequently or, like the Sultan, purchased large numbers of female slaves. The seventeenth-century poet Fenani was once asked by the Sultan if there was a pleasure the Sultan did not enjoy. 'Yes,' was the reply: 'that of suddenly repudiating four legitimate wives; it is the greatest pleasure in the world. It is truly a pleasure of kings.' Provided he had the means to treat them equally, a Muslim could take up to four wives at a time, and divorce them when he wished. Even if he did not practise divorce, he could buy as many women as he wanted to serve in his household. Only a very wealthy or beloved wife dared threaten to return to her father's house.[41]

Some wives lived in harmony in the same house, agreeing to give precedence to the first wife as head of the harem. Others lived in separate households in different districts. One old man in the 1840s kept one wife in Constantinople, another in Tophane, a third in Uskudar and the fourth up the Bosphorus, so that wherever he was in the city, he could always sleep at home with a wife to cook his pilav. Wealthy women could learn, by accident, that their husband had for years been keeping another wife in another house. The present author has met a woman of Istanbul, whose great-aunt, wife of the commander of the Sultan's bodyguard Tahir Pasha, asked the identity of a beautiful new visitor in her favourite hamam. 'She is the wife of Tahir Pasha' was the reply.[42]

Whereas Ottoman princes remained secluded in Topkapi, the largest houses on the Bosphorus belonged to the Sultan's sisters and daughters, who were distinguished from other women by the suffix *Sultan* after their first name (Ayse Sultan, Fatma Sultan and so on). The fortunes of their husbands, the leading pashas of the day, were consumed by the expense of maintaining their wives in imperial style – as the Sultan intended. The Grand Canal in Venice was visible evidence of the wealth and power of patrician families like the Gritti, Contarini, Mocenigo by whose palaces it was lined; the Bosphorus, however, reflected the over-powering presence in the city of one family: the Ottoman dynasty.

The princesses' husbands were considered the slaves of their wives. On the wedding night the husband, when or if admitted to his wife's bedroom, dared to approach her only from the bottom of her bed. The husbands were sometimes sent away from the capital to govern a province. The princesses never, with one exception, consented to join them.* The size of their palaces reflected their status, not the number of their children. To remove potential rivals to the Sultan, after 1607 princesses' children were generally killed at birth. By 1842 the Sultan wanted to abolish this tradition. His concubines, more Ottoman than their master, overbore him and arranged the death of a son just born to his sister Atiye. They are said to have excused themselves with the words: 'What was one infant's life, in comparison with the horrors of fifty civil wars?' The princess died of grief two months later.[43]

Some princesses enjoyed happy marriages. Thus in the seventeenth century Kaya Sultan, a daughter of Murad IV, who once gave her the entire annual tribute of Egypt, was a pious Muslim, and a clever manager of her household. The historian Evliya Celebi often talked with her through a latticed window (a sign that sexual segregation was less strict for older women). He wrote: 'She never took pleasure in the company of women, preferring to withdraw to a corner of solitude and busy herself with devotions. In fact she and the pasha [Melek Ahmed, her husband] used to perform the five daily prayers together . . . In the end she loved the pasha and driving away all of the corrupting female companions from her company spent all her time conversing with the pasha.' They enjoyed 'nice wrestling matches' in bed forty-eight times a year, and she helped him obtain high office. After her death her

---

*In the nineteenth century one woman from the Sultan's harem, who had taken refuge in the British embassy, vowed that she would sooner marry a *hamal* (porter) than leave Constantinople.

widower was remarried to another princess, the aged Fatma Sultan. He told Evliya: 'The tortures I have suffered from that wife of mine during this nuptial night are not visited on the Malta captives [Muslim prisoners of the Knights of St John on Malta, whose treatment was a byword for barbarism]. God forgive me, what a shameless immodest extravagant woman!'[44]

Yet even these most powerful and privileged of Ottoman women might be tortured by jealousy. Adile Sultan, daughter of the great nineteenth-century reformer Mahmud II, married an army officer, Mehmed Ali Pasha. They were in love. One day at the fashionable meeting-place up the Golden Horn called the Sweet Waters of Europe, she attracted his attention. Since she was thickly veiled, he did not know who she was. He dropped a scented handkerchief at her feet. That night the Pasha found the handkerchief on the pillow beside his sleeping wife.

On another occasion she went to a distant mosque to pray. Needing to rest on the way, she called at a mansion and was politely welcomed. Offered coffee and sherbet by her hostess, she asked her name: the lady replied that she was the wife of Mehmed Ali Pasha. Adile Sultan expressed her thanks and left. Thereafter she lived in seclusion, writing poems of increasing sadness. When she died in 1898, she was buried beside her husband. They never referred to his infidelity.[45]

Less well-bred households knew storms of jealousy. Men could treat the slaves as sexual provender. They sometimes applied to the imam for permission not to obey the Koranic injunction to wash after intercourse, as such ablutions aroused their wife's wrath against the female slaves. Lady Blunt wrote: 'Every hanoum [wife] I have known would go down to the laundry regularly to rinse with her own hands her husband's clothes after the wash, fearing that if any of her slaves performed this duty she would have the power of casting spells to supplant her in her husband's affections.'[46]

One of the greatest of modern Turkish writers, the leader of Constantinople's first wave of feminists, Halide Edib, wrote of her father's household, in the city's last golden age before 1908: '[Polygamy] was a curse, a poison which our unhappy household could not get out of its system . . . The constant tension in our home made every simple ceremony seem like physical pain, and the consequences hardly ever left me. The rooms of the wives were opposite each other and my father visited them in turn . . .'[47]

One distraction in the harem was to offer hospitality to women friends, Greek, Jewish and Armenian as well as Muslim. There was a constant exchange of visits among harems: visits of enquiry, of inspection, of salutation, of congratulation, of condolence. Visitors often spent the night. A well-connected woman could spend the entire year visiting. Visitors acted as postmen and gossip columnists, relating the news of the city. Professional saleswomen also went from house to house, buying and selling clothes and embroidery.

Some sultans, however, tried to enforce strict seclusion. Osman III (1754–7) forbade women to go out on more than four days in the week; Mustafa IV (1807–8) decreed that they should never go out. Some women learnt to fear men so much that, if trapped in a fire, they chose to burn to death, rather than be saved in the arms of a neighbour or a Janissary. At times women were criticized even for such traditional activities as going to the markets 'among men', or visiting graveyards. Women usually prayed at home. In mosques, they prayed in special galleries or behind barriers, not in the main part of the mosque. A woman as powerful as Hurrem is said to have gone out into the city only at night – although she did make journeys to the provinces to see her sons. The Buyuk Valide Han, built by Kosem, could only be visited by members of her sex with the permission of, and escorted by, the intendant.

In the imperial harem, even in the relative freedom of the nineteenth century, most ladies led severely segregated lives. They fell in love with men they had not seen: a voice heard singing one moonlit night on the Bosphorus; a violinist playing in the distance. In both cases the girls remained in love, while knowing nothing of the beloved, for years. When, in *Don Juan*, Byron wrote that for the Turks wedlock and a padlock meant the same, he was scarcely exaggerating.[48]

However there were avenues of independence. In the West husbands controlled their wives' fortunes. Even that ferocious figure, Sarah Duchess of Marlborough, could manage her extensive properties only through a trust established by her husband, the trustees of which were guaranteed to obey her wishes. Partly to prevent one wife's dowry being spent on another, Islam ensured that women retained control of their own property. In Constantinople women administered their properties either directly or through stewards. Some women owned shops in the bazaar. Others, like their husbands, lent large sums to government officials or foreign ambassadors. Legal records show that in 1548 one woman, Nefise bint Kemal, owned a water-mill; in 1804, Hoshyar Hanim was proprietor of a bakery. Women were also, as will be seen, particularly effective slave-dealers.[49]

Architecture was one of the main indulgences of wealthy Constantinople women. Of the 953 mosques in and around the city in 1962, sixty-eight, or 7 per cent, had been built by or for women. Of the 491 Ottoman fountains surviving in Istanbul in the 1930s, whose sober grey marble façades are as characteristic of the city as swirling white baroque fountains are of Rome, 28 per cent had been commissioned by women.[50] On a fountain at Beshiktash built by Turhan Sultan (whose first name was Hatice), passers-by could read:

> Hatice Sultan who is the crown of the chastity of the well-guarded
> and the mother of Mehmed Khan, Sultan of the Sultans,
> the order of sovereignty and the community, pure of character,
> Caused this sublime fountain to flow freely
> so that the thirst of the whole universe might be slaked.

A fountain finished in 1741 has the inscription: 'When the mother of Ali Pasha Vezir in the reign of Sultan Mahmud quenched the thirst of the people with the pure and clear water of her charity, Riza of Beshiktash, a Nakshibendi dervish, uttered the following epigram: Come and drink the water of eternal life from this fountain.'[51] Matriarchy rules: but the commissioning woman is defined by her son.

A few women of Constantinople challenged the rules. The poet Hubbi Hatun remained at court under Selim II after her husband's death and was rumoured to be a confidante of the Sultan and the mistress of several of his courtiers. At the beginning of the seventeenth century a woman of the city called Leyla wrote love poems:

> When I am in your arms, do not make me suffer any more:
> Paradise is there; it cannot become a hell.

In the eighteenth century Fitnat Hanim, sister, niece and granddaughter of Seyhulislams, was encouraged by her family to write poetry. She addressed a sonnet to the cultivated Grand Vizier, Ragib Pasha, and even visited his literary salon. Women could be musicians or calligraphers. One calligrapher separated from her husband wrote out nine descriptions of the Prophet, works of art which she considered as substitutes for children.[52]

Poorer women lived more like housewives in the West, although segregation of the house between male and female quarters was observed, if only by a curtain hanging in the middle of a room. They could be seen, often unveiled, with their husbands, shopping, sitting together in the evening on their doorstep – or dragging the husband out of a tavern. Some women sold what they had made at home – sausages, linen, embroidered towels – at weekly markets for women held in different quarters of the city.[53]

Outside household tasks, the chief occupation of the women of Constantinople was embroidery – as, in rural Anatolia, it was carpet-making. No other empire has put so much energy into needle and thread. In the mid-seventeenth century a French visitor, Jean Thévenot, claimed: 'Their only occupation at home is crochet and embroidery. All the housework is done by female slaves.' A hundred years later one of the greatest of Ottoman historians, Mouradgea d'Ohsson, wrote: 'All the women set great store by embroidery which adorns not only their own clothing but all the linen employed in ordinary household chores. Handkerchiefs, towels [embroidered towels were used as prizes in archery competitions], table napkins and cloths. In fact everything down to pants and sashes is embroidered.' In the early twentieth century Lucy Garnett, an ethnologist who lived many years in the Balkans, wrote: 'Needlework especially is held in great estimation and for many years before marriage a girl finds occupation for her leisure hours in embroidering the sheets, towels, quilts, napkins and other articles which will later on figure in her trousseau and deck the bridal chamber.'

Using some of the flower patterns observable in Iznik tiles and velvet kaftans, embroidery was applied to every available object, from the cradle to the coffin: bed covers, cushion covers, turban covers, wallets, horse trappings, prayer rugs – and, the most precious embroidery of all, the covering sent every year to Mecca for the Ka'aba. Embroidery also covered the pieces of cloth in which, since paper envelopes were not used until the nineteenth century, letters and objects were sent from one person to another. The richer the embroidery, the greater the compliment paid to the recipient. In wealthy households, coffee-drinking could also lead to a display of embroidery. The first server wore a round cloth hanging over one shoulder. Made of silk or velvet, it was heavily embroidered in gold thread, and occasionally jewels; the tassels were sewn with pearls. Its sole purpose was to display beauty and wealth.

Embroidery also covered clothes – as can be seen in the imposing dresses, as stiff with gold thread as herald's tabards, on display in the Sadberk Hanim Museum in Buyukdere. From the sixteenth to the nineteenth centuries they changed little. Lady Mary Wortley Montagu admired the brocaded damask petticoat and kaftan and jewel-encrusted girdle of an Ottoman lady: but what most 'grieved her eyes' were the embroidered table-cloths and napkins. In winter rich women could wear a robe of satin lined with ermine or sable, the head-dress generally velvet, embroidered with pearls or diamonds. On one side of the hair was a bouquet of jewels arranged to look like flowers: pearls represented buds, rubies roses, diamonds jasmine. When women went out, they wore headscarves of thin white muslin, with a gap for eyes, and *feraces* or voluminous cloaks, covering everything from neck to toe.[54]

The cult of embroidery, like folk religion and imperial processions, united the different communities of the city. In 1673 Signor Tersia, the dragoman of Venice, a Catholic of Pera, displayed his daughter's dowry to his friends. It consisted principally of dresses, handkerchiefs, kaftans, bedspreads, all richly embroidered 'in the fashion of the country' with gold or silver thread, pearls or crystal, *toutes de prix*. Jewish Torah curtains and prayer shawls were embroidered in the same style, with the same flower motifs, as Muslim textiles. Synagogues used rugs looking like Muslim prayer rugs, with 'the shape of the opening where the Ishmaelites [Muslims] pray'.[55]

The fame of Turkish embroidery reached another citadel of luxury, the court of France. In the 1570s Catherine de Medici and fifty years later Marie de Medici summoned girls from Constantinople to practise embroidery in their household. Even when the city had, in almost every domain, embraced Western styles, embroidery remained the preferred present for distinguished visitors to the capital. The first presents given by the Valide Sultan to the Empress Eugénie, wife of Napoleon III, on her visit to Constantinople in 1869 were traditional embroidered handkerchiefs.[56]

5

City of Gold

Jews, Turks and Christians several Tenets hold.
Yet, all one GOD acknowledge, that is, GOLD.
from *Letters Historical and Critical from a Gentleman in Constantinople*
to his Friend in London, 1730

There is no city of fairer aspect than Constantinople or better adapted for trade.
Ogier Ghislain de Busbecq, 1555

IN THE HEAT of the summer the Sultan frequently moved down
from the palace to kiosks overlooking the sea. There, cooled by the
breeze, he was able to enjoy a view so spectacular that many at first
doubted its reality: the great sweep of water formed by the junction of
the Golden Horn and the Bosphorus, covered in a constantly moving
pageant of boats. There were so many that at times, as Melchior
Lorichs's view of 1560 suggests, masts and sails almost concealed the
water. Between the larger vessels a mass of small boats (about 15,000 in
all worked in the port) skimmed along the surface like flies.[1] Binding the
outskirts of the city to the centre in a web of daily human journeys, they
moved nearly as swiftly as the seagulls swooping overhead or the dol-
phins leaping through the water. The rowers' yells and whistles made
the port noisier than Naples. Constantinople, more than London or
Lisbon, combined the roles of capital and port. The sea not only came
into – it was – the heart of the city.

The view across the water to the right of Palace Point showed
Uskudar, a confusion of villages, mosques and palaces, where white
domes and minarets stood out against the green of gardens, cypress
groves and the first hills of Asia. On the left, directly across the Golden
Horn from the palace, was the city of Galata, an amphitheatre of red-
roofed houses, garlanded in green vegetation, crowned by a grey tower.

Stretching for one and a half miles to the left of Galata, was the centre of the Sultan's naval power, one of the largest naval complexes in the world: the imperial arsenal and dockyards. Yet another city within the city, enclosed by a high wall, the arsenal had sheds with room for building up to 200 galleys at a time. In a view of 1650 it looks like a row of red-roofed bus garages. Beside the arsenal were gunpowder and munitions factories and, after the transfer of the headquarters of the Ottoman navy from Gallipoli in 1516, the palace of the Kaptan Pasha, or Lord High Admiral. He soon became one of the principal officials in Constantinople, with the right to sit in the Divan, and authority over the Aegean islands and Galata itself. The navy was manned by Turks, Greeks and Dalmatians. They were called *levents*, from the Italian word *levantino* (Levantine), and the boats, whose construction was often based on Venetian models, had semi-Italian names like *Patrona, Riyala (Reale), Kaptan.*[2]

Beside the arsenal was the sinister edifice known as the *bagno*, surrounded by a high wall. The main inhabitants were two to three thousand slaves captured as a result of the warfare and piracy endemic in the Mediterranean, between the Knights of St John and the Algerian corsairs. The horror of the slaves' life, building and rowing the Sultan's galleys, was tempered by the presence of Catholic and Orthodox chapels, offering salvation in 'the infinite world', and the efforts of Christian ambassadors and religious orders to obtain their release. The galley slaves added another *lingua franca* to the polyphony of Constantinople. Most came from Spain, Italy or France, and spoke a mixture of those languages called *Franco*.[3]

Every 6 May, on the feast of the great Muslim saint Hizir, Constantinople celebrated its role as a sea capital in a day of ritual theatre. Watched by the rest of the city from kayiks and sailing-ships, the Kaptan Pasha and the chief officers of the fleet slowly sailed from the arsenal, down the Golden Horn to the Yali Kiosk on the palace waterfront. There they were formally received by the Sultan, surrounded by his household. He invested them with kaftans and wished them a safe journey and success. Saluted by a deafening cannonade from the shore forts, and the sound of martial music played on board each galley by its band, they then took the fleet for a tour of inspection and tax collection, in the Aegean islands. In 1583 the first English ambassador William Harborne saw the departure of the Kaptan Pasha, 'bounde to the sea with sixe and thirty gallies, very fairly beautified with gilding and painting and beset with flags and streamers'.[4] The ceremony was as grandiose as the 'wedding of the sea' every 8 May, when the

Doge of Venice was rowed in his gilded galley, the Bucentauro, accompanied by hundreds of smaller ships, to throw a wedding ring into the Adriatic. The similarity of date, purpose and splendour suggests that the influence of Venice permeated most aspects of naval life in Constantinople.

Merchant ships anchored to the right of the naval headquarters, along the wharves and jetties of Galata and Eminonu opposite and below the palace. The harbour is so deep and sheltered that even the largest boats could unload directly on to the shore, using wooden planks: the quality of its port had been one reason for the first Greek settlement of the site. Once a ship had landed, the captain presented notification of cargo to Ottoman customs officials, who then checked the goods for themselves. A Janissary stayed on board until customs duty of 5 or 3 per cent had been paid. After he had been given a receipt of payment, goods could be unloaded. The taverns and markets of Galata and Eminonu were the centres of the life of the port: merchants, porters and sailors came there every day in search of drink and work. In the winter, while the 120 or so ships of the Ottoman navy were in dry dock in the arsenal, the behaviour of the levents in the taverns of Galata became a byword for debauch.

Constantinople was the largest city and one of the largest ports in the Mediterranean. All roads and most trade routes in the Ottoman Empire led to the capital: from Poland via Wallachia, from central Europe through Belgrade and Edirne, and from Venice down the Adriatic to Dubrovnik, and over the brigand mountains of the Balkans. At least once a month caravans containing up to two thousand mules and camels arrived at Uskudar. They came from Persia; from the great port of Basra at the head of the Persian Gulf; and from Syria. By sea Constantinople was the destination for trade routes from Marseilles, Venice, Alexandria and the Crimea. The Black Sea was for the Ottoman Empire what South America was for the Spanish. From 1592 to 1774 its commerce was reserved for Ottoman subjects.[5]

Imperial ideology, as well as self-interest, favoured trade. A fifteenth-century pasha advised one Sultan:

> Look with favour on the merchants in the land; always care for them; let no one harass them; let no one order them about, for through their trading the land becomes prosperous and by their wares cheapness abounds in the world; through them the excellent fame of the Sultan is carried to surrounding lands and by them the wealth within the land is increased.

In the sixteenth century the imperial government conducted wars with Persia for control of the silk trade and with Portugal over the routes taken by spices from the Indies to Europe, and ran a state merchant marine.[6]

To strengthen the empire, the Ottomans wanted all products, as well as races, available in Constantinople. One Florentine merchant in cloth and silk wrote from Galata in 1502, of Bayezid II: 'The Sultan bestows on us every favour and wishes that we may do our business in his country.' Indeed the palace was the merchants' best customer for foreign luxuries. The presence of foreign merchants helped Constantinople to retain its character as a world city. Liberal trading privileges, known as 'capitulations', enabled foreign merchants to live in Constantinople, and other Ottoman cities, under the jurisdiction and protection of their own ambassador. Capitulations were granted by the Sultan to Venice in 1454, France in 1569, England in 1581, the Netherlands in 1612. Florence and the republic of Dubrovnik had them before the fall of the city. The Holy Roman Empire, Russia and Sweden obtained them in the seventeenth century, Denmark in the eighteenth.

Trade was one of the principal reasons why so many embassies were sent to Constantinople; for Venetians 'the principal burden of a Bailo of Constantinople is the defence of the nation's trade'. Whilst both the English and Ottoman governments hated Spain, it was above all shared love of commerce which led to the establishment of diplomatic relations between them. Murad III wrote to Elizabeth I on 7 March 1579:

> Just as the people of Franja, and Venedik and Leyh [France, Venice and Poland] which are sincerely devoted to our Sublime Porte have come and carried on trade, so shall the merchants of the domain of Anletar [England] also come and go [and] whilst coming and going and travelling around in our divinely protected dominions by way of trade, let no one ever hinder [them].

The first English ambassador, William Harborne, was also a merchant who imported lead, tin and cloth to Constantinople and exported Malmsey wine and currants. Until the nineteenth century the Levant Company, which he helped found, rather than the British government, paid the ambassador's salary. By 1640 there were twenty-five English firms in Constantinople, principally dealing in cloth.[7]

However, it was not England but France, a political ally of the Ottoman Empire since 1535, which became its main Western trading partner. The French 'Levant trade' (that is, trade with the Ottoman

Empire), controlled by the chamber of commerce of Marseilles, was believed to comprise half all French maritime commerce by the early seventeenth century. In the eighteenth century it was one of the factors which contributed to France's influence in the Ottoman capital. In 1789 the Ottoman Empire was the third in importance of France's markets after Spain and America, and France controlled about half all European trade with the empire. Constantinople imported cloth, paper, leather and glass from France. It exported raw wool, hides, silk and luxury goods – caviare, fine yellow wax, and processed goat's hair, to become wigs on the heads of Europe. Two products peculiar to the city were shagreen (dyed shark skin, whose hardness was appreciated in sword handles and book bindings), and marbled paper, called 'Turkey paper', which was pasted inside the boards of books.[8]

In the empire's golden age in the sixteenth century the course of trade ran smoothly – as is suggested by the dramatic rise in the popula- tion of Constantinople, from 80,000 to 400,000 between 1477 and 1530. The Venetian Bailo wrote in 1523: 'I know of no state which is happier than this one; it is furnished with all God's gifts. It controls war and peace with all, it is rich in gold, in people, in ships and in obedience: no state can be compared to it.' In the seventeenth century, for many reasons, the empire was weaker and terms of trade moved against it. Foreign merchants in Constantinople began to be subjected to fines called *avanies* (literally 'insults') levied by the Ottoman government in return for the renewal of the capitulations (which in theory had to be renewed by each Sultan) – or simply to raise revenue. Ottoman resent- ment of the systematic corruption practised by foreign merchants and ambassadors was another reason for these penalties.

The Ottoman government struck few gold coins. Its silver *akce* and copper *piastre*, always decorated with the *tughra* of the reigning Sultan, and the seal of the Kayi tribe of Turks, were, after 1584, often reduced in weight and devalued. As a result, despite repeated government inter- dictions, Ottomans often preferred to use foreign coins rather than their own in commercial transactions. Constantinople was so open to foreign trade that Venetian, Dutch, Austrian, Spanish, even Polish coins were in use there. After 1650 secret mints sprang up in Avignon, Orange, Monte Carlo and Livorno, specializing in counterfeiting European coins, with 30 or 40 per cent less precious metal content, for use in the Ottoman Empire. By this means foreign merchants could make profits of up to 600 per cent. The French and the Dutch were per- sistent counterfeiters. One French merchant, the Chevalier Chardin, wrote of the Turks: 'They are naturally rather simple and dense, people whom one can easily deceive. So the Christians play an infinite number of dirty tricks and cheats on them. One deceives them for a time but they open their eyes and then they strike harshly and retaliate for everything at one time.' In desperation, at the end of the seventeenth century, the Ottoman government itself made imitations of foreign coins.[9]

Trade was encouraged by the order maintained in the city by the Ottoman government. Most foreign merchants lived peacefully in Galata or on a vine-covered hill above, noted for its good air, called Pera (Greek for 'beyond' – 'beyond' the Golden Horn). To deflect local hostility, Western merchants often wore Ottoman dress and beards: it was said that the Dutch and the English could pass as Turks but the French always gave themselves away. However, by the seventeenth century, Western clothes were habitual. To his ambassador's surprise the French traveller Jean Thévenot, who hired a house in Pera in 1650, had no problems roaming around the city. In Constantinople itself, some children threw apple cores at his party; however, 'some Tradesmen coming out of their Shops ran after them and dismissed them'. Commerce united what religion divided.

Compared to the turbulent cities of London and Paris, where thieving and riot were common, Constantinople was relatively law-abiding. Good order was believed to be directly related to the fear inspired by the Sultan. An Irish traveller a century later, Lord Charlemont, agreed:

> There is not, I believe, in Europe any city where the police is so well regulated as at Constantinople. Housebreaking and street robbery, crimes so unfortunately common in our great towns as to render the dwelling in them unpleasant and unsafe,* never happen in the Turkish metropolis [unlike the forests outside], and a man may walk its streets at all hours of the night or even sleep in them with his pocket full of money, without the smallest fear or danger of molestation. No murders, no assaults, no riots ever happen here, nor are those brutal acts of violence by which our impetuous and ill educated young men are so fond of signalizing themselves ever so much as heard of.

This happy state of affairs was in his opinion the effect of 'the salutary rigour of frequent acts of execution'.[10] An English visitor wrote that people in the streets were 'much civiller than we English would be to them'. They were stared at, the occasional stone was thrown (treatment frequently dealt out to foreigners and well-dressed Englishmen and

---

*With the exception of the period 1920–80.

women in London), but they could visit ordinary eating-houses. In a private room, they ate 'cabbobs which is little bits of meat, as big as Walnuts, stuck on long iron-skewers'. In the seventeenth century the streets were filthy and badly paved. In 1730 they were 'paved and though not so clean as those at the Hague are not so dirty as those were in London'.[11]

In 1662, at the age of 19, the Hon. Dudley North, a younger son of Lord North, realized that he had few prospects of inheriting wealth. Forward and handsome, he decided to join a 'house of factorage' in Constantinople, 'there not being a greater emporium upon the face of the earth than Constantinople, the seat of a vast empire and where a merchant of spirit and judgement cannot fail of being rich'. Renting a house in Pera from a rich Muslim, he learnt the Ottoman language and Ottoman law and made a fortune as a banker, jeweller and dealer in 'trumpery goods'. He lent at 20 or 30 per cent to the pashas, and supplied jewels to the palace. His opinion on Ottoman corruption is based on first-hand experience, and his friendship with an old *kadi* or judge. He believed that small presents were the equivalent of fees, without which the judge felt defrauded: 'The judge will not commonly do flat injustice for any present; and if neither side slights them, however unequal soever the presents are, they will determine according to right.'

Many Turks lived isolated from local Christians, let alone foreign merchants, surrounded by a wall of disdain. The diary of a seventeenth-century dervish records a peaceful, well-regulated existence: days were marked by alms-giving and social calls, coffee parties, visits to grave-yards and barber shops; he loved his wife; not one non-Muslim is mentioned. Compared to his contemporary Pepys, he is complacent and uncritical.[12]

On the other hand, outside the closed world of the pious, liquor and lucre drew Turks to foreign houses and taverns. Dudley North kept open house for his Turkish friends, including the chief customs official, to whose house he in his turn was invited. To his friends' attempts to convert him to Islam, he replied that he was 'bred to drink wine and eat hog'. In 1680, much richer than when he arrived, he decided to leave Constantinople. His friends were incredulous. 'Why Gaour [*gavur* – a pejorative term for a non-Muslim] are you mad? Can you be so sense-less as to leave this Place?' In London, an advocate of free trade and strong monarchy, he became a commissioner of the Treasury, and an MP. He died in 1691.[13]

*

Although foreign merchants could make vast profits, the Ottoman economy was not dominated by foreign trade. Until the nineteenth century, the Ottoman Empire was an economic microcosm in which Muslims were the most active traders. Only 8.5 per cent of a group of ships leaving Constantinople in the eighteenth century went to Europe: the rest left for ports in the Ottoman Empire. Of a group of ships' charterers in the eighteenth-century city 71.5 per cent were Muslim (of whom seven-eighths were Turks, the rest being Arabs), 24.5 per cent Christian and 3.5 per cent Jews.[14] Turks dominated the most important trade in the city: food.

The task of satisfying the hunger, and quenching the thirst, of Constantinople preoccupied sultans and grand viziers even more than protection of the pilgrim route to Mecca. Suleyman brought the city's water supply to a peak of efficiency, ordering his architect Sinan to rebuild the old Byzantine aqueducts and water towers in 1563–4. In the forests and valleys north of the city the complex of dams, reservoirs and aqueducts built by successive sultans surpasses in size, utility and elegance those built by their Byzantine predecessors. Like Roman emperors, the Ottoman sultans also supplied their capital with cheap food: documents frequently contain phrases such as 'the grain supply being one of the primary considerations of my imperial government'. The wording of a price regulation of 1676 suggests why the Ottoman government tried so hard:

> Those who have charge of the State will apply themselves in person to the operations of fixing maximum prices and will continuously inform themselves of the conditions of life of the inhabitants, for the application of maximum prices forming one of the elements in the tranquillity of the people, it is fitting that the affairs of the people of the souks and markets are regulated.

The government could not be sure of the 'tranquillity of the people'; every Wednesday the Grand Vizier himself inspected the markets of the city. In the nineteenth century a young English diplomat saw a government official comparing traders' weights, escorted by two files of Janissaries with white wands. A trader detected with light weights was taken away by one of the Janissaries to receive his punishment. Other culprits were led through the city with a board of jangling bells fastened to their neck.[15]

Along both shores of the Golden Horn, warehouses were erected to store the meat, grain and other foods shipped to the capital. Fish was sold by the quays of Galata in what was called by the French traveller Jean Thévenot 'the finest fish market in the world'. The vendors were almost all Turks and stood ranged around the square with fish piled up on mats on the ground or upon long tables, around which buyers haggled and dogs yelped. Mullet was fished in the Bosphorus, sometimes from huts erected on wooden stilts. Oysters came from the Sea of Marmara, mackerel from the Black Sea. Sword fish, sardines, and salted tunny-fish also had devotees.*

On the south side of the Golden Horn, beside the Yeni Valide Cami, to which it paid rent, was the spice bazaar, a long low T-shaped building with a distinctive smell of garlic, pepper, saffron and frankincense. It was also called the Egyptian bazaar, as most spices and perfumes came from Egypt, with a cargo of rice, coffee, lentils, incense and henna, in the annual 'Cairo caravan' of ten or more vessels. Its organization was one of the principal duties of the governor of Egypt and its arrival as important, for Constantinople, as the annual arrival of the 'Atlantic fleet' from America for Seville.[16]

While Egypt supplied spices, the city's meat came from Anatolia and the Balkans. Supplies were ensured by a complex system of assigning quotas to registered rural farmers, sending officials called *celebs* to buy at officially registered low prices and checking numbers on arrival in the city. From 1544 until 1829, the Voivodes (Princes) of Wallachia and Moldavia had to send 100,000 (and often more) head of sheep a year to Constantinople. Later the system slipped out of the hands of the state and into those of 'the merchants and rich men of Constantinople'. The seventeenth-century historian Naima wrote that they 'were in the habit of advancing sums of money to every new voivoda on the condition of collecting from the peasantry articles of the above description'.[17]

The annual consumption of sheep by the palace (probably including the eighty to a hundred thousand state employees living in the capital) was prodigious. In 1489/90 it amounted to 16,379 sheep. By 1573/4 the figure had risen to 38,226, by 1669/70 to 99,120, by 1761/2, including the Janissaries' consumption, to 211,116, and by 1803/4 to 336,000. The stomachs of the citizens of Constantinople were so privileged that on one occasion, in 1577, all slaughter of mutton and lamb in the Balkans

---

*Fishermen on the Bosphorus were so skilled that in 1723, as part of a programme to revive French fishing, the artist Jean-Baptiste Vanmour was commissioned by the Minister of the Marine to paint twelve pictures showing their methods of fishing.

was forbidden. They were reserved for the capital. Provincials could eat goat or beef.

The feast of Hizir, the day the Kaptan Pasha sailed out to sea, was also a feast-day for butchers, when they were given permission to begin the slaughter of lambs (most slaughter-houses were near that human slaughter-house, the castle of the Seven Towers). Owing to the state's insistence on providing cheap meat for the city, butchers' profit margins were low and they frequently faced bankruptcy. By the late sixteenth century wealthy notables from Anatolia or the Balkans were being forced to become butchers in Constantinople, and often entered government service in order to avoid such a fate. The victim was taken under armed guard to the capital, having been compelled to sell his goods in order to ensure he had enough money to invest in butchering. His reluctance was, in part, due to the risks attending his new profession. In the 1650s Mehmed IV went around the markets incognito followed, at a distance, by executioners. Thévenot wrote: 'Sometimes he would go to a Baker's shop and buy bread and sometimes to a Butcher's for a little meat; and one day a Butcher offering to sell him Meat above the rate which he had set, he made a sign to the Executioner who presently cut off the Butcher's head.'[18]

Meat was not the only tribute exacted from Wallachia and Moldavia. They supplied Constantinople with honey, cheese, ox-hides, tallow for candles, wheat and barley for the imperial stables. Butter and salt came from the Crimea; sugar from Cyprus; soap from Syria. Fresh fruit and poultry were produced in 'the orchard of the Ottoman Empire', the district stretching east along the Black Sea coast. Raisins, almonds, figs and bees-wax arrived from the district of western Anatolia around the great port of Izmir. By 1650, because of its geographical position and relative freedom from government interference, Izmir, 'the Pearl of the Levant', was beginning to rival Constantinople itself as a trading capital, and continued to do so until 1922.[19]

By 1700 Constantinople was consuming about four million sheep, three million lambs and 200,000 cows a year, and 500 tonnes of wheat a day. In winter each of the city's 133 ovens had to have a reserve of three months' supply of wheat to ensure cheap bread. Coffee and rice were forbidden to leave the city 'so that abundance shall reign in Constantinople'. Government policy, and the system of feeding the poor through the mosques, kept Constantinople one of the best fed cities in Europe. Lord Baltimore wrote in 1763: 'Provisions are always in great plenty, very cheap and very good.'[20] The dearth and famine familiar in France and Ireland and Bohemia, the food riots which changed the course of history, in Paris in 1789, and Petrograd in 1917, were almost unknown in the Ottoman capital.

Like other trades, the food trade was run by guilds which probably had their origin in the Byzantine corporations. By the mid-seventeenth century, according to Evliya Celebi, there were 1,100 guilds, organized in 57 groups. Not only butchers, bakers and kaftan-makers, but also thieves and prostitutes had guilds of their own. Outside the service of the state, they were the main form of communal identity in the city. Guilds regulated admission to a trade. They had their own funds, and provided a form of social security for the ill and a source of loans to members who wished to expand their business. Prayer meetings at Eyup, distributions of food to the poor, and festivals outside the city wall, which also acted as trade fairs, were organized by guilds.[21] The dynasty asserted control over the city's economic life by placing an official of the imperial household over every trade in the city: the jewellers were under the *kuyumcubasi* or chief imperial jeweller, the physicians under the *hekimbasi* or chief imperial physician, the tailors under the *terzibasi* or chief imperial tailor.

After Muslims, Greeks were the main merchants in Constantinople. The expanding free trade area of the Ottoman Empire and its frequent wars with the Greeks' old economic rival Venice gave them a stronger trading position than in the last centuries of the Byzantine Empire. In 1476 leases on the wharves of Gallipoli and Galata were awarded to a Greek consortium, including two members of the Palaeologus dynasty, relations of the last Byzantine Emperor. It had outbid Muslim rivals by offering the massive sum of 450,000 ducats. In 1477 two Greeks purchased the right to administer customs duties on the import of wheat into the city for one million *akces*.[22] Success in commerce was a substitute for ruling an empire.

The career of Michael Cantacuzenos illustrates the prizes and perils awaiting a Greek merchant in Constantinople. Born about 1515, he was a direct human link between the Byzantine and Ottoman capitals. He was descended from the Emperor John Cantacuzenos who, in the fourteenth century, had invited the Ottomans into Europe and had married his daughter Theodora to Orhan, the second Ottoman Sultan. One Cantacuzenos died as Grand Domestic at the siege of 1453. Michael Cantacuzenos, described as 'the honour of the Greeks by his words and deeds', and almost certainly his son, died of plague on 25 June 1522 and was buried at the church of St Paraschiva in Haskoy. They were the most prominent Greek family of the city. One relation, Theodore Cantacuzenos Spandugino, published an early account of the Ottoman Empire, much used in this book, in 1515.

The son of Michael Cantacuzenos, also called Michael, was at once furrier to the Sultan, a customs farmer, the power behind the patriarchal throne and an intimate of the Grand Vizier Sokollu. He lived in Constantinople and in a palace on the Black Sea, served by a princely train of servants, slaves and pages. In Constantinople according to the German prisoner Gerlach, 'a jovial old man, he travels in the city on a horse draped in black velvet, six men leading the way, one more modestly dressed closing it'. Like the Phanariot Greeks discussed in the following chapter, he combined pride in the Byzantine Empire with service to the Ottoman. He stamped letters with the double-headed eagle of the Byzantine Empire, but built twenty galleys at his own expense for the Ottoman navy after its defeat by the Holy League of Venice, Spain and the Papacy at Lepanto in 1571.

His greed won him the name *Seytanoglu*, the son of Satan, from the Turks: Greeks considered him a leech and a thief. All rejoiced when, on 3 March 1578, the Sultan ordered him to be hanged at the entrance to his country palace, without time to see a priest or make a will. He had been trapped in two webs of intrigue: the conflict between the Ottoman vassal principalities of Moldavia, Wallachia and the Crimea, in which he was personally involved, since his brother had married a daughter of a Voivode of Wallachia; and, in Constantinople itself, an underground struggle for power between Sultan Murad III and the Grand Vizier Sokollu. Sokollu was stunned by his death, but was able to protect his son and widow.

At the sale of Cantacuzenos's possessions outside the palace walls, buyers chose from 'an almost infinite number of silk, velvet and brocade clothes, sometimes having golden buttons framing rubies and turquoises, magnificent sable furs, superb horses, of which the Sultan kept twenty for himself'. The phrase 'I bought it at the Cantacuzenos sale' entered the lore of the city. The university of Tübingen and the wealthy Orthodox monasteries of Mount Athos competed for his Greek manuscripts. The Cantacuzenoi left Constantinople for Wallachia in the early seventeenth century – the first link in the connection between the Ottoman Greeks and the Danube principalities, which was to reach its apogee in the eighteenth century.[23]

Below such merchant princes were thousands of Greek traders, shopkeepers, tavern-keepers, boatmen. Greeks were so eager for business that they continued working in Constantinople even when plague drove other traders into the country. Greek-dominated guilds, with the synod of twelve bishops and the notables of the city, particip- ated in the election of the Patriarch until the middle of the nineteenth century. The fur trade, crucial to the etiquette of the palace and the rise of Seytanoglu, was regulated by a powerful guild, which paid for the maintenance of schools and hospitals in the capital, and the church of the Holy Sepulchre. Thus Constantinople subsidized Jerusalem as well as Mecca.[24]

A blend of tension and toleration characterized the economic, as it did the religious, relations between Muslims and Christians and Jews in the city. In Vilna in Lithuania before the twentieth century, because different races monopolized different professions, Yiddish was used to address the coachman, Polish the schoolteacher, German the dentist and Lithuanian the maid. In Constantinople, however, such specialization was unnecessary. No trade, not even that of mosque- building, was the monopoly of one community. Of the 3,523 crafts- men who worked on the Suleymaniye mosque in the 1550s, 51 per cent were Christians. Of 331 butchers in Constantinople in 1681, 215 were Muslims, 70 Christians and 46 Jews. Of twenty-eight surgeons permitted to operate in 1700, twelve were Greek, eight Jews, four Muslims, two English, one French and one Armenian. Although most guilds had Muslim patrons – such as David for armourers, or Jonah for fishermen – many were composed of both Muslims and non- Muslims.[25]

Relations between Christians and Jews in Constantinople were worse than between Christians and Muslims. In certain Greek districts, if a Jew appeared in the streets during Holy Week, boys would grease his beard with tar and set fire to it. Good Friday processions included a figure of Judas dressed in the costume of a local rabbi. Boys hurled dirt at it, screaming – one Greek remembered – 'a litany of the coarsest abuse'. At every Christian house the procession stopped to be given money or Easter eggs. The former bought wood to burn 'Judas'; the latter were eaten to celebrate his death.

The Muslim population of the city, on the other hand, was tolerant, or indifferent, towards Jews. In 1492 in the aftermath of the fall of Granda, Jews were expelled from Castile; Aragon and Portugal fol- lowed suit. The Ottoman Empire opened its frontiers. In a famous, possibly apocryphal comment, Bayezid II remarked that King

Ferdinand could not be as clever as reputed, if he expelled so many industrious subjects to enrich a rival monarch.[26]

After 1502, the Ottomans also welcomed Arabs from Granada. Given the choice by the Catholic Kings of conversion or emigration, many left, not for Arab cities nearby, but for Constantinople: they seized the Catholic church of St Paul, in Galata, and transformed it into the Arap Cami, or Arab Mosque, as it is still called today. Receiving more 'Grenatini', as persecution worsened in the late sixteenth and early seventeenth centuries, Galata became a centre of Arab sailors, who wore Arab dress and introduced Arab sweets and drinks.[27] For Jews and Arabs – and for the stream of Christians who left western Europe for the Ottoman Empire until the nineteenth century – Constantinople was a city of refuge. It offered three advantages: toleration, prosperity and, as capital of an empire frequently at war with the states which had rejected them, revenge.

The great port of Salonica, known as 'the new Jerusalem', where Jews soon became a majority, was the bastion of Ottoman Judaism. However, there were 8,070 Jewish households in Constantinople by 1535, five times the figure in 1477. The names of the city's synagogues – Lisbon, Cordova, Messina, Ohrida – and families – Sevilia, Toledano, Leon, Taranto – reveal the diversity of their origins. Constantinople was a city of double identities. Sephardic Jews, however, had three: Jewish, Ottoman and 'Sephardi', or Spanish. A new language was heard in the streets of Constantinople: an artificially embalmed Castilian called Ladino (the written version) or Judezmo (the spoken language).

Ladino was of little political or commercial use. The main reason for its survival was religious. It was the language in which the scriptures were read and chanted at home and in synagogue. In Constantinople (despite the persistence of Greek-speaking 'Romaniot' congregations), Jews and the Spanish language were synonymous: many Turks called the latter *yahudice*. As late as 1869, during a visit of the Empress Eugénie, the Grand Rabbi of the Ottoman Empire addressed her in her native Spanish. In 1873, when the first railway lines opened near the city, Jews could not work on them: they did not know the language of the country where they had been living for over three hundred years.[28]

In prosperous households in the Jewish districts of Balat and Haskoy either side of the Golden Horn, Jews listened to the *turkito* ('little Turk' – muezzin) on the *verandado* (large first-floor hall). At *convitas* (parties), they ate dishes like *Piskado reynado* (fish with walnuts), and sang *romanceros* (songs) lamenting their exile from Spain. Poorer families lived in a *cortijo*, a low building containing residences and shops, where two or three families might share one room.[29]

In the realms of business and medicine, a symbiosis developed between Jews and Muslims – closer than that of either with Greeks and Armenians. A prominent Spanish Jew, Moses Hamon, a favourite doctor and dentist of Suleyman the Magnificent, helped procure a firman in late 1553 or early 1554 decreeing that all accusations of ritual murders of Christian children by Jews be referred to the Imperial Divan. Such accusations, made by Christians in the Ottoman Empire with psychotic frequency until the twentieth century, led to riots by Greeks against Jews as late as 1874 in Constantinople itself.

A physical symbol of Muslim-Jewish tolerance is the proximity of a small synagogue and a mosque on the first floor of the Buyuk Corapci Han, the han of the sock-makers built under Suleyman the Magnificent in the commercial district of Eminonu between the bazaar and the Golden Horn. Helped by their knowledge of Western languages and accounting methods, the Jews of the city scaled new heights in the sixteenth century, to the detriment of Italian merchants. A French diplomat who lived in Constantinople under Suleyman the Magnificent, Nicolas de Nicolay, wrote enviously:

> They now have in their hands the most and greatest traffic of merchandise and ready money that is conducted in all the Levant. The shops and stalls best stocked with all the varieties of goods which can be found in Constantinople are those of the Jews. They also have among them very excellent practitioners of all the arts and manufactures, especially the Marranos not long since banished and expelled from Spain and Portugal who to the great detriment and injury of Christianity have taught the Turks several inventions, artifices and machines of war such as how to make artillery, arquebuses, gunpowder, cannon-balls and other arms.[30]

Because of their medical knowledge, Jews served as doctors in the palace until the nineteenth century.

The Nasi family were the most famous of Constantinople's Jews. Their odyssey illustrates, both in time and space, the spread of intolerance across the face of Renaissance Europe – until it reached the Ottoman frontier. In 1492 they left Castile for Portugal, where they were forced to convert to Catholicism. In 1536 they moved to Antwerp, financial capital of Europe, in 1544 to Venice, and in 1550 to Ferrara. In each city they met persecution and restriction (a ghetto had been established in Venice in 1515). In 1553, partly as a result of letters written to the Doge of Venice by Suleyman the Magnificent himself (on the prompting of Moses Hamon), the head of the family, Dona Gracia Nasi, was able to leave for Constantinople. A few months later *La Señora*, as she was known, made a triumphant entry into the city, followed by forty cavaliers and four carriages of servants. Using her personal fortune, and deposits she attracted from Muslims, she operated as an independent business woman and tax-farmer. With her nephew Joseph, she paid cash in advance for concessions for supplying the city with lumber and wine. She also ran an import–export business, exchanging pepper, wheat and raw wool for European cloth.[31]

Joseph Nasi was a courtier, banker and international entrepreneur. Known as João Miques to the Portuguese, Juan Miguez to Spaniards, Jehan Micquez to the French, and 'the Great Jew' to his enemies, he had been born in Lisbon in 1526. After the family's move to Antwerp, he was educated at the university of Louvain, where the future Holy Roman Emperor Maximilian II was a fellow student. A German resident noted Nasi's entry into Constantinople in 1554 with 'over twenty well-dressed Spanish servants. They attend him as if he were a prince. He himself wore silk clothes lined with sable. Before him went two Janissaries with staves, as mounted lackeys, as is the Turkish custom, in order that nothing should happen to him . . . He is a large person with a trimmed black beard.' In Constantinople, he soon, in the words of a Spanish doctor, became 'one of the Devil's own' – converted to Judaism.

Three thousand guests came to Nasi's wedding to his wealthy cousin Reyna. They lived in the style of the Spanish nobility, in a palace called Belvedere overlooking the Bosphorus above Ortakoy. In his carpet-lined library, he discussed politics with the French ambassador, the science of dreams with Rabbi Almosnino, astrology with the Oecumenical Patriarch. Attached to his palace, he maintained a printing press, an academy, a synagogue and a jousting ground.[32]

Nasi soon became a friend, jeweller and banker of the heir to the throne, Prince Selim, to whom he supplied both wine and cash. A Venetian diplomat reported: 'His Highness drinks much wine and the said Don Joseph sends him many bottles of it from time to time, together with all manner of other delicacies.' On Selim's accession to the throne, he made Joseph Nasi duke of the former Venetian-dominated Duchy of Naxos in the Aegean, with the rank of *sancakbey*. Thus success in the Ottoman capital enabled a Jew to give orders to Catholic nobles (who still owned much property in the Aegean). How sweet it must have been for this outcast from Catholic Europe to issue orders under the form:

> Joseph, by the Grace of God Duke of the Archipelago, Lord of Andros etc. . . . Given in the Ducal Palace of Belvedere near Pera at Constantinople, this eleventh day of July 1577 . . .
>
>> At the Duke's mandate.
>> Joseph Cohen, Secretary and Amanuensis.[33]

Nasi's businesses continued to expand. He began to export Cretan wine to Poland and acquired a monopoly of the wax trade. The Ottoman government acted as his debt collector in a long dispute with the French government over money he had lent to French ambassadors: Suleyman the Magnificent wrote no less than three letters to the King of France on behalf of 'the model of the notables of the Mosaic nation and one of the *muteferrik* [official companions] of my son Selim'. His favour with Selim was well known. Maximilian II sent him three gold drinking flasks, while the King of Poland, to whom he lent money, called him 'Excellent Sir and well-beloved Friend!'

His contacts in western Europe enabled him to maintain an international intelligence network which helped him obtain revenge on Spain and France. It is possible that, from the banks of the Bosphorus, he encouraged the revolt of the Netherlands against Philip II of Spain. An envoy from the rebel leader, the Prince of Orange, came to see him in 1569. The historian Famianus Strada wrote: 'As regards the Flemings, Miches's [i.e. Nasi's] letters and persuasions had no little influence on them.' However no letters have come to light.[34]

Nasi was a player in the faction-fighting of the court, and hostile to Venice on account of its treatment of Venetian Jews. Sokollu Mehmed Pasha, who had his own Jewish diplomatic agent (his doctor Rabbi Salomon Ashkenazi) and favoured peace with Venice, tried to ruin him. However, the Bailo of Venice wrote that Nasi 'has always managed to save himself, the Grand Signor himself excusing him and defending him on several occasions'. Nasi encouraged the empire's war of 1570 against the Papacy, Spain and Venice – possibly in the hope of becoming King of Cyprus, or helping the Dutch rebels. After the peace of 1573 and the death of Selim II in 1574, Nasi's influence declined. However he laughed last. Cantacuzenos was hanged. Possibly at the Sultan's instigation, Sokollu was stabbed to death by a dervish in the Divan chamber in the palace. Nasi died peacefully in his palace.[35]

Nasi and his relations promoted specifically Jewish causes. In 1556 they tried to save twenty-four Ancona Jews whom the Pope had ordered burnt to death. The Sultan wrote a personal letter to the Pope – in vain. The Nasis and other of the city's Jews were so influential that Venetian diplomats believed that the outcome of peace talks depended on Venice's treatment of its Jewish community. The Nasis founded a famous rabbinical academy at Tiberias in Galilee, rebuilt the city walls and encouraged Jewish settlement there.[36] However, like most Constantinople Jews, they were content to be subjects of the 'Sultans of mercy' as they called their sovereigns. They did not plan a Jewish state.

After their golden age in the sixteenth century, Jews remained extremely influential. Firmans permitting the construction of synagogues were renewed in 1604, 1693, 1744 and 1755. So many Jews worked in the city's customs office that trade came to a standstill during Jewish holidays. A French traveller called Michel Febvre wrote in the late seventeenth century: 'There is no family of consideration among Turks and foreign merchants [local Christians are, significantly, not mentioned] which does not have a Jew in its service either to estimate the value and quality of merchandise, or to serve as interpreter or to give an opinion on everything that is happening.'[37]

From 1700 on, however, the position of Jews began to decline at the same time as the empire they had served so well. Some of the city's synagogues fell into debt. The number of Jewish books printed in Constantinople fell every decade. Rich and well-protected European traders began to take over the commerce of the city.[38]

The Jews' decline was hastened by the rise of a rival merchant community: the Armenians. From the early seventeenth century Armenians had begun to arrive in Constantinople in large numbers, fleeing rebellions and wars in eastern Anatolia. At first they had humble jobs such as porters, broom makers and sellers of bread and a dried meat called *pastirma*. Soon they moved into other trades, helped by protection from the palace: both Murad IV and 'Mad Ibrahim' had favourites of Armenian origin. The eighteenth century witnessed growing Armenian confidence and energy. In 1727 the ancestor of a dynasty of architects which was to change the face of the city, Sarkis Kalfa Balian, was a palace architect. In 1757, in place of the Jewish Yago Bonfil, a member of the Armenian Catholic family of Duzian was appointed superintendent of the imperial mint, a position which remained in his family, with a gap of thirteen years, until 1880. Soon most of the employees were Armenian, and the records were kept in Ottoman in the Armenian alphabet, which few but Armenians could read. The Duzian also became keepers of the Sultan's jewels.

Regarded as particularly honest and trustworthy, Armenians replaced Jews as the chief bankers of the city. The last Jewish banker of a Grand Vizier was Jesova Soncino in 1746–7; the last Greek banker, Scanavi Capsaloni in 1770–1. Thereafter Armenians took over. Between 1770 and 1840 they played a pivotal role in financing provincial governors and organizing tax collection. The rate of interest they charged varied between 18 and 24 per cent.[39]

The Armenian bankers or *amiras* were called 'leaders of the nation', 'bright princes' or 'princes of great honour'. Visibly part of the Ottoman élite, with the right to wear quilted turbans and fur coats, and to ride horses in the city, they claimed descent from the ancient kings of Armenia. No doubt they wanted to compete with Greeks' pretensions to descent from Byzantine emperors.[40] The Serpos family, which arrived from Sivas around 1700, by 1750 had a banking empire stretching from Venice to India, and enjoyed the diplomatic protection of Britain or Sweden. One Serpos was chief banker of two grand viziers from 1732 to 1746. Another arranged the transfer of the Ottoman subsidy to Sweden, via Hamburg, in 1789 when both countries were fighting Russia.[41]

The *amiras* dominated the Armenian Patriarchate, and helped select the Patriarch. By 1700 the Patriarch had despotic powers over his flock, its schools, churches and printing presses. The announcement, 'the Holy Father would like to see you', struck terror into members of his flock. On fast days – and no community fasted more rigorously than the Armenians – the Patriarch's servants went through the streets, sniffing like dogs for the smell of meat. The guilty were fined and sometimes imprisoned or sent to a lunatic asylum. During one service, 'lunatics' chained in a cellar below the church rattled their chains and uttered woeful cries to such effect that a wealthy Armenian offered to construct a hospital for them outside the city.[42] Whether the *amiras*' wealth would be translated into power in the city of Constantinople, as well as their own community, was one question facing the capital at the beginning of the nineteenth century.

All the merchants of the city, whether Muslim, Greek, Jewish or Armenian, met in the bazaar on the brow of the hill between the Golden Horn and the Sea of Marmara. The streets of Constantinople were unusually quiet. The bazaar, however, greeted visitors with a rush of heat, colour, perfumes and noise: 'Buy my fine cloth, one thousand kurush! Buy my fine cloth, two thousand kurush!'

The bazaar is an immense stone edifice, so large that it was said that no native of Constantinople ever saw it all. Surrounded by high grey walls and surmounted by a roof of cupolas perforated with holes to let in light, it contains a labyrinth of arcaded alleys, crowned by plaster vaults stencilled in elaborate Ottoman blue and red arabesques. Each alley was lined on both sides by stalls, known as *dolaps*, about seven or eight feet wide and three to four foot deep, decorated with flowers and pious messages from the Koran. There were some 4,000 stalls, about a tenth of all those in the city as a whole. Each *dolap* had a bench in front where the vendor displayed his wares. Most stall-keepers were Muslims and built a small recess for ritual ablutions, where they retired before performing their prayers on the bench. The bazaar was a miniature city with its own mosques, courtyards and fountains: one was erected by an imperial princess 'in honour of a shoemaker who sent home his work punctually'.

The bazaar was opened every morning at about half past eight with prayers for the Sultan and his soldiers and the souls of all past members of the bazaar, and an injunction: 'There will be no cheating! There will be no hoarding! There will be no sale of goods without security!' The tradesmen then filed in. The stalls closed at about 6 in the evening.[43]

The nucleus of the bazaar was the Bedestan, or covered market, now called the Old Bazaar, built by Mehmed II in 1456–61. By 1473 there 124 shops inside and 72 outside the Bedestan. Over two thirds were Muslim-owned. The Bedestan was surrounded by four gates, of the skullcap-sellers, the cloth-sellers, the jewellers and the second-hand booksellers. The latter's reputation for meanness was such that the phrase 'worse than a second-hand bookseller' entered bazaar lore. Outside the Bedestan every product had its particular street. In the street of the arms dealers, the sixteenth-century French traveller Philippe du Fresne Canaye was entranced by 'harnesses in silver gilt with very fine carving, a lot of golden vases, very rare plumes with rubies and turquoises in such quantity that it is impossible to regard them fixedly . . . In short one sees so many beautiful things there that it is very difficult to leave without putting one's hand in one's purse.' The rents from the Bedestan went to the *vakif* or endowment which supported Aya Sofya.[44]

The bazaar also contained state-designated safes built behind the stalls, where individuals deposited jewels and money. It was probably more free of crime than markets in the West. Merchants could leave stalls unattended; pastry-sellers trusted members of the public to pay for the wares they left on a small round tray. In 1591 a robbery of safes in the Grand Bazaar was an unprecedented horror. The culprit was a young man who worked for an Armenian jeweller – he hid the goods under the straw matting on the shop floor. He was hanged in the Sultan's presence. It was not until the nineteenth century and the advent of modern tourism that the bazaar acquired a reputation as a nest of vultures.[45]

The bazaar combined the roles of shopping centre, stock exchange and bank. It was also a club where merchants met to plan transactions and voyages. Dudley North missed the bazaar more than anywhere else in Constantinople, for he had found there 'almost any kind of thing that any man desires or uses'. Above all it was a meeting-place. In London, despite the coffee-houses and the Exchange, 'those that wanted him, could not find him, any more than he them'.

The bazaar was surrounded by twenty-one hans, like the Buyuk Valide Han, built to foster trade. Consisting of two or three arcaded storeys around a tree-filled courtyard, the hans accommodated goods and animals on the ground floor, and craftsmen and merchants on the first and second floors. Unlike most houses in the city, hans were made of stone. By 1700 the Buyuk Valide Han had become the commercial and religious centre of the city's Persians (most of whom came from Azerbaijan). Several thousand lived there and it was compared to a small independent state. Capitulations, far from being confined to European communities, were also enjoyed by Persians. In the nineteenth century a Persian pilgrim, passing through Constantinople on his way to Mecca, noted: 'Legal recourse for Iranians is entirely through the embassy; they are never under the jurisdiction of Constantinople.'

Attitudes towards the Shi'i branch of Islam had relaxed since the sixteenth century. The main Shi'i mosque of Constantinople was in the middle of the first courtyard. Every 10 Muharram a ceremony in commemoration of two Shi'i martyrs, the Prophet's grandsons Hasan and Huseyin, affirmed the piety and identity of the Persians of the city. First there were prayers in the mosque. Then, by the light of torches, to the sound of drums and cries of *Hasan! Huseyin!*, watched by up to 20,000 spectators, a long procession of white-shirted men flagellated themselves in unison with truncheons, and with recently sharpened swords. Blood streamed down their sides: their heads and chests resembled raw meat. They then proceeded to other hans to perform the same ritual. The next day they crossed over to Uskudar to a stream in the cemetery where doctors waited with bandages.[46]

Whereas the Buyuk Valide Han was devoted to the commerce of a certain area, other hans were dominated by a particular trade: carpenters, goldsmiths and so on. The Suleyman Pasha Han south of the bazaar specialized in one of the most profitable commodities in the Ottoman capital: humans. Constantinople was the centre of a slave trade with supply lines starting in Poland, the Caucasus and the Sudan. The government levied a tax on each slave entering the city (four gold ducats a head in the sixteenth century) and, like modern London auction-houses, on both buyers and sellers. Males, who could be exposed naked, were also sold in the Old Bazaar. In 1547 the French traveller Jean Chesneau saw dealers leading 3-year-old children through the bazaar, crying their price in public. Circassians were especially prized, followed by Poles, Abaza (from another Caucasus district) and Russians. The men from western Europe were thought too soft, and the women too hard. Blacks were also on sale: Pushkin's great-grandfather was an Ethiopian, bought in Constantinople by the Russian ambassador.

Prospective purchases were tested like cattle. Buyers spat in their face to see if make-up came off, and felt 'teeth, legs, thighs and the most secret parts. The poor things, men as well as women, let themselves be mistreated with lowered and expressionless eyes.' Absence of teeth, beauty or virginity lowered the price. In 1600 a young virgin cost a hundred ducats, a woman of 60 thirty-six. Before he bought a female, a purchaser could take her home for the night to see if she snored.[47] Until the twentieth century, women were especially prominent in the slave trade, purchasing young girls, after the usual physical examination and financial bargaining, from independent female slave-dealers going from harem to harem. The girls were taught deportment, sewing and singing, and then sold on at a profit.[48]

Domestic slaves in Muslim households (in theory no Christians or Jews were allowed to own slaves) were relatively well treated – better than slaves in the Americas or many free servants in western Europe. Slavery could act as a form of kinship, and thus, as the Janissaries well knew, as a means to social advancement. If slaves did not like their master, they could, in theory, petition judges to be sold. Some slaves earned the money to buy their freedom by manning ferries between Uskudar and Europe. However other slaves were bought for physical pleasure. A seventeenth-century Ottoman called Latifi wrote:

> Among them are girls and boys of such exceptional beauty that people lose all
> self-control and squander their whole fortune, declaring that money is of no
> importance compared with the soul and love ... As the poem says: the most
> valuable thing in the world is union with beauty, otherwise what are people of
> love seeking in this bazaar?

Men who had spent all their money on slaves could not resist returning to the slave-market, despite the pain of being able to see, but no
longer to buy, the beauties on sale. Including the Sultan's slaves of the
Gate, slaves formed a large proportion of the population of
Constantinople – up to 20 per cent, according to Halil Inalcik, compared to about 3 per cent of the population of Venice in 1600.[49]

If humans were among the principal imports of the capital, they were
also one of its main exports. Soldiers, officials and *ulema* left the city
every year in thousands to guard or govern the empire. Few achieved
greater prominence than the members of the great families, Koprulu
and Mavrocordato.

6

Viziers and Dragomans

If Prince Kaunitz is prince of the Holy Roman Empire, I am prince of the very holy Ottoman Empire . . . I am the master; I am a prince born of a family which has reigned for two hundred years, a reigning sovereign, I will say what I please; I fear neither the Emperor nor Prince Kaunitz.

Alexander Mavrocordato, Prince of Moldavia, to the Austrian consul Stefano Raicevich, 30 November 1784

B Y 1622 THE 17-year-old Sultan Osman II had defied the traditions of his dynasty and the interests of his capital. Instead of restricting himself to slave consorts, he had married three free women, including a daughter of a Mufti of Constantinople. Going to prayers one Friday, he wore a kaftan of pale pink Venetian material, and used 'very light' horse trappings. The English ambassador, Sir Thomas Roe, wrote that he made himself 'cheap and vulgar, by night walks, and in disguised habits haunting taverns and by-places and there exercising the office of a constable'. Janissaries found in taverns were drowned in the Bosphorus. The entire corps, which had performed badly in a recent campagin against Poland, was reputed 'apt to mutiny and dissolution' and had its pay cut.

Against the advice of the Grand Vizier, the Sultan planned the ultimate sacrilege: to leave the city, perform the pilgrimage to Mecca and raise an army in his Arab provinces to counterbalance the Janissaries. The Mufti issued a fatwa, declaring 'The pilgrimage is not necessary for sultans. It is preferable that they stay in their place and dispense justice. This is lawful since disorder might ensue.' It had no effect.

On 7 May the imperial tents and treasure began to be taken out of the palace and across the Bosphorus into Asia. Threatened in their pride and their pockets, and manipulated by leading pashas, Janissaries assembled on the Atneydan the next day and cried: 'In the name of the Law we want to have Sultan Mustafa Khan' – the Sultan's uncle and predecessor, whom he had imprisoned in a vault with two naked black women, since Mustafa could not abide the opposite sex. Finally, on 9 May, Janissaries stormed the palace, seized Osman II and took him to the Seven Towers wearing nothing but a white shift. The crowd's abuse along the way reduced him to tears: 'Yesterday I was Padishah. Today I am naked.' The new Grand Vizier, who had helped plan the rebellion, ordered Osman II's death, from a combination of strangulation and compression of the testicles. When his orders were questioned, he said: 'It matters little who is Sultan so long as the world order is not disturbed.'[1] In appearance the Sultan was absolute master of the city and the empire, and the viziers were his slaves. In reality constraints on his rule were as brutal as those imposed, at the same period, by courts, nobilities and parliaments on Western monarchs. If sultans had grand viziers executed, viziers could also execute back.

The power and status of this élite were visible on the streets of the city. In the opinion of one seventeenth-century observer, Paul Rycaut: 'One may guess at the greatness of this Empire by the Retinue, Pomp and number of Servants which accompany Persons of Quality in their Journeys.' The purpose of these households was not only to impress the public but also to control the central government. In 1656 Sultan Mehmed IV admitted that he owed his accession to the throne to God's will, his own abilities and the consent of the civil officials and the religious scholars.[2]

At the apex of the official hierarchy was the Sultan's 'absolute deputy', His Highness the Grand Vizier, served by a household of 2,000, modelled on the Sultan's, and protected by a guard of 500 Albanians. In western Europe, outside royalty's sacred circle, only Richelieu and Mazarin, who enjoyed both the power of a principal minister and the rank of a cardinal (equal to that of prince of the blood), had comparable status.

The Grand Vizier was also in effect mayor of Constantinople. For the capital had no independent institutions of its own, no *hôtel de ville*, no guildhall. All depended on the state. Before the Grand Vizier's inspection of the markets every Wednesday, he held a meeting in the Divan on the affairs of the capital. He was assisted in its administration by the four *kadis* or judges for Stanbul, Galata, Uskudar and Eyup. They were appointed by, and had direct access to, the Sultan and enjoyed virtual autonomy in the administration of the *sheriat*. They supervised the market-place and tried to ensure that the Muslims of the city lived truly

Muslim lives. Under the kadis an army of lesser officials inspected goods, prices and tradesmen, and levied taxes on shops, markets and products entering the city.[3]

Owing to a run of feeble sultans and the complexity of Ottoman government, from 1650 the Porte replaced the palace as the centre of power. This shift received architectural confirmation in 1654, when the Porte obtained a permanent home in a pasha's house, down the hill from the palace, on the present site of the offices of the Governor of Istanbul, and part of the Ottoman state archives. At the Sublime Porte, entry was 'free to all the world and he [the Grand Vizier] gives Audiences even to the meanest of the Poor'. Lord Charlemont, who was shown over the building in 1749, was impressed by the magnificence of the Grand Vizier's 'large, lofty and well-proportioned' private apartments, furnished with English clocks, French mirrors and Persian carpets.

The Porte housed an efficient bureaucracy of scribes and clerks (869 in the late eighteenth century), serving the Grand Vizier, his deputy the *Reis Efendi* (Secretary of State) and other pashas. It contributed as much as the dynasty and the army to the survival of the empire. Lord Charlemont wrote:

All the Ministers who hold their offices at the Porte have beside their apartments, chambers adjoining, which serve as secretary's offices in which their clerks write. I went into five or six of them and was astonished at the multitude of the clerks, the singular attitude in which they write [on their knees, without desks] and the great expedition and regularity with which business is carried on . . . The registers of precedents are the most exactly kept of any in the world and such is their precision and regularity that any memorial or any fact whatsoever of a hundred years standing may be found in the space of half an hour.

(At the end of the nineteenth century an official of the Porte boasted that in four hundred years it had never lost a document.) In this over-centralized empire, every provincial governor constantly addressed copious written reports to Constantinople. The abundance of documentation is, indeed, one obstacle facing historians working in the Ottoman archives.[4]

Some grand viziers became so powerful that they were able to pass on status and wealth to their descendants. Sokollu Mehmed Pasha, who was said to have paid for the construction of 300 mosques, died owning four palaces in Constantinople, a 360-room palace in Edirne, and eighteen million gold piastres. His son by Ismihan Sultan, daughter of Selim

II, Ibrahim Hanzade, inherited part of his father's wealth. In one document he describes a section of his father's palace in Uskudar:

> The exterior court enclosed by high walls contained a large reception hall and a chamber of petitions beside it, which was flanked by two rooms, two privy chambers and a hall, two corridors and an exercise terrace and an ablution room which faces a garden and a fountain, and a large faienced room with fine metal wire and mother-of-pearl inlaid windows . . . this was the extent and the entirety of the palace I inherited from my father, the house of the late Mehmed Pasha.

Ibrahim Hanzade held several offices in the palace and the government such as chief gatekeeper and superintendent of the Sultan's kitchens: his Hanzade descendants lived in the Kadirga district of Constantinople in a palace designed by Sinan, off the income of estates at Edirne, Belgrade, Višegrad and Aleppo. On their tombs around Sokollu's stately, semi-royal mausoleum at Eyup, they were often called *beyefendi* or lord. Like courtiers in the West, they could be social companions of the monarch. The Sultan paid them visits, allowed them access to his person, and employed them as his hereditary chief huntsmen. Like the Sultan they reproduced themselves through concubinage rather than by marriages. A British ambassador described them as 'infinitely respected by the people'. They were so rich that in 1696 Ibrahim Ali Bey, a member of this family, was expected to contribute 500 soldiers to the imperial army – like a great lord in sixteenth-century France or England.

Another branch, the Sokolluzade, descended from Sokollu Mehmed Pasha's union with another consort. Many served as chief treasurer, *reis-ul kuttab* (head of the imperial chancery) or provincial governors; at the end of the eighteenth century one Sokolluzade was responsible for the construction of a dam for Constantinople's water supply.[5] The mother of Dinc Bilgin, owner of one of the most successful Turkish newspapers of the 1990s, *Sabah*, is a Sokollu.

The power of the Porte, and of a dominating but unofficial élite, was confirmed by the appearance of one of the ablest ministerial dynasties in the history of Europe – the only family which has produced five chief ministers (and two others who were close relations). The Koprulu appeared at the appropriate moment.

Since the late sixteenth century the Ottoman Empire had experienced a crisis of confidence. In 1622 Sir Thomas Roe the English ambassador, who called the empire 'a sinke of men and sluttisheness', was convinced it was close to collapse. Writers from the élite blamed the educational system and looked back to a mythical golden age under Suleyman the Magnificent. The public criticized rampant official corruption. In 1624 Cossacks of Ukrainian origin had sailed down from the Black Sea into the Bosphorus and burnt and looted the village of Yenikoy.

Despite a recovery under Murad IV in the 1630s, by 1656 catastrophe appeared imminent. For the third time in ten years the Venetian navy – from whom the empire was trying to conquer Crete – had blockaded the Dardanelles. Four thousand Christian galley slaves fled to join them. People left Constantinople in search of a better life in Anatolia. Food prices soared. Mutinous Janissaries shouted at the Sultan: 'We linger in the corners of the hans hungry and improverished and our stipends are not even enough to cover our debts to the proprietors of the hans.' In despair the Valide, Turhan, who had been appointing grand viziers since the murder of her rival Kosem five years earlier, turned to an unpopular old man of 80 called Koprulu Mehmed.[6]

Born in the village of Ruznik, in what is now Albania, Koprulu Mehmed was probably of Albanian origin. Possibly recruited through the *devshirme* system, he worked in the palace kitchens, whence he was dismissed for pride and temper. He received the name Koprulu from his wife, who came from the small town of Kopru in Anatolia. After holding a variety of offices – superintendent of the guilds, inspector of the arsenals, provincial governor – he returned to palace service.

Through his contacts with the chief architect and palace tutor, also Albanians, he secured a secret audience with the Valide Sultan Turhan on 13 September 1656. Since the government was in chaos, Koprulu Mehmed was able to impose four startling conditions – the Porte's judgement on decades of rule by the palace and the harem. First, all his requests should be granted by the Sultan; secondly, there should be no pressure to grant favours – 'such unreasonable requests are the source of all disturbances'; thirdly, there should be no independent military viziers; and finally, the Grand Vizier should be immune from denunciation – 'for everyone wants to share in the affairs of state'. Turhan accepted the conditions. The ceremonial surrounding the Sultan was a façade. Even his mother did not believe that he should exercise the reality, as well as the appearance, of power. On 15 September 1656 Koprulu Mehmed Pasha became Grand Vizier.[7]

In the provinces people said: 'Just see what an evil day the Ottoman state has reached when we get as Grand Vizier a miserable wretch like

Koprulu, who could not even give straw to a pair of oxen!' Others were more prescient: 'This Koprulu is not like other grand viziers. He has seen much of the hot and cold of fate, he has suffered much of poverty and penury, distresses and vicissitudes, he has gained much experience from campaigning and he knows the ways of the world.'[8]

Indeed Koprulu soon restored the central government to a degree of efficiency unknown since the days of Sokollu Mehmed Pasha. He appointed his own men as Mufti and treasurer, cut state pensions and established a network of informers throughout Constantinople. Venice was defeated, Lemnos retaken and a rising in Anatolia – always more rebellious than the Balkans – suppressed. He ruled through terror. One state executioner calculated that he alone had consigned 4,000 corpses to the water. A letter from Koprulu to a provincial governor reveals Koprulu's style of government:

> It is true that we were both raised together in the imperial harem and are both protégés of Sultan Murad IV. Nevertheless, be informed that from this moment if the accursed Cossacks pillage and burn any one of the villages and towns on the coast of Ozu province, I swear by God the Almighty that I will give you no quarter and will pay no heed to your righteous character but I will cut you into pieces as a warning to the world.

He had two Oecumenical Patriarchs and one Armenian Patriarch executed on suspicion of treasonable contacts with foreign powers.[9]

The Grand Vizier's critical weapon was the readiness of the young Sultan Mehmed IV, who called him 'father', to be a symbol rather than a ruler. Mehmed IV was described as 'a very swarthy man, his face shining and pretty full eye, black and sparkling . . . He hath a great deal of Majesty in his countenance, and terror, too when he please to put it on.' A passionate hunter, he could stay in the saddle from before dawn to after dusk. His favourite falcons received bejewelled collars; his beaters, however, sometimes froze to death. One Bostanci Pasha laid out their corpses in silent reproach. The Sultan merely cursed him for hiring such rotten men. It was said that the Grand Vizier deliberately turned the Sultan's love of slaughter towards animals, in order to protect his subjects – and to allow the Grand Vizier to govern undisturbed. More powerful than any chief minister in the West, the Grand Vizier even told the Sultan what to say to officials paying homage at Bayram receptions. Remembering 'Mad Ibrahim', there was a rhyme in Constantinople about his son:

The father was mad for the cunt,
The son is mad for the hunt.[10]

Despite profound differences from other European dynasties, the Ottoman dynasty was subject to some of the same problems, such as religious extremism and biological weakness, often at the same time. Owing to a coincidence of weak or youthful monarchs, Valide Sultans exercised power in the same century, 1560–1660, as the Queen Mothers of France, Catherine de Medici, Marie de Medici and Anne of Austria. In the Ottoman Empire, as in other monarchies, royal love of the hunt caused the court to leave the capital for extended periods. Edirne offered the Ottomans as many pleasures as Constantinople, without its problems. Surrounded by hunting forests, it became the counter-capital. Its mosques rivalled, or in the case of the Selimiye mosque built for Selim II surpassed, those of the capital itself. On the edge of the city by the banks of the River Maritza, the Edirne palace was another Topkapi of pavilions, kiosks and courtyards, surrounded by a park. Edirne was also a better assembly point for an army before a campaign in Europe, since it avoided lodging thousands of soldiers in the capital. Suleyman the Magnificent, who took his duties as Sultan so seriously, had spent winters in Edirne, according to Busbecq, the Imperial ambassador, 'because he has there his Seraglio which opens upon a chase and he goes hunting almost every day'. He returned to Constantinople only when the croaking of the frogs at night, on the river by the palace, made sleep difficult.[11]

Mehmed IV abandoned Constantinople at the same time as Louis XIV Paris, and for the same reasons: love of the hunt and fear of sedition. He said that rather than return to Constantinople, where his predecessors had been victims of so many rebellions, he would set it alight with his own hands and would watch with joy as the city and the palace were consumed by flames.

The challenge to Koprulu Mehmed came from the mosques, not the palace. Islamic conservatism had become more aggressive in Constantinople since the sack of the Sultan's observatory in 1580. The last remaining Christian frescos in Aya Sofya were covered in 1609. Scientific and medical schools declined, as Muslim students turned to religious studies. In the mid-seventeenth century relations between Muslims and Christians deteriorated to the point where they established different lodges in the same guild; Christian members complained that they were made to pay for Muslim festivals.

Starting in the 1630s mosque preachers, known as the *kadizadeliler*, had begun to proclaim what were called 'extremist notions'. They denounced not only coffee, tobacco, silk and dancing, but also such dervish practices as pilgrimages to tombs. All innovations since the era of the Prophet – even minarets – were to be eradicated. Constantinople should become the new Medina. Like their contemporaries the English Puritans, Muslims were expected to 'seek out' sinners and force them back to the 'true path'. The Janissaries were infected: attacks on Sufi lodges began. The extremists, whose headquarters were in the mosque of Fatih, were so threatening that for most of 1651 the Oecumenical Patriarch took refuge in the French embassy – an early example of the use of the embassies as asylums, which was to reach a peak in the late nineteenth century. Finally in 1656 Koprulu had the *kadizadeliler* banished to the island of undesirables, the Australia of the Ottoman Empire, Cyprus.[12]

On 31 October 1661, as Koprulu Mehmed lay dying in Edirne, the Sultan himself came to pay his respects. The Vizier's last words of advice to his master were: not to listen to women; to fill the treasury, even by oppressing the people; always to keep the troops employed on campaign; to change senior posts frequently; to punish the slightest mistakes by death; and – showing the conscious use of Islam as a polit-ical weapon – to give Ottoman government 'an appearance of religion and justice'. In a break with tradition, he also said that the appointment of his own son as Grand Vizier would be the best way to preserve the empire from chaos. The Sultan agreed. After a promising career as a provincial governor, Koprulu Fazil Ahmed found himself Grand Vizier at the age of 27. He proved to be the youngest, and one of the ablest and longest serving, of Ottoman grand viziers.

According to the former palace official Bobowski, in contrast to his ruthless father 'the present vezir . . . governs in a most gentle fashion and pardons people easily.' He cut purse-strings, not throats. The father could barely read or write; the son was a poet and a patron of poets. During his vizierate the Ottoman establishment took its first steps towards reestablishing contact with modern scientific knowledge. In 1675–85 a protégé of Koprulu Fazil Ahmed from Damascus, Abu Bekr, translated into Turkish a recent work of geography, the *Atlas Major* of the Dutch geographer Johan Blaeu. The English chaplain, Dr John Covel, wrote:

He is but a little man and goes (as I often afterwards saw him) a little lamely, and something stooping thereupon, which they say is from many issues which he hath about him for the Sciatica. He hath a small round face, a little short thin black beard, little eyes, little mouth, without any wrinkles in his lips; a smooth round forehead and an erected brow, with thick, but very short, hair on it. He is pockbroaken much. In summe, he hath an acute but morale and serious look; and, if I can judge anything, I should think him a subtle cunning man.

He could not be bribed. A war leader with the reputation for finishing what he started, he conquered Podolia in southern Poland and the island of Crete. The empire was larger than it had ever been.[13]

Koprulu Fazil Ahmed also won a reputation for justice and mercy, demonstrated in the strange case of the mystical Messiah. Traumatized by massacres of Jews in the Ukraine in 1648, the worst until this century, some Ottoman Jews believed that the Messiah was a handsome and engaging 39-year-old Jewish merchant of Izmir, Sabbatai Sevi. On 30 December 1665 Sevi sailed to Constantinople, announcing his intention to depose the Sultan. The Jewish community became delirious. A Catholic priest wrote of 'transports of joy such as one can never understand unless one has seen it'. Merchants gave him regal garments; women entered into trances and began to prophesy. Convinced that 'the Crescent and all the royal crowns in Christendom' were about to fall, some Jews prepared to leave Constantinople for the promised land. The prospect of release from the rabbis' tyranny was another reason for their elation. At the same time as Islam was becoming more rigorous, Jewish life too had become more constrained. Jewish women were told not to walk beside the sea or in public places; games and entertainments were forbidden. Sabbatai Sevi, on the other hand, preached a doctrine approaching free love – even within the family. For commercial rather than religious reasons – trade in the capital was languishing – Sabbatai Sevi was imprisoned in February 1666. On 16 September he was received by Koprulu Fazil Ahmed in Edirne.

Struck by his intelligence, his dignity and his Arabic, the Grand Vizier gave him the choice of death or conversion. He turned Muslim. Aziz Mehmed Efendi, as he was now called, received a pension and a place as gatekeeper in the place; his wife Sara was known as Fatma Kadin. However, they soon relapsed. They lived up the Golden Horn at Kagithane, attending sometimes a mosque, sometimes a synagogue. Having become a focus of pilgrimage, in 1672 'the obstinate infidel', as Koprulu now called him, was exiled to Albania, where he died four years later. However his followers, known as *Donme*, formed, and still form, another distinct community in the Istanbul mosaic. Most live as conventional Muslims. Some privately maintain certain Jewish traditions, such as reciting prayers in Hebrew. The smallest group awaits the return of Sabbatai Sevi as the Messiah.[14]

Fazil Ahmed's prudence, firmness, wisdom and discretion impressed the Venetian ambassador. He said that, if he had a son, he would be given no school of politics other than the Ottoman court. The Koprulu ended the Ottoman crisis of confidence that had overtaken the court in the first half of the century. Fazil Ahmed's deputy could write, in 1667: 'Our empire has always been the same since its origin; until now its strength and its power have continually increased; God willing, it will always be so and our empire will only finish at the day of judgement.' The Ottoman Empire was strong enough to pose as the protector of weaker nations, even if they were Christian. To the Chancellor of Poland, Koprulu Fazil Ahmed wrote that the most glorious and powerful of all padishahs would defend the oppressed Ukrainians, who had appealed for help to the refuge of the universe. However, he died of drink at the age of 41 in 1676.[15]

Like the *ulema* élite, the Koprulu had a sense of caste. The five sisters of Koprulu Fazil Ahmed Pasha married pashas in high official positions, such as head of the navy or the treasury. Two Koprulu married imperial princesses. The Koprulu family ran the empire with as much confidence as the great political clans of the eighteenth century, such as the Pitts and the Grenvilles, ran England. Since there were no official aristocratic institutions to restrain them, their power was in some ways superior. A truly Ottoman family, they served as provincial governors, owned estates, and raised buildings throughout the empire, from Hungary to Egypt. European nobles built houses and palaces to enhance the pleasure and standing of their own families; Koprulu grand viziers built for the public – mosques, schools, markets, fountains, baths, inns and bridges. Near the Constantinople bazaar Koprulu Mehmed had built the three-floor arcaded Vizir Han. Comparable in size and function to a modern shopping arcade, today it is full of workshops and offices. His son, like the contemporary English chief minister, Lord Clarendon, ordered the construction of a library. The domed Koprulu library, far smaller than the Clarendon Library in Oxford, can still be visited beside the family mausoleum in Divanyolu, between the mosques of Sultans Ahmed and Bayezid. Fazil Ahmed also built a commercial complex in the rising trading-port of Izmir, as well as mosques in his two conquests, Crete and southern Poland. His cousin Amcazade

Huseyin built five fountains, a slaughter-house and two water viaducts in Constantinople alone. Such buildings had a fourfold purpose. They demonstrated the builder's success to his contemporaries; preserved his fame for the future; ensured an income for his descendants; and served the empire.

Pashas' households were nurseries of statesmen, like the palace school or the households of great nobles in France and England before 1600. In the late seventeenth century over 50 per cent of senior Ottoman officials had previously served in the households of viziers or pashas, compared to 29 per cent who had served in the palace or the army: a sign of the grip of the ruling élite over the state machine. One product of the Koprulu household was Kara Mustafa Pasha, who succeeded his cousin and brother-in-law Fazil Ahmed as Grand Vizier in 1676. His violence and avarice won him the hatred both of the army and of the citizens of Constantinople. In 1683 the Ottoman army surrounded the Red Apple – Vienna. It was saved only by a European coalition of the Holy Roman Empire, the Papacy, Venice and Poland. After the Ottoman defeat at Vienna, the Grand Vizier was executed in Belgrade. The Austrian advance continued. Buda fell in 1686, Belgrade in 1688. In Constantinople, fear that a Christian army was about to appear outside the walls caused a collapse in house prices. As in 1656, many fled with their belongings to Asia. The Sultan's extravagance and indifference to affairs of state began to be criticized.[16]

A younger brother of Fazil Ahmed, Koprulu Fazil Mustafa had become a vizier in 1680 at the age of 43. Demetrius Cantemir, a former resident of the city, wrote in his history of the Ottoman Empire published in 1727, that Koprulu Fazil Mustafa was 'a man famous above all the rest of the Turks for holiness of life, integrity, prudence and courage'. He was also extremely rich, since he had inherited the wealth of his brother and father, which had – exceptionally – escaped confiscation by the Sultan. A son-in-law and former slave of Koprulu Mehmed, Syavus Pasha, led a rebellion against Mehmed IV which gave the Koprulu household its opportunity to recover power.

It is often claimed that Islamic history is distinguished by an absence of representative assemblies, which had functioned continuously in the West since the eleventh century or earlier. Constantinople, however, was a law to itself. Since the reign of Suleyman the Magnificent, the Sultan and Grand Vizier often summoned an assembly of viziers, notables and *ulema* known as 'the high consultative council', to legitimize, and deflect responsibility for, decisions.* However, the Ottoman élites lacked the inherited taste for liberty and privilege which was a crucial force behind the Dutch revolt, the English revolutions and the outbreak of the French revolution. Silence, or a demand for further orders, was the usual reply to the government's request for advice. This silence, bred of fear of the Sultan's power of execution, is one of the distinguishing marks of the Ottoman capital. Assemblies in Western countries might be distinguished by radicalism or conservatism, particularism or patriotism. They were rarely silent.[17]

In Aya Sofya, on 8 November 1687, Koprulu Fazil Mustafa convoked an assembly of *ulema*, to whom he read out a petition asking for the Sultan's deposition. Silence. Koprulu Fazil Mustafa then said: 'Since the Padishah, as the petition says, thinks only of enjoying himself hunting, and since, when the empire was under attack on all sides, we have only seen him dismiss the men capable of remedying these misfortunes, can you still doubt, gentlemen, that the dethronment of a Padishah who conducts government business in such a manner is legitimately permitted? Why then do you remain silent?' The silence continued. The Pasha then led the assembly to the palace. The Sultan was deposed and his brother Suleyman appointed. Fear also dominated the palace. Having spent forty years in an apartment in the harem, the new Sultan was convinced that executioners were waiting outside. At first he refused to leave.

In response to popular pressure, 'rather from a popular opinion of his integritie than any inclination of the Seraglio', in the words of the English ambassador, Koprulu Mustafa became Grand Vizier a year later. Like other Koprulu grand viziers, he had a utilitarian attitude to the Ottoman dynasty. To prevent a restoration of Mehmed IV, or his sons, in 1691 Koprulu Mustafa selected the third brother as Sultan. Ahmed II, 'said to be an idiott and to divert himself chiefly by beating of a drum', was another malleable weakling who had spent his life in the palace. When the French ambassador asked the Ottoman Empire not to recognize as King of England France's enemy William III, who had deposed James II, a later Grand Vizier replied that it was absurd for Ottomans, who had so often deposed their own monarchs, to dispute other nations' right to do so.[18]

---

*Thus when the first Ottoman written constitution was introduced in 1876, the newspaper *Vakit* described it as a wise return to the past.

1. *Mehmed II, conqueror of Constantinople, confers ecclesiastical concessions on the Oecumenical Patriarch Gennadios in 1453*. Print from an original oil painting, said to be by Girolamo Galazzi da Santacroce (1500–50). The Patriarch and the Sultan are shown as near-equals. This depiction of the event which governed relations between the Ottoman government and the Greek community was made into a print in the nineteenth century, with captions in Ottoman, French, Greek and Armenian, in order to promote religious harmony.

2. Gentile Bellini, *Mehmed the Conqueror*, 1480. Gentile Bellini lived in Constantinople at the Sultan's request from 1479 to 1481. He painted not only this portrait but also erotic frescos for the Sultan's private apartments. Although much overpainted, this picture is an accurate likeness of the conqueror of the city. The three crowns symbolize his conquests in Trebizond, Anatolia and Rumelia.

3. P. Coecke Van Aelst, *Procession of Suleyman the Magnificent, c.* 1533. The Sultan, on the right, is riding through the city, preceded by pashas and guards. This view, possibly commissioned by the Grand Vizier Ibrahim Pasha as a design for a tapestry, shows the Roman columns and obelisks remaining in the Ottoman city before the expansion of the mid-sixteenth century. On the left is the mosque of Fatih.

4. Jean-Jacques-François Le Barbier *l'aîné, Procession of the Sultan to the Sultanahmed mosque, c.* 1780. The Sultan is going to the mosque preceded by *solaks* – guards with feathered head-dresses. Janissaries have lined up beside the mosque. On the right is the obelisk erected in 390 by the Emperor Theodosius in what was then the Roman hippodrome.

5. Paolo Verona, *Abdulmecid I going to mosque in Eyup*, c. 1840.
The Sultan, a patron of reform, wears a Western-style uniform and cloak.
This picture may depict his inauguration in 1839.

6. Fausto Zonaro, *Dervish ceremony*, c. 1900. Watched by European ladies, a *seyh* of the
Rufai order is about to heal old men prostrate on the floor by walking on them.
Nearby young girls also wait to be healed. On the left chanting Rufai dervishes include
the artist, himself a dervish, fifth from left. On the right Zonaro has shown, contrary to
probability in a Rufai *tekke*, a Mevlevi dervish playing the *neyh* or flute. This is one of
the finest representations of dervish fervour, frequently reproduced today in books
about them or hung on the walls of their *tekkes*.

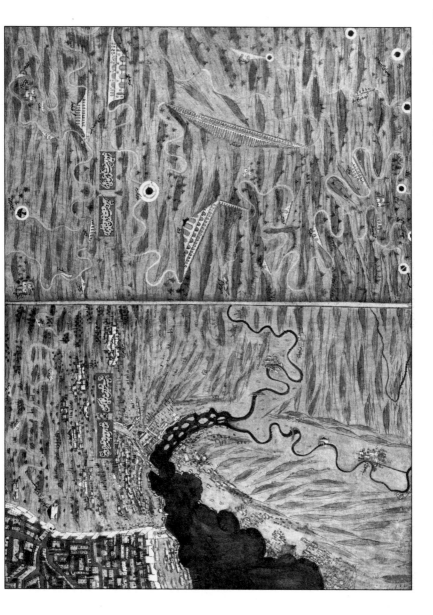

7. Panorama of the upper Golden Horn, 1580. This view comes from a panegyric of Suleyman the Magnificent written for his grandson Murad III. It shows the western walls of the city; the shrine of Eyup at the head of the Golden Horn; the stream which 150 years later became the site of Sa'adabad; and on the right some of the cisterns and aqueducts built by the sultans to boost the city's often inadequate water supply.

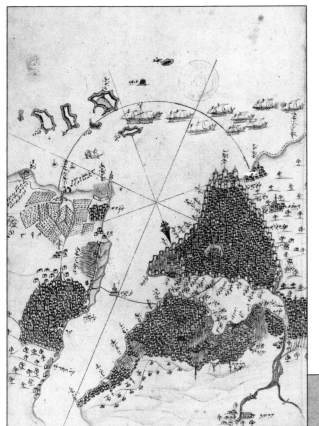

8. Map of Constantinople, *c.* 1600. Uskudar is on the left of the Bosphorus. On the right are Galata, the Golden Horn (the arsenal is on the indentation on the Galata side) and, occupying the peninsula, the city proper. The fortress of the Seven Towers is conspicuous at the top, where the city walls meet the Sea of Marmara.

9. *Suleyman praying at the grave of the Prophet's companion, Abu Ayyub, at Eyup,* painted for Murad III *c.* 1580. Eyup was the holiest Muslim site in Constantinople, and scene of the inauguration of the sultans from 1600 to 1918.

10. Jan van der Steen, *View of Constantinople from Pera*, c. 1770. Left to right: Uskudar, the junction of the Bosphorus and the Golden Horn, the palace, the mosques of Aya Sofya and Sultanahmed; in the distance the snow-capped mountains of Anatolia. This is the classic view of the city, which made an Ottoman poet write that heaven itself gasped with envy and which Western visitors called the finest view in the world.

11. Cornelis Loos, *The Palace, c.* 1710. The palace is shown as it appeared from the other side of the Golden Horn. The central tower is the 'Tower of Justice' near the council-chamber. In the kiosk nearest the Golden Horn the Sultan received the Kaptan Pasha before the fleet's annual tour of inspection in the Aegean. The artist was a Swede employed by King Charles XII of Sweden, then a refugee on Ottoman territory.

12. Jean-Baptiste Vanmour, *Audience of the Dutch ambassador Cornelis Calkoen with Sultan Ahmed III, 14 September 1727.* The Grand Dragoman Alexander Ghica (with his back to the artist) is about to read out his Turkish translation of an Italian version of the speech which the ambassador has just delivered in Dutch. The audience appears to be a collision between two civilizations. The Europeans are obliged to wear Ottoman kaftans; the Sultan stares ahead, silent and immobile. In reality the ambassadors in Constantinople represented the conjunction of political, commercial and occasionally military interests between the empire and European states. Vanmour and his imitators often painted this scene for ambassadors, since it showed the supreme honour – presentation to the Sultan in his throne room. An ambassador never spoke to him again.

13. Konstantin Kapidagi, *Bayram reception in the second courtyard of the palace, c. 1800.* Sultan Selim III sits on his throne in the Gate of Felicity, surrounded by the Grand Vizier, chief black eunuch, sword-bearers and other dignitaries. On the left is the palace guard of *peyks* in gilded helmets. On the right another palace guard, the *solaks*, in feathered helmets. This picture by a Constantinople Greek shows the growing influence of Western art under Selim III.

14. Courtyard of the favourites in the imperial harem. The imperial harem is one of the few places where seventeenth-century civilian Ottoman architecture of wood and wattle and protruding windows is preserved. This courtyard was overlooked by the apartment where imperial princes were immured and the 'golden road' between the Pavilion of the Holy Mantle and the courtyard of the Valide Sultan.

15. Artist unknown, *Fête given for the Valide Sultan in the Palace in the presence of Madame de Girardin Ambassadress of France who had it painted on the spot and brought it to Paris, c.* 1689. On the left is a black eunuch. Women and dwarfs dance, play music and serve refreshments. Monsieur de Girardin was French ambassador from 1686 to 1689, when both countries were united in hostility to the House of Austria.

16. Antoine de Favray, *Greek women visiting the bazaar,* c. 1765. Christian women, unlike Muslims, could go around the city unveiled. At their feet are some of the dogs which divided the city into zones controlled by rival packs. In contrast to other capitals, women could walk in Constantinople with little fear of molestation.

17. Jean-Baptiste Vanmour, *Turkish Wedding.* The artist has shown a bride, hidden in a litter, escorted by friends and relations and preceded by *ulema*, musicians, a 'wedding palm' and children. On the other side of the Bosphorus is the great fort of Rumeli Hisari, constructed, and in part designed, by Mehmed the Conqueror in 1452 to close access to Constantinople before his siege.

18. Artist unknown, *Murad III, c.* 1590. Murad III was one of the first sultans to spend most of his time in the capital rather than fighting on the frontier. He wears one of the opulent kaftans now preserved in Topkapi Palace Museum.

19. J. Toorenvliet, *Koprulu Mehmed Pasha,* 1660. The first of the five Koprulu grand viziers, Koprulu Mehmed Pasha, who governed from 1656 to 1661, restored order in the empire and repulsed the Venetian fleet from the Dardanelles.

20. Ferdinando Tonioli, *Abdulhamid I, c.* 1780. The Sultan wears jewels and a robe lined with the black fox-fur prized in the palace. Tonioli was a painter in the suite of the Venetian ambassador.

21. Jean-Jacques-François Le Barbier *l'aîné, The Sultan in the hamam, c.* 1787. The several hundred women in the Sultan's harem could provide personal servants as well as sexual partners. This drawing is based on interviews with husbands of former harem inmates.

22. L. N. Cochin, *Celebration of the Feast of Mevlud in the mosque of Sultanahmed*, 1787. Raised on the left is the Sultan's closed tribune, where he prays hidden from the faithful. In the middle, below the alcove or *minbar* indicating the direction of Mecca, sits the Grand Vizier. Before him are *ulema* and Janissaries. Mevlud was one of the greatest festivals of the Muslim calendar, formalized in Constantinople in 1588 to celebrate the birth of the Prophet by the recitation of panegyrics in Arabic and, unusually, Turkish. It was held in the mosque of Sultanahmed in order to provide enough space for the Sultan's household.

23. Artist unknown, *View of Sa'adabad*, *c.* 1770. The palace, the fountains and avenues of trees are clearly visible. Sa'adabad, on the city's European side, was a popular pleasure resort from its construction in 1721 until 1914. This picture is one of eighty painted for the Swedish ambassadors Ulrik and Gustaf Celsing.

24. Jean-Etienne Liotard, *Hélène Glavani and the English merchant, Mr Levett, c.* 1740. Hélène Glavani, on the left, wears the costume of the Tartars of the Crimea, where her father, member of a prominent Pera family, had been French consul. Levett, a friend of Liotard, wears fur-lined Ottoman costume to indicate his wealth, and desire to adopt Ottoman customs. The great artist Liotard, who lived in Constantinople between 1738 and 1742, has also drawn artefacts symbolic of Ottoman pleasures: a *cura* or lute on the left, and a perfume-sprinkler and incense-burner, set on a writing box inlaid with tortoiseshell and mother-of-pearl. Mlle Glavani plays a *tanbur* or guitar; Mr Levett holds a long jasmine-wood pipe.

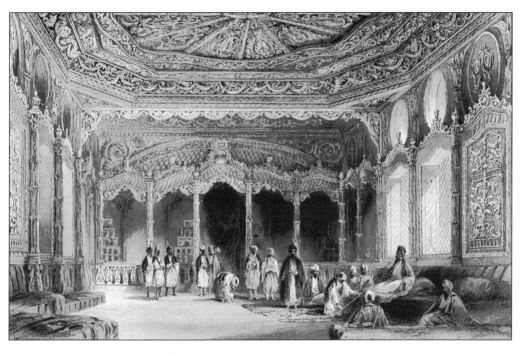

25. Thomas Allom, *Apartment in the palace of Esma Sultan in Eyup, c.* 1840. This print shows the heavy gilded interior, low divans and *sofa* – a lavishly decorated raised area in a reception room – characteristic of grand houses in the city. The princess owned at least four other palaces in and around Constantinople.

26. Jean-Baptiste Vanmour, *Patrona Halil.* Patrona Halil was leader of the popular revolt which deposed Ahmed III on 1 October 1730. Brandishing his sword in triumph in front of the Imperial Gate of the palace, he wears the fur-trimmed robe of a successful Ottoman, rather than the dishevelled clothes which had been his trademark. On 24 November, on the orders of the new Sultan Mahmud I, he was murdered in the second courtyard of the palace.

27. J. G. Wolfgang, *Nicholas Mavrocordato, Prince of Wallachia*, 1721. The prince wears fur-lined robes and a jewelled crest to indicate his rank in the Ottoman hierarchy. Below him are the arms of Wallachia and Moldavia, crowned by a single princely coronet – revealing his ambition to present himself, in the heraldry of dynastic Europe, as ruler of both principalities.

28. Madame Eynard, *Prince Alexander Mavrocordato*, Geneva, 1819. Even in western Europe, Mavrocordato wears the costume of the empire he was plotting to overthrow. He defended Missolonghi in 1822–3 against the Ottomans, and was subsequently four times Greek Prime Minister.

29. Antoine de Favray, *The Comte de Vergennes in Ottoman costume*, 1768. Ambassadors and travellers often commissioned portraits of themselves in Ottoman dress to mark the success of their embassy or journey. Painted the year of Vergennes' departure, showing him leaning against, as well as wearing, fur, and holding a pipe, this portrait commemorates one of the most able French ambassadors to the Porte.

30. Antoine de Favray, *The Comtesse de Vergennes in Ottoman dress*, 1768. The Countess, a Savoyarde previously married to a Pera merchant, had lived publicly with the ambassador and borne him two sons before their marriage, which may have precipitated his recall. They never saw the city again.

Koprulu Fazil Mustafa won the reputation of never committing a crime or saying an unnecessary word. He abolished the practice of pashas giving presents to the Sultan at Bayram and established councils of notables in provincial cities. To prevent Christian subjects supporting the invading Venetian and Austrian armies, Koprulu Mustafa lowered their taxes and improved their status. More churches were said to have been built during his vizierate (1689–91) than during the fifty-year reign of the Emperor Justinian. In 1691, as *seraskier* or commander-in-chief, accompanied by the sacred banner of Muhammad, Koprulu Fazil Mustafa led the Ottoman army into battle against the Austrians. To set an example, he marched with the troops on foot. However, he died at Slankamen on the Hungarian plain, possibly killed by his own soldiers.[19]

Ottoman armies suffered more defeats. Finally in 1697 another member of the family, Koprulu Huseyin, a first cousin of Fazil Ahmed, and a former provincial governor and Kaptan Pasha, was appointed Grand Vizier at the age of 53. He told the Sultan: 'My uncle and my cousin were grand viziers of your father Sultan Mehmed Han for twenty years and they were contented and so was he. If you ignore the advice of others and if you give me independence in the government, God willing, I will serve much better than they.'

'If you are loyal to me,' the Sultan replied, 'I will give you independence.'

The new Grand Vizier was another Koprulu prodigy. One of the foremost Ottoman historians, Naima, dedicated his history of the empire to 'that perfectly instructed vezir whose all-tranquil bosom is the treasure-house of wisdom and learning and whose lofty-disposed heart is the storehouse of truths and certainties'. Understanding the need for peace and reform, through the mediation of the Dutch and English ambassadors, he made peace with Austria, at Carlowitz near Belgrade, in 1699.[20]

The Peace of Carlowitz is a watershed in Ottoman history. It is considered to represent the closing of the Ottoman frontier in Europe and the transformation of the empire from an offensive to a defensive state (although some Ottomans saw it as no more than a truce: the main Ottoman negotiator Rami Mehmed Efendi claimed that 'a temporary peace is the equivalent in meaning to the *jihad*'). A portent of a new age of peace and pleasure was the entertainment the Grand Vizier gave in his *yali*, or seaside house, on the Asian side of the Bosphorus, for the ambassadors of England, the Netherlands and the Holy Roman Emperor.

Built in 1698, and painted rust red on the outside, the yali is still owned by a Koprulu family *vakif*, which, in 1995, benefits 117 of Koprulu Huseyin's descendants. It has suffered years of neglect. In the late nineteenth century it was occupied by Muslim refugees from the Balkans. In this century most of the harems and out-houses were demolished to allow a road to be widened. Bungalows for the Grand Vizier's descendants have been built – illegally – in the garden: housing estates cover nearby hills.

One reception room survives, decorated with a central domed rotunda above a marble fountain. For ninety years it has been in a state of imminent collapse. The waters of the Bosphorus gleam through holes in the floor. Thorns and bindweed have invaded from the garden. The wooden panels on the walls have faded and fallen. In 1700, however, the panels were painted with brilliant bouquets of flowers arranged in the blue and white Kutahya vases then fashionable in Constantinople. Above a marble fountain the ceiling was a masterpiece of arabesque patterns. The room was as elaborate as a boudoir at Versailles, but more serene. In this house of flowers and pleasure the Grand Vizier received his guests.

With a victor's arrogance, the Imperial ambassador Prince von Oettingen Wallerstein swept up the Bosphorus with a large suite and his own band, in three galleys. The sound of the music was drowned by the rattle of the chains fastened to the galley-slaves rowing in the hold below. The ambassadors were entertained by displays of archery, wrestling, juggling and dancing, and by a Persian singer. Finally dinner was served: pigeon, pheasant, roast chicken, stuffed vine-leaves, many kinds of pilav, pastries. It did not last long. For the servants quickly cleared the dishes, in order to devour the remains themselves. Either they were out of control, or the host wanted to end this distasteful entertainment as rapidly as possible.[21]

The Grand Vizier was known as *amcazade* 'the cousin', *Mevlevi* because he was a member of that dervish order, or *sarhosh*, 'the drunk': integrity was not the only Koprulu tradition he continued. He had permission to miss official business in the evening because he was taking treatment for lame feet: in fact he was drinking spirits so strong that one drop burnt the throat. In 1702 he resigned and retired to a farmhouse near Edirne. He died a year later from the physical shock of renunciation of alcohol. His tomb can still be visited in an elegant mosque complex he constructed near Fatih, beside his town palace.

The last Koprulu Grand Vizier, Damad Fazil Numan Pasha, son of

Fazil Mustafa Pasha, was born in Constantinople in 1670. Head of the family foundations, he enjoyed an income of over 100,000 escudos a year. A vizier since 1700, in June 1710 he was appointed Grand Vizier. The British ambassador described him as

> a man very much famed for justice and integrity, and very far in the Esteem and affections of the people, insomuch that his promotion to the Vizirat hath caused an universal joy. He is a man very learned in and a great Observer of the Law, exceedingly curious and inquisitive into the situation and interests of Foreign Countries, and esteemed to be well skilled in them as well as in the interests of this Empire for which he is very zealous.

Thousands descended on the city, from both Anatolia and Rumelia, in search of justice. However Damad Fazil Numan Pasha was too honest for the corrupt and cruel Sultan Ahmed III, who was reasserting the power of the palace over the Porte. The Sultan resented remarks from his Grand Vizier such as 'The troops should be paid with the revenues of the empire, not the blood of the people'. The Grand Vizier's policy of peace with Russia was opposed by a faction favouring the fugitive Charles XII of Sweden. Moreover he was an eccentric who believed that there was a fly at the end of his nose. Whenever he brushed it away, it returned. Dismissed after two months, Damad Fazil Numan Pasha died as governor of Crete in 1719.[22]

Thereafter the Kopruluzade lived in Constantinople in and around a large family house near the Koprulu library, another near Suleymaniye and two yalis on the Bosphorus. They enjoyed the revenues of Koprulu estates and foundations scattered throughout the empire. No longer producing men with the skill or luck to win high office, crippled by the absence of primogeniture, the Koprulu declined in wealth and status. Koprulu Ahmed, son of Damad Fazil Numan Pasha and a talented calligrapher whose work is now in the Koprulu library, was governor, successively, of Selanik (Thessaloniki), Crete, Belgrade, Izmir, Bosnia, Euboea, Aleppo and Egypt. Provincial governorates were rotated in order to prevent governors establishing local power-bases. Indeed it was said of another Koprulu official in Izmir that he 'considers himself almost as an equal to the Sultan'. Subsequently they held minor positions in the central bureaucracy. However, in a radically different role one Koprulu, Fuad, would return to prominence in the twentieth century.[23]

The services of such empire-builders as the Koprulu help explain the survival of the Ottoman Empire. Moreover the Ottoman army remained a formidable force, still capable of defeating Western armies. In 1711 Peter the Great himself was defeated by Ottoman armies and obliged to make an unfavourable peace. Through force of arms the empire recovered the Pelopponese from Venice in 1718, and Belgrade from Austria in 1739. The very success of the Koprulu recovery, however, was dangerous. Rather than introduce the radical measures which transformed the French and English governments in the seventeenth century, they restored the old machine to efficiency. In 1689 the English ambassador reported that Koprulu Fazil Mustafa Pasha 'has already declared his intention to settle this government according to their antient methods'. He would not set price maximums as they were not in the Koran.[24] The élite believed that tradition held the answers.

The Koprulus' tolerance of Christians and grasp of foreign affairs was due not only to their own judgement but also to the presence at their side of a man who combined the roles of Grand Dragoman (chief translator) of the Porte, Councillor of State of the Empire, and confidant of European ambassadors: Alexander Mavrocordato. The Mavrocordato family are a signal example of the way Greeks, like Ottomans, used Constantinople as a means of promotion – and were transformed, in their turn, into servants of the Ottoman Empire. The history of their family is the history of south-eastern Europe.

Language was the reason for Mavrocordato's eminence. In the 1520s Ibrahim Pasha had dealt with some Austrian ambassadors in Serbo-Croat. After 1580, with the closing of the Ottoman mind, few Muslims knew any languages other than Ottoman, Persian and Arabic. With its elaborate sentence structure and complex vocabulary, the Ottoman language erected a wall between the empire and the outside world. Grand viziers therefore needed an interpreter to deal with ambassadors. Educated Greeks were among the few people who knew both Ottoman and Western languages. It was not unusual to choose members of a minority to serve the state. Referring to the French monarchy's use of Protestants and Italians, J. H. Elliott writes: 'A seventeenth-century statesman had to find his men, his money and his professional experties where he could.'[25]

Years later, when they had attained the rank of temporary royalty, the Mavrocordato claimed to date from the reign of Justinian. In reality, they first appeared in Constantinople in the seventeenth century. A Greek merchant called Scarlattos or Iskerletoglu, who had made a fortune in the customs farms and food supply of the city, left a million piastres when he was murdered by a Janissary in 1631. His wealthy daughter Roxana, widow of a prince of Wallachia, fell in love with and married John Mavrocordato, a handsome silk merchant from Chios, one of the richest islands in the Aegean. Their son Alexander was born in 1641. His father died three years later.

Roxana Mavrocordato ensured that Alexander was one of the first citizens of Constantinople to be sent to the West for his education. He was educated first at the Greek college in Rome, founded by exiles from Constantinople in the early sixteenth century, then at the universities of Padua and Bologna where he wrote a thesis on the circulation of the blood. He was an Ottoman citizen at ease in Western culture. At the age of 58, he discussed medicine, botany and styles of Greek pronunciation with the French botanist Piton de Tournefort, who found him 'well inform'd in foreign Affairs and no stranger to the Interests of the princes of Europe'. However, he confessed that he was too old to imitate 'the Boldness of the European Physicians', and 'his head running solely upon Politicks he wonder'd I came so far only to hunt for new Plants'. In Constantinople power and money, not scientific exploration, were motives for travel. Lack of intellectual curiosity was the curse of the city. Some inhabitants of Galata never took the trouble to cross the Golden Horn.[26]

From 1665 to 1672 Alexander Mavrocordato directed the Patriarchal Academy. Tall and eloquent, author of works of syntax, rhetoric and history, he encouraged the revival of learning among the Constantinople Greeks which had been gathering pace since the nadir of the late sixteenth century, when high Greek culture had almost disappeared from the city. The family coat of arms, a phoenix rising from the ashes, may refer to the rebirth, not of the Byzantine Empire but of Greek learning. From 1668 until his death in 1709 he always held one of the offices of the Patriarchate: he was successively Grand Orator, Grand Chartophylax, Grand Skevophylax and Grand Logothete.

In 1670 he married Sultana Chrysocoleos, a woman of sweet nature and great wealth. Through her descent from Stephen the Great, Prince of Wallachia, she was related to many noble families of Wallachia and Moldavia. Medicine helped him rise in the Ottoman hierarchy. Already the doctor of many pashas, in 1671 he became secretary of Panagios Nicousios, doctor and Grand Dragoman to the Grand Vizier Fazil Ahmed Pasha. On his death in 1673 Mavrocordato succeeded as Grand Dragoman. Thereby *Iskerletzade Iskander*, as his Ottoman masters called him, had the right, denied to other Greeks, to wear an ermine bonnet, to ride on horseback and to be accompanied by armed guards. In appearance he was almost an Ottoman. He was only 32.[27]

Thereafter his fortunes were linked to those of the empire. After the Ottoman defeat at Vienna in 1683, he was taken to prison in chains and fined 300 purses – twenty purses more than the entire annual tribute of Wallachia: his wife and mother were imprisoned and beaten, and his mother died six months after her release. However his knowledge of Europe and its languages made him indispensable. A Venetian renegade called Seferaga, recommended by the French ambassador, proved an incompetent dragoman. In 1687 Mavrocordato returned to office.

He was imprisoned again that year, and fled for safety to the French embassy for a few weeks in 1688. Nevertheless Mavrocordato, on the orders of Koprulu Huseyin, helped arrange the Peace of Carlowitz between the Ottoman and the Habsburg empires, persuading each proud empire that the initiative came from the other. His letters in Italian to the English ambassador and mediator Lord Paget show a politeness excessive even in that formal age:

> Most Illustrious and Excellent Signor and Patron,
>
> I cannot say how happy I am to receive Your Excellency's most pleasant and polite letter of 10/20 February 1699 from Belgrade carrying the desired news of your very good health which means that we too live in health, because of the strong links which bind us together, through the obligations we feel . . . the Most High Supreme Vizier our most blessed Signor was pleased with the cordial greetings and the sincere wishes of Your Excellency . . .
>
> Your Most Devoted, Most Ready Servant,
> from Adrianople 23 February 1699,
> Alessandro Mavrocordato

In a later letter he claimed: 'The attraction of Your Excellency is so great that staying so long deprived of your sweet company and gentle features is almost unbearable.' The Porte was so pleased with the services of Lord Paget that he was asked to remain in Constantinople. He did not finally prise himself away until 1703 – four years later than planned.[28]

As a reward for the successful peace negotiations, in 1700 Alexander Mavrocordato became Councillor of State. He was given an ermine robe by the Sultan, Byzantine manuscripts by the Holy Roman Emperor. In 1703 when the capital had fallen into rebellion, he again took refuge in the French embassy and again had to pay 200 purses to return to office. Alexander Mavrocordato died in January 1710, leaving 500 purses in cash and a reputation as a dangerous enemy but an extremely useful friend. One epitaph called him

Des Grecs et des Latins le père,
Le grand oracle des Osmans,
Des visirs l'étoile polaire,
Le prototipe des scavans.[29]

It is natural to ask where lay the final loyalty of the man described by a French diplomat as 'one of the best actors in Europe': with the Ottoman Empire which imprisoned and beat him? With Greek and Russian dreams of a new Byzantine Empire? In 1672 Alexander Mavrocordato read a study of the strengths and weaknesses of the empire to a French scholar called Antoine Galland, the first translator of *The Arabian Nights*. The empire's force lay in the blind obedience of its subjects and the flexibility of its career structure. Its weaknesses were the sumptuous households of the Sultan and pashas; the annual ravages of the plague; the defective currency and legal system; the lack of capable officers; and habits of pillage. He clearly hoped that it would collapse. Twenty-five years later, during the negotiations at Carlowitz, Alexander Mavrocordato took large bribes from Austria, his preferred foreign power, and denounced the 'instability and perfidy and other barbarous and cruel vices of the Turks'. He also secretly sent Vienna copies of his instructions from the Porte. The French ambassador, on the other hand, considered him sympathetic to Russian ambitions to 'reestablish the former Greek empire', and ready to serve the Greeks 'even to the prejudice of the interests of the Porte'. In secret correspondence he called Mavrocordato 'Ali' and used him as a source of military information, in return for which 'Ali' received a pension of 2,400 livres a year, later increased. Mavrocordato could thus be seen as a quadruple agent, working for the Ottoman Empire, Russia, Austria and France. On the other hand, it is possible that he received his fees, or bribes, and sold information with the Grand Vizier's knowledge. In 1699 his diplomacy kept more territory for the empire than might have been expected. In the age of Mazarin and Marlborough, and in a city like Constantinople, his corruption and indiscretion were by no means exceptional.[30]

Moreover the Ottoman Empire brought the Mavrocordato family advantages on such a scale that, whatever the sums they received from foreign powers, their final loyalty was Ottoman. Like the Irish 'castle

Catholics' who served the British Empire before 1922,* the Mavrocordato believed that, while the Ottoman Empire existed, they and their fellow Greeks might as well benefit from it. By his influence at the Sublime Porte Alexander Mavrocordato helped the Orthodox Patriarch and monks recover from their Catholic enemies dominance in the two principal Christian shrines, the churches of the Holy Sepulchre in Jerusalem and of the Holy Nativity in Bethlehem. From 1675, in return for payment of 1,000 piastres a year to the mosque of Sultanahmed in Constantinople, the Orthodox Patriarch in Jerusalem controlled the decisive trinity of keys, candelabra and carpet, which were to be the cause of so much tension before the outbreak of the Crimean War. As well as holding lucrative offices, Mavrocordato lent money at 20 per cent interest. He became so rich that he could write to the Oecumenical Patriarch: 'If you ever need money I can with pleasure give whatever sum is necessary.' Mavrocordato was also able to renew the privileges of the island of Chios, his family base, which enjoyed a period of peace and prosperity thereafter, until the outbreak of the Greek War of Independence.[31]

The elevation of his son Nicholas Mavrocordato, in 1709, to the throne of Wallachia was still more gratifying. Born in 1680, Nicholas Mavrocordato was a polymath who knew Greek, Latin, Ottoman, Arabic, Persian, Italian and French – all learnt in Constantinople for, unlike his father, he did not attend a Western university. From 1700 to 1709 he was Grand Dragoman. Since he could always supply, from memory, the source of a quotation, his father called his son his 'library'. La Motraye, the Huguenot refugee who helped to teach him French, wrote: 'I have never seen a man with such a vast and well-trained memory as he.'

There were precedents for the appointment of a native of Constantinople to the throne of Wallachia or Moldavia. The connection between the Constantinople Greeks and the Danube principalities had been growing closer since the mid-sixteenth century. The princes had started to copy Byzantine ritual in their inaugurations and to pay the Oecumenical Patriarch's debts. Greeks such as the Cantacuzenos family had moved from Constantinople to Moldavia or Wallachia, out of desire for wealth and longevity. Like other international dynasties, such as the Habsburgs (at once Holy Roman Emperors, Kings of Hungary,

---

*Including one British ambassador to the Ottoman Empire, Sir Nicholas O'Conor, who died *en poste* in Constantinople in 1908.

Kings of Bohemia, and much else besides), or the Hanovers (Electors of Hanover and after 1714 Kings of Great Britain and Ireland), the Mavrocordato were able to play different roles, in different homelands, at the same time. They would have regarded as senseless the twentieth-century conviction that, as Raymond Aron has written, 'no one can have two countries'. Far from being prisoners of one identity, the Mavrocordato, Cantacuzenos and other families emphasized whichever – Ottoman, Greek, Wallachian – seemed most useful at the time. Like other educated Europeans, they regarded a nationality as a career, not a cause.

In apparent despair at his son's elevation, Alexander Mavrocordato beat his head and tore his hair, proclaiming that it was the ruin of his family. He was practising Talleyrand's maxim, that words are given us to hide our meaning. Husband of a descendant of Stephen the Great, having married all his children, including Nicholas himself, to the children of princes of Wallachia or Moldavia, clearly Alexander Mavrocordato, like ambitious princes in the Holy Roman Empire, had a 'royalty strategy'. For although the princes of Wallachia and Moldavia were appointed by the Sultan, and ruled for limited periods, they did so 'by the Grace of God', enjoying such attributes of royalty as a guard, a court, and the nomination of bishops. The courts of Europe acknowledged their rank of Most Serene Highness. In the Ottoman hierarchy they almost ranked with the Grand Vizier. At the centre of intrigues between the boyars (the local nobles), the Porte, the palace, Russia, Austria, France and the Crimea, condemned to satisfy the Porte's hunger for cash, the princes of Wallachia and Moldavia lived between death and the throne. The risk was acceptable. One prince said: 'Let death come when it will. I have lived long enough, since I have been a prince.' After the execution of another prince, his mother asked: 'Is it not better that my son should die in such a manner than if he had quietly awaited death in bed?'[32]

Like previous princes before him, Nicholas Mavrocordato was anointed Prince of Moldavia in Constantinople – the princes of Wallachia and Moldavia are the only rulers to have been anointed in a country of which they were not sovereign. The ceremony was a visible assertion of the treble identity of the Phanariot nobility, so called from the Phanar district where they inhabited ancient brick and stone houses, with corbelled upper stories jutting into the street. First the new prince or *voivode* (his official title, from a Slav word for lord) arrived by kayik at the Sublime Porte. There he received Ottoman marks of honour: a kaftan of cloth of gold, less sumptuous kaftans for his attendants and a *cuka* or jewelled crest with ostrich feathers. The prince then proceeded, on horseback and escorted by Janissaries, to the church of the Phanar. He was received by the Patriarch, the clergy and Greek notables of the city. Outside the church the Grand Vizier's footmen proclaimed: 'May the most high God grant a life of many years to our Padishah and our Prince Efendi and may he long live in prosperity.'

As the Prince Efendi entered the church, he moved out of the Ottoman into the Byzantine empire. The choir struck up a hymn to the Virgin Mary. He ascended a throne. Prayers were said that 'our most pious, most serene and most excellent Lord Nicholas Mavrocordato, may he be crowned with strength, victory, stability, health and security and may the Lord our God further cooperate with him, guide him in all things and put all his adversaries under his feet!' He then laid his head on the altar, to be anointed with holy oil by the Patriarch 'reciting the prayers that were used at the inauguration of the Orthodox emperors'.

A few days later, in his own house, Ottoman ceremonial reasserted its authority. While the Sultan's band played Ottoman music, a banner was presented to the prince. He kissed it and said: 'May the blessed and great God grant the most potent, most gracious and most just Emperor long life and multiply his days.' Days passed in ceremonial visits from or to the patriarchs and even the Mufti. Meetings with the bankers and businessmen of the capital, who regarded the Danubian principalities as their Peru, were another consecration ritual. Finally, escorted by boyars and Janissaries, the prince rode to the Sultan's palace. He received a fur-lined robe and another *cuka*, and was ceremonially feasted by the Grand Vizier. In the throne room, accompanied by four of his boyars, he prostrated himself three times before the Sultan. In the Sultan's name the Grand Vizier declared: 'Since his faithfulness and sincerity has reached the ears of my Majesty, I graciously confer on him as a reward the principality of Wallachia. It is also his duty not to fail in his fidelity and services for the future. Let him protect and defend the Provinces under his subjection and dread to commit any thing against or beyond my Mandate.'

The prince replied: 'I vow on my life and head to lay out my whole endeavours in the service of my most just and gracious Emperor, so long as he does not withdraw the aspect of his clemency and Majesty from the Nothingness of his Servant.' He then left the palace on horse-back, saluting and scattering money in the street. Three horse-tails on poles were ceremonially deposited in a corner of his throne room, and he distributed kaftans to Ottoman officials. The ceremonies had emphasized his power in the Ottoman hierarchy, and the links between the empire and its Orthodox subjects.

During the following weeks an interminable procession of Greeks, Turks and boyars, accompanied by a band, Ottoman flags and horse-tails on poles, proceeded from Constantinople over the Balkan mountains to Bucharest or Jassy. As the bells in the city pealed in joy, the new prince was crowned and anointed for a second time, in the cathedral, and then escorted to his palace to the sound of trumpets and drums. In his throne room the Sultan's decree was read out in Ottoman and translated into Romanian. The prince was robed with a kaftan and installed on his throne by an Ottoman official. Cannons fired. The Sultan's messengers cheered. Nobles kissed the prince's hand. The celebrations were closed by a splendid feast and ball.[33]

Clearly, the Ottoman government was elevating the Phanariots in order to defuse at a stroke the threats both of Danubian aggression and of Greek discontent. Native Moldavians and Wallachians were unreliable. In 1600 Prince Michael of Transylvania, Wallachia and Moldavia had dreamed of saying mass in St Sophia. 'As being descended from the imperial family', Serban Cantacuzenos, Prince of Wallachia from 1679 to 1688, had won a promise from the Tsar to be Emperor of the Greeks; at the same time the Patriarch was encouraging a Russian attack. Cantacuzenos's son-in-law Demetrius Cantemir lived in Constantinople from 1688 to 1710 as a hostage for the good behaviour of his father the Prince of Wallachia. He was an Ottoman scholar and composer, who built for himself an elegant palace overlooking the Golden Horn. Regarding the Sultan's court as 'the greatest court in the world', he dedicated to Ahmed III the *Book of the Science of Music as Explained in Letters*, in which he transcribed 351 Turkish, Persian and Arabic tunes according to his own system of notation. He was appointed Prince of Moldavia in 1710. Yet despite the rewards of his Ottoman identity, he deserted to Russia a year later, in return for a promise of the throne of Moldavia under Russian suzerainty for himself and his descendants.

In Constantinople, as some viziers knew, lying below the Ottoman surface like the Christians' subterranean holy fountains, was a secret world of plots and dreams of liberation by the 'emperor protector', the Tsar. The Grand Vizier told the British ambassador in 1710 that Peter the Great 'promised himself to be one day Master of Constantinople and that he had said he hoped to be buried in the Church of Sancta Sophia'.

The princely titles were rotated frequently enough to satisfy Greek families – and the Ottoman treasury, to which each new prince had to pay large sums. Constantinople made almost as many princes as Vienna. From 1710 to 1821 six Mavrocordato, five Ghika, four Callimachi, three Soutzo, three Racovitza, two Mourousi, two Ypsilanti and one Mavroyeni reigned as princes in Bucharest or Jassy. (In addition, four Mavrocordato, four Ghika, four Soutzo, four Callimachi, two Ypsilanti, five Mourousi were Grand Dragoman, and a further office, Grand Dragoman of the Fleet, also conferred power and wealth on Phanariots.) These families had come to the city, by 1650, from many different regions: Albania (Ghika), Epirus (Soutzo), Trabzon (Ypsilanti and Mourousi), Romania (Callimachi and Racovitza), the Aegean (Mavroyeni). Originally merchants and shipowners, they succumbed to the city's siren call of grandeur, and began to claim Byzantine descent (as Armenian bankers did from King David). Temporary royalty on the Danube tied them to the empire, satisfying their personal longings for money and power as well as their patriotic desire to help Greek causes. It gave them the means to build churches and schools and to enrich the Patriarchate. At the height of Phanariot power, to the benefit of the Oecumenical Patriarchate and the detriment of Arabic-speaking Orthodox, Greek-speaking clergy won control of the patriarchates of Antioch and Jerusalem, and the monastery of Mount Sinai. The separate Serb and Bulgarian archbishoprics at Peč and Ohrid were abolished, in 1766 and 1767 respectively. Henceforth Arabs and Slavs received religious instruction in Greek.[34] Some Phanariots compared their role in the Ottoman Empire to the Greeks' civilizing role under the Romans.

In Bucharest or Jassy, sole citadels, in the Balkans, of inherited wealth and luxury, the prince entered a new world, at the intersection of three cultures – Catholic, Orthodox, Muslim – and three empires – Habsburg, Russian, Ottoman. He was served by officials with grandiloquent offices, all held, at different times, by members of the Mavrocordato family: Grand Postelnic (prime minister), Grand Spatar (chief of police), Grand Hetman (chief justice). The palaces were furnished in a style which was half oriental and half European and the boyars led a life of idleness, interspersed by balls, visits and love-affairs. By the eighteenth century Ottoman influence had become so strong that they ate Ottoman food and wore Ottoman costume.

At the end of the century the court of the Prince of Moldavia, a later Alexander Mavrocordato, at Jassy delighted a writer and courtier who epitomized civilized Europe: Charles-Joseph, Prince de Ligne. In his opinion it had 'enough of the oriental to have the piquant of Asia and enough civilization to add to it some European graces'. The prince gave his men friends a 'carte blanche of pleasure', allowing them to 'visit' the women in his wife's household – provided they first underwent a medical examination. 'Mavrocordato saw only happy faces. People took each other and left each other, there was neither jealousy nor bad temper.' Ligne admired the alabaster arms and transparent dresses of the ladies, reclining on divans – and such asides in their conversation as 'here my father was massacred by order of the Porte, and here my sister by order of the Prince.'[35]

Nicholas Mavrocordato's life illustrates the rewards and risks of the thrones of Wallachia and Moldavia. Replaced as Prince of Moldavia on 27 November 1710, on his return to Constantinople, like his father before him, he took refuge in the French embassy until a large contribution to the Ottoman treasury released him from corruption charges. Appointed Prince of Wallachia in 1716, Nicholas proved his loyalty to the Ottoman Empire by enduring two years' imprisonment by the Austrians during the war of 1716–19. He encouraged his subjects' loyalty by reminding them of the persecution of Orthodox Romanians in Transylvania by the Catholic Habsburgs.[36] His reward was to reign again as Prince of Wallachia, from 1719 until his death in 1730.

His father had been a traditionalist who believed that Moses was the greatest of historians. Nicholas Mavrocordato, however, was a citizen of what contemporaries called 'the Republic of Letters' – the intellectual community of western Europe. In Bucharest he founded schools and libraries, and patronized Greek and Arabic printing presses. In the eighteenth century Bucharest and Jassy, more than Constantinople or Mount Athos, were centres of Greek culture. The prince himself amassed a superb library, bringing some of his father's books from Constantinople, buying new books from Amsterdam and old manuscripts from Mount Athos. Many works now in the libraries of Romania are inscribed *Ex bibliotheca Alex Maurocordati Constantinopolitani* (not Ottoman, not Greek, *Constantinopolitan*). After a copious dinner boyars would sleep for at least two or three hours. Rarely spending more than half an hour over a meal, Nicholas Mavrocordato would then retire to his library, to study botany, learn Hebrew, read the latest French books or correspond with the Archbishop of Canterbury.[37]

In the freedom of the principalities, Nicholas printed his father's works. With his own, they provide a window into the Phanariot mind.

Alexander Mavrocordato wrote in classical Greek, not what he called 'the dialect of the market-place' – the Greek of the people. His *Book of Duties*, much admired by contemporaries, avoids the temptation of idealism. He praises the simulation of virtue as a means to avoid scandal. Poverty is the greatest of ills. There is no talk of liberty:

Do not do what you want, nor what you can, but what serves your interests.

I have succeeded by dint of great exertion in winning one vizier's favour; but now he has fallen and another has taken his place and then another. Each time I have to start afresh.

If you visit a government office, you should enter blind and leave deaf.

Nicholas Mavrocordato's advice to his son in 1727 displays the same worldliness:

Do not promise; but if you make a promise keep it.

Anger is a fatal passion; gentleness has strength.

Do not be generous, be economical. Do not be avid but manage well what you have. Stretch your legs as far as your cover allows.

Unthinking charity leads to great ills and to a life of public waste; by doing good to an ill-intentioned person you do harm to the whole community.[38]

Between 1717 and 1720, Nicholas Mavrocordato wrote the first modern Greek novel, *The Leisure of Philotheus*, set in Constantinople. Friends walk in the Atmeydan, meet three men dressed as Persians, visit Galata, and converse among the kiosks, fountains and 'voluptuous perfumes' of an Ottoman garden. They discuss everything: atheism, Muslim women's love for Christian men, the nature of jealousy, the heroes of antiquity, the Maxims of La Rochefoucauld, the career of Charles XII of Sweden. Mavrocordato condemned the superstitious practices of Ottoman Islam, and the lack of 'a more solid philosophy based on the senses'. The Phanariot dilemma is obvious. The narrator says, 'We were as Greek as it is possible to be'. At the same time he praises the religious toleration of Constantinople, the return of learning and, perhaps ironically, the courage, magnanimity and wisdom of Ahmed III: 'His prudent spirit encompasses the whole spirit of the monarchy which functions and is animated by his remarkable genius.' There is no mention of the horrific ends in 1714 of four sons and a son-in-law of Constantine Brancovan, Prince of Wallachia. Executed for high treason, their bodies had been exposed before the imperial gate of the palace, and then thrown into the sea. Nor does Nicholas Mavrocordato refer to the execution, two years later, of no less than ten members, of all ages, of the Cantacuzenos family. His silence may have been due to the fact that he himself had denounced these relations and rivals to the Ottoman authorities.[39]

The monastery of Vacaresti, built by Nicholas Mavrocordato in 1716–22 in a wood outside Bucharest, was a symbol in stone of the Mavrocordatos' dynastic ambitions. Covering 180,000 square metres, the largest monastery in south-east Europe, grander than any of the Koprulu foundations, it consisted of a church, a monastery, a palace and a library. Whereas in Constantinople no church bells were permitted, Vacaresti had an impressive bell-tower. In the church two sets of frescos showed the prince and his second wife Smaragda, surrounded by their children and boyars. Their pose, holding models of the church in their hands, is Byzantine. Their fur-lined robes are Ottoman. The crowns on their heads are Wallachian.

On a white marble sarcophagus in the church, crowned with the emblems of Wallachia and Moldavia, the prince's epitaph read:

> The sight of you, O tomb, fills me with wonder, for you cover Nicholas, Prince first of Moldavia then of Wallachia. He divinely erected this church of the three suns, the very wise, the very learned, the mirror of the learned by his studies, of the illustrious line of the Scarlatti. His father was Alexander the Privy Councillor of the Ottoman Empire. He whom the Muses have crowned with laurels of glory is now crowned by a sepulchre of marble, for he succumbed to the cruel scourge of the plague leaving his children to an unbearable sorrow, as well as his wife and the crowd of his relations. Let us praise him according to his merits, let us implore the Almighty God to place his soul in green gardens.[40]

In 1986, on the orders of President Ceausescu, the monastery, long used as a prison (of which the President may have once been an inmate), was demolished. A park now covers the Escorial of the Mavrocordatos.

Such barbarism may be explained by the Romanians' memory of their exploitation by the Porte and the Phanar. Throughout the eighteenth century Constantinople received increasing quantities of gold and food from the principalities: as much as two thirds of government revenue was spent outside the provinces. The money for Nicholas Mavrocordato's library came from exactions from the Wallachians.

Local chroniclers complained that there were so many Greeks from Constantinople in Bucharest and Jassy that the Phanar was deserted. Mavrocordato ruled Moldavia through pomp and fear, in the style of the Sublime Porte, 'not as a real prince but as a wild lion . . . this prince inspired such terror that simply at sight of him one trembled.'[41]

The Phanariots and the Patriarchate, on the other hand, felt renewed loyalty to the Ottoman Empire. The spirit of cooperation between Greeks and Ottomans can be judged by the letters sent by the Patriarch to the Sultan, requesting permission to imprison or exile priests accused of heresy or other crimes. He addressed his letters directly to 'your honour, my all-powerful Sultan, may His Highness remain in good health', and signed them 'your servant the Greek Patriarch of Constantinople'. Greeks felt sufficiently free to riot in front of the Sublime Porte if they disapproved of a new Patriarch. Elizabeth Santi Lomaca, daughter of a Greek dragoman working in the Sublime Porte, married a French cloth merchant called Louis Chénier: the poet André Chénier was their son. Like most Greeks, she was in two minds about Ottoman rule. She praised Sultan Mahmud I (1730–54) as merciful, cultivated and worthy of the epithet 'the Great'. On the way to Friday prayers he could be petitioned by any of his subjects, male or female, Muslim or Christian. His favourite saying was: 'The powerful are never so great as when they go to the help of the weak.' Yet she also described the Greeks as 'enslaved and subjected by a barbarian people'.[42]

While the Koprulu sank into obscurity, the thrones of Moldavia and Wallachia kept the Mavrocordato rich and powerful. Nicholas's son Constantine, born in 1711, was elected Prince of Wallachia by the boyars in 1731 at the age of 20. He ruled for a total of twenty-six years: six reigns in Wallachia between 1731 and 1763, four in Moldavia between 1740 and 1769. He is the only person to have been able to say: 'when I started my seventh reign' or 'towards the end of my ninth reign'. Less brutal than his father, he issued decrees in 1746 and 1749 attempting to ease the peasants' intolerable burden of serfdom, taxation and forced labour. Some lived in holes in the ground and were bought and sold by landowners like slaves in the markets of the capital. Constantine Mavrocordato was no fanatic for Greek culture. He spoke Romanian, commissioned the first Romanian grammar and made Romanian, rather than Slavonic or Greek, the language of the Church. By the end of the century every town had a Romanian as well as a Greek school.[43]

Like his father and grandfather, Constantine lived between the throne, prison and the safety of the French embassy. Since he had failed to pay the Porte's latest demands, and was accused of treachery, he was imprisoned down a well on the island of Lemnos in 1749, and in the Seven Towers in 1758 and 1763. Although he spent so much time in Moldavia or Wallachia, he also maintained a house in Galata, where his library became a source of pride to the Greeks of Constantinople. When foreign ambassadors offered to buy it, 'all the Greek nation united to ask him to keep it'. However, in 1757 he had to sell his house, and much of his library, to pay a sum of 300 purses demanded by the Porte. In 1769, Constantine Mavrocordato was imprisoned for the last time, in Jassy by a Russian army invading at the start of a Russo-Turkish war. Loyal, or frightened – two sons were hostages in Constantinople – he told the Russians: 'The Turks will return tomorrow and will chase you from here like dogs.' He died that year and was buried in Jassy cathedral.[44]

Constantine's son Alexander, Prince of Moldavia from 1782 to 1785, known as *Deli Bey*, or 'the mad lord', remained true to the family tradition of Ottomanism. His outraged retort to an Austrian consul who refused him the title Most Serene Highness is the epigraph to this chapter. To a Russian officer offering him an independent principality, he replied that his family had always been loyal to one sovereign. 'I prefer poverty with honour to the riches of Croesus with dishonour. It is better that Her Majesty [Catherine II] regard me as a friendly Turk, which does not detract from my quality as a Christian, but on the contrary my Christian faith even orders me to be faithful to my Emperor.' Deposed as a result of Austrian and Russian pressure, he died in Constantinople in 1812. Other Greeks were satisfied by their growing prosperity, and the rise in the numbers of Greek schools and ships. One Greek wrote: 'The prevailing god of all the inhabitants of Constantinople is financial self-interest and everything is secondary where this is concerned. This is the depth to which slavery has reduced the nation of the Romans.'

God, as well as Mammon, justified the Ottoman Empire. In 1798, when the armies of the French Republic invaded Egypt and threatened the empire itself, the Patriarch of Jerusalem – or the Oecumenical Patriarch Gregory V using his name – published, in Constantinople, a Greek apologia for the Ottoman Empire entitled *The Paternal Exhortation*. God had

> raised up the empire of the Ottomans higher than any other kingdom . . . so as to be to the people of the West a bridle, to us the people of the East a

means of salvation. For this reason he puts into the hearts of the sultans of these Ottomans an inclination to keep free the religious beliefs of our Orthodox faith and, as work of supererogation, to protect them even to the point of occasionally chastising Christians who deviate from their faith.

The restriction on building new churches merely recreated the holy poverty of the early Church. Liberty was 'a destructive poison destined to precipitate the people into catastrophe and disorders'. It had even destroyed, the previous year, Constantinople's ancient rival the republic of Venice (conquered by the French Republic). The Patriarch ended with a cry from the heart: 'We have not here an abiding city. We seek after the city which is to come.'[45]

However, for some Greeks, even privileged princes of the Mavrocordato family, loyalty to the empire of the Ottomans was beginning to seem treachery. The power of Russia under Catherine II raised expectations. A younger brother of Deli Bey, Demetrios Mavrocordato, Grand Hetman of Moldavia in the 1780s, instead of returning to Constantinople, remained in his new homeland, where he founded the Romanian branch of the Mavrocordatos. Another Alexander Mavrocordato, a former Grand Dragoman who had become Prince of Moldavia, earned the name *firari*, the fugitive, by fleeing to Russia from Jassy on 25 January 1787. In Constantinople his wife Zamfira had to sell her own clothes to survive – although she later rejoined him. They settled in Moscow, where 'the fugitive' began to write poems encouraging Greeks to obtain liberty through their own efforts rather than those of foreign powers. Nineteen years later, in 1806, the Mavrocordatos' cousins the Ypsilanti family – secretly in touch with Russian agents for decades – also fled to Russia. In 1813 John Cam Hobhouse, who had toured the area with Lord Byron, noticed the depth of Greeks' hatred of Turks: 'All their [the Greeks'] hopes are directed towards the restoration of the Byzantine kingdom in the person of any Christian, but more particularly of a Christian of their own church.'[46] The Phanariots were leaving the familiar universe of dynastic ambition for the new world of nationalism. The city had ceased to satisfy. One Ypsilanti called it not *Constantinopolis* but *Barbaropolis*.[47]

7

Cushions of Pleasure

Let us visit Sa'adabad, my swaying cypress tree, let us go!

Nedim, *c.* 1725

T HE VIEW WAS the greatest pleasure of Constantinople. The combination of water and architecture was so arresting that poets called
the Bosphorus a diamond between two emeralds, the jewel in the ring
of universal empire. Love of the view affected the design of the city's
houses. The English architect C. R. Cockerell wrote: 'The rooms are all
contrived as to have windows on two sides at least, and sometimes on
three, and the windows are so large that the effect is like that of a glass
house. The Turks seem to be the only people who properly appreciate
broad sunshine and the pleasure of a fine view.' Bow-windows, jutting
out like the prow of a ship in order to provide a better view, were considered so essential that they were the principal local feature incorporated in the houses built there in European styles in the nineteenth
century.[1]

In this city of views, sight was a form of communication as frequent
as speech or script. From the terrace of Topkapi palace, the Sultan often
looked at Galata through a telescope. The inhabitants of Galata, when
they dared, trained telescopes on the palace. On one occasion the flash
of sunlight on the French ambassador's telescope nearly led to a suspension of diplomatic relations. In the nineteenth century princesses of
the imperial family were 'adept at hiding the glasses [binoculars] amidst
the folds of lace and satin of the window curtains in order to look at
neighbours and visitors. Very little went on which the women of the
harems did not know or see.' (Binoculars remain essential household
equipment on the Bosphorus today.)

The prevalence of gardens distinguished Constantinople from other water cities like Lisbon and Venice. Swathes of green stood out against red-tiled roofs and grey stone mosques. The Slav proverb 'Where the Turk trod, no grass grows' is a slur. If the physical image of heaven for Christians is a shining city on a hill, for Muslims it is a garden of delight, with ever-flowing springs and rivers. The annual festival of the Muslim saint Hizir Elyas in early May was a celebration of flowers and greenery. The Grand Vizier regularly sent presents of flowers and fruit to the Sultan, the harem, and foreign ambassadors. Du Fresne Canaye observed that Ottomans treated flowers as holy relics. They often had one in their hand or their turban. Seeds, bulbs and flowers were sold, as they still are, in courtyards beside the spice bazaar. Flowers and gardens were the principal motif in the tiles, the embroidery and the poetry of the city. One sixteenth-century poet wrote: 'Why should I contemplate the garden? My heart is a garden for me.' For the great poet Baqi, 'In the garden of the world happiness, no more than roses, cannot last an endless year.'[2]

Ottomans created many different styles of garden in Constantinople: the inner paradise garden with flowerbeds; the pleasure garden outside a house; terraced gardens shaded by trellised vines; fruit and kitchen gardens known as *bostanlar*; sunken gardens, dug in the earth, for cool in the summer. In 1690 a French visitor, the historian Jean du Mont, was impressed by the garden of the Grand Vizier's *kaimakam* (deputy): 'The paths are sanded and bordered in some places by orange trees and in others by fruit trees. The squares of the gardens are not laid out like our parterres, but only separated by boards and filled with flowers which the Turks love very much.' Trees also grew in the streets and walls of Constantinople. Vines and wistaria were, and are, draped over houses, and trailed across streets on ropes – making even the poorest districts less squalid than slums in other cities.[3]

The Sultan possessed sixty-one gardens along the Sea of Marmara and the Bosphorus. Avoiding the rigid patterns of both Western and Iranian gardens, they were scattered with flowers, 'eye-caressing' Judas trees, poplars and cypresses. During visits by his harem, the gardens were surrounded by lattices to shield the ladies from alien eyes. The imperial gardeners, the Bostancis, were one of the chief units at the court: an account book of 1580 records the expense incurred by their renewal of 'the jasmine pergolas near the terrace of the House of Felicity in the palace gardens'.[4]

One form of garden was peculiar to Constantinople: the flowering graveyards stretching across the hills and valleys outside the city. Cypresses, flowers and creepers grew between Ottoman tombs, or out of holes carved in the middle of them. The tombstones, of which there were said to be enough to rebuild the entire city, were scattered haphazardly rather than arranged in orderly rows. The funerary flowerbeds were so agreeable that they became a favourite picnic resort for families on Fridays. Cafés were built in, or overlooking, graveyards. Franks assembled every evening to talk and promenade in a graveyard in Pera, with a magnificent view across the Golden Horn, which they called *le Petit Champ des Morts*.[5]

Once brightly painted in blue, gold and red,* years of wind and rain have turned the tombstones white or grey. Flowers or a shawl are carved on the headstone of a woman's grave; stone turbans mark the official rank of a dead man. Inscriptions confirm the place of the garden in Ottoman imaginations:

> Him the Eternal!
> My Sadika has gone,
> Alas, alas!
> My darling child has left me.
> Alas, alas!
> Sadika the light of my eyes,
> the rose garden of my hopes,
> has gone to paradise.
> Pray a Fatiha† for Sadika,
> the daughter of Osman Bey
> AH 1256.

Him the Eternal!
Scarce had I become a mother and seen my new-born child,
When the arrow of destiny sent my soul into Eternal Life:
I left the garden of this world for that of Paradise.
Say a Fatiha for Ayse, wife of Orman Efendi.[6]

Jasmine, irises, roses, lilies, carnations and hyacinths were favoured in the gardens of the capital. No flower, however, was more Ottoman than the tulip: it was particularly cherished since the letters of its Turkish

---

*In 1904 the French novelist Pierre Loti reerected and regilded the tomb of his beloved Aziyade, heroine of his novel of that name, outside the land walls.
†The opening verses of the Koran, the standard Muslim prayer.

name, *lale*, are the same as those of Allah. The Ottoman Empire was scoured for tulips for the gardens of Constantinople. In 1574 Selim II wrote to an official near Aleppo: 'I need about 50,000 tulips for my royal gardens. To bring these bulbs I send you one of the chiefs of my servants. I command you in no way to delay.' In 1577 Murad III ordered 300,000 tulip bulbs from the Crimea. They were given names like Dwarf's Purple, Glitter of Prosperity, Beloved's Face, Rose Arrow; their colour, stalks and stamens were subjects of discussion and emulation. Pointed petals are a characteristic of Turkish tulips. A perfect tulip was described as 'almond-shaped, needle-like, ornamented with pleasant rays, her inner petals like a well, as they should be; the outer petals a little open, thin too, as they should be'. In summer they might be shaded with linen to prevent scorching by the sun. From Constantinople in the sixteenth century tulips spread to central and western Europe.[7]

By the eighteenth century the Bosphorus was lined with vineyards, gardens and orchards. Different villages specialized in different fruits: Rumeli Kavak in cherries; Ortakoy in cherries; Beykoz in walnuts; Mecidiyekoy in mulberries. In the seventeenth century Melek Ahmed Pasha and his guests gorged on 'juicy ruby-coloured cherries' in his twelve *yalis* or wooden waterfront houses along the Bosphorus and Golden Horn.[8]

Yalis soon became an essential part of life in Constantinople. In Paris, after the mid-seventeenth century, in order to avoid fires, construction of wooden houses was gradually forbidden. Most houses in the Ottoman capital, however, after the sixteenth century, were built of wood. The reasons were not merely the practical advantages of availability (Anatolia was covered in forest), cheapness, and speed of construction – it took only two or three months to build a large house – but also the particular geography and aesthetical sensibility of the city. Constantinople was built on a fault-line, frequently devastated by earthquakes: the worst occurred in 1509 ('little doomsday'), 1648, 1719, 1766, 1894. Since wood bends, it resists earthquakes better than stone (as traditional architects in Tokyo also found). Constantinople was also a city of water, and wood absorbs humidity better than stone. The choice of wood also reflected love of the view: walls of wood permit more and larger windows than walls of stone.

From the outside, the yalis and *konaks* (the name for large houses not built beside the water) looked less appealing than the surrounding gardens. They were generally painted rust-red, with few distinguishing features. Surviving old houses, like the Koprulu Yalisi, the Sadullah Pasha Yalisi at Cengelkoy on the Asian side of the Bosphorus or a grandiose four-storey wooden skyscraper built for Christian ship-owners, the Kavafyan Evi in Bebek, show that exteriors were under-stated compared to the great stone palaces lining the Grand Canal of Venice. Dynastic power was, predictably, the cause. Owners feared the Sultan's disapproval or envy, as he was rowed up the Bosphorus or the Golden Horn. Occasionally, particularly if the owner was Christian, sections of the same house were painted different colours in order to make it appear several separate properties. In theory, on the shore, Christians and Jews had to build houses two feet lower than Muslims – although they frequently bought exemption from this rule.

The principal room inside a yali was called the *sofa*: a large reception room on an upper floor, or, in such a room, a bay raised a foot from the ground, covered with particularly sumptuous carpets and lined with a divan. The ceilings, windows, frames and walls were carved and decor-ated with brightly coloured and gilded flower motifs, rosettes and arabesques; niches in the walls held pots of flowers or incense-burners. Flowers were displayed either in bunches in blue and white vases or, as individual stems, in long-necked Venetian glasses. The same style of interior was used by Christians, Jews and Muslims. According to the Anglo-Dutch designer Thomas Hope, author of the great Phanariot novel *Anastasius* (1818), Greek houses of the Phanar contained 'rooms furnished in all the splendour of eastern magnificence. Persian carpets covered the floors, Genoa velvets clothed the walls, and gilt trelliswork overcast the lofty ceilings. Clouds of rich perfumes rose on all sides from silver censers.' Many rich Greek houses, like their Muslim neigh-bours, had separate quarters for men and women.[9]

Perhaps as a reflection of the Ottomans' nomadic past, there was little furniture, apart from braziers, stools (on which large circular trays were placed for meals) and, around the walls, embroidered divans. Mattresses stored in cupboards in the walls and rolled out on the floor at night served as beds. Jewels and textiles – carpets, wall hangings, cushion covers – were the main note of luxury. After visiting the houses of the Grand Vizier and the Kaptan Pasha, a Russian diplomat wrote: 'However simple their houses are on the outside, on the inside luxury and magnificence reign. Gold, rich fabrics, pearls and precious stones are there in an abundance of which it is difficult to convey an impression.'

Lady Mary Wortley Montagu shared his opinion. In 1718 she visited the palace of Ahmed III's 14-year-old daughter Fatma, widow of Ali

Pasha, whose first marriage had been celebrated with such splendour in 1709, now married to the Grand Vizier Ibrahim Pasha. It was built on the site of what is now the Ciragan palace:

> It is situated on one of the most delightful parts of the canal [the Bosphorus] with a fine wood on the side of a hill behind it. The extent of it is prodigious; the guardian assured me there is 800 rooms in it. I will not answer for that number since I did not count them but 'tis certain the number is very large and the whole adorned with a profusion of marble, gilding and the most exquisite painting of fruit and flowers.

The room in which the Sultan was entertained

> is wainscotted with mother-of-pearl fastened with emeralds like nails; there are others of mother-of-pearl and olive wood inlaid and several of japan china. The galleries which are numerous and very large, are adorned with jars of flowers and porcelain dishes of fruit of all sorts, so well done in plaster and coloured in so lively a manner that it has an enchanting effect. The garden is suitable to the house where arbours, fountains and walks are thrown together in an agreeable confusion.

The kiosks in the gardens of the yalis were especially pleasing. According to Cockerell: 'The most charming things are the kiosks . . . They are entirely of wood and even the most extensive are finished in about two months.' Decorated with cupolas and gilded wordwork, they were 'such as you might imagine from reading *The Arabian Nights*'. Exterior lattices created a green tapestry of vines, jasmine and honeysuckle.[10]

Proximity to water distinguished the yalis of Constantinople. Since there is no tide, rooms could be built on the same level as the Bosphorus. The sight and sound of the water through the windows, its reflection on ceilings, gave some yalis the feeling of floating on the water. Some rooms were traversed by channels of water cut in the floor. On the floors of domed sofa rooms, marble fountains threw up spouts of water. Wall fountains produced both coolness and a dashing sound as water tumbled from one marble cup to another. Gardens contained marble cascades, pools and winding canals. Imitated in such provincial cities as Kastoria, Safranbolu and Damascus, reproduced on frescos throughout the empire, as well as on documents like Jewish marriage contracts, the yalis of Constantinople became preeminent symbols of the 'Ottoman way'.

*

Naturally food and drink were among the inhabitants' principal pleasures. William Harborne, the first English ambassador, recorded the meal served to him in the palace in 1582: 'Mutton boiled and roasted, Rice diversely dressed, Fritters of the finest fashion and dishes daintily dight with pretty Pappe, with infinite others I know not how to expresse them . . . Our drink was made with Rose water and Sugar and spices brewed together.' The principal dish, and the first test of every new cook, was pilav, rice cooked in meat juice. The pages in the palace school had it as a treat every Thursday. The poor lived off bread, water, fruit, vegetables, yoghurt, rice and if lucky, chicken or mutton and pilav, eaten after work towards 5 p.m. The rich ate black caviare, the poor red.[11]

Drawing on Mediterranean, Middle Eastern and central Asian traditions, in time Ottoman cuisine became one of the most sophisticated in the world. Many former inhabitants of Istanbul miss its food more than any other aspect of the city. Long after he had left the city in his person, the millionaire Calouste Gulbenkian continued to inhabit it through his palate, since he retained an 'oriental' (Turkish, Greek or Armenian) cook to prepare the dishes he had enjoyed in his youth. Among them were Circassian chicken, prepared with walnuts and paprika; mackerel stuffed, without breaking the skin, with rice, currants, pine nuts and onion; chicken pudding – chicken breast beaten into a smooth pulp and flavoured with milk, sugar and cinnamon; and special kinds of halva (a sweet made from sesame seeds) cooked to make peace between quarrelling friends, or to revive returning war heroes. In wealthy households, cooks used only left legs (right legs were considered tough, since animals stand on them more).

Vegetables were the glory of Ottoman cuisine, prepared with a subtlety rarely devoted to them in other countries. Some dishes, especially those based on 'the king of vegetables', the aubergine, required days of preparation. Two sets of vegetables were served at meals: cold vegetables cooked in oil and hot vegetables cooked in butter. Fruit juices were made from the hips of wild roses, violets, mulberries or tamarind, chilled with ice brought from the mountains above Bursa and stored in cisterns. Nuts, spices and mint added flavour. Preserved fruit and jams were another speciality. From its colour and richness, one jam was called the conserve of rubies – although we need not believe the claim of Dr James Dallaway, in the late eighteenth century, that it also contained pounded rubies. *Pekmez* or grape treacle was made every year in Constantinople households as a flavouring for other dishes.[12]

Greeks, Armenians and Turks shared the same food as well as the same city. With the partial exception of Sephardic Jewish cuisine, there were no separate cuisines like those of Chinese and Indians in late twentieth-century London, or of Jews and Italians in early twentieth-century New York. Differences of materials and preparation owed more to wealth or region, than to race or religion (although Christians had special Lenten foods such as dried fish).[13] Hence the similarities between late twentieth-century 'Greek', 'Turkish' and 'Armenian' cook-books, despite their wilful nationalism.

Meals were followed by the pleasures of tobacco and coffee. English merchants introduced tobacco to Constantinople, from America, in 1601. At first it was denounced in mosques as an abominable innovation. The contemporary historian Ibrahim Pecevi accused smokers of poisoning the air: 'Puffing in each other's faces, they made the streets and markets stink.' In 1633 Murad IV forbade smoking on pain of death. As the severity of his interdiction increased, according to another historian Katib Celebi, 'so did people's desire to smoke, in accordance with the saying "Men desire what is forbidden", and many thousands of men were sent to the abode of nothingness.' In desperation smokers inhaled the aroma of crushed tobacco leaves. Finally in 1647 the Mufti of Constantinople allowed tobacco. By the end of the eighteenth century it was not only one of the principal exports of the Ottoman Empire, but also one of the principal means, after costume, to convey or deny status and recognition. The length, beauty and intricacy of a pipe and its mouthpiece signalled the smoker's rank and wealth. Mouthpieces might be of amber, ivory or hippopotamus tooth: pale lemon amber was especially fashionable. The pipe-bearer had such an important task that he became a confidential household official. The pipe became 'the alpha and omega of oriental etiquette', even if the visitor did not smoke. In 1841, at a moment of unusual tension in Franco-Ottoman relations, the French ambassador threatened to leave Constantinople until he received a formal apology for his failure to obtain the honours of the pipe in the Sultan's palace.[14]

Coffee arrived from Yemen in the mid-sixteenth century. Two Syrians established the first public coffee-house in 1554 – a hundred years before coffee-houses appeared in London or Paris. After three years they returned to Syria with a small fortune. Coffee-houses rapidly became the principal centres of male social life in the capital. Men spent hours, even days, there, playing cards or dominoes, or smoking – as some still do.* They were supplied with pipes by the coffee-house, but brought their own mouthpieces and tobacco. Pictures of smart coffee-houses show carved and gilded interiors, equipped with fountains, carpet-covered benches, large windows through which to contemplate the view. Men are smoking, writing letters or playing draughts. In poorer districts, and around the bazaar, men treated the café as a labour exchange, somewhere to wait for offers of work. Muslims and non-Muslims frequented the same coffee-houses, but there were also separate Greek, Albanian, Persian and Janissary coffee-houses.[15]

As in nineteenth-century Vienna, some coffee-houses were frequented by wits and writers. Pecevi wrote:

> Some read books and fine writings, some were busy with backgammon and chess, some brought new poems and talked of literature . . . even great men could not refrain from coming there. The imams and muezzins and pious hypocrites said: 'People have become addicts of the coffee-house: nobody comes to the mosques!' The *ulema* said: 'It is a house of evil deeds: it is better to go to the wine tavern than there.'

Bans were imposed, but soon lifted. Instead of lending money at high rates to the government, viziers invested in coffee-houses.[16] By the early nineteenth century, according to one estimate, there were 2,500 in and around the city.[17]

Coffee became as characteristic of Constantinople as tulips. The French traveller Thévenot who stayed in the city in 1655, wrote that Turks considered coffee to have medicinal properties: 'There is no one poor or rich, who does not drink at least two or three cups of it a day.' Until the 1960s the largest cafés were frequented by professional musicians and story-tellers. Musicians sang of love:

> With the hawk of thy eyes thou hast caught the bird of my heart . . .
> The luscious balm of thy lips makes me long for sipping it,
> Oh my sweetheart!

Story-tellers frequently began: 'Once upon a time God's servants were many, very long ago the camel was a pedlar, the mouse a hairdresser, the donkey was the bearer of the king's stamp and the mule an armourer.' Stories dwelt on the trials of marriage, the peculiarities of foreigners and minorities. Those about the legendary Turkish idiot hero, Hoca

---

*In the small suburb of Kuzguncuk, on the Asian side of the Bosphorus, where much of this book was written, the main street is lined with ten cafés. They are never empty.

(teacher) Nasreddin, were the equivalent in Turkey of 'shaggy-dog stories'.

Every feast of Hizir, on 6 May, the day the Kaptan Pasha took the fleet to the Aegean and butchers started to slaughter lambs, the people of Constantinople used to go into the country to enjoy the spring flowers, taking a picnic of lamb, dolma and pilav. Their usual destination was one of the two wide green valleys, the 'Sweet Waters of Europe' at the end of the Golden Horn, or the 'Sweet Waters of Asia' halfway up the Bosphorus on the Asian side. One year the Hoca had been given a lamb. Taking advantage of his simplicity, his friends told him to roast it for them, as the following day was the Day of Judgement. They all went to the Sweet Waters of Asia and while the meat was roasting on a fire, lay down for a nap. When the fire burned low, the Hoca took their cloaks and clothes and threw them on. They woke up and complained. He replied: 'As the day after tomorrow will be the day of resurrection, none of you will need any clothes.'[18]

Jam and perfume, in addition to tobacco and coffee, were served to honoured visitors to a grand household. Jam was eaten with a gilt spoon. From a narrow-necked silver bottle, musk-scented rose-water was sprinkled on the hands. A silver urn containing burning perfumes scented the room, and if held under coat or kaftan, the visitor's entire person. This was the perfume of power. For in Constantinople, as in Versailles, rank was indicated by smell as well as dress and manner. When Lord Charlemont learnt how to hold the urn under his kaftan, 'the Reis Efendi laughed heartily and with great good humour told me that he was pleased to see me begin to accommodate myself to their customs, to which he hoped I should not long be a stranger'. The manners and customs of Constantinople, like the splendour of the palace and the glory of the mosques, were part of the city's message to the outside world.[19]

Other pleasures, however, were kept from foreign eyes. The four 'cushions on the sofa of pleasure', in Pecevi's phrase, were tobacco, coffee, opium and wine. Opium, although forbidden by Islam, was sold in a street by the Suleymaniye mosque. Every sunset, looking like ghouls risen from the grave, trembling and stuttering addicts congreg-ated there to buy opium pills. Some took as many as four, swallowed with water, and enjoyed visions of kiosks of pearls, or the houris of paradise. An evening concert of monotonous, melancholic Turkish music, in a grandee's house, would be heightened by the pleasures of opium and tobacco, until the silent spectators were 'intoxicated with a languishing Enthusiasm'. The Sultan's opium was often mixed with perfumes or powdered pearls.[20]

The prohibition of alcohol was the Muslim tradition least observed in Constantinople. Jews imported wine from Germany and Spain, but the most popular was the sweet wine of the Aegean islands, such as Samos or Crete, celebrated since classical times: there were sound economic reasons for Venice and the Ottoman Empire to spend thirty years fighting over Crete in the seventeenth century. It was after the conquest of Crete, as he relaxed on Chios, that Koprulu Fazil Ahmed acquired the taste for wine that led to his early death. Grapes were grown, and wine produced, along the Bosphorus, even on land belonging to Muslim *vakifs*.

As early as the reign of Bayezid II (1481–1512) poets frequented disreputable taverns along the Golden Horn. By the seventeenth century, according to the historian Evliya Celebi, there were 1,400 taverns in Constantinople. Compared to the soaring mosques of stone, they looked small and sordid but, in the words of one poet:

> From outside the tavern seems a dingy place
> But inside it is airy, charming, full of space.[21]

In moments of puritanism or insecurity, or to set the appropriate tone at the beginning of a reign, wine was forbidden and taverns closed, even to Jews and Christians.* Pleasure-seekers exchanged the crystal of the wine glass for the porcelain of the coffee cup. However, there was a local saying that the Sultan's order lasts from midday to one o'clock. The Aga of the Janissaries and the Bostanci Pasha administered and benefited from taxes on taverns. They soon reopened.[22]

Sultans and muftis often drank in private what they forbade in public. No Christian dynasty, except perhaps the Stuarts, has drunk as deep as the Ottoman sultans (who were, however, outdrunk by their fellow Muslims, the Mogul emperors). Suleyman the Magnificent himself drank wine until the last decades of his reign. One of his poems uses wine as a metaphor for love, for wine was part of the poetry as well as the reality of the capital:

---

*Taverns were closed, by Bayezid II, Suleyman the Magnificent and in 1613, 1622, 1670, 1747, 1754.

> Let the taverns celebrate those ruby lips of yours to the core,
> Night and day let no one put the cups down; let them drink and
>   adore . . .

His son Selim II, known as the Sot, died from a fall in a hamam – probably while drunk. Murad IV drank wine in front of Evliya: 'Evliya you are now initiated into my secrets; take care not to divulge them.'

Poets celebrated wine, not sherbet. They cried: 'O cup-bearer where is the life-giving bowl?' and hoped that tulip-hued wine would replace blood in the bloodstream. A seventeenth-century Mufti wrote:

> In the mosque let hypocrites indulge in their hypocrisy –
> Come to the tavern where you'll neither sham nor shammers see . . .
> Let them henceforth call this meeting-place a grogshop if they will
> Give here the goblet, server, and let them call me drunk.
> Let them say 'he never sobered up'.[23]

A kadi and a mufti, known to be in the words of the great Austrian historian Hammer-Purgstall 'free thinkers addicted at once to wine and to infamous debauchery' ran their own taverns. In the morning the judge got drunk at the mufti's; in the evening the mufti at the judge's. In the eighteenth century an Ottoman ambassador to Persia complained: 'In Turkey we drank oceans; in Persia cups of tea.' Humbler citizens drank a sort of beer called *boza*, of which Evliya wrote: 'It is permitted to drink *boza* as it gives strength even to soldiers of the faith.' 'Potato spirit', a type or schnapps made by Jews in Haskoy, was drunk there in taverns with wine and fried oysters. By the nineteenth century 'raki evenings' were commonplace. The sort of food still provided in Istanbul restaurants was served: nuts; cheese and melon; fish roe and spiced meat; cold vegetables such as eggplant or salads; grilled or fried fish; mussels; liver cooked in Albanian style; cheese or meat cooked in pastry, known as *boreks*. Male guests drank the aniseed-flavoured liqueur and recited poems until the arrival of a plate of fruit signalled that it was time to leave.[24]

Wine increased the appetite for sex. Since adultery could be fatal, written evidence for love affairs is tenuous. However, despite all the pressures of religion, custom and fear, some women did have love affairs with men to whom they were not married. If they could not leave the house, lovers communicated through salesmen and women, often Greek, Jewish or Armenian, going from house to house. As the nineteenth-century poet and memorialist Leyla Hanim wrote: 'They were terrible *intrigantes*, who sometimes practised the most disreputable trades.' Flowers, thrown in the street to the loved one, expressed a secret language of love. Holding a daffodil meant 'Can you love me?' Pulling a rose bud in two asked the question: 'Would you die for my sake?' 'I would submit my neck to the bow-string without a murmur' was conveyed by pulling the head off a violet. Love also had a rhyming code: 'Perhaps a pistachio nut, called in Turkish *fistik*, is sent; the rhyme to which it alludes is *ikimize bir yastik*, Let us both have the same pillow . . . A thread of silk, in Turkish *ipek*, has a reference to the rhyming expression *seni seviyorum pek* "I love you with rapture".'[25]

Azizi, who worked in the Seven Towers and died in 1585, wrote poems which suggest that lovers enjoyed considerable licence. 'Long-haired Zeman, a many-headed torment of the Earth', had as many lovers as hairs on her neck. 'Cemila of the Fair Hands', 'Ayse of the Ankles', knew where to find pleasure. Many women had the opportunity to pay visits to other harems, to hamams or the bazaar. In the street, shrouded in cloaks and veils, they were in a world of their own, with opportunities for what a later harem inmate called 'intrigues and clandestine intercourse'. They could talk with their eyes, as well as their tongues – luminous, staring eyes.

The poet Baqi wrote:

> If ladies when they are abroad are always veiled, appears it strange?
> For highway robbers shroud the face when forth in quest of prey
>   they range.

Wearing daring purple veils, some women went noisily from shop to shop in the bazaar, testing shopkeepers with such questions as: 'Do you have anything suitable for me? If you have good merchandise I am interested but you must measure me up.' The more the shopkeeper saw their hennaed fingers, the more excited he became.

Stories were related of Turkish women hiring private rooms in Pera taverns – or brothels – where they could 'gratify their voluptuous desires and reward their gallants according to their personal merit'. Young men could be smuggled into harems dressed as girls. According to the Baron de Tott, a Turkish-speaking officer of Hungarian origin who lived in the city from 1755 to 1776, women were often murdered by their lovers. Their bodies might be seen, stripped and mangled, 'floating in the Port, under the very windows of their Murderers'.[26]

Some women, however, turned to each other for love and friendship. Lesbians had the reputation of being well-read and loyal. They were 'the graceful ones', and often showed their love by wearing coordinated colours or perfumes. The following letter from a maid called Feleksu written to Behice Sultan, a daughter of Sultan Abdulmecid, in 1875, when Feleksu was suffering from a bout of malaria, shows the strength of feeling between women, whether physical or unphysical:

> My little lioness, I love you very much and you said you loved me a bit too. In this world you are the joy of my heart. From your health I too find health. Honestly it is not because you are Princess Behice. There are many princesses – God bless their lives. You know I love you, you show me much kindness, I love you, I love you, in short I love you, I honestly do. Truly I do. There I have said I love you and I do; that's all there is to it . . .

Behice Sultan died a year later, having been married only two weeks.[27]

In contrast to the secrecy imposed on Muslim women, Christian women openly maintained the lascivious traditions of Galata. Greek women could be hired by the month, through an arrangement known as *mariage à la cabine*, from a Turkish word for a form of temporary marriage called *kabin*. One eighteenth-century British ambassador was said, by his successor, to have spent his twelve years in Constantinople 'upon a sofa with the women'. According to Lord Charlemont, 'the women are exceedingly handsome and well-dressed and their manners are remarkably pleasing, a probable indication that they are no foes of love'. Since 'it is the duty of the traveller to leave nothing unseen', he visited brothels licensed by the Aga of the Janissaries and the Bostanci Pasha. Inmates were either Christian or Jews, 'many of whom are extremely beautiful and well skilled in all the necessary arts and allurements of their calling'. On one visit the 'matron of the house', a Greek,* surrounded him with eight or ten naked 'goddesses' who reminded him of Hera, Athene and Aphrodite. At the end of the eighteenth century the best brothel was beside the British embassy. Independent operators entertained clients in graveyards – where unaccompanied women were assumed to be visiting the graves of dead relations.[28]

Constantinople offered one freedom hard to find in western Europe: freedom from sexual conformity. Homosexuals in western Europe

---

*Today 'Madame Mathilde', the queen of the red-light district in Istanbul beside the Galata Tower – and one of the highest tax-payers in Turkey – is Armenian Catholic.

might suffer prison or death. Fatih, however, had promised his soldiers both 'very beautiful women, young and good-looking' and 'boys too, very many and very beautiful and of noble families'. Radu, brother of Vlad the Impaler, Prince of Wallachia, original of Dracula, was the Sultan's own most famous favourite. Radu had arrived as a hostage at the Ottoman court at the age of 7, 'no taller than a bouquet of flowers'. At first he refused the Sultan, wounding him with a sword and escaping up a tree where he spent the night. After he became the Sultan's lover, he was rewarded with his brother's throne.[29]

A century later a French visitor wrote that Turks 'are also very subject to the vice of Sodom, the grandees more than the ordinary people, there being hardly a captain without one or more *bardacè*'. Coffee-houses and taverns kept 'beautifull boyes who serve as stales [prostitutes] to procure them customeers', acording to an English traveller. Two hundred years later Charles White denounced 'the disgusting spectacle of the Greek dancing-boys of Galata . . . revolting even to the coarsest mind'. In harems and hamams, to the music of lute, guitar and castanets, teams of dancing girls, often dressed as men, entertained women. In Janissaries' and sailors' taverns – and at the winter halva parties of the grandees – richly clad, long-haired dancing boys, with names like Golden Ball, Curly, New World, danced in a way which left nothing to the imagination.[30]

Such diversions may explain why foreigners resident in Constantinople often wrote of Turkish 'freedom and pleasures', or 'the ease and freedom of an Eastern life'. They referred not only to the lack of a rigid class structure, but also to the range of pleasures on offer. Venetian boys under 16 were forbidden to travel to Turkey, for fear that they would 'turn Turk'. Many Venetian diplomats and students, seduced by the *lussúria del viver turchesco*, decided to become Muslim and remain in Constantinople. No Ottoman Muslim settled in Venice.[31]

The city's poets wrote love poems to 'the fawns of Istanbul' – often bath attendants or dancing boys. The old Roman hippodrome by the Sultanahmed mosque, the Atmeydan, was 'the favourite resort of beautiful youths'. Their bodies were compared to cypresses, their faces to the moon, their lips to rubies. They were candles, their lovers moths drawn to the flame. The poet yearned for his face to be the mat on the floor of his loved one's hamam.

> Each night you let outsiders hold you to their hearts' content
> Ah tyrant, I too have a heart! How can you be so cruel?

You come, O vintner's lad, a rose in one hand, in the other wine,
Which shall I choose? Is it the rose, the wine or you will give content?[32]

One reason for the celebration of youths was that it was socially
acceptable: explicit reference to women, in writing or conversation, was
considered shocking. Some poets pretended that such loves were pure.
Yet in many cases the love was neither pure nor a substitute. In the
palace Murad IV would occasionally recite, according to his courtier
Evliya:

I have nothing to say against the one with clean skirts
A thousand curses a day on the unclean catamite.

He looked the little sword-bearer Mustafa in the face: 'What do you
think about this poem, Mustafa?' and the sword-bearer turned red in
the cheeks. The Sultan then gave him a sable robe of honour. A
hundred years later the poet Nedim wrote that all the *ulema* were
enamoured of boys; not one remained who enjoyed female love.[33]

The bisexuality of Constantinople received its clearest expression in
the work of Fazil Bey (1759–1810). Born in Safed in Palestine, son and
grandson of Arab rebels, he was brought to Constantinople and educated in the palace school. He continued to live in the city, except for
a spell of exile in Rhodes in 1799–1804, until he died destitute in
Beshiktash in 1810. In his *Zenanname* (The Book of Women), written
in the 1790s, he claimed that beauty is God's revelation of himself, that
God is the ultimate object of a lover's passion. Below this façade his
books are a paean to pleasure: the women of Constantinople have
pink skin and walk in such a refined manner that the whole world
would like to emulate them. Some women are so secluded they would
not even be seen in the afterlife; like parrots in a cage 'the sun has
never shone on their faces, nor has the wind blown their hair'. Others
are more adventurous. In Ottoman fashion, Fazil Bey lists them by
nationality: Persians are well-read, with intoxicating eyes; Sudanese
women have faces of the night; Hejazis are beautiful but empty-
headed, with blue lips and hooked nostrils; Jewish women have bad
complexions; Armenians are badly behaved and badly dressed, but not
all ugly; Greeks are gracious and seductive: 'We have to have lovers
like these.' Circassians were even better: 'A lover can find all that he
can hope for in a Circassian woman.' He also described Yemeni,
Spanish, Dutch and an English woman:

Her red cheek to the rose doth colour bring,
Her mouth doth teach the nightingale to sing.

In the *Khubanname* (The Book of Beauties) he celebrated, although
with fewer details, young men of the same nationalities: his current
lover had threatened to turn to women unless he wrote out a list. His
own heart, he wrote, has been a tiltyard whence king has driven out
king. Persians are tall and beautiful; they have eyebrows like a bow, red
cheeks and round faces and are masters of flirtation. Baghdad boys 'like
torturing' and never keep appointments. The French are beautiful, but
clumsy in bed. Armenians are good against the cold: 'Keep Sarkis for
the winter as his body is like a field of hair.' Albanians have unappealing
voices, big bellies and thick necks. Greeks' silver chests and white skins
captivated him: 'Their bodies are so beautifully proportioned that the
whole world is amazed.' Even at 50 he would fall into the deepest well
for their love.[34]

During the nights of Ramadan when Muslims broke the fast they had
been observing all day, Constantinople was ruled by pleasure. The firing
of a gun announced the setting of the sun. The streets, normally so quiet
in the evenings, came to life in a frenzy of food, drink and music: 'For a
few minutes the Turkish city is nothing but a monster with a hundred
thousand mouths that eat and drink.' Verses from the Koran were strung
from one minaret to another in letters of flame. In the streets below, the
public was entertained by snake-charmers, jugglers, fortune-tellers and
the shadow puppet theatre known as *Karagoz*, in which figures about
fifteen inches high enacted (often highly obscene) tales of love and battle.
Pashas' households would hold recitations of the Koran in the courtyard.
Others staged comedies by troupes of Greeks or Jews, 'mimicking the
different Officers of the Empire and executing their functions in such a
manner as to turn them into ridicule' – not sparing the Sultan and Grand
Vizier. The poor could go from house to house, watching the entertainments and eating as much as they wished.[35]

The city's cult of pleasure reached a peak during the 'tulip age' in
the early eighteenth century – with the reign of Suleyman the
Magnificent and the mid-nineteenth century, one of the Ottoman city's
three golden ages. Mustafa II (1695–1703), who loved hunting, had
resided almost exclusively in Edirne. Ambassadors and merchants
moved to Edirne; princesses built palaces there; Constantinople
was outraged. In 1703 a rebellion of Janissaries, encouraged by the

ulema and the Koprulu household, led to the deposition of Mustafa II. The new Sultan, his brother Ahmed III, promised never to live in Edirne.[36]

Ahmed III was not only an avaricious tyrant who ordered the executions of the Cantacuzenos and Brancovan families, but also a cultivated bibliophile. At about the time other European monarchs were beginning to prefer private to state apartments, Ahmed III complained to his Grand Vizier about the etiquette at Topkapi: 'If I go up to one of the chambers, forty privy chamber pages are lined up. If I have to put on my trousers, I do not feel the least comfort. The swordbearer has to dismiss them, keeping only three or four men so that I may be at ease in the small chamber.' In his quest for informality, he began to build smaller kiosks and palaces around the capital, which he used in preference to Topkapi palace: the House of Eternal Gaiety in Defterdarburnu and the House of Eternal Honour in Uskudar. The Venetian Bailo wrote: 'It is not easy to find an earlier example of a Sultan being away from the royal palaces for so long a time.'[37] The spirit of the age was epitomized in one of the inscriptions placed by the Sultan on a kiosk in Topkapi:

> May Allah bless this kiosk and may there be rejoicing here,
> May this Kiosk of Happiness be replete with happiness!

His most famous palace, called Sa'adabad or Eternal Happiness, was built at a traditional place of recreation, along the stream leading into the Golden Horn at Kagithane (which Europeans called the Sweet Waters of Europe). Sa'adabad was influenced by prints of Versailles which are still in the Topkapi library, and by advice from Mehmed Said, who had accompanied his father's embassy to France in 1721 – to learn about French fortresses, trade, customs, and to strengthen the alliance between the two empires. Architects were summoned from Europe. The garden was planted in the style of Versailles, with straight rows of trees, and square flowerbeds. Under the personal supervision, and at the expense, of the Grand Vizier, the Sultan's son-in-law Ibrahim, construction of the palace lasted from June to August 1722. Part of the stream was straightened into a marble-banked canal 1,100 metres long, lined with pools, cascades and gilded baldachins. Despite the French influence, the palace and kiosks at Sa'adabad were also very Turkish, with wide projecting eaves, golden domes, walls painted bright blue, red or green – among the freedoms enjoyed by Constantinople was freedom of colour. Water poured from dragon-headed bronze fountains into marble pools. To celebrate completion, and the palace's name, the Grand Vizier composed a couplet: 'Let it be blessed to Sultan Ahmed to have eternal happiness [*Sa'adabad*] in the State'. Two hundred Ottoman dignitaries were asked to build different coloured residences nearby, which were decorated with symbols of their functions: cannons for the chief of artillery, birds for the head falconer. Architecture and garden design were not the only aspects of French culture which pleased the Sultan. One thousand bottles of champagne, and 900 bottles of burgundy were ordered from France.[38]

Sa'adabad was celebrated by the most original of Ottoman poets: Nedim, 'the boon companion'. Member of an *ulama* family, born in Constantinople around 1680, he was librarian and friend of the Grand Vizier Ibrahim. With a pagan zest for life, he sang the pleasures of wine, love and the passing moment. His most famous poem is addressed to a friend:

> Let us give a little comfort to this heart that's wearied so,
> Let us visit Sa'adabad, my swaying Cypress, let us go!
> Look, there is a swift caique all ready at the pier below,
> Let us visit Sa'adabad, my swaying Cypress, let us go! . . .
>
> Get permission from your mother, say you're off to Friday prayers.
> We should steal a day at least from destiny and all its cares!
> Going by secluded back-streets till we reach the harbour stairs.
> Let us visit Sa'adabad, my swaying Cypress, let us go!
>
> Let us laugh, let us play and take pleasure from the world!
> Let us drink the waters that the springs of Eden bring!
> Let us watch life's waters as they leap from dragons' mouths!
> Let us go to Sa'adabad, my moving cypress tree!

Nedim also wrote a panegyric to the capital, in the well-established tradition of city eulogy.

> O city of Istanbul, without equal and without price!
> I would sacrifice all Persia for one of your stones.
>
> You are a jewel engraved on two seas,
> You are like the sun warming the whole world.

Istanbul is the seventh heaven, the Garden of Eden, a mine of happiness. The brocade of knowledge is sold in its bazaars. Its mosques are oceans of light, its inhabitants are amiable and refined.

Istanbul the fortunate and prosperous,
We have cause to be proud of you!

We can say that your palaces, your hills and your banks
All breathe joy, pleasure and sensuality.

Can we ever describe you, O Istanbul? No,
I only want to praise the excellent Grand Vizier . . .

In fact your slave Nedim has drowned, O Lord of the Worlds,
In an abyss abounding in graces, rewards, favours and benefaction![39]

During this interlude of pleasure, the use of death as a dynastic weapon was relaxed. The Sultan had a Jewish doctor, Daniel de Fonseca. Born in Oporto in 1668, he lived in Constantinople from 1702 to 1730, and was frequently consulted on Ottoman policy by foreign ambassadors. In 1724 he wrote that the Grand Vizier was not only a good courtier and clever politician but also a 'very great gentleman [*très honnête homme*] . . . since the Grand Vizier entered the ministry this land is almost entirely rid of the former barbarity and ferocity. Today all flourishes and lives for pleasure, everything is full of *politesse et agrément.*' Lady Mary Wortley Montagu agreed: 'I am almost of opinion that they have a right notion of Life; they consume it in Music, Gardens, Wine and delicate eating, while we are tormenting our brains with some Scheme of Politics or studying some science to which we can never attain or if we do, cannot persuade people to set that value upon it we do ourselves.'[40]

The cult of tulips became a frenzy, like the 'tulip craze' which had peaked in the Netherlands in 1637. Up to 1,000 gold coins could be paid for one bulb until the government issued official price lists. A council of flower experts under the presidency of the Sultan's chief florist judged new varieties of tulip and, if they were found faultless, awarded them an official name.[41] The Grand Admiral Mustafa Pasha created forty-four new varieties, the Grand Vizier six. A total of 839 was listed in a special register in the palace. In the tulip garden created by the Sultan in the fourth courtyard of the palace, he held a fête every spring at which the colour of the tulips matched the colour of the guests' clothes and the liquid filling decorative vases. One evening the ladies of the harem ran booths in a mock bazaar: the Sultan was the only shopper.[42]

The Bosphorus had become a focus of city life. A tradition arose by which people moved to their yalis up the Bosphorus around the feast of Hizir (6 May) and returned to town on Ruz-i Kasim (7 October), which was also the traditional end of the campaigning season. The Patriarch of Jerusalem, the Mufti of Medina, the wealthy Armenian families of Kumurcuyan and Duzoglu, the great *ulema* family of Durrizade, the Mavrocordato and the Koprulu, all had houses on the Bosphorus. Mehmed Efendi Durrizade lived in such state that when Sultan Mahmud I (1730–54) paid a surprise visit to his house in Uskudar to break fast during Ramadan, the Sultan's train of 150 was also welcomed and fed.[43]

Constantinople had become a way of life – the only city to be both resort and capital, Bath and London, Spa and Paris. The shared pleasures of food, wine, music, the tavern, the coffee-house and the Bosphorus, united Muslims and non-Muslims. In the paintings of Jean-Baptiste Vanmour, and the drawings executed by Jean-Etienne Liotard in the four years he spent in the capital from 1738 to 1742, the Greeks, Armenians and Franks of the city not only look like Ottomans but are doing Ottoman things. A lady in stilted clogs and an ermine-lined robe is about to enter a bath. Ladies reclining against cushions play a game called *mankah*, a version of backgammon, or make music. Others are embroidering or drinking coffee; clothes, cushions, coffee-pots are entirely Ottoman. Only their portrayal by a man shows that they must be Greek or Frank. The role of Constantinople as a city of pleasure is confirmed by the words it gave the outside world: sofa, kiosk, coffee, kaftan, turban.

Constantinople was a world of its own, convinced of its superiority over provincial cities. The poet Nabi, for example, had written: 'Nothing teaches the inferiority of the provinces more than the sight of Constantinople. Heaven in vain revolves around all the world. It sees nowhere a city like Constantinople. See how she gleams with a beauty all her own as the sea laughingly caresses her!' Its empire of taste was as absolute as the Sultan's political dominion. With his quick courtier's eye, the Prince de Ligne wrote: 'Constantinople sets the fashion for Jassy as Paris does for the provinces, and the fashions arrive even quicker. Yellow was the sultanas' favourite colour. In Jassy it became every woman's. Long pipes of cherry wood had replaced in Constantinople pipes of jasmine wood. We boyars now only have cherry-wood pipes.'[44]

The city became a destination on the Grand Tour, for visitors in pursuit of pleasure, as well as scholars in search of knowledge. The British were coming: in 1724, a Jacobite, Lord Garlies; the Earl of Radnor in 1730; John Montagu, 4th Earl of Sandwich, and William Ponsonby in 1738; Richard Pococke and the Marquess of Granby (drawn by Liotard) in 1740. Many were portrayed wearing Turkish dress. Lord Charlemont reported:

> The mode of living at Constantinople is to a young man as pleasant as in any great city whatsoever. That quarter of the town which is called Pera and which forms itself a large city is entirely peopled with Franks and Greeks who live together in the most sociable manner and, with the public Ministers [ambassadors] form a society as pleasing as possible. The pleasures of the table are well understood and frequent and scarce an evening passes without balls, concerts or assemblies at all which the intercourse between the sexes is as easy as can be wished.

The Dutch ambassador was dismayed that Dutch merchants 'far from being content with an honourable way of life . . . want to vie with foreign diplomats in appearance, retinue and style of life; their wives and daughters daily indulge in festivities, balls and pleasurable excursions to all agreeable resorts.' Casanova came for three months in 1745. He seduced no one, but was himself 'surprised' in a kiosk, as he watched ladies bathing, by a Turk called Ismail.[45]

Did the indulgences of Constantinople save parts of Europe and India from becoming Ottoman provinces? They clearly sapped the fighting-will of the empire. Both in 1514 and 1517 the Janissaries forced the redoubtable Selim I to return to the city. In 1771, while the Ottoman Empire was fighting a war with Russia, Constantinople was preoccupied with another struggle: a dispute between a company of Janissaries and some levents over a 14-year-old dancing boy had begun in a Galata tavern. Business was interrupted, cannon deployed. Fifty people were killed. The Grand Vizier commented: 'So much bravery at Galata and so much cowardice on the Danube shows plainly that Turks are only afraid of hats.'* It took four days to restore order and the Grand Vizier had to promise that the boy would belong to neither side. He was hanged instead.

After the puritan outbreaks of the seventeenth century, greater individual licence returned to the city in the eighteenth. Levni's paintings of the reign of Ahmed III, with their strongly characterized faces, use of perspective and humour are a new development in Ottoman art.

---

*A term for Christians. Muslims wore turbans; hat brims interfered with the act of prostration during prayer.

Another change was the birth of printing by and for Muslims. There were two patrons: Mehmed Said Efendi, the designer of Sa'adabad, and a Unitarian from Transylvania, Ibrahim Muteferrika.

Captured in the wars in about 1693, the latter had freed himself from slavery by converting to Islam. He then became a *muteferrik* – one of a group of guards and honoured companions in the palace, described as 'men of all nations and all religions'. He is said to have known French, Italian, German, Latin, Turkish, Hungarian (and was later used by the Porte as a translator of diplomatic documents). In 1726 he submitted a treatise on printing to the Grand Vizier and the *ulema*. Claiming that it would help literacy, stop Europeans printing Islamic books and make Ottomans sole leaders in the world of Islam, he requested that the 'act of printing be declared by the Seyhulislam as commendable and useful for the Muslims and in accord with the glorious *sheriat*'. He also emphasized its practical advantages: cheapness, accuracy, the increase of learning. A fatwa was issued permitting books to be printed on all subjects except Islam – despite the opposition of a group of *ulema* who claimed, according to Ibrahim Muteferrika, 'that the aforesaid invention would be dangerous to public order and to the conduct of religion; it would place more than the necessary amount of books in circulation.' The concept of a 'necessary' amount of books is a chilling insight into some Ottoman official minds. Opposition also came from professional calligraphers, who staged a demonstration near the palace.[46]

Functioning in Ibrahim Muteferrika's house, the press was a multinational enterprise. *Ulema* served as proof-readers. Jonah ben Jacob Ashkenazi, a Jew from near Lvov who had started a Hebrew printing press in Constantinople in 1711, may also have helped. Printers, engravers and typesetters came from Vienna. The first book printed on 31 January 1729 was an Arabic dictionary, followed by an edition of the Ottoman historian Katib Celebi and a Turkish grammar, by Père Holdermann, for the use of French students and merchants.

In 1731 Ibrahim Muteferrika submitted to Mahmud I *Rational Bases for the Politics of Nations* in which he asked the question which has haunted Muslims ever since: 'Why do Christian nations which were so weak in the past compared with Muslim nations begin to dominate so many lands in modern times and even defeat the once victorious Ottoman armies?' He referred to the parliamentary system in England and the Netherlands, to the Christians' expansion in America and the Far East and even mentioned that, while Ottomans were governed by the *sheriat*, Europeans had 'laws and rules invented by reason': 'We remain in a state of utter unpreparedness . . . it has now become an evident and urgent need to collect information about the details of European affairs in order to repel their harm and to prevent their malice.' Military reform was his solution to the problem of Ottoman decline:

> Let the Muslims cease to be unaware and ignorant of the state of affairs and awaken from the slumber of heedlessness . . . Let them act with foresight and become intimately acquainted with new European methods, organization, strategy, tactics and warfare . . . All the wise men of the world agree that the people of Turkey excel all other peoples in their nature of accepting rule and order. If they learn the new military sciences and are able to apply them, no enemy can ever withstand this state.[47]

The tulip age ended in a popular revolt. By 1690, judging by figures for the poll tax paid by Christians and estimates by foreign residents, the population of Constantinople had reached between six and seven hundred thousand. It was the largest city in Europe and the Middle East – to use a metaphor beloved of the Ottomans themselves, an ocean of men and women. In the 1720s the population continued to grow as immigrants in search of work flooded in from Anatolia. The Sultan had to build seven new wheat stores near the arsenal, so that the city's bread supply could keep pace with its population.

At the same time, many of the immigrants, refused admission to the city's guilds, began to form an embittered under-class. The Sultan's extravagance led to salary cuts and tax rises. In July 1729 a fire described by the Venetian Bailo as 'greater than any other seen within the memory of men or described in registers' destroyed 400 houses, 130 mosques and caused 1,000 deaths. The weakening of some barriers between the sexes fuelled popular resentment. At one party at Sa'adabad, the Grand Vizier tossed gold coins down the dress of the wife of the kadi of Constantinople. Pleasure grounds were opened on the Atmeydan and at Sa'adabad, where 'the bird-brained women' met young men. 'And they would claim that these were human rights and would leave for the amusement parks and would force their husbands to give them money and if not would ask for divorce and would take this matter into their own hands and so there were no more than five honest women left in any one quarter.' The city was ready to explode.

Outraged by the innovations of the court, the Mufti of Constantinople and certain members of the *ulema* encouraged rebellion. A recent treaty with Russia and an impending war with Persia were

denounced in sermons in Aya Sofya: 'The war between those who turn
to Mecca is unjust.' Rebellion broke out on the morning of 28
September 1730. The leader, said to have been of Albanian origin, was
known as 'Patrona' Halil, since he had served on the ship *Patrona*. After
a spell as a Janissary, Halil had turned to selling clothes in the streets.
Like the *sansculottes* ('without breeches') of revolutionary Paris, he wore
ostentatiously ripped clothes. With his cronies Muslu the fruit-vendor
and Ali the coffee-seller, he led about thirty rebels into the bazaar and
asked people to join in 'implementing the *sheriat* of Muhammad'. It was
Thursday, a day of rest. The *kaimakam* was at his summer house, plant-
ing tulips. The Sultan and the army had moved in pomp to Uskudar on
the Asian side of the Bosphorus, in preparation for war with Persia.
Having seized weapons from the Janissaries, the rebellion soon spread
until it became the first large-scale social, religious and political revolution in the history of Constantinople.[48]

The Sultan was indecisive and ill-informed. Patrona Halil, on the
other hand, was a good public speaker. On Friday the rebels recruited
many followers at mosques; but Greeks, Armenians and gypsies also
joined. The eighteenth-century symbiosis between Turks and Greeks
had worked not only for Phanariot princes but also lower down the
social hierarchy. Patrona Halil's drinking companion, a Greek butcher
called Yanaki, lent him money at the start of the revolt. Soon shipyard
workers, government officials, and the Kaptan Pasha himself rallied to
the winning side. Patrona Halil demanded the head of the Grand Vizier.
On 30 September the Grand Vizier's corpse was flung out of the palace
and abandoned to the dogs in the streets. The Sultan's sense of guilt was
assuaged when fifty-four chests of gold coins were found among the
Grand Vizier's treasures.

On 1 October Ahmed III received rebel emissaries who told him:
'Your reign is finished, your subjects no longer want you as master.' He
accepted his fate and kissed the hand of the next Sultan, his nephew
Mahmud. His last advice was: 'never to put too much affection and
trust in his Grand Viziers . . . but to govern according to his own
enlightened ideas, asking for counsel, but never completely relying
upon anyone'. The poet Nedim died from a fall as he fled over roof-
tops, pursued by a band of Halil's followers, or (according to another
account) by the enraged parents of one of his favourites. The administration collapsed: rebels and *ulema* reigned. Their triumph was demonstrated by the presence beside the new Sultan, on his way to Eyup for
his inauguration, of Patrona Halil and Ali the coffee-seller, throwing

pieces of gold to the crowd. Yanaki briefly became Hospodar of Moldavia. Despite Mahmud I's opposition, rebels destroyed some of the hated new houses and gardens at Sa'adabad. The Sultan planned revenge with senior Janissary officers and the Khan of Crimea, who was visiting Constantinople. On 24 November Patrona Halil and twenty-eight followers were lured to the palace, with the promise of new honours. They were killed by guards in the council room and their corpses flung outside the imperial gate, like that of the Grand Vizier two months earlier.[49]

Yet for a long time order could not be restored. On 25 March 1731 another rebellion broke out, led by another Albanian, called Black Ali. Several thousand rebels were executed. Albanians and Laz – Muslim Georgians from the Black Sea – were banished from the city, and some pursued as far as Albania. Coffee-houses were closed and strict controls on entry into the city, even on urgent business, were imposed. In revenge more fires broke out, and the people demanded a change of Grand Vizier and chief eunuch. The British ambassador Lord Kinnoul wrote that 'the diabolical spirit of the people . . . is so very great that they are continually throwing papers about the streets threatening never to desist doing mischief till they have burnt all Constantinople.' In September, after another rebellion, many thousands of rebels were sewn up in sacks and drowned in the Bosphorus.[50] The 'diamond between two emeralds' was also a graveyard.

8

Ambassadors and Artists

Our high-windowed Hall has ever been open and unveiled to friend and enemy alike.
Murad III to Elizabeth I, 17 March 1579

Il n'est point de Cour où le rang des ambassadeurs soit mieux marqué qu'à la Porte.
Marquis de Ferriol, French ambassador, 26 February 1700

NO OTHER CAPITAL welcomed so many embassies. Ambassadors came to Constantinople from London and Paris, Stockholm and Samarkand, Goa and Fez. In 1628, by no means an exceptional year, ambassadors from Vienna, Warsaw, Moscow, Isfahan and Delhi arrived to pay their respects to the Sultan.[1] Power was the draw. The Ottoman Empire was at once a European, Middle Eastern, African, Black Sea, Mediterranean and Indian Ocean power. It stretched from Morocco to Mesopotamia and Poland to Yemen. It had more neighbours – more matters for dispute or negotiation – than any other state.

The presence of permanent embassies in Constantinople from the mid-sixteenth century, soon after their establishment in Western capitals, shows that, in diplomatic terms, the Ottoman Empire was part of Europe. Ambassadors there were not treated as aliens, like ambassadors in Moscow before Peter the Great and after 1918. More than elsewhere, ambassadors played a role in the internal life of the capital, as well as the external relations of the empire.

In practice, whatever zealots on both sides might claim, there was no holy war between Islam and Christianity. The theory existed; hatred for 'infidels' was frequently expressed in Constantinople and Paris. Yet such hate was applied with even greater force to heretics within Christianity or Islam – whether Protestants, or Persian believers in the Shi'i form of Islam. Despite Ottoman devotion to Persian culture, disputes over religious doctrine, geographical frontiers and the access of

Shi'i pilgrims to Mecca and Medina (issues which still poison Iran's foreign relations today) made Iran the most persistent enemy of the Ottoman Empire. Persians were known as *kizilbash* or redheads, from their distinctive red headgear. After the Safavid shahs adopted Shi'i Islam as their state religion in 1506, they started to flood eastern Anatolia with *kizilbash* missionaries who found an enthusiastic response. Persian ambassadors were the only ambassadors executed in Constantinople – in 1524, and again in 1729. In 1549, the Mufti of Constantinople declared of a war with Persia: 'Yes, it is the greatest of holy wars and a glorious martyrdom.'[2] Wars broke out with vicious regularity until the nineteenth century.

Between 1556 and 1748 embassies were occasionally exchanged with the other great Muslim monarch, the Mogul Emperor in Delhi. However there was a clash of grandeur. Both monarchs called themselves 'Caliph', 'shadow of God', 'refuge of the monarchs of the universe'. Ottoman authorities behaved with insolence to Mogul emissaries in Constantinople. The Moguls, for their part, never forgot their descent from the great Timur, who had captured the Ottoman Sultan in 1402. Mogul emperors in the sixteenth and seventeenth centuries claimed that their capital Agra was the 'abode of the Caliphate'; Constantinople was merely 'seat of the Ottoman sultanate'. Thus, despite sharing enemies such as Portugal and Persia, and despite a common interest in the safety of the *hajj* (the pilgrimage to Mecca and Medina) and the protection of central Asia from Russia, relations between the Ottoman and Mogul empires were rarely cordial and never close. Geography and ambition led the Ottoman Empire into the European state system and away from contact with other Muslim monarchies. The journey between the two empires took between six and eight months; between Constantinople and Venice three to six weeks. Neither the Mogul Empire nor Persia maintained permanent embassies in the Ottoman capital.[3]

In his account of *The Muslim Discovery of Europe* (1982) Bernard Lewis not only laments the Ottomans' superficial and inaccurate knowledge of Europe, but also finds that 'the idea of an alliance with Christian powers, even against other Christian powers, was strange and, to some, abhorrent.' In fact European alliances were among the oldest traditions of Ottoman government. Ottoman soldiers had first crossed into Europe as allies of the Byzantine Emperor and the city of Genoa. The ceremonial governing the reception of ambassadors in Constantinople not only exalted the Sultan but also honoured the ambassador. He rode to the palace on the Sultan's horses, was admitted with a numerous suite into the second courtyard of the palace, dined alone with the Grand Vizier, and received an impressive number of kaftans and, finally, the privilege of admission into the Sultan's throne room. Ambassadors were, in theory, the Sultan's guests. They received a daily living allowance from the Ottoman government and were invited to ceremonies such as the circumcision of imperial princes. Some ambassadors accompanied the Sultan on campaign.

For the Ottoman Empire never lacked European allies. Fatih had been a friend of Florence; Suleyman supported France. They enjoyed the greatest bond: a shared hatred of the House of Austria. By 1526, the head of the House of Austria, Charles V, was Holy Roman Emperor, King of Castile and Aragon and sovereign of the Low Countries; his brother Ferdinand was King of Hungary and Bohemia and Archduke of Austria. Like their descendants the Spanish and Austrian Habsburgs, they fought the Ottoman Empire for mastery of the Mediterranean, the Balkans and Hungary. Thus when François I of France was defeated and captured by Charles V at the battle of Pavia in 1525, he sent a letter pleading for help to Suleyman the Magnificent.

The first permanent French ambassador arrived in Constantinople in 1535. Thereafter the French ambassador had precedence over others; his master, in Ottoman documents, was generally called Padishah, like the Sultan. Despite arrogance and misunderstanding on both sides, the friendship lasted until 1798. On one occasion, in 1639, the Venetian ambassador threatened the Ottoman government with the wrath of Christendom. The Grand Vizier's deputy replied: 'You make me laugh when you try to frighten me with the forces of Christianity. It is a chimera with nothing terrible except its name.' However the King of France, conscious of his titles of 'Most Christian King', 'eldest son of the Church', fearful of the criticism of Catholic Europe, evaded the written alliance repeatedly requested by the Porte.

The 'union of the lily and the crescent' became one of the fixed points in European politics. Both Muslim and Christian zealots were offended. Partly to defuse criticism, the legend arose in Constantinople, as early as the sixteenth century, that the two dynasties were related through the mother of Mehmed II, daughter of a King of France. For their part, French ministers and diplomats pretended, to themselves as well as to European opinion, that the first motive of their friendship with the Ottoman Empire was to protect and propagate Catholicism within its frontiers. The increase of French commerce was the second.

The principal motive, however, was, as one ambassador was instructed in 1724, to ensure that 'the power of the Turks always remains an object of fear for the House of Austria'.[4] At the height of Franco-Habsburg hostility, the French ambassador in Constantinople arranged for French ships to refit in the port of Constantinople in 1538 and for the Ottoman fleet to winter in Toulon in 1543–4. He personally instructed Ottoman artillery during the war against Persia in 1548–50, and organized joint Franco-Ottoman naval operations against Spain in the Mediterranean in 1551–5.[5]

France was not the Ottoman Empire's only Christian ally. Since before 1453 Poland had enjoyed closer diplomatic ties with the Ottoman Empire than with France or England. In 1533 the two monarchies signed a treaty of 'perpetual friendship and alliance'. On the death of King Sigismund I in 1548, Suleyman said: 'We were like two brothers with the old king and if it please God the Merciful we will be like father and son with this king.'[6]

Thus when an ambassador went to see the Grand Vizier, in the Porte or a private kiosk, it was a meeting between men who wore different costumes, spoke different languages and followed different religions. However, they shared the same interest in monarchy, power and trade. At times, locked in negotiation in the Porte or the palace, a certain friendship could arise between the Grand Vizier and European diplomats, sealed by presents and entertainments. The Imperial ambassador Baron de Busbecq called the vizier Ali, a Christian from Dalmatia recruited into the Janissary corps, 'a kind and intelligent Turk if ever there was one. He bade me regard him as a friend on every occasion and not to be afraid to address myself to him when I needed anything. His acts fully accorded with his promises.' Ali told Busbecq that the souls of princes were like mirrors which reflected the advice of their councillors. 'Good ministers should try to conciliate all interests just as good cooks try to prepare dishes to suit everyone and not just such and such a guest.' Turks began to complain that, while the Grand Vizier was closeted with Christian ambassadors, they had to wait in the antechamber. Twenty years later, however, another Imperial ambassador called the Sultan 'the hellish wolf'. All depended on the balance of fear and need between governments at a particular moment.[7]

If Constantinople was one of the most important of diplomatic posts, it was also the most alarming. The presence of ambassadors was considered a mark of submission to the Porte – 'the asylum of kings . . . the refuge of the world', as Suleyman described it to François I.

Ambassadors were hostages, responsible to the Porte for the good behaviour of the monarch who had sent them. There was no diplomatic immunity in Constantinople.

If the Sultan was displeased by a foreign government's declaration of war, or evidence that it was surreptitiously helping an Ottoman enemy, its ambassador might be imprisoned in the Seven Towers. Such was the fate of the Imperial ambassadors in 1541, 1596 and 1716; the French in 1616, 1658, 1659, 1660 and 1798; the Venetian in 1649 and 1714; the Russian in 1768 and 1787.[8] The ambassador could not be certain that he would emerge alive – although all did. Ambassadors were also, on occasion, humiliated. Ottoman arrogance reached its height in the seventeenth century. Suleyman and Selim II had talked to ambassadors. After 1600 the Sultan hardly looked at them. Even relations with Poland deteriorated; in 1634, Murad IV drew his sword halfway out of his scabbard and rose from the throne as if to strike the Polish ambassador in the middle of his speech. The Janissaries guarding the ambassadors were sometimes called 'swine-herds'. The Janissaries themselves showed respect to the ambassador they escorted in public; they would have been punished, if they had not. When they saw him inside the embassy precincts, they rarely deigned to rise.

Regarding their capital as the centre of the universe, Ottomans wanted foreigners – craftsmen, merchants, ambassadors – to come to the city, not the other way around. They did not follow the Koranic injunction to travel in search of knowledge as far as China. The Sultan did send embassies abroad – to Paris in 1582, to invite King Henri III to the circumcision feast of his son Mehmed; to Stockholm in 1657, at the time of Sweden's invasion of Poland. Between 1384 and 1600, 145 temporary envoys, usually *cavus* (messengers) from the Sultan's household, were sent to Venice.[9]

However, the Porte regarded the maintenance of permanent embassies in foreign capitals as expensive and embarrassing. For much of the time it relied on Christian or Jewish merchants from the city for news of western Europe: thus in 1492 Andreas Milas, a merchant of Galata travelling to Italy on business, informed Bayezid II about the fates of his brother Cem and of the Muslims of Granada. Agents maintained by the Princes of Wallachia and Moldavia in Germany, Poland and Russia were another source of information. In 1774 the Grand Vizier knew of the death of Louis XV five days before the French ambassador. Foreign ambassadors resident in Constantinople were also interrogated about European politics. There were so many, and their policies were so opposed, that one of them could always be relied upon to supply the Porte with information about his colleagues. The Dutch ambassador, considered the most objective, was often consulted.[10]

The arrogance and occasional brutality of the Ottoman government towards foreign ambassadors were equalled, and sometimes surpassed, by the arrogance of the ambassadors themselves. Constantinople (like most other capitals) was the scene of status wars which took centuries to resolve. The claim of ambassadors, as personal representatives of their sovereigns, to equality of status with the Grand Vizier led them to remain standing in his reception room, in order to avoid rising on his entrance. They then sat down simultaneously. A portent of future strife was the refusal of the first Russian ambassador, in 1497, to conform to Ottoman ceremonial about wearing a kaftan, dining and communicating with the Grand Vizier rather than directly with the Sultan.[11]

At first diplomats lived in a special han in Constantinople itself. By 1600 most were established in Pera on the hill above Galata, with a direct view across the Golden Horn to the Sultan's palace. Until the mid-eighteenth century the embassies were built *alla turca* in wood, with a large upper reception hall or *sofa* off which other rooms opened. Embodiments of their country's identity, on the first modern map of Constantinople, printed by a member of the French embassy in 1786, they are simply marked *Angleterre*, *France*, *Russie*. By then Pera had begun to resemble a small western European city, built around a main street known as the *Grande Rue de Pera*.

In letters and despatches they were called palaces – Palazzo di Venezia, Palais de France, the British Palace. For, if in other capitals ambassadors lived like princes, in Constantinople they lived like kings. Each embassy was a miniature court: pages, equerries and gentlemen attendants served the ambassadors, ladies-in-waiting their wives. According to official Ottoman records, in 1750 the Dutch embassy had a staff of 38, the British 55, the French embassy 78, the Venetian 118 (including 50 priests): embassy chapels, alone of Constantinople's churches, could toll their bells. The French embassy had a throne room lined with portraits of kings of France and ambassadors, and a larger permanent staff than any other French embassy.[12]

The ambassador issued ordonnances sealed by *notre premier secrétaire, chancelier et sceller de nos armes, au Palais de France, à Pera de Constantinople,* and was often described as going to church *avec toute sa cour*. When he went to mass on Easter Sunday 1673, he was preceded by footmen,

Janissaries, dragomans and *jeunes de langue* (youths sent to Constantinople, after 1669, to study oriental languages). Since the streets were narrow and the hill on which Pera was built exceptionally steep, he did not go by carriage. He rode on horseback, escorted by four footmen *vêtus à la grecque*, followed by his household and the French merchants of the city 'in a very great number'. The embassy precincts contained, in addition to an observatory, a printing press and the church of Saint-Louis des Français, a law-court and prison. For the capitulations system, by which foreigners lived under their own laws, gave the ambassador powers of life and death over French subjects. A body sometimes swung from a gallows erected outside the main gate.[13] The French ambassador also had the power to equip a twenty-cannon ship, whose duties were to protect French shipping in the Aegean and, above all, to make money from *la course* – privateering. English vessels were frequent victims.[14]

Ambassadors visited each other in the evening in semi-royal state, escorted by guards, running footmen bearing flambeaux 'and a numerous train of attendants and servants . . . they are particularly scrupulous in observing the forms which have been established to distinguish their different degrees of rank and precedency, and according to the number of times a bell tolls it announces an ambassador, an envoy or a chargé d'affaires.'[15]

Entries of ambassadors into Constantinople, escorted by servants and guards, with bands playing and flags flying, were the acme of ostentation. A Polish embassy of 300 nobles, priests, footmen, hussars, and *heiduks* (military footmen) in flame-coloured livery with heron plumes in their caps, arrived in the city at the height of Ottoman-Polish tension, in 1677, six years before the siege of Vienna. The horses wore silver horseshoes, loose enough to drop off before the awestruck crowd. The Grand Vizier Kara Mustafa Pasha commented that the embassy was too small to besiege Constantinople, but too large to kiss the threshold of the Sublime Porte. He feared that it would be soiled by the contact of so many Christian lips. The Sultan, he added, would have no difficulty in feeding 300 Poles, when he already owned 3,000 Polish galley-slaves.[16]

Clashes between grand viziers and French ambassadors show each monarchy's determination to win the status war. Relations between the two nominal allies had deteriorated since the 1620s, in part because French ambassadors tended to treat their embassies as private business ventures. One fell into debt while trying, from Constantinople, to manage the customs farm of the Aleppo province. Others speculated, generally unsuccessfully, in the wheat trade.

French ambassadors were also crippled by *folie de grandeur*. Monsieur de Marcheville, sword in hand, charged a group of unarmed Janissaries, who had not made way for him with sufficient celerity. The Ottoman authorities declared him mad and read out (although they did not enforce) the ambassador's sentence of death in the presence of his Venetian, Dutch and British colleagues. Another ambassador, the Comte de Césy, fired so many cannon to celebrate the birth of the future Louis XIV in 1638 that the ladies of the imperial harem, visiting an imperial garden near the arsenal, took fright and thought that the Cossacks had landed – or that the Christians had risen. In the 1650s relations deteriorated further, because the French government, while professing friendship for the Ottoman Empire, supplied men and money to Venice and the Holy Roman Emperor in their wars against it. More than most of his predecessors, Louis XIV liked to pose as the champion of the Catholic Church. Koprulu Fazil Ahmed said: 'The French are perhaps old friends but we always find them with our enemies.' Too wise to declare war, he obtained revenge on another battlefield.

In conversation with the British ambassador he was 'very free and affable'. However, he addressed monosyllables or insults to the French ambassador. One French ambassador was hit on the head with a *tabouret*. When the Marquis de Nointel presented his respects to the Sultan in 1671, the messengers forced down his head so violently that he fell before the throne. Such behaviour, so revealing of the mentality of the period and the city, did not prevent the renewal of French capitulations on a favourable basis in 1673.[17]

The Ottoman government under Koprulu Fazil Ahmed, perhaps worried by the growing power of European monarchies, was particularly brutal to diplomats. A Russian ambassador who refused to prostrate himself was expelled from the imperial palace with blows; for not bending low enough, the Polish ambassador was assaulted; an Austrian dragoman received a bastinado. The power and wealth of the Ottoman Empire made most governments endure such treatment. *L'affaire du sofa*, however, almost ended relations with France.

In the seventeenth century a Grand Vizier had allowed ambassadors to sit on stools on his *sofa*, the raised platform of honour in his reception room. The most xenophobic of grand viziers, Kara Mustafa Pasha, was determined to stop this outrage. Alexander Mavrocordato said that ambassadors had won the privilege only because an indisposed Grand Vizier had been unable to hear one ambassador from the normal distance. On 2 May 1677 the Marquis de Nointel was prevented from placing his stool or *tabouret* on the sofa. He said the Grand Vizier could dispose of his seat but not his person. Ottoman officials shouted, 'Go away, go away! Leave, infidel!' For a few days the ambassador was under house arrest. Five months later Nointel agreed, under duress, to have his *tabouret* placed below the sofa. He was soon recalled by Louis XIV, who was also dismayed by the ambassador's habit of levying taxes on French merchants, to subsidize his grandiose *train de vie* at the embassy.[18]

The Comte de Guilleragues arrived as French ambassador in 1679, with instructions to ensure that Louis XIV was respected as 'the greatest, the most powerful and the most glorious of Christian princes', and to preserve 'the alliance which has existed for a long time between the two greatest and most powerful empires in the world'. France, however, continued to behave as an enemy rather than an ally. In 1681, in retaliation for acts of piracy by ships from North Africa, a French fleet bombed the island of Chios, damaging a mosque and killing 250 Ottoman subjects. Guilleragues sent information of Ottoman battle plans in secret to the empire's enemies in Malta and Poland. Rather than sit below the sofa, Guilleragues remained standing. Kara Mustafa threatened him with the Seven Towers. He replied that Louis XIV would come to open its gates for him. An *avanie* of 250,000 ducats was levied on French merchants.

However, in 1683 the Ottoman armies besieging Vienna were defeated, and Kara Mustafa himself executed. The next year, in one of those gestures which proclaim the end of a world, like the Prince of Salina in *The Leopard* inviting the local mayor to dinner as the Kingdom of the Two Sicilies collapses, ambassadors obtained the right to sit on the sofa. They won another victory at their audiences in the Sultan's throne room: most ambassadors henceforth stood firm when their escorts tried to make them prostrate themselves before the Sultan, 'and keep themselves upright with all their strength'.[19]

Austrian successes after the Ottoman defeat before Vienna in 1683 revived the friendship between France and the Ottoman Empire. Both monarchies were enemies of the House of Austria, and Louis XIV had formally forbidden ambassadors to levy taxes on French merchants. The Franco-Ottoman alliance affected most aspects of European politics. One reason why Louis XIV launched an attack across the Rhine in 1688, thereby leaving William of Orange free to invade England from the Netherlands and replace James II on the throne, was desire to relieve Habsburg pressure on the Ottoman Empire. Relations between the two monarchies were so close that one French ambassador, Monsieur de Chateauneuf (Mahout to his Ottoman friends), not only moved to Edirne in order to be near the Sultan and Grand Vizier, but generally wore Ottoman costume.

In 1699, after the conclusion of the Treaty of Carlowitz between the Ottoman and Habsburg empires, he was replaced by the Marquis de Ferriol, who had served with Ottoman armies during their campaigns against the Austrians in the 1690s. His hopes of restoring French prestige were not helped by *l'affaire de l'épée*. Possibly to embarrass his successor, Chateauneuf had recorded that he had gone to his audience with the Sultan wearing a dagger under his coat. At his audience with the Sultan on 5 January 1700, Ferriol therefore insisted on wearing a sword, as if he were a courtier at Versailles – although no one in the Ottoman palace, not even the Grand Vizier, appeared armed in the presence of the Sultan.

The ambassador ate with the Grand Vizier, put on a kaftan and proceeded towards the Sultan's throne room. The Grand Dragoman Mavrocordato, in a trembling voice, requested him to remove his sword. Ferriol swore that he would fight to the last drop of his blood if anyone tried to remove it. He considered himself to be defending the honour of his master, and of all ambassadors at the Porte. The Grand Vizier Amcazade Huseyin Pasha replied, that 'in well-regulated courts such an usurpation of ceremonial was not allowed': the voice of the courtier down the ages. For an hour different high-ranking Ottoman officials assured Ferriol that no previous French ambassador had worn a sword. He was obdurate, saying that his life was a matter of indifference the moment the dignity of an ambassador and the execution of the orders of the King of France were at stake. A few metres away, the Sultan, who had come especially from Edirne for the audience, was waiting on the throne.

Finally the Grand Vizier tried subterfuge. Ferriol was informed that he could proceed to the throne room. In a vestibule the chief doorkeeper swooped down to remove the offending weapon. The ambassador hit him in the stomach. Normally so silent, the Gate of Happiness resounded with argument. Ferriol shouted in indignation to Mavrocordato: 'Is it thus you violate the law of nations? Are we friends or are we enemies?' Trembling in fear and dismay, Mavrocordato whispered: 'Friends, but you cannot enter with your sword . . . you must adapt to the ceremonies and manners current in the country where you are.' Finally the chief white eunuch told the ambassador to retire. The ambassador and his suite removed their kaftans, took back the clock and mirror they had brought as presents and returned to the French embassy, through crowded streets. Until his departure eleven years later, Ferriol never returned to the palace.[20]

Such was his *folie de grandeur* that he ordered the construction of a kayik like the Sultan's, decorated at one end with a gilded pavilion lined with purple silk. When it first appeared in the harbour, the Bostanci Pasha ordered its destruction, and had the crew beaten. Thereafter each time the ambassador went from the embassy to the Sublime Porte, he made a lengthy journey by land around the Golden Horn, rather than cross it in a less regal vessel. Yet Ferriol loved the Ottoman world: inside the French embassy, even attending mass, he wore a turban and Ottoman costume.

One reason why Ferriol was so excitable was that an embassy in Constantinople was a position demanding exceptional skills. It attracted ambassadors of the calibre of Hoepken (Sweden), Vergennes and Thouvenel (France), Thugut (Austria), all of whom later became foreign ministers in their respective countries. In 1707 Ferriol wrote: 'I find myself here in the centre of the world. I have to deal with the affairs of Hungary, Persia, the Crimea, those of politics, religion, commerce, and questions throughout this empire, in Poland, Muscovy, Italy etc.' He also, like his colleagues, had to deal with fugitive slaves seeking asylum in his embassy (they were often smuggled on to ships in the port and then away to freedom). A later ambassador deplored: 'In Constantinople one is never finished with a piece of business. What is simple elsewhere is complex here.'

Religion was one of the principal preoccupations of a French ambassador. In the early seventeenth century Constantinople became a battleground between Protestants and Catholics, as well as between the Ottoman Empire and its enemies. The French ambassador, backing Jesuit attempts to dominate the Patriarchate, opposed the Dutch and British ambassadors, who favoured links with Protestantism. The British ambassador had the Jesuits temporarily expelled. Jesuit intrigues contributed to riots in the streets of Galata, the destruction of the Greek printing press in 1626 and the murder of the Patriarch Cyril Lucaris, on the Grand Vizier's orders, in 1638.[21]

After 1660, however, Catholics tried gentler methods. Missionaries converted Armenians into Armenian Catholics – keeping the Armenian rite but acknowledging the supremacy of the Pope. Armenians were attracted because they thereby paid their priests less, and needed to fast for forty, rather than 240, days a year. Swiftly taken under the protection of the French embassy, by 1691 Armenian Catholics rejoiced at French victories as if they were French themselves. The Armenian Orthodox were horrified. In 1707 the Armenian Patriarch Avedik launched an accusation in the Grand Vizier's divan against a priest called Gomidas, who had turned Catholic: 'There is great danger that soon all the nation will attach itself to the nation of the Franks and will constitute in your empire an interior enemy.' The priest was executed. Ferriol retaliated, in 1707, by having the Patriarch kidnapped in Constantinople, taken to France and imprisoned. In 1710 Ferriol returned to France. When a later Grand Vizier was told that Ferriol had gone mad, he replied that Ferriol had been mad when he arrived.[22] Yet the 'madness' may have been a device to enable this tactless ambassador to be withdrawn without loss of face.

After Ferriol's departure, a succession of able ambassadors helped France to resume its role as principal Ottoman ally. In 1724, at a series of conferences held in Constantinople, the French ambassador mediated peace treaties for the Ottoman Empire with both Russia and Persia. The Grand Vizier was so impressed that he proposed a league between the empire, France and Russia. That year in the Divan chamber in the second courtyard of the palace, the Grand Vizier told the new French ambassador, the Vicomte d'Andrezel,

> that I was very welcome, that the Empire of France had been for an infinite time linked by a close friendship with the Gate of Felicity which was linked with eternity . . . Truly, he said addressing himself to his Kiaya [deputy], France's affairs and our own are common and if there is any difference between us it is only Religion. I have, he continued, a particular respect for the Emperor of France with whom we are related by blood, because one of our first sultans married a princess of the royal blood of France, and I will seize all opportunities to please his ambassador and his other subjects.

Laughing, he caressed the ambassador's two sons, who had been allowed to sit on the sofa, ordered a servant to tie two embroidered handkerchiefs around their necks 'and gave a thousand blessings to the King to whom he wished a reign as long and fortunate as that of King Louis XIV'.[23]

France assisted the Ottoman war effort against Russia and Austria in 1736–9, as a result of which the Ottoman Empire recovered Belgrade. From 1740 twenty-two French gunners helped introduce modern artillery tactics into a branch of the Ottoman army, under the guidance of the brilliant and eccentric Ahmed Pasha. Born the Comte de Bonneval, he had served successively France and the Habsburg monarchy, until in 1729 he fled to the Ottoman Empire and converted to Islam. In 1731 he had been given the task of reforming the corps of bombardiers. From his house in Pera, Bonneval also advised the French and Swedish ambassadors and, in meetings at the Porte, the Grand Vizier and Reis Efendi over the course of Ottoman diplomacy. The expansion of Russia under the successors of Peter the Great was their main preoccupation.

Fear of Russia had already led the empire to befriend Charles XII of Sweden.* His successor King Frederick I had served in the Austrian army with Bonneval in the early eighteenth century. In letters sent from Constantinople to Stockholm between 1733 and 1745 (he died in 1747), Bonneval preached an Ottoman-Swedish alliance, and war against Russia and Persia, in cooperation with the Mogul Empire and the Uzbek khans. Clearly confused over his own identity, he wrote long, flattering letters to the King or the Swedish Foreign Minister, signing himself either: *le comte de bonneval; le très humble et très obéissant serviteur le comte de bonneval, beylierbey de karamanie*; or *le très humble et très obéissant serviteur, ahmet pacha, Beglierbey de Caramanie, vulgo le comte de bonneval.*[24]

At the same time the French government tried to use the count, in conjunction with the French ambassador, to persuade the Porte that it was in its interest to attack the Habsburg monarchy, with which France was at war from 1740 to 1748. Bonneval and the Porte, however, realized that France desired the entry of the Ottoman Empire into the war only in order to be able to make a better peace itself. Moreover the Porte felt humiliated by French refusal of its offer of mediation in the War of Austrian Succession in 1745.[25]

Unlike many foreign diplomats, Bonneval did not underestimate the empire, praising its well-stocked treasury and, in 1735, referring to 'an empire as solid as the Sultan's'. A treaty between the Ottoman Empire and Sweden was signed in 1740. At the Swedish ambassador's audience in 1744, the Sultan said that 'the King and Kingdom of Sweden' – a

---

*Charles XII governed Sweden from his refuge on Ottoman territory, Bender in Moldavia, between 1708 and 1715.

phrase revealing his knowledge of the King's limited power compared with the parliament's – were not in his heart like other Christian princes, 'but much more intimately'.[26]

The Comte de Vergennes was one of the most remarkable of French ambassadors to the Ottoman Porte. At his first audience in 1755, the Sultan called Louis XV 'the oldest and the most faithful ally of the Ottoman Empire'. However it was no longer an alliance between equals. The Ottoman Empire was falling behind European states in military technology and economic power. In 1766 Vergennes warned the Foreign Minister the Duc de Choiseul that, unless the empire reformed itself, it would fall into 'an abyss of misfortune, contempt and division'. However, Paris and Constantinople shared the same fears. Like Bonneval, Choiseul considered that the balance of power in Europe, and the security of France's allies Poland and Sweden, were threatened by the rise of Russia. Vergennes was ordered to persuade the Ottoman Empire to attack its northern neighbour.

In reality in early 1768 both the Sultan himself and public opinion in the capital – an increasingly potent force – were outraged by a massacre by Russian troops of Muslims on Ottoman territory, and by the continued presence of several thousand Russian troops in Poland and Warsaw. Without need of French encouragement, a 'high consultative council' declared in favour of war. On 6 October, having been kept waiting half an hour, the Russian ambassador was received by the Grand Vizier with words which, in the next two centuries, could have been said with equal truth by each of Russia's neighbours: 'Traitor! Perjurer! . . . do you not blush before God and before men at the atrocities which your compatriots are committing in a country which does not belong to you?' The ambassador was imprisoned in the Seven Towers, though later released through the intervention of the French ambassador.

The external weakness of the empire soured relations between communities in the city. At the beginning of the campaign in March 1769, Austrian diplomats watching the Sacred Banner of Muhammad paraded through the streets of Constantinople were almost lynched by a frenzied mob. As the Austrians were hurried back to Pera by their Janissary guards, the mob – for the first time – turned on local Christians. Many were killed: shops were looted.

The war was a disaster for the Ottoman Empire – and for Poland which suffered its first partition, between Austria, Prussia and Russia. In August 1769, as punishment for incompetence and corruption, the heads of the Grand Vizier, the Prince of Moldavia and the Grand

Dragoman were exposed in front of the palace. In 1770 Russian armies took Moldavia and Wallachia. A Russian fleet swept into the Aegean, encouraged a Greek rising in the Peloponnese, destroyed the Ottoman fleet near Chios and blockaded the Dardanelles. For the first time since 1656 Constantinople itself was under threat. The taverns rocked with discontent.[27]

A Hungarian protégé of Vergennes, the Baron de Tott, trusted and housed by the Sultan, helped to organize the defence of the city. He supervised the modernization of forts guarding the entrances of the Bosphorus and the Dardanelles and the construction of defensive batteries. In order to stop the Ottoman government making a disastrous peace with Russia, the French ambassador the Comte de Saint-Priest helped organize the city's wheat supply, bypassing the Russian blockade of the Dardanelles. With the help of a Scottish convert to Islam, Archibald Campbell, known to Turks by the inappropriate name of 'Ingiliz Mustafa',* Baron de Tott also established foundries for making cannon, and a school of mathematics for the navy.

The Okmeydan was a valley north of the arsenal strewn with elegant marble posts commemorating the distances the sultans had shot arrows in archery contests. From 1773 it echoed, not with the hiss of arrows but with the roar of modern artillery. Practice sessions were watched by crowds of citizens, the French ambassador and Sultan Mustafa III himself. The arrival of a Russian fleet outside the city had been prevented; but for how long? The Baron de Tott told the Reis Efendi that the next war might lead to the expulsion of the Ottomans from Constantinople. According to Tott, 'He immediately looked through the Window and, after glancing at the Coast of Asia, "there are some pleasant valleys, replied he, turning to me, with a Smile: we shall build delightful Kiosks."'

Energetic and accessible, a frequent visitor to the offices of the Porte, Mustafa III realized that the army needed radical reform. The Baron de Tott describes him as: 'Entirely devoted to business and perpetually buried among his papers . . . when his favourites represented to him that such continuous attention was injurious to his health, he answered: "My application is necessary since none of you understand how to conduct Business."'[28] In a conversation in verse with his advisers, the Sultan expressed alarm:

---

*Described by an embassy official as 'a worthy clever fellow', he had come to Constantinople 'no one knows for what'.

The world is in decay. Do not think it will [come] right with us.
Base fate has given over the state to the mean.
Now the men of rank about us are all cowards.
Nothing remains for us but immortal compassion.

The Mufti denied responsibility:

Truly the worldly state is grasped by the mean,
Order no more comes to hand by honest thinking;
Even the leaves and rain are the cowards' loot.
May the *sheriat's* waters right the garden of the state!

The Grand Vizier revealed despair:

What are these your restless world desires?
The wheel turns on its eternal cycle.
Fear not, O my heart, the coward finds a moment's joy,
The Creator gave a mean world to the mean.

The decline of the empire was reflected in the rise in the power of ambassadors in Constantinople. Both the French and Austrian ambassadors were consulted by the Grand Vizier at secret night-time meetings at kiosks on the Bosphorus, as well as during daytime audiences at the Sublime Porte. By selling honorary consulships granting protection to wealthy members of the minorities, Western ambassadors were weakening the Sultan's authority over his own subjects. In 1774, after the conclusion of peace through Austrian mediation, a Russian embassy entered Constantinople like a conquering army. The ambassador Prince Repnin was accompanied by 600 courtiers, servants and guards 'with banners unfurled, music playing, drums beating, infantry officers with rifles at shoulder arms, the cavalry with carbines on the knee, infantry with fixed bayonets, the cavalry with rifles instead of swords but without bayonets'. Seventy six-oared kayiks, and one with fourteen oars for the ambassador, conveyed the embassy from Galata to the Sublime Porte on the other side of the Golden Horn.[29]

Russia and Austria made no secret of their designs on the Ottoman Empire. In 1779, in pursuit of ancient Russian dreams, but above all her personal desire for glory, Catherine II gave her second grandson a name which was a political programme in itself: Constantine. He was given Greek nurses; and from 1780 she discussed with the Holy Roman Emperor Joseph II her 'Greek project': to divide the Ottoman Empire in Europe between them, and revive the Byzantine Empire at Constantinople under Constantine as Emperor. The Russian threat was confirmed in 1783 by her annexation of the Crimea – which Ottomans considered the gateway to Constantinople.[30] the Black Sea was no longer an Ottoman lake. Henceforth Russian interest in the Ottoman capital was sharpened by the growth of Russian trade through the Bosphorus and the Dardanelles.

Louis XVI and Vergennes, by now French Foreign Minister, reacted, in 1784, by sending as ambassador to Constantinople an erudite young courtier, the Comte de Choiseul-Gouffier. He had inspired the misanthropic epigrammatist Chamfort to write: 'He is one of those beings who by their virtues and their contact have helped to reconcile me to the human race.' For Talleyrand, he was 'the man I have loved most' – the only friend he never betrayed. He was, however, a surprising choice as French ambassador in Constantinople, since he was suspected by the Grand Vizier of being pro-Austrian. Moreover, he was a classicist in love with the Greek past. In the *Discours préliminaire* of his book of travels in Greece, published in 1782, he had called the 'Greek project' *ce noble et grand dessein* and asked : 'How can one see without indignation the stupid Muhammadan resting on the ruins of Sparta and Athens, tranquilly levy the tribute of bondage?' His British colleague, Sir Robert Ainslie, naturally felt obliged to draw the sentence to the attention of the Grand Vizier. In an expensive act of repentance, Choiseul-Gouffier substituted a different preface, printed on the embassy press. All other copies, he claimed to the Porte, were counterfeit.

Moreover the ambassador loyally followed the policy of Louis XVI and Vergennes. They were determined to support the Ottoman Empire, as Vergennes wrote, 'by all the means which will be in his [the King's] power'. Louis XVI and Vergennes had a vision fifty years ahead of their time. In his official instructions Choiseul-Gouffier was told to 'give impetus to the revolution and accustom the Turkish government to look for the instruction it needs and to obtain educated men from abroad until the nation is educated'.[31]

Choiseul-Gouffier brought a military and naval staff of thirty officers to help the Ottoman Empire modernize its armed forces (and two artists, Jean-Baptiste Hilair and Louis-François Cassas, for whom he paid out of his own pocket). In 1783 a modern military engineering school was started with French instructors; fortifications courses were sometimes attended by the Kaptan Pasha himself, and French engineers strengthened the forts defending the entrance to the Bosphorus. Works on naval manoeuvres, the art of war and Ottoman grammar were printed in Ottoman on the French embassy press. Two engineers, Kauffer and Le Chevalier, completed the first accurate map of the city in 1786. French engineers began to work in the arsenal on the Golden Horn, and helped build a modern ship, launched in the Sultan's presence on 30 May 1787.[32]

Choiseul-Gouffier proved an able diplomat who became so popular that, when there was question of his recall, the Grand Vizier wrote to Louis XVI, praising his zeal for 'the friendship which reigns between this august empire and the court of France' and asking for him to stay. Choiseul-Gouffier could keep his composure in the most testing circumstances. During one conference the Kaptan Pasha's pet lion put its head on Choiseul-Gouffier's lap. The ambassador murmured, '*Il est beau, fort beau*', and carried on talking.[33]

On 17 August 1787 the Porte, again driven by public opinion in the city, and encouraged by what Choiseul-Gouffier called *les perfides Conseils du Chevalier Ainslie*, declared war on Russia. The *ulema* in the 'consultative council' had been bribed with 80,000 Dutch ducats to give their consent. One reason for the outbreak of war was Russia's refusal to return Alexander Mavrocordato, Prince of Moldavia, whose flight from Jassy earlier that year had been organized by the Russian consul. The French government, which had recently begun a rapprochement with Russia (hence Ainslie's enthusiasm for an Ottoman attack on that empire), was dismayed.

Louis XVI had revealed his realism, and preference for peace, in a letter of 20 May 1787 to the young Selim Efendi, heir to the throne, with whom Choiseul-Gouffier was in secret communication: 'We have sent at our cost to Constantinople artisans and officers to give the Muslims demonstrations and examples of all aspects of the art of war ... War has become a very difficult science. To undertake it without being put on the level of one's adversaries is to expose oneself to certain losses.' Choiseul-Gouffier feared that war would be a disaster for French commerce in the Levant, and the thousands who lived off it in the Midi, and repeatedly warned the Reis Efendi of the likely consequences. The Ottoman official thanked him for his advice.

However, denunciations of Russian 'insolence', 'insatiable ambition' and 'revolting bad faith' prevailed over realistic assessment of the balance of power. Already the fall of the Ottoman Empire was, at least as a rhetorical device, anticipated at the Sublime Porte. According to Choiseul-Gouffier the Reis-ul Kuttab told him that, if God had decided on 'the ruin of this empire, at least the Muslims were prepared to perish with energy and to prefer a glorious death to the point of degradation to which they were to be brought, to the long and painful tortures which the perfidy of the Russians was preparing for them'.[34]

French officers were withdrawn from Constantinople in mid-1788, six months after Austria had also declared war on the Ottoman Empire. The war and the outbreak of violent revolution in France in 1789 ended Louis XVI's plan for peaceful revolution in the Ottoman Empire. The war ended in 1792 with the Ottomans' defeat and the loss of the great Black Sea fort of Ochakov. The frontier of Russia was moving nearer to Constantinople.

On 24 September 1792, after the overthrow of Louis XVI, Choiseul-Gouffier resigned as French ambassador, expressing his regret, gratitude and 'devotion to the Sublime Porte'. He barricaded himself in the Palais de France and awaited events surrounded by Albanian guards. After a vote by the French merchants of the city accepting the French republic, he left in 1793, with his antiquities and the embassy silver, for St Petersburg, where he became Director of the Imperial Library and President of the Academy of Fine Arts.[35]

In 1795, three years after losing the French monarchy, the Ottoman Empire lost another ally. The last remnant of the Polish commonwealth was partitioned between Austria, Prussia and Russia. For years the last official relic of Poland's existence was the former Polish embassy dragoman in Constantinople. A former Janissary guard at the Polish embassy conducted him to and from the Sublime Porte. Ottomans said: 'There is a ghost of a *cavus* [guard] fulfilling his duties to a ghost of a dragoman of a dead embassy.'[36] The old European order, whose divisions had helped the empire to rule a quarter of the continent for four centuries, was disappearing. The empire was now surrounded by neighbours as expansionist as the empire itself had once been.

The embassies in Pera would have been able to achieve little without the swarm of spies, interpreters, doctors, missionaries, and merchants living in the surrounding side-streets. The embassies were the centre of their world, providing justice, protection, employment, entertainment and news. In Constantinople there was no court in the Western style, with a ritual of receptions signalling to the outside world who was or was not presentable. The embassies filled the gap. Until 1914 failure to be invited to embassies, for the city's Christians, was social death. One nineteenth-century visitor wrote:

> The society of Pera is as brilliant as that of which I have just written [Pera low life] is hideous. In no place in the world, except Paris, are so many savants, artists, travellers and men of taste of every kind found together . . . the large

receptions offer a charming mixture of the most diverse national qualities, blended with an exquisite taste and amiability. The soirees of the palais de Russie were above all magnificent; those of the ambassadors of France and England were distinguished by more taste and less richness; but the formal dinners at the Austrian embassy effaced all else.[37]

Ottomans also frequented the embassies of Pera. The French traveller and unofficial diplomat, Nicolas de Nicolay, noted in the 1550s that Ottoman officials enjoyed dining with the French ambassador, Monsieur d'Aramon: 'as much for the delicious meats as for several kinds of good wines, malmsey and muscat [from the Greek islands] with which they filled themselves so abundantly that most often while returning to their houses the largest streets of the city were very narrow for them, so well do they know how to perfume themselves with such sweet septembral and bacchic liquor.' Both in the seventeenth and eighteenth centuries French ambassadors to Constantinople visited the Mufti: one Mufti asked that the son of the Marquis de Villeneuve, French ambassador in 1729–40, be named 'Constantinopolitan', after the city. When the Russian ambassador was entertained to lunch by the Grand Vizier at the Sublime Porte in 1775, he was asked to behave as master in his own house. He watched 'dancing in the Asiatic tradition and that of the various Greek islands', and boys singing Arabian songs. Whereas most Ottomans still ate with their fingers, he used utensils of gold set with diamonds. Five other banquets and entertainments followed, provided by five different officials in their residences.[38]

Ottomans attended even those receptions given by a victorious enemy. At a ball in honour of St Catherine's day, the feast-day of the Empress, at the Russian embassy in 1793, a Russian diplomat noted:

The apartments were barely big enough to contain this brilliant reunion. All the women were covered in diamonds and jewels . . . Our old friend the Kapici Pasha [head of the palace gate-keepers] and several other Turks of distinction were present at this reception . . . Seeing the sparkle of the delicious wines they were offered, they began to drink to the health of the Prophet and ended by partaking in all the pleasures of this fete until the end.

In the summer, the embassies, like other wealthy inhabitants, left to enjoy the cooler climate of the villages of Buyukdere, Tarabya and Belgrade up the Bosphorus. Life was more relaxed: one traveller found Tarabya 'a place of great gaiety'. At times there were, according to a British officer, so many Greeks serenading their mistresses at night that sleep was impossible: it seemed that 'the deity of love had made it his favourite residence.' A few Turks joined in the Sunday reunions with Greeks, Armenians and Jews, when 'everyone who belonged to society' met under lime-trees in a plain outside Buyukdere.[39]

Espionage, inevitably, was one of the main occupations of the embassies. In the sixteenth century the church of St Francis in Galata was a favourite meeting place for Venetian diplomats and their agents, since Janissary guards did not deign to enter a church: under cover of worship, they could talk unheeded. Discovery, however, was fatal. On 26 April 1571, during the war of the 'Holy League' of Venice, Spain and the Papacy against the empire, the impaled body of a Venetian spy, Fra Paolo Biscotto, was raised on a pole outside the window of the Bailo of Venice, and left to rot – *pour encourager les autres*.[40]

A century later Count Jacob Colyer, Dutch representative at the Sublime Porte from 1683 until his death in 1725, was a 'perfect master' of Ottoman and Greek. Cantemir wrote: 'As he freely entertains at his house the courtiers, that are extremely greedy of wine, there is nothing so secret in the Vizir's court but what he can sist [extract] from them by that means.' The Imperial ambassador in the mid-eighteenth century, Heinrich Christoph Penkler, also spoke excellent Ottoman and employed paid informers at every level of Ottoman society and in foreign embassies. His successor Baron Thugut was himself recruited by the French ambassador the Comte de Saint-Priest to work for France in 1771 – although since the information he supplied was of little value, his treason may have been a double-bluff. Thugut complained that in Pera secrets did not last more than a quarter of an hour: 'Everyone seems to know everyone else's comings and goings.'[41] They still do.

The inhabitants of Pera were called not Perotes but pirates. A popular song went: *Pera, Pera, dei scelerati il nido* ('Pera, Pera, the nest of scoundrels'). The gossip of Pera ladies sitting round the *tandour*, or brazier, was said to be worse than that of the worst French provincial town.[42] However Pera also had the allure of cosmopolitanism. Until this century many of its inhabitants could speak five or six languages. In 1718 Lady Mary Wortley Montagu compared it to the tower of Babel:

In Pera they speak Turkish, Greek, Hebrew, Armenian, Arabic, Persian, Russian, Slavonian [Serbo-Croat], Wallachian, German, Dutch, French, English, Italian, Hungarian; and, what is worse, there is ten of these languages spoke in my own family. My grooms are Arabs, my footmen, French,

English and Germans, my Nurse an Armenian, my housemaids Russians, half
a dozen other servants Greeks; my steward an Italian; my Janissaries Turks.

Pera attracted Jews, Orthodox and Protestants as well as Catholics. It
was a city where, more even than in Vienna, Rome or Valetta, capital of
the Knights of Malta, Europe was visible and audible.[43]

Europe was a reality not only in the streets but in the careers of the
Catholics of Pera. For six centuries the name of the Testa family was
rarely absent from the annals of the city's diplomacy. Originally merchants and notaries, they had arrived from Genoa in the thirteenth
century. One Testa is said to have signed the treaty by which the
Byzantines recovered Constantinople from the Latins in 1261. In 1436
Tomaso de Testa and his wife Luchineta di Spinola were buried in the
church of St Paul (the present Arap Cami of Karakoy: their gravestone
is now in the Archaeological Museum). In 1513 Andrea de Testa helped
pay for the rebuilding of the church of St Francis after the great earthquake of 1509; in 1561 his son Angelo witnessed the donation of the
church of St Peter and St Paul to the Dominicans. Like three other
members of his family in the next three hundred years,* he was Prior of
the Magnifica Communità di Pera – the body of twelve counsellors
which managed the affairs and churches of the Catholic community of
about 500 people. Like other prominent families, the Draperis, the
Salvago, the Testa lived in considerable splendour, in Galata, beside the
Franchini Han.[44]

From the second half of the seventeenth century, since they knew
Ottoman, Italian, Greek and other languages, the Testa began to act as
interpreters for Western embassies. In the eighteenth century they
made the decisive change in status from locally hired interpreters to
subjects and ambassadors of European governments. Gaspard Testa
(1684–1758) was dragoman of the Dutch embassy. His son Jacques,
Jonkheer de Testa (1725–1804), became Dutch chargé d'affaires in
Constantinople. His descendants became Dutch and served the
Netherlands in the family profession of diplomacy, in Constantinople,
Tokyo, Madrid and elsewhere; one branch of the family lives in the
Netherlands today. Thus the family's most precious possession, the
thorn from the Crown of Thorns saved by Francesco Testa from a fire
which destroyed the church of St Francis in 1660, is no longer seen in

---

*Bartolomeo Testa in 1568, Gaspare Testa in 1651, Bartolomeo de Testa in 1778–92.
Francesco Testa was sub-prior in 1683.

religious processions in Istanbul but is sealed in a niche in the church of St Agnes in Amsterdam.

An austere bachelor when he arrived in Constantinople, Vergennes had fallen in love with Anne Viviers, widow of Francesco Testa, a merchant cousin of Jacques de Testa. She bore Vergennes two illegitimate children. In 1760, five years after his arrival, he risked his career by promising, in writing, to marry her. Seven years later, to the horror of the French government and Pera society, he fulfilled his promise at the church of Saint-Louis des Français. He wrote to the Baron de Tott: 'I am very happy with my new state; my wife, who has the honour to be known to you, is dearer than she has ever been to me and I adore my children.' Louis XV, in shock, recalled him from Constantinople. Louis XVI proved more tolerant. Thus as Madame la Comtesse de Vergennes, wife of the Minister of Foreign Affairs, an elderly Perote with 'a past' had the duty of presenting foreign princesses at the court of Versailles.

Like the Mavrocordato, the Testa refused to be imprisoned in one nationality. They were an extreme example of a once common phenomenon: Europeans who regarded a country as a career rather than a cause. Hereditary diplomats, they worked in Constantinople because it was a centre of diplomacy as, in the eighteenth century, foreigners worked in Paris because it was the centre of fashion (intellectual, artistic and vestimentary). The Testas' primary loyalties were to the city of city. Constantinople, the Catholic religion, and whichever power they were serving at the time. In addition to the Netherlands, Testas served, at different times, France, Sweden, Austria, Prussia, Poland, Venice and the Ottoman Empire (visitors shocked by Perote cosmopolitanism said that they knew the languages of five nations and had the soul of none). Constantinople's relaxed attitude to nationality, class and sex shows that it was at once very traditional and remarkably modern.

Carlo de Testa (1753–1827) began his career as a dragoman of France, where he had been educated. He boasted that he was *aussi bon patriote qu'aucun français* but, like the Sultan and the Porte, was horrified by the execution of Louis XVI in 1793, and resigned his post. Thereafter he served, first Sweden, then Austria, as First Dragoman. Baron Ignace de Testa (1812–73), Tuscan chargé d'affaires in Constantinople, edited the *Recueil des traités de la Porte Ottomane avec les puissances etrangères depuis 1536 jusqu'à nos jours*. Begun in 1864, the eleventh and last volume was published in 1911 – eleven years before the work's subject, the Sublime Porte, ceased to exist. Unfortunately no private letters, diaries or memoirs have been discovered in – or released from – the family archives. The Testa view of Ottoman diplomacy would be very different from that enshrined in the archives of European ministries and the Sublime Porte. The dragomans of Pera believed that they were the incarnation of diplomatic skill. Ambassadors were puppets, manipulated at the dragoman's wish.[45]

The Pisani were another famous diplomatic family of Pera. They claimed to be a younger branch of the Venetian noble family of that name, which came to Constantinople from Crete after its conquest by the Ottomans in 1669. They soon became dragomans for the British embassy, one Pisani receiving the title 'His Majesty's Translator for Oriental Languages' in 1749. It was well deserved. In 1754, within fifteen days of the arrival of Louis XV's secret letter to the Sultan asking him to join the *secret du roi*, the secret anti-Russian alliance linking France, Sweden and Poland, the British ambassador had obtained copies through Pisani.[46]

The almost daily letters to Sir Robert Liston in 1794 of a First Dragoman called Bartolomeo Pisani, famous for the excellence both of his manners and his English, are those of an experienced estate agent to a landowner arriving at a recently acquired property, where he does not speak the language. Pisani tells Liston when to write to the Sublime Porte, relates news of other ambassadors, the movements of ships and European politics, discusses visits to the Grand Vizier and the Kaptan Pasha. Phrases recur like 'if Your Excellency pleases', followed by a suggestion, or: 'I shall always think it a duty to convey to Your Excellency any intelligence I may receive which may affect His Majesty's Service or be interesting for Your Excellency's private information.' The daily and financial business, as opposed to the high policy, of the embassy was in Pisani's hands.

The following letter of 24 October 1794, sent from Pera to the ambassador who was still in the suburb of Belgrade, shows Pisani's confident, managing style, and the close relations of friendly embassies with the Ottoman government:

Dear Sir,
    I do myself the honour of acquainting Your Excellency for your information that the Captain Pashaw having previously obtained the accustomary permit from the Sultan to return with his Fleet to the Arsenal; his own Kirlanghiz with some other small Craft have already left the Canal [the Bosphorus], and anchored before the Divanhane this morning. The large

ships will follow between this and Sunday next when, I am told, the Pashaw will take up his residence at his office, without the formality of a publick ingress, as generally observed on the return of the Fleet from a distant Expedition.

Monday or Tuesday, therefore, your Excellency might, if you please, send to pay him the usual compliment on his supposed return to the Capital for the Winter Season.

I shall keep in Town to receive your Excellency's Commands in the event, that it may be your wish to be among the first in paying His Excellency that usual act of publick attention.

I understand that an excellent good intelligence passes between Hussein and the new Prime Minister.

I have the honour to be with the truest respect and very sincere Attachment,

Dear Sir,
Your Excellency's
most devoted and much
obliged humble Servant
B: Pisani.[47]

He was devoted to his profession. He served two years in prison in 1807–9 when Britain and the Ottoman Empire were at war. Lady Hester Stanhope, Pitt's niece who wintered in Constantinople in 1810–11 on her way to Lebanon, reported that Pisani had 'talent and integrity and [is] more feared and loved than His Excellency'. Lady Liston admired Pisani's skill in interpreting between her husband and the Kaptan Pasha: 'I have been surprised to observe upon several occasions how very lively these conversations are, by means of interpreters who often enter into the humour of them.'[48] When the British ambassador Sir Stratford Canning came to visit him on his sick-bed on 8 September 1826, the excitement was fatal. The dragoman died as he took off his nightcap. Of his nephew, Stratford Canning's dragoman Frederick Pisani, who retired in 1877, a later British ambassador Sir Austen Layard, the archaeologist of Assyria, wrote: 'He actually seemed to live in the Chancery, in the midst of despatches and papers of which he was the most trustworthy and jealous guardian and in which his whole existence, all his pleasures and hopes seemed to be concentrated . . . a more simple-minded, trustworthy and honest creature never lived.'[49]

Long after the wars, treaties and trade agreements contrived in the embassies of Constantinople have been forgotten, their cultural patron-

213

age remains one of the glories of European diplomacy. Their protection made the foreign scholar asking questions, or the artist drawing views, familiar figures in the streets of the city. The Baron de Busbecq bought Greek manuscripts from the Sultan's doctor Moses Hamon for the Imperial Library in Vienna. His own letters (although, like Lady Mary Wortley Montagu's, reworked at a latter date) remain a classic account of the empire at the end of the reign of Suleyman the Magnificent. Like those of Lady Mary Wortley Montagu, they are free of what Edward Said has called 'the essence of orientalism': 'the distance between Western superiority and oriental inferiority'. They exaggerate the virtues of Ottoman society, in order to criticize their own, and are less condescending than many Western accounts of other Western countries. Busbecq praises the discipline of the Ottoman army and the career open to the talents. Lady Mary Wortley Montagu praises the ease and elegance of Ottoman life, the practical advantages of Islam, the freedom of Muslim women and the beauty of their embroidery.

A former Venetian Bailo, Giovanni Batista Donado, wrote the first study of Ottoman literature in a Western language, *Della letteratura de' Turchi* (Venice, 1688). Count Marsigli, author of the most comprehensive account of the organization, weapons, discipline and uniforms of the Ottoman army and navy, *L'Etat militaire de l'Empire Ottoman* (2 vols., The Hague–Amsterdam, 1732), had lived in Donado's embassy in 1679–80, at a time when it was in effect a school of Ottoman studies. His work was based on Ottoman records, which he obtained through intellectuals such as Huseyin Efendi Hezarfenn. The Abbé Toderini was able to write another, longer history of Ottoman literature, because he lived between 1781 and 1786 *alla splendida corte di S.E. Agostino Garzoni, Bailo Veneto alla Porta Ottomana.*

The French embassy, more than others, provided a framework for scholarly and artistic exploration of the Ottoman Empire. In this case Edward Said's thesis that orientalism was essentially a projection of Western will 'to govern over the Orient' is especially misleading. For France was the power which, for reasons of *realpolitik*, was most interested to strengthen the Ottoman Empire. Nicolas de Nicolay accompanied a French embassy to Constantinople in 1551. While his book *Discours et histoire véritable des navigations, pérégrinations et voyages faits en Turquie* (Lyons, 1567) owes much to previous travellers' accounts, the woodcuts with which it was illustrated were probably the first accurate visual images of the Turks to reach the West. The treaty of 1604 between Henri IV and Ahmed I was the second book printed in

Ottoman, in Paris in 1615, thanks to a cultured Ottoman-speaking French ambassador Savary de Brèves, who had brought back from Rome Ottoman, Arabic, Persian and Syriac printing types (the first book, printed in Rome in 1587, was a work on Euclidean principles of commerce). However Savary de Brèves did occasionally advocate the destruction of the Ottoman Empire.[50]

The Swedish embassy inspired the chief literary monument to the diplomatic life of the city. Its author was an Armenian Catholic of Constantinople, born in 1740, called Mouradgea. A dragoman at the Swedish embassy from 1763 to 1782, he lived in a kiosk in the garden of the Palais de Suède. In 1780 he was ennobled by Gustavus III as Mouradgea *d'Ohsson*, from his Turkish sobriquet *tossun* or stout. He was a historian as well as a diplomat. The Swedish ambassador, Gustaf Celsing, persuaded him to write a description of the empire rather than, as originally planned, a history of the reign of Selim II. The result, *Tableau général de l'Empire Ottoman* (3 vols., Paris, 1787–1820, later translated into English, German and Russian), is just as useful for study of the Ottoman Empire, as the monument of the French invasion, Denon's *Description de l'Egypte*, for study of Egypt. It is a survey, with 233 illustrations, of every aspect of the empire: Islam, the palace, costume, government, army, the legal system, morality, the harem.

Mouradgea d'Ohsson spent twenty-two years on research, enjoying access to government registers, and conversations with ministers and with husbands of former inmates of the harem: he later wrote that it cost him more money and effort to learn about the imperial harem than about all the rest of the empire. He hoped both to lessen popular prejudice about the East in the West, and to bring Western knowledge to the East. He called for a new Suleyman the Magnificent who would 'maintain more intimate relations with the Europeans, adopt their tactics, in fact absolutely change the face of their empire'. The book was dedicated to Gustavus III, an ally of the Ottoman Empire in its war against Russia in 1788–90, and printed in Paris (where Mouradgea lived, to supervise publication, between 1784 and 1791) at the *Imprimerie de Monsieur*, the future Louis XVIII, like most Bourbons a friend of the Ottomans.[51]

Another of the city's learned dragomans was Joseph von Hammer-Purgstall, who worked in the Imperial embassy as a *sprachknabe* (language student), and later as an interpreter, from 1793 to 1799 and 1802 to 1806. Often wearing Ottoman dress, he learnt Arabic, Greek, Persian and Ottoman in Constantinople, visited its monuments, and missed no chance to buy books and manuscripts for his history of the Ottoman Empire – still the best by a foreign historian. Remembering the library where he researched, he later wrote: 'In no other library where I later worked did I work with such zeal and uplift as I did in the library of Abdulhamid.'[52]

Embassies provided the framework for the artistic commemoration, as well as scholarly investigation, of Constantinople. Before 1600 ambassadors commissioned from Western or Turkish artists albums of drawings and sketches of the city's political hierarchy, daily life, costumes and ceremonies: the Sultan in procession, scenes of wrestling, archery, whirling dervishes.[53] Thereafter they preferred pictures. Moscow and Madrid were exotic. Vienna, Venice and Rome were imposing. Paris was the capital of European culture. Only Constantinople, however, inspired so many 'embassy pictures'.* They were not only tributes to the power and glamour of the city and to the desire of ambassadors to provide visual proof of their success to contemporaries and descendants. They also, either consciously or unconsciously, filled a gap.

There were no great picture collections in Constantinople. Religious tradition prevented either the sultans or the viziers from commissioning or purchasing pictures, as opposed to calligraphy or illuminated manuscripts. Christan families such as the Mavrocordato or the Testa showed neither the inclination nor the courage to collect pictures in Constantinople (although the former did so in Wallachia and Moldavia). Thus the best pictures of seventeenth- and eighteenth-century Constantinople hang not in the city itself but in 'Turkish rooms' in Swedish manor houses, Austrian castles and French chateaux, belonging to ambassadors' descendants.

The favourite subject is the ambassador's reception in the imperial palace by the Sultan and the Grand Vizier – although some pictures depict particular events such as imprisonment in the Seven Towers, or the renewal of capitulations. Two seventeenth-century Imperial ambassadors, Siegmund von Herberstein and Freiherr von Kuefstein, and Vergennes and his wife a hundred years later, had themselves painted in Ottoman costume. All three ambassadors also commissioned spectacular pictures of scenes from daily life, such as a wrestling match or a visit to the bazaar, as well as views of the city.

---

*However, between 1703 and 1741, Carlevarijs, Joli, Richter and Canaletto painted spectacular ceremonial pictures of ambassadors arriving by gilded barge at the Doge's Palace in Venice on the way to present their credentials.

The principal embassy artist was Jean-Baptiste Vanmour. Born in Valenciennes, he arrived in Constantinople at the age of 28, in 1699, in the suite of the Marquis de Ferriol, and remained there until he died in 1737. Clearly in love with the city, he wrote that he wanted to '*m'instruire à fond de toutes les particularités qui concernent les mœurs et usages des turcs*', and was permitted to accompany ambassadors to their official reception. His formal scenes of the Sultan or the Grand Vizier and their suites, signed and dated 1711, or of the reception of the French ambassador in 1724 and of the Dutch in 1727, were much admired for their vivacity and naïvety. Contrasts of faces and costumes are piquant. Placid Dutchmen walk past Janissaries rushing for pilav: the French ambassador's minuscule sons in full-bottomed wigs are addressed by a turbaned Grand Vizier. Vanmour's pictures were so appealing that they inspired similar representations, by less skilled hands, of the reception of other (British, Polish, Swedish, Venetian) ambassadors. Many of his views of Constantinople were commissioned by the Dutch ambassador Cornelius Calkoen and, having been kept together as a collection by the terms of his will, now hang in the Rijksmuseum.

Ferriol may have been an absurd ambassador. Lovers of Constantinople will always be grateful that in 1707 he commissioned Vanmour to paint one hundred pictures of different officials and races in their respective costumes: the chief eunuch; a court messenger; a Jewish woman taking goods to Turkish harems; a Turkish man cutting himself to show his love for his mistress; the Oecumenical Patriarch; the Armenian martyr Gomidas; Albanians, Bulgarians, Greeks, Wallachians, Persians, Arabs. In France, Ferriol helped arrange the publication of one hundred prints of these pictures: *Recueil de cent estampes représentant différentes nations du Levant* (1714). So great was the appetite for knowledge about the Ottoman Empire that it was quickly reprinted in French, translated into German, Italian, English and Spanish, and became the principal source of *turqueries* for artists such as Watteau, Guardi, Van Loo. In official recognition of Vanmour's talents he was granted the unique, but despite his protests unpaid, post of Peintre ordinaire du Roi en Levant in 1725. When he died on 22 January 1737 the household of the French ambassador and 'the whole French nation' attended his funeral in the church of Saint-Benoit in Galata.[54]

The most impressive cycle of embassy pictures is in Biby in the heart of Sweden, the property of the Celsing family. They transform a rust-coloured Swedish manor-house into a shrine to eighteenth-century Constantinople. Two bachelor brothers Gustaf and Ulrik Celsing, sons of an agent of Charles XII in the Sublime Porte in 1709–11, served in the Swedish embassy as secretaries, residents and ambassadors between 1745 and 1773 and 1756 and 1780 respectively. They both knew Ottoman and, thanks to the shared fear of Russia, were able to keep Ottoman-Swedish relations as close as in the days of Ahmed Pasha. Ulrik Celsing sent back to Sweden, by land and sea, an important collection of oriental manuscripts, which he left to Uppsala University Library on condition that it was kept in a cupboard inscribed *Collectio Celsingiana Librorum Orientalium*, and 102 pictures of Constantinople.

The most remarkable are neither the scenes of their reception by the Sultan, nor the portraits of different craftsmen and officers of the city, nor the family tree where Ottoman sultans are shown literally grafted on to a tree. They are the twenty-five hypnotizing panoramas of the Golden Horn, the city, the palaces and boats of the Bosphorus and, above all, the blue and green kiosks and gilded pavilions of Sa'adabad, of which they are the best visual record. The pictures are unsigned; the artist may have been A. Steen, who dedicated some drawings of Constantinople, also in the Celsing collection, to *Monsieur Gustaf de Celsing, Président du Conseil Royal de Commerce de S.M. le roy de Suède, Envoye Extraordinaire à la Porte Ottomane et Chevalier de l'Ordre Polaire.*[55]

The European embassies in Constantinople sponsored archaeologists as well as painters and writers. The city's past as a Roman imperial capital might have been expected to contribute to its fascination. In the eighteenth century classical ruins, such as the Forum and the Colosseum, were the principal attraction of its sister-city Rome for foreign visitors and artists. In Constantinople, however, admiration and excavation were equally impossible. As early as the 1540s a French scholar, Pierre Gilles, had observed that the area within the old Roman walls of the city was almost entirely covered with modern houses: 'During the time I lived in Constantinople [1544–7], had I not seen so many ruined churches and palaces and their foundations, since filled with Mahometan buildings, so that I could hardly discover their former layout, I would not so easily have guessed what destruction the Turks had accomplished since they took the city.' With his own eyes he saw the great bronze equestrian statue of Justinian carried into 'the melting-house' – for transformation into Ottoman cannon. Classical pillars were used in the construction of Ottoman mosques. Emperors' tombs were placed as trophies in the garden of the Sultan's palace. Visitors to Constantinople came for the Ottoman present not the Roman past.[56]

However, the archaeological treasures in the rest of the empire – successively ruled and built on by Assyrians, Greeks and Romans – became a major preoccupation of diplomats stationed in the city. Their passion for antiquities was so great that a play was performed at the French embassy called *L'Antiquaire français*. Choiseul-Gouffier employed a French merchant, Louis-François-Sebastien Fauvel, to explore – and pillage – the antiquities of Greece. British ambassadors, oddly reluctant to commission pictures, showed a greater appetite for antiquities. In the 1620s, working for the Earl of Arundel, Sir Thomas Roe stole segments of the Golden Gate, which are now in the Ashmolean Museum, Oxford. The French invasion of Egypt in 1798, and the alliance against France signed in January 1799 between the empire, Russia and Britain, placed the British ambassador, Lord Elgin, in a position to surpass Choiseul-Gouffier. Owing to the skill of Bartolomeo Pisani and the 'friendship, sincerity, alliance and good will subsisting *ab antiquo* between the Sublime and ever durable Ottoman Court and that of England and which is on the side of both those Courts manifestly increasing', Lord Elgin obtained a firman to excavate and remove fragments from the Parthenon. Greatly exceeding its original terms, he took sculpture from any section of the Parthenon, and any building in Athens, he wished. 'The Elgin Marbles' arrived in London in 1806. The controversy thus generated, which lasts to this day, owes its origin to an embassy in Constantinople.[57]

9

The Janissary's Frown

The Sultan trembles at a Janissary's frown.

Lady Mary Wortley Montagu, April 1717

CONSTANTINOPLE WAS A battleground not only between different embassies, nationalities and religions, but also between the Sultan and his guard. Between them was a shifting balance of fear and need, power and weakness, blood and gold – until, at the end of the empire, the last Sultan fled under protection of a foreign guard. The cause of the soldiers' power was the absence of independent civilian institutions. In an absolute monarchy barriers against political intervention by the armed forces are weakened. As Suetonius wrote of the Praetorian Guard: *'Quis custodiet ipsos custodes?'* (Who is to guard the guards themselves?) On eight occasions in Russia between 1725 and 1825, units in the Imperial Guard decided who should rule as monarch or regent. Napoleon also felt the danger. He said: 'Palace troops are terrifying and become more dangerous as the sovereign becomes more autocratic', and advised other monarchs to avoid them.[1]

The principal military force in Constantinople were the Janissaries. The Janissaries were composed of 196 *ortas*, or units, in theory of 100 men each. In the sixteenth century they formed one of the most effective armed forces in Europe, and certainly the best fed, enjoying regular rations of soup, mutton and rice. Food played such a central part in their life that the commander of each *orta* had the title *corbaci*, or soup cook, and as a sign of his rank wore a soup ladle hanging from his belt. Each *orta* had its own flag, displaying such symbols as a lion, a mosque, a pulpit or a ship. Janissaries wore uniforms of blue cloth and a majestic pleated white head-dress like a giant sleeve, sometimes decorated with plumes and jewels. When Janissaries bowed their heads at the same time, they were compared to a field of ripe corn rippling in the breeze.

The sixtieth, sixty-first, sixty-second and sixty-third *ortas* composed the Sultan's personal bodyguard, known as *solaks*. Their ample plumed head-dresses made the Sultan appear to be floating on clouds as he rode to mosque. Other *ortas* also had specific palace duties. The sixty-fourth was responsible for the Sultan's hunting dogs, the sixty-ninth for his greyhounds and falcons. Janissaries also, with the Bostancis, acted as the policemen, fire watchers and customs officials of the capital. They were responsible for checking the identity of immigrants coming into the city, or expelling recent immigrants when the Sultan considered the city overcrowded. The complex of Janissary barracks between the Suley-maniye mosque and the Golden Horn was one of the power-centres of the city, together with the palace, the Porte, the mosques, the patri-archate and the embassies. Their supreme commander, the Aga of the Janissaries, lived there in a palace so splendid that Suleyman the Magnificent once sighed: 'If I could be Aga of the Janissaries for just forty days!'

Compared to the noisy and unruly troops of Western monarchs before 1700, Janissaries were at first models of sobriety. Their pay-day on Tuesdays, every three months, was a solemn occasion in the second courtyard of the palace, witnessed by the Grand Vizier and on occasion a foreign ambassador. The money was placed in small leather bags and given out to each company in turn: at the end the senior officers entered the Divan and kissed the corner of the Grand Vizier's cloak.[2]

A web of ritual, apparently trivial, in reality expressive of the mar-riage between a ruler and his guard, brought the distant and majestic figure of the Sultan into the Janissaries' world. The Sultan enrolled in the sixty-first *orta*, received its pay and returned it, heavily augmented, to the commander. After his inauguration he visited the Janissary bar-racks saying: 'We will meet again at the Red Apple' – Rome or Vienna. When he passed the barracks, he paused to drink a glass of sherbet, and returned the emptied glass filled with gold to his grateful comrades. He often watched Janissaries shooting, drilling and wrestling in the big square near the mosque of Sultan Bayezid, and then handed out prizes. Every Ramadan the ladies of his harem prepared trays of baklava for them. The Janissary corps was repeatedly flattered in imperial proclamations. In 1750, for example, they were called 'a great corps composed of brave champions of the faith, on which rests the blessing of him who is shadow of God on earth and the consideration of the men of God . . . our august and numberless favours tend daily to augment their dignity and consideration.'[3]

Below the surface harmony, however, Janissaries had a vested interest in changing sultans, since a new Sultan meant an accession 'bonus'. In the absence of a representative institution like a parliament or senate, the Janissaries sometimes acted as an equivalent. They not only, on occasion, expressed the social, economic and political discontents of the populace but might also be manipulated by viziers or *ulema* as a means to achieve their political ends. Years later when one minister was asked his opinion about the dissolution of the Janissaries, he said: 'But then how are we going to stop any lion [Sultan]?' Janissary rebelliousness was increased by the corps' close affiliations with the Bektashi order of dervishes which had Shi'i sympathies.[4]

The booming sound of Janissaries overturning their pilav cauldrons was a signal of mutiny. The cauldrons were then set up on the Etmeydan, a large open space near their barracks, and used as rallying points. The cry 'Long live the brother!', 'We want the brother!' was the Ottoman equivalent of politicians deserting the King's court for that of the Prince of Wales in eighteenth-century England. Both reminded the monarch unpleasantly of a dynastic alternative to his rule.

On the accession of Selim II in 1566 Janissaries did not receive the customary bonus. At Belgrade, possibly with the encouragement of the Grand Vizier Sokollu Mehmed Pasha, who was dismayed by the influence of the new Sultan's courtiers, they insulted the corpse of Suleyman the Magnificent and threatened his son Selim II. On 9 December the new Sultan's procession entered Constantinople. It came to a halt by the Edirne gate since the front of the column had stopped in the middle of the city, and refused to advance further. The viziers asked what was wrong. 'A hay cart is blocking the way and stopping the procession' was the Janissaries' reply – their cryptic expression of discontent. The Kaptan Pasha said: 'Soldiers! This is disgraceful!' They shouted: 'What is it to do with you, poor sailor?' and beat him up. Finally the Grand Vizier and his officials threw them coins. The procession started again. When it reached the first courtyard of the palace, Selim II promised: 'The gratuity and the rise in wages are granted in accordance with the usage transmitted to me by my ancestors.' Thus at the height of Ottoman power, the son of Sulyeman the Magnificent had had to purchase his way to his own palace.[5]

The decline of the *devshirme* system of recruiting Janissaries from Christian families in the Balkans and Anatolia decreased the Janissaries' dependence on the Sultan and increased their unreliability. From the mid-sixteenth century the flower of Balkan youth began to be replaced by the sons of Janissaries and even by local tradesmen. In 1582 Murad III is said to have let thousands of entertainers, acrobats and wrestlers into the corps as a reward for the success of his son's circumcision celebrations. By 1650 pashas were enlisting their servants as Janissaries in order to transfer the cost of their households to the state. Janissaries became part of the economic fabric of Constantinople, infiltrating guilds of boatmen, butchers or slave dealers. The fourteenth *orta* became bakers, the eighty-second butchers. As late as 1673 Bostancis in Constantinople talked to each other in Serbo-Croat. However from 1700 Janissaries were essentially a power group representative of the male population of the capital. Their pay-slips were speculated in as if they were stocks and shares. The last known firman issued to levy children for the *devshirme* dates from 1703.[6]

In 1528 the Janissaries numbered 27,000; in 1591, 48,088. In the following century numbers were reduced under Murad IV and the Koprulu grand viziers; but thereafter they steadily rose, with the greatest increase coming at the end of the eighteenth century, when from 43,403 (1776), and 55,256 (1800), they rose to a total of 109,971 (1809).[7]

Pay, as well as power, caused unrest in the corps. They were often paid in bad coin, owing to inflation and debasement of the coinage: as in other armies officers frequently kept the troops' salaries for themselves. The Janissaries were a symptom and cause of the Ottoman crisis of the seventeenth century, 'the sixty-year sleep of the House of Osman'. At the end of the sixteenth century one Ottoman complained: 'No discipline remains; nobody heeds prohibitions. The cruel ones . . . pillage the honour and property of Muslims and Christians. Among those who commit this crime, the majority is constituted by those who are called the *kuls* [slaves] of the Sultan.'

At times Janissaries represented the specific interests of Constantinople, pulling the Sultan back to the capital. By threatening mutiny, even firing on the Sultan's tent, they forced Selim I, in 1514, to abandon an attack on Persia. In 1529 they obliged Suleyman to raise the siege of Vienna – in both cases because they wanted to return to the city. Unlike most of its subjects, the Ottoman dynasty was prepared to experiment with new cultures and countries. Two sultans tried to strengthen links with their Arab subjects. Selim I wanted to stay in Cairo after its conquest in 1517: the Janissaries forced him to return to Constantinople. Osman II's plans to leave for Mecca in 1622 led to his deposition and murder.[8]

For much of the period 1622–32, Janissaries ruled the city, killing Murad IV's ministers and his favourite Musa, and threatening the Sultan himself with the cry: 'We want the princes!' Murad IV had a good memory. Having changed viziers, he returned terror with terror. Janissary numbers were cut. The true reason for the closure of coffee-houses and taverns in 1633 was not their novelty, but 'to terrify the general populace'. According to the seventeenth-century historian Naima, they were meeting-places where the people of Constantinople 'would spend the time criticizing and disparaging the great and the authorities, waste their breath discussing imperial interests connected with affairs of state, dismissals and appointments, fallings-out and re-conciliations, and so they would gossip and lie'.[9] Murad IV patrolled the city by night, executing anyone found with a pipe or a cup of coffee: according to Bobowski he took particular pleasure in beheading men with fat necks. Corpses were left in the street, for removal the next morning. The only execution of a Mufti of Constantinople in Ottoman history took place on 1 January 1634 on Murad IV's orders. Murad IV imposed such terror that 'no man could say a word about the Padishah, not even in his own home.' In disgust some people began to abuse him as 'the slave's son'. In 1635 the Sultan, the most ruthless of his dynasty, even planned to execute the Armenians who had begun to move to Constantinople in large numbers: he was dissuaded by his Grand Vizier.[10]

In shaping the balance of terror, fire, as well as insurrection,* was a weapon used by the people and the Janissaries against the Sultan. The wooden houses of the capital brought death, as well as the pleasures of nature, close to daily life. Every few years the domes and minarets of Constantinople were outlined against a flame-red sky as another district was devastated by fire. '*Yangan var!*' – 'There is a fire!' – yelled by Janissaries hurrying to the scene, was a familiar cry. Another answer to the question 'where did the wealth of the Ottoman Empire go?' is: it burnt. In the words of an Ottoman proverb, 'Were it not for the fires of Istanbul the thresholds of its houses would be paved with gold.' The frequency of fires in the city explains why so few old houses remain.

The day the Imperial ambassador Busbecq arrived in 1555 there was

---

*Janissary revolts also took place in 1651, 1655, 1687, 1703, 1730, 1733, 1734, 1740, 1742, 1743 and 1783.

a fire. In his opinion it was started by soldiers or sailors, eager to loot and rape in the resulting panic. Fires were also begun to express dissatisfaction with the Sultan's policies, to blackmail him into changing ministers – or simply to hurt the rich. The arrival of modern fire-fighting equipment from Amsterdam in 1725 changed little. In 1755 for example a fire began near the palace. Despite prompt action by the Sultan and Grand Vizier, who both arrived on the scene, it was spread by a strong north wind. The lead on the dome of Aya Sofya melted. The city seemed like an ocean of fire, fed by rivers of lava. An entire corps of Janissaries was burnt alive. The fire lasted thirty-six hours, and devoured a seventh of the city, including the Porte and the offices of the treasury and the chancellery.[11]

Public opinion – with its weapons, fire and the Janissaries – was particularly powerful in the eighteenth century. The people were assuming a right to criticize – often yelling abuse at the Sultan when he came to the scene of a fire. Foreigners wrote of *une populace devenue souveraine*. Vergennes told the French Foreign Minister, 'They have greater liberty, one could almost say licence, than any other civilized people in Europe.'[12]

After 1700, owing to recurrent plagues, Constantinople was also the most dangerous city in Europe, from a medical point of view. The plagues had not, at first, been exceptional. London, for example, experienced five outbreaks of plague between 1563 and 1603, in the last of which up to a fifth of the population died. However, long after plague had been eliminated in Europe (the last major outbreak killed half Marseilles in 1720) by the use of quarantines, 'the angel of death', as plague was called, paid almost annual visits to Constantinople, from its strongholds in the arsenal, the prisons and the hans. In 1778 possibly a third of the population died of plague; business was at a standstill. Among British ambassadors, Lord Winchilsea lost a daughter, Hussey died of the plague in 1762, Grenville had to flee from the embassy at a moment's notice in the middle of the night because a servant of his household had developed the fatal symptom, and in 1813 Liston and his whole family were kept prisoners in their house for over three months, not even a servant going out of the gate because of the plague. In that year entire streets were depopulated and estimates of the number of dead varied between 100,000 and 250,000. The catastrophe was regarded as divine retribution for the sins of the people. Bachelors, in particular, were considered worse than brigands; one street where special bachelor quarters had been established, called 'Where angels do not tread', was demolished and a mosque erected on its site, to expunge its memory. Until the 1830s outbreaks of plague were one of the causes of the deterioration of the empire's political and military position. In the eighteenth century France, Austria and Russia grew in population by over a third. The Ottoman Empire did not.[13]

As a precaution against plague, Christians, Jews and members of the Muslim élite soaked themselves and their surroundings in perfume or vinegar. They also closed up their houses, or fled to the less insalubrious surroundings of Buyukdere or Tarabya. Most Muslims, however, were fatalistic. In 1555 Busbecq was informed of Suleyman's attitude to the plague: 'Did I not know that pestilence is God's arrow, which does not miss its appointed mark? Where could I hide so as to be outside its range? If he wished me to be smitten, no flight or hiding place could avail me. It was useless to avoid inevitable fate.' What some called fatalism, others called courage. Three hundred years later a Muslim of the city, Ali Nami Bey, wrote in a defence of Islam: 'Never has any people, as much as ours, shown a more total contempt for death.'[14]

Constantinople no longer deserved its epithet *al-mahmiyya*, the well-protected – by God against disorder, by the Sultan against injustice. One Sultan found on his return from a nocturnal promenade through the city that no one was on guard at the middle gate of the palace. Presents were refused by pages of the privy chamber as being too small. Even the harem was out of control. By the eighteenth century, for reasons unknown and unrecorded, a harem schedule had emerged, which the Sultan had to keep: one girl was executed for selling her 'night turn'. If he tried to break the schedule, he was subject to 'dangerous jealousies and harassing clamours'. There is a pleading tone in a letter from Abdulhamid I (1774–89) to a harem girl called Ruhsah: 'Mistress, I am for you a slave in chains. If you want, beat. If you want, kill. I have given myself to you. Come tonight, I beg you.' The Sultan begs! In order to see the women they wanted, some sultans were driven to hire rooms in secret in the city.[15]

Fire, plague, a disastrous war, disobedient guards, economic decline, a restless populace, ambitious minorities, aggressive neighbours and religious fundamentalism combined to render the position of Selim III in 1789, when he succeeded his uncle Abdulhamid I at the age of 27, as perilous as that of his correspondent Louis XVI. Already Abdulhamid I had complained of sleepless nights: 'God help the Sublime State.' Selim III said: 'I am ready to content myself with dry bread for the state is breaking up.' Like many of his predecessors, he began his reign by expelling immigrants and reimposing restrictions on dress, coffee-houses and taverns. He prowled the streets in disguise to inflict mortal punishment on law-breakers. The French ambassador Choiseul-Gouffier reported: 'In fifteen days the enthusiasm which he had inspired has turned into general consternation. All trembles in this capital.'[16]

Aware of the need to remedy the empire's ills, he asked twenty-two senior officials – including members of the *ulema* – for specific proposals. One of those approached was Mouradgea d'Ohsson, who had returned from Paris in 1792 with copies of the first two volumes of the *Tableau général*, which delighted Selim III when they were presented to him, with translations from the French. In Constantinople, wearing European dress, and full of enthusiasm for the French revolution, he presented a memoir to the Sultan advocating radical reform of the army. He said that once change was decided there should be no retreat. Rome – an interesting model for the Ottoman Sultan – was successful because it learnt from its neighbours. Everything in the universe is the will of God: but God has given mankind the power to think and rulers the power to protect. The *sheriat* did not forbid Muslims to borrow laws and technology from other cultures. If religious opposition was countered by use of science, Selim III could be as successful as Fatih, Suleyman and Murad IV. An academy to teach military science, with a modern library and curriculum, and French as well as Turkish teachers, was built in Haskoy. However, contrary to Mouradgea's suggestions, no Christian pupils were admitted.[17]

The Kadiasker of Rumeli presented a long memoir on the need to galvanize the economy, and to lessen the burden of taxation on the poor and the minorities. Like Mavrocordato over a hundred years earlier, he also considered the size of the pashas' households and their luxurious way of life a cause of the empire's weakness. But the Janissaries were the heart of the problem. Another official, writing on the Sultan's orders, denounced them as the dregs of the populace, 'pastry-cooks, sailors, fishermen, owners of coffee-houses and brothels'. For yet another official they were rats whose principal characteristic was insubordination. They blackmailed food merchants and ships' captains into paying protection money. They adulterated coffee beans with chickpeas, and raped women while rescuing them from fires. Moreover they mocked the hierarchy of the state. When a vizier and his train of servants passed in front of a Janissary guard-house, instead of rising and saluting, Janissaries played guitars in a mocking manner. During Easter celebrations Janissaries harassed Christians, forcing them to sit and drink and hand over money. Janissaries' worst crime was their failure to defeat the Russians on the battlefield. In the war of 1788–92 many Janissaries had never held a gun before. They frightened everyone except the enemy.

After the peace of 1792, the Sultan began to create a new infantry force called the *Nizam-i Cedid* or New Order, intended to 'perpetuate the duration of the sublime government even to the end of the world'. By 1807 about 27,000 troops had been trained in modern European drill and tactics. To defuse the affront of novelty, they were called Bostancis like the imperial gardeners, and were stationed outside the city, near Buyukdere and at Uskudar. The Sultan often visited their barracks, in effect separate military cities with their own shops and houses; at the Uskudar barracks a printing press with Latin and Arabic types was set up. The Nizam-i Cedid's performance on the battlefield was soon better than the Janissaries'.[18]

Selim III also reestablished a consultative council of about 300 notables and *ulama* to advise on policy and discuss questions of war and peace. The balance of fear had turned so sharply against the Sultan and Grand Vizier that the council's real purpose was to shield them from blame if government decisions led to disaster. The Grand Vizier kept written records of meetings as an insurance, not at the Sublime Porte but in his personal archives. A Phanariot informer told the Russian ambassador that 'the ministers, relieved by the establishment of the perpetual *musavere* [council] which has created here a sort of aristocracy, from the personal responsibility which weighed on each of them individually, are neither mad enough to take responsibility for events themselves, by voicing an opinion contrary to that of the *musavere* nor influential enough to enforce it.'

In part to instruct the Nizam-i Cedid, about 600 advisers came from Britain, Sweden, Austria and, above all, France (both émigrés and republicans). The arsenal and the naval and military engineering schools founded under de Tott were modernized. Sir Robert Liston wrote: 'The fashion of the day is strongly in favour of European imitation in every rank of society' – but the high salaries of the foreigners were unpopular.[19]

Despite his desire for reform, Selim III lacked the ruthless energy of a Peter the Great. He succumbed to the pleasures of the city. According to Sir Robert Liston, he spent much of his time moving from palace to palace, demolishing, rebuilding, enjoying excursions which were 'blamed by the publick and regarded as inconsistent with economy and with that attention to business which becomes the monarch'. He appreciated the less demanding aspects of European culture: dance, music, French wine, Italian comedians, English prints. Yet he did not abandon traditional Ottoman culture. Constantinople remained a city where it was possible to enjoy the best – and worst – of different worlds. Selim III painted on muslin handkerchiefs, and was a skilled calligrapher and composer of traditional Ottoman music. Under the pseudonym *Ilhami*, 'the inspired', he wrote poems whose ideals he ignored:

> O Ilhami, do not be indolent and do not trust in the things of this world.
> The world stops for no one and its wheel turns without ceasing.[20]

The palaces of Constantinople began to show the effects of Western influence. Despite the weight of traditional Ottoman culture, the Ottoman élite was returning to the broadmindedness evident in the years before 1530. Already details in the Nuru Osmaniye mosque built at the entrance to the bazaar in 1748–55, such as capitals, arches and mouldings, showed baroque influence. From 1770 on the walls of some Bosphorus yalis, the imperial harem, and the Gate of Felicity itself, fantasy Italianate landscapes of woods and rivers, ships and bridges, curtains and columns, had replaced the gilded arabesques and Iznik tiles of the past. Selim III employed a miniature painter to record the women of his harem, while illustrations to Fazil Bey's books on female and male beauties, *Zenanname* and *Khubanname*, show strong Western influence.

A young artist from Baden, Antoine-Ignace Melling, became more familiar with the Ottoman palace than any Western artist since Gentile Bellini. Melling, who arrived in Constantinople around 1785, was a protégé of the Pera embassies. A member of the Russian ambassador's household, he drew pictures for the ambassadors of Britain and the Netherlands, and was known to Baron Hubsch von Grossthal (German for 'big valley', a mistranslation of the Turkish Buyukdere, which means 'big stream'), minister of Saxony, banker to the Russian embassy, and personal friend of many Ottoman ministers.[21] Hatice Sultan, sister and confidante of Selim III, who told her of his plans to familiarize his subjects 'with the arts and civilization of Europe', visited the European garden of Baron Hubsch's splendid houses at Buyukdere. She decided that she wanted one herself. Baron Hubsch recommended Melling as a garden designer.

As a result Melling was in his own words 'attached for several years to Hatice Sultan as artist and architect' – so closely 'attached' that he was given an apartment in her husband's quarters in her palace. Pera and the palace, long familiar with each other at a distance, became intimate. Having created a labyrinth of roses, lilacs and acacias for the princess, he began to redecorate the inside of her palace. Adding the arrogance of a decorator to the condescension of a European, he wrote: 'An elegant simplicity was substituted for a luxury of gilding and colours which left no rest for the eye.' The interior pleased the princess so much that she asked him to design her a palace. Despite persecution by her servants and eunuchs, who considered European styles contrary to the Koran, a neoclassical palace for the princess soon arose at Defterdarburnu. Melling also designed dresses, cutlery and furniture for the princess, and kiosks for Selim III and his mother at Beshiktash.

The princess sent Melling letters in Ottoman written in the Latin alphabet. The tone is the same as those of Nurbanu two hundred years earlier:

> Kalfa Melling,
> . . . Is my knife pretty? And the place-mat. I want to have it too today. Show me how you work. You must absolutely ensure that the place-mat is ready today. I also want the dark blue ornament today. When will I receive the mosquito net? I absolutely must have it tomorrow. Has the furniture maker begun? I want it quickly.
>
> *mercoledi matina ora 3.*

Melling's drawings of the city and the Bosphorus, Buyukdere, Bebek, the port, the arsenal, the palace, originally done for the Sultan and his sister, are masterpieces of accurate observation. They include what is probably the sole accurate representation of the interior of an imperial harem (that of the summer palace on Seraglio Point). Melling knew 'the hot and cold' of harem life. One night he was rowed back from dinner on one of the Princes' Isles. Because there was a bright moon, he could see, by the sea walls of the palace, Bostancis putting stones in a sack containing two women. They then put the sack in a boat and rowed out to sea, accompanied by a eunuch (to report back to the chief eunuch that the mission had been accomplished). As Melling's boat continued its journey, for a long time he was followed by the cries of the two women. Silence fell after the sack was pushed overboard.

The French invasion of Egypt, possibly exacerbated by a personal quarrel, forced Melling to leave the princess's service in 1798. He did not finally leave Constantinople until 1802 – with a Levantine wife (Françoise-Louise Colombo), a child and the drawings which were finally published, with the support of the French government, as *Voyage pittoresque de Constantinople et des rives du Bosphore* in 1819.[22]

While the Sultan was enjoying life on the Bosphorus, his empire was falling apart. The Sultan's weakness, the disintegration of the Ottoman army, and the inhabitants' longing for decent administration, enabled governors and local landowners to carve out semi-independent domains in the provinces: Muhammad Ali in Egypt; Ali Pasha in northern Greece; the Karaosmanoglu family in south-west Anatolia; Pasvanoglu in what is now Bulgaria. In 1802 the latter threatened to besiege Constantinople itself and had to be bought off with an additional provincial governorship. In 1804 there was a rising in Serbia against the reign of terror practised by Janissary regiments: within two years a semi-independent Serbian state, while acknowledging the Sultan's suzerainty, had taken Belgrade and given itself a constitution. The cruellest blow was the emergence of a fundamentalist sect, the Wahhabis, in Arabia. In 1803 they conquered Mecca from the Sherifs, and prevented the arrival of the pilgrim caravan from Constantinople. The Sultan Caliph could not guard the Holy Places! As provinces fell away, less revenue reached the capital; Janissaries' arrears and aggression increased.

Foreign governments were also closing in on the city. The French ambassador Jean-Baptiste-Annibal Aubert Dubayet in 1796 had been the first to refuse to appear at the Gate of Happiness except in military uniform. After the period as ally of Britain and Russia in 1799–1805, Selim III switched his support to France. When François-Horace-Bastien Sébastiani arrived as Napoleon's ambassador in 1806, he became the favourite of the Porte, while the Russian ambassador was obliged to leave (the first enemy ambassador to avoid imprisonment in the Seven Towers).

Alarmed at the prospect of a Franco-Ottoman alliance, the British government despatched a fleet from Malta to Constantinople: Malta's change of role in 1799–1800, from headquarters of the Knights of St John to British naval base, had changed the balance of power in the Mediterranean in general, and would, in the future, affect the destiny of Constantinople itself. On 21 February 1807, having forced the Dardanelles (the feat of which the Russian navy had proved incapable in

1770), seven British men-of-war anchored within bombarding distance of the palace – the first foreign force to approach Constantinople since the Cossack raid of 1624. In the fright and confusion the Sultan suggested that Sébastiani leave the city. The next moment the Sultan himself, with Sébastiani beside him, helped dig fortifications along the sea, beside thousands of workmen, to whom he distributed generous gratuities. Soon the walls had been repaired and were defended by 300 cannon. The British ships withdrew to the islands and on 3 March, much damaged by fire from batteries on the Dardanelles, to the Aegean.[23]

After the shock of invasion, chaos returned. In the streets of the capital, sailors supported a pro-French reform group; the Nizam-i Cedid and the artillery backed a British faction, while Janissaries and *ulema* favoured the faction of the Valide Sultan. Riots between the rival groups fostered popular distaste for reform. On 25 May 1807 a revolt broke out at Rumeli Kavak, a small fort up the Bosphorus. One of the Sultan's chief advisers was Mahmud Raif Efendi, who had grown up with him as a slave companion in the palace, and had served as secretary to the first Ottoman ambassador in Britain in 1793 and as Reis-ul Kuttab, chief deputy to the Grand Vizier, in 1800–5. An enthusiastic Westernizer, he believed that the Ottoman Empire was always especially brilliant after changes to its 'political constitution'. He was instructing the troops to wear European-style uniforms, when he was murdered by a soldier shouting, 'It is not a Muslim but the infidel *Ingiliz Mahmud* whom I kill.' The troops stormed other Bosphorus forts and marched on Buyukdere and Ortakoy. The Nizam-i Cedid troops were confined to barracks.

The Sultan lurked, indecisive, in Topkapi palace. His reputation for softness and Westernization, and the fact that their pay was low and late, had earned him the Janissaries' hate. On 28 May at a meeting in the supreme symbol of Ottoman imperial power, the Suleymaniye mosque, the Janissaries, possibly encouraged by conservative pashas, declared that the Sultan had consorted with infidels, scorned their corps and disdained the *ulema*. They joined the rebels. Shops shut in panic. The Mufti rallied to the rebels. Too late, the Sultan dissolved the Nizam-i Cedid.[24]

In the palace Selim III ordered some of his friends executed – to spare them a worse fate at rebel hands. At the Porte on 29 May the Mufti read out a fatwa authorizing the Sultan's deposition. The Sultan's secretary Ahmed Bey was slashed to pieces and his head despatched up the hill to the palace. The Sultan understood the message, and abdicated in favour of his brother Mustafa IV. As rebels paid homage to the new Sultan on the throne in the second courtyard, the old one was confined to an apartment in the harem.[25]

Mustafa IV was weak and reactionary. With Wallachia and Moldavia under Russian occupation from 1806 to 1812, the capital's food supply deteriorated. As the Sultan went to mosque, women protested at the cost of living. At the head of 15,000 troops, a provincial governor, Mustafa Pasha Bayrakdar, took control of the city, with the ultimate intention of restoring Selim III. On 28 July 1808 he surrounded the Porte and the palace. Taking the Mufti to legitimize their acts, a large party moved on the palace. At the Gate of Happiness Mustafa IV, in a rage, sent back messengers who had urged him to abdicate. Not knowing whom to obey, the Mufti wandered in the third courtyard, 'like a dog between two villages'.

Out of respect for the imperial sanctuary, Bayrakdar hesitated to go further. When Mustafa IV asked his courtiers, 'And now what is to be done?' they knew the answer. Twenty courtiers and Bostancis rushed to Selim's apartment and, after a prolonged struggle, murdered him. Another intended victim, his young cousin Mahmud Efendi, was saved by his servants' loyalty. A female slave threw a pail of hot ash from the hamam over his assailants' heads. In the confusion Mahmud was taken up a chimney, out on to the palace roof and then down a ladder of knotted sashes into the gardens.

After his fatal hesitation, Bayrakdar stormed into the third courtyard. He was met by silence, an absence of courtiers, and finally the sight of Selim's massive, mutilated corpse lying on a stone bench near the throne room. He cried and cursed the Sultan's murderers, and licked his master's wounds in grief. His staff brought Mahmud to him from the garden, saying, 'It is our lord the Sultan Mahmud and it is on you, Pasha, that the protection of the Caliphate depends.'[26] In reality it was on the new Sultan that all depended. Would he, as many assumed, be the last of his line? That year, planning the partition of the Ottoman Empire in St Petersburg with the French ambassador, Tsar Alexander I claimed Constantinople for Russia: 'It is the key to the door of my house.'

Born in 1785, the only son of Abdulhamid I, Mahmud had received a better education than most princes: from May 1807 to July 1808 he had been instructed inside the harem by the deposed Sultan Selim III. The first year of his reign was one of the most horrific in the history of

Constantinople. On 15 November 1808, during a Janissary attack on the Sublime Porte, Mustafa Bayrakdar, who had become Grand Vizier, blew himself up, to avoid surrender and death. For weeks the city endured riots and fires, started by the Janissaries. Breaking their promises to the Sultan, they hunted down and killed members of the disbanded Nizam-i Cedid.[27]

In the struggle with the Janissaries, Mahmud II had one advantage, as important to a monarch as a good television image to a modern politician. He looked a Sultan. At an audience in Topkapi in 1810, John Cam Hobhouse noticed that, while the Janissaries were 'in appearance the very scum of the city', the Sultan, dressed in yellow satin, his milk-white hands 'glittering with diamond rings', had an 'air of indescribable majesty'. An American missionary had the same reaction, before '*such an eye* that I always felt overawed'. To a British general he looked decidedly handsome, with intelligent black eyes, 'a complexion which tells more of the bivouac than of the luxurious effeminacy of the harem, great breadth of shoulders and a large open chest' – although his legs were short. 'His beard is one of the finest and the blackest I ever saw.'[28]

The Sultan's greatest asset was his will-power. The opposite of a fatalist, he said that, while everything was ultimately in the hands of God, God had made everything depend on human endeavour. Far from degenerating into a race of *rois fainéants*, some of the last Ottomans suffered from too much energy and an inability to delegate. From the beginning of his reign, Mahmud II broke with the past. Whereas most books claim that the Sultan left the sanctuary of tradition, the palace of Topkapi, in 1839 or 1853, in reality Mahmud II did so from 1808. In the winter he lived at Beshiktash, where Dolmabahce palace is today, in the summer at Beylerbey, Ciragan and Sa'adabad – in wooden palaces, now gone, whose columned and pedimented façades recalled Carlton House rather than Topkapi. They were rebuilt for the Sultan by the imperial court architect Krikor Amira Balian, an Armenian whose father had already served as an imperial architect. Beshiktash was a seat of government which contained, behind the Western façade, a traditional Ottoman complex of pools, fountains, baths, banqueting pavilions, kitchens, an armoury and a chamber of the Holy Mantle like Topkapi. Some government offices and the palace school continued in Topkapi; the Sublime Porte remained below the palace. However, the Sultan's residence had moved up the Bosphorus – away from predominantly Muslim districts.[29]

Sir Robert Liston was impressed by the Sultan's

imperious command over government and his freedom from all scruples as to the means of removing the obstacles that may stand in his way . . . From what I have learnt of the *character* and what I have witnessed of the *conduct* of the Sultan I should be inclined to say that he will sooner hazard his throne and his life than abandon the contest [with the Janissaries]. Those who know him say he has considerable abilities, a vigorous and active mind, with such an idea of the elevation, perhaps of the sanctity of his station, and so strong a feeling of personal superiority that he deems all opposition criminal, all resistance vain and ultimate disappointment on his part impossible.

Mahmud II once obliged the Kaptan Pasha to spend the winter in the Aegean, rather than return with his fleet to Constantinople, since he had not brought back a rebel governor of Anatolia. He used Muhammad Ali, the governor of Egypt, to destroy Wahhabi power in Arabia: Mecca reverted to the dominion of the Sherifs and the Sultan in 1813. In 1818 rebellious Wahhabi sheikhs were paraded through the streets of Constantinople, then killed and their heads exposed in the first courtyard of the palace.

Mahmud II had a Churchillian need for 'action this day'. A ship launched from the arsenal stuck in the mud. As Sir Robert Liston recorded:

> The Sultan sullenly retired saying he should return in the morning (the launch had taken place in the afternoon) when he trusted he should see her move into the middle of the channel. Crowds of workmen were instantly employed and the Terzan Emini himself (an officer whose duties are a combination of those of the minister of the marine with those of commissioner of the dock-yard) was seen labouring all night in the water by torch-light. When His Highness appeared the next day the ship floated into the middle of the stream as he had directed.

He once went to the Porte at 8 a.m. and called for the Reis Efendi. The official was not present. Nor were any ministers except the Grand Vizier, who lived on the premises. 'His Highness staid about half an hour, when some of the other publick officers began to drop in, and received from him an admonition which the subalterns at least have not forgotten.'[30]

More than most of his predecessors, Mahmud II used terror as an instrument of government. Possibly as many as 200 women of Mustafa IV's harem were drowned in the Bosphorus, to prevent them producing a son (a dynastic rival whom the Janissaries could use against the

Sultan). One of those diplomatic decisions in Constantinople which transformed the balance of power in Europe was the treaty signed in 1812 between Russia and the Ottoman Empire. Both empires needed peace, and Napoleon had alienated the Ottoman Empire by discussing its partition with Alexander I at Tilsit and Erfurt. Russia gained Bessarabia – and freedom to turn most of its army against Napoleon's invasion that summer. The empire recovered Wallachia and Moldavia. However Prince Mourousi, the Grand Dragoman, was blamed for the peace terms. Summoned to the Sublime Porte from his yali on the Bosphorus, he was sentenced to be executed. Seizing the executioner's sword, he succeeded for a long time in defending himself, but succumbed in the end.[31]

It was clear to foreign diplomats and dragomans – although the number of the Janissaries' friends in the government prevented such plans from being recorded – that the Janissaries were destined for similar treatment. They reacted with insolence. In 1814 a paper was stuck to the palace gate for the Sultan's attention, representing him as a dog led by a Janissary: 'You see how we use our dogs; as long as they are useful to us and suffer themselves to be led, we use them well, but when they cease to be of service, we cast them into the streets.' A year later, as a warning to the Sultan, the Janissaries threatened to burn the city. The disorder in the capital was such that, as one Grand Vizier told them, Constantinople had become the laughing-stock of Europe.[32]

The Greek insurrection of 1821, which led to protracted and indecisive fighting in the provinces, delayed the final reckoning. However the need for reform was confirmed by the Janissaries' poor performance against the Greek rebels. The Sultan was compared to a mole working in silence and darkness – or a scorpion, concealing its sting until the right moment. In accordance with the Sultan's plans, their Aga, Huseyin Pasha, a former gang leader in the city streets, began to weed out the most dangerous Janissaries, and planted spies in their taverns and coffee-houses.[33]

In 1826 the Sultan began to modernize the army. Since the fifteenth century the Ottoman army had frequently adopted foreign tactics, particularly in the field of artillery. The navy had been modernized under Selim III. Mahmud II did not at first threaten to abolish the Janissary corps. However the Janissaries were so intractable, and so opposed to change, that in May 1826 Mahmud II first obtained a fatwa from the Mufti, stating that the new drill and uniform were not European, but 'modern Muslim'; he also secured signed engagements of approval from 208 senior officials. On 11 June 1826 in the large drilling ground near the Janissary barracks, the Etmeydan, occurred one of the most decisive events in the history of Ottoman Constantinople. Four drill-masters (one Egyptian, three veterans of Selim III) began to drill 200 Ottoman soldiers, wearing modern uniforms, in the European fashion.[34]

On 13 June, on the same spot, 20,000 Janissaries gathered, shouting: 'We do not want the military exercises of the infidels!' The bombardiers, marines and engineers remained loyal to the Sultan. Competing armies swept through the streets of the city shouting: 'Muhammad and Haci Bektash!' (the dervish patron of the Janissary corps) or 'Muhammad and Mahmud!' Certain of their invincibility, Janissaries stormed the palace and harem of their Aga and threatened Topkapi. The Grand Vizier tried to appease the mutineers, saying: 'The new military system which we have adopted is both sensible and in accordance with our Holy Book and religious precepts. It has the consent of the *ulema*. We wish to carry it out for the honour and strength of the Ottoman family. We will not permit a single stone to be removed from this sacred structure.'

Mahmud II arrived at the palace by boat from Beshiktash, in a state of exhilaration. He had been waiting eighteen years for this moment. He believed: 'Either the Janissaries will all be massacred or cats will walk over the ruins of Constantinople.' In the circumcision chamber in the palace he handed the Sacred Banner of the Prophet to the Grand Vizier and the Mufti, saying in tears: 'I want to join you and fight in the midst of the true Muslims to punish the ingrates who offend me!'

However, they begged him to stay in the safety of the palace. He directed operations from the chamber above the imperial gate. Messages were sent to the prayer leaders of each district in the city, inviting Muslims to hurry to the Sultanahmed mosque to protect the Sultan Caliph. The city was eager to fight the guard: many Muslims wanted revenge for the Janissaries' numberless acts of murder and theft. They were handed swords, rifles and cartridges from the palace arsenal. The Sacred Banner was unfurled in the pulpit of the Sultanahmed mosque. The Grand Vizier and senior officials lived in the mosque, sleeping in tents in the courtyard.

Loyal troops soon recaptured the Etmeydan. The role of the artillery, as in Paris at the fall of the Tuileries palace in 1792 or St Petersburg in the suppression of the Decembrist revolt in 1825, was crucial. At first the gunners hesitated. Then a confidant of the Sultan known as Kara

Gehennem, 'the black infernal', rushed forward and lit the cannon fuses. Thousands died in the subsequent slaughter. Many Janissaries perished by the weapon they themselves had frequently used. Their barracks were set on fire, and their charred bodies were found in the ruins the following morning.[35]

Mahmud II was a dynastic revolutionary, who caused more bloodshed in Constantinople than the Committee of Public Safety in Paris. On 16 June the British dragoman Bartolomeo Pisani wrote to the ambassador, Sir Stratford Canning: 'Every corner of the town is searched and every Janissary and officer that is caught is conducted to the Grand Vizir and by him ordered to death and executed *ipso facto* when the corpse is thrown in the middle of the Hippodrome to remain three days. All the public offices are shut up; the markets suspended and no business of any sort attended to.'

On 17 June, the Janissary corps was formally abolished by an ordinance stating that, to serve 'the Ottoman monarchy which should last as long as the world', science was an element of success more certain than numbers or courage.[36] By 22 June Canning believed that 6,000 Janissaries had been executed and 5,000 exiled: 'The entrance to the Seraglio, the shore under the Sultan's window and the sea itself are crowded with dead bodies – many of them torn and in part devoured by the dogs.'[37] The official account, accepted and corrected by the Sultan himself, describes one rebel's end in a room underneath the Sultanahmed mosque: 'The executioners fastened around his neck a snakeskin noose. "Pull, my hearties," he told them and he died with ferocious courage.'

Constantinople was a city of long historical memories, where figures such as the last Emperor Constantine, the Conqueror Fatih, the saintly Eyup were part of everyday consciousness. June 1826 was a settling of accounts between the dynasty and the Janissaries, after three hundred years. The official history enumerated acts of insubordination by the corps stretching back to the reigns of Selim I and Suleyman, as well as recent outrages, including attacks on Christians. Many Janissaries were hanged, on the Grand Vizier's orders, from the same tree in the Atmeydan where Janissaries had hanged a Grand Vizier one hundred and seventy-eight years before.[38]

The 'purging of the garden of the empire of savage and useless weeds', also known as 'the Blessed Event', was consciously seen as the dawn of an era. Saying he no longer needed vast sums to pay the Janissaries, the Sultan abandoned his right to confiscate or inherit private property: 'I no longer want the drum of iniquity and the cries of spoliation to be heard in my court, asylum of justice.'[39]

On 20 June the outer courtyard of Topkapi palace echoed to the sound of Western drums and fifes. Two thousand Turks appeared

> in various dresses, but armed with muskets and bayonets, arranged in European order and going through the new form of exercise. The Sultan, who was at first stationed at the window within sight, descended after a time and passed the men in review. His Highness was dressed in the *Egyptian* fashion [i.e. in a modern uniform] armed with pistols and sabre and on his head, in place of the imperial turban was a sort of Egyptian bonnet

– a change in the monarch's appearance as decisive as Mustafa Kemal's adoption of the hat a hundred years later.[40] Ottoman dress had once possessed such prestige that it was copied as far as Buda and Warsaw. Status now came to Constantinople from the West. The Sultan's new clothes sent out the message that his empire was opening to Western culture.

Continued executions in July and August terrorized the city. Accused of debauch, impiety and criminal intelligence with the Janissaries, the Bektashi order of dervishes was proscribed, its members hunted down, its *tekkes* destroyed. European merchants were threatened; an Austrian dragoman was beaten to death. Fires, probably started by ex-Janissaries, devastated part of the city at the end of August. An English inhabitant noted: 'Much strangling. General discontent. Reaction hoped for even by quiet Turks.' Finally the only force capable of stopping the Sultan – the women of the city – marched to the palace in protest. The slaughter slowed. However the vendetta was not over. Years later a British general watched with his own eyes as the Sultan supervised workmen striking the Janissary bonnets off gravestones in a Pera burial-ground.[41]

10

Mahmud II

Heaven is under the shadow of swords.

Mahmud II

MAHMUD II HAD applied the same ruthlessness to Greeks as to Janissaries. In 1814 a secret society called the *Philiki Etairia*, the Friendly Society, dedicated to the destruction of the Ottoman Empire and the freedom of 'the sacred and wretched fatherland', had been founded in the flourishing Russian Black Sea port of Odessa. The first members, merchants on the verge of bankruptcy, deceived other Greeks into believing that they enjoyed the support of the Tsar and his Foreign Minister, Count Capodistrias – a Greek from Corfu. In Moscow in 1816 they were joined by Alexander Mavrocordato, 'the fugitive'. In 1818 their headquarters moved to the house of a merchant, Emmanuel Xanthos, in Constantinople. However, the city was too commercial and too Ottoman to make an effective centre of revolution. According to one member 'the *eforia* [council] of Constantinople . . . was expected to play the major role. It could have, had the spirit of its members not been consumed by their trade and their own self-interest.' Only 9 per cent of the 946 members of the Philiki Etairia came from Constantinople. Most Phanariots remained loyal or subservient, their ambitions directed towards the principalities.

Nevertheless, in some quarters, there was a change of heart. In 1807, as the British fleet hovered off Seraglio Point, the author of the Patriarchal Exhortation of 1798 which had urged loyalty to the Ottoman Empire, Patriarch Gregory V – staff in hand, and accompanied by 1,000 Greeks – had helped Selim III repair the fortifications. When he learnt of the society several years later, however, he expressed sympathy. Although he refused membership ('If his name was found on the Etairia's books of membership the entire nation would be endangered'), one of his secretaries joined – perhaps in order to keep His All-Holiness informed.[1] Meanwhile in the diaspora and the Pelopponese the movement was gaining strength.

In St Petersburg in 1820, Alexander Ypsilanti, a Phanariot prince who had become an ADC of Tsar Alexander I, unbalanced, romantic and poor, agreed to lead the society. On April 1821 Ypsilanti crossed the River Prut into Moldavia at the head of the Sacred Legion, mainly composed of Greeks. He believed the Ottoman Empire was a volcano about to erupt. In reality most Romanians were more anti-Phanariot than anti-Ottoman. Alexander Soutzo, Prince of Wallachia, thought the rising a catastrophe for the Greeks. Michael Soutzo, Prince of Moldavia, however sent letters to the Philiki Etairia in Constantinople, via a Russian diplomatic courier, which reveal the conspirators' delusions: 'Let fire consume the capital. Encourage the sailors to take control of the arsenal. Try every means to seize the Sultan at the moment he goes to the fire. Let the voice of the fatherland be heard . . . Success is very near.' Greeks rose against the Ottoman Empire in the Pelopponese and Epirus.[2]

News of the revolts and of the threat in Ypsilanti's manifesto – that the crescent would be cast down and the cross would rise again – terrified the Ottomans in the capital. Masks fell. The synthesis which had enabled Christian and Muslims to live side by side for centuries dissolved. Muslims regarded Greeks as scorpions capable of every mischief, and were told to carry arms. The best account comes from the British embassy chaplain, the Revd Robert Walsh. 'On my return to Pera I found a total change had taken place in a few hours in the appearance and manners of the people.' Armenians withdrew to their houses in the greatest alarm. 'The Turks were walking slowly about, holding one hand on the hilt of their yataghans and with the other twisting their moustaches; while the Greeks and Jews, whenever they met them, got out of their way into some store or coffee-house that happened to be open.' Greeks were killed and western Europeans attacked by Muslims in the street. An anathema on the revolt, composed by the Patriarch after five hours of consultation with the Sultan, and signed by the Holy Synod, was read out in every church.[3]

However the Sultan suspected the Patriarch, rightly, of knowing more than he admitted. On 22 April, the Saturday before Easter, during a packed service in the patriarchal church at the Phanar, the anathema was again read out.

The people were about to disperse, strongly impressed with what they had heard, when suddenly some chaoushes [guards] entered the patriarchate, and having with difficulty forced their way through the mass, who thought no more of them than as persons sent as usual to keep order in a crowd, they rudely seized the Patriarch, who had just given his benediction to the people, and his officiating bishops; and dragging them along by the collar into the courts, they tied ropes round their necks.

The Patriarch was taken to the gate of the Phanar courtyard, hanged from the top and left to die. Since he was an old man who weighed little, his agony lasted many hours. Two chaplains and three archbishops were hanged in different parts of the city – to spread the message of retribution and contempt. After three days the Patriarch's body was removed and, in order to foster intercommunal hate, was given to Jews to drag through a dirty market down to the Golden Horn. It was flung into the water where, bloated with putrescence, it soon floated to the surface. A few days later it was secretly removed for burial in Odessa.

Kites and vultures wheeled above the bodies of Christians murdered in the streets; but dogs got them first. 'Indeed it was impossible to conceive a more dismal scene of horror and desolation than the Turkish capital now presented.' A Greek architect, Comnenos Kalfa, was beheaded as he was finishing inspection of the office he had designed for the Ottoman navy at Galata. Outside the imperial gate of Topkapi palace, there were piles of heads. When the British ambassador went to present his credentials to Mahmud II on 22 May 1821, his party saw mounds of ears and noses, 'like small hay-cocks', trophies of victory sent by Ottoman generals in the Pelopponese, and boys kicking heads in the street. Inside, before the immobile Sultan, the new dragoman, Stavraki Aristarchi, trembled so violently, and dripped so much sweat on to the ambassador's letter of credentials, that he had difficulty making out the words.[4]

Of the seventy-six Greek churches in and around Constantinople – their increase since the sixteenth century a sign of the growth in Greek prosperity – one was demolished and thirteen looted by Janissaries. The fountain of St Saviour by Topkapi palace, where Sultans had once watched Greeks dance and sing, was walled up for ever.[5] Only on 5 July, after ten weeks, was a proclamation issued against killing Christians 'without provocation'. The markets reopened and some degree of security returned to the city.[6] However Muslims, even young boys, were allowed to remain armed. Although Armenians showed little sympathy for their fellow Christians, the government, eager to divide and rule, ordered them to suspend all relations with the Greeks, to keep no Greek servants and not to wear Frank dress.[7]

A hecatomb of Phanariots signalled the end of their era. The Mourousi and Callimachi palaces in Tarabya were looted and destroyed. Constantine Mourousi was executed in his official dress as dragoman outside the Alay Kiosk. Nicholas Mourousi, Grand Dragoman of the Fleet,* who had encouraged the Pelopponese to revolt while tranquillizing the Turks, was executed at the arsenal. Other victims were two former grand dragomans, John and Charles Callimachi, and Stavraki Aristarchi: he had had reason to tremble. Many of the city's Greeks were hanged, exiled to Anatolia, or fled to Russia. The streets of the Phanar were covered in books looted from Greek libraries, until they were gathered up on the Sultan's orders and sold to the diplomats and Catholics of Pera. Most Phanariots broke with their Ottoman background and left for Greece. The Ypsilanti, the Caradja and the Soutzo fought in the Greek War of Independence. In his memoirs Prince Nicholas Soutzo admitted that he had enjoyed learning Ottoman, Persian and Arabic as a boy in Tarabya. 'But soon after, having left Constantinople and the Greek revolution having come to change the course of my ideas, I no longer had the occasion to cultivate in any way studies which had not had the time to consolidate themselves, and finished by losing all knowledge of them.'[8]

The Mavrocordato, the most famous of all Phanariot families, also broke with the Ottoman Empire. George Mavrocordato, a former Grand Hetman of Wallachia and Grand Ban of Moldavia, was hanged in Constantinople on 17 April 1821 – the first of his family to suffer the death penalty. The career of his cousin Alexander Mavrocordato symbolized the Phanar's conversion to Greek nationalism. Born in Constantinople in 1791, in 1812 he had accompanied his uncle John Caradja, Hospodar of Wallachia, to Bucharest. He joined the Philiki Etairia. In 1818, as Grand Postelnic or minister of foreign affairs, he had paid his respects to Alexander I, on a tour of his southern provinces, telling Capodistrias that 'as Greeks they longed to hear the Russian armies had crossed the River Prut.'[9]

---

*The original purchaser of the Venus de Milo until its seizure, on the island of Melos, by the second councillor at the French embassy, the Vicomte de Marcellus, and abduction to France.

The same year he followed his uncle, forced into exile by accusations of corruption and misgovernment. After visiting Geneva and Paris, he moved to Pisa to attend the university – the first Mavrocordato to be educated in the West since the 1650s. This polyglot cosmopolitan, at ease in four cultures (Ottoman, Greek, Romanian, Western) became so impregnated with nationalism that he was the first person to anticipate the transformation of the Ottoman Empire into a Turkish national state. Throughout the Balkans and Anatolia the mix of races and religions was as complex as in the capital itself. No region was less suited to the creation of national states. Massacres of Muslim and Jewish civilians in the Pelopponese were among the first acts of the Greek insurrection in 1821. Yet, disregarding history, demography and geography, Alexander Mavrocordato wrote: 'This power [the Ottoman Empire] is rushing to its fall . . . it should either be replaced by a [Turkish] national government like that of the Greeks or invaded by the Russians', or 'a young and vigorous power' – a new Greek empire – should arise.[10]

At Pisa, with his huge 'moustachio' and romantic expression, Mavrocordato charmed his neighbours, the Shelleys. Shelley dedicated the violently Ottomanophobe poem *Hellas* (its epigraph, 'Prophet I am of noble combats') 'to his Excellency Prince Alexander Mavrocordato, late Secretary for Foreign Affairs to the Hospodar of Wallachia . . . as an imperfect token of the admiration, sympathy and friendship of the author'. Mavrocordato taught Mary Shelley Greek. She taught him English, which he learnt with Phanariot speed.

In 1821, while Mavrocordato's mother and sisters fled from Constantinople hidden in bags of flour on a Greek ship which took them to safety in the island of Aegina, Mavrocordato left Pisa for Marseilles – then centre of a wealthy Greek colony. On 18 July, having collected recruits, money and weapons, he sailed for Greece. On 11 August 1821 he arrived at Missolonghi. On 1 January 1822 he became President of the Executive Power. Thereafter, until his death in 1863 he was at the centre of Greek national life, as a minister, prime minister – and, on occasion, ambassador to Constantinople.[11]

At the same time as fighting the Greeks in the Pelopponese, Mahmud II, after the destruction of the Janissaries in the 'Blessed Event', had embarked on the creation of a new Ottoman army. As in Peter the Great's reformed Russian army, the Sultan's guard had a crucial role as training school and power-base. The Bostancis, and two ceremonial guard units, the *solaks* and *peiks*, were formally reorganized on 31 August 1826. Called Trained Imperial Gardeners, they served directly under the Sultan rather than under the commander-in-chief and had their own officers' school and command structure. A court battalion was also founded, to train the Sultan's slaves and grandees' sons as officers in the new army. By the end of 1826 there were about 25,000, by 1828 30,000 in the new army.[12] It was paid for out of the confiscated *vakifs* of the Janissaries.

From 1829 Constantinople began to resemble other great military capitals such as Berlin or St Petersburg. Janissaries had lived in wooden barracks near the Suleymaniye or in their own houses in the city. In different quarters of the city stone barracks in the simple, dignified Ottoman neoclassical style, distinguished by wide windows, marble columns and stark yellow walls, were constructed by Mahmud II's architect, Krikor Amira Balian. They were larger and generally cleaner than the equivalents in other capitals: all had a special pavilion (*hunkiar kasri*) for the Sultan's visits – a sign of his power and ubiquity.

The Selimiye barracks in Uskudar, overlooking the Bosphorus, built in wood for Selim III in 1794–9, were rebuilt in stone from 1826 and inaugurated on 1 February 1829. A vast towered quadrangle, a cross between the Escorial and Sandhurst, it is so large that two soldiers are said to be able to live there for a year without meeting: it is the headquarters of the First Istanbul Military District today. Balian also built a naval school and barracks on the island of Heybeli in the Sea of Marmara; another barracks in what is now Taksim square; and Davud Pasha barracks, outside the city.[13]

Henceforth, a common sight in parade-grounds around the city, day after day, whatever the weather, was the Sultan, simply dressed in a plain dark blue mantle, 'cossack trowsers' and boots, drilling his troops with 'an expression of firmness and self-confidence and of haughtiness not unmixed with a degree of ferocity'. He often slipped into the barracks in disguise to inspect their condition. The rifle with which one conscientious secretary butted the intruder in the stomach was plated in silver, to honour such obedience to orders, and can be seen today in the Istanbul Military Museum. By the end of the Sultan's reign about 46,000 soldiers, sailors, marines and artillerymen were stationed in and around Constantinople.[14]

The Sultan was assisted by loyal officers like Huseyin Pasha, Ahmed Fathi Pasha, colonel of the guards (an office which replaced Bostanci Pasha), and two foreigners. Having served Napoleon on Elba and at Waterloo, Giuseppe Donizetti, brother of the great composer, found promotion difficult in Restoration Europe. Arriving in Constantinople in 1828, he taught Ottoman bands Western marches, including the *Mahmudiye*, the first official Ottoman march, composed in honour of the Sultan. The parade-grounds of Constantinople resounded to the music of Rossini and Donizetti. The Ottoman dynasty had begun its long love-affair with Western music. Donizetti Pasha, as he became, worked in the palace (teaching both the Sultan and the ladies of the harem Italian music) and the School of Imperial Music, until his death in 1856.[15]

The foreigner most trusted by the Sultan was a Piedmontese called Calosso. This former officer in the Napoleonic army, implicated in liberal conspiracies in Piedmont in the 1820s, had failed to make his fortune in Constantinople as a brewer. He was close to penury when, in 1827, his skill in mastering a horse which had thrown every Turk brought him to the Sultan's notice. It was Calosso who taught Mahmud II to make the transition from traditional Ottoman to modern Western horsemanship. In the former there were 'huge saddles like cradles and short and almost immovable stirrups that tuck up the knees in close contact with the groin'; in the latter small saddles and long stirrups. Whereas the Sultan adapted to them with ease, his guards cursed them as the invention of the devil. In 1828 Calosso told an English visitor that 'the Sultan could manoeuvre [cavalry squadrons] as well as any European major or captain of long standing.'

Good-looking, with a 'fine military tournure and an easy elegance of manner', Calosso soon reached 'an unrivalled degree of favour'. He drilled the new troops, saw the Sultan every day and was given one of the best houses in Pera. Dragomans and ambassadors who had ignored him now greeted him with 'a quiver of reverence' and a deluge of invitations. Calosso, who learnt to speak fluent Turkish, admired his master for his 'inexorable will' and what he called 'the absence of prejudices of this prince so superior to his entourage'. At the departure of the Sacred Caravan one year, the Sultan had Calosso, a Christian, stand beside him in the second courtyard of Topkapi palace.[16]

A sign of Mahmud II's desire to modernize his empire was the head-dress he imposed on his army and administration: the crimson wool fez. The physical prostration required during prayer makes headgear particularly significant for Muslims. Already some of the new troops of Selim III had worn a small red skull-cap like that used by some Greek islanders and North Africans. In 1826 the Sultan adopted it and in 1827, after some hesitation, 50,000 were ordered from Tunis for the Sultan's troops. In 1829 it was extended to all government employees. Thousands of red cones henceforth added colour to the streets of the city. The fez replaced the turban on Ottoman gravestones. It was less grandiose but more unifying than the turban. The latter had been restricted to Muslims: the fez was worn by all government employees, finally by all who wished, even porters in the street, no matter what their creed – although until the 1840s small badges distinguished the Christian from the Muslim fez.

In 1832 an imperial fez factory was founded in Eyup, employing first Tunisian, then 3,000 Turkish and Armenian workers to make the fez – a complicated process involving dyeing and stiffening the wool. From the crown of the fez hung a tassel of blue silk or wool, so long and intricate that combing fez tassels became a new profession on the streets of the city. In 1845 'the tasselled curse', as it was called, was exchanged for a short black tassel.[17]

The spread of the fez showed the prestige of Constantinople and the Ottoman Empire. By 1860 it had been adopted by the Muslim or Muslim-ruled élite from Bosnia to Java. In the twentieth century it was worn by Bosnian troops in the Austrian army,* Kenyan troops in the British army, and, until 1953, the Egyptian army. The fez symbolized the Ottoman way of modernization: it was adapted to Islam, since it was adopted on the initiative of the Sultan and practicable for use during prayer; but it was not exclusively Muslim. The fez became part of daily life and, in the words of the nationalist writer Falih Rifki Atay, 'part of the Turkish soul'. The way it was worn could indicate wealth or morals. Local Christians and foreigners working in the region – Gordon, Kitchener, Rimbaud, Loti among others – wore the fez when they wanted to show respect for, or deflect the hostility of, the Muslim population.[18]

The Sultan's reforms did not help the Ottoman Empire in its struggle against the Greek revolt. The success of the Greek revolt was sealed by the destruction of the Ottoman fleet at Navarino by the fleets of France, Britain and Russia on 20 October 1827. From Constantinople the British ambassador Sir Stratford Canning had encouraged the Allied commander to fight the Ottoman government. In an effort to persuade the Ottoman government to recognize Greece, European ambassadors,

---

*Bosnian officials at Sarajevo, in the last photographs of the Archduke Franz Ferdinand, wear the fez.

who felt physically threatened in Constantinople, left the city for the island of Poros between December 1827 and June 1829. The Reis Efendi had told them: 'The Porte does not need foreign medicines. The sword will reply to the sword. There is no place for mediation.' The Straits were closed to foreign ships. In 1829 Russia declared war. The Sultan's new troops proved no better at winning victories than the Janissaries. On 20 August 1829, the Russians entered Edirne, the second city of the empire. The Russian Black Sea fleet hovered off the mouth of the Bosphorus.

The people of Constantinople, by no means enthusiastic about the Sultan's reforms, appeared ripe for revolt; Russian control of Wallachia and Moldavia and the collapse of the government-controlled food monopolies increased the threat of famine in the capital. Calosso claimed that some *ulema* prayed for the foreigners to overthrow the infidel Sultan. Even a sober politician like the Duke of Wellington was convinced of the impending dissolution of the Ottoman Empire, and planned the reconstruction of the Greek empire in Constantinople under a prince of Orange or Prussia.[19]

However, one advantage of the strategic situation of the Ottoman Empire and in particular Constantinople was that no great power could hope to conquer them without arousing the opposition of the others. Moreover the statesmen then ruling the great powers were too fearful of the political consequences to desire the collapse of the empire. Far from being a conflict of East and West, the history of the 'Eastern Question' shows the desire of Western powers, and even Russia, to avoid the destruction of the Ottoman Empire for as long as possible. The British Foreign Secretary Lord Castlereagh had said: 'Barbarous as it is, Turkey forms in the system of Europe a necessary part.' In Russia a secret government committee had concluded in 1828 that 'the advantages of the preservation of the Ottoman Empire outweigh its disadvantages' (since it would probably be replaced by powers under the influence of Britain or France). When he recovered from his initial fear in August 1829 that the empire would collapse, Wellington revealed the great truth: 'The Ottoman Empire stands not for the benefit of the Turks but of Christian Europe.' Metternich pronounced the preservation of the Ottoman Empire in Europe 'a political necessity for Austria'. For the next hundred years it was such opinions, together with the resilience of the Ottoman army and the loyalty of its Muslim subjects, which kept Constantinople Ottoman.

The Sultan and his ministers knew how to turn European interest to their advantage. On 9 September 1829, after consultation with the Ottoman government, both the British and French ambassadors, Sir Robert Gordon and Comte Guilleminot, wrote to the Russian commander: 'The Sublime Porte has formally declared to us, and we do not hesitate to attest the truth of the declaration, that in that case [a further Russian advance] it will cease to exist.' Both ambassadors received the authority to summon the French and British naval squadrons which had appeared before the Dardanelles, if they were needed to help maintain law and order in Constantinople. On occasion foreign embassies guarded the city more effectively than its walls. In fact the Russian government had already decided not to attack the capital. Peace was signed at Edirne on 14 September. Russia made extensive gains in the Caucasus, while Ottoman control of the principalities was loosened.[20] The fate of Constantinople had, not for the last time, been decided between the Porte, the Russian army and the Royal Navy.

Thereafter the powers tried to preserve the empire through acts as well as words. From 1834 Russia, Prussia and Britain sent military and naval officers to Constantinople to reform the Ottoman army and fleet. Four times – in 1834–5, 1836, 1853 and 1878 – the British ambassador to the Porte was granted the power to summon the fleet to the Bosphorus to protect Constantinople, if the Sultan requested.

The combination of massacre, invasion and fire – another fire, possibly started by former Janissaries, devastated Pera in 1831 – could have made Constantinople after 1826 as sombre and repressed as Madrid in the grey decades following the Spanish Civil War. On his return in 1832, Stratford Canning wrote: 'The general tendency is evidently towards decay and depopulation.' Pera was 'a perfect wreck'; the empire 'evidently hastening to dissolution'.[21]

Events disproved the ambassador. Incapable of doubt or despair, fortified by dynastic pride, Mahmud II cheerfully transformed his capital, his government and himself. It seemed that only the Janissaries had delayed the empire's return to the openness of the reign of Fatih and the early sixteenth century. After 1830 Mahmud II's palaces not only looked European from the outside, but were furnished with Sèvres china, French tables, chairs and clocks – although in reminiscence of their habit of lying on cushions, pashas still rested their legs on the rungs of the chairs, rather than the floor. Coffee was served in the palace 'quite in the Frank manner with saucers, spoons, sugar and even sugar tongs'. The Sultan ate two meals a day, at eleven and towards sunset, not in the traditional manner on a tray raised on the floor but on a table with a cloth, fork and knife. A large bottle of champagne was set beside him at dinner. Unkind observers attributed his ruddy complexion not to hours of drill in the open air but to hours of drink in the palace. His doctors wrote: 'He liked to see his table covered with the finest dishes, the best wines of France . . . his meals were those of a gourmet and sometimes he indulged himself rather generously.' In the evening his palace resounded to the sound of music. Dancing boys and, what shocked courtiers more, Greek girls from outside the palace appeared.[22]

The best informed man in his empire, with eyes and ears everywhere, he was the last Sultan to visit coffee-houses 'incognito' (although always in reality recognized) to test public opinion. With royal confidence, he talked to the discontented in barracks and mosques, pardoned rebels, played with his children and joked with the dragomans. At Tarabya he danced with Baroness Ottenfels, wife of the Austrian ambassador (inconceivable audacity in an empire where dancers were considered little better than prostitutes), and hunted with mixed parties of Ottomans and Europeans. The habits of centuries, even the Sultan's right of summary execution, were disappearing in a decade. The last example of summary executions was the death of two of his ministers, Pertev and Vassaf, in 1837. When an English visitor, Sir Grenville Temple, asked a palace attendant if heads still adorned the imperial gate of Topkapi, he received the regretful reply: 'Formerly very often, now rarely.'[23] It was the Sultan's reason, and his determination to save his monarchy, which drove him to modernize. There is no hard evidence for the story that his mother Nakshidil, Valide Sultan from 1808 until her death in 1817, was a cousin of the Empress Josephine and influenced her son to Westernize. As Valide she could have established contact with the outside world. Such rumours, like later stories about Ataturk's mother, reveal Western unwillingness to attribute successful modernization to a Turk.[24]

In 1826 Sir Stratford Canning had undergone the traditional ambassador's reception in Topkapi. In 1832 in Beshiktash he wore diplomatic uniform without a kaftan – as in a Western court. He was 'received very graciously by the Sultan and with circumstances of more than usual distinction. All the gentlemen with me were admitted into his presence and introduced separately to him, and he gave me a diamond snuff box and a horse etc.'[25]

Mahmud's II's embrace of European customs was followed by his ministers. They said that, since brandy and champagne did not exist in the Prophet's day, he could not have forbidden them. Breakfasting in Uskudar on the morning of the departure of the Sacred Caravan for Mecca in 1834, Sir Grenville Temple received from the leader of the caravan, as well as the traditional pipe and coffee, fruit, fish, yoghurt and brandy. On 25 January 1835 a grand ball in 'the palace of England' was attended by several pashas. The band of the imperial guards, composed entirely of Turks, played quadrilles, waltzes and cotillions. The commander-in-chief of the Ottoman army opened the ball by 'walking' a polonaise with the French ambassadress. English guests could not help admiring the 'incredible celerity' with which bottles of champagne and bordeaux disappeared. Constantinople had acquired a new identity, as a metropolis of modernization. That year Prince Milos Obrenovich of Serbia, on a visit to his suzerain the Sultan in Constantinople, dropped his traditional Ottoman costume for the new fez and the Ottoman frock-coat or *stambouline*. At dinner with the Grand Vizier he had his first taste of French food and champagne.[26]

The central government was transformed at the same time as the court. New ministries of the interior, justice, the treasury, were created in 1836. The Reis-ul Kuttab became Minister of Foreign Affairs. The translation bureau, created in 1821 to fill the gap left by the disloyalty of the Phanar, educated some of the great reformers of the future. Henceforth the Grand Vizier was less of an 'absolute deputy' of the Sultan and more of a prime minister. The new Sublime Porte building, finished in 1844, with Italianate arches and pediments, resembled a British government building in Calcutta.[27]

In November 1831 the first Ottoman newspaper, an official journal called *Takvim-i Vekayi* (Calendar of Events), or *Moniteur Ottoman*, appeared in both Ottoman and French editions. As the best educated of Ottomans, the *ulema* were often in the vanguard of reform and the printing was supervised by a member of the *ulema* called Sheyhzade Essed Mehmed Efendi and a Frenchman from Smyrna, M. Blaque. In order to ensure that the news was widely understood, there were later editions in Greek, Armenian, Persian and Arabic. It was said that the Sultan himself checked and wrote articles. The British embassy chaplain, the Revd Robert Walsh, wrote: 'The paper made its way to the coffee-house and the same Turk that I had noticed before dozing half stupefied with coffee and tobacco, I now saw actually awake with the paper in his hand, eagerly spelling out the news.'[28] The Sultan was giving the city new life.

He also changed the principle, although not immediately the reality, behind the treatment of minorities. In a speech in 1830 he promised: 'I distinguish among my subjects, Muslims in the mosque, Christians in the church and Jews in the synagogue, but there is no difference among them in any other way. My affection and sense of justice for all of them is strong and they are all indeed my children.' The horrors of 1821 did not end the ancient mutual need of the Ottoman government for Greeks, and of Greeks for access to Constantinople and the Ottoman Empire. The Ottoman government had no desire for a purely Muslim capital. In May 1821 the Patriarch who had replaced Gregory V presented a solemn memorial assuring the Sultan of his countrymen's 'inviolable allegiance and fidelity'. In August 1821 a proclamation of the Ottoman government invited Greeks to return to the city, assuring them that none would be punished.

If Constantinople was a place of long memories, memories were also conveniently selective. Walsh wrote:

> When I left Constantinople [in 1825] the unfortunate Greeks were in a state of miserable alarm and depression, seldom appearing abroad, and when they did they seemed to shrink from notice, and walked along with that look of suspicion and alarm which intimated very truly the state of insecurity and suspicion under which they laboured. On my return [in 1831] I found them as noisy, active and gay as ever.

Their revival was visible on the streets. They 'took the wall' of Turks – that is, made them walk on the outside of the pavement. On religious festivals they danced through the streets in their best clothes, preceded by music, before retiring to taverns which they filled with shouting and laughter. After 1830 twenty-five new Greek churches were built while many sacked churches, such as the shrine of Balikli, were rebuilt on a bigger scale. In 1831 a Greek commercial school was founded on the island of Halki, with courses in English, French, German and Turkish. From 1834 the Patriarch again received investiture directly from the Sultan, as he had until his predecessor's treason in 1657. In 1838 a hospital called the National Philanthropic Institution was built at Balikli, for which the Ottoman government provided free food.[29]

A 'second Phanar' emerged, led by the families of Aristarchi, Mavroyeni, Karatheodory. Lucie Mavrocordato, a cousin of Alexander Mavrocordato, linked the two. Born in Constantinople in 1812, she died there in 1884. Her husband, Mahmud II's doctor Stephane

Karatheodory, who was said to be able to read the Bible in eighteen languages, founded a dynasty of Greeks in the Sultan's service. The English writer Julia Pardoe watched the 'second Phanar' at a ball given by a wealthy Greek merchant in the long gallery of his house in the Phanar during the carnival of 1836. The guests retained an Ottoman sense of colour: 'Such bright blues, deep pinks and glowing scarlets I never before saw collected together; and this glaring taste extends even to their jewellery which they mix in the most extraordinary manner.' She danced with Nicholas Aristarchi Bey, courteous, flashing eyed, with 'the whitest teeth I ever saw'. He was son of the dragoman killed on the Sultan's orders in 1821; his mother and sisters had suffered exile and penury. Yet he served both the Sultan, as a foreign-policy adviser, and the Patriarch, as Grand Logothete. The ball united different countries and epochs. The band was Wallachian. At least two thirds of the young spoke French. Aristarchi, who had a well-justified reputation for being pro-Russian, wore Western clothes but, as befitted his Ottoman status, was followed on to the dance floor by servants who kept him continuously supplied with clean handkerchiefs, a luxurious pipe, and a chair on which to sit.[30]

The Armenian community also benefited from Constantinople's short memory. In 1819 flaws had been discovered in the accounts of Artin Duzian, Director of the Mint. Without the opportunity to return any money, four members of the family had been forced to sign confessions of embezzlement and then hanged from the windows of their luxurious mansion on the Bosphorus (later given to Huseyin Pasha, the Sultan's lieutenant in 'the Blessed Event'). Yet the family recovered the post of director of the mint in 1834, and held it until 1890. In 1830, after a long and agonizing struggle with the Armenian Orthodox, which had led to riots in Kumkapi and exile in Anatolia, Armenian Catholics were recognized as a separate *millet*, or religious community. Thereafter the Armenian community entered a golden age. Armenian churches built in the 1830s can still be seen in and around Constantinople. An Armenian councillor of Mahmud II, Haroutian Amira Bezdjian, often went to the palace while the Sultan himself visited his modest house in Yenikapi. During the war of 1829, he advised the Sultan to deregulate the food supply, and rely on market forces – an act which prevented the city from starving. He also helped to found Armenian schools, churches and the St Saviour national hospital, which still survives. When Bezdjian died in 1833 his ashes were placed in a casket in a boat and rowed past Beshiktash palace, so that the Sultan could say farewell.[31]

Under the sultans control of industry passed to the faithful, hard-working Armenians, who were more exposed to Western culture and languages than Muslims, while the latter continued to run the government and the army. The army was the reason for the introduction of factories, as it was for so much else in Constantinople. By the 1780s local gunpowder was so bad and scarce that foreign gunpowder was imported, in secret, from Spain and England. In the desire to achieve 'European standards', or 'English standards' – phrases constantly recurring in official letters – new gunpowder factories were opened, from 1795 on, at Yesilkoy, where the airport now is, Bakirkoy and Azadli. They were managed by the great Armenian dynasty of Dadian, a force in the life of Constantinople for the next hundred years. Arakel Amira Dad, who had come to Constantinople from Anatolia in 1767 at the age of 14 to stay with a rich uncle, soon received the title of *Barutcubasi* or Chief Powder Maker. From 1805, in an attempt to stem English imports, they started looms for weaving cloth. In 1810 Mahmud II wrote: 'Arakel Usta is honest and hard working. God bless them all!'

Arakel's son Hovhannes Amira Dadian, born in 1798, ran the gunpowder mills; a paper mill at Beykoz, founded in 1804; and a spinning mill at Eyup, founded in 1827. His new methods of rifle production were demonstrated in the presence of the Grand Vizier himself on 29 June 1827. He became an international entrepreneur who knew, and worked in, Ottoman, Armenian, Greek and French.* At government expense he visited France and England in 1835–6 and 1842–3, to study the latest industrial techniques, and purchase steam engines. In the 1830s and 1840s more state factories were founded in and around Constantinople, some using steam power. Guns and rifles were produced in a factory near the imperial palace at Dolmabahce; boots, muskets, leather, copper and wool in what was almost an industrial park west of Yedikule. In 1837 Mahmud II was so pleased with the gun factory at Dolmabahce that he said to Hovhannes Dadian: 'Ask. What do you want of me?', and granted his request that Christian children should no longer be drafted in from Anatolia to work in factories in Constantinople. However there were rumours of incompetence and corruption. An American missionary called the Dadian 'bold, skilfull, daring, energetic men whose distinction consisted in knowing how to handle men. Every man has his price was one of their principles, and

---

*Descendants still possess his three signet rings, each engraved with his name in a different alphabet: Ottoman, Armenian, Latin.

they found few men whom they could not bend to their purpose.' Some of the Dadians' factories closed because they could not compete with Western imports. The only factories which worked well, in this city of textiles, were those which produced the fez, textiles and carpets. In the imperial palaces built later in the century, among the few products made in the empire would be the silk coverings of walls and chairs, woven in a state factory at Hereke on the Sea of Marmara.[32]

Both physically and mentally, Constantinople was being forced into the industrial age. On 20 May 1828 astonished crowds lined the banks of the Bosphorus, to watch the arrival of the first steamboat, the English vessel the *Swift*, promptly bought by the Sultan. In 1831 another symbol of progress and prosperity, a theatre, was opened on the Grande Rue de Pera, opposite Galatasaray, by a Syrian Catholic called Mihail Naum Efendi: Donizetti Pasha soon organized an annual opera season there. Finally fulfilling a project discussed in the early sixteenth century with Leonardo and Michelangelo, a bridge across the Golden Horn was constructed in 1836. The Sultan, who was the first to cross, repeatedly drove up and down in another European novelty: a carriage.[33]

A school for medical and naval surgeons was founded in the same year, on the site of the old pages' school at Galatasaray: professors came from Vienna, instruction was in French. To shocked Muslims brought up to believe in the superiority of Islamic medicine, Mahmud II said that the reason for learning French was to incorporate as quickly as possible recent European scientific advances. Europeans 'have facilitated the methods of teaching these subjects greatly and have added their new discoveries. Therefore the Arabic works seem to me somewhat defective in comparison . . . my purpose in having you study the French language is not to teach you French as such but that you may learn medicine – and in order to incorporate that science step by step into our own language.' Open to Ottomans of every religion, by 1847 the school had 300 Muslim, 40 Greek, 29 Armenian and 15 Jewish pupils. Polytechnic, military, administrative and engineering schools were also founded, which were to be the basis of Constantinople's emergence, after 1850, as a modern educational capital.[34]

French began to replace Persian as the second language of the Ottoman élite. It was soon the language of the military academy and of despatches from Ottoman diplomats abroad to the Foreign Ministry in the capital. Nicholas Aristarchi taught it to the heir to the throne, Abdulmecid Efendi. French was so popular that by the twentieth century there were 5,600 borrowings from French in Turkish: words like *makillaj*, *noter*, *ruj* (for *rouge* – Communist). French gave the Ottomans a vehicle for communication, with the city and the world, more effective than their own language. Few non-Muslims had learnt to write Ottoman. French, however, was the second language of Greeks, Armenians, the embassies of Pera and educated Europe. From 1835, for example, the French translation of Hammer's great history of the Ottoman Empire was on sale at French-language bookshops through-out Europe, including Constantinople, which had a better international bookshop (J.-B. Dubois) in the 1830s than it does today.

Henceforth Constantinople was in continuous direct communica-tion not only with Mecca and Cairo, but also with Paris and Vienna. After the hiatus of the Revolution and the Empire, Paris had resumed its role as the capital of science and medicine, literature and pleasure. It was 'the cradle of the new Europe, the great laboratory where world history is formed', according to a German visitor.[35] An Ottoman poet agreed:

> Go to Paris, young sir, if you have any wish;
> If you have not been to Paris, you have not come into the world.

The great reformers Mustafa Reshid Pasha, Ali Pasha and Ahmed Vefik Pasha served or were educated there. It is nineteenth-century Paris, not 'the sublime principles of 1789', which changed Constantinople.

Another reform due to Mahmud II was the introduction from 1836 of the full apparatus of quarantine and plague hospitals, to combat the spread of plague. Until 1914 a sanitary council of two Turks, five foreign doctors living in the city and five representatives of foreign embassies administered the quarantine regulations. The council's official language was French. By 1850 plague began to disappear. However moderniza-tion and Westernization were by no means synonymous: the former often occurred despite, rather than because of, Western influence. Although foreign embassies helped to administer quarantine regula-tions, the British ambassador Lord Ponsonby feared that quarantine regulations would interfere with trade and, despite capitulations, lead to searches of foreigners' houses by the authorities. Putting privilege and profit before life itself, he wrote in January 1839: 'I am averse to these measures.'[36]

The transformation of the city was reflected in a change in the status of women. Their march of protest on the palace in 1826 has already been mentioned. Soon their freedom was such that official edicts denounced 'women of iniquity' for wearing 'all kinds of innovations' and forbade them to employ ornately dressed young coachmen and grooms. The thin gauze *ferace* (cloak) was so transparent that it was *une coquetterie de plus*. At the procession of the Sacred Caravan, 'whilst they studiously concealed their eyebrows and faces, all save their eyes, they carelessly let fall their ferigees, and evinced no scruples in exhibiting more of their persons than is usually exposed even by the least scrupulous of London and Paris'.

No woman was as free as the Sultan's favourite sister Esma Sultan, equally famous for the beauty of her slaves and the looseness of her morals. Born in 1778, she had been widowed at the age of 25 and, unlike most other princesses, never remarried. At night her palace on the Bosphorus attracted kayiks of all sizes, moored outside to hear the music of her celebrated female orchestra. The Prince de Joinville, son of King Louis-Philippe, was more impressed by the sight of the aquiline-featured princess and three ravishing attendants, flying across the Bosphorus in a kayik rowed by boatmen whose gauze shirts and breeches barely contained their athletic figures, than by Aya Sofya itself.

The princess's visits to the Sweet Waters of Europe or Asia were slave raids. In those valleys of light and shade and water, among playing children and groups of brightly dressed women sitting in the shade of ancient lime trees, her approach resembled that of a bird of prey hovering above flocks of defenceless fowls. Every man trembled lest he should attract her attention, for she would then despatch a servant to summon him to her palace. Refusal was impossible. After she had obtained her desires, she was said to order the exhausted male to be drowned in the Bosphorus.[37]

Her palace at Ortakoy (she also had palaces at Macka, Eyup and Sultanahmed), built at the end of the sixteenth century, contained apartments 'heavy with gilding and gloomy with cornices'. The grand saloon was covered with Persian carpets and lined by forty porphyry pillars. Julia Pardoe – one of the many European visitors who came to observe and record Mahmud II's revolution in Constantinople after 1826 – observed: 'The sleeping chamber, hung with crimson and blue satin and scattered over with perfumes and objects of taste had an air of comfort and inhabitation almost English.' The Sultan's apartment combined Ottoman luxury and English comfort: it contained incense-burners of gold, studded with precious stones; a Koran written by the Sultan and 'bound in gold with the imperial cipher wrought upon each corner in brilliants'; and a European bed hung with flowered muslin.[38]

For Esma Sultan was one of the richest women in Constantinople, with such influence on 'my angel lord', as she called her brother, that Muhammad Ali of Egypt addressed letters to her in the hope of affecting the Sultan's decisions. Some of her most profitable estates were mastic groves on the island of Chios. In 1822 massacres of Greeks by Ottoman forces on the island had led to a glut of Greek slaves in the streets and markets of the capital. Terrified young girls, handled 'like cattle at an English fair', presented to Robert Walsh 'the most deplorable picture of human suffering I ever beheld'. Indignant both at the loss of life and her own loss of revenue, Esma persuaded the Sultan to dismiss the officers responsible for the massacres. She also freed some slaves and returned them to Chios at her own expense.[39]

The beauty of his sister's slaves, as well as the quality of her advice, provoked the Sultan's visits. He had male favourites. A good-looking fat young man, Mustafa Efendi, had been 'noticed' serving in his father's café in Bebek. Having started as a page, he rose to be director of the Sultan's household, and private secretary, and earned a reputation for avarice, frivolity and dissipation.[40] However the Sultan also liked women, in particular his sister's graceful freckled slave Nazip, who had a laugh which was 'the very echo of joyousness'. She felt so happy in Esma's palace that, as was her right as Esma's adopted daughter, she thrice refused the Sultan himself. Another beautiful slave girl presented by Esma to her brother, called Bezm-i Alem or Ornament of the Universe (who as Valide in the next reign was to be a notable benefactor of the poor and the women of the city), bore Mahmud II two sons, Abdulmecid and Abdulaziz. For the first time since 1808 there was more than one male in the dynasty and the Ottoman throne did not depend on one life. Dynastic biology had stabilized.[41]

Mahmud II's modernization programme was a revolution from above, which gave his subjects a feeling of insecurity and vulnerability. Moreover the price of food was rising since, after the treaty of 1829, Wallachia and Moldavia were no longer forced to supply Constantinople with cheap food. A commercial treaty with Britain in 1838 abandoned government monopolies, opened the empire to a flood of British goods and ruined many Ottoman crafts. Beggars became more common on the streets of the city. The soldiers in the new army, many of whom had been conscripted from rural districts, showed their discontent. A Prussian officer serving with the Ottoman army, Helmuth von Moltke, the future victor of the Franco-Prussian War, found the

Sultan and senior officials and officers courteous. However, women and children in the streets occasionally insulted foreigners: soldiers obeyed, but refused to salute, their foreign officers. Marshal Marmont, a former marshal of Napoleon I and Charles X, thought the Sultan's troops as bad as could be: 'They are not troops, they are a reunion of men the character of whose general appearance is a miserable and humiliated air. It is clear that they are aware of their weakness.' For Julia Pardoe, in contrast to the outward magnificence of the barracks and workshops of the imperial guard, the soldiers themselves were 'very bad', 'mere boys, dirty, slouching and awkward . . . as unlike Household Troops as can well be imagined'.[42]

Popular resentment extended to the Sultan himself. Greeks claimed that they had seen a portent of the Sultan's impending conversion: the cross of Constantine (which the founder of the city had seen before his conversion 1,500 years earlier) hovering above Aya Sofya. Muslims said: 'The Franks are turning the head of the Sultan and he will soon be as they are.' In 1837, as the Sultan was crossing the bridge over the Golden Horn, he was denounced by a dervish known as the Hairy Sheikh, as *gavur padishah* (infidel Sultan): 'You shall be responsible to Allah for your impiety.' When the Sultan called him mad, the dervish screamed: 'Mad, I mad! It is you and your base counsellors who have lost your reason!' When the dervish was executed, he was hailed as a martyr. A brilliant light was soon seen shining above his tomb.[43]

Constantinople began to lose confidence in itself. On a visit to an Ottoman house, ladies continually remarked to Julia Pardoe 'how much I must find everything in Turkey inferior to what I had been accustomed to in Europe'. Aware of the rude comments of Westerners each time there was a fire, the great reformer Reshid Pasha wrote to the Sultan in November 1836 advocating the introduction of stone buildings, and streets planned by European architects 'according to the rules of geometry'.[44]

The most dangerous opposition to Mahmud II came not from his subjects in the Ottoman capital but from a political genius in Cairo: Muhammad Ali, Pasha of Egypt. Muhammad Ali was Egypt's revenge for three hundred years of subordination and tribute to Constantinople since its conquest by Selim I in 1517. One of the ablest rulers of the nineteenth century, probably of Albanian origin, from 1820 Muhammad Ali began to modernize Egypt and to send Egyptians to be educated in Europe. His son Ibrahim Pasha, who dreamt of an Arab caliphate independent of the Ottoman Empire, created an effective army, which was one of the models for the Sultan's forces after 1826. In 1818, reminiscing on St Helena about his expedition to Egypt, Napoleon had said: 'The East only awaits a man.' Was the Pasha, not the Sultan, 'the man' for whom the East was waiting? In 1832, Egyptian troops took Syria. In 1833 they invaded Anatolia and on 2 February reached Kutahya, only 150 miles from Constantinople. Since Egypt had close relations with France, the Sultan in desperation turned to the Ottomans' traditional enemy, Russia. On 20 February Russian ships anchored in the Golden Horn. For much of that year 14,000 Russian troops camped along the Bosphorus. French protests were answered with the remark: 'He who falls into the sea embraces even a serpent.' The aggressively anti-Russian British ambassador, Lord Ponsonby, told the Sultan he was throwing his crown into the lap of the Emperor Nicholas and reminded him of the power of the British fleet to stop Muhammad Ali and Russia.[45]

A compromise was reached later that year whereby Muhammad Ali was appointed governor of Syria. Russian forces withdrew. Soon the Pasha wanted hereditary possession of Egypt and Syria for his family, and the removal of his personal enemies from the central government. Claiming, by virtue of his energy and courage, to be the most effective defender of 'the cause of Islam and the integrity of the Ottoman Empire', Muhammad Ali won many admirers in Constantinople, even in the palace.

In 1839 he launched another attack on the Anatolian provinces. The Sultan became thin with worry about his army and his fleet, and had to have his clothes taken in. There were rumours that he was drinking pure alcohol, or wine fortified with brandy, and that he had delirium tremens. On 24 June, at the battle of Nezib in Anatolia, the Egyptian army again routed the Ottoman army. On 29 June the Sultan died in Esma Sultan's house in Camlica, aged 54. On 15 July the Kaptan Pasha Ahmed, a former oarsman in the imperial kayik, sailed into the port of Alexandria, leading most of the Ottoman navy over to Muhammad Ali.[46] In one month the Ottoman Empire had lost a fleet, an army and a Sultan.

I I

City of Marvels

Has the French ship arrived? What is the news from Europe?
First telegram sent in Constantinople, by Sultan Abdulmecid, 1847

MAHMUD II WAS succeeded by his son Abdulmecid (1839–61). As in 1829, Europe helped rescue the Ottoman Empire. Ottoman, British and Austrian ships and troops, partly organized by the ambassadors in Constantinople, defeated Muhammad Ali's forces in the eastern Mediterranean. In 1841 he agreed to cede Syria, to return the Ottoman fleet and to increase tribute payments, in return for hereditary governorship of Egypt for his house. The Straits were to remain closed to all foreign warships. Thereafter the delights of Constantinople contributed to the transformation of the House of Muhammad Ali from rebels into apparently loyal vassals of the Sultan. In the heat of the summer the ruling family, and increasing numbers of wealthy Egyptians, left Egypt to spend several months in palaces on the Bosphorus. In 1846 Muhammad Ali himself visited the city; in 1848 a palace at Beykoz was finished for his son Ibrahim Pasha. In 1858 one of the Sultan's daughters married a grandson of Muhammad Ali in Constantinople. The Egyptians' extravagance and European tastes were blamed by conservative Ottomans for raising prices and inspiring 'new trails of debauchery' in the capital.

With the preservation of the Ottoman Empire Constantinople entered its third golden age. More diverse than the reign of Suleyman or the 'tulip age', it was a time when the city was torn between contradictory forces: between dynasticism and nationalism; capitalism and the pre-industrial state; Islam and Christianity; the Russian army and the Royal Navy. Sitting on his golden throne at the Gate of Felicity in

Topkapi palace, Abdulmecid received the homage of the dignitaries of the empire, while his band played tunes from *L'elisir d'amore*.[1] His second eunuch would visit the judge of the British Supreme Consular Court, Edmund Hornby, for a pipe and a few hours' conversation in fluent, if high-pitched, French. An old madman, regarded as a saint, could walk totally naked, chatting to his friends, through the streets of Constantinople, even on occasion visiting the Sublime Porte; and the conversation of Ottoman ladies dressed in the height of Paris fashion (blue cashmere *robe de matinée*, rose wreaths, *crêpe lisse* ruffs), and reading the latest French novels, made a foreign visitor feel that 'the revolution' must come soon.[2]

Constantinople was the last bastion of the sedan chair – a conveyance suited to a city of steep hills and cheap labour. Caravans of camels still arrived from Europe and Asia. Yet the city also experienced a communications revolution. There were regular steamer services to Odessa after 1833, to Izmir after 1834, to Marseilles after 1837, and between the city and its suburbs after 1851: ferry schedules were difficult to keep since different households meeting at a ferry-stop insisted with scrupulous politeness that the other board first. The journey from Marseilles was shortened from six weeks to six days. The number of boats arriving in the port of Constantinople increased fivefold in thirty years, from 7,342 in 1837, to 39,901 in 1868. By then there were so many coal-driven steamboats using the harbour that a black smog often hid the kayiks scurrying below.[3]

After 1855 the Sublime Porte had its own telegraph office, thereby greatly facilitating both its control of the provinces and access to Europe. From 1872 a network of horse-drawn trams stretched from Yedikule (no longer a prison but a menagerie) in the west of the city to Pera in the north – although service and trams were inferior in the Muslim districts. Trams brought the life and noise of Europe to the streets of the Ottoman city. As one travel-writer, the Italian Edmondo de Amicis, recorded: 'You are startled by the sound of a horn and the trampling feet of horses; you turn and can hardly believe your eyes. An omnibus of large dimensions, rolling forward on two iron rails that had escaped your notice, and full of Turks and Franks, with its conductor in uniform.'

The hub of the city was the kilometre-long bridge built across the Golden Horn in 1845, between the pushing, yelling crowd of touts and porters on the quays of Galata and the majestic calm of the Valide Sultan mosque on the Constantinople side. Inverting the Ottoman proverb that the world was a bridge, the bridge was the world. The growth in communications brought more nationalities to Constantinople in the nineteenth century than before – and all crossed Galata bridge. To a Japanese visitor, it was the 'Bridge of Ten Thousand Nations'.

Greeks in flared white kilts walked beside Kurds in embroidered jackets and Arabs in burnous and kheffiyeh. Albanians in white breeches, whose orange sashes bulged with pistols, sold lemonade or *boza** to Laz – Muslims of Georgian origin from the Black Sea coast – in tight black costumes and pointed shoes. Hamals in brown jackets staggered past under massive burdens (on occasion a porter might carry a piano or a carriage on his back). Blind beggars rattled tin cups, crying *Allah! Allah!*, as Europeans in the latest fashions, or an ambassador's carriage preceded by running footmen in livery, passed by. In 1847 the sight of a black Ottoman officer on horseback, followed by white attendants on foot, bewildered visiting Americans.[4]

From the viewpoint of Pera and the palace, traditional Ottoman dress had become a curiosity, to be worn at a fancy dress ball or, in the case of old Janissary uniforms, displayed in a museum on the Atmeydan (some of these uniforms can still be seen today, in the Istanbul Military Museum). Ottoman officials wore Western-style uniforms or, more frequently, the *stambouline*, the cut-away frock-coat resembling that worn by Victorian clergymen, adopted after 1839. Provincial or old-fashioned Turks, however, still wore flowing robes and turbans of flowered muslin. Beside European ladies in hats, Ottoman ladies displayed intensely coloured *feraces* – apple green, scarlet, bright blue – replaced, later in the century, as Western tastes strengthened their hold, by less vivid colours: gold, bronze or crimson. Whatever the colour, Western economic dominance was such that, after 1850, almost all were manufactured abroad.[5]

The bridge reflected the rise and fall of empires, and changes of hour and season. F. Marion Crawford wrote: 'There is nothing like it in the whole world, from San Francisco to Peking – nothing so vivid, so alive, so heterogeneous, so anomalous and so fascinating.' At noon it was packed, at night deserted. During the Crimean War, fought against Russia in 1854–6 by the Ottoman Empire, France and Britain, the bridge was packed with English and French soldiers (called *Johnny!* and

*A drink of fermented millet: still on sale by the Istanbul end of the bridge.

Dis donc! by the city's street vendors). The cool way they looked at Muslim ladies in their carriages caused many an attendant eunuch to mutter *gavur!* and flick his whip.[6]

Circassians in sheepskin head-dresses as tall as a guardsman's busby, and narrow-waisted black tunics, reflected, on the streets of Constantinople, the advance of Russian armies in the Caucasus – or their desire to sell daughters and sisters in the best market. The advent of steamers increased the numbers of pilgrims passing through the city. During the Hajj Persians and Bokharans in brightly patterned wadded coats arrived on their way to Mecca. Their stories of Muslim resistance to Russian advance in central Asia electrified the coffee-houses of the capital. A wooden *tekke* of Uzbek dervishes on a hill above Uskudar, founded in the eighteenth century, acted both as the pilgrims' hostel and Bokhara's embassy in Constantinople. Russian pilgrims on their way to Jerusalem came through every year before Easter: later in the century, Nicholas II built a hostel for them in Galata, with an onion-domed chapel on the fifth floor. Traffic on the Galata bridge was so great that it was enlarged in 1863, in 1878 when a row of shops and restaurants was built under the bridge at either end, and again in 1912.[7]

The crowd on the bridge symbolized the open spirit of the reign of Abdulmecid. He loved wine, women and reform. In 1847 the city's slave market was closed: the slaves, landed by night on the shores of the Sea of Marmara, were henceforth on sale in private houses around Tophane and Suleymaniye. The Sultan's verdict on slavery, delivered to the British dragoman Frederick Pisani in 1851, revealed an apparent change in Ottoman attitudes: 'It is a shameful and barbarous practice . . . for rational beings to buy and sell their fellow creatures. Though slaves in Turkey are treated better than elsewhere, yet they are sometimes very ill-used. Are not these poor creatures our equals before God?' However, slavery remained legal until the end of the empire. Nor did the Sultan stop the acquisition of slave women for his own harem, although he allowed them exceptional licence: their veils were the thinnest in the city, and they conversed with young men from their carriages or the palace windows 'in the most lively manner'.[8] A favourite of the Sultan, Safinaz Hanim, hid a secret lover in the imperial garden of Yildiz, on the hill above Ciragan palace. When the Sultan found out, his rival was not executed, but merely sent to Bursa.

A young member of the Dadian family once scolded the Sultan for smoking while visiting the Hereke carpet factory, despite the prohibitions pasted on the wall. The Sultan told the boy's father, 'Your son is

right', and threw away his cigarette.[9] The Ottoman government continued its traditional role as protector of the Jews against Christian prejudice – a prejudice so ingrained that anti-Jewish riots took place in
Christian districts until the end of the century. A *hatt-i sherif* (imperial
decree) of 6 November 1840 renewed denunciation of the Christian
'blood libel' and declared that 'The Jewish nation will be protected and
defended.' The Sultan personally ordered a kosher kitchen and 'sabbath
leave' at the Imperial Medical School, in order to encourage Jews to
enrol.

Nineteenth-century Constantinople owes its grandeur to its defiance
of nationalism. Abdulmecid, and some of his ministers, had a vision of
the empire as a rampart against nationalism. He told Lamartine in 1849
that he wanted to create one people out of diverse races and religions:
'in one word to nationalize all these fragments of nations who cover the
soil of Turkey, by so much impartiality, gentleness, equality and tolerance that each one finds its honour, its conscience and its security interested to cooperate in maintaining the empire in a sort of monarchical
confederation under the auspices of the Sultan'. He paid this ideal a
monarch's ultimate compliment. He created a bodyguard of chiefs'
sons, two from each race of the empire – Kurdish, Syrian, Druze,
Circassian, Albanian. All were over six feet tall and wore their respective
national costumes on ceremonial duty in his palaces and during his
Friday prayers.[10]

The effective rulers for most of the period 1839–76 were a trio of
able if autocratic pashas, Reshid, Fuad and Ali. Reshid Pasha, noticed as
clever and promising by Mahmud II, had served as ambassador in
London and Paris. Between 1837 and his death in 1858 he was six times
Grand Vizier and three times Minister of Foreign Affairs. He was celebrated not only for his commitment to reform but also for the number
and luxury of his houses on the Bosphorus. Fuad Pasha, son of a
famous poet, was educated at the medical school before serving in the
translation chamber at the Porte and as a diplomat in Europe. With the
reputation of 'a man who in all matters liked invention and innovation',
he was twice Grand Vizier and five times Foreign Minister between
1852 and his death in 1868. He believed that 'Islam was for centuries, in
its setting, a marvellous instrument of progress. Today it is a clock
which has lost time and which must be made to catch up.'[11] Ali, son of
a poor bazaar merchant, shared the same beliefs, until his death in 1871.

Under their aegis, the two great imperial decrees of 1839 and 1856
were issued, forming the basis for what was known as *tanzimat*: the

policy of reform followed by the Ottoman government after 1839. They promised Christians and Muslims equality before the law in place of their separate legal systems, equal liability to military service and access to government positions, freedom from confiscation and, in the words of the 1856 decree, 'the attainment of full happiness for all classes of our imperial subjects who are bound to one another by the heartfelt bonds of a common patriotism and are all equal in our equitable compassionate view'. The last execution of a convert to Islam, who had reverted to Christianity, took place on 4 October 1843. Despite the protests of the five European ambassadors, alerted by the victim's relations, an Armenian was decapitated in public and his body flung into the street. Thereafter the law lapsed. Mixed courts to judge cases involving both religions came into existence in 1847. In 1850 a commercial code based on French law was enacted. The power of kadis to regulate morals and markets, declining since 1826, was transferred to a new police ministry, also based on the French model. By 1876, largely under the influence of France, Ottoman law had been transformed, and the powers of the Patriarchs over the Armenian and Orthodox communities had also diminished.[12]

These reforms were designed both to modernize the empire and to forestall foreign intervention. Having helped to save the empire in 1839–41, confident of their military and technological superiority, the embassies were beginning to give orders to the Sublime Porte. They were known as 'the sixth great power' or (after the creation of united Italy in 1861) 'the six kings of Constantinople'.* Ambassadors arrived at Constantinople on warships called *Thunderer* or *Charlemagne*, and sped in ten-oared embassy kayiks between their winter embassy in Pera and their summer residence in Tarabya: soldiers presented arms at each guard-post they passed.

Ambassadors enjoyed power as well as influence. In 1840 an agent of Muhammad Ali's son Ibrahim Pasha was told that the British ambassador 'Lord Ponsonby is he who today directs the policy of the Ottoman cabinet'. Decisions were sometimes made by the Grand Vizier, not in the palace or the Porte but at meetings with the European ambassadors in the British embassy. Conferences of the ambassadors in Constantinople met to decide the future of Serbia, Egypt or the empire itself. In 1869 'the embassies' and the Porte jointly appointed

---

*In 1857, his French colleague, discounting the others, called the British ambassador, Lord Stratford de Redcliffe, 'the sixth great power'.

the international commission for the reorganization of the port.[13]

Most of the embassies in Pera were rebuilt after the great fire of 1831, in a style epitomizing the power and character of the nation it represented. The Russian embassy, constructed between 1836 and 1843, is a red Romanov palace looming above the Bosphorus, with ten reception rooms, including a white colonnaded ballroom, decorated with views of St Petersburg. The architect was Gaspare Fossati, who later restored Aya Sofya for Abdulmecid, inserting an imperial tribune – a reassertion of Ottoman authority in a shrine which many Christians, especially Russians, expected soon to be theirs.[14]

The Palais de France, built between 1839 and 1847, covered in the LP monogram of King Louis-Philippe, looks from the outside like a large provincial prefecture. Within it is furnished as a palace with gilded *tabourets*, Gobelins tapestries, Aubusson carpets, Sèvres vases, portraits of sultans, kings and ambassadors. The British embassy is a replica of the Reform Club in Pall Mall, designed by W. J. Smith and Sir Charles Barry and built in 1844–51. A square block thirteen windows wide, its high walls, ample courtyard and green lawns made it an oasis of calm amid the turmoil of the city.

The embassies' arrogance could be useful to the empire, protecting it against external enemies and strengthening the reformers at the Porte against the conservatives. Reshid Pasha wanted further embassy 'surveillance' – his own term – and more foreign warships stationed in the Bosphorus, to force the Sultan to reform at a quicker pace.[15]

However, ambassadors' influence increased the Ottoman sense of outrage at the system of foreign capitulations. Consular courts began to claim the right to try foreigners accused of criminal acts against Ottoman subjects, and many foreigners and Ottoman citizens – possibly some 10 per cent of the population – used diplomatic protection to avoid paying taxes. The Ottoman government began to regard capitulation as the greatest hindrance to their country's progress. In 1847 European inhabitants themselves petitioned the Sultan against the crimes countenanced by their embassies; they had little effect. In 1848 Lord Stratford de Redcliffe blustered to Palmerston: 'While lamenting the irregularities that have been taking place, we nevertheless have insisted on the British right to full trading privileges.'[16]

Working ten or twelve hours a day quill in hand, handsome, irascible, detested by his staff, Stratford Canning was intoxicated by his sense of infallibility. When he survived a riding accident, his staff is said to have drunk a toast to 'Better luck next time'. Three times Ali Pasha asked London to recall the ambassador since he tried to take all credit for reforms to himself, and would not permit the Sultan to reign as his equal. It was a private joke between the ambassador and his wife to call the Sultan, not Padishah but 'Paddi'. The Austrian ambassador, Count von Prokesch-Osten, who believed that if the Austrian and Ottoman empires did not hold together they would simultaneously come to grief, said that Canning behaved not as an ambassador but as a sovereign. Canning's anti-Russian bellicosity, fuelled by Palmerston, London journalists and British public opinion, was a contributory cause of the Crimean War.[17]

Another factor was the desire of Napoleon III, who had recently proclaimed himself Emperor, to challenge the Vienna settlement of 1815 and divide Austria and Russia. Religion was his chosen instrument. In December 1852 the ultra-Catholic French ambassador, the Marquis de Lavalette, temporarily won the right for Catholic priests to have the keys of the church of the Holy Nativity in Bethlehem. Tsar Nicholas I did not share the territorial ambitions of his grandmother Catherine II. However he was intent on resisting French demands over the Holy Places and on establishing a Russian protectorate over the Orthodox Church, even claiming the right of Russian officials to 'give orders' in churches in Constantinople and elsewhere. He hoped in the long term, in concert with the other powers, to partition the Ottoman Empire in Europe and transform Constantinople into a free city. Russian troops would be stationed on the Bosphorus, Austrian at the Dardanelles. The Tsar's language was unusually aggressive.[18] In early 1853 he made a famous remark to the British ambassador in St Petersburg: 'We have a sick man on our hands, a man gravely sick' (not so sick, however, that large numbers of the Tsar's own Muslim, Catholic and Old Believer subjects did not choose to leave the Russian empire and go to live in the Ottoman).

On 23 February 1853, watched by a crowd of excited Greeks, the Tsar's special envoy, Prince Alexander Menshikov, an arrogant professional soldier accompanied by the chief of staff of the Russian Fifth Army, landed at Constantinople. His mission was to enshrine in a formal convention not only all the traditional rights of the Orthodox Church but also, misreading the terms of the treaty ending the war of 1768–74, the right of Russia to intercede with the Ottoman government on behalf of its Orthodox subjects. In the seventeenth century the Ottoman government had expressed its arrogance by physical assaults on Russian envoys to the Porte. In the nineteenth, on the same battle-field of ceremonial, the Russian humiliated its victim by less violent means. During a courtesy visit to the Grand Vizier, Menshikov wore civilian costume rather than diplomatic uniform. He calmly walked past the office of the pro-French Foreign Minister Fuad Pasha, pretending not to see him, despite the efforts of the protocol officer to lead the ambassador through the open door to the waiting minister. Yielding to Russian pressure, the Sultan replaced Fuad Pasha by Rifat Pasha.[19]

International prestige, not the Orthodox Church, was the issue in Constantinople. The bishops, aware of the tsars' cavalier treatment of the Russian Orthodox Church, feared that 'protection' would mean 'slavery'. They told a Russian diplomat: 'We are now rich and strong. Nine million souls in the hands of the Patriarch, his synod and seventy bishops. You with the right of protectorate will deprive us of every-thing.' Moreover the Russian government was in reality prepared to modify nearly all its demands.[20]

However, in March 1853 the situation worsened with the despatch of the French Mediterranean fleet to Greek waters. In April Stratford Canning, recently raised to the peerage as Viscount Stratford de Redcliffe, returned to Constantinople with the intention, as he wrote to his wife, 'to make the P[orte] stand by me'. Like previous British ambas-sadors, Ainslie and Ponsonby, in the intoxicating atmosphere of the Ottoman capital he was ready to risk war with Russia – and he had the power to summon the Mediterranean fleet if the Sultan desired. When Menshikov visited Reshid in his yali, Stratford waited outside in his kayik, in order to discuss Russian demands as soon as they had been made.[21]

Even for Constantinople the diplomacy of these months was unusu-ally fevered. The Ottoman government used the prospect of French and British support to engineer a war with Russia under more favourable circumstances than those of 1829, 1787 and 1768. Demonstrations by *softas* (students from the *medreses*) in August 1853 were used to request the arrival of the French and British fleets, then anchored off Besika Bay near the Dardanelles, to protect foreigners' lives and property. On 26–28 September a 'grand council' of repres-entatives of the law, the army, the navy and the guilds, summoned by the Sultan, voted in favour of war. According to an observer from the British embassy, so different was Abdulmecid from his predecessors, and so quickly had Ottoman society changed, that instead of staying silent or requesting further orders, the grand council of 120 resembled in its disputations a meeting of the House of Commons. Having secured a favourable fatwa the Sultan declared war on Russia on 4 October 1853. On 22 October, a joint Franco-British naval squadron anchored off the Golden Horn.[22] On 28 March 1854 war broke out between Russia and Britain and France.

Volunteers streamed into Constantinople, among them a Kurdish contingent led by an unveiled and unmarried heroine called Black Fatima, who became the talk of the coffee-houses. To the dismay of many inhabitants of the city, French troops camped outside the walls and beside Aya Sofya. The hills of Uskudar were covered with the snow-white tents of their British allies. They were quickly surrounded by another army, of money-lenders, horse-dealers, street-vendors and 'rogues of all nations'.[23] French and British troops roamed the streets of the city; officers were stabbed, shops ransacked. Britain and France imported their own policemen to keep order. At one point the British consular jail overflowed and the British locked their criminals on a hulk in the Bosphorus. The war and capitulations enabled foreign tradesmen to attack the monopolies of the city guilds, still potent forces in Constantinople's economic life. By the end of 1855 several hundred Slav and Maltese boatmen were working in the harbour, and foreign wine shops had opened in many corners of the city. 'Worse ruffians than the keepers of these shops or worse dens of vice and crime than the shops themselves do not exist,' wrote an American political observer, Nassau Senior, in October 1857.[24]

The Crimean War turned Constantinople into a city of the wounded. In addition to traditional Ottoman hospitals, there was an efficient French hospital in Pera, two floating British hospitals in the Golden Horn, and a British naval hospital at Tarabya. The barrack hospital established in the Selimiye barracks in Uskudar cared for over 2,000 British casualties. The superintendent was Florence Nightingale, who lived in one of the towers, now the Florence Nightingale Museum. When she took charge, the filth, disease and overcrowding in the hospital made it worse, in her opinion, than the poorest house in the worst district she had seen. Nearby was the general hospital and the cemetery (now the Crimean Memorial Cemetery, the principal graveyard of the city's British community). Among her problems was lack of support from the British embassy.[25] Lord and Lady Stratford de Redcliffe were better at giving parties than visiting the sick.

By early 1856 Russia was close to defeat and peace negotiations were about to open in Paris. The triumph of the Crimean alliance was celebrated by a ball at the British embassy, attended by the Sultan himself. On the night of 8 February 1856, below the illuminated names of *Victoria* and *Abdulmecid*, artillery, Grenadiers and Highland troops waited in the courtyard for the Sultan. Cannon salutes and the sound of 'God Save the Queen' greeted the arrival of the Sultan, escorted by English lancers. He was met by Lord Stratford de Redcliffe at the carriage door. Lady Stratford de Redcliffe, in eighteenth-century dress, received him at the top of the staircase. After a pause for rest in an antechamber, the Sultan entered upon a scene which rivalled one of Queen Victoria's *bals costumés* in Buckingham Palace. In the brilliantly illuminated ballroom, the embassy staff wore costumes from the reigns of Queen Anne or George III. They were outshone by the traditional costumes of such local guests as the Greek Patriarch, the Grand Rabbi, Turks, Greeks, Persians, Albanians and the wives of wealthy Greeks and Armenians, blazing with diamonds. The chief black eunuch walked about on the arm of another black, their swords clattering on the floor. Alexis Soyer, the famous chef, arrived with a performing bear – who turned out to be a friend in disguise.

The Sultan, who wore a plain dark blue frock-coat, moved through the ballroom, 'bowing on both sides and smiling as he went', stared at like a wild animal and followed by a 'gorgeous array of pashas'. Instead of sitting on the raised chair prepared for him, he remained standing to watch the quadrilles and waltzes, and to receive the presentation of diplomats' wives. He then walked through the rooms, ate an ice, expressed particular admiration for the Highland troops and English cavalry lining the staircase, and departed. The pashas stayed to eat and drink until morning.

The behaviour of a Turkish lady veiled in a grey *ferace* caused amazement. She went up to British officers, examining their stars and orders 'in the most bold and impudent manner', upbraiding passing pashas with threats of freedom: 'No more cages for us. We are going to see the world and judge for ourselves and love whom we like. What fine tall fellows these English officers are!' Further remarks followed. Finally Fuad Pasha insisted that the lady reveal her identity. She was the best Turkish speaker of the ambassador's secretaries – the Hon. Percy Smythe.[26]*

*

---

*In the Crimean Memorial Church below the Grande Rue de Pera, the first neo-Gothic

At the peace of Paris in May 1856 the Ottoman Empire was formally admitted to 'the advantages of the Public Law and System of Europe'. Its integrity and independence were guaranteed by all the signatories. The Dardanelles and the Bosphorus remained closed to warships of all nations; and Russia was forbidden to maintain a fleet in the Black Sea. Further celebrations followed Abdulmecid's move to his new palace of Dolmabahce on 7 June 1856. Ministers and ambassadors were happy to indulge, indeed encouraged, the sultans' passion for palaces – a passion which makes Constantinople, like Vienna and St Petersburg, an imperial power statement of the nineteenth century: Dolmabahce (1849–56), Beylerbey (1861–5), Ciragan (1864–71) and many kiosks, hunting lodges and private palaces were built along and above the Bosphorus. The architects were again members of the Balian family: Karabet Amira Balian and his Paris-trained sons Nikogos and Agop Balian. Topkapi was deserted, a palace of tears for discarded harem ladies and white eunuchs. The Sultan visited it only for his inauguration or, once a year, to venerate the relics of the Prophet. The mid-nineteenth century was the apogee of 'occidentitis'. The embroideries of the Topkapi throne room were, on the Sultan's orders, melted down to yield 88,345 kilos of silver and 912 kilos of gold. In 1871 the legendary shore pavilions and summer palaces, already badly damaged by fire, were levelled to make way for that supreme symbol of progress: a railway line.[27]*

No monarch had palaces as modern and luxurious as the Ottoman Sultan. Abdulmecid supervised the architecture and decoration of Dolmabahce during daily visits to the construction site. It is the apotheosis of Ottoman grandeur. In keeping with Ottoman tradition, the gates, carved with a frenzy of urns, rosettes and garlands, are like triumphal arches. The majestic façade, 284 metres long, stood out as a beam of white marble between the green of the trees above and the blue of the Bosphorus.

Within are 304 rooms, filled with gilded mirrors, overpowering pelmets, porcelain fireplaces, crystal torchères rising six feet from the floor, a double flying staircase with banisters of red crystal. The relative simplicity of the Ottoman imperial tradition had been exchanged for a

---

building in Constantinople, his 'loved and loving wife' erected a memorial tablet after his death in 1869, on which he was praised for 'never relaxing his attachment to the Turkish Empire'.

*The line connected Constantinople to the suburbs and Edirne, and after 1888 directly to western Europe.

style which Théophile Gautier called *Louis XIV orientalisé*: much furniture in Dolmabahce was supplied by Sechan of Paris and William Gibbs Rogers of London.

The surrounding complex of stables, kitchens, theatre, barracks and ministries transformed nineteenth-century Beshiktash into an Ottoman court suburb: a row of terraced houses for pashas imitated a London street. The palace retained traditional Ottoman elements, such as the division into *selamlik* and *haremlik*, and large central halls or *sofas*, off which other rooms opened. But its architecture and furnishings are essentially European. The walls are hung with European royal portraits and a collection of orientalist paintings, of harem ladies, the Hajj, the Sweet Waters of Europe and Asia, which appealed to the last Ottoman sultans as much as to the European élite. The gardens consisted of French parterres tended by European gardeners. No traditional Ottoman garden remains in Istanbul. None of the 1,500 cultivated varieties of Ottoman tulip survived there.[28]

In the middle of Dolmabahce, towering two storeys above the rest of the palace, is the largest throne room in the world. Fifty-six Corinthian columns support an exuberant *trompe l'œil* ceiling, frescoed like a backdrop for Italian opera, with pillars, clouds, curtains and garlands of flowers. The room is thirty-six metres high, forty metres wide and fifty metres long. The throne room became the ceremonial focus of the empire, in replacement of the Gate of Felicity in Topkapi palace. It was here that the gilded imperial throne, especially transported from the treasury in Topkapi, was placed when the Sultan received the congratulations of court, government and harem at the end of Ramadan.

On 22 July 1856 a banquet for 130 guests celebrated both the completion of the palace and the victory over Russia. The Grand Vizier Ali Pasha and the Foreign Minister Fuad Pasha received the guests. They were presented to the shy and smiling Sultan, who then retired: the Ottoman court was not yet so westernized that the Sultan Caliph could eat with guests in state. At the banqueting table in the throne room, lit by a giant chandelier burning 400 jets of gas, the Grand Vizier sat in the place of honour, Lord Stratford de Redcliffe on his right; on his left Maréchal Pelissier, victorious commander of the French army in the Crimea. Among the guests were the Ottoman commander-in-chief Omer Pasha, Stratford's indispensable Count Pisani and Sardinian, Prussian and Austrian diplomats. The imperial band played the *Mecidiye* march, followed by the French and British national anthems. When a storm broke outside, the band was so frightened by the peals of thunder and flashes of lightning that it ran away, and half the candles were blown out since they left a door open: the guests, although impressed by the palace, could not resist comparing the banquet to Belshazzar's feast, and prophesying, for Constantinople, the doom of Babylon.[29]

Surviving menus show a mixture of European and Ottoman dishes characteristic of the late Ottoman palace: *borek, pilav, kadayif* and *baklava* are interspersed with *potage Sévigné, paupiette à la reine, croustade de foie gras à la Lucullus.* Some dishes may be new creations, another local synthesis of East and West: *croustade d'ananas en sultane, suprême de faisan à la circassienne, bar à la valide.*[30]

The rash of splendid palaces was built for reassurance as well as display. The dynasty was losing self-confidence. Before the visit of the Empress Eugénie in 1869, on her way to open the Suez Canal, the Sultan's chief maître d'hôtel, M. Marco, was sent to Paris to hire chefs, footmen and tableware, as if the Ottoman palace's standards were no longer acceptable.[31]

Outside the palaces, the modernization of the city was extremely rapid. Equality with Christians and Jews was not only visible, since they could wear the same clothes, but audible. After 1856, for the first time since 1453, church bells rang in Constantinople. Some Muslims complained that the *hatt-i humayun* (imperial decree) of 1856 was 'a day of weeping and mourning for the people of Islam'. Many Greeks preferred the former superiority of Islam to the unwelcome novelty of equality with Jews. In 1859 a conspiracy against 'innovation' was led by the *seyh* (elder) of the Bayezid mosque. However, most *ulema* had been well rewarded from the spoils of the Janissaries. Fearing similar annihilation if they opposed the government, they kept silent.[32]

Moreover the government was careful to maintain Islamic appearances. The *selamliks* of Abdulmecid had had a note of frivolity. Accompanied by a band playing Rossini or the Marseillaise, the Sultan had sometimes looked so shattered from the pleasures of the previous night that spectators feared that he would fall off his horse. The *selamliks* of Abdulaziz, who came to the throne on his brother's death in 1861, were more solemn. He generally went by imperial kayik to the mosque at Ortakoy, built in 1853–4 on the Bosphorus north of Dolmabahce. Sir Henry Woods Pasha, one of the Englishmen employed in the Ottoman navy, remembered the Sultan speeding down the Bosphorus, 'a proud haughty-looking man with lowered brows and a sombre expression upon his somewhat dark visage, looking straight before him'. The oars 'worked in perfect unison, dipping and rising as one single pair. There was no splashing but as the oars came out of the water the drops fell from the blades glistening like diamonds in the bright sunshine.' Along the banks of the Bosphorus bands played, troops presented arms, and people made low reverences. Cannon saluted the Sultan from forts and warships, and as he passed kayiks crowded around to obtain a better view.[33] The Sultan, the city and the sea united to celebrate God and the empire.

The traditional world of the holy city, in whose mosques and *medreses* students were obliged to study the Koran and the Hadith in traditional dress, was not destroyed by the government of the Tanzimat – although ministers knew the *medrese* needed reform. In Constantinople Western and Ottoman cultures lived side by side. Abdulmecid loved both Western opera and traditional calligraphy: examples of his own calligraphy hang in the Hirka-i Sherif, a mosque with an interior like an Italian opera-house which he built near the mosque of Selim I. Far from evaporating in face of modernization, the dervish orders flourished. The Mevlevi *tekke* of 1855, on the Grande Rue de Pera, is a characteristic combination in style of East and West. With Corinthian columns and green wooden floor, it looks like an Irish ballroom. The Bektashi order, proscribed by Mahmud II, revived under his son, and new orders such as the Nakshbendi arrived. The reforms of this period, stressing the equality of religions and the importance of modern science and philosophy, were felt to have the same principles as Sufi teaching. A later sufi, Riza Tevfik, a leading intellectual at the end of the empire, wrote: 'There is no difference between the spirit of Sufism and that of modern science.' By 1900 Constantinople contained 350 *tekkes*, each with mosque, meeting hall and library.[34]

The presence of new French-speaking schools, where Muslim students read Voltaire, and the influence of Ottoman students returning from Paris, caused a cultural revolution in the capital. The first non-official Ottoman-language newspaper was founded in Constantinople in 1861 by a former student in Paris, Ismail Sinasi, dedicated to reforming the Ottoman language. The number of books published yearly in Ottoman rose from eleven in 1820–39 to 43 in 1840–59, 116 in 1862–76, 286 in 1877–1908, and 650 in 1909–20. Among them were works like the first modern Ottoman play *The Marriage of a Poet* (1860), and the first novel *The Love of Talaat and Fitnat* (1871), which attacked such pillars of traditional Ottoman society as arranged marriage and slavery. Most revolutionary of Ottoman writers was Namik Kemal, known as 'the Angel of Death of the solecism'. He began to eliminate the Persianisms which throttled the Ottoman language, and consciously to Turkify it. Referring to the publishing revolution and the change in mentality, E. J. W. Gibb wrote in his history of Ottoman poetry: 'In 1859 the Turks were still practically a medieval community. In 1879 they had become a modern nation.'[35]

An example of the rapid intellectual transformation of part of the Muslim élite of Constantinople was the writer and statesman Ahmed Vefik. Born in Constantinople in 1818, he attended the Lycée Saint-Louis in Paris in 1834–7, when his father was Ottoman ambassador to France. After a few years in the translation bureau at the Porte (which his grandfather had headed after the execution of Stavraki Aristarchi in 1821), he served both in the diplomatic service, in London, Tehran, Bucharest and Paris, and in Constantinople as a member of the high court and a lecturer to the Ottoman Scientific Society.

His father, according to their friend the archaeologist and diplomat Austen Layard, was 'a perfect Turkish gentleman of the most refined manners and of very dignified appearance with his snow white beard and his turban and robes'. He lived in an old-fashioned wooden house near the Suleymaniye mosque, containing fine carpets, divans covered in Bursa or Damascus silk and little else. Ahmed Vefik, however, was a new 'Istanbul Efendi', plump, dark and beardless, wearing fez and *stambouline*, equally at ease in Western and Ottoman culture. In his agreeable, disorganized house in a garden behind Mehmed II's fortress of Rumeli Hisari, across the Bosphorus from the Koprulu Yalisi, he maintained the traditional division between male and female quarters, but had only one wife. He is said to have known sixteen languages, among them Persian, Arabic, Greek, French and English, and to have owned the most cosmopolitan library in Constantinople (in the catalogue published after his death, of 3,854 books and manuscripts only 1,366 are in Arabic, Persian or Ottoman). He liked the Bible, Shakespeare and Dickens. 'A perfect store of information on all manner of subjects, Western and Oriental . . . the most cheerful, the most merry and the most entertaining of companions' according to Layard, he was an intermediary between Constantinople and the West. He translated Victor Hugo and Molière into Ottoman, and helped Charles White, correspondent of the *Daily Telegraph* in Constantinople – the city had entered the age of journalism – to write 'the best and most complete account of the manners and customs of the various inhabitants of the Turkish capital': *Three Years in Constantinople* (3 vols., 1845).[36]

Most Ottoman documents, books and newspapers, were still written in language as ornate as the gates of Dolmabahce palace – quite different from the simple Turkish of the street. Letters of ladies of the imperial harem are only slightly less elaborate than in the sixteenth century. It is not surprising that many French-educated 'Istanbul efendis' were alienated from their own culture and were satirized in the earliest Turkish novels. In Ahmed Midhat's novel *Felatun bey ile Rakim efendi*, published in 1876, its central character, Felatun Bey, loves Western furniture and despises Ottoman poetry: '*quelle bêtise, quel scandale que tout cela!*' His Greek valet announces meals with the phrase: '*Monsieur est servi.*' He moves near Pera, and enjoys going to its modern cafés. His sister stops making traditional embroidery and buys machine-made goods. The old Ottoman cohesion was disappearing.

However Ahmed Vefik retained his Ottoman culture, and pride. He read Hafiz and Omar Khayyám and wrote a history of the Ottomans and an Ottoman dictionary which tried to simplify – and Turkify – the Ottoman language. At dinner in the British embassy, Lord Stratford de Redcliffe was raging about the arrest of a British-protected criminal and asked what the authorites would do if he himself went with his *cavass* to effect their release. Vefik replied: 'Why, they would probably put you and your *cavass* in the prison to join him – and they would only be doing their duty!'[37]

One link between the Ottoman and western European élites was their shared imperialism. On his journeys in the Sultan's service Ahmed Vefik called Wallachia 'a new Sodom', and was horrified by 'those terrible people one calls the Christians of Syria'. The Ottoman Empire was a European necessity: 'Belgrade [remaining Ottoman] is worth an army of one hundred thousand men and I say one hundred thousand for the defence of European interests. The Serbs in possession of the Gates of Iron would be an inconvenient power for everyone.' However he occasionally succumbed to despair. In 1857, sitting by Rumeli Hisari, symbol of the Ottoman conquest of Constantinople, he bemoaned the empire's weakness towards Europeans: 'Perhaps we are justly punished. We were insolent and unjust in our dealings with foreign nations in our day of power. Now in our adversity you trample on us. It is the will of God.'

The state of Greece led Vefik to comment that there was 'no Greece, there are only Greeks'.[38] In chaotic, nationalistic Athens Alexander Mavrocordato, head of 'the Mavrocordato faction' or the English party, was said to be the only Greek politician who 'wanted a regular government as it is understood in Europe'.[39] Preferring the Ottoman Empire to independent Greece, many Greeks voted with their feet and emigrated to Constantinople. According to the census of 1881, over 50 per cent of the 200,000 Greeks in Constantinople were born outside the city.

The most prominent of the city's Greeks in this period were the 'Galata bankers'. While the Phanar became a backwater, as clean and quiet as the ecclesiastical quarter of a French provincial town, they lived in Pera and Tarabya and worked in Galata. Distant cousins of the Mavrocordato, called Mavrogordato, left Chios in the 1830s to be bankers in Constantinople. Their success was such that their former town house off the Grande Rue de Pera looks like an *hôtel* of the Faubourg Saint-Germain. The prominence of Greeks in Ottoman banking was not due simply to Greeks' preference for their own race – as the managers of the first Turkish banks set up in the 1920s would learn. Few Muslims were trained in modern banking techniques or ready to start at the bottom; by tradition they entered government service or the army. In 1871 and 1872 alone ten new banks started in Constantinople: the city was called 'the new California'. Bankers borrowed in Europe at between 3 and 4 per cent and lent at between 12 and 18 per cent to the Ottoman government – increasingly desperate for cash to pay running expenses and interest on the government debt.[40]

The rise of Constantinople as a banking capital is shown by the career of the Baltazzi family. Like the Mavrogordato they arrived in Constantinople from Chios about 1830. Bankers and tax farmers based on the Baltazzi han in Galata and a house in Tarabya, they soon won the reputation of being the richest individuals in the empire. Greek women, continuing Pera's tradition of seduction, often married foreign husbands.* In 1864, at the age of 17, Helene Baltazzi married the Austrian consul, Baron Vetsera, in Constantinople. Her brothers took the money they had made on the Bosphorus and, through their love of horses

---

*In the nineteenth century Amedeo Preziosi, a Maltese artist, and Guillaume Berggren, a Swedish photographer, both living in Constantinople, married Greek wives. Eurydice Aristarchi, Princess of Samos, conducted a love affair with Sir Henry Bulwer, the British ambassador, in the 1860s. He built her a castle on an island in the Sea of Marmara, which he had bought in order to develop as a market garden. According to Sir Henry Drummond Wolff she was 'a woman of great charm and accomplishment . . . much courted by the different Embassies, being intimate with the harem of the Sultan . . . she was the only woman who could argue coldly on political matters.' She was expelled as a Russian agent in 1877.

and the patronage of Prokesch-Osten, transformed themselves into Viennese aristocrats.[41] The Vetseras' daughter Mary brought the licence of Pera to the palaces of Vienna; it was with her that Crown Prince Rudolf of Austria chose to commit suicide at Mayerling in 1889.

The most important Galata banker was a rival of the Mavrogordato and the Baltazzi, George Zarifi. Educated in Greece, Zarifi made a fortune in Constantinople during the Crimean War, supplying the Allied fleets with coal. In 1864, with Baltazzi, another Greek banker called Ralli and a Jew, Count Albert de Camondo, he founded a bank called the Société Générale de l'Empire Ottoman. In 1875 the *Levant Herald* wrote that he 'enjoys a financial reputation second to none in the Levant and is beyond all question a financial power'. He was as influential with the Ottoman government as any eighteenth-century Phanariot: it was said that 'when Zarifi, Christakis and Agop Efendi want to carry through a transaction, that deal has to be made no matter what.' A generous benefactor to Greek schools throughout the empire, as well as to the Great School in the Phanar, which he helped rebuild, he was also a true Ottoman. Banker of Abdulhamid Efendi, the most intelligent of the sons of Abdulmecid, he travelled on his Ottoman rather than his Greek passport. When a French customs officer called him Greek, he replied: 'I am an Ottoman.' Although closely linked with the National Bank of Greece, in 1867 he refused to subscribe to a Greek government loan, raised on the Constantinople market, on the grounds that it was destined to cover military expenditure. In a letter of 5 April 1867 he wrote: 'Of course some ardent patriots will say that, with the loans armies will be formed and Turkish provinces will be gained. I say that in this way it is impossible to gain provinces. The only way is to build bridges, to do away with brigandage and to balance the budget.'[42] He wished Greece, 'my country', well; but his interests were centred in Constantinople. The loan failed.

The Greek community flourished under the protection of the Galata bankers. On the initiative of Ali and Fuad Pashas, however, the Patriarchate and the Holy Synod were reorganized under the 'National Regulations of the Nation of Romans', drawn up in 1858–9 by an assembly of Greeks and approved by an imperial firman in 1862. The old Greek guilds closed in face of the new capitalism sweeping into the empire; their wealth was transferred to the eighty-eight Greek schools in and around the capital. Among the most famous were the Zographeion, built by a successful Greek banker, Christaki Zographos Efendi, in a markedly Greek neoclassical style which stands out beside the more sober appearance of the Imperial Ottoman School of Galatasaray, which it overlooks. In 1861 a literary society, the Filologikos Syllogos, was founded by Zographos and the Sultan's doctor, Stephane Karatheodory, in a building off the Grande Rue de Pera. Unable to restore the Byzantine Empire politically, the Syllogos could at least commission the first scientific excavations of the Great Palace of the Byzantine emperors near Sultanahmed.[43]

Despite the prosperity of the 'second Phanar', after 1860 Athens was the intellectual and political capital of the Greeks. Greek children were sent from Constantinople to Athens to be educated, not the other way around. It was also in Athens that the 'great idea' of a revived Byzantine Empire, with its capital at Constantinople, became an indestructible passion, carried from the cradle to the grave. In 1844 the Prime Minister Collettis in a speech to the constituent assembly revealed the place of Constantinople in Greek hearts and minds: 'There are two great centres of Hellenism, Athens and Constantinople. Athens is only the capital of the kingdom; Constantinople is the great capital, the city, the attraction and the hope of all the Hellenes.'[44] Pictures of the Oecumenical Patriarch hung on Greek walls beside the King and Queen of the Hellenes – and Aya Sofya, without minarets.

Closely linked to the Janissaries, whose finances they alone had been said to understand, the Jews had suffered from the 'Blessed Event'. Behor Isaac Carmona, head of the community and banker to Esma Sultan, had been strangled; the next decades were the nadir of the Jewish community in the city. Oscanyan, an Armenian resident, wrote of them – and his observations are supported from other sources:

> They live in such places as no one else would inhabit. Their houses are like beehives, literally swarming with human life; even one single room serves for the only home of several families – and the streets of their quarters are almost impassable from the collection of garbage and all sorts of refuse, which are indiscriminately thrown from the windows of their dwellings.

After 1850 the most prominent of the city's Jews was Albert Camondo, later ennobled by the King of Italy as Count Albert de Camondo, known as 'the Rothschild of the East'. Born in Ortakoy in 1785, he was a friend and banker of Mustafa Reshid Pasha. In 1854 he helped to found the first secular Jewish school, providing the startling novelty of Turkish and French lessons. Among its pupils were David

Molho, who would be first translator of the imperial divan from 1880 to 1908. Infuriated rabbis opposed reforms, including Turkish lessons. Camondo was excommunicated and assaulted. On his way to Friday prayers in Eyup in his state kayik, Sultan Abdulaziz was suddenly surrounded by boatloads of rabbis and their followers, chanting sacred songs. They obtained the release of the rabbi who had led the attack on Camondo. Finally the imposition of a relatively liberal constitution by the Porte in 1864 gave the Jews their own assembly and reduced the power of the rabbis and the religious courts. Camondo, however, left for Paris in disgust. Their own conservatism, and the absence of a modern state education system, prevented the Jews of Constantinople from experiencing a cultural explosion comparable to that of the Jews of Vienna.[45]

The role of Constantinople as a modernizing metropolis is confirmed by its impact on Bulgarians. Until 1876 Constantinople was the capital of the Balkans. Drawn by the growing wealth of the city, and the increasing ease of communications, Croats and Montenegrins, 'as honest and faithful as they are handsome', came to work as watchmen or construction workers. After a few years in the capital, they returned to their mountains with their earnings. Every spring, as they had for centuries, two to three thousand Bulgarians, 'strong rude men' in brown jackets and sheepskin caps, drove flocks of lambs and goats into the city. During the summer they worked in the fields outside as milkmen and gardeners – and tortured passers-by with the scream of their bagpipes.[46]

With 40,000 Bulgarian inhabitants, Constantinople became the Bulgarians' largest city. In 1845, encouraged by the Tanzimat reforms, Bulgarian residents, for the first time acting as a separate national group, chose two representatives, Ilarion Makariopolsky and Neofit Bozveli, who asked for a Bulgarian church in Constantinople, and Bulgarian bishops in districts with a Bulgarian majority. The Oecumenical Patriarchate, wholly Greek despite its title, arrested the two Bulgarian leaders and imprisoned them on Mount Athos. However, a Bulgarian press opened in Constantinople in 1847. From 1848 to 1861 a Bulgarian newspaper, *Tsarigradski Vestnik*, published in a han by the Galata bridge, played a crucial role in Bulgarian cultural and educational life, having among its contributors the foremost Bulgarian teachers and writers of the day.[47]

The leader of the community was one of those multi-faceted notables characteristic of Constantinople, like Camondo, Zarifi, the

Dadians. Stefanaki Vogoridi was born in 1782. An Ottoman dragoman in the early years of the century, he was also a confidential agent of the British embassy in its dealings with the palace: Stratford de Redcliffe was rowed across the Golden Horn to the Phanar in the middle of the night for meetings in the Vogoridi house. Lord Ponsonby would talk for three or four hours at a time with the official he considered 'perhaps the best informed man in this country', enjoying 'a large power over the Sultan's mind', and speaking to him more boldly than any minister. It was a sign of the Sultan's trust that, having been Kaimakam of Moldavia in 1821–2 at the beginning of the Greek revolt, in 1833 Vogoridi became first Prince of Samos,* the Aegean island which for the Greek élite supplied some of the status and profit previously provided by Wallachia and Moldavia. Patient, discreet and loyal, he opposed the introduction of legal equality between Muslims and Christians on the grounds of haste (and perhaps because it threatened the Patriarchate's power). In 1851 Sultan Abdulmecid himself attended the wedding of Vogoridi's daughter to John Photiades Bey, a Constantinople Greek sufficiently trusted to occupy the uncomfortable post of Ottoman minister to Athens.[48]

Vogoridi was Grand Logothete of the Patriarchate, and the Patriarch regarded him as Greek. However Vogoridi's mother spoke Bulgarian and wore Bulgarian dress. Stefanaki Vogoridi was also Stefan Bogoridi, a Bulgarian who encouraged Bulgarian cultural revival and ecclesiastical independence. He remained a loyal, above all a realistic, Ottoman. He told the British ambassador that experience of Russia ensured that 'the Bulgarians would be the warmest defenders of the Turks *against* Russia if they could see a chance of success.' As the behaviour of other minorities, and indeed of the Turks themselves, would show, the ultimate determiner of loyalty to the Ottoman Empire was its performance on the battlefield.

Having moved to a spacious house in Arnavutkoy up the Bosphorus, Vogoridi allowed the first church services in Bulgarian in Constantinople to be held in his house in the Phanar. During the 1860s vicious disputes with the Patriarchate were interspersed with concessions made too late for effect. Bulgarians used the Sultan against the Patriarch. On Easter Day 1860 they sang a special hymn of praise to Abdulmecid, but omitted the Patriarch's name from the liturgy. Finally in 1870, at the urging of the Russian ambassador, Count Nikolai

---

*Its wealth and fleet had won it autonomy, under princes appointed by the Porte.

Ignatiev, a firman created a Bulgarian ecclesiastical authority based in Constantinople: the Exarchate. An impressive Bulgarian church, built in a mixture of 'Russian' and neo-Gothic styles, was consecrated on the Golden Horn beside the Phanar. The Oecumenical Patriarch placed an anathema on the Exarch and his bishops, which was not lifted until 1945. Tension between Bulgarians and Greeks was so great that Greeks demonstrated in the streets of Constantinople: 'Long live the Schism! We won't be absorbed by the Slavs; we won't let our children be Bulgarized!'[49] This factionalism satisfied the aims of the Porte in granting greater freedom to its Christian subjects – by meeting their demands, it kept them divided.

In addition to the Exarchate, a new school, Robert College, helped reassert Bulgarian identity. The foundation stone was laid near Rumeli Hisari on 1 July 1869, on land given by Ahmed Vefik, despite the opposition of Muslim neighbours led by the wife of the local imam. When it opened on 4 July 1871, the language of instruction was English. Run by American missionaries, it attracted large numbers of Bulgarian students and was the direct ancestor of Bogazici University, the best in Turkey today. Constantinople was becoming an international educational capital, like London and Paris. However, far from being, as the American ambassador had hoped, proof of 'the universal brotherhood of mankind', Robert College bred nationalism. There were fights between Greek and Bulgarian students and, only a few years later, in 1876, Bulgarians educated at Robert College would lead revolts against the Ottoman Empire.[50] No city, not even London, has educated more leaders of nationalist revolts against the empire of which it was capital.

The modernization of Constantinople was quickened by the arrival of approximately 100,000 immigrants from western Europe. Their presence turned Constantinople in the period 1839–80 – for the only time since 1453 – into a city with a Christian majority. Some immigrants were attracted by the moral anarchy of the city: others were Polish and Hungarian refugees, fleeing Russian and Austrian repression after the revolutions of 1848. True to its finest traditions, the empire caused a diplomatic incident in 1849 when it refused to permit their extradition; Austria and Russia briefly closed their embassies.

Thus if the Ottoman élite embraced Western culture, the relationship was not one-sided: many western Europeans continued, as they always had, to prefer Constantinople to their own homeland. Renewing the ancient Ottoman-Polish friendship, Constantinople was, after the failed

Polish rising of 1831, one of the centres of Poland in exile: shared hatred of Russia was stronger than differences of religion. Indeed the Polish revolutionary, Constantine Bozecki (1828–77), converted to Islam and, as Mustafa Celaleddin Pasha, was to be an early advocate of political reform and Turkish nationalism. Fiercely anti-Russian, he taught cartography at the military academy, and proposed a national assembly with seats allotted by race and religion. He married a daughter of Omar Pasha, a former Croatian soldier in the Austrian army, who had become commander-in-chief of the Ottoman army during the Crimean War.[51]

Poland's national poet, Adam Mickiewicz, likewise felt at home in Constantinople, where he appreciated the honesty of the tradesmen. The Turks' habit of living among a crowd of dogs and hens reminded him of his home town in Lithuania: 'We Poles cherish the Turks for not having yielded to force in front of our enemy.' He died there in 1855, during the Crimean War, from cholera caught while organizing a Polish legion to fight with the Ottoman army against Russia. (In another force, known as the Sultan's Cossacks, Poles and Old Believers served under a flag containing both a cross and the Ottoman star and crescent.) Another Pole, Stanislas Chlebowski, was court painter to Sultan Abdulaziz; he worked in a studio in Dolmabahce from 1864 to 1876, painting scenes of Ottoman glories past and present. His pictures, such as *The Entry of Fatih into Constantinople* and his frescos of the Sultan's battleships, still decorate the palaces today.[52]

Most 'Franks', however, came in search of wealth not freedom. Businessmen overburdened with the regulations and taxes of western Europe found it easier to make money in the Ottoman Empire, especially after the treaty with Britain of 1838 which lessened state control of the economy. Capitalism flourished on the ruins of the old economic order. Between 1838 and 1847 land values in Pera rose by 75 per cent; between 1820 and 1850 rents in the Grand Bazaar fell by 90 per cent. Of the 1,159 names of merchants and bankers in the *Indicateur Constantino-politain* of 1868, only 222 kept premises in Constantinople proper rather than Pera and Galata – and only 3.6 per cent were Muslim.[53]

The banks in the Bankalar Caddesi in Galata are a monument to this phase of Constantinople's history. Neither the cultural map of the city, nor Western love of Ottoman profits, had changed since the fifteenth century. Nineteenth-century Western bankers worked in the same street where, four centuries earlier in the Palazzo del Podestà, Genoese merchants had met to discuss the rise and fall of prices and pashas. Like their counterparts in the City of London, the banks are built in styles as various as the bankers' nationalities: neo-Mameluke, neo-Venetian, neo-classical. The street façade of the Ottoman Bank, in pillared 'Banker's Renaissance', symbolizes triumphant European capitalism. The rear façade is late Ottoman composite. The architect of the bank (and of other nineteenth-century buildings of Constantinople, the Caisse de la Dette, the Cercle d'Orient and the Imperial Museum) was Vallaury, son of a *patissier* on the Grande Rue de Pera. In keeping with its architectural dualism, the bank, established in 1863, was both a private Anglo-French bank and the official bank of the Ottoman Empire, with sole power to issue bank notes.

French, German and British communities emerged in Constan-tinople, each with its own chamber of commerce and post office: few foreigners trusted the Ottoman postal service started by Mahmud II. The British community worked in the embassy, the banks, 'Her Majesty's Supreme Consular Court', the British Seamen's Hospital by Galata Tower, the Imperial Ottoman Mint and the British High School for Girls, founded by Lady Stratford de Redcliffe on the Grande Rue de Pera. Before the Greeks had their Syllogos, the British Literary and Scientific Institution was opened in Pera in 1860. One of the leading authorities on the Ottoman language was John Redhouse, who lived in Constantinople from 1826 to 1853, serving both the Porte and the British embassy as an interpreter. He wrote *The Turkish Campaigner's Vade Mecum* (1855), for soldiers in the Crimean War; the first English-Turkish dictionary, of which a version is still in print in Istanbul; and, in 1877, a *Vindication of the Ottoman Sultan's title of Caliph*.

From the 1860s until the 1950s merchant dynasties – Whittalls, Barkers, La Fontaines – prospered in Constantinople in the import–export business. However long they had lived there, their sons were always sent to school back in England. There were regular cricket matches between 'the Embassy', 'Constantinople' and, later, 'Bebek' and 'Moda'. The latter, a village on the Asian side within easy reach of good 'rough' shooting, was home of the many branches of the Whittall family. They lived in large houses on 'The Avenue' and went to work every day in 'Con' by steamer.*

By 1878 the British community contained about 3,000 people and, in

---

*Sir James W. Whittall (1838–1910) established the family firm of J.W. Whittall and Co., specializing in the export of grain, nuts and opium, in 1873, and helped found the British Chamber of Commerce in Constantinople in 1887.

the words of one consul-general, was 'rather over-parsoned'. The embassy chapel was select and official; the Crimean Memorial Church tended to ritualism; there were also in Constantinople Presbyterian, Church of Scotland, Free Kirk, and American churches, many of whom tried to make converts; and All Saints, Moda, founded in 1876.[54] Despite persecution by the Armenian Patriarchate and the Russian embassy, some Constantinople Armenians ventured to become Protestant.

While much of the Muslim city remained relatively unchanged, the European influx helped transform Pera and Galata into a modern Western city. The twenty years after the end of the Crimean War were decisive. A memorandum establishing the Commission for the Regulation of the City proclaimed the desire to imitate 'foreign ways' and 'the best European cities', in order to deflect foreign criticism of 'the threshold of Happiness', as Constantinople was still called in official documents: 'In Istanbul the state of buildings, lighting and cleanliness of the city is second rate . . . it has been decided to make use of the knowledge of Ottoman and of foreign families long resident in the city and familiar with foreign ways to form a municipal commission.' Seven of the first thirteen members were foreigners. In 1865 the worst fire in the history of the city destroyed much of the area between the Sea of Marmara, the Golden Horn and the mosques of Bayezid and Aya Sofya. Thereafter streets were widened, in some cases incorporating sections of cemeteries. In the same year street names were extended throughout the capital. Regulations about the quality of building materials were gradually enforced. However Constantinople avoided the brutal urbanization, the imposed visual unity, fashionable in other capitals. It had no Ringstrasse, no sad straight boulevards like those driven through the historic heart of Paris by Baron Haussmann and, in direct imitation, through Cairo by the Khedive Ismail.[55]

In 1857 the sixth municipal district, with power to levy local taxes, was established in Galata and Pera by the Ottoman government under the presidency of a brother-in-law of Fuad Pasha. Records were in French and Ottoman, but French was the language of deliberation. A few years earlier, according to Ahmed Vefik's friend Charles White, Galata had still presented 'a picture of dissoluteness and profligacy not to be paralleled by any city in the world'; it was so filthy you had to wear galoshes. In 1858–9 it was both metaphorically and literally cleaned up. Shops and houses were pulled down, streets widened and paved, drains laid, traders and prostitutes evicted, in some cases by force. Prostitutes moved up the hill to side-streets off the Grande Rue de Pera. According to *Les Amours dangereuses*, by Raouf d'Orbey, published in Constantinople in 1874, some of the city's brothels resembled those of Paris, with marble staircases, powdered lackeys, pink satin sofas: *ivresse et plaisir!* In 1856 gas lights came to the Grande Rue de Pera (two hundred years after street lighting had been introduced to Paris): gas was supplied by the Sultan's personal factory. In 1864–5 most of the old Genoese walls of Galata were demolished. The cemeteries of the Grand and Petit Champ des Morts were transformed into municipal gardens; in 1864–9 the public park at Taksim was laid out.[56]

Pera became self-consciously Parisian. The chronicler of its golden age, Said Naum Duhani, great-nephew of the founder of the Theatre Naum, wrote that it was at once Montmartre and the Faubourg Saint-Germain (since it contained places of entertainment and the residences of the élite). The Grande Rue de Pera was lined with shops and restaurants whose names evoked the boulevards: *La Maison des Modes Françaises, Bon Marché, Grand Hôtel de Londres, Café Chantant Parisiana*. In the summer, when prosperous families moved to lodgings up the Bosphorus, many husbands, Muslim and Christian, used deliberately to miss the last ferry home. They would rush to the post office, send an apologetic telegram to their wives – and then spend the night 'on the town'. *Ivresse et plaisir!* Pera became a synonym for corruption, like the court in anti-courtier diatribes. 'When a man goes to Pera, you know what he is going for' was a remark requiring no explanation. 'Even the good Lord is different in Pera,' said one sad mother to her son, who refused to leave Pera to visit her in Uskudar.[57] Running off the Grande Rue de Pera were covered passages lined with shops, typical of nineteenth-century Paris and Constantinople. When the luxurious Cité de Pera (the present Flower Passage), was opened in 1876, the newspaper *La Turquie* called it 'a monument of which even Paris would be proud'.[58]

By 1882 the population of Galata was 237,293, one quarter of that of Constantinople as a whole. The total population of the city had risen from about 391,000 in 1844, to 430,000 in 1856, 650,000 in 1878 and 873,565 in 1885. Three quarters of the population of Galata were Christians, living mainly under the protection of foreign passports. Poor Jews and Muslims had been driven out by economic and social pressures.

The contrast between the darkness and decay of Constantinople and the light and prosperity of Galata, the growth in the Christian population, the accumulation of modern European buildings and artefacts in

the city, led both Ottomans and foreigners to draw political conclu-
sions. Ziya Pasha wrote in the new Ottoman newspaper *Hurriyet*, on 16
November 1868: 'We have remained mere spectators while our commerce, our trades and even our broken-down huts have been given to
the foreigners . . . Soon it will not be possible to make a living and it will
be necessary for them [the people of the city] to move to Bursa or
Kutahya or Konya and in this way Istanbul will be empty and the
European will reside in our places.' Six years later Edmondo de Amicis
wrote:

> Upon the immense façade of the city is presented in architecture and in
> columns the great struggle that is being fought out between the Christians
> who reconquer and the children of Islam, who defend with all their strength
> the sacred soil. Stamboul, once a Turkish city only, is now slowly assailed on
> every side by Christian quarters which slowly eat into it along the shores of
> the Golden Horn and the Sea of Marmara; on the other side the conquest
> proceeds with fury; churches, palaces, hospitals, public gardens, factories,
> schools are crushing the Mussulman quarters, overwhelming the cemeteries,
> advancing from hill to hill.

No one could tell which side would win.[59]

Another population, shorter, hairier and uglier than Constantinople's
human inhabitants, also lived there. Since the sixteenth century, thousands of dogs had divided the city into districts, each controlled by one
pack under a leader. Living street-sweepers, they scoured the streets for
food and offal. Like birds and cats, they were fed by the inhabitants,
particularly the Muslims, who gave them bread, meat (liver or spleen
sold by itinerant Albanians) and water. A large soft loaf resembling a
thick pancake was baked on purpose to fling to them. In Pera and
Galata, however, they feared the sticks and poison of Christians.

Each pack killed or expelled beasts from rival packs who trespassed
on its territory. The dogs were not afraid to sleep in the middle of a road
and cause the entire population of a quarter to turn aside. Mark Twain
saw three dogs remain lying in a street, without moving, as a herd of
sheep walked over them. The first trams had to be preceded by men
with sticks, to chase dogs out of the way.[60]

As the sun set, making the Horn truly Golden, Constantinople faded
into darkness, like a country village. In Pera and Galata gas lamps were
lit; the dogs began to howl. An English visitor in 1850 wrote: 'The
yelping, howling, barking, growling and snarling were all merged into
one uniform and continuous even sound, as the noise of frogs becomes

when heard at a distance.' If you returned home on foot at night, a stick, as well as a paper Chinese lantern, was essential. A drunken English sailor fell down in a Galata street one evening. Next morning only his bones remained.

There is a Middle Eastern proverb that a city where dogs do not bark at night is a dead city. Dogs were part of the life – many believed of the luck – of the city. They could defy the Sultan himself. Abdulmecid once had them taken to an island in the Sea of Marmara.[61] The public outcry was so great that he was obliged to ship them back to Constantinople.

12

The Road to Tsarigrad

Will mass be celebrated at St Sophia in the presence of the Tsar?
Théophile Gautier, 1852

O N 17 JANUARY 1875, the first day of the great Muslim festival celebrating Abraham's sacrifice of Isaac, Kurban Bayram, a short underground funicular railway was opened between Galata and the Grande Rue de Pera on the hill above. After the inaugural journey, Ottoman ministers and European ambassadors were served 'a sumptuous *déjeuner à la fourchette* with champagne and other choice wines' by Vallaury, the Pera confectioners, on elegantly decorated tables on both sides of the platform at the Pera station. Mr Albert, the railway manager, proposed the health of His Imperial Majesty the Sultan Abdulaziz. He then made a speech in which, to loud applause, he expressed the hope that the line (which still functions today) would be 'a new link of fraternity to cement the friendship between the Eastern and Western elements which met in Constantinople'. The *Aziziye* march, composed in honour of the Sultan, was played. Since the railway company was English-owned, the guests then drank the health of the Queen of England, 'the most ancient ally of the Sultan', and listened to 'God Save the Queen'.

The speech suggests that there was a wider cultural question besides the dominant political concern – whether Russia would take the city. Would Constantinople link East and West? Or were the city's Muslims and Greeks, Armenians, Jews and Europeans as divided as the rival packs of dogs in its streets, and so likely to make the city easy prey for a foreign power?[1]

A series of vital urban institutions – opera, bourse, school, masonic lodge – provided one answer. They showed that, on one level, Constantinople had become truly cosmopolitan. No aspect of Western culture aroused greater enthusiasm in the Ottoman palace than Western classical music. The personal interest of Mahmud II and Abdulmecid led members of the imperial family and ladies of the harem to form their own orchestras. Princes and princesses composed for the piano. After Friday prayers Abdulmecid sometimes went from the mosque to the opera, at the Theatre Naum in Pera. Performances were in Italian, but Friday matinees were in Ottoman and the programmes generally contained plot résumés in Ottoman. The flash of jewels behind latticed screens indicated the presence of Ottoman ladies in the audience. Constantinople's opera-house was on the European circuit: *Il Trovatore* was performed there in 1853, before it reached London. In 1846 the great composer of traditional Ottoman music, Ismail Dede Efendi, had died in Mecca, where he had gone on pilgrimage, possibly in disgust at diminished appreciation in his native city.

As in other cities the opera served the double purpose of entertaining the social hierarchy and advertising its wealth and sophistication. When the Prince and Princess of Wales, on an official visit in 1869, went to *L'Africaine* with Abdulaziz, the celebrated journalist W. H. Russell was impressed by the dress and jewels of the Armenian and Levantine ladies in the audience: 'It needed an effort to believe we were in Constantinople, so brilliant and Europeanized was the spectacle.' The city had been transformed since his last visit during the Crimean War in 1855: 'The "sick man" to the outward eye has shaken off all signs of the incurable disease from which he was supposed to be suffering so dreadfully.'[2]

Another theatre, the Theatre Ottoman (Tiyatro-i Osmani) in Gedikpasha, beyond Divan Yolu, was opened by Gullu Agop, an Armenian convert to Islam, in 1868. It employed seven Muslim and nineteen Armenian actors and eighteen Armenian actresses – whose Ottoman accent was not always above reproach. Dikran Tchoukhadjian, son of the chief clock-keeper to the Sultan and a founder of the Oriental Music Society, wrote *Arif*, the first opera in Ottoman. After its successful première at the Theatre Ottoman on 9 December 1872, Tchoukhadjian wrote three more Ottoman operas in 1873, 1875 and 1890, and songs and pieces for piano, inspired by the city, such as *Souvenir de Constantinople, Retour de Kiathane, Tour de Léandre*. Constantinople had become a city with two musical traditions.[3] Guatelli Pasha, director of the imperial band from 1861 to 1899, while teaching

Western music to Ottomans, used oriental tunes in the marches he wrote for Sultans Abdulmecid and Abdulaziz, and arranged Ottoman music for publication in the West.

The Theatre Ottoman also put on plays. On 1 April 1873 Namik Kemal's patriotic play *Vatan*, about an Ottoman victory in the Crimean War, galvanized audiences, and led to a demonstration in favour of the popular heir to the throne, known for his advanced ideas, Murad Efendi, son of Abdulmecid, and nephew to the reigning Sultan Abdulaziz. Its appeal to defend the empire at all costs showed the strength of the Ottoman bond:

> The enemy's dagger is thrust in the breast of our motherland.
> Is there no one here to save our unfortunate mother?
> If I should die before my country prosper
> Let them write on my grave, my country is grieved and so am I![4]

Constantinople was as imperialist as London or Vienna. From 1865 the first advocates of constitutional monarchy, known as 'Young Ottomans', were driven in part by fear that the government was too ready to cede outlying portions of the empire to Christian states. Indeed in 1867 the last Ottoman troops left Belgrade.[5]

With the exception of Muslims, reluctant to try new forms of commerce, the different communities in Constantinople shared a love for the stock market. A modern bourse was founded in 1854 in the Havyar (Caviare) Han in Galata. According to the 1867 *Statuts de la Bourse de Constantinople*, 'The bourse is administered by a committee of thirteen members, to be elected every year, of whom five will be Greek, four Armenian, two Catholic and two Jewish.'* Speculation resisted constraints of time or space. Stocks were bought and sold on the streets of Galata, in beer-halls and during intervals at the opera.

In 1868, despite the opposition of Pope, bishops and rabbis, the interdenominational imperial lycée of Galatasaray opened, with the help of a grant from the French government. Its buildings on the Grande Rue de Pera are still used, by what is now Galatasaray University. The first pupils included 147 Muslims, 48 Armenians, 36 Orthodox, 34 Jews, 34 Bulgarians, 23 Catholics, 19 Armenian Catholics. The principal language of instruction was French.

---

*In fact many Muslims speculated through third parties. The Chamber of Commerce founded in 1882 had eight Armenian, six Greek, five Muslim and two Jewish members.

In 1869 the school system was reorganized and began to be secularized: the state rather than the mosque was now considered responsible for Muslim education. The first modern Muslim girls' schools were founded. In 1870 a modern university opened, in a massive classical building built by Gaspare Fossati beside Aya Sofya in 1846: the 450 students were mostly Muslims from *medreses*. In his opening speech the Minister of Education admitted the tragedy of Ottoman Constantinople:

> If the encouragement, respect and protection bestowed upon the men of sciences and arts in the first two centuries of Ottoman history had continued for another two hundred years – if contact with the civilized nations of Europe had been established and maintained and the pace of progress had been kept alongside those nations – the Turkey of today would be in a different state. It is therefore necessary for all classes of the empire to adapt themselves to the requirements of the time and to enter upon the road of progress in all branches of the sciences and arts.

If the government had practised what it preached, however, the Sultan and the pashas would have built fewer palaces and more schools – and the university, first planned in the 1840s, would not have taken thirty years to open.[6]

The élite of the capital also joined the same club and lodges. From 1884 the Cercle d'Orient, one of the main centres of news and gambling in the city, was housed in a magnificent building on the Grande Rue de Pera. It was open to men of every race and religion, and viziers were members *ex officio*. Freemasons had existed in Constantinople since the eighteenth century; the Bektashi order had remarkable, and remarked on, similarities with the Masons, perhaps due to contacts with France through Bonneval Pasha. The masonic message of universal fraternity and abolition of religious and national differences seemed especially appropriate to the Ottoman Empire. The lodge *Le Progrès*, founded in 1868, held meetings in Ottoman and Greek. It was joined by men of different religions: Namik Kemal; Edhem Pasha, the last Grand Vizier to have been a slave (he had been purchased after the massacre of Chios in 1822); Stephen Mavrogordato, a banker; the American diplomat and expert on dervish orders, John Porter Brown. In another lodge called the *Union d'Orient*, in 1866, a French atheist cried, perhaps for the first time in Constantinople: 'God does not exist! He has never existed.'

Another member of Le Progrès was a commodities broker, Cleanthes Scalieri, a Greek who believed in the Ottoman Empire, a radical in touch with the great reforming vizier Midhat Pasha, the British embassy, and the heir to the throne himself. Scalieri was even allowed to lunch in Murad Efendi's harem. In 1872 Murad Efendi, who often roamed the city in disguise, joined Le Progrès, at the house of a lawyer called Louis Amiable in Kadikoy. Next year Murad wrote to the Grand Orient of France, the main masonic lodge in Europe, promising to follow masonic ideals: 'By fraternization our peoples of the Orient above all, so divided by diverse religions and different nationalities, will also be able to place themselves at the service of veritable progress.'[7]

The household could be as cosmopolitan as the school or the lodge. Large households, like embassies since the days of Lady Mary Wortley Montagu, were mirrors of the multinational empire. Nurses tended to be Circassians or African, servants Greek, stewards Armenian, cooks from Bolu (a small town between Constantinople and Ankara famous for its food), boatmen Turks or Greeks, gardeners Albanians, *agas* of harems African, governesses French or, later, Russian. All nationalities, Ottoman and foreign, liked Greek servants, because of their reputation for cleanliness: hence the Whittalls of Moda spoke better Greek than Turkish.

Different households might follow different specializations. In a large house at Camlica, an hour's drive from Uskudar, on a hill with splendid views over the entire city, lived one of the many Hashemites settled in Constantinople in the nineteenth century, Sherif Ali Haydar. Enjoying a large income from Mecca and a pension from the Sultan, he employed black slaves and eunuchs. The cook and the steward were Turks. A Kurd kept the poultry. The nurse and the *kayikci* were Greek; and the coachman, Jim (Hasan Aga), was an Englishman who had converted to Islam. Arabic, Ottoman, French and English were spoken in the household. The Sherif's sons by his first, Turkish wife attended, first the English high school, then Darulfunun University. His daughters by his second, Irish wife, Isobel Dunn (daughter of an officer in Ottoman service), were taught English by Miss Petala, French by Mlle Boutan and Turkish by Amin Efendi.[8]

Language itself shows that Constantinople was a mixture of antitheses and syntheses. Most official or commercial announcements, and the envelopes of letters, were written in Ottoman, French, or both. However, calendars, theatre programmes, commercial invoices, and later political cartoons and trade union rules, were printed in four or more languages: Ottoman, French, Greek and Armenian, with the occasional addition of Ladino. Even the municipal ticket placed on water-sellers' glass containers, to show that they were licensed to practise their trade, was often in Ottoman, Greek, Armenian and French. The people of Constantinople shared the same way of life and tastes; but no single language.

The supreme example of the city's cosmopolitanism in print was the popular calendar *Almanach à l'usage du Levant*. On the same page the almanach recorded the date according to the Muslim, Jewish, Old Style Christian (Orthodox and Armenian), New Style Christian (Catholic and Protestant) and Rumi calendars (the latter a special financial calendar in operation in some government departments). The almanach bid the believer rejoice, according to his or her creed, over the Immaculate Conception, the Prophet's night flight to heaven on a winged horse or the dedication of the Temple of Jerusalem – all three episodes being commemorated on the same date. The languages used were Ottoman, Ladino (in Hebrew letters), Greek, Armenian and French, with a short phrase up the middle in Bulgarian. The different means of telling the time of day, from sunset for Muslims and Jews, from midnight for Christians, were also recorded in the almanach. To be able to tell both Ottoman and European time, some residents carried two watches, or a watch with two dials. Steamers operated by Ottoman time, trains by European.[9]

The press also reflected the cosmopolitanism of the city. After 1860 a new sound could be heard among the street-vendors of the city: the sound of newsboys hawking papers. The number published in Constantinople rose from 14 in 1850, to 49 in 1876 and 57 in 1902. In 1876, there were papers in Turkish (13), Greek (9), Armenian (9), French (7), Bulgarian (3), Hebrew (2), English (2), Arab, Ladino, German and Persian (1 each).[10]

Many newspapers were published near the Sublime Porte, from which most of them received subsidies: *Bab-i Aali* became a synonym for the Constantinople press as well as the Ottoman government. One of its newspapers helped to modernize Persians as *Tsarigradski Vestnik* had modernized Bulgarians. *Akhtar*, published in Constantinople from 1876 to 1896, was a decisive agent in presenting modern ideas and Ottoman reforms to its Persian readers. Mirza Husayn Khan, from 1858 to 1869 ambassador to the Porte, there observed the reforms of costume and ministerial organization which, as chief minister from 1870 to 1880, he was to attempt to introduce in Persia. Some

Constantinople journalists were figures as cosmopolitan as George Zarifi or Stefan Bogoridi. A French-educated Greek journalist, Teodor Kasap (1835–1905), adapted Molière for the Theatre Ottoman and edited *Diyogen*. The first Ottoman humorous magazine, it appeared at different times in Ottoman, Greek, Armenian and French. Another of his magazines, *Hayal*, was famous for its caricatures. In a street scene which could have occurred in 1995, a traditionally clad woman confronts another in modern dress:

> 'My daughter, what kind of costume is that? Are you not ashamed?'
> 'In this century of progress it is you who should be ashamed.'[11]

The cosmopolitanism of Constantinople was a heroic contrast to the strident nationalism which dominated the political, intellectual and emotional life of other European capitals. With few exceptions 'liberal' opinion adopted nationalism with rapture. Citizens for whom nationalism was irrelevant – like the Greeks who left Greece for the Ottoman Empire – expressed themselves in acts rather than words. 'Every nation a state', the creed of Mazzini, one of the creators of the new Italy, expressed the spirit of the age. He believed that nations were divinely ordained. A state based on a dynasty, a religion or a region appeared an anachronism. Despite the primary importance of cities in human lives, since there were no more city states, there was no rival ideology of urban loyalty to weaken the grip of nationalism. Even in Constantinople's old rival, Venice, which had so much reason to grieve for its past independence, urban particularism had lost its political dimension. Both in 1848 and 1866 Venetians voted for union with Italy.

Perhaps the only city which aroused feelings of proprietary nationalism of equal intensity to Constantinople was Prague. After 1850 the Czech and German cultures of Prague separated. By 1890 Czechs and Germans frequented different cafés, listened to rival orchestras, attended different universities (using the same library on different days) and elected rival deputies. There were street fights between Czech and German youths. The poison also infected the rest of the Habsburg monarchy, which survived, in one of half of its territory, by making a compromise with Hungarian nationalism and, in the other, by drawing closer to German nationalism. Hungary imposed a policy of Magyarization on non-Magyars after 1867. The refusal of German speakers to learn Czech led, in 1897, to riots which almost caused a revolution in Vienna. German-, Italian- and French-speaking, Vienna had once been a trilingual city with aspirations to be the capital of Europe. From 1900 every immigrant who applied for citizen's rights had to swear 'to preserve the German character of the city'.[12]

Meanwhile, in a switch particularly relevant for Constantinople, Russia was turning from pan-Orthodoxy to pan-Slavism, from protection of the Greeks to a Balkan policy favouring Bulgarian nationalism. From 1870 the newspapers of Constantinople were filled with reports of nationalistic insurrections – in Dalmatia and Bosnia, Bulgaria, Albania, Mesopotamia.[13]

Inside Constantinople itself, many Ottomans began to succumb to nationalism. The social, economic and cultural bonds created by living in the same city could not outweigh the emotional satisfaction, the sense of righteousness, solidarity and self-sacrifice, provided by nationalism. The city was not enough: many inhabitants yearned for a state of their own. A prominent Paris-educated Armenian intellectual, Krikor Odian, writing in Constantinople, declared that love of the nation 'corresponds to the strongest and most natural feelings. The love and respect that one feels for one's father and mother, the charity and compassion that one feels for one's blood brothers and the inifinite love and tenderness that one feels for one's children are all contained and summed up in the love of the nation.' Nation, for him, meant the Armenian community, not the Ottoman Empire. There was a critical difference between the Armenian and Ottoman texts of the constitution granted in 1863 to the Armenian *millet*, at the same time as the Greek and the Jewish. With two councils, one for religious and one for secular affairs, elected by universal suffrage, it had represented a victory for the city's guilds and intellectuals over the Church and the *amiras* (notables). In Armenian it was called 'the national constitution of the Armenians', in Ottoman 'regulation of the Armenian Patriarchate'.[14] Abdulmecid's hope that Ottomans would lose their identity in their empire, like immigrants in the United States, was not fulfilled.

The Armenians reflected the struggle in Constantinople between dynasticism and nationalism. Valued disseminators of Western culture, they taught in military schools, served as ministers' bankers, secretaries and doctors and dominated the customs administration. The Balian clan built the Sultan's palaces; the Dadian made his gunpowder. Armenians were official treasurers, doctors, printers, photographers and embroiderers to the Sultan. No other minority has enjoyed such a degree of royal favour.[15]

Abdulmecid was so fond of the Dadian family that he gave them the privilege of wearing his gold *tughra* on their fezzes. Like his father, who had visited them in 1832, he stayed in the Dadians' luxurious seaside mansions at Yesilkoy, for visits of two to eight days, in 1842, 1843, 1845 and 1846. For a sovereign to stay with a subject was an exceptional honour in any country; in the Ottoman Empire the barriers between religions made the honour doubly striking. The silver basin and ewer used by the Sultan to wash his hands are preserved in the Armenian church of St Stephen in Yesilkoy.[16] One Dadian boasted in 1867 of the Ottomans' 'almost unlimited confidence' in the Armenians. Many Muslims, however, resented their success.[17]

The Armenians of Constantinople, particularly the rich, were happy with their situation. Krikor Odian was a realist as well as a nationalist. To the enthusiastically nationalistic Khrimian, known as 'little father' or 'the iron Patriarch', Krikor Odian said: 'Don't surround yourself with false hopes, beloved son of our dear fatherland. A new phoenix will not arise from the ashes. Here we have grand palaces erected by the hands of masters. Leave those ashes – return, come hither, so that your eyes may rest upon golden vestments.' The voice of the capital down the ages.[18]

However the palaces of Constantinople were one cause of what Khrimian called 'the woes and wounds of Armenia'. Provincial governors, determined to live well in the capital, extracted massive bribes from the areas they misgoverned. The American political journalist Nassau Senior wrote in 1857: 'There is not a palace on the Bosphorus that has not decimated the inhabitants of a province.' Marauding Kurds were a more physical danger. In the oppressed provinces of the East, divided between Turks, Kurds and Armenians, many Armenians turned to insurrection, and Russia. In Constantinople itself Armenians learned the habit of riot – against their own leaders in 1820, 1848 and 1861, and in 1863 outside the Porte itself, in order to speed ratification of their constitution. Moreover they were seduced by revolutionary liberal nationalism and the model of France, 'the beloved country', 'the promised land', 'the paradise of the idea', whose language almost all learnt to speak.[19] Caught between the attraction of a revolutionary solution, like that admired in France, and the reality of overwhelming weakness in the event of armed conflict, they were entering a situation they could not win.

If the Armenians were discontented, in the Greek community there was a conviction that time was on the side of 'the Great Idea'. Christianity was thought synonymous with progress, Islam with decay.

In Athens George Mavrocordato, a cousin of Alexander Mavrocordato and a future minister of foreign affairs, wrote: 'The conquering race is on the road to ruin; the Greek race is superior to all other races.' To attend a meeting of the Syllogos in Constantinople, and hear the expressions of national pride in every speech, was to understand the strength of Greeks' fanaticism for their fatherland.[20]

Bulgarians were also increasingly hostile to the Ottomans. One revolutionary leader, Lyuben Karavelov, wrote in 1869: 'A Turk is a Turk and neither God nor the devil can make a human being of him.' In 1875 some Bulgarian revolutionaries planned to set fire to Constantinople; others were preparing insurrection in Bulgarian provinces. A few Muslims were also beginning to hear the call of nationalism and to call themselves not Ottomans but Turks. They were encouraged by a feeling of solidarity with Turkish-speaking victims of Russian expansion in central Asia – large numbers of whom took refuge in Constantinople. An able young officer called Suleyman Pasha, born in the metropolis in 1852, director of military schools and author of a Turkish grammar, wrote in 1876: 'The term Ottoman is only the name of our state, while the name of our nation is Turk. Consequently our language is the Turkish language and our literature is Turkish literature.' He also favoured the introduction of a constitution.[21]

Protected by Ottoman strength and the European balance of power, the people of Constantinople, outside the governing class, had led a sheltered existence. The shocks of the reign of Mahmud II had been followed by an interlude of stability. After 1875, however, the city was threatened by an excess of history. Ancient ambitions revived, in Petersburg, the Armenian centre of Echmiadzin, Sofia, Athens – and Mecca.

The empire was challenged internally by the rise of nationalism, externally by the deterioration of its international position. After 1866 Austria-Hungary turned to the Balkans as an area of expansion to compensate for its expulsion from Italy and Germany. The emergence of the new states had brought two new embassies to Constantinople. The Italian embassy was off the Grande Rue de Pera; the German embassy a neoclassical palace built on a hill above the Bosphorus. German eagles spread their wings on each corner of the building. Sultan Abdulaziz said that he could feel their beaks pecking at his brain.

Abdulaziz was an eccentric with a passion for ram-fights and camel-wrestling. During his reign money borrowed to fund dams and railways was spent on the construction of further palaces, in addition to Dolmabahce. Until 1871 the Sultan had had the sense to be guided by Fuad and Ali Pashas. After their deaths, with his new Grand Vizier Mahmud Nedim, he fell under the influence of the redoubtable Russian ambassador, Count Ignatiev, a diplomat beside whom Stratford de Redcliffe seemed weak. He imprisoned or kidnapped enemies of Orthodoxy such as Armenian Protestants and Bulgarian Catholics, financed Bulgarian insurrections and helped create an anti-Ottoman Balkan League between Greece, Serbia and Romania. He was also the first pan-Slav in Russian government circles. Among his nicknames in Constantinople were *menteur pacha*, 'the vice-Sultan' and Satan.[22]

His writings reveal his fear and hatred of the Ottoman Empire: 'Improving gradually, the Turkish government, in spite of all its defects, constantly increases and develops its military forces, whereas the Christians get weaker and lose their warlike spirit.' He wanted 'to prepare the autonomy of our Christian co-religionists' and 'energize the destructive action of the Christian populations'. The Oecumenical Patriarch should be truly Oecumenical, rather than eternally Greek. Russia was stifled by the limits on her access to the Straits imposed after the Crimean War. Constantinople should be a free city ruled by a Grand Duke, and capital of a Balkan confederation, until finally it was annexed to Russia. His views, at first rejected by the Russian Foreign Ministry, found a more sympathetic audience after the defeat of France in 1870. Dostoevsky, for example, wrote in 1876: 'It goes without saying that sooner or later Constantinople should be ours.' Nevertheless both Sultan and Grand Vizier came to trust Count Ignatiev.[23]

The Ottoman Empire began to spiral downwards. In 1871, its radicalism alarming the authorities, the university was closed. In 1873–4 the empire was devastated by drought and famine. Between 1854 and 1881, for loans to the theoretical value of 94 million pounds sterling, the government received only 45 million: the rest went in commissions to Galata bankers, in bribes to pashas – and in loans to the Sultan's mother. The largest item of expenditure was the armed forces. The Sultan made the Ottoman navy the third largest in the world: so fond was he of battleships that he had Chlebowski paint them on the palace ceilings. By 1875 the Ottoman army was equipped with the best modern field-guns and rifles. By then, however, over half Ottoman expenditure went on servicing debts. On 3 October 1875 the Ottoman government reduced payments for service of the debt by half – a fatal blow to government solvency.[24]

Zarifi and other Greek bankers secretly entered into communication with Murad Efendi. Constantinople seemed like a madhouse on the edge of a precipice. In May 1876 the Greek and Muslim workers in the arsenal, who had been unpaid for many months, went on strike, possibly the first strike in the history of the city. The Sultan flitted restlessly between Dolmabahce and his new palace of Ciragan, which was lined on the outside with neo-Gothic windows and pink marble columns like the Doge's Palace, and inside contained consciously 'oriental' rooms decorated in ivory, porphyry, marble and mother-of-pearl.[25] Hated as 'the devourer of the people's substance', he was said to eat hard-boiled eggs, since they were the only food he trusted. Ignatiev hired extra Croats to guard his embassy – and advertise the panic in the city. On 9 May the religious students in the *medreses*, the *softas*, bought large quantities of guns. Since much of the army was away fighting Bulgarian rebels, the *softas* were now a formidable armed force, and were in touch with the reforming ex-Grand Vizier Midhat Pasha. At mass meetings in the Suleymaniye mosque they demanded a change of Grand Vizier and Mufti. Koranic texts circulated stating that the Sultan's absolutism was contary to the *sheriat*. Not for the last time, the forces of 'the holy city' and of political reform had joined sides. In Bulgarian provinces, as a result of the Bulgarian insurrection, several thousand civilians were butchered by irregular Ottoman troops. The number of victims in 'the Bulgarian atrocities' was exaggerated by diplomats and journalists in Constantinople, some of whom were manipulated by Ignatiev. Gladstone took up their cause.[26]

On 12 May the *softas* took to the streets. Shops closed: Muslims and Christians took refuge behind the iron doors of the hans. To please the *softas*, Mahmud Nedim was dismissed as Grand Vizier and a week later Midhat became a minister. Although foreign Christians claimed to be frightened, in fact the *softas'* target was their own government. The élite – Krikor Odian, Midhat, the new Grand Vizier Mehmed Rushdi, and the Seyhulislam – wanted to depose Abdulaziz and proclaim a constitution.[27]

Huseyin Avni, the Minister of War, a personal enemy of the Sultan, and the reformer Suleyman Pasha, won guards officers to their side and maintained communication with Murad through a Mason, his doctor Capoleone. The Seyhulislam, Hairullah Efendi, legitimized the Sultan's deposition. He was asked: 'If the commander of the Faithful exhibits folly in his conduct, not having the political knowledge necessary for good government; if his personal expenditures are beyond the endurance of the empire; if his maintenance upon the throne will lead to unhappy consequences, is it necessary, yes or no, to depose him? The Holy Law says yes. Hairullah, to whom may God be merciful.'

At 3 p.m. on 30 May, followed by two companies of soldiers, Suleyman Pasha entered Dolmabahce. Murad, his servants and his mother had been forewarned. Suleyman Pasha told him: 'Please, we are awaiting your presence. The soldiers are waiting for you.' Feigning ignorance in order to absolve himself of responsibility if the plot failed, Murad was escorted out of the palace. He was then taken by kayik to Constantinople and received homage as Sultan, not in Topkapi palace but in the imperial chamber of the War Ministry. The soldiers and people in the streets, with tears of joy in their eyes, cried: 'Long live our Padishah! Long live the nation!' *'Bin yasha!'* and, if Greek, *'Zito, Zito!'* However there was already a split between the absolutists and constitutionalists. The Grand Vizier told the ministers: 'My good fellows, it does not do to give these people privileges. As soon as you do, they always ask for more.'[28]

The simple manners and evident goodwill of Murad enchanted his new subjects. Poems in his praise filled the newspapers. Meanwhile in Dolmabahce Abdulaziz had been woken by the sound of cannon saluting his nephew's accession. When he looked out of the window and saw ships facing his palace, he quietly said: 'They have enthroned Murad.' He was then taken by kayik to Topkapi, where he was lodged in the room where Selim III had been murdered. With his mother, his maids and members of his family, he was next removed to an annexe of Ciragan called Feriye. Humiliation increased his nervous tension. One officer prevented the Sultan, so fond of building palaces, from inspecting repairs in the garden: 'It is forbidden to stop here. Go inside!' He spent much time reading the Koran. On the morning of 3 June he asked his mother for a pair of scissors with which to trim his beard. She dared not deny the request. A few minutes later he was found in a pool of blood, having slashed his wrists. Despite a certificate of suicide from eighteen doctors, rumours soon circulated, with the encouragement of the Russian embassy, that the suicide was murder.[29]

On 15 June a Circassian officer, whose sister had been one of Abdulaziz's consorts, burst into a ministerial meeting and, in revenge, killed Huseyin Avni and the Foreign Minister and wounded others. Never especially stable, Murad V took refuge in drink and morphine. Soon he was incapable of receiving ambassadors or discussing business. Doctors agreed that a recovery was unlikely. On 30 June Serbia and

Montenegro declared war on the Ottoman Empire. The ministers turned to the Sultan's able younger brother Abdulhamid, who promised to observe a new constitution and to follow their advice. On 31 August, meeting in the domed chamber in Topkapi, where the Grand Vizier had once held his divan, a grand council took the oath of loyalty to Abdulhamid. He was 34.

On his way to his inauguration at Eyup, he passed the kayik of Julien Viaud, a young French naval officer soon to win fame – in part due to the novels he set in Constantinople – as Pierre Loti. He noticed the new Sultan's expression of youth and energy: 'He was thin and pale and sadly preoccupied, with large black eyes surrounded by dark patches; he looked intelligent and distinguished.' At this stage, the Sultan said: 'My policy is to obey the ministry. When I have learnt what is needed, I shall change my policy and make the ministry obey me.' A commission including Midhat, Namik Kemal, Suleyman Pasha, Odian and Karatheodory drew up a liberal, bicameral constitution, modelled on the French constitution of 1814 and the Belgian of 1831.[30] Instead of a synthesis of East and West, the new constitution represented the triumph of Western ideas over the traditional Ottoman absolutism, balanced by the influence of the *ulema* and the fear of deposition.

A diplomatic conference was called in Constantinople to discuss the situation in the Balkans. On 23 December 1876 the opening session in the imperial chamber of the naval ministry was interrupted by the sound of cannon proclaiming the Sultan's approval of the new constitution. Its promulgation twenty-nine years before Russia was granted a modern constitution, and only twenty-eight years after Austria and Prussia had received theirs, was the culmination of the role of Constantinople as a modernizing metropolis. It was the first modern constitution in a Muslim country (except for an interlude in an Ottoman vassal, Tunisia, in 1864–6).

The text was read out in heavy rain in front of the Sublime Porte, in the presence of Midhat Pasha, by then Grand Vizier, the Mufti, the Greek and Armenian Patriarchs, and a joyful crowd of all religions and races. The Sultan promised a bicameral legislature, and 'the blessings of liberty, justice and equality' for all his subjects without distinction. Thousands of copies of the text of the constitution were distributed throughout the city. Houses and shops were illuminated as for a Ramadan night. Students and money-lenders celebrated with torchlight processions in front of Dolmabahce palace and the other power centres of the city, the European embassies, shouting, in Greek and Turkish:

'Long live the Sultan!', 'Long live the Constitution!', 'Long live Midhat Pasha!'

Midhat took the unprecedented step of visiting the Armenian and Greek Patriarchs. The latter greeted him as 'the resuscitator of the Ottoman Empire'. At the elections for the first parliament five Muslim deputies and five non-Muslims (three Armenians, two Greeks and a Jew) were selected for Constantinople. Elections went smoothly, although Greek newspapers denounced a Turco-Armenian plot to reduce Greek representation. However the Sultan feared that Midhat's constitutional views threatened his power: indeed Midhat had sent Krikor Odian, the Armenian intellectual and politician who had become one of his closest advisers, to London to request a guarantee by the great powers of the Ottoman constitution and reforms. On 5 February 1877 Midhat was dismissed and sent into exile on the imperial yacht.[31]

On 19 March 1877, in the throne room of Dolmabahce where Abdulmecid had held his inaugural banquet in 1856, councillors of state, pashas, sherifs, patriarchs, rabbis, deputies, generals, diplomats and journalists assembled to witness the opening of the first Ottoman parliament. Of the total of 115 deputies, sixty-seven were Muslim and forty-eight non-Muslim. They included speakers of Ottoman, Persian, Arabic, Greek, Armenian, Bulgarian, Serbo-Croat, Bosniak (the form of Serbo-Croat spoken in Bosnia), Albanian, Vlach, Kurdish, Syriac, Hebrew and Ladino. When one journalist told his neighbour he was trying to work out each deputy's race and religion, the answer was that they were neither Muslim, Greek nor Armenian but were all Ottomans.

The Sultan entered, followed by his brothers and his ministers, and stood before the gold-plated throne, his plain dark blue frock-coat a contrast to the heavily embroidered uniforms of the pashas around him. There was a deep obeisance, and silence for the monarch still called 'the auspicious Caliph Our Gracious Lord the Sultan . . . the glorious monarch . . . the glory of the Heavens and the earth'. After prayers by the *ulema*, the Sultan's speech was read by his first secretary, while the Sultan stood, 'his left hand resting on the hilt of his sword, the right now and then, more or less unconsciously, stroking his chin and twirling his moustache, a weary look, a somewhat anxious expression gradually settling on his face'. The expression of youth and energy which Loti had noticed eight months earlier had already vanished. The speech promised application of the constitution and administrative reforms. It ended with the claim: 'I have a firm conviction that from this moment all my subjects will unite in their efforts to make the name Osmanli retain the force and power hitherto surrounding it.' Neither the splendour of the setting, nor the salutes from the battleships outside, could hide the implausibility of the Sultan's words.[32]

The only ambassador absent had been Ignatiev. On 23 April crowds on the Grande Rue de Pera could watch the great double-headed eagle above the entrance to the Russian embassy being folded back behind the parapet: the architect, anticipating all eventualities, had mounted it on hinges. The embassy archives and staff left by ship. The next day, Russia declared war. Swept by the first popular nation-wide movement in their history, Russians saw the war as a crusade on behalf of their Slav brothers against the Ottoman Empire.

The next year was the most terrible since 1826. Sitting from 19 March to 28 June and 13 December 1877 to 14 February 1878, in the former university building by Aya Sofya, the parliament rejected any cession of Ottoman territory; but, despite the presidency of Ahmed Vefik, it preferred to criticize the government's corruption and inefficiency, and to cross-examine ministers, rather than to suggest practical solutions to problems. Tunisians, Egyptians, Greeks, Tartars, Bokharans and Malays poured into the city to join the Ottoman army. Guerrillas known as *zeibeks*, from south-west Anatolia, wearing short white breeches and blue jackets, brandished their knives and pistols in the concert halls of Pera.

The Ottoman army fought better, and the Russians worse, than expected. But the great Ottoman fortress of Plevna south of the Danube, in what is now Bulgaria, fell on 10 December, after a heroic resistance of six months. The words massacre, refugee, orphan entered the everyday conversation of the city. Railway trucks and ox-carts, loaded with refugees (Greeks as well as Muslims) fleeing the Russian advance, began to appear in the streets.[33] A total of 300,000 – equal to half the population of the city – passed through. The government moved as many as possible into Anatolia or more distant provinces. However, a refugee town of tents sprang up around the railway-station below Topkapi. Others were housed in mosques.

While the price of bread rose fivefold, Circassians stole everything they could, including children. Private houses, even Ciragan palace, were opened to refugees and the wounded. By January 1878 the people had begun to lose hope. Ministers no longer dared show themselves in the street. An old imam told an American resident that the pashas were worse enemies of the country than the Russians or English: 'Our nation is destroyed, our nation is ruined.' On 21 January the Russians entered Edirne (where they completed the destruction of the old Ottoman palace begun during their invasion in 1829). Despite snowstorms and sub-zero temperatures, Russians continued to advance. Their commander, the Grand Duke Nicholas, wrote to his brother the Tsar: 'We must go to the centre, to Tsarigrad, and there finish the holy cause you have assumed.'[34]

At this moment of horror, for the fourth time in the century, as in the years 1829, 1839 and 1853, Constantinople was saved by the concert of Europe. Austria-Hungary was prepared to fight Russian control of the Straits. Britain believed that Russia's expansion in the Balkans, the Caucasus and central Asia threatened the British route to India; the role of Constantinople as a world city meant that its occupation by Russia might also threaten British control in India. Since the eighteenth century, Indian Muslim attachment to the Ottoman Empire, the last Muslim great power, had been increasing. The Sultan was acknowledged as Caliph: prayers were conducted in his name. Some rulers, such as Tippu Sahib in 1786, had begun to send embassies to Constantinople to secure investiture from the Sultan Caliph. Indian respect and interest had increased since the end of the Mogul Empire and the imposition of direct British rule in 1856. The Viceroy of India warned the British government in early 1877 that if Constantinople fell to Russia, Britain's loss of prestige, and the outrage of Indian Muslims at the attack on the Caliph, would cause India to swim in 'a bath of blood'.[35]

From July 1877 the British government, regarding a Russian occupation of Constantinople as a *casus belli*, kept part of the Mediterranean fleet near the Dardanelles. The embassy's military attaché and British engineers advised on improvements to the fortifications of the city and the Straits. British public opinion swung from sympathy with the Bulgarians to support of the Ottomans. Two British officers in Ottoman service, Admiral the Hon. Augustus Hobart Pasha and Valentine Baker Pasha, distinguished themselves in command of the Black Sea fleet and an army division in the Balkans respectively. Constantinople became a British cause. The Stafford House Committee, the Grosvenor House Committee, the Turkish Compassionate Fund, the British National Aid Society sent bandages, money and relief workers to the city, and opened hospitals there. Many individuals became disillusioned by official disorganization and corruption; but nurses found Turkish men 'more delicate in their relation with females than the average of male patients in our English hospitals'.

The British embassy, under Sir Austen Layard, the only European ambassador remaining in the city (the others had been withdrawn in January 1877 after the Ottoman rejection of European demands for reform) functioned as a medical supply-centre. Secretaries, attachés and guards learnt to roll bandages. The Russian ambassador wrote that London was so overwrought that 'one would really think oneself at Constantinople'. Constantinople, which could inspire aggression in most nationalities, gave the English language the word *jingoism*. Waving the Ottoman flag in Trafalgar Square, crowds sang:

> We don't want to fight,
> But by jingo if we do,
> We've got the ships,
> We've got the men,
> We've got the money too.
> We've fought the bear before,
> And if we're Britons true,
> The Russians shall not have Constantinople![36]

On 31 January 1878 an armistice was signed between Russia and the Ottoman Empire. On 8 February, after much hesitation in London, ships of the British Mediterranean fleet were ordered to proceed from their anchorage at Besika Bay through the Dardanelles, under the pretext of defending the lives of foreigners in Constantinople. On 13 February six British iron-clads anchored off the Princes' Islands in a snowstorm, at the spot where Admiral Duckworth had moored in his attempt to intimidate the city seventy-one years before. Meanwhile the Ottoman parliament had called for the trial of the War Minister and certain generals. On 14 February Ahmed Vefik, who had become Prime Minister (as the Grand Vizier was called under the new constitution) and favoured absolutism, read out a decree for the suspension of the Ottoman parliament. It was not recalled for thirty years.[37]

Infuriated by the news of the arrival of the Royal Navy, the Tsar telegraphed to his brother on 10 February, instructing him to enter Constantinople: 'I leave to you the numbers and moment to occupy.' Ignatiev, who was at the Grand Duke's headquarters, also urged occupation. The Ottoman government was losing its nerve. Ahmed Vefik had become a tearful old man obsessed with the fate of the refugees. He wrote notes to his old friend Layard, whom he saw almost daily, urging him to save the empire. In January: 'We cannot commit suicide.' In

February: 'You said nothing to me and I do not know what to do at the council.' Again: 'We are ruined and how to resist one more year?'

The Sultan, who had an acute sense of his own vulnerability, had already, a year earlier, moved out of Dolmabahce into a palace called Yildiz, on a hill above Ciragan, since it was less easy to attack from sea or land. When the Grand Duke threatened to occupy Constantinople unless the Ottoman fleet was handed over, the Sultan said: 'I would rather die first, and my children perish with me, than let one Russian soldier into the city. Before the Russians enter the city they will pass over my dead body.' In reality, in the case of a Russian entry, he had already negotiated a guarantee of escape for himself and his family on the British embassy vessel, HMS *Antelope*. It remained moored off Ciragan's marble quay, and visible from Yildiz, to demonstrate to the Sultan that he had a means of escape.

In the end a Russian advance was prevented by logistics. There were only 40,000 ill-equipped and exhausted Russian troops between Edirne and the city. Outside the walls of 'Tsarigrad' was a formidable obstacle of 30,000 Ottoman troops. (By May the numbers on each side had risen to about 90,000.) Moreover the Grand Duke Nicholas feared that if he tried to enter the congested capital, riots would break out and the Sultan would flee to Bursa.[38]

Nevertheless the Ottoman government agreed to let a few thousand Russian troops advance to Yesilkoy, six miles outside the walls of the city but within sight of its domes and minarets. On 24 February the Grand Duke Nicholas Nicholaievich arrived by train from Edirne. He was met by the Ottoman Minister of War, Ottoman generals and Orthodox priests. By arrangement with the Ottoman authorities, he lived and conducted negotiations in the mansions of Arakel Bey and Artin Pasha Dadian. (On seeing one of their luxurious kiosks prepared for dinner, he is said to have exclaimed: 'The Winter Palace is no finer!') On 3 March the peace treaty of San Stefano, creating a greater Bulgaria stretching from the Black Sea to Albania, was signed by Ignatiev and Ahmed Vefik Pasha in the Villa Nerriman, beside the Sea of Marmara. However, Russia was alarmed by the outrage at the terms which swept Britain and Austria. Fear of the Royal Navy and the Austrian army led to Russian agreement to suspend the Treaty of San Stefano and attend the Congress of Berlin.[39]

While negotiations continued in Berlin from 13 June to 13 July, Constantinople displayed a characteristic combination of tension and solidarity. The Ottoman army had been defeated. The Russian army was provocatively close to the city, and Russian officers were in the habit of visiting the city. Demonstrations or appeals for help by local Christians could have given the Russians a pretext for occupation. Yet none took place. Shopkeepers contented themselves with visiting the Russian forces with overloaded supply-carts and returning with bulging wallets.

Constantinople proved more resilient than the only other great European capital to witness an enemy army outside its walls between 1815 and 1940: Paris, during the Franco-Prussian War of 1870–1. After the defeat of the French army, the Second Empire was overthrown and a republic proclaimed. During the German siege, some inhabitants were reduced to eating rats. Bread riots were common. After Paris capitulated, German forces paraded triumphantly through the city. Finally social tensions exploded in the civil war between the French government and the Paris Commune. Excluding soldiers, the total number of Parisian civilians who died in what was known as *l'année terrible* was about 20,000, many shot in cold blood. During its *année terrible*, the military and government machines of Constantinople proved more stable, helped by the charity and discipline of Islam, and the realism and cohesion of the Ottoman élite.

However, the minorities were unreliable. There were many protestations of loyalty in public, the Armenian Patriarch declaring: 'If this great state is destined to be demolished, we consider it our duty to be buried under its ruins.' However an American reported that, in private, Armenians were delighted by the success of Armenian generals in the Russian army: 'To the Turks the Armenians are unwilling but cringing servants; the Greeks double-faced friends; Bulgarians enemies under a thin disguise. As to the Jews, they at once utilize and dislike the Turks but always side with them in controversies with Christians.' Few local Christians volunteered to join the forces raised under 'flags of brotherly love', with the Ottoman star and crescent in the middle, and a white cross in each corner. As the imperial dragoman Stefanaki Vogoridi had said, all depended on the outcome on the battlefield. On 7 December when Ottoman resistance seemed successful, the Armenian general assembly in Constantinople voted to serve in the civic guard recently created by the government. On 17 December after the fall of Plevna, despite the Patriarch's advice and the advantage of bearing arms in their own city, the Armenian ecclesiastical council decided that Armenians should not serve.[40]

In search of autonomy for the provinces inhabited by Armenians from Cilicia to Lake Van (where Armenians, although the largest and least contented group, were nowhere a majority), the Armenian Patriarch repeatedly visited the Grand Duke and Ignatiev at San Stefano. He also sent his own delegation to the Congress of Berlin to ask for autonomy and European gendarmes. When the Sultan expressed his outrage, the Patriarch replied: 'Go and tell the Sultan that I myself sent these delegates to secure remedies for the woes of my communities and I will not recall them even if he means to hang me at the door of the patriarchate, as the Greek Patriarch was hanged half a century ago.' When the Congress of Berlin granted nothing more than empty promises of reform, while part of Bulgaria secured self-government, the Patriarch warned European delegates: 'The Armenian delegation will return to the East, carrying with it the lesson that without struggle and without insurrection [such as the Bulgarians had launched] nothing can be obtained.'[41]

The Bulgarians of Constantinople were no more loyal than its Armenians. The Vogoridi family, who had risen so high in the Ottoman Empire, turned against it. Putting his Bulgarian identity before his Ottoman loyalty, Alexander Vogoridi resigned as Ottoman ambassador to Vienna in 1877. Eventually, like so many who had enriched themselves in Constantinople, the Vogoridi family retired to Paris.[42]

The Greeks were divided. The Patriarchate and the Galata bankers remained loyal, or prudent. When a general sent by the Grand Duke called at the Phanar, he was told that the Patriarch was too ill to receive him. Alarmed by the possible non-repayment of their loans if the Ottoman Empire disintegrated, the Greek banker George Zarifi organized a defence loan and loans for the purchase of arms, from which he and his colleagues made large profits. In May 1878, at the empire's lowest point, Zarifi also obtained the right to collect the city's customs revenue. However, the Greek Syllogos of Constantinople sent a memorandum of monumental arrogance to the Congress of Berlin, deriding the Bulgarians as 'an agricultural people *par excellence* almost totally lacking in a spirit of concentration'. After 'a struggle of four hundred years against the Turkish conquest', the Syllogos hoped for 'a Greek state from the Ionian Sea to the Bosphorus'.[43]

Adding internal conflict to external defeat, in May 1878 a Young Ottoman called Ali Suavi launched a bid to liberate Murad V. Inside Ciragan palace, the former Sultan had begun to recover his mental balance. Already one conspiracy had been organized by a lady of the harem called Nakshidil, and by his old friend and lodge brother

Cleanthes Scalieri. They had been in touch with Murad through colour-coded washing hung on a nearby balcony, and had even entered Ciragan through pipes leading from a water cistern outside the palace walls. The plot had been discovered and the conspirators had fled to Athens.

Ali Suavi had a combination of motives: a desire to return to the purity of early Islam, with himself as Seyhulislam; outrage at the humiliating terms agreed with Russia; republican liberalism. He may also have been secretly encouraged by the Grand Vizier and members of the imperial family. Since his English wife burnt all his papers, little is certain. At 11 a.m. on 20 May 1878, 300 refugees from the Balkans attacked the palace from land and sea. Ali Suavi entered the palace from the landward side and stormed up the harem staircase. Servants guided him to Murad's apartment. The ex-Sultan had been forewarned, although he had not been told the date fixed for his liberation. Ali Suavi and a fellow conspirator began to lead him down the arabesque staircase, holding him by both arms and shouting, 'Long live Sultan Murad!' Murad's sole recorded words were the crucial question, asked by so many candidates for the Ottoman throne in the past: 'What have you done to my brother?'

However, regular troops from Beshiktash soon arrived, and guided by servants' cries quickly overpowered the rebels. Ali Suavi was clubbed to death by a soldier loyal to Abdulhamid. Severed limbs and corpses littered the staircase. Murad was taken to the Malta pavilion in Yildiz park, under his brother's unforgiving eye.[44] The Sultan, who distrusted his own attendants, could not sleep for fear of assassination. After one audience Layard thought he might go – had gone – mad: 'He walked rapidly up and down the room in great agitation, talking of his children.'

At the Congress of Berlin, with the backing of Austria and Britain, the Ottoman Empire salvaged much of the Balkans. Cyprus was occupied by Britain, whose main motive was desire for a convenient military base if Constantinople was again threatened. On 18 August, after a farewell review at Yesilkoy watched by thousands of spectators from Constantinople, the Russian troops sailed home. In March 1879 the ships of the Royal Navy sailed back through the Dardanelles.[45]

The cohesion of Constantinople and the support of Europe had prevented the Tsar from hearing mass at St Sophia. Nevertheless Ottoman control of Constantinople remained uncertain. There were frequent fires, and fears of 'an imminent disorganization of the body politic'. Abdulhamid was the twenty-eighth Sultan to reign in Constantinople, and people remembered an ancient prophecy that the thirtieth Sultan would be the last. One evening in 1880 a young English diplomat called Edgar Vincent, who was to be a prominent figure in the city for the next twenty years, went down to the Galata bridge to take a steamer. Looking at the mosques and minarets standing out against the sunset, he asked himself the question on all minds: 'How long will the Ottoman Empire last?'[46]

13

Yildiz

Nothing escapes the vigilance and the activity of H.I.M. the Sultan. Indeed no monarch has better deserved the blessings of his subjects than H.I.M. Abdulhamid.

Moniteur Oriental, 31 August 1896

IF THE GALATA bridge was the supreme expression, in flesh and dress, of Constantinople's role as a meeting-place of East and West, the palace of Yildiz, residence of Abdulhamid from 1877 until 1909, was its equivalent in stone and wood. Fashionable European tastes were everywhere evident. The large kiosk called the Buyuk Mabeyn or Great Between (because it was between the Sultan's private quarters and the public domain), as well as the stables and the green Malta Pavilion further down the hill, had been built by Abdulaziz in a simple classical style. The palace was hung with views and portraits by Abdulhamid's court painter, Fausto Zonaro from the Veneto, who saw himself as the successor of Gentile Bellini. Kiosks were added in art-nouveau style by the Sultan's ultra-fashionable architect, the Ligurian Raimondo d'Aronco. In 1893 the Sèvres of the Ottoman sultans opened in the park – a china factory where Swiss and French experts taught Turks the techniques of making and painting on porcelain. On official buildings, like the massive neo-Turkish general post office in Constantinople and the ferry-stops along the Bosphorus, there was a return to traditional Ottoman motifs. In the plates and vases made in Yildiz, flowery Dresden patterns and human portraits predominated.

However, Yildiz was also very Ottoman. The textiles on the walls and chairs were made at Hereke, the silk factory founded by the Sultan's father in 1843. It maintained the traditional Ottoman use of vibrant contrasting colours and in 1886 opened its own shop on the Grande Rue de Pera – a sign of that recovery of Ottoman manufactures which was taking place, at the same time, in other industries. Ottoman taste was discernible in the elaborate arabesque patterns on walls and ceilings, and in the glassy blue-green landscapes of Yildiz, innocent of human figures, painted for the Sultan by Seker Ahmed Pasha and Ahmed Ziya.

Moreover, Yildiz reverted to the traditional Ottoman palace pattern. Like Topkapi, and unlike Dolmabahce and Ciragan, Yildiz was a mosaic of separate buildings – pavilions, kiosks and workshops – surrounded by gardens and a towering wall. As in Topkapi, few structures were more than two storeys high; and government was conducted in the outer courtyard.

The Buyuk Mabeyn housed most of the Sultan's secretaries and advisers. On the opposite side of the first courtyard was a long low building for his officers, with fretwork roofs like a Swiss chalet. In the second courtyard were the Sultan's private quarters, a house ten windows wide called the Kucuk Mabeyn ('Small Between'). With walls of 'Maria Theresa yellow' and an interior of white and gilt rococo *boiseries*, it would not have been out of place in the suburbs of Vienna. Here, and in adjoining buildings since burnt, the Sultan lived with his women and his eunuchs. The Sultan trusted the eunuchs so much that he raised the chief eunuch to the rank of Highness, on a level with the Grand Vizier, the Seyhulislam and the Emir of Mecca.

Yildiz was a museum-complex and industrial park as well as a palace and government compound. Within the grounds were one museum of natural history and another for the Sultan's pictures and antiquities. A furniture factory with sixty workmen made the elaborate late Ottoman high-backed gilded or inlaid palace furniture. The Sultan's personal photography laboratory, library and carpentry workshop revealed his favourite forms of relaxation: he was a skilled carpenter who made desks for his daughters and walking sticks for his wounded soldiers. Yildiz also contained four hospitals, an observatory, a pharmaceutical laboratory, a printing press, an embroidery workshop and a zoo.[1]

The gardens, 500,000 square metres planted with trees and flowers from all over the world, were the glory of Yildiz. In the inner garden behind the Kucuk Mabeyn, according to the wife of the orientalist Max Muller, 'Exquisite shrubs and palms were planted in every direction, whilst the flower borders were a blaze of colour. The air was almost heavy with the scent of orange blossom and gardeners were busy at every turn sprinkling the turf, even the crisp gravel walks, with water.'

Through the green of the gardens flashed the red fezzes of the

Sultan's guards. The Sultan's fear of assassination is in part explained by the deposition of his two predecessors and the assassination by nihilists or anarchists of, among other contemporary rulers, the Tsar of Russia (1881), the President of the French Republic (1896), the Empress of Austria (1898) and Kings of Italy (1900), Serbia (1905) and Portugal (1908). The Sultan trusted few people: some of his personal gold-inlaid rapid fire revolvers can be seen in the Istanbul Military Museum today. Turkish, Arab and Albanian guards were stationed in barracks around Yildiz. His inner guards were ferocious-looking Albanians over six foot tall. Their commander, Tahir Pasha, had come to Constantinople as a young man to lay the paving stones still known as 'Albanian paving'. Hostility between Albanians and Serbs was ferocious in the capital as well as in the Balkan mountains, and one day Tahir killed a Serb in a duel. The driver of the carriage which took him away told Hamid Efendi, as the Sultan then was, of the Albanian's prowess. Hamid met him, liked him and offered him a job as a bodyguard: his fortune was made.[2]

Guards were not the only force protecting the Sultan. It was said that he paid one half of his empire to spy on the other, and that in every large household either the cook or a slave was spying for the Sultan. Sons would denounce their own fathers to the palace. The Sultan was suspicious of anyone who used the same tailor as his brother and heir Reshad (who was housed in a kiosk in the park at Yildiz); and he scrutinized, for evidence of conspiracy, lists of guests at parties given by his relations, the Cercle d'Orient and the English Club. When the Oecumenical Patriarch held a meeting with two bishops in the Phanar, he asked them how many people were in the room. They replied, 'Three.' He provided the correct figure: seven – the three ecclesiastics and the four walls.[3]

Although Abdulhamid rarely left Yildiz, he was more accessible than contemporary monarchs like Queen Victoria or Alexander III. Anyone suitably dressed, with business to discuss, could enter the Buyuk Mabeyn. In order to win a favourable impression for the Ottoman Empire, the Sultan broke with precedent and began to provide regular entertainment for members of the élite as in Western courts. He entertained to dinner a stream of royal visitors, ambassadors, generals and tourists who visited Constantinople in its last years of imperial glory. Although the Sultan knew more French than he pretended, his Grand Master of Ceremonies, Munir Bey, intepreted, salaaming all the time. The other guests were pashas, who behaved like slaves before their master. When the Sultan went in to dinner, they bowed from the waist, until he passed: their bent backs were so even that a child could have run along them. The dining room had, for an American guest, 'the air of a sumptuously furnished European drawing room, one in which the style and taste of the last of the Napoleons still reigned in the heavy gilt mouldings of window cornices and mirror frames'. Guests were waited on by servants in red and gold livery, and ate off gold plate. Whether the food was Ottoman or European – the Max Mullers in 1894 were served *potage Windsor*, *boreks* (meat or cheese cooked in pastry), turbot, lamb, chicken, quails, asparagus, pilav and pineapples *à la Victoria* – it was cold and bad, as it had been reheated after a long journey from the palace kitchens. As in the sixteenth century there was generally 'complete silence' in the Sultan's presence unless he spoke. The Sultan himself did not drink alcohol; however, his guests were served excellent claret and potent punch.[4]

After dinner the Sultan sometimes entertained his guests and his harem with operas performed in the cream, gold and turquoise palace theatre, built by Sarkis Bey Balian in 1888–9. Like much of Yildiz, from the walls of the mosque to the covers on the chairs, the theatre ceiling is decorated with gold stars on a blue background, in keeping with the palace name (*yildiz* is Turkish for 'star'). After 1893 the Sultan employed the travelling company of an Italian from Gaeta, Arturo Stravolo, which included Stravolo's wife, daughter, sister, brother and father. The frequent pregnancies of Signora Stravolo made her implausible in young female roles. The Sultan merely remarked that he looked forward to the new member of his chorus.

Yildiz was the Sultan's private world, which he manipulated as he pleased. For performance in the theatre he changed the plots of plays and operas, and inserted episodes invented by himself, in order to avoid unhappy dénouements. *La Traviata* became *Madame Camélia*, with a new ending: a doctor arrives and restores Violetta to health. *Rigoletto*, the Sultan's favourite, was renamed *L'Opéra de la fille du roi*.[5] On other evenings the Sultan offered traditional Turkish entertainment: either Turkish music, or massive shaven-headed wrestlers, 'naked to their waists, bare even below that conventional line . . . oiled till even their trousers shone like satin'. He must have enjoyed watching the expressions of his European guests.

An evening at Yildiz had, in the words of an American writer, Anna Bowman Dodds, a 'peculiarly electric quality', due to the magnetism of the short, slim, simply dressed, black-bearded Sultan. Like Yildiz itself, he was a collection of antitheses, subtle and silly, brave and frightened, cruel and tolerant, modern and traditionalist, listening one moment to the Koran, the next to the adventures of Sherlock Holmes (read to him at night from behind a screen, in specially commissioned translations). To the Hungarian scholar Arminius Vambery, the Sultan was 'one of the greatest charmers that ever was'. Lady Dufferin, wife of a British ambassador, agreed: 'The Sultan has a very good face and pleasant manner.' He struck matches for his guests' cigarettes himself.[6]

Constantly smoking, he would talk for hours through an interpreter, praising Japan (a role model for the Ottoman Empire as a modernizing monarchy and enemy of Russia), or justifying his dismissal of the parliament in 1878 on the grounds that it did not represent the country. He assured a French journalist, Henri de Blowitz, of his determination to solve the country's financial problems, and move with the times: 'But the excess of a liberty to which none is accustomed is as dangerous as complete absence of liberty. A country to which liberty is given is like a man entrusted with a gun which he does not know how to use.' Education was the answer and he founded many new schools. Prize pupils of his school of civil administration served on his staff in Yildiz. The Sultan believed that 'none of our ills is incurable and we have in us qualities and forces which make us capable of a complete recovery. We do not have many friends, yet this must be a fine country since so many countries want it and pursue a policy whose sole aim is to discredit us so as to make us easy prey.'[7]

Power was the key to the Sultan's magnetism. Although the constitution was still theoretically in force, no parliament met in Constantinople. At a time when other palaces were losing power, Yildiz ruled the capital and the empire. In 1880 Layard was told: 'His Majesty reigns supreme as hitherto, everything and everybody being more than ever under his absolute management and control.' In 1895 the French ambassador wrote: 'The Sultan has ended by absorbing everything . . . Everything is decided at the palace, the most insignificant as well as the most important affairs.' The Sultan's ministers were summoned to Yildiz at any time of the day and night; he was said to read all his correspondence personally and to keep his papers in such order that he could find anything he wanted in the dark. Sacks of incoming letters were sterilized in a special machine before being sent to the Sultan's desk.[8]

The Sultan's absolue power was demonstrated in 1881 at the trial, in a tent in the outer garden of Yildiz, of the great constitutionalist Midhat Pasha who was charged with having organized the 'murder' of

Abdulaziz. The dead Sultan's mother herself gave witness. Midhat was found guilty, and exiled to Taif south of Mecca, where he was murdered in 1884.

In defiance of the nationalism corroding the empire outside the palace walls, in Yildiz the Sultan employed the most international bureaucracy that existed prior to the European Commission – Turks, Greeks, Armenians, Arabs, Germans, Poles and Italians. Their daily access to the Sultan soon gave them more power than the ministers working in the Sublime Porte. The head of the palace service – and a strong opponent of the West – from 1878 to his death in 1900, was Field Marshal Gazi Osman Pasha, hero of Ottoman resistance at the siege of Plevna. Two of his sons married two of the Sultan's daughters. The Sultan's first secretary was Turkish: Sureyya Pasha, replaced in 1894 by another Turk, Tahsin Pasha, 'indefatigably conscientious, always at his post, a loyal and unquestioning servant of his sovereign'. It was said that Tahsin Pasha never took a holiday in twelve years, and only knew of the arrival of summer, when strawberries were brought for him to eat. Under his authority twenty secretaries, graduates of the school of civil administration, had to be ready to work day or night. The Sultan's confidant Lutfi Agha, master of the robes, was also a Turk: to pay him to dream a 'favourable dream' could be extremely rewarding – it was the means by which Ferdinand Prince of Bulgaria won the rank of Ottoman Field Marshal. Other Turkish officials were chosen, like some court officials of Louis XIV, in order to placate and keep under surveillance within the monarch's palace potential malcontents. The radical writer and former editor of *Diogen*, Teodor Kasap, for example, became a palace librarian.[9]

Special offices in the palace dealt with Albania, with Balkan affairs, with the army and with espionage reports. One translation office translated the detective stories which delighted the Sultan. The selections from the European press translated by the other office, under the Armenian Nishan Efendi, usually caused displeasure: one French newspaper called him *le grand saigneur*. Agop Pasha Kazarian, the Minister of the Civil List (a post always held by an Armenian), helped Abdulhamid acquire a private real estate empire, including petroleum-bearing lands in Mesopotamia.

Spiridion Mavroyeni, a great-nephew of Nicholas Mavroyeni, the only Phanariot to have become an Ottoman general, had an office in the palace as the Sultan's doctor and intermediary with the Patriarchate. Senator, vizier, inspector-general of the civil and military hospitals, three times president of the Greek Syllogos, he entertained no high opinion of his master. In 1892, writing in Yildiz itself, he called him 'that absolute despot, selfish, suspicious, who in no way resembles his glorious ancestors'. They frequently quarrelled, and Mavroyeni once took refuge in the Russian embassy.

Alexander Karatheodory Pasha was the most important Greek in the palace. Born in 1833, the son of Stephane Karatheodory, doctor of Sultan Abdulmecid, he was a polyglot who served as Ottoman pleni-potentiary at the Congress of Berlin, Minister of Foreign Affairs in 1878–9, Prince of Samos from 1884 to 1894, governor of Crete in 1895–6 and 'First Translator of H.I.M. the Sultan'. Abdulhamid trusted him so much that he called Karatheodory 'a man with remarkable ability, not only the cleverest diplomatist in Turkey but one of the cleverest in Europe', and gave him an apartment in Yildiz. Saying that he had daughters to marry off, Karatheodory showed little interest in Greek nationalism. In 1901 he formed part of the Ottoman delegation to the funeral of Queen Victoria, whilst a Greek cousin was a member of the Greek delegation. The Greek was delighted to see Alexander Karatheodory Pasha, and immediately started telling him news of his many Greek relations. The Pasha, pretending to have met his cousin for the first time, merely said 'Thank you, thank you' with an embarrassed air. His funeral in 1906 at Arnavutkoy, conducted by the Patriarch and all the Holy Synod, marked the end of Phanariot tradition begun by his Mavrocordato ancestors.[10]

After 1895 an Arab from Damascus called Ahmed Izzet al-Abid rose in the Yildiz hierarchy until he was second secretary, with a patron-age base in Syria and a reputation as the most influential man in the palace. The Zionist leader Theodore Herzl, who made six visits to Constantinople under Abdulhamid in his attempts to buy Palestine, compared Izzet to a tiger ready for the pounce. A man of slight build and medium height, 'his tired, wrinkled but intelligent face leans toward ugliness. Large nose; dark, fluttering, half-length beard; shrewd eyes.' Head of a commission on treasury reform, he made a fortune out of serving the Sultan. Yet like Mavroyeni he did not hide, before intimates, his contempt for his master. When visited by Herzl in 1896, Izzet had a small, dingy office in the Great Between with two desks, a few arm-chairs and a curtained four-poster bed (in case he had to spend the night); 'that is all,' wrote Herzl. 'But a window opens on the broad and laughing beauty of the Bosphorus, on the white minarets of the Selamlik mosque, and far off on the haze-wrapped Princes' Islands.'

One of the achievements of Izzet and the Sultan was the Hejaz railway built to take Muslim pilgrims from Damascus to Mecca. Funded by Muslims throughout the world, despite the problems posed by building a railway in a desert, by 1908 it reached as far as Medina. To the dismay of Bedouin who had lived off the protection-money, the Holy Caravan of presents and pilgrims which left Constantinople every year could thenceforth go much of the way by rail.[11]

The Hejaz railway was an outward manifestation of one of the principal policies of the Sultan: the revival of Islam. As a weapon against the expanding empires of Europe, as a means of giving hope and union to his impoverished and dispirited subjects, Islam was the choice of the monarch who chose Greek and Armenian confidants and watched Italian operas. As he wrote to his chief secretary in 1892, 'The only way to fight against them [the missionaries funded by 'wealthy and fanatical' Christians] is to increase the Islamic population and to spread belief in the Holiest of Faiths.' During his reign, Yildiz was the Muslim Vatican. Already, under Abdulaziz, Constantinople, renewing its role as capital of Islam, had attracted Muslim refugees from Russian and British imperialism. They ran newspapers, extracted Ottoman subsidies and preached revenge and holy war. After 1876 a stream of Muslim preachers, dervishes, students and *ulema* came to Constantinople. Bearing Korans and Ottoman flags, they were then sent as far as Zanzibar, Siberia and Java, where they urged Muslims to support the last independent Muslim monarch, the Sultan Caliph of whose power and glory they gave glowing accounts.[12]

Islam received weekly expression when the Sultan left Yildiz to pray in the Hamidiye mosque fifty yards down the hill. Built by Sarkis Bey Balian in 1886, it is in an elaborate Ottoman neo-Gothic style, with a suggestion of the Alhambra. The walls are painted with red, blue and gold arabesque patterns and hung with calligraphy roundels decorated with mother-of-pearl: the lectern was carved by the Sultan himself. In 1884 Wilfrid Blunt had called the ceremony of the *selamlik* 'a very simple affair, a couple of companies of rather ill-groomed soldiers, a few men on seedy horses, half a dozen dust-carts filled with sand to sprinkle the road, two carriages full of ladies who did not enter the mosque, about fifty officials in uniform'.[13]

Within ten years Abdulhamid's *selamlik* became the best Ottoman opera of all. As regiment after regiment – infantry, cavalry, artillery, lancers, marines – arrived outside the palace, words of command and the thud of marching troops were punctuated by the spirited music of the *Hamidiye* and other Ottoman marches. The fezzes on the soldiers' heads turned Yildiz hill into a sea of red. Ambassadors in full dress, foreign and local notables, and secret agents watched from a specially constructed terrace and kiosk overlooking the road to the mosque. Smiling aides-de-camp made sure they had good places; servants circulated with golden trays of coffee, tea, sorbet, cakes, sandwiches, and cigars stamped with the Sultan's monogram.

Troops presented arms. Out of the palace gate came harem carriages, escorted by eunuchs, followed by the chief eunuch; pashas on horseback; the palace secretaries under Tahsin Pasha; and the Sultan's sons. Finally trumpets announced the Sultan. When he appeared in an open victoria drawn, very slowly, by a pair of grey stallions, the soldiers shouted 'Long live our Padishah!' The spectators inclined in respect. After the acclamations, sudden silence, as the carriage passed below the diplomatic terrace. Every eye was fixed on the Sultan. As he passed, his lids opened and he flashed a glance of scrutiny to check who was there.

In the mosque courtyard, he exchanged smiles with his sons. A muezzin with the finest voice in the city sang the call to prayer and a reminder to the Sultan that he was no more than a man. He entered the mosque. After half an hour of prayer he returned, driving himself and his favourite son Burhaneddin Efendi in a smaller phaeton, followed by pashas and secretaries running panting up the hill. His descent had displayed the Ottoman Sultan as a modern European monarch: his return was a symbolic recreation of the Ottoman Sultan leading his army into battle.[14] In keeping with Ottoman tradition petitions from the people, who watched from beyond the cordon of troops, were collected after the *selamlik*, and taken to a special office in the palace. Most petitions received an answer.[15]

After the *selamlik* the Sultan disappeared into the Hedge Kiosk, where he received ambassadors or prominent foreigners. These audiences could be a useful means of obtaining or providing information, and he often made notes in ink on his wrist of what he planned to say. Herzl, for example, offered the Sultan enough money to free the Ottoman Empire from the Debt Control Commission, in return for an autonomous Zionist entity in Palestine. The Sultan appeared undecided, since he wanted to use Herzl's press contacts in order to improve the Ottoman image in Europe. In reality he never wavered in his opposition to Zionism: 'I cannot sell even a foot of land for it does not belong to me but to my people . . . The Jews may spare their millions.

When my empire is divided, perhaps they will get Palestine for nothing. But only our corpse can be divided. I will never consent to vivisection.' 'When my empire is divided . . .' Official year-books published in Constantinople still proclaimed that the Ottoman dynasty was one of the oldest in the world and would last 'until the end of time'. The Sultan, like many inhabitants of the city, feared that its division was only a matter of time.[16]

Some of the guards at the *selamlik* were the famous *zouaves à turban*, Arabs from Tripolitania who wore green turbans. Many of the spectators on the terrace were Arab leaders once at war with the Sultan, now his guests clothed in Ottoman robes of honour. Under Abdulhamid, the Ottoman Empire still included almost all the Arab world, and Constantinople was both an Arab capital and an Ottoman weapon. Since the sixteenth century there had been Arab teachers, poets and merchants who had preferred Constantinople to the backwaters of Baghdad and Cairo. Arabs had introduced the city to the pleasures of coffee in the sixteenth century, and opera in the nineteenth. Abdulhamid was the first Sultan to use Arabs as political agents. He appointed a *seyh* (religious elder) from Aleppo, Abu'l-Huda, as an instructor in doctrine at Yildiz and *Rumeli kadiasker* (chief judge for the European provinces). Abu'l-Huda wrote as many as 212 books and pamphlets, stressing that absolutism was natural to Islam. God, the Koran and the Prophet commanded obedience to the Sultan Caliph. Pious and just, he cared for the welfare of his subjects. It was a duty to submit to his commands, especially in times of war against oppressive enemies and of struggle against dissenters. Constantinople was the new Baghdad.[17]

While Abu'l-Huda rallied Syria, Seyh Zafir al-Madani from Tripolitania was in charge of pan-Islamic policy in North Africa. From 1892 the great Islamic modernizer and advocate of union against the West, Jamal al-din al-Afghani, also lived in a house in the grounds of Yildiz, receiving food from the Sultan's kitchen and use of one of the imperial carriages: he had been invited from London by the Sultan, to prevent the British government using him to advocate the Caliphate of a Sherif of Mecca. From the comfort of Yildiz, he wrote to Shi'i dignitaries in Iran urging them to support Sunni Islam and the Ottoman Caliphate, in return for presents and salaries from the Sultan. He helped inspire the assassination of the Sultan's detested rival the Shah of Persia, in 1896. Mirza Riza, the assassin, revealed during his interrogation that, at a meeting in Constantinople in 1895, al-Afghani had expressed the desire to draw all Muslims 'towards the Caliphate and make the Sultan the Commander of the Faithful over all Muslims' and had encouraged him to kill the tyrant (the Shah). Al-Afghani died in Yildiz, officially in disgrace, in 1897.[18]

Schools were an additional instrument in the Sultan's Arab policy. The sons of provincial notables were brought to Constantinople to be educated in military or administrative colleges. A School of Nomadic Tribes was founded near Dolmabahce in 1892. The intention was 'to enable the tribal people to partake of the prosperity that emanates from knowledge and civilization and further to augment their well-known natural inclination towards and love for the great Islamic Caliphate and the sublime Ottoman Sultanate'. After five years in Constantinople, they would return to their provinces as teachers or officials. Boys from further afield – Java, Morocco, Persia and Bulgaria – were also brought to be educated at the Sultan's expense in modern schools in the capital. They often returned advocating pan-Islamism and expecting their colonial masters to treat them as Europeans.[19]

Abdulhamid also strengthened Ottoman ties with the great Arab dynasty of the Hashemites, who, from their semi-independent power-base in the Hejaz, had been both subjects and rivals of the Ottomans since 1517. In the early nineteenth century, as Ottoman power weakened, Hashemite hostility increased. A French traveller found 'an invincible antipathy, an irreconcilable enmity of Turks and Arabs'. The Ottoman government reacted by strengthening Ottoman forces in Jeddah and inviting Hashemites to Constantinople.

From 1816 some Hashemites were given handsome salaries, wives and houses in the capital. At once prisoners and honoured guests, they were treated as part of the Ottoman élite. At a dinner at Reshid Pasha's in October 1857, one guest was a handsome, grave young man of about 30, called Sherif Abdullah. He came from a junior and more deferential branch of the dynasty, the Devi Aun, whom the Ottoman government played against the senior branch, the Devi Zeyd. When asked why he did not wear the green turban of a sherif, he replied: 'I wear it sometimes, but our pedigree is too well known to need a badge.'

On the other hand their presence in Constantinople was a two-edged weapon. By revealing the Sultan's weakness in the face of European interference and technological superiority, residence there might increase the rebelliousness, rather than the loyalty, of his subjects. When Sherif Abdul Muttalib returned from Constantinople during the Crimean War, he told the *ulema* in the Hejaz that the Ottomans were doomed apostates and launched a 'holy war' against the Ottoman governor, whose efforts to stop the slave trade had outraged the local population.[20]

Abdul Muttalib was defeated and brought back to Constantinople, where he lived from 1856 to 1880. A friend of Midhat, he attended the inauguration of Murad V in 1876. Forty years before a sherif launched the Arab revolt in Mecca with British encouragement, there was already talk in the British embassy in Constantinople, and in Arab provinces, that 'the state of things was wholly hopeless for the Turks' and the Caliphate would 'some day return to Arabia'. In 1880 the Sultan's friend Sir Austen Layard saw 'an Arab gentleman' who told him that 'discontent with Turkish rule prevailed amongst the Arab populations in all parts of the Ottoman Empire. They were ready, he declared, to emancipate themselves if they could depend upon the support of England . . . all true Mussulmans now looked to the Sherif of Mecca as their real religious head.' That year, having been proclaimed Emir and Sherif of Mecca in state at the Sublime Porte, Abdul Muttalib again returned to Mecca: the Sultan thought this friend of Midhat and Murad V even more dangerous in Constantinople than in Mecca.[21]

Nevertheless under Abdulhamid sherifs continued to be among the most respected inhabitants of the city. The grandson of Abdul Muttalib, Ali Haydar, born in Constantinople in 1866, was educated in the palace school, in a kiosk in the grounds of Yildiz, with Ottoman princes, descendants of the Khans of Crimea, and pashas' sons. He became a friend of Seyh Abu'l-Huda, and of Abdulmecid Efendi, a son of Sultan Abdulaziz. When he complained about the school, his grandfather said: 'If you do not go straight to school I will send you back to Mecca.' In the nineteenth century the Prophet's family considered Constantinople as home, and the holy city of Mecca as banishment.[22]

In 1893, another Hashemite, Sherif Huseyin from the Devi Aun branch, who had been born in Constantinople in 1853, returned to live there, in a handsome yali in Yenikoy on the European side of the Bosphorus, with his sons Ali, Abdullah and Faisal. An absolutist said to spy for the Sultan, he was a member of the council of state, an institution which functioned as a substitute parliament. Already married to an Arab cousin, in Constantinople he married a granddaughter of Reshid Pasha, Adile Hanim, by whom his last and favourite son Zeid was born in 1898. A few years later he moved from Yenikoy to a kiosk which he built on a thickly wooded hill above Buyukdere – 'far from the Sultan and his spies'.

Both Sherif Huseyin and Sherif Ali Haydar and their families maintained two identities, Ottoman and Arab. The sons of the former were forced, by teachers provided by the Sultan, to speak Turkish — which, to the end of their lives, they used as oral cipher when surrounded by Arabs. In his memoirs Sherif Huseyin's second son Abdullah (by then King of Jordan), while praising 'the beloved Arab calls, palm trees and Arab buildings' of the Hejaz, was more enthusiastic about Constantinople, the 'seat of the Caliphate . . . fascinating beyond description, a city of great beauty enthralling in every season, summer and winter alike. How pure are its springs, how fine its fruits! . . . It contains Muslims of every walk of life, of different fashions and tongues, yet nobody and nothing seems strange and you can find anything you want from any country.'[23]

Sherif Abdullah remembered the Bosphorus with particular pleasure. While the Sultan ruled from behind the high walls of Yildiz, the Bosphorus experienced a second golden age. Every May the road over the hills from Constantinople to Tarabya was dotted with ox-carts taking furniture to villas on the Bosphorus. Leaving early in the morning, the servants could have their master's new residence ready by the time he arrived in the evening. The air on the upper Bosphorus was so pure that it was described as 'tonic to the body and exhilaration to the spirit'. Louis Rambert, who worked in the Ottoman Bank in the reign of Abdulhamid, was enthralled: 'What light! What sunshine! From the month of May to the month of November the summer season follows its course, almost without a cloud, filling the air with intense clarity, reflected by the great blue mirror. The arrival every morning in the capital and the departure in the evening of the Bosphorus boats end by engraving on your imagination a spectacle of real enchantment.' The *douceur de vivre* of pre-1912 Constantinople, like that of Paris before 1789, was never forgotten by those who knew it.[24]

A continuous line of yalis stretched along both shores of the Bosphorus. The largest were those of the imperial princesses beside, but at a respectful distance from, the imperial palaces. In Tarabya a succession of green parks edged down to the white wooden yalis of the ambassadors and the blue of the Bosphorus, where the embassy *stationnaires* (each embassy was allowed to keep one ship in the Bosphorus) were moored. In the afternoon the quay at Tarabya was an international promenade. Journalists learnt or spread the latest rumours. Diplomats and bankers planned tennis tournaments, polo matches (the

Constantinople Polo Club, of which Harold Nicolson was secretary in 1913, was in Buyukdere), balls, and much else besides. The chronicler of the late Ottoman city, Said Naum Duhani, son of a senior official in the Ministry of Foreign Affairs, wrote:

> Lovers, financiers, complaisant husbands, aspiring seducers, made signs to each other which only the initiated could interpret correctly. For the Levantine *gratin* [Mavrogordatos, Zarifis, Testas, Ostrorogs] of both sexes this promenade exhibition was a useful occupation, likely to obtain for men a business deal, for an unmarried young girl as good a way as any to catch in passing an embassy attaché whom she would turn into a husband.[25]

Tarabya was European and Levantine. Kayiks were the focus of a more traditional pattern of life. One of the greatest of modern Turkish novelists, Yakup Kadri, in *Nur Baba* (1921), described kayiks waiting on the enamelled Bosphorus as if suspended in a blue void, outside the yali of a wealthy court official, Safa Efendi: 'The whole bay would be flooded in light and harmony as if on a night of festive illumination. All the *sandals* [rowing-boats] that set out nimble and quivering in shoals and swarms from both shores of the Bosphorus, from Bebek and Kandilli to Sariyer and Cubuklu, in pursuit of pleasure and enjoyment would always make a stop here.' So many kayiks were moored close together listening to the music that men and women could exchange glances, or flowers.

On moonlit nights, utterly absorbed, Safa Efendi never left his window, or put down his binoculars, at the same time speaking very slowly to his friends:

> Wonderful binoculars these! Hasene Hanim is right here in front of me. If I put out my hand I could touch her! Look at the man in the next boat! He never leaves her side for a moment. They look as if they were stuck together. Ah-ha, the ladies of the court have turned their backs on him. What hair styles, what hair styles, what hair styles! They are real old bags! . . . and here are Faik Bey's daughters! My! My! What flighty young things they are! Drifting around from morning to night! I am beginning to think there is something between them and the boatmen! They're so familiar and free and easy in the way they talk and laugh together! That is funny! This evening I can't see the Egyptian Raksinaz Hanimefendi anywhere! I hope she hasn't come and gone already.

On other nights kayiks containing musicians and trays of food and drink would meet in the bay of Kalendar. Others would circle around to listen, forming a shifting mass of boats like a single raft. In the reign of Sultan Abdulaziz 'when hearts were gayer, emotions were more intense, muscles stronger, life more leisurely and purses heavier', it was said that as many as a thousand boats would drift from bay to bay down the Bosphorus until dawn, hypnotized by the beauty of the night and the sound of the music.

In Egypt, where he had commissioned *Aida*, the Khedive Ismail had shown a taste for Western music. In Constantinople, where he retired at the end of his life, he reverted to the tastes of his childhood. On moonlit nights a chorus of a hundred female slaves sang oriental music in his yali at Emirgan. Kayiks gathered to listen outside formed a bridge of boats stretching from Emirgan to the Asian shore of the Bosphorus. One of his slaves had a voice that carried from Emirgan to the other side where, striking the hills above, it produced double or triple echoes. However the Sultan feared both large gatherings and the Pasha's popularity. Claiming that it was unsuitable to listen to Muslim women's voices in public, an order from Yildiz banned the entertainments.[26]

One palace on the Bosphorus was out of bounds to every vessel. In Ciragan the deposed Sultan was a perpetual threat, and reproach, to his brother in Yildiz. After 1876 – like Mary Queen of Scots and Elizabeth I – Murad V and Abdulhamid II were rival dynasts who never met. Murad V lived in the separate harem section, now a school, to the left of the palace, surrounded by a wall of secrecy as impenetrable as the walls of his palace. An entourage of sixty, including his children and harem, shared his imprisonment. His household consoled itself with amateur theatricals and classical and Ottoman music. Guatelli Pasha, director of the imperial music, told Abdulhamid, of Murad V's children and grandchildren in Ciragan: 'Your Majesty, I go to listen to them, not to teach them.' Murad V read, wrote poetry and music (among his compositions are a march and a polka), scanned the Bosphorus with binoculars, and drank cocktails of brandy and champagne. He never performed the Muslim prayers. Sometimes he told his children and grandchildren of his visit to France and England with Abdulaziz in 1867: 'One day we will be free and I will take you to all these countries in a boat.'

As no dentist was admitted, Murad V learnt to pull his own teeth. He rarely received new clothes, so his harem made them. A chamberlain was sent every day from Yildiz to enquire if Murad V wanted anything. He was too proud to ask. On one occasion he yielded to his harem's reproaches and requested a calendar. The chamberlain refused.

Abdulhamid hated his brother. Fatwas from the Seyhulislam permitting the Sultan to execute Murad V have been found; but dynastic fratricide no longer seemed appropriate in the late nineteenth century. This liberal prince, who might have turned the Ottoman Empire into a constitutional monarchy, died in 1904 at the age of 64, after twenty-eight years in captivity.[27]

Below the magic microcosm of the Bosphorus, the city looked increasingly modern. With its emphasis on flowers and curves, art nouveau particularly appealed to Ottomans. Among buildings by the Sultan's Italian architect Raimondo d'Aronco were the massive Haydar Pasha Military Medical School finished in 1895 (built on the Asian side, possibly to remove students from the corrupting influence of Pera), the Casa Botter at the end of the Grande Rue de Pera of 1901, and the Italian summer embassy at Tarabya of 1905.[28]

On the Galata bridge, European dress was the rule, not the exception. An intelligent young Muslim called Halil Halid refused to study in a religious *medrese*, since students had to wear traditional gowns and turban and 'like most of my countrymen I was seized with the ambition of appearing up to date and of dressing in a more modern manner'. Simple houses continued to be decorated with framed pieces of calligraphy, low divans, and little else. However, members of the Ottoman élite, such as Osman Hamdi Bey, the director of the imperial museums and the school of fine arts, Nigar Hanim, the poet who lived in a yali by Rumeli Hisari and entertained men in her salon, or the Shakir Pasha family, resembled less their own parents than their counterparts in London or Paris in costume, gestures and furniture. The old rituals of pipe and perfume (but not coffee) began to disappear. Every smart household had a piano. Meals were served in the French style, on a table with forks and knives, rather than on a tray on the floor; in place of the eldest in the family, women were served first. Only the fez the men kept on their heads, even in the most intimate settings, indicated that they were Ottomans. Some female members of the Halim branch of the Egyptian ruling family were so confident of their own modernity that they launched a fashion for wearing traditional Ottoman dress and jewellery.[29]

Family relationships themselves began to change. With his desire for control, Abdulhamid commissioned the most accurate statistics in Ottoman history. Only 2.16 per cent of married men in the city in 1907 had more than one wife. The population of Constantinople was the first

Muslim group to practise contraception on a large scale. The wide-spread use of abortion as a means of family limitation alarmed the Sultan. Contraceptive pessaries relying on soap or lemon juice as spermicides were also common.[30]

Ottomans began to abandon Arabic and Persian: 'It was the French language and culture above all things which was responsible for my awakening,' wrote one intellectual, Huseyin Cahid. Another Constantinople writer, Ahmed Midhat, felt that the Ottoman language was so rotten that whatever part of the structure was touched fell down.[31]

There was an obvious antithesis between the forward-looking élite and the Sultan's traditional autocracy, between the city and the palace. Abdulhamid defied the two most important movements of the age, industrialization and nationalism. In order to prevent further inroads into the economy being made by European firms, almost no large factories were permitted in Constantinople. By 1891 in addition to government factories like the Fezhane on the Golden Horn, where fezzes were made, and the textile and gunpowder factories, the city contained no more than ten privately owned factories making silk, bricks, tiles and glass and two gasworks. Electricity was permitted in Izmir and Salonica, and in the separate world of Yildiz, but not in Constantinople itself except in hospitals, embassies and the Pera Palace Hotel.[32] Before 1876 Constantinople had been relatively modern. Under Abdulhamid it was a city in a time warp.

According to a tax list of 1887, 287 traditional guilds were still operating in the capital. Every guild – of boatmen, butchers or porters – had a chamberlain at its head, thereby strengthening Yildiz's control of the city, and the guilds' own power. The guild of port workers could force large boats to anchor far out to sea and use the workers' small boats – thereby diminishing the profitability of the port. The modernization of the port facilities, planned by the government and a group of foreign investors since 1890, was delayed. After 1895 the guild was transformed as Kurds replaced Armenians from eastern Anatolia as the main source of members.[33] For national conflicts in the provinces had begun to cause bloodshed on the streets of Constantinople.

In the 1880s, as Patriarch Khrimian had prophesied, some Armenians chose violent revolution. In 1887 the Hunchakian party was founded in Geneva. The first revolutionary Marxist party in the area, influenced by Russian populism and nihilism, it recruited 700 members in Constantinople, mainly among Armenians working for foreign companies.

Three years later in Tiflis another Armenian revolutionary party, soon known as the Dashnaks, was formed. The Armenian cause lost the sympathy of the Tsarist government, but gained revolutionary ardour and organization. Hunchaks and Dashnaks began to assassinate Armenians in the Sultan's service.

Fear and distrust transformed the government's attitude to Armenians. In conversation with a Hungarian agent of the British government, the historian and Turcologist Arminius Vambery, in Yildiz in 1889, the Sultan became so angry that he several times lifted his fez: 'Tell your English friends and in particular Lord Salisbury, for whom I have great consideration, that I am ready to cure the evils in Armenia but I will sooner allow him to sever this head from my body (and here he grew very excited) than to allow the formation of a separate Armenia.'[34]

Archives from Yildiz show that the Sultan and his officials regarded Armenians as 'impostors', full of 'evil intentions' to the 'Sublime State'. The eastern provinces, according to the Sultan himself, should rightfully be called Kurdistan, since more Kurds than Armenians lived there. To impose reforms in Armenia would be like 'holding one's beard in one's left hand and cutting one's throat with the other'.[35]

On Sunday 27 July 1890 the 'Kumkapi affray' outside the Armenian patriarchate in Kumkapi, opened a cycle of horror. A Hunchak revolutionary group, mainly from the Caucasus, surrounded the cathedral, molested the Patriarch and read out a manifesto against the Sultan. The police opened fire and killed about twenty Armenians. Two policemen were also killed – the first time since 1453 that Christians had dared attack Ottoman forces in Constantinople. In protest against both the police and the terrorists, the Patriarch resigned. The crowd, crying 'Long live the Hunchak committee! Long live the Armenian people! Long live Armenia!' sided with the Hunchaks. Some of them hoped for a massacre in the belief that it would provoke the intervention of the great powers. The following year the Armenian constitution was suspended. On 25 March 1894 the Patriarch was again wounded by a young Armenian terrorist at Kumkapi.[36]

On 18 September 1895, after months of preparation by Hunchak revolutionary committes, about 2,000 Armenians, many armed with knives and pistols, moved from Kumkapi towards the Sublime Porte crying 'Liberty or death!' and singing revolutionary songs 'to make the Sublime Porte fully aware of the miseries of the Armenians'. The Patriarch had been terrorized into accompanying the demonstration. The Armenians linked their cause to European imperialism. A letter was sent to the embassies asking for reforms (freedom of speech and assembly, permission to bear arms, an end to massacres), and a police force under a European governor-general, in the six 'Armenian provinces' in the East. They asked for greater European economic penetration, but at the same time threatened that, if no help came, the protests of Armenians might 'find an echo in the toiling classes of your own countries'.

The Ottoman reaction was brutal. Police opened fire on the crowd. The government, to use a phrase suited to Constantinople under Abdulhamid, 'unleashed the mob', employing genuine Muslim popular outrage for its own political purposes. Muslims were allowed to beat Armenians to death in the street, not only near Kumkapi but in many other districts of the city. The police were either passive or participant: some Armenians were clubbed to death in police courtyards. Attacks started at the same time; and the mob was careful, with some exceptions, to spare foreigners, their Armenian servants, and Armenian Catholics and Protestants. Massacres lasted for two days, in some quarters for two weeks. Poor Armenians – hamals and dock-workers – suffered most; as recent immigrants from the East, they could be recognized by their costume and their accent. More prosperous Armenians took refuge in their houses or in churches. The Patriarch fell ill from shock.[37]

Greeks showed little more sympathy for Armenians, in 1895, than Armenians had for Greeks in 1821. Prince Nicholas Mavrocordato, son of the leader in the Greek War of Independence, like other Phanariot descendants had become a Greek politician and diplomat. In 1894 he returned to the city of his forefathers as ambassador from Greece. Although he became a well-known figure in the city, and president of the Cercle d'Orient, like his father he was an ardent Greek nationalist who called the principle of the integrity of the Ottoman Empire 'a vain and ridiculous formula'. In 1895 he wrote that the Ottoman authorities tried to divide Armenians and Greeks, assuring the Greeks that they were regarded as 'sincere friends', releasing Armenians who were servants in Greek households. The Oecumenical Patriarch tried to give moral support: 'the Greeks, however, acting wisely, see to it that they go through these agitating days peacefully'. Indeed on 10 September some Armenians at Ortakoy had attacked Greeks. Worse massacres devastated Armenians in the East. The foreign ambassadors finally intervened with a collective note. The Sultan signed a reform decree, which remained a dead letter.[38]

On 26 August 1896 horror returned to Constantinople. Armenian revolutionaries of the Dashnak party launched a series of well-planned bomb attacks throughout the city, especially in Galata and Samatya. The most dramatic occurred at 1 p.m. Twenty-five Armenians, disguised as porters, seized one of the power centres of Constantinople: the head office of the Ottoman Bank in Galata. It was chosen because its solid construction would enable it to resist a siege, and its financial importance guaranteed European publicity. Having killed two employees, and taken 150 staff and customers hostage, they threatened to dynamite the bank unless their demands for Armenian autonomy under European protection were met. Edgar Vincent, who had become governor of the bank, escaped from his top-floor office through a skylight in the roof. After long negotiations, conducted through embassy dragomans, the terrorists were allowed to leave the city on Vincent's yacht. They then travelled to Marseilles on a French embassy boat and were later released.

The Ottoman government again unleashed the mob. *Softas* and thugs started attacking Armenians in Haskoy, Tophane and Galata. The army and the police stood by, or assisted. Most people shut themselves up in their houses or behind the heavy iron doors of the hans. An official of the Ottoman Bank, Louis Rambert, wrote in his diary: 'All Armenian houses are attacked and their little shops, people enter and pillage everything. It happens almost without a sound [since the killers used clubs, not guns]. Every Armenian found in the street is killed' – even on the Grande Rue de Pera. Carts took the corpses away. With his own eyes he saw the murder of rowers of a kayik, watched with visible pleasure by a large crowd on Galata bridge.[39]

Recording the events, an English diplomat wrote:

Meanwhile bands began to appear, composed partly of the low Turkish population of the quarter but partly of individuals wearing turbans and long linen robes rarely seen in this part of the town [religious students from the *medreses*]. They killed all the Armenians whom they met in the streets and looted many shops in Galata. The work of destruction was however fiercest in the quarters of Kassim Pasha and Hasskoy, where the Armenian population had been almost annihilated. In the latter district the Jews, who are very numerous, sided with the Turks against the Christians . . . I also saw the mob, who were in high spirits and laughing like children on a holiday, rush down to the bridge connecting Galata and Stamboul and satisfied myself that the ostentatious efforts made by the police to disarm them were a simple farce.

In a visible manifestation of the concert of Europe on the streets of Constantinople, embassies landed soldiers and marines from their *stationnaires* – not to help Armenians but to protect their nationals' lives. The French, British and Russian dragomans went to Yildiz, bringing a menacing note from their ambassadors and, as proof of events in the city, a club and an assailant. Tahsin Pasha replied, as if there were no soldiers or policemen in Constantinople, that it was natural for Muslims to retaliate when Armenians were attacking innocent people with knives and dynamite. The Austrian ambassador told the Minister of Foreign Affairs that, if the Ottoman government could not keep order, European opinion would demand a 'remedy'. The Russian ambassador threatened to summon Russian ships to bomb Buyukdere. On the evening of 27 August, clearly on government orders, the assailants handed in their clubs to police stations and returned to work, as if nothing had happened. For several days, however, Armenian revolutionaries continued to throw bombs and to fire on people from houses. In Constantinople, in the course of 1896, about 6,000 people died.[40]

In 1895–6 both the Sultan and the Armenian revolutionaries treated the Armenians of Constantinople as pawns, without regard for human life. The revolutionaries were warned by the orientalist Max Muller that their acts would cause many deaths. They replied with the claim: 'Those who die will do so as true patriots and martyrs.' The French ambassador deplored their death-wish as 'one of the most remarkable effects of national sentiment'.[41]

The newspapers surpassed the Sultan himself in defying reality. To mark their horror, ambassadors, for the first time in the Sultan's reign, refused to illuminate their embassies in honour of his accession day. On 2 September, however, the *Moniteur Oriental* reported that, on the island of Buyukada the Persian ambassador Malkum Khan, himself Armenian, married to a Dadian, had given a splendid dinner in honour of the occasion. In his residence 'The salons decorated with rare flowers and plants were crowded with the high-life of the island . . . The ladies were noticeable for their graceful toilettes competing in elegance and good taste.' On 19 September the same paper wrote: 'We have no cause for alarm either in the present or the future for – under the auspices of H.I.M. the Sultan – Ottoman authority is always prepared to maintain public order and security.' On 8 October 1896 it noted, cruelly, that Armenians were leaving Constantinople 'without even realizing half their fortunes'. Below the political struggle between the Sultan and the revolutionaries there was a financial calculation: the wealth of the Armenian élite disgusted both Christian and Muslim enemies.

One Armenian who left was a young man of 26 called Calouste Gulbenkian. He had been advising his fellow Armenian Agop Pasha Kazarian, Minister of the Sultan's Civil List, on petroleum prospects in Mesopotamia. From his new base in London, he kept his interest in petroleum, and an office in the Demir Han in Galata. With Ernest Whittall of the famous English trading family, he helped establish in 1912 the Turkey (later Iraq) Petroleum Company, combining British, Dutch and German interests but retaining 5 per cent of the share capital for himself: hence his name 'Mr Five Per Cent' when it started producing oil in Iraq after 1927.[42]

A representative of the lost Ottoman-Armenian synthesis, Artin Pasha Dadian, was the last link between the palace and the Armenian revolutionaries. A son of Ohannes Bey Dadian, born in 1830, he had lived in Paris as a student and as a diplomat. Able, pious and rich, Artin Pasha Dadian had three identities. He was a trusted servant of the Sultan, whom he had known personally since childhood, as a result of Abdulmecid's frequent visits to the Dadians. He served in the Ottoman Foreign Office as under-secretary of state in 1875–6, 1883–5 and 1885–1901. He was also a European figure, a pasha who spoke better French than Armenian and received decorations from Russia, Austria, Prussia, Italy, the Netherlands and Greece. He was often summoned to Yildiz to translate the latest telegrams from Europe and in 1884, as censorship became more strict, he became head of the bureau established to censor 'harmful' private telegrams from Europe. In 1885, on the occasion of the visit of Crown Prince Rudolf of Austria, Artin Pasha's 17-year-old daughter Yevkine (Eugenie) became official interpreter to the imperial harem.[43]

Artin Pasha Dadian was also a prominent figure in the Armenian community: he had helped draw up the constitution of 1860, and in 1871–5 was president of the Armenian National Council. At once Armenian, Ottoman and European, he was one of the last defenders of Ottoman cosmopolitanism. In *Nécessité du maintien de la domination turque en Orient*, he praised the tolerance of the Ottoman government, and cited, as proof of the empire's viability, some Christians' preference for veiling and for using Muslim law-courts. 'No government in the world has distinguished itself as much as Turkey [*sic*] for the talent of reuniting around the imperial throne the many scattered nationalities of the Orient'; under 'the domination of the conquering Muslim race', they have 'almost always observed a calm attitude without letting themselves be swept away by those brusque and violent revolutionary torments which so many times have shaken European countries composed of diverse disparate nations like Turkey.' Many Ottomans, in the second half of the nineteenth century, paid back European arrogance by expressing pity and contempt for the socialism and anarchism growing stronger in western Europe, but not in the Sultan's 'well-guarded domains'.

In 1896 the Sultan appointed Artin Pasha Dadian president of a commission to resolve the conflict between the empire and the Armenian revolutionaries. Having secured an amnesty and the liberation of 1,200 political prisoners, he sent his son to Geneva to talk to the exiles. He himself claimed to work for reforms in the East 'at once as an Ottoman civil servant and as an Armenian'. When an Armenian radical smiled at the phrase, he said: 'I know that you young Armenians, you do not believe in my patriotism and believe me a Turkish zealot. That is false. I know that their fear was not completely without foundation and I am convinced that, in a dangerous situation such as our feeble nation lives in, it is our duty to work faithfully for the state and fear movements of revolt so as not to suffer terrible punishments.' He ended with a cry from the heart: 'Prudent patriotism, is it not also patriotism?'

In a letter of 1898, intended for the Dashnak party, he is lucid and prophetic:

I suggest that today we have nothing but patience and tolerance. First, Europe shows complete indifference and says there is no Armenian case as far as they are concerned. Second, the threat of the complete annihilation of the Armenian nation has not yet entirely passed, and third, the people are tired of revolutionary deeds and are ready to patch up their differences with the government in order to remain safe from further terrible events such as have almost wiped out our people from the face of this earth. Fourth, various organizations are fighting different causes, each in their own way, and in the middle of all this stands one pitiful Artin Pasha, who on the one hand begs the Sultan for mercy by telling him that this would be the best thing for his empire and on the other hand fights base individuals who in order to attain their selfish aims are even willing to sell their nation . . . I believe it will be proper, as I have mentioned countless times before, for our people to patch up its differences with the Sultan.[44]

However Armenian revolutionaries believed in justice and revenge, not prudence. In 1897 they tried to blow up the council of ministers, in

1903 to assassinate the Armenian Patriarch. At the *selamlik* of 21 July 1905 a gelignite bomb fitted to a carriage by Dashnaks missed the Sultan by a few minutes. As he returned from the mosque to the palace, he appeared equally unmoved by the attack and by the cheers from the crowd.[45]

In addition to the Armenian catastrophe, the evolution of the Albanians shows nationalism's tightening hold. Already in 1878 there had been risings in favour of autonomy in some Albanian regions. The Frasheri brothers, sons of an Albanian chief who had moved to Constantinople, helped to define Albanian nationalism. In 1879 a central committee for the defence of the rights of Albanian nationality had a brief existence in Constantinople under Abdyl Frasheri, a former deputy in the Ottoman parliament. His son Midhat Frasheri, although working in the Porte, was a patriot who translated into Albanian the life of the national hero of another mountain people which had fought for independence, William Tell.

Abdyl Frasheri's brother Sami remained both Albanian and Ottoman. Born in 1850, he came to Constantinople at the age of 22. To the end of his life Sami Frasheri, known in Ottoman as Shemseddin Sami, remained an Ottoman civil servant. He was the leading Turcologist of his day, author of works in Turkish such as *Universal Dictionary of History and Geography* (Constantinople, 1894) and a Turkish-French dictionary.* However, he was in clandestine communication with activists in Albania and abroad and the Société des Lettres Albanaises, founded under his presidency in 1879 in Constantinople, became a focus of nationalism. Their enemies were Greek as well as Ottoman. Anyone using the reformed Latin alphabet created by Sami Frasheri, instead of the Greek alphabet, was threatened with excommunication by the Oecumenical Patriarch. His pamphlet *Albania, what she was, is and will be* (published in 1899 in Bucharest) is a plea for a bicameral legislature and a prime minister nominated from Constantinople, eventually leading to independence under a republic. That year he was placed under house arrest.

His brother Naim Frasheri, who worked in the Ottoman railways, wrote poems in praise of Scanderbeg, the anti-Ottoman Albanian hero

---

*Dictionnaire Turc-Français par Ch. Samy-Bey Fraschery. Approuvé par la Commission du Ministère de l'Instruction Publique. Constantinople Imprimerie Mihran. Rue de la Sublime Porte No. 7. 1885.

31. Artist unknown, *Janissary patrol by night, c.* 1590. Such patrols apprehended robbers and ensured that inhabitants were inside their houses. The Aga of the Janissaries rides his horse, and his soldiers carry lanterns, in front of the city walls.

32. J. N. de Lespinasse, *A public office in the Sublime Porte,* 1787. The Ottoman Empire was a paper empire, held together by a meticulous and efficient bureaucracy, as well as by the might of its army. Twenty-five such offices dealt with financial matters alone.

33. Antoine-Ignace Melling, *The Palace of Hatice Sultan at Defterdarburnu, c.* 1800. The French artist Melling has shown the classical-style wing he added to the already large palace of his employer Hatice Sultan. Their relations were sufficiently close to arouse the jealousy of her staff.

34. Luigi Mayer, *View of a bonfire lit by Greeks on the eve of the feast of St John in Tarabya, c.* 1790. After 1780 Tarabya was one of the main pleasure resorts of the city and the ambassadors' summer residence. The houses have wide Turkish eaves and projecting upper floors. Such scenes show Greeks' freedom to celebrate their festivals. Mayer was a professional artist employed at 50 guineas a year by Sir Robert Ainslie, British ambassador from 1776 to 1792.

35. Artist unknown, *Mahmud II, c.* 1830. The Sultan was convinced of the value of portraits of himself in modern uniform and ordered them to be hung in army barracks.

36. David Wilkie, *Abdulmecid I,* 1840. The Sultan, a patron of reform, wears a modern uniform and few jewels.

37. Ahmed Vefyk Pasha. Ahmed Vefyk Pasha, an important cultural mediator between Constantinople and the West, was twice Grand Vizier. He wears the *stambouline,* standard dress for the Ottoman élite from the 1840s to the early twentieth century.

38. General Ignatiev, Russian ambassador in Constantinople from 1864 to 1877. While winning the confidence of the Sultan by advising him not to grant a constitution, Ignatiev turned the Russian embassy into the headquarters of a hidden army of Slav insurrectionaries. In 1878 he urged the Russian army to occupy the city.

39. Sébah and Joailler, mosques of Sultanahmed (*left*) and Aya Sofya (*right*), *c.* 1890. The Byzantine sea walls are clearly visible. Between the mosques is a classical building, designed in 1846 by the Swiss architect Gaspare Fossati, who also built the Russian embassy and supervised the restoration of Aya Sofya. Like many buildings in the city it was used for a succession of different purposes: as the Ministry of Justice, the university, a hospital for French troops during the Crimean War, a home for Circassian refugees after the Russo-Turkish war and as the Ottoman Parliament in 1877–8 and 1908–10. It burnt down in 1933.

40. Sébah and Joailler, photograph of Tarabya on the Bosphorus, with the German *stationnaire* 'Loreley'. Tarabya was the principal summer resort for Europeans and Levantines before 1914. On the right a ferry is about to leave. On the left is the German embassy boat. Each embassy could keep one, and after the massacres of 1895 two, boats on the Bosphorus for the use and protection of its nationals.

41. Abdullah Frères, Dolmabahce palace. Inaugurated in 1856, it symbolized the dynasty's taste for grandeur and modernization. The central block houses the throne room; beyond are the quarters of the harem and the heir apparent. Dolmabahce was the residence of the Sultan from 1856 to 1877 and 1909 to 1918, and of the last Caliph from 1922 to 1924. Abdullah Frères were Armenians who came to Constantinople from Kayseri in the 1850s and won the title of Photographers to the Sultan and the right to display his *tughra*. They lost both when they sought the patronage of Grand Duke Nicholas, commander of the Russian army outside the city in 1878.

42. Departure of the *mahmal* from Dolmabahce palace, *c.* 1910. Every year a sacred caravan of pilgrims and presents left Constantinople for Mecca and Medina. The Sultan sent a gold-embroidered covering or *mahmal* for the Ka'aba in Mecca on the back of a heavily decorated camel, shown here in front of the ornate imperial gate of Dolmabahce palace. Overdressed women were frequently compared to such camels.

43. M. Jourdain, 'Inauguration of the Dolmabahce palace theatre', *L'Illustration*, 25 June 1859. The palace theatre was built in 1851–8 by the Parisian decorator Charles Séchan and, although smaller, was considered more luxurious than the palace theatre at Versailles. The official opening on 12 January 1859 showed the growing taste of the Ottoman dynasty for court life in the Western sense, in which the monarch shared his pleasures with members of the élite. The Sultan and his guests – princes, viziers, ambassadors, 'the most elegant ladies of Pera' and, behind trellis screens, of the imperial harem – watched two acts of *Scaramuccia* by Luigi Ricci and a new ballet called *Chasse de Diane*. No more operas were performed there after the Sultan's death in 1861 and the opera house was pulled down in the 1940s.

44. Opening of the first Ottoman Parliament, March 1877, *Illustrated London News*.
The ceremony takes place in the new ceremonial centre of the empire, the throne room
of Dolmabahce palace. Abdulhamid II stands before the gold-plated throne transported
from the treasury in Topkapi palace for the occasion.

45. Thomas Allom, *Entrance to the Divan*, *c.* 1840. The gate is the Sublime Porte, the entrance to the offices of the Grand Vizier and the Ministry of Foreign Affairs. On the left a man threatens a pack of dogs; on the right are soldiers in the new uniform, and the Alay Kiosk, from which Sultans watched processions.

46. Amedeo Preziosi, *The Bazaar*, 1851. Preziosi was a noble from Malta who married a Greek wife and worked in Constantinople as a professional artist from 1842 until his death in 1876. He has shown the variety of goods and costumes visible in the bazaar. Some men wear a turban, others a fez. On the shield hanging on the left is a Sultan's *tughra*.

47. M. Tancoigny, *Refugees in Aya Sofya*, 1878. As a result of the Russo-Turkish war thousands of refugees fled to the city. Many were housed in mosques, pictures of misery in the midst of majesty. After typhus broke out in Aya Sofya, the refugees had to leave and the mosaics were hosed down with carbolic.

48. Fausto Zonaro, *The Bridge of Galata*, c. 1900. The bridge is a turmoil of ships and people. The smoke from the former almost obscures the Valide Cami. Zonaro painted several hundred pictures of Constantinople and its inhabitants during his residence there between 1893 and 1910. His picture of the élite Etughrul cavalry regiment crossing this bridge won him the title Painter to His Imperial Majesty the Sultan in 1896.

49. A street in the Phanar, *c.* 1900. These substantial brick and stone houses near the Oecumenical patriarchate were formerly the residences of the Phanariot élite.

50. A street at Beykoz, 1885. A typical Turkish neighbourhood, as here photographed, had wooden houses and narrow winding streets.

51. Postcard. Patriarch Joachim III, c. 1905. Patriarch from 1878 to 1884, when he resigned in protest at the government's attempts to restrict the Patriarchal courts, and from 1901 until his death in 1912, Joachim III won the respect of the Sultan as well as his own flock. His dual loyalties are displayed on his chest: he wears Ottoman orders founded by Sultans Abdulmecid, Abdulaziz and Abdulhamid, and the Greek orders of Well-Being, of George I and of the Phoenix. Having preached submission to the Ottoman Empire for most of his pontificate, by the end he advocated the 'great idea' of a new Greek Empire.

52. Fausto Zonaro, *Design for a fan*, c. 1895. The fan has been signed by members of the diplomatic corps in Constantinople: on the left the ambassadors of the great powers and Persia; in the centre the British ambassador Sir Philip Currie (*en poste* 1893–7) and his staff; on the right representatives of lesser powers. The numbers and prominence of the British contingent suggest that they were the hosts of, or occasions for, the festivity. In 1908 the question whether the *agent diplomatique de Bulgarie*, whose signature is at the bottom of the list on the far right, was indeed a member of the foreign diplomatic corps, or the agent of an Ottoman provincial governor, would provoke a diplomatic incident, and the proclamation of Bulgarian independence.

53. A page from the *Almanach du Levant*, 20 April 1911. The almanach records the date, the times of sunrise and sunset, and the relevant religious festival in Ottoman, Greek, French, Ladino (Spanish in Hebrew letters), Armenian and Bulgarian. It also prints a concordance of Turkish and European hours. On 20 April 1911, midnight *à la turque*, the start of the day by the Muslim calendar, is at 6.49 p.m., shortly after sunset.

54. Ironmonger's bill, Artin Chahmirian, Galata, Rue Mahmoudie No. 80, 21 June 1927. Hassan Baloukli owes 1,702 piastres. The shop's name and address are printed in Turkish (in the traditional alphabet, one year before the change to the Latin alphabet), French, Greek and Armenian, but the bill is written in French and annotated in Greek.

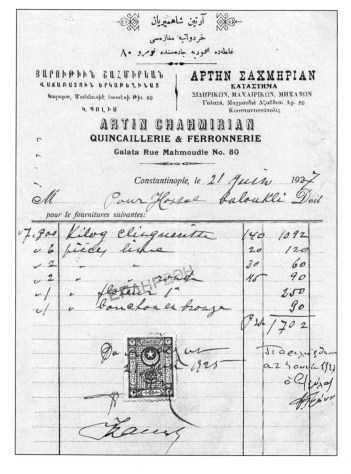

55. Eunuchs with officers of the 'Action Army', Yildiz palace, 25 April 1909. The 'Action Army' from Salonica has just occupied the city and overthrown Sultan Abdulhamid. Some of the officers were Europeans appointed to try to keep the peace in Macedonia.

56. Fausto Zonaro, *Enver Bey*, 1909. Surrounded by Macedonian 'irregulars' who had accompanied his army, stands Enver, the hero of the Young Turk revolution.

57. Accession ceremony of Mehmed VI, July 1918. Officials have formed in line to pay homage to the last Sultan, Mehmed VI, who stands before the gold-plated imperial throne in the Gate of Felicity of Topkapi palace. To the right of the throne stand the Mufti; an unknown official; Enver Pasha, deputy Commander-in-Chief and Minister of War; and Cemal Pasha, governor of Syria. The Sultan detested them and worked for their overthrow.

58. A group in the park of the house of Sherif Ali Haidar, Camlica, 1919. On the bench, left to right, Sherif Ali Haidar, of the senior, pro-Ottoman branch of the Hashemites; Durushehvar Sultan and her father Abdulmecid Efendi, the last Caliph (1922–4); and Said Halim Pasha, Grand Vizier in 1913–17. Behind Abdulmecid Efendi stand his son Omer Faruk Efendi and courtiers and officers. It is the end of their world. The city is under foreign occupation: a nationalist revolt is about to erupt in Anatolia. In March 1920 Said Halim Pasha will be interned on Malta by the British government, and two years later shot dead in Rome by an Armenian. Ali Haidar, Abdulmecid and Omer Faruk will die in exile in Beirut, Paris and Cairo, in 1936, 1944 and 1969 respectively. The sole survivor today, Durushehvar Sultan, lives in London.

59. HMS *Hibiscus*, 20 March 1920. Allied forces have occupied the city. Among the 150 prominent Ottomans arrested, some in their night-clothes, are the Ministers of Marine, the Treasury and Defence, here shown on a British ship. They were later interned on Malta – where many Turks had been imprisoned in previous centuries by the Knights of St John.

60. A modern Istanbul family, the Shakirs of Istanbul, c. 1927. Emin Pasha (*left*), an officer who had joined the nationalists, with the widow and descendants of Shakir Pasha, a prominent Ottoman officer. Many of the children later distinguished themselves in the arts. Among them (fourth from right) is Fahrelnissa, who would marry the Emir Zeid, son of Sherif Huseyin, and become a painter of the School of Paris.

of the fifteenth century, and tried to remove foreign elements from the Albanian language. Every Friday and Sunday friends gathered in his house in the suburbs to discuss Persian literature and Albanian independence. Thus by 1900 privileged chiefs' sons, well treated by the Ottoman Empire, had turned against it. By the banks of the Bosphorus, they dreamt of 'liberating' their homeland.[46]

The rising power in the Balkans was Bulgaria, ruled from 1887 by the able and ambitious Prince Ferdinand of Coburg. In theory an Ottoman vassal, in 1896, six months before the Armenian massacres, he visited Constantinople to receive the Sultan's recognition as ruling prince – the crucial step in legitimizing his status in Europe. In Aya Sofya, he deliberately stood on the slab of porphyry where Byzantine emperors had been crowned. For Bulgaria was merely a step in his dream of Byzantium. Bulgarian ambition, as well as Bulgarian atrocities in Macedonia, explain why, at dinner in Yildiz in 1900, the Sultan advised Prince Nicholas of Greece, in his soft, kind voice: 'We have the same enemies.'[47]

While some Armenians and Bulgarians chose violence, most Greeks were too prosperous to fight for 'the Great Idea'. They felt that while the Ottomans reigned, Greeks, through their banks and commerce, governed. In the words of one Greek businessman: 'We lend them the vivacity of our intelligence and our business skills; they protect us with their strength, like kindly giants . . . I have one certainty. The future belongs to the Greeks; distant no doubt but peoples can wait.' Indeed a secretary in the Greek legation, Jon Dragoumis, who worked with a nationalistic 'Constantinople Organization', complained of lack of interest from the city's Greeks. Some were so levantinized that they sent their children to Catholic schools: 'The marbled king will stay marbled for ever . . . we are losing the city completely.'[48]

A short Greco-Turkish war in 1897 barely affected Greco-Ottoman relations in the city – although some Constantinople Greeks fought on the Greek side. The Ottoman army won easily. *The Attack*, a graphic depiction of Ottoman troops killing Greeks, by the Sultan's court painter Fausto Zonaro, was hung in the ambassadors' waiting room in Dolmabahce. In 1895 and 1896 Abdulhamid had let the streets run with blood. In 1897 he reinforced patrols in the city and ensured that order was undisturbed. That year the Patriarch, who had visited Yildiz to congratulate the Sultan on the anniversary of his accession to the throne, received the Grand Cordon of the Order of the Osmaniye.[49]

His successor was a Patriarch whose memory is revered to this day. For a visiting journalist, 'The present Patriarch Joachim III is without exception the most imposing personality I have ever met. His massive frame in its simple blue robe is surmounted by a noble head with the traditional flowing beard which marks the Eastern clergy. Even the slight limp with which he moved across the room to meet me had the air of deliberate stateliness.' Rather than confronting Ottoman authorities, he cooperated with them. In an architectural expression of the rising tide of 'Hellenism' in Constantinople, he received permission to open an *ayazma*, or holy well, in the wall of Topkapi palace, opposite the Sublime Porte. He also restored and expanded the patriarchate buildings in the Phanar. As at the beginning of the empire, the Patriarch was again received by the Sultan in person, and had the privilege of addressing him in Greek. On the great Muslim festival of Sheker Bayram marking the end of Ramadan, Joachim III visited Izzet Pasha in Yildiz to offer his congratulations and assurances of the Greek community's satisfaction. (It was the custom, until the end of the empire, for officials, whatever their religion, so to mark each others' religious festivals.) The Sultan replied by sending the Patriarch a eunuch bearing messages of satisfaction and a token of favour: a pineapple grown in a palace hothouse. The Patriarch raised the pineapple to his lips, kissed it and reiterated, in Turkish, expressions of the loyalty and gratitude of the Greek nation and its leader.[50] Such gestures and phrases were not meant to be sincere; but they did show, on both sides, a desire for a *modus vivendi*.

In addition to the Balkan states, the great powers were taking an increasingly aggressive attitude towards the Ottoman Empire. Britain was as confident of its imperial destiny as the Ottoman Empire had once been. It had staked a claim to preeminence in the Gulf and was increasing its power in Egypt, which it had occupied in 1882. The British occupation of Cairo neutralized Constantinople's main rival for leadership of the Muslim world. However, it also made Cairo the focus of British policy in the Middle East. With Egypt a 'bird in the hand', Constantinople no longer seemed indispensable to the defence of the route to India. After the first Armenian massacres in 1895 the Cabinet, despite the urgings of the Prime Minister Lord Salisbury, refused to risk a war with Russia by sending the fleet to the Bosphorus.

Russia, equally sure of its imperial destiny, had not abandoned its designs on Constantinople. From 1882 Nelidov, the Russian ambassador to the Porte, advocated a surprise landing at Buyukdere and a march on the city to turn it into a 'Russian Gibraltar'. During a visit to

Balmoral in 1896, Tsar Nicholas II also revealed his ambition that Russia should take 'the key to her backdoor': Constantinople. Lord Salisbury expressed only limited opposition.* Four years later the Tsar's ministers agreed that seizure of the Bosphorus was Russia's 'most important task in the twentieth century' – although, given the weakness of Russia's finances and its Black Sea fleet, action was not yet possible.[51]

The Sultan's response to the threats to his empire was to concentrate more power in, and invite a new friend to, Yildiz. A new kiosk, the Chalet Kiosk, asserted the grandeur and modernity of the Ottoman Empire and its equality with the powers which were so eager to devour it. Today it is so well preserved, and so rarely visited, that visitors find no difficulty in imagining that they are, not tourists in the 1990s, but the Sultan's guests a hundred years earlier. The Chalet Kiosk began as a pre-fabricated chalet erected in 1880. New sections were added in 1889 by Sarkis Bey Balian, and in 1898 by Raimondo d'Aronco. Despite its alpine name, it is a sumptuous, sixty-room Ottoman palace divided, according to tradition, into female (*haremlik*) and male (*selamlik*) sections. The Chalet Kiosk is decorated with heavy European-style furniture (some carved by the Sultan himself), parquet floors, elaborate flowered fabrics and neo-rococo wall-panelling. Vases and wash-basins are made of *yildiz porselan*. The Sultan, who used gold-tooled field glasses and ate in private with a gold knife and fork, had inherited the Ottoman taste for luxury. He entertained guests to dinner in the blue hall, with mother-of-pearl doors, neo-Islamic ceilings, startling blue silk chair covers from the imperial factory at Hereke and Puginesque chandeliers. Like some of the glowing red, blue and gold arabesque rooms in other late Ottoman palaces, this room has the enigmatic appeal of the sculpture of Palmyra or Gandhara – of the meeting of East and West in the same artefacts.[52]

The reason for the kiosk's expansion was the need to accommodate the Sultan's new ally the Kaiser, who visited Constantinople in 1889 and 1898. The alliance with Germany at last gave the empire a European ally with no territorial ambitions in the area. Another architectural memorial to the alliance is a railway station of unmistakably northern European appearance at Haydar Pasha on the Asian side. It was built as

---

*Russia's designs on Constantinople met widespread acceptance. In 1915 the British Prime Minister, Asquith, wrote that Constantinople's 'proper destiny' was to be Russian.

a terminus for the Berlin to Baghdad railway,* encouraged by the Kaiser and financed by the semi-official Deutsche Bank. By 1908 the railway reached Adana. It not only strengthened the Sultan's military control over his empire, since troops were easier to transport by rail, but also brought to Constantinople grain from a new source: the plains of Anatolia.

One reason for the success of the German-Ottoman friendship was the skill and tact of the First Dragoman of the German embassy, Charles de Testa, the last of his family to play a major role in the city. The mid-nineteenth century had been the heyday of the Testa. In Constantinople in the 1840s they had provided Austria, Prussia, Sweden, the Netherlands and Tuscany with dragomans, the Netherlands with a minister, Reshid Pasha with a secretary and the Pope with a vicar-general. However after 1850, they too turned towards modern European nationalism. Branches of the family found it more attractive to leave Constantinople and live in France, Austria or the Netherlands.

Although Charles de Testa stayed on in the city, he served Germany and acquired German nationality. A founder member of the Cercle d'Orient, he visited Yildiz every day, working 'with the patience, the supple spine and the oriental wiles of a great dragoman of the old school'. As president, in Constantinople, of the Anatolian, the Baghdad, and the Salonica–Constantinople railway companies, director of the Haydar Pasha Port Company and German representative on the Council of the Ottoman Public Debt Administration, he fought ardently for German economic interests, sometimes in opposition to the Ottoman government. The German Foreign Office thought so highly of him (Chancellor Prince von Bülow called him 'one of the best authorities on Turkish conditions') that, at a time when Morocco was a focus of great power diplomacy, he was promoted to be German minister in Tangier.[53]

After 1898 Yildiz continued to expand. A school for railway engineers, now Yildiz University, was built on one side of Yildiz hill. Like Fatih, who built pavilions representing different realms in the garden of Topkapi palace, Abdulhamid built in the park of Yildiz a Japanese pavilion, one called Petit Trianon, and, in honour of a visit from the new Shah of Persia, a Persian pavilion. New stables for the Sultan's white Arabian stallions, were built by Raimondo d'Aronco in 1895–1900, in

---

*Sometimes known in Germany as BBB: Berlin–Byzantium–Baghdad.

an idiosyncratic combination of art nouveau and neo-Gothic. A memorial mosque and fountain to the Sultan's religious adviser for North Africa, Seyh Zafir, at the bottom of Yildiz hill, built in 1903, looks like a smaller version of the *Sezession* building in Vienna – but for the presence of a carved *tughra* of Abdulhamid. By 1908, according to one estimate, 12,000 people inhabited the palace city. So much food was prepared in the palace kitchens, that the cooks built houses for themselves out of the profits made from selling the left-overs.[54]

Yildiz had become so powerful that 'the palace' and 'the Porte' were sometimes compared to two separate states. Torn between the two, Ferid Pasha, Grand Vizier from 1903 to 1908, said he would prefer to be a hamal on the quays of Galata. The palace and the Porte had different attitudes to the rule of law. The Bedir Han family, rich and powerful Kurdish notables brought to the city by the Sultan, assimilated metropolitan habits without losing their own. When asked by a bridge partner if the Kurds were thieves, Abdul Razzak Bedir Han, a master of ceremonies at Yildiz, replied: 'Madame, we are brigands if you wish, but not thieves.' In 1906, after a dispute between the prefect of Constantinople and two of the Bedir Hans, the prefect was shot dead on a railway platform. To the fury of his government, the Sultan, without following due process of law, merely sent the Bedir Han family into exile.

One of the Sultan's secret police forces was managed by his wet-nurse's grandson, a fat pink-cheeked psychopath called Fehim Pasha. His agents subjected both men and women to torture, extortion and abduction. Finally, when German subjects received such treatment, the German ambassador, Baron Marschall von Bieberstein, a former Foreign Minister over six foot tall and broadly built, known as 'the giant of the Bosphorus', confronted the Sultan with evidence of Fehim Pasha's crimes. He was exiled to Bursa.[55]

Lack of money was another problem. Since 1879 there had been a four-cornered struggle for control of Ottoman revenues between the Sultan, the banks, the foreign bond-holders and the Public Debt Administration established in 1881 to manage the Ottoman debt. The Sultan was forced to lease, first to Zarifi, Mavrogordato and Camondo, then to the Public Debt Administration, a portion of the customs revenues and taxes on salt and tobacco. The Public Debt Administration, housed in a massive neo-Turkish building near the bazaar, helped the government obtain new loans on more favourable terms, and introduced many Turks to modern management. However it was essentially a means of 'opening up', and controlling, the Ottoman economy in the interests of European investors. It was run by foreigners, mainly British and French: the Ottoman representative, Osman Hamdi Bey, could attend, but not vote at, board meetings. By 1912 it employed over 5,500 full-time officials, more than the Ministry of Finance itself.[56]

Throughout the reign of Abdulhamid, government expenditure remained higher than revenues. The diary of Louis Rambert is full of references to the treasury being 'empty', 'living from day to day', unable to pay the troops. In a once famous novel based on the life of Edgar Vincent, *L'Homme qui assassina* (1902), Claude Farrère wrote that 'between the Bank and the Debt, the Golden Horn is strangled.' The roofs of the Public Debt building threatened the domes and minarets of Constantinople. Greeks, Syrians, Armenians and Jews were gathering for the kill. The empire was *un pays foutu*. In 1907, in order to modernize the port, the government was forced by foreign investors to ban the restrictive practices of the guild of port-workers. A vital link between the people and the palace was cut.[57]

The Sultan's appearance symbolized his empire's weakness. To Herzl he looked frail, with a dyed beard, long yellow teeth, protruding ears and bleating voice. He was like the captain of a beleaguered town. The troops were close to mutiny; half the inhabitants were in a state of sedition; and the envoys of the besieging force were lodged inside the walls.

Revolts in the provinces also alarmed Yildiz. On an average day in 1896 news arrived of riots in Crete, a rising in Lebanon, and an incursion of Armenians from Russia into eastern Anatolia. After 1900 the Macedonian question – how to govern a region inhabited, and coveted, by Muslims, Greeks, Bulgarians, Serbians and Albanians – haunted the palace, and the chancelleries of Europe.[58]

The atmosphere, and actions, of autocracy at bay gave Constantinople an aura of evil. Other large European cities, particularly since the industrial revolution, had been frequently denounced as new Babylons, intrinsically evil on account of their assumed depravity, poverty, ugliness and over-crowding. Shelley, for example, wrote: 'Hell is a city much like London.' Smog and disease earned it names like 'the great wen', 'the smoke', 'desolation'. Le Corbusier called Paris a cancer.[59] Constantinople's undisputed beauty, the prevalence of gardens and scarcity of factories, saved it from such excoriation. It was the people, and the government, which tainted its reputation.

Louis Rambert wrote: 'Nowhere else do human turpitudes have a finer stage on which to flourish.' A pious Muslim student who had grown up in the mountains of Kurdistan had a similar reaction. Bediuzzaman Said Nursi had imagined 'the seat of the Caliphate to be a beautiful place. I arrived in Constantinople [in 1896] and saw that the hatred which persons nourished against one another made them all into well-dressed savages . . . I saw and understood that Islam was behind, far behind the civilization of our times.' The most powerful denunciation came from the poet Tevfik Fikret, who had been editor of the great cultural review *Servet-i Funun*, before becoming Professor of Turkish Literature at Robert College. A hundred and seventy years earlier Nedim had compared Constantinople to the sun warming the entire world. Tevfik Fikret wrote that it was a city shrouded in fog: 'This veil suits you so well, O realm of all the oppressions, cradle and tomb of magnificence and splendour.' The eternally attractive Queen of the East was in reality a senile sorceress, poisoned with hypocrisy, jealousy and greed. It was a city of spies and beggars, fear, lies, injustice and dishonour:

> Veil yourself then, O tragedy, yes, veil yourself, O city.
> Veil yourself, and sleep for ever, whore of the world

– a cruel reference to the Ottoman epithet 'refuge of the world'.[60]

The beauty of Constantinople appealed to Sherif Ali Haydar: the sound of the wind sighing in the pine-trees, like waves on the seashore; his quiet life with his second wife, Isobel Dunn, and their children, reading, playing music, riding through the countryside. However, his hatred of the regime turned him against the city: 'Stamboul began to suffocate me and I grew weary of the place where every kind of cruelty, mental and physical, was practised.'[61]

Ahmed Vefik was a loyal Ottoman. After four successful years as Governor of Bursa in 1879–82, he returned to Constantinople. Having served as Grand Vizier again, for three days, he retired to his house at Rumeli Hisari where he died in 1891 at the age of 70 – one of the few pashas to die poor. Wearing an old-fashioned gown and a square fez from the reign of Mahmud II, in 1884 he had told Wilfrid Blunt that Abdulhamid should be deposed. He was '*un misérable et un fou*. He is out of his mind with fear and jealousy . . . he cares only for intrigue and for being cleverer than all those he meets and for outwitting them . . .' In reality the Sultan was not mad. He improved the city's water supply (better in 1900 than in 1995), reopened its university, doubled the number of schools. His rejection of industrialization made his subjects' lives, in the opinion of Pierre Loti, resemble the Golden Age compared to those of factory workers in the West. Economic historians estimate that wages in Constantinople were not much lower, given the difference in the cost of living, than in the United Kingdom. If the Ottoman élite on the whole disliked the Sultan, the poor and the minorities (except the Armenians) supported a ruler 'whose charity is proverbial and who really takes care of his subjects as far as this lies in his power'. He avoided wars and bankruptcy. However, his traditionalist autocracy was no substitute for the systematic modernization and industrialization occurring at the time in Japan.[62]

Constantinople had once been a city which received exiles. Now it generated them. The first 'Young Turk' conspiracy had broken out in the military medical college in 1889, and been easily suppressed. A series of secret revolutionary societies spread through the military, the administrative, the veterinary and the naval colleges, and the army itself. Since they used the 'cell' system, many conspirators were unknown to each other. Even the Sultan's tribal school was affected. It was dis-banded in 1907, ostensibly on account of a rebellion caused by bad food. However the Sultan's police was too effective in the capital for conspiracies to succeed. Liberals like Odian Efendi, Ahmed Riza, a nephew of the Sultan called Prince Sabaheddin, fled to Paris or Cairo. Discontented students were sent into exile in distant provinces like Tripolitania. For them Abdulhamid was the Red Sultan, the scourge of God, the bloody hangman.

The most powerful secret society, the Committee of Union and Progress, was based in Salonica, where the Sultan's police was weaker and censorship was looser. Eagerly waiting at Sirkeci station on the Golden Horn, people often paid double the cover price for Salonica newspapers, since they were so much freer than their Constantinople equivalents. Initiates to the Committee of Union and Progress, includ-ing Mustafa Kemal, swore oaths against autocracy by 'the holy light of liberty and justice'. Their fervour was heightened by a meeting between Edward VII and the Tsar, to seal the Anglo-Russian entente, on 9–10 June 1908. A reconciliation between two imperialist powers, from whose rivalry the empire had so greatly benefited, proved that the Sultan was no longer safeguarding the empire. Moreover the Sultan's police was on the trail of the conspiracy. On 3 July 1908 some officers took to the hills in Macedonia. To universal surprise, both in Constantinople and abroad, the revolution spread rapidly. 'Young Turk' propaganda had been effective; and so many troops had been unpaid for so long that the Sultan could no longer rely on them.[63] On 24 July, following the advice of the council of ministers meeting at Yildiz, and Seyh Abu'l-Huda, the Sultan abolished censorship and announced a political amnesty and elections to a new parliament for the autumn. For a day people hesitated, fearing a police trap. Then Constantinople exploded with joy.

14

Young Turks

We need an *advanced* and *modernized* Turkey. Constantinople would then be a source of light where Muslims would come without any prejudice to learn ideas of science and civilization.

Abdullah Cevdet, 20 August 1908

CONSTANTINOPLE AFTER THE Young Turk revolution for once justified the name Gate of Happiness. Some provincial cities regretted the end of the Sultan's absolutism: in the capital, long mined by Young Turk propaganda, people embraced each other in the street. Caught in an ecstatic crowd, Sherif Ali Haydar experienced 'the sweetest moments in my life. Only those who have lived through years of oppression and bondage can appreciate this.' Halide Edib, daughter of one of the Sultan's chamberlains, and a future feminist and writer, remembered a human tide flowing across the Galata bridge 'radiating something extraordinary, laughing, weeping in such intense emotion that human deficiency and ugliness were for the time completely obliterated'. The city had found a new role. It was both the capital of an empire and the headquarters of a revolution.[1]

By restoring the constitution so quickly, the Sultan could play the role of a father delivered from evil councillors. On 26 July, sixty thousand people massed in front of the entrance to Yildiz. They carried banners reading, in French and Ottoman, *Liberty, Equality, Fraternity and Justice*, and wore 'liberty cockades' in red and white (the colours of the Ottoman flag), aping the tricolour cockade of Paris in 1789. When the Sultan appeared at a balcony, there were cheers of 'Long live our Padishah!' He replied: 'Since my accession I have devoted all my efforts to the happiness and salvation of my fatherland. My great desire is the happiness and salvation of my subjects whom I do not distinguish from my children. God is my witness.' More cheers. Years later the Sultan's

346

painter Fausto Zonaro wrote: 'Never in all my life had I heard such a cry. Never had I seen so many exulting people.' Symbolizing the conviction that the revolution was a new dawn for the empire, postcards appeared showing the sun rising above Constantinople's domes and minarets, or Abdulhamid smiling above the words, in French and Ottoman, *Liberté, Egalité et Fraternité*.[2]

Under a new Grand Vizier, the skilful and industrious Kamil Pasha, Yildiz lost some of its luxuries and most of its power. The Sultan's spies disappeared like snow before the sun. Aides-de-camp, gardeners, and Arturo Stravolo's opera troupe were dismissed. Fehim Pasha was lynched. A new set of refugees from Constantinople arrived in Cairo: former grand viziers and ministers, like Izzet Pasha, replaced the Young Turks who had lived there before 1908. When Young Turk leaders and officers returned to the capital in triumph, it seemed as if the entire population was lining Galata bridge and the quays in order to greet them.

For a capital suddenly granted freedom after thirty years of despotism, Constantinople appeared remarkably calm. However, real power lay, not with the official government under Kamil Pasha but with the Committee of Union and Progress, led by three patriots who would dominate the government for the next ten years: Enver, Cemal and Talaat Pashas. The first was an idealistic young officer, who believed himself the idol of the nation and capable of realizing its dreams; the second was an energetic and progressive administrator; Talaat, a burly former postal official in Salonica with a sweet smile, was the most ruthless of the three. While deliberately staying in the background, members of the Committee paid weekly visits to the Grand Vizier and the ministers, to inform them of its views – in other words to give instructions. The palace appeared to accept the new order unreservedly. Without waiting for 'the usual translation', the Sultan 'with singular loud laughter' told the Austrian ambassador, the Marchese Pallavicini (known from his frequent prophecies of doom as 'the Cassandra of Pera'), that he had no desire to withdraw the constitution, 'not in five, not in ten, nor even in fifteen years'.[3]

That autumn the elections were celebrated by dramatic rites of liberty, fraternity and flowers. Voting booths, set up in the courtyards of mosques, churches and police stations, were decorated with chrysanthemums, magnolia and bay. On 25 November, in pouring rain, flower-strewn ballot boxes were carried in palace landaus to the Sublime Porte as if they were battle trophies. The processions were headed by mounted troops and bands of drummers, escorted by carriage-loads of brightly dressed schoolchildren singing patriotic songs, and followed by the populace on foot, also singing, and waving the red Ottoman flag and green Islamic banners.[4]

The city celebrated fraternity between religions, as well as free elections. In July Muslims and Christians attended requiem services at Taksim and Balikli Armenian cemeteries for the victims of the 1895 and 1896 massacres. Prince Sabaheddin, who went to the Phanar to reassure the Patriarch that Greek privileges would be preserved under the new regime, called Hellenism in Turkey an indispensable element of order and progress. In December the last ballot boxes were escorted over Galata bridge by Kurds, Laz, Georgians, Circassians and Arabs, wearing national dress and weapons, a contrast in costume, but not sentiment, to the uniformed Ottoman officials, and mullahs, priests and rabbis, beside them. Before the elections there had been disputes over some Greek voters' inability to produce proof of Ottoman citizenship: they had taken Greek or foreign nationality, in part to avoid taxation. A crowd of angry Greeks marched down from Pera across the Galata bridge to the Sublime Porte and demanded, and received, from Kamil Pasha a written assurance that their complaints would be investigated. However mullahs, Greek and Armenian priests and rabbis were photographed side by side, surrounded by Ottoman soldiers, in commemoration of their successful organization of the elections. Of the deputies elected in 1908, 142 were Turks, 60 Arabs, 25 Albanians, 23 Greeks, 12 Armenians (including four Dashnaks and two Henchaks), five Jews, four Bulgarians, three Serbs, one Vlach. The Young Turks, the colloquial term appropriated by followers of the Committee, had about 60 deputies. Others included *ulema* opposed to secularization, conservatives, and liberals in favour of decentralization.[5]

On 17 December parliament was opened, not in an imperial palace as in 1877, but in the parliament building beside Aya Sofya. Excited crowds swamped the surrounding area. Pigeons and seagulls were displaced from the roof of Aya Sofya by men and women eager for a view of the ceremony below. Cheers rose at the appearance of the Seyhulislam, a noted supporter of the constitution, and the most popular deputies. Suddenly the band switched from playing the newly composed Constitution March to the *Hamidiye* march, so familiar from the *selamliks* at Yildiz. Two hours late, the Sultan arrived, escorted by lancers of the guard. Stooping, pale as death, he did not walk but shuffled to a tribune above the deputies. Senator Alexander Mavroyeni, son of the Sultan's doctor, wrote: 'He looked like a man hunted by the enemy, almost a corpse, who while moving his lips cannot make himself heard.' In a loud voice the chief secretary read his speech, with its pretence that, since the level of education had finally made elections possible, the Sultan had called them of his own free will. That night mosques, palaces, ministries, yalis and ships were illuminated in honour of the new era.[6]

The Sultan was now a spent force. Deputies invited to dinner in Yildiz – in the main room of the Buyuk Mabeyn – on 31 December became humble and respectful within the palace walls. They kissed his hand and coat-sleeve, as tradition demanded, rather than merely making a deep bow, as the Committee preferred. His chief secretary assured him that he was one with his people. The Sultan wept tears of joy and said that he had never been happier.[7]

Meanwhile, in part because of what became known as 'the Gueshov incident', the Young Turk government had suffered a loss of prestige. The Sultan, always wary of contacts between his subjects and foreigners, had discouraged diplomatic dinners. On 14 September the Foreign Minister Tevfik Pasha, an amiable old man famous for a composure which no crisis had been known to disturb, gave a dinner for diplomats in his house by the German embassy. M. Gueshov, the Bulgarian *agent diplomatique*, received no invitation, a signal that the Ottoman government still considered Ferdinand Prince of Bulgaria governor of an Ottoman *vilayet*, not an independent sovereign. Enraged by this display of Ottoman grandeur, the Prince proclaimed himself independent Tsar of Bulgaria on 5 October. An entire diplomatic timetable was upset. Austria was led to announce its annexation of Bosnia-Herzegovina (also still in theory an Ottoman province), ahead of a schedule the Austrian Foreign Minister had agreed with his Russian colleague, who in compensation had intended to obtain Ottoman consent to open the Straits to Russian warships. Russia was humiliated. Austro-Russian relations deteriorated; the rush to 1914 accelerated. The Ottoman Empire lost two tributary provinces (and a third, Crete, the same year). A boycott of Austrian goods and boats was launched by the patriotic tradesmen of Constantinople. Austrian ships were unable to unload their cargoes on the quays of Galata. The boycott was lifted only after the payment of a substantial indemnity by Austria to the Ottoman government.[8]

At the same time as a revolution of 'Liberty, Equality, Freedom and Justice', Constantinople experienced a movement resembling modern

fundamentalism. A preacher called 'Blind Ali' denounced the constitution in the mosque of Fatih. On 7 October 1908 he led a large Ramadan
crowd to Yildiz to see the Sultan, who appeared at a window. Blind Ali
told him: 'We want a shepherd! A flock cannot exist without a shepherd!' The fundamentalists demanded the rule of *sheriat*, the prohibition
of taverns, theatres and photography, and an end to Muslim women's
freedom to walk around the town. It was a programme as puritanical as
that of the Muslim zealots, the *kadizadeliler*, in the seventeenth century,
a sign that the Islamic life of the city had its own momentum, independent of revolutions and constitutions. Blind Ali was sentenced to
prison.

The fundamentalists were not alone. Discontent infected many of
the troops stationed in the city – even revolutionary troops transferred
from Salonica to Constantinople to strengthen the new order. They
were not only pious Muslims attracted to fundamentalism but also
dynastic favourites outraged by a reduction in their privileges. Time formerly spent in prayer was allotted to military drill. Officers who had
been promoted from the ranks by the Sultan were replaced by graduates
of military school who supported the Committee. Guards accustomed
to an easy life at Yildiz mutinied at the prospect of service in the Hejaz.
The inhabitants of Constantinople itself faced loss of their traditional
tax privileges and freedom from conscription.[9]

A fundamentalist newspaper, *Volkan*, was started in November with
the programme 'to spread the light of divine unity in the capital of
the Caliphate'. The Sultan's piety and charity were celebrated; the
Committee was accused of forgetting that 'Constantinople is not Paris'.
The harmony of the summer of 1908 disappeared. On 9 February
Kamil Pasha, who had wanted to depoliticize the army and draw closer
to the palace, resigned in face of pressure from the Committee. On 3
April 1909 the Society of Muhammad was established and held meetings in Aya Sofya hostile to the Committee: 'Forward! If we fall as
martyrs, do not retreat!' Many sufis and imams supported it; senior
ulema remained loyal to the constitution.[10]

On 7 April the editor of an anti-Committee newspaper was murdered on Galata bridge, a favourite murdering-place since the killer
could easily disappear in the crowd. On the night of 12/13 April soldiers and NCOs mutinied, crying 'We want *sheriat*!' They overpowered
their officers, and marched on the parliament building beside Aya
Sofya. Their demands were: application of *sheriat*; dismissal of the
Unionist ministers and officers; restriction of Muslim women to the

home. While they invaded the parliament building, the Sultan quickly accepted their programme. His chief secretary was sent to read a proclamation to the chamber, and the soldiers and *hocas* (Muslim teachers) milling around it. According to his memoirs the following dialogue took place:

> 'Please go back to your barracks and be comfortable, my sons, the Sultan forgives you.'
> 'Tell the old man young boys are kicking us and blaspheming our religion and slandering the Sultan.'

Tevfik Pasha became Grand Vizier. The Sultan had not instigated, but had probably foreseen, and certainly exploited, the mutiny. He recovered control of the crucial ministries of the army and the navy. While some parliamentarians continued to meet in Constantinople, others fled to the San Stefano yacht club, near where the Russian army had camped in 1878. Soldiers sacked the officers of pro-Committee newspapers such as *Tanin*, and killed the Minister of Justice and some of their officers. The incident showed both the revolutionaries' ignorance of the feelings of the people and the army, and Constantinople's dynastic conservatism. It was more loyal to the monarch than St Petersburg or Tehran, both of which had recently (in 1905 and 1906 respectively) supported revolutions.[11]

After the first bloodshed the troops returned to discipline. However, the Young Turks in Salonica refused to accept the authority of the new government. A note of specifically anti-metropolitan feeling appears in their writings. Abdulhamid considered the possession of Constantinople one of the four pillars of the empire, with Islam, the House of Osman and guardianship of the two holy cities. Young Turks denounced 'the intrigues woven in the miserable environment of old Byzantium', and determined to 'cleanse' the capital.[12]

A force called the 'Action Army' advanced on the capital from Salonica under the command of Mahmud Shevket Pasha, a Young Turk general of Arab origin, an admirer of German tactics and French literature (his translation of *Manon Lescaut* had been published in Constantinople in 1879). The streets of the city, even the Galata bridge, emptied. The Sultan's government, which may have expected to resume power without resistance, had no will to fight. He had the support of the people but not the élite. The *ulema* persuaded most of the mutineers not to resist, and issued a manifesto saying that *sheriat* was compatible, not with absolutism but with the constitution. Reassured by messages from Shevket that deposition was not planned, the Sultan rejected the request of loyal officers for permission to resist.

At Abdulhamid's last *selamlik* on 23 April the troops and the spectators had never appeared more enthusiastic, nor the Sultan more smiling and gracious: his cheeks had been rouged and his beard dyed for the occasion. An innovation – and sign of despair – was the imam's exhortation to Muslims to remain faithful to the Caliph. Some spectators felt that he would somehow weather the storm. However one look from his carriage showed him that there were no ambassadors on the diplomatic terrace: Europe had gone over to the winning side.[13]

During the night of 23/24 April and throughout 24 April, troops from Salonica occupied the city. Soldiers in the barracks at Taksim and Fatih, and at the Sublime Porte, resisted for several hours, leaving the Porte with cannon-holes in its walls. However, on the night of 24/25 April the guards at Yildiz surrendered or fled across the Bosphorus. Gas and electricity were cut, plunging the palace in darkness. Courtiers and servants streamed out carrying bundles of linen and jewels. The Sultan's sons fled to their married sisters' palaces. The eunuchs and ladies had hysterics. Finally, according to the Sultan's unmarried daughter Ayse, 'in this great palace there were only women'.[14]

On 25 April Shevket imposed an emergency law. On 27 April in closed session the National Assembly decreed the Sultan's deposition. The Seyhulislam composed the necessary fatwa. That day four deputies (Essad an Albanian, Karassu a Jew, Aram an Armenian and Arif Hikmet a Laz) came to Yildiz to tell the Sultan that he was deposed on grounds of oppression, massacres, infringement of the *sheriat*, and responsibility for the recent uprising. The Sultan, a broken man, replied that he had tried to serve the nation. He reminded them of his victorious war against Greece in 1897 and declared that he was not the cause of the recent mutiny. He asked to live in Ciragan, but the Committee had decided to send him to Salonica. At 2.45 a.m. on 29 April the Sultan, with his immediate family and a few servants, left the city by train from Sirkeci station beside the Golden Horn.[15]

The palace city of Yildiz was dismantled. The first eunuch and some mutineers were hanged on Galata bridge. On 27 April, 300 frightened, dishevelled palace servants – eunuchs, cooks, coffee-pourers – had been led through the streets of Pera, over the bridge, to prison in Constantinople. Two hundred and thirteen harem women were taken from Yildiz by carriage to the abandoned palace of Topkapi. Some were collected by relations from the mountains of Circassia and Anatolia, who were 'dazzled by the beautiful faces, the graceful manners and the rich apparel of their kinswomen'. In other cases relations arrived, only to learn that their daughter or sister was no longer alive. For some women no one came.

Yildiz fell prey to looters. The library, which the Sultan used to visit every day, was given to Darulfunun University, where it still is. Finally in July, the palace was opened to the public. At a sale organized by the Young Turk government in Paris in 1911, the Sultan's jewels realized seven million francs. Among them was a necklace of 154 pearls; a pair of binoculars decorated in gold and diamonds; and a gold cigarette case on which the route of the Berlin to Baghdad railway had been engraved in sapphires, rubies and diamonds.[16]

Despite the fall of the old Sultan, the dynasty remained embedded in the hearts and minds of Muslim Ottomans. The new Sultan was Abdulhamid's brother Reshad, a Mevlevi dervish and the last Sultan to write Persian poetry. His known sympathy for liberal ideas had long inspired hope in Young Turks and fear in the Sultan. He took the name Mehmed Reshad, as a sign that, like his ancestor Mehmed Fatih, he had conquered Constantinople – through the constitutional army. Like Fatih, he held his first Friday prayers in Aya Sofya. The simplicity of his manners astonished the city. He lived in Dolmabahce, with a reduced household. According to the memoirs of one of his secretaries: 'Almost absolute silence now reigned in the enormous palace . . . if a plate fell and broke in the dining room the crash resounded throughout the whole building like the crack of doom.' Fat and well-meaning, Reshad appeared content to do what the Committee or the Porte required. The constitution was rewritten to reduce the powers of the crown in matters of legislation, foreign policy and electoral procedure.[17]

With the accession of the new Sultan, Constantinople resumed its role as a modernizing metropolis, never wholly suspended under Abdulhamid. The Ottoman parliament sat every year until 1918, debating laws, budgets, the competence of ministers. A deliberate attempt was made to found a modern Muslim capitalist society. From 1909 the slave trade was (in theory) banned, although the institution of slavery survived until 1926, or later. Guilds were abolished in 1910, to the delight of the city's chamber of commerce, which had long complained of their restrictive practices. In 1910–11 a new shipyard and grain mill, and new beer, shoe and cement factories were built.[18]

The Société Anonyme Ottomane d'Electricité began to bring electricity to the city. Telephones were installed by the Société Anonyme Ottomane des Téléphones de Constantinople, founded in 1911 – although there had been a few privileged telephone owners under Abdulhamid. *Stamboul 42* was the number of the Sublime Porte; Dolmabahce palace was *Pera 24*. Soon Taksim gardens, according to the *Moniteur Oriental*, was a modern resort containing 'every pleasure': a restaurant, an open air cinema, a *théâtre de variétés* and a *cabaret de nuit montmartrois*, with a *bar ultra-sélect fréquenté par le high life de la capitale*. Throughout the city different cafés attracted particular clienteles: sailors, pilgrims, Greeks, Turks, Persians or Albanians. Conspicuous by their lavish jewellery and brilliant neckties, eunuchs patronized a café near the Galata bridge. The 'very large and very European' Hotel Tokatliyan had been founded by an Armenian family in 1892, in a large columned classical building on the Grande Rue de Pera. Its café became an important political centre, patronized by politicians, officers, journalists and spies of all nations, and 'all kinds of ladies except Turkish ladies'. Waiters were said to know at a glance whether a client required coffee, beer, cognac or raki.[19]

Under the Young Turks the city was also liberated from its dogs. In May 1910 they were collected off the streets and deposited on the island of Sivriada in the Sea of Marmara. At first they came to the shore in hope as boats sailed past. Then a terrible howling was heard across the Sea of Marmara for several nights – fifty years later old men still remembered it. Finally, the survivors tore each other apart. For several months Constantinople slept soundly. Then a few squeals were heard, as puppies emerged – the offspring of stray survivors in the outskirts of the city. By 1913 dogs were again visible on the streets. Turks who blamed the empire's latest misfortunes on their expulsion were relieved.[20] Today, despite repeated 'cullings', in some areas dogs can still render sleep impossible and pavements impassable.

Both Europe and the Middle East were hypnotized by the Young Turk revolution. Illustrious foreigners came to observe the new capital: the inevitable Loti, André Gide (who loathed it), Le Corbusier (who preferred the old Muslim city to the *allures new-yorkaises* of Pera); the Kings of Bulgaria, Serbia and Montenegro; Winston Churchill. A flood of books appeared on the story of the year: *The Fall of Abdulhamid, Turkey in Revolution, Jeune Turquie, Vieille France*. Since they record events, and Young Turks' opinions, without the benefit of hindsight, some are valuable historical sources. No foreign visitor, however, had as great an effect as a Marxist journalist with a Russian Jewish background, Alexander Israel Helphand. A friend of Lenin and Trotsky, a leading figure in the revolution of 1905–6, from his arrival in Constantinople in 1910 Parvus, as he called himself, connected the Young Turks to the Second International.

The city appeared ready for socialism. Within a few days of the Young Turk revolution, workers in the docks and trams, bakers and newspaper employees had gone on strike for higher wages – which they won. In May 1909, a few days after the overthrow of Abdulhamid, a group of socialists calling themselves the Socialist Centre had arrived from Salonica to educate 'the labouring classes of Constantinople'. In 1910 journalists, teachers and students founded the Ottoman Socialist Party, with branches in Constantinople and Paris. Parvus began writing articles urging economic liberalism and the creation of a national (Muslim) bourgeoisie, not only in European newspapers but also in a Young Turk journal called *Turk Yurdu*, of which he became economics editor. He had arrived poor but within two years was a prosperous businessman supplying the capital and the army with grain.[21] In a speech in November 1910 to the Socialist Centre, he admitted: 'Today the workers of the Ottoman Empire are divided by religion, patriotism and ethnic hate', but he hoped that they would unite in face of the capitalists united against them. In fact Jews, Armenians, Bulgarians, Greeks and Muslims from Daghestan and the Crimea were prominent in the Ottoman socialist party. The first unions formed in Constantinople in 1910–12 (of building workers, commercial employees and dockers), although Greek-dominated, attracted workers from different nationalities and printed notices in four or five languages. The typographers union had Bulgarian, Greek, Armenian, Turkish and French sections.

However the Committee was more interested in strengthening the empire than fostering revolution. In late 1910 the Socialist Centre was closed. In early 1911 many socialist were exiled to Anatolia, joined two years later by Huseyin Hilmi, who had founded the newspaper *Ishtirak* (Participation) in 1908.[22]

The Young Turk revolution also brought the beginning of female emancipation. Abdulhamid had been particularly conservative in this domain. In 1889, not for the first time, he had issued orders to women to wear the *charchaf* (resembling the modern Iranian *chador*) rather than, as hitherto, the more revealing *yashmak* and *ferace*. He also forbade Muslim women to leave the home in the company of any male, even their own father. Nevertheless women refused to be suppressed.

A traveller wrote in 1895: 'Strict as the Sultan's ordinance is, there is not the slightest pretence of obeying it and in the great majority of cases a thin white veil barely covers the forehead and is but loosely drawn together under the chin.' A Bektashi woman poet wrote around 1900:

> Did not God create us too?
> Is the female lion no less a lion?

Women had been enthusiastic in support of the revolution of 1908, showing their face in public, as a sign of celebration, on 17 December 1908 at the opening of parliament, and on 30 April 1909 at Reshad's first *selamlik*.[23] Some members of the élite began to end the division in their houses between *haremlik* and *selamlik*, and to allow their wives to meet male visitors. They began to say in public, what they had long been saying in private, that female seclusion was 'the curse of our country', that Turkey would never be a modern nation until women emerged from behind the lattices of the harem and the folds of the yashmak.[24]

In the city's Turkish Hearth, a club founded by Young Turk intellectuals, women lectured to men and men to women; Halide Edib, the writer and feminist who had become a prominent teacher, frequently spoke there. Another leading Young Turk intellectual, Murris Tekinalp (originally Moiz Cohen, a Jew from Salonica) wrote: 'The general opinion is that the liberation of women will take place in a comparatively short time.' The first modern girls' lycée was opened in 1911. From 1913, there were several women's organizations in Constantinople: Ottoman Womanhood, and societies for the Elevation of Women, Employment of Women and the Defence of the Rights of Woman.[25]

Constantinople was a laboratory brewing new drugs for the Middle East: not only socialism and feminism, but also Kurdish and Arab nationalism. The boast of a Young Turk, Riza Tevfik, in the Ottoman parliament that Muslims were less nationalistic than Christians, Enver's claim that 'in Islam nationality does not exist', were not true.[26]

Approximately 30,000 Kurds lived in the capital. Not all were Kurdish nationalists. The great theorist of Turkish nationalism Ziya Gokalp, who taught sociology at Darulfunun University and edited *Turk Yurdu*, a short fat dark man with, according to Halide Edib, 'strange eyes looking beyond and away from the people and things that surrounded him', had Kurdish blood and spoke Kurdish before Turkish. However he became so Turkish that he wanted Turks to return to their roots. He boasted that he derived inspiration from Attila and Genghiz no less than Alexander and Caesar and wrote poems in praise of *Turan*, the legendary Turkish homeland in the East. (Halide Edib also wrote a visionary political novel called *Yeni Turan*.) Other Kurds wanted autonomy, or more, in the East. In 1908–9 prominent Kurds in Constantinople such as Abdulhamid's favourites the Bedir Han family, and Sayyid Abdulkadir, future president of the council of state, founded *Kurdistan*, a bilingual Turco-Kurdish paper, the Kurdish Society for Progress and Mutual Aid, the Society for Propagation of Kurdish Education, and a Kurdish school. In 1912 a deputy of Kurdish origin, Lutfi Fikri, advocated radical measures: secularization of the state, equal rights for women and Latinization of the alphabet.[27]

After 1908 Constantinople also became a centre of Arab nationalism, more important than Beirut or Cairo. Arab-Turkish tensions had been increased by Abdulhamid's use of Arabs as spies, officials and body-guards. Hostile remarks in the Turkish newspaper *Ikdam* regarding Arab 'loyalty' led to an attack on its printing press by Arabs. As a riposte the Society of Arab-Ottoman Brotherhood was founded in the Variété salon of Pera on 2 September 1908: it aimed 'to unite all Ottoman communities without distinction of race or sect and to consolidate their solidarity in a way which would enable them to serve and to reform the Ottoman state.' At the opening ceremony, after speeches in Arabic and Ottoman, the following lines were cheered: 'From now on our path is justice, fraternity, equality, freedom. Long live Sultan Abdulhamid Khan, the padishah of the government of constitution and consultation!' A clubhouse below the Grande Rue de Pera was open every evening. However some feared a hidden agenda behind the loyal façade. Some Arabs were beginning to ask that government schools in Arabic-speaking provinces should teach in Arabic – not, as hitherto, in Ottoman.[28]

In the summer of 1909 the Society was replaced by Al-Muntada al-adabi, the Literary Club, founded in Constantinople by officials and deputies from Damascus and Jerusalem. It organized plays and lectures in its clubhouse and soon had a membership of thousands throughout the Fertile Crescent. Two secret societies with more nationalistic aims were also founded: Al-Kahtaniya, around 1909, and Al-Ahd, for the army, probably in 1914. Of 498 Arab officers in the Ottoman army 315 had joined Al-Ahd by 1914.[29]

A sign of the success of Abdulhamid's Arab policy was that, in contrast to 1880, few Arabs now favoured any programme more drastic than decentralization or, as one party put it, 'an Ottoman government neither Turkish nor Arab, a government in which all the Ottomans have equal rights and equal obligations'. They still considered the Caliphate a sacred trust in the hands of the Ottoman dynasty, and the empire the Arabs' first line of defence against the West. Constantinople itself was another argument for Ottomanism. Al-Ahd believed 'that Constantinople is the head of the East. The East cannot survive if it is stripped off from it by a foreign state. Therefore the association is especially concerned with defending it and preserving its security.' In an effort to strengthen ties between the empire and the Arabs, in 1910 Mahmud Shevket Pasha arranged the first marriage between a Hashemite and an Ottoman. A granddaughter of Murad V brought up in Ciragan, Rukiye Sultan, married Sherif Abdulmecid, elder son of Sherif Ali Haydar.[30]

Sherif Ali Haydar admired Mahmud Shevket and Talaat, who frequently visited him at his property at Camlica, on the Asian side of the Bosphorus. To Arab friends he said: 'The Young Turks are opening a new page in the history of our nation and all will come right with time. Do not attempt to break away from the Ottoman Empire when the general condition of the world is in a state of upheaval.' His ultimate goal was an Arab-Turkish dual monarchy resembling Austria-Hungary, with a second capital and parliament in Baghdad or Medina.[31]

Ali Haydar's cousin and rival Sherif Huseyin, although he disliked the 'usurpers' of the Committee of Union and Progress and the revival of the constitution, also remained loyal to the Ottoman Empire. Appointed Sherif and Emir of Mecca by Abdulhamid, to the fury of Ali Haydar (no doubt disqualified by his Irish wife), he had left Constantinople for Mecca in November 1908. Married to a Turkish wife, with relations and property in the capital, he pursued a pro-Ottoman policy, despite disputes with the *vali* (Governor) caused by the Sherif's opposition to such Ottoman reforms as the prolongation of the Hejaz railway to Mecca and the abolition of slavery. His sons Abdullah and Faisal visited Constantinople for the annual sessions of the Ottoman parliament, in which they sat as deputies for Mecca and Jeddah respectively. He himself helped the Ottoman Empire reconquer the province of Asir, south of the Hejaz, in 1911.[32]

A force potentially more deadly for the Ottoman Empire and its capital than Kurdish or Arab nationalism was Turkish nationalism. Long after Armenians, Greeks and Bulgarians, Turks were finally yielding to the spirit of the age. Dynastic and religious loyalties were weakening.

Already under Abdulhamid Ottoman intellectuals had begun to write in praise of 'the services of the Turks to the sciences and the arts', and to show an unprecedented interest in the Turks of central Asia and Anatolia. Cevdet Pasha told the Sultan that 'the Turks are the real force behind the Sublime State'.[33] From 1908 Ottoman rather than the quadriga of Ottoman, French, Greek and Armenian was compulsory on official forms. Intellectuals in Constantinople began to believe 'we are Turks and we need Turkish', and to substitute Turkish words for words of Arabic or Persian origin. They considered the name Ottoman no more appropriate for Turks than the dynastic name Umayyad for the early Arabs: 'There can be neither an Ottoman nation nor an Ottoman language.'[34]

Such growth in nationalism was intended to counteract a long history of racial denigration. Not only did the Ottoman ruling class use the word Turk to mean lout; Arabs claimed cultural superiority. A Perote novelist called Turks *un peuple enfantin*. According to a book published by a European inhabitant of the city in 1915, 'The Turks have neither intellectual aspirations nor patriotism; the people is utterly amorphous.'[35]

The growing attraction of Turkish nationalism is reflected in the career of the most distinguished modern representative of the Koprulu family, Fuad Koprulu, founder of modern Turkish historiography. He never mentioned his ancestry, and his son Orhan Koprulu remembers him saying, 'In our country we do not have any nobility.' However, although his branch of the family descended from a daughter, rather than a son, of the first Koprulu grand vizier, they used the name Kopruluzade. In the eighteenth century they served in the army; in the nineteenth in the administration – Kopruluzade Ahmed Ziya Bey was ambassador in Romania in 1890–2. He was father of Ismail Faiz Bey, a civil servant who married a refugee from Bulgaria. Their son Fuad Koprulu was born in 1890 and brought up in a family property opposite the Koprulu mausoleum and library on Divan Yolu. Other élite families were leaving their mansions in Constantinople for modern houses or flats in the new districts of Shishli and Nishantash, beyond Pera, made fashionable by their proximity to the imperial palaces of Dolmabahce and Yildiz. However, around 1900 the Koprulu built a kiosk in the traditional district south of Sultanahmed. Between the sea and the old Byzantine walls, beside a mosque built in the year of the Ottoman conquest and the railway line to Europe, it was an ideal setting for a historian.

Fuad Koprulu was educated in the modern school system started in the 1840s, and also taught himself at home. He soon knew French better than his teachers, as well as Greek, Ottoman, Persian and Arabic. Always slightly above ordinary life, he was never happier than when spreading books around him on the floor in a circle, and trying to read them all at once. In his case books, rather than the city or its inhabitants, made the link with French culture. Familiar with both Ottoman and Western literature, like many members of Constantinople's élite, he subscribed to the *Revue des Deux Mondes*. He liked the scientific point of view and clarity of modern French thinkers, especially the founder of modern sociology, Emile Durkheim, who held that there were no individuals, only society. Fuad Koprulu was a positivist who believed in the value of science. His principal intellectual achievement, in a career in which he wrote a torrent of articles and a total of seventy-five books, would be to apply modern scientific methods to the study of Turkish culture and history. He did not perform the five daily prayers and rarely went to mosque.[36]

His first published work had been a dynastic poem in honour of Abdulhamid's sixty-third birthday in 1906, but after 1908 he was a whole-hearted nationalist. He joined the Turkish Association, founded in 1908 'to study the past and present achievements and activities and circumstances of all the people called Turks'. With the great poet Yahya Kemal and other friends such as Talaat Pasha, he went every Friday to Buyukada for dinner in the house of Ziya Gokalp. This island, a summer resort for people from Constantinople, whose towering art-nouveau wooden houses and horse-drawn carriages still evoke the atmosphere and smell of the late Ottoman city, was largely inhabited by Greeks. Yet it was there that modern Turkish nationalism was constructed. Gokalp was a romantic nationalist haunted by dreams of Turan and determined to save the Ottoman Empire. Defining the nation not by race but by a 'common bond of culture and sentiment', Gokalp wanted a Turkish land where the Koran was read in Turkish and 'ideals, customs, tongue, belief all are one'.[37]

Gokalp, Koprulu, and other intellectuals like Abdullah Cevdet, believed there was no choice but to accept Western culture in entirety, 'with its roses and its thorns'. Forgetting the Ottoman heritage of multi-nationalism, art, religion, poetry, and manners and customs, they were convinced that 'civilization means European civilization.' Even some aspects of Islam came under attack: in 1913 a newspaper called *Free Search*, edited by Abdullah Cevdet, published articles declaring war on theologians and debating whether the Prophet was epileptic.

Nationalism was one aspect of Western culture Koprulu accepted without hesitation. He believed that Turks had forgotten their own history and language. If they acquired national consciousness and purpose, the Ottoman Empire would revive as Germany and Italy had done. In a famous article of 1913 in *Turk Yurdu*, he wrote:

> Turkish nationalists are neither reactionary nor visionaries nor separatists but simply believe that the preservation of Ottomanism and Islamism depends upon the awakening and development of Turkism. Only when the Turks come to possess a national consciousness of their own will Ottomanism and Islamism obtain the necessary force of attraction to preserve the empire. Only then will the various elements making up the empire be able to pursue their national development in full harmony with the empire.

Denying the multinationalism of Ottoman history, and his own family's Albanian roots, he wrote: 'The central force of the empire is Turkish as it always has been . . . the empire is above all else a Turkish Islamic sultanate.' He had little love for, and few friends among, the minorities. In 1912 he wrote that they were able to monopolize trade with the West since 'the Christian population escaped the exhaustion brought about by military service in defence of the empire'.[38]

Some Young Turks even began to discuss a revolution in language and the adoption of the Latin in place of the Arabic alphabet; 'we are no more Arabs than the French are', they maintained. Mustafa Kemal, an ambitious young officer who had served in the 1909 Young Turk campaign, sometimes wrote in Turkish in Latin letters to a Pera friend called Corinne. Halide Edib denounced the Ottoman alphabet: 'What do you expect from a medium of instruction that requires almost six years study and practice before you can write it?'[39]

One result of the birth of Turkish nationalism was the creation on 25 March 1912 of an association of 'Turkish Hearths', open to Turks but not to foreign Muslims. Soon it was an extensive network of clubs, welcoming Turkish refugees from the Balkans and working 'for the national education of the Turkish people, which forms the most important division of Islam, [and for] the raising of her intellectual, social and economic standards, and for the perfection of the Turkish language and race.' In its clubhouse and library in Constantinople, the Turkish Hearth organized evening classes, public lectures – particularly on heroes of Turkish history and art – 'literary and artistic evenings'. Ziya Gokalp and Fuad Koprulu were present most evenings.[40]

The growth of Turkish nationalism was an intellectual fashion restricted to a small circle. The 1,800 members of the Turkish Hearth did not make a mass movement. Islamic newspapers specifically attacked the use of terms like 'Turkish government' and 'Turkish army'. Suleyman Nazif wrote: 'In our veins there is only Ottoman blood.' Ahmed Naim called nationalism 'a foreign innovation as deadly to the body of Islam as cancer is to man'. They rejected any connection between the Ottomans and central Asia. Most Muslims in the empire continued to call themselves Osmanli and to use the word Turk to mean lout. In 1915 in the bazaar a passer-by told the American journalist John Reed: 'You must not call us Turks. Turk means rustic clown, rude as you would say . . . We are Osmanlis, an ancient and cultivated race.' Constantinople remained a multinational city, with a government which, however attracted to Turkish nationalism, practised multinationalism in deeds as well as words. The Young Turk army from Salonica had been accompanied by bands of Bulgarian, Greek and Albanian guerillas, who terrified the shopkeepers of the capital. Demetrius Mavrogordato Efendi, of the banking branch of the family, was appointed Minister of Commerce and Agriculture (in other words, as a Christian, given an unimportant portfolio in token at once of goodwill and distrust).[41]

Moreover in 1912 the dynasty reasserted its power over the Committee. The dynasty's most forceful member was a son of Abdulaziz called Abdulmecid Efendi, a prince of imposing appearance and wide sympathies who during Abdulhamid's reign had lived in a house above Uskudar, forbidden to visit Constantinople. He told Pierre Loti that he had spent twenty-eight years in a tomb.[42] Like Fuad Koprulu, Abdulmecid was a product of the Ottoman élite's marriage with French culture. He spoke Ottoman, Arabic, French and German, and called France a second fatherland. He had spent his seclusion composing classical music, reading the complete works of Victor Hugo and the latest numbers of the *Revue des Deux Mondes* and cultivating his park. Like many educated Ottomans, such as Osman Hamdi Bey and Halil Pasha, he painted in a modern Parisian style, mainly *peyzaj* (landscapes) and scenes from Ottoman history such as the instruction of Shehzade Mahmud by Selim III, or the deposition of Abdulhamid II.

At once cosmopolitan and patriotic, Abdulmecid Efendi also encouraged the revival of Turkish culture. His house was in the neo-Turkish style with wide eaves, brightly painted walls and fireplaces lined with Kutahya tiles: he himself designed the neo-Seljuk gate. After 1908 he held gatherings of Turkish writers and musicians, and put on plays by Abdulhak Hamid in his garden. A friend of Tevfik Fikret, author of *The Fog*, and described as 'the Maecenas of poor Turkish poets and artisans', he became an active patron of the schools of music and painting in Constantinople.

In 1911, in many interviews with the Sultan, Abdulmecid and his cousins begged him 'in the name of the dynasty' to recall the former Grand Vizier Kamil. The party hatred between the Committee and its rival the Liberal Union, which advocated decentralization, gave him room for manoeuvre. The Sultan was encouraged by a by-election victory in Constantinople in December 1911 of Tahir Hayreddin, son of the Grand Vizier of 1878, over the Committee's candidate. On 21 July 1912 the Sultan formed a new government under Gazi Ahmet Muhtar Pasha, with three former grand viziers. The pro-Committee first secretary in the palace was dismissed, greater autonomy promised to Albanians and army officers were obliged to take an oath not to interfere in politics.[43]

However, at this point new disasters hit the empire and Constantinople. The empire was a victim of the general rise in aggression and inter-state rivalry in Europe before 1914. Inspired by the model or fear of Germany, general staffs had begun to change their war plans from defence to attack and massively to increase their expenditure on armaments. In October 1911, Italy attacked the Ottoman province of Tripolitania in North Africa. In April and July 1912, the Italian navy blockaded the Dardanelles, in an effort to force the Ottoman Empire to make peace. The Ottoman government replied by closing the Straits. As a result Russian exports – between a third and half of which passed through the Straits – collapsed and there was a run on Russian banks. Russia now desired possession of Constantinople and the Straits for economic, as well as strategic, religious and imperial, reasons.[44]

One of the achievements of Abdulhamid had been to keep the Balkan powers divided. After 1908 the prospect of a reforming and constitutional Ottoman Empire, enjoying the sympathy of Europe, united them in horror. One Bulgarian newspaper warned its readers 'to keep their gunpowder dry and their eyes fixed on Constantinople'. Russian diplomats and *The Times* Balkan correspondent J. D. Bourchier, known to Bulgarians as 'our Bourchier', helped the formation of a Balkan League. Bourchier visited Constantinople in September 1911 in order to effect a reconciliation between the Oecumenical Patriarch and the Bulgarian Exarch. Hitherto they had devoted much of their energy to publishing reports detailing Bulgarian or Greek atrocities in Macedonia.[45] Now they turned on the Ottoman Empire. Serbia and Montenegro joined in for the kill.

War broke out on 17 October 1912. The Ottoman generals were too optimistic, and too eager to protect the Muslim population in Macedonia, to stick to a realistic plan of campaign. Their supply system was abysmal. The officer corps was divided between supporters and opponents of the Committee. The result was catastrophe. Provinces which had been Ottoman for five centuries were lost in five weeks. To shouts of 'Christ is risen!', a Greek army entered Salonica on 19 November. 'Hellenization' began at once. Churches which had become mosques at the Ottoman conquest reverted to their original dedication – a warning of the fate Greeks reserved for Aya Sofya. Turks and their families sailed away: Abdulhamid and his household were brought back to Constantinople and installed in the palace of Beylerbey. Subjected to the same treatment he had inflicted on his cousins, the ex-Sultan was within sight of, but forbidden to visit, Yildiz.

The old Ottoman order was disintegrating. An Albanian district had elected as deputy in the Ottoman parliament Ismail Kemal Bey, a former official in the Sublime Porte who had turned into an Albanian nationalist. Soon after the war started, like many other nationalist politicians in the following decade, he sailed away from Constantinople to found a new country. On 28 November 1912 in Valona (Vlonë) in Albania, he proclaimed Albanian independence. The former official of the Sublime Porte became president of the first Albanian national government. It was the beginning of the end of Constantinople's connection with the race which had provided it with grand viziers and generals, as well as street-sellers and pavement-layers.

By 15 November the Bulgarian army had conquered all Thrace except Edirne and had reached the Catalca lines, the stretch of earthworks and fortifications thrown up in 1877–8 twenty-two miles west of the city. Despite Abdulhamid's inexplicable neglect, they remained a formidable barrier. Tsar Ferdinand had not forgotten his Byzantine ambitions. He was said to have declared: 'We shall dictate the peace in Constantinople' and to have carriages and an imperial costume ready for his entry through the Golden Gate. The Russian Foreign Minister, annoyed by Bulgaria's success, reiterated Russia's traditional policy: that on the Bosphorus there could only be Turks or Russians.[46]

The Ottoman soldiers who had marched proudly through the city at the start of the war, returned famished and blood-stained. Constantinople became a traffic jam of ox-carts, in which Muslim families fleeing the atrocities of the advancing Balkan armies sat weary and emaciated on the straw. Sultanahmed became a refugee camp, Fatih a hospital, Aya Sofya a cholera infirmary. A Museum of Vakifs (ancestor of the present Museum of Turkish and Islamic Art) was founded in order to house the carpets, calligraphy and wood-carving which had to be removed from the mosques. Camels reappeared on the streets of Pera, since the army had requisitioned all the horses. Every night fires were started: the ancient gesture of urban discontent.[47]

Embassies suspended their receptions. The German embassy became a hospital. Across the Sea of Marmara in Moda the Whittalls tore up their sheets to make bandages for the Ottoman wounded. But the ballrooms and theatres of Pera, and fashionable restaurants like the Tokatliyan and Marquise, remained busy. Wounded soldiers staggered up the hill past the Pera Palace Hotel, to the sound of waltzes being played within for the daily *thé dansant*. According to Odette Keun, who wrote a novel of these years, Perotes remarked, between cups of tea: 'The Turks no longer even know how to fight.'

Many Greeks abandoned Ottomanism and reverted to their ancient ambition, to realize the Great Idea. In 1910 the poet Kostis Palamas had written, in Greece, *The King's Flute* – a poem which is a tribute to the magic of Constantinople, and the myth of the last Byzantine Emperor hidden in marble below the Golden Gate in the walls of the city:

> King, I shall arise from my enmarbled sleep,
> And from my mystic tomb I shall come forth
> To open wide the bricked-up Golden Gate;
> And, victor over the Caliphs and the Tsars,
> Hunting them beyond Red Apple Tree,
> I shall seek rest upon my ancient bounds.

Formerly so prudent, the Oecumenical Patriarch Joachim III was transformed by Ottoman defeats into as ardent a nationalist as Fuad Koprulu. Forgetting the Phanar's successful use of the Ottoman Empire, over three centuries, to strengthen both its ecclesiastical authority and Greek cultural hegemony over eastern Christendom, the Patriarch who had once kissed the Sultan's pineapple told a French Philhellene that the Ottoman Empire was a power which is foreign to my race, to my religion, to my nation . . . I represent an idea. And that is what gives me in my material weakness, incalculable strength. The virtue of the idea will sooner or later be victorious over the brutality of the *fait accompli* . . . Nothing will be able to triumph over the idea. It is living. It is immortal. It is it which has sustained us for four centuries.

Most of his flock shared his feelings (although Leonidas Zarifi, one of the Greek bankers, gave the ground floor of his house in Pera to the Red Crescent). If there was news of a Turkish victory, Greeks stayed at home. At the first news of defeat, they were out on the Grande Rue, laughing and confident.

Pera filled with journalists, and those rumours of massacres 'on which every true Perote is brought up', in the words of Odette Keun.[48] Such fears became an instrument of Ottoman policy when the Grand Vizier Kamil Pasha threatened foreign ambassadors with massacres in the city if the Bulgarian army entered. The last military expression of the concert of Europe which had regulated the Continent since the defeat of Napoleon (except during his nephew's reign) could be seen on the streets of Constantinople in 1912–13. On 12 November with Ottoman permission, fourteen foreign warships carrying 2,700 sailors anchored in the Bosphorus to reassure the Christian population. On 16 November a delegation from the Armenian Patriarchate asked the embassies for protection. On 18 November, the sailors landed with machine-guns. The French took up position in Galata, the British in Pera, Austrians and Germans in Taksim, and Russians along the quays.[49]

On 17 November windows began to rattle, and the ground to shake, as Bulgarian and Ottoman guns opened fire along the Catalca lines. The Whittalls could hear the noise eighty miles away at Moda. Mary Poynter, an Englishwoman living in Nishantash, wrote in her diary:

> It is a warm still autumn day with a soft south wind, the sun veiled by light clouds. Sound carries far on these damp days and though the battle seems near, they tell us it must be at least twenty miles away . . . Early this morning the artillery firing sounded like distant thunder, then it came in low ominous growls as the currents of air varied, then in heavier reports that made the earth vibrate.

The roofs and balconies of Pera filled with spectators, some of whom had faces white with fear. They soon learnt to distinguish between the sharp, dry sound of shots fired from Ottoman ships in the

Sea of Marmara and the 'strange muffled thudding', as Harold Nicolson, Third Secretary of the British Embassy, described the sound of the guns on land. Despite war outside the walls, and fear within, the only disturbances in the city came from the foreign sailors sent to prevent them – particularly from brawls between the French and the Germans.[50]

Constantinople's geographical position, at the end of a peninsula far from other centres of population, was an advantage in 1912, as in 1878. By the time both the Russian and the Bulgarian armies had approached the prize, they had exhausted their strength and overstretched their supply lines. Despite the ravages of cholera and dysentery, Ottoman troops, well supplied with food and guns, fought with renewed vigour in defence of 'the seat of the Caliphate'. On 18 November the Bulgarians failed to storm Catalca. On 3 December an armistice was signed. Peace negotiations opened in London.[51]

When Enver returned from Tripolitania, where he had been leading resistance to the Italians, he was enraged by the fear and apathy in the city. Hatred between supporters and enemies of the Committee seemed as strong as hatred between nationalities. In accordance with the advice of the great powers of Europe at the London conference, the government intended to cede Edirne, second city of the empire, to the Bulgarians. Convinced that he dominated 'all the hearts of the nation', Enver wrote to a German friend on 14 January: 'I would not like to act as a revolutionary but I do not know where it will all end . . . To save the fatherland or to die with honour I will try to overturn everything [*tout bouleverser*].'[52]

At 3 p.m. on 23 January 1913, accompanied by Samuel Israel, chief of the political section of the police, Talaat, Cemal, and some fifty or sixty people waving liberty banners and Islamic flags, Enver led an attack on the Sublime Porte. They had cut the telephone line and arranged for a pro-Committee battalion to be on guard. It saluted as they entered. Crying 'Death to Kamil Pasha!', they swept up the stairs into the Grand Vizier's office. One of his ADCs, Captain Kibrisli, and the Minister of War and another ADC, were shot dead. The Grand Vizier resigned. Enver appointed new army commanders and made Mahmud Shevket Pasha Grand Vizier. After twenty minutes, a smiling officer emerged to tell the crowd of 500 outside, 'We have had a little revolution.' A group of Indians – their presence a sign of the empire's continued appeal in the Muslim world – harangued the crowd, saying that India was heart and soul with Turkey. The Sultan, at first incredulous, despatched his first chamberlain from Dolmabahce to check the news. As Enver desired, the empire reentered the war. Enver boasted that he was working thirty-six hours a day and could guarantee victory. He had formed a new government without the foreigners' knowledge and was strong enough to face the entire Bulgarian army.[53]

In February cannonfire at Catalca could again be heard in the city. However the Ottoman army could not save Edirne. Constantinople observed a day of mourning on 26 March 1913 when its old rival fell to the Bulgarians; and though Enver won the admiration of the empire when leading the army which recaptured Edirne on 22 July, its recovery was due rather to the diversion caused by an attack by Bulgaria on Greece and Serbia than to Ottoman military might.

The empire's weakness strengthened the great powers' anti-Ottoman bias, which had been growing since the 1890s. Before the war, in the expectation of Ottoman victory, they had issued a declaration against changes to the *status quo* in the Balkans. After Ottoman defeats, they helped Balkan states divide the spoils. Unofficial economic protectorates were marked out, for Britain in Mesopotamia, for France in Syria, for Russia in northern Anatolia, for Germany along the Berlin to Baghdad railway. The British ambassador wrote: 'All the powers including ourselves are trying hard to get what they can out of Turkey. They all profess to wish the maintenance of Turkish integrity but no one ever thinks of this in practice.' A feeling that the Ottoman Empire was entering its death-agony permeates private letters as well as diplomatic despatches. A few Committee members were reported to favour a republic. The ousted Grand Vizier Kamil Pasha, rightly known as 'Ingiliz Kamil', called for 'some adequate foreign control . . . in regard to the administration in Turkey'.[54]

In an effort simultaneously to modernize the armed forces and remove them from politics, the Committee summoned British officers to reorganize the navy, Germans the army, French the gendarmerie. The British munitions firm of Vickers, under the name Société Impériale Ottomane Co-intéressée des Docks, Arsenaux et Constructions Navales, obtained a thirty-year lease on the bastion of Ottoman sea-power, the arsenal on the Golden Horn.[55] General Liman von Sanders arrived on 14 December 1913 at the head of sixty officers, and was given his own office in the War Ministry. Fear of the Germans in Constantinople was the principal cause of tension between Germany and Russia on the eve of the First World War. Enver, who had become Minister of War and was known as Germany's friend, was an increasingly dominant figure. The last independent Grand Vizier, Mahmud Shevket Pasha, had been shot on 11 June 1913, driving through Bayezid square, in one of the few motor cars then on the streets of the city (henceforth the car in which Enver sped through the streets of Constantinople was followed by another containing heavily armed ADCs). A relation of the imperial family and a brother of the successful Liberal deputy in 1912 were blamed and executed. The new Grand Vizier, Said Halim Pasha, a descendant of Muhammad Ali of Egypt, a man of luxurious tastes and a constant visitor to the Cercle d'Orient, was said to be a cipher in the hands of the Committee. Enver married Naciye Sultan, a favourite niece of the Sultan, on 2 February 1914 – one of the few marriages in history between a revolutionary and an imperial princess. They lived in luxury in a yali in Kuru Chesme.[56]

Trouble with the Greeks added to the empire's woes. The resettlement of approximately 400,000 Muslim refugees from the lost provinces of the Balkans heightened tensions. There may have been a government attempt to terrify Greeks into emigration. In early 1914 some houses were demolished on government orders in Greek villages near the capital. In June the Patriarch announced the closure of Greek schools and churches. Behaving as if the Phanar was as powerful and independent as the Vatican, he sent memoranda to foreign embassies, visited the Greek legation in person, and demanded exemption from military service for some of his officials.[57]

Relations with Arabs also deteriorated. One of the leading Arab nationalists was Aziz Ali 'al-Masri', a graduate of Constantinople's military college who owed his conversion to Arab nationalism more to personal rivalry with Enver than race or language: he was a Circassian who had taken part in the Young Turk revolution. On 9 February 1914, rightly suspected of planning rebellion, he was arrested leaving Hotel Tokatliyan after lunch. After a long trial he was released through British pressure, and sailed away to Egypt – another future leader of a nationalist revolt to leave the capital. Sherif Abdullah, the deputy for Mecca, who loved Constantinople so deeply, was already planning Arab independence, and making overtures to Lord Kitchener, when he stopped in Cairo on his journeys between Mecca and Constantinople.[58]

The outbreak of war in July 1914 gave the Ottoman Empire an opportunity to strengthen its position. Neutrality could increase its economic prosperity and diplomatic weight. However the Triumvirate (as Enver, Cemal and Talaat were sometimes called) were convinced that the empire needed an alliance. Tentative approaches by Talaat to Russia and Cemal to France respectively had led nowhere. On 2 August in Said Halim Pasha's yali at Yenikoy, without the rest of the cabinet's knowledge, Enver and Talaat signed a secret alliance with Germany, which he had been negotiating since 18 July. The Ottoman Empire swore to enter the war on Germany's side. For the time being it remained neutral but mobilized its army. That summer, the most decisive in the history of the empire, the British and German embassies in Constantinople struggled for influence over the Ottoman government.

In 1908 Britain had been celebrated as the home of liberty, and Germany blamed as the friend of Abdulhamid. After the restoration of the constitution, the new British ambassador's carriage had been unhorsed on Galata bridge and pulled up the hill to his embassy by a delirious crowd. This popularity had been thrown away by ambassadors and dragomans convinced that the Committee was run by Jews and Masons, and by a government which refused the Ottoman Empire's offers of alliance. The British government was afraid of the effect on its Muslim subjects in Egypt and India of a successful parliamentary regime in Constantinople. The Young Turk revolution had a long reach: in 1911 the Emir of Bukhara had been forced to grant a constitution by pressure from 'Young Bukharans', inspired by the example of Constantinople.

In August 1914 the British government lost further popularity by confiscating for its own use two Ottoman battleships which had been paid for by public subscription in the Ottoman Empire, and built in British yards (the confiscation was not early enough, however, to prevent Enver using the ships as bait to lure a reluctant Germany into the 2 August alliance). On 10 August two German battle-cruisers, the *Goeben* and *Breslau*, which had already visited Constantinople as part of the international fleet in November 1912, arrived in the Sea of Marmara after a bungled pursuit by British ships in the Mediterranean. On 15 August the ships were officially handed over to the empire, which was deemed to have 'purchased' them, by their brilliant and aggressive commander, Admiral Wilhelm Souchon, who in turn became commander-in-chief of the Ottoman navy. The crews of the *Yavuz Sultan Selim* and the *Midilli*, as they were renamed, remained German but, on public occasions, wore the fez. Public opinion became even more favourable to Germany. British officers employed in the Ottoman navy were confined to shore duty.[59]

The German ambassador was Hans, Freiherr von Wangenheim, a

Thuringian giant much respected in Constantinople. During the summer of 1914, on days of good news from Germany, he could be seen sitting on a bench outside his summer embassy at Tarabya, reading diplomatic despatches. The British ambassador, Sir Louis Mallet, a bachelor with a passion for Italian gardens, had been on leave in August. Although an expert on 'Eastern Questions', he was ineffective and pessimistic. He failed to use the Entente's investments in the empire (much greater than Germany's) and control of the Ottoman Bank and Debt as a weapon. At the end of August Britain, France and Russia offered to guarantee the integrity and independence of the empire in return for its continued neutrality. However, on 6 September Mallet telegraphed the Foreign Secretary Sir Edward Grey that 'to guarantee integrity and independence of Turkey was like guaranteeing the life of a man who is determined to commit suicide.' His tactlessness was in part due to anti-Ottomanism in the embassy: his dragoman Andrew Ryan wrote, 'If the Turks weather the European war without getting involved in it themselves, they may give a lot of trouble in the future.'

Showing that neutrality increased the empire's leverage, the Greek schools and churches reopened at the end of August. On 8 September the government abolished the capitulations, which had enabled so many foreigners to flaunt their wealth and crimes in Constantinople. On 9 and 10 September drum-beating torchlight processions celebrated this Ottoman triumph in front of the houses of Talaat near Aya Sofya, and of Cemal in the new area of Nishantash, at the Sublime Porte and Dolmabahce palace. Huseyin Cahid Bey, editor of the Young Turk newspaper *Tanin*, proclaimed: 'We were not the owners of the country. It was the foreigners.' The Grand Vizier gave a banquet for 300 in the Hotel Tokatliyan. The government announced that from 1 October 1914 foreign post offices would close.[60]

War and peace hung in the balance. While Germany fought on the Marne, General Liman von Sanders was frustrated by the inaction on the Bosphorus. In effect under Ottoman not German control, Souchon felt like a chained lion. The Russian ambassador Giers knew of the struggle between opponents and supporters of war inside the Ottoman cabinet, as he had bribed an employee in the Ottoman post office and could read the Austrian ambassador's cipher telegrams. On 14 September Enver was obliged by his colleagues, led by Said Halim, to cancel instructions to Souchon to lead his ships into the Black Sea and attack Russia.

However, as the attack on the Sublime Porte had shown, Enver's military control of the capital was decisive. The road from Tarabya to Constantinople that summer was covered not with pleasure-seekers' carriages but with army tents. In early September German officers and engineers began to arrive by train, to strengthen the Dardanelles forts and overhaul the Ottoman fleet. Mallet telegraphed on 17 September: 'So long as the army is mobilized and the Minister of War is Generalissimo, Cabinet is not in a position to enforce its will and must temporize to some extent.'[61] Only irresistible quantities of Allied gold, or a *coup*, could have stopped Enver.

On 17 September the British naval mission left, and the Sultan reviewed the battle-cruisers *Yavuz Sultan Selim* and *Midilli* at Buyukada. Yet the Sultan himself, like most of his subjects, wanted peace. Andrew Ryan, who saw him on 21 September, wrote: 'The old gentleman, who is usually so gaga, astonished us by his liveliness and intelligence. He told us he was going to be neutral and he didn't want war, and it wasn't his fault that Admiral Limpus went off without seeing him and he loved the ambassador.' As late as 16 October the British ambassador telegraphed: 'I cannot give up hope that if we still continue to exercise patience and if we still have successes [in the war] as I do not doubt we may pull it off.'[62]

However, so many Germans were serving in the Ottoman army and navy that neutrality would have been difficult to maintain. On 23 September Souchon received effective command of the Ottoman navy. On 26 September, a British ship stopped an Ottoman torpedo boat containing German sailors – as most Ottoman ships now did – from leaving the Dardanelles and entering the Aegean. In retaliation General Weber Pasha, German commander of the Dardanelles forts, closed the Dardanelles to all shipping. Russian grain ships piled up in the Sea of Marmara and eventually returned home. By 12 October, as Enver had demanded, two million Turkish pounds in German gold had arrived by special train from Berlin as a 'soft' loan – in effect, a bribe. The next day Enver drew up a war plan. On 27 October, the two new Ottoman war-ships under Souchon entered the Black Sea. On 29 October, at about 3.30 a.m., without a declaration of war, they bombarded Odessa and Sebastopol. When the news reached the Cercle d'Orient, Cemal Pasha said: '*Si ce cochon de Souchon a fait cela, que le diable l'emporte!*' In reality Cemal supported the decision. On 2 November, soon followed by Britain and France, Russia declared war. Four Ottoman ministers resigned: the Grand Vizier, who had threatened to do so, was persuaded to remain in office.[63]

The last British and French in the city prepared to leave. A German acquaintance said to Sir Edwin Pears, forty years a lawyer in the city and a historian of the Byzantine Empire: 'Sir Edwin, you have written *The Destruction of the Greek Empire*; I think you are going to live to write the destruction of the Turkish Empire . . . I like the Turks but I think they are committing suicide.'

On the many previous occasions when the Ottoman government had declared war on Russia, Constantinople had been enthusiastic. In 1914, however, it was Enver's war, not the dynasty's, nor the people's. No delighted crowds massed in front of the palace to cheer the outbreak of war, as they had in London, Berlin and St Petersburg. The Sultan was reputed to have said: 'To make war on Russia! But its corpse alone would be enough to crush us.' Implicitly criticizing Enver, he later told an American journalist, in Dolmabahce palace: 'My people is no longer what it once was. It has gone through too many wars. It has bled too much . . . I did not want this war. Allah be my witness. I am sure that my people did not want it.' In the palace of Beylerbey Abdulhamid snorted: 'We have sacrificed ourselves for two boats.'[64]

Holy War was proclaimed at Fatih on 9 November. The Mufti of Constantinople issued an appeal to Muslims in Russia, India and Algeria to rise against their imperialist masters: 'O Muslims, true servants of God! Those who will share in the Holy War and come back alive will enjoy a great felicity; those who will find in it their death will have the honour of martyrdom.' Few heeded the call. A crowd chanting 'Death to Russia!' celebrated the entry into war by sacking the Hotel Tokatliyan, the owner of which was a Russian subject.

Constantinople became a war capital. By early December, compared to their normal activity, the bridge and the port were deserted.[65] Army patrols hunted for young men dodging conscription. The price of bread multiplied thirty-eight times over the next four years – far faster than salaries. Queues formed outside bread shops, crying 'We don't care for victories. Give us bread!' The little bread there was tasted of straw. Dried raisins were used to sweeten tea, as there was no sugar. The water supply often failed and two gas companies shut down. Trams were so crowded that women compared travelling in them to the horrors of the trenches.

From Constantinople Parvus began to organize Ukrainian and Georgian revolutionary activities against Russia. In January 1915 'the Merchant of Revolution', as he was called, was recruited in Constantinople by the German ambassador, von Wangenheim, to arrange the alliance between Imperial Germany and Russian revolutionaries which would bring Lenin to Russia, with German help, in 1917.[66] The city's principal contribution to the war effort of the Central Powers, however, was neither the proclamation of Holy War nor the recruitment of Parvus, but the closure of the Bosphorus and the Dardanelles to shipping. The resulting dislocation of the Russian economy helped provoke the revolution of 1917. The desire to reopen the route to Russia, as well as to knock the Ottoman Empire out of the war, and bring in the neutral states of Greece, Bulgaria and Romania on the Allies' side, led to the enthusiastic decision of the British War Council on 13 January 1915 to prepare a naval expedition 'to bombard and take the Gallipoli peninsula with Constantinople as its objective'.

Never did the city inspire so much rivalry as in its last years as an imperial capital. Both King Ferdinand of Bulgaria and King Constantine XII of the Hellenes (the choice of numeral indicated that he was successor of the last Byzantine Emperor, Constantine XI) hoped to enter it as conqueror. In St Petersburg Nicholas II had issued a manifesto in November 1914 calling for the 'fulfilment of Russia's historic mission on the shores of the Bosphorus'; and Russia was formally promised the city and the Straits by its allies in March 1915. In London the First Lord of the Admiralty, Winston Churchill (who had visited Constantinople in 1910, and knew the Young Turk leaders), supported the plan for the attack on the Dardanelles with the words: 'Think what Constantinople is to the East! It is more than London, Paris and Berlin all rolled into one to the West.' In the elation of war he discounted his own belief, and that of the British General Staff, before 1914, that an attempt to force the Dardanelles by the navy alone was 'no longer possible'. An Allied fleet of eighteen battleships and 200 smaller vessels, including submarines, assembled off the Greek island of Lemnos, forty miles from the Dardanelles. Across the sides of some ships men scrawled such slogans as 'Turkish Delight' or 'To Constantinople and the Harems'.[67]

The Allied naval bombardment of the Dardanelles fortifications began on 19 February. Three British battleships were sunk, and many other ships damaged, by floating mines at the Dardanelles. On 25 April Allied troops landed on beaches near Gallipoli. The resulting butchery needs no retelling. In all 539,000 troops were engaged on the Allied side, and 310,000 on the Ottoman. Several times an Allied breakthrough, either on land or sea, was likely. The price of wheat in Chicago fell in the expectation that Russian wheat would be exported through the Straits again. Panic swept Constantinople when a British submarine broke through the Dardanelles and started sinking ships in the Bosphorus: by the end of the year Allied submarines had brought daytime traffic on the Sea of Marmara almost to a halt. At times the Ottoman government planned to move to Bursa, or beyond. The final Ottoman victory was helped by the terrain, Allied incompetence and the skill of the Ottoman commanders, Liman von Sanders and Mustafa Kemal. However, in the opinion of one German officer Hans Kannengiesser Pasha, it owed most to the psychological factor: the Ottoman troops' 'firm will, stubborn devotion and unshakeable loyalty to their Sultan and Caliph'. The last Allied troops withdrew in January 1916.[68]

During the fighting at Gallipoli, a greater cataclysm was decided in Constantinople. The Committee had at first enjoyed relatively good relations with Armenians. Between 1909 and 1914 both the Armenian national assembly and congresses of the Hunchak party had met in the capital. An Armenian, Gabriel Noradoungian, a protégé of Ali Pasha, had briefly been Minister of Foreign Affairs in 1912–13 (he left for Paris soon after). From 1913, however, plans for reform in eastern Anatolia caused a rise in tension. In 1914 some Armenians helped Russian troops in Anatolia against Ottoman forces. There was an Armenian rising in Van. In Constantinople itself some Armenians were seen gloating over the first Russian victories. The Committee decided on a policy of extermination. In Anatolia, between six and eight hundred thousand Armenian men, women and children died during deportations, epidemics and massacres (many thousands of Turks and Kurds also died in the same region during the war). From Constantinople itself 2,432 men, the élite of the Armenian community, were deported. Among them were seven senators, twelve deputies including Krikor Zohrab, deputy for Constantinople, who had given shelter to Talaat during the counter-revolution of April 1909. Few were seen again.[69]

The 'special organization' which concerted the deportations and massacres, was run from Constantinople. Its work of destruction was well known. On 25 June 1915 the German ambassador, informed by German consuls in the East, reported that deportations had begun from areas not threatened by Russian invasion. 'This fact and the manner in which the relocation is being carried out demonstrates that the government is really pursuing the aim of destroying the Armenian race in Turkey.' On 7 August, according to the diary of an American journalist, George Schreiner, Halide Edib had said to him at tea in the school she ran in a traditional quarter of Constantinople: 'It's all too bad! I wish the government could find some way out of the situation. Now the poor things are being taken to Mesopotamia. I have heard there have been massacres. I can't believe it!' The decision to kill Armenians was not only due to fears in the Ottoman government following its first defeats (after an Arab revolt one year later, there was no hecatomb of Arabs). The American ambassador wrote in his diary that Talaat, the Minister of the Interior, had told him that the government wanted to make the Armenians 'powerless', because they were rich, wanted an independent state, and encouraged the empire's enemies. Three times the ambassador warned Talaat that he was making a serious mistake. Talaat said that he never had regrets. On 30 September 1915 the interim Austrian ambassador reported: 'It appears that the plan to exterminate the Armenian race has largely succeeded. Talaat gleefully told me recently that there are no more Armenians in Erzerum, for example. Turkey today is in a maniacal state for having implemented with impunity the extermination of the Armenian race.'[70]

The old Ottoman order had gone. The last Sacred Caravan of pilgrims to Mecca, led by Enver's father, set out from Uskudar in 1915. The following year the journey was not possible. After a hesitation of four hundred years, a Sherif decided to break with the Ottoman Empire. Despite his Ottoman connections, Sherif Huseyin, alienated by the Young Turk government, tempted by British offers of gold and recognition, launched an Arab revolt in Mecca on 10 June 1916. Yet his proclamation showed how Ottoman he remained. It denounced the Committee as heretics who allowed Ottoman newspapers to publish impieties and prevented the Sultan from naming his own chief secretary. Despite the Emir's revolt most Arabs, including his own brother Sherif Nasser who lived in Constantinople, remained loyal. Arab troops helped defend the capital at Gallipoli in 1915. The Ottoman government riposted by proclaiming his cousin Sherif Ali Haydar Emir of Mecca in his place. The last celebration of Ottoman Arabism took place before a large crowd outside the Sublime Porte on 18 June 1916. Ali Haydar, wearing the white turban of a sherif, his black and gold uniform and Ottoman decorations, arrived in the Sultan's state landau, accompanied by an Arab bodyguard and the Sultan's band. Ministers, sherifs, Ottoman princes watched as his firman of appointment was read out. However, he got no further than Medina and returned to Constantinople in 1918.[71]

War enabled the government to pursue a policy of Turkification and modernization. Laws were passed insisting on the use of Turkish in private offices as well as on official documents. Non-Muslims finally began to learn a few words of Turkish. A cartoon in *Servet-i Funun* showed a Turk asking a European why he looked so sad:

'Because in order to get along a little in Turkey, I now have to understand a little Turkish.'
'Well, up to now I, a Turk, had to behave like a European in order to get along in my own homeland.'

Change was very rapid. In 1916 the Seyhulislam was removed from the cabinet and *sheriat* courts and *medreses* were transferred from his jurisdiction to the Ministry of Justice. The Family Law of 1917 recognized the right of women to initiate divorce. Muslim women began to work in government labour battalions and, in some cases, shops. The Inspector of Constantinople and head of the guild of hamals, known as Kara Kemal ('Black Kemal'), regulated first the food supply, then the entire economic life, of Constantinople. He encouraged the nationalization of the economy, creating a Muslim Merchants Association and National Bakers and Cloth companies, in 1916–17.[72]

The wartime alliance turned Constantinople into a magnet for Germans. A German naval base was established at Istinye on the left bank of the Bosphorus. The sailors, who renamed it *Steniatal*, kept pigs nearby so that they could eat roast pork for Sunday lunch. Workers from Krupps served in munitions factories; among the German officers stationed in Constantinople were Von Papen and Ribbentrop. Enver's chief of staff in the War Ministry was the able General Hans von Seeckt, the future reorganizer of the German army after 1919. Abdulmecid, the artist prince, painted pictures of a harem lady reading Goethe and members of the imperial family playing Beethoven – tributes at once to modernization and to the wartime alliance. By the end of the war there were about 9,000 German and 1,000 Austrian troops in and around Constantinople. Some German officers talked of the empire becoming a 'German Egypt'. One German said he liked sitting on the balcony of the Hotel Tokatliyan, as it was a comfortable position from which to spit on Turks in the street. However, watching the sun set over the Golden Horn from the *Gartenbar* in the Petit Champs, Merten Pasha, commander of the Dardanelles forts, said: 'There are times when I would prefer being a beggar in Constantinople to anything anywhere else.'[73]

The alliance with Germany destroyed the empire. As Constantinople became more Turkish, so by default did the Ottoman Empire: Baghdad fell to Allied forces on 11 March 1917, Jerusalem on 9 December, Damascus on 1 October 1918. Allied troops broke through on the Salonica front. Allied planes began to bomb Constantinople. Suddenly the Young Turk government realized it had lost the war.

The Allied navies in the Mediterranean and troops on the Salonica front were now masters of the situation. Constantinople could still provoke aggression in London, although not of the same intensity as in 1878. On orders from the Admiralty, British admirals in the Aegean excluded French colleagues from armistice negotiations, despite France's overall naval command in the Mediterranean. At meetings in Paris, Clemenceau and Lloyd George had some of their worst arguments of the war. On 25 October 1918 Clemenceau wrote one of many letters of protest to Lloyd George, referring to the French-led victories on the Salonica front and French investments, financial and cultural, in the empire: 'In Constantinople France has the greatest sum of interests.'[74]

The British government did not yield. On 30 October, on HMS *Agamemnon*, at anchor off Mudros on the island of Lemnos, the Ottoman Minister of the Marine, Rauf Bey, signed an armistice with the commander of the British Mediterranean fleet, Admiral the Hon. Sir Somerset A. Gough-Calthorpe: no Frenchman was present. The armistice ordered Ottoman demobilization and gave the Allies the right to occupy 'any strategic points in the event of a situation arising which threatens the security of the Allies'. Calthorpe assured Rauf Bey that the Allies would occupy, in and around Constantinople, the dockyard and the Bosphorus forts, but not the city itself. When Rauf Bey asked for a written guarantee, Calthorpe told him that there was no time to refer back to London. Rauf Bey trusted the admiral. He assured a press conference on his return to the city that 'not a single enemy soldier will disembark at our beloved Istanbul.' On 1 November Enver, Talaat and Cemal fled on the last German submarines out of the Bosphorus.

Back in London the War Cabinet was persuaded by a former Viceroy of India, Lord Curzon (who, like Churchill and other arch-imperialists such as Catherine II and Count Ignatiev had a fixation on Constantinople) that, since there was no specific exemption, the occupation of Constantinople was desirable 'from the point of view of the mentality of the East'. The terms of the armistice were dismissed as implacably as French participation in their negotiation. The city was victim of its glory and its geography. Having for so long been considered a symbol of imperial and Islamic greatness, the British Cabinet, and Curzon in particular, believed that its occupation would raise British prestige in the Near East and India. Its geographical position made its occupation desirable and, unlike that of the other enemy capitals Berlin, Vienna and Sofia, feasible.

Constantinople's war, which had begun on 27 October 1914 with two German warships leaving the Bosphorus to shell Russia, ended on 13 November 1918, with a long line of Allied (predominantly British, but also French, Italian and Greek) warships entering the Bosphorus. In the preceding one hundred and fifty years many powers had considered Constantinople an object of desire.[75] At the height of its world power, its confidence renewed by victory, its forces stationed throughout Ottoman territory, Britain had won the prize.

15

Death of a Capital

Istanbul located at the junction of two great worlds, the ornament of the Turkish nation, the treasure of Turkish history, the dearest object of the Turkish nation, has a place in the heart of every Turk. The suffering of the city under unfortunate events caused bleeding wounds in the heart of all Turks.

Mustafa Kemal, Istanbul, 1 July 1927

CONSTANTINOPLE'S LAST YEARS as a capital were the most international in its history. On 13 and 14 November 1918, 3,626 British, French and Italian troops landed from the Allied ships. The Ottoman government protested at the violation of the armistice. The British representative calmly replied that Constantinople had been chosen as British headquarters. The Ottoman official was too taken aback to reply.

The commander of the Allied troops was General Sir Henry Maitland Wilson, and 2,616 of them were British. In the following weeks, while German and Austrian troops were being repatriated to their respective countries, Constantinople acquired a variety of British-controlled authorities. The headquarters of the Allied corps in the city was the English Girls School, 181 Grande Rue de Pera; that of the separate Allied Army of the Black Sea, which also controlled forces in south Russia and the Caucasus, was in the Ottoman Military School in Harbiye. From 11 January 1919 an International Police Commission under a British president assumed 'executive control' of the city police. The Allies also established a separate inter-allied police force (one third British, one third French, one third Italian), and their own system of military courts, and put their own guards outside the city's prisons, hospitals, banks and embassies. The Allied occupation brought costumes unknown even to Constantinople to the streets of the city: the uniforms of French troops from Senegal and Indo-China, and of British troops from India, and of the forces of another victorious ally, Japan.[1]

On 8 February 1919 Allied control received consecration through street theatre, and the French government at the same time delivered its riposte to British domination. Marshal Franchet d'Espérey landed at the quay at Galata from Salonica to take up command of another Allied force, the Allied Army of the Orient. In a vengeful echo of the entry of Fatih in 1453, the Christian conqueror rode to the French embassy on a white horse presented by a Greek. The Grande Rue de Pera was lined with Allied flags and troops and cheering Greeks and Armenians. After a visit to the Phanar, where he was received to the sound of peeling bells, Franchet d'Espérey proceeded to his new residence, Enver Pasha's yali at Kuru Chesme.[2]

For the next four years the three Allied representatives, called High Commissioners, were more powerful than the Sultan himself – the culmination of the ambassadors' steady rise in power since the seventeenth century. The Allied occupation was the most naval, as well as the most international, period in the history of Constantinople. The Bosphorus was black with battleships. Commander-in-Chief Mediterranean Station, Admiral the Hon. Sir Somerset Gough-Calthorpe, who lived on HMS *Iron Duke*, moored off the Princes' Islands, was also British High Commissioner. France, Italy and Greece were also at first represented by admirals. Tophane became a British naval base; Vickers-Armstrong (of which a Constantinople Greek, the enigmatic Sir Basil Zaharoff, was a senior director) recovered control of the imperial Ottoman docks and arsenal.

Like Berlin and Vienna after 1945, the city was divided into zones. The French were in Constantinople proper, south of the Golden Horn; the British in Galata and Pera; the Italians in Uskudar; and a small Greek contingent in the Phanar. Some streets were patrolled by groups of four policemen: one Turkish, one British, one French and one Italian. In what they called 'Constant:', the British had the largest and, according to survivors, worst behaved contingent. British troops rolled drunk through the streets of Pera. British officers lived in the Pera Palace Hotel or the Grand Hotel de Londres, or were billeted in the hitherto inviolable sanctuary of the Muslim home (one outraged hostess killed her unwanted guest before fleeing across the Bosphorus). British military intelligence, which had many agents in the city, worked from the Hagopian Han in Galata. All day people dropped in there to gossip with the British intelligence officer, J. G. Bennett: at night he was visited by 'very secret agents'.[3]

Sport played as large a part as drink in the lives of British troops.

Soldiers and sailors played rugby by the Sweet Waters of Europe and cricket at Beykoz. Twenty years after he left 'Constant', Nevile Henderson, who served on the staff of the High Commission, remembered: 'One of the High Commission's most successful efforts was to organize a cricket team, though it meant calling up almost every available man.' To some British officers, Constantinople's pleasures could not compare with hunting foxes and jackals in Thrace. 'Billy' Fox-Pitt, a 26-year-old captain in the Welsh Guards, called Constantinople 'this ghastly town', 'the dirtiest and most dilapidated . . . that I have ever been in'. Soon after he arrived, he became whipper-in for one of the two British hunts. He wrote to his father: 'I think this place will become a bit boring when the novelty has worn off, as the hunting is a good way off and there won't be much else to do when the weather gets bad.'[4]

Imperialism, vengeance and anti-Communism were the principal motives for the occupation. The Allies wanted to control the capital of the Ottoman Empire in order to expedite its disarmament and partition. Until May 1919, in accordance with the armistice, munitions poured in from the provinces, to be impounded by the Allies in stores in the capital and the Straits. The Allies intended to prove that Gallipoli had been worth the lives lost in 1915, and to punish the Ottoman Empire for joining the Central Powers. Both Curzon and Lloyd George claimed – with no evidence – that the Ottoman Empire's entry into the war had prolonged it by two years. Britain and France also wanted a 'gate to the East', a supply centre for the White Russian troops in south Russia and the Caucasus whom they were helping against the Bolsheviks.[5]

In 1919, drunk with victory, the Allies were about to impose a vindictive peace on the Central Powers, and to remodel Europe on nationalistic lines. The defeat of the Ottoman Empire was so total that some Allied statesmen hoped to inflict worse terms on the Ottoman Empire than on Germany, including the loss of Constantinople. The British prime minister Lloyd George was a believer in Mazzinian nationalism, passionately pro-Greek and an intimate of Sir Basil Zaharoff. In 1918 he had promised that Constantinople would remain Ottoman; in 1919 he declared: 'Stamboul in the hands of the Turks has been not only the hot bed of every sort of Eastern vice but it has been the source from which the poison of corruption and intrigue has spread far and wide into Europe itself . . . Constantinople was not Turk and the majority of the population was not Turkish.' In the disruption that followed the war, statistics were particularly hard to compile. However, according to an estimate from British officers on the spot, the population in 1920 consisted of 560,000 Muslims, 206,000 Greeks and 83,000 Armenians. Of approximately 150,000 foreigners, a large number were Greeks with Hellenic, rather than Ottoman, nationality. Nevertheless Constantinople had a Muslim, Turkish-speaking majority.

The US delegation to the Paris peace conference agreed with Lloyd George: 'Constantinople and the narrow straits upon which it stands have occasioned the world more trouble, have cost humanity more in blood and suffering during the last five hundred years than any other single spot upon the earth.' Lord Curzon, the man behind the Allied occupation, went further, in a paper circulated to the British Cabinet on 7 January 1919. Forgetting both the Foreign Office's traditional appreciation of the Ottoman Empire's contribution to the European balance of power, and the recent record of Balkan states such as Serbia in 1914, Curzon claimed: 'For nearly five centuries the presence of the Turk in Europe has been a source of distraction, intrigue and corruption in European politics, of oppression and misrule to the subject nationalities and an incentive to undue and overweening ambitions in the Muslim world.' He denounced 'the polluted coulisses of Constantinople' (although British-protected merchants and criminals had been among the most energetic polluters): 'An opportunity of cutting out or getting rid for ever of this plague spot such as has not arisen for centuries has now presented itself.' The city was too 'vast and perilous a charge' for Britain to rule alone. Nor was it suitable to be capital of the League of Nations. Claiming that only 40 per cent of the population was Turkish, he advocated occupation and administration of the city and the Straits by an international commission. The city would become 'the cosmopolis or the international city of the Eastern world'. The Sultan would retire to Bursa or Konya.

The idea of Constantinople as a city state had first been advocated in the 1820s. However, the age of the city state was past (even Shanghai would revert to stricter central government control after 1927). Above all, in 1919 more than ever, Turks, Greeks and Armenians each wanted a state of their own, not a shared city.

Curzon's fixation about 'this plague spot' led him into a militant Christianity which, when governing India, he had rejected. An essay on the Emperor Justinian had won him a prize at Oxford, and forty years later he wrote: 'Justinian's great Byzantine fane of St Sophia which was for 900 years a Christian church and has been for little more than half that period a Mohammedan mosque would naturally revert to its original dedication.'[6]

The city's last years as an Ottoman capital were the culmination of its role as a battleground. Curzon was not alone in considering it 'natural' to make Aya Sofya a church. A 'redemption agitation' spread from Greece to Britain, where a 'St Sophia Redemption Committee' was formed. The Catholic Church also staked a claim to Aya Sofya. An Italian deputy stated that, since the city had been founded by a Roman emperor, and contained Genoese buildings, it should be Italian. The Ottoman government posted soldiers with machine-guns in the mosque to prevent a Christian *coup de main*.[7]

More than personal prejudice, Constantinople's role as capital of Islam was the reason for Curzon's wish to rebaptize its main mosque, and to drive out the Sultan Caliph. To his Cabinet colleagues he claimed that 'the Indian Mohammedans have never attached any particular sanctity or reverence to Constantinople.' In reality they had done so since the eighteenth century, and the pro-Ottoman Khilafat movement, one of whose purposes was to help Turkey and keep Constantinople Muslim, was about to sweep India. Curzon himself wrote confidentially to the Secretary of State for India that pan-Islamism was 'the only real and latent danger to our rule in India from the Mohammedan population'.[8] He believed that British prestige in India would be strengthened by diminishing the Muslim presence in Constantinople.

Realpolitik, as well as emotional imperialism, drove British policy. In 1919 many people (although not Curzon himself) believed that Greece was the power in the eastern Mediterranean most likely to shield the British route to India. It was 'strong enough to save us expense in peace, and weak enough to be completely subservient in war', wrote one of Curzon's officials, Harold Nicolson (whose dislike of the Ottomans, acquired *en poste* in Constantinople in 1912–13, was expressed in his novel *Sweet Waters* published in 1923).

Greeks believed that, as a result of the Allied victory, the Great Idea was about to become reality. The Greek Prime Minister Eleutherios Venizelos promised a Greece 'on two continents, washed by five seas' (the Black, Marmara, Aegean, Mediterranean and Ionian Seas). He told King Alexander, who had succeeded his father King Constantine on the latter's forced departure due to alleged German sympathies: 'We shall take the City.' From the moment of Ottoman defeat, some Constantinople Greeks dropped their mask of Ottomanism and behaved as conquerors. In his novel *Leonis, a Greek of Constantinople*, George

Theotokas, a native of the city, remembers the occupation as a perpetual party. The blue and white Greek flag was flown from the patriarchate, and from private Greek houses. A colossal picture of Venizelos was erected in Taksim.[9]

An aggressive new acting Patriarch, committed to Greek 'irredentism', was elected in October 1918. On 16 March 1919, an official declaration by the Patriarchal Council ended all cooperation or communication with the Ottoman government. Greeks were requested not to vote in Ottoman elections or teach Turkish in their schools, and to resign from posts in the Ottoman administration. For the next three years, with Allied approval, the Greek and Armenian Patriarchates issued their own passports to their 'subjects', in place of Ottoman passports.

Petitions and telegrams flooded in to London and Paris from Constantinople, declaring the yearning of 'unredeemed' Greeks for the expulsion of the Sultan and 'the liberties of a national regime'. Nothing, they asserted, could bridge the gulf which separated the Greeks from the Turks as a result of the persecution of centuries.[10] The compromises of centuries were forgotten. The acting Patriarch, who sent his own delegation to the peace conference, denounced 'an intolerable yoke of 466 years' under which seven (in reality three) patriarchs had been killed. 'As long as Constantinople is not Greek, the Eastern Question will not be definitely resolved.' In its memoir for the peace conference, the Syllogos claimed that Turkish 'inferiority' in Constantinople was numerical as well as intellectual, since many Turks were officials and soldiers who would leave when Hellenism was reintegrated in its 'imprescriptible rights'.[11]

Rejection of the Ottoman Empire was visible on the streets of its capital. Many Ottoman Christians discarded the fez and bought hats: some even tore the fez off others' heads. The great Turkish comic writer Aziz Nesin remembers a Greek shopkeeper on one of the Princes' Islands throwing his fez on the ground and jumping up and down to grind it in the mud, crying '*Zito Venizelos! Zito Venizelos!*' 'Who'd have thought such a thing, he was such a nice man,' said Nesin's mother. However, some Greeks, like Nesin's mother, remembered the Ottoman compromise. They did not throw away their fezzes, but wrapped them in tissue paper and put them in a drawer – in case of future need.[12]

While Greeks rejoiced, Turks felt strangers in their own city. Halide Edib wrote: 'We were no longer a nation of empire builders who were unconscious of their own superiority complex as we had been not long ago . . . instead we had now become one of the people who suffer from the superiority complex of other great empire builders.' In the struggle for Constantinople, its Ottoman monuments were one argument advanced for the city's remaining in Ottoman hands – thereby revealing one motive for their construction: the desire to demonstrate the city's Ottoman identity. The Prefect of the city protested to the House of Commons against Curzon's proposal to make Constantinople a free city, since it was 'full since centuries with their historical monuments and buildings and with the tombs of their ancestors'.[13]

No argument aroused greater fury among the Greeks. The acting Patriarch told Lloyd George that the monuments of the city proved that it was eminently Greek, even after centuries of 'Turanian vandalism'. It was not a 'holy city of Islam': Muslim pilgrims went from, not to, Constantinople. Greeks were blinded by nationalism: they could not see the Ottoman skyline of domes and minarets, the Muslim pilgrims at Eyup, the palaces lining the Bosphorus. They saw only the entry of a triumphant Greek army through the Golden Gate, Aya Sofya shorn of minarets, the priest emerging to resume the mass interrupted in 1453. One petition to 10 Downing Street described the return of St Sophia, Kariye Cami and St Irene to Christianity as 'an elementary act of justice'. In another petition, stamped with the seals of 99 Greek and 7 Armenian parishes of the city, their presidents wrote:

> As for the tombs of their sultans, the Osmanlis can be assured that we will respect them scrupulously when the high justice of the great civilized nations added to our irreducible wish will reintegrate us in our right to this soil which has contained the desecrated tombs of our emperors and which contains the remains of those of our patriarchs who have not been drowned or hanged.[14]

A financial contest accompanied the political and religious struggle. Greek banks inflated the value of the drachma against the Ottoman lira, in order to help Greeks buy property in Constantinople. From May 1919 the Ottoman government reacted by offering high prices for properties on sale. On the bourse Greek stock-brokers tried to lower Ottoman funds, and Jews to support them.[15] The fate of the city hung in the balance.

Between 1918 and 1924, Constantinople was the setting for two historic dramas: the game of nations between the Ottoman Empire, the Greeks and the West; and the power game between the Ottoman dynasty and its Muslim subjects. The principal protagonist was, at first, the new Sultan Mehmed VI Vahideddin, who had succeeded to the throne on the death of his elder brother Reshad on 3 July 1918. After his inauguration at Eyup, he had begun to recover power from the Young Turks. Military defeat in 1918 led to the deposition of the Habsburg and Hohenzollern dynasties, since they were blamed for their empire's entry into war in 1914. The Young Turks, however, not the Ottoman dynasty, were blamed for the Ottoman defeat. The 'sick man of Europe' outlived the Russian, German and Austrian empires. On 22 December 1918 Mehmed VI dissolved parliament.

Ugly, thin, drooping-shouldered, Mehmed VI, a good horseman in his youth, was by 1918 a worried old man in uncertain health. The future Field Marshal Alexander, stationed in Constantinople in the Irish Guards, called the Sultan 'terribly ill, very old, very unimpressive, a pathetic figure'. In 1920 Admiral de Robeck, who had commanded the British naval attack on the Dardanelles, replaced Calthorpe as High Commissioner in Constantinople. He wrote to Lord Curzon from the *Iron Duke*: 'The Sultan, though well-dressed and generally well-groomed, presents a somewhat shrunken appearance.' At the beginning of the audience he brought out his words 'with a hesitancy which was almost painful' and displayed 'extreme nervousness'.

The Ottoman throne was losing its carapace of splendour. The Sultan lived in Yildiz, now a shadow of its state under his elder brother Abdulhamid. Bayram receptions in Dolmabahce had once been impressive occasions lasting several hours. At a 1919 reception, the senator Alexander Mavroyeni (one Greek who did not obey the Patriarchal injunction to cut ties with the Ottoman Empire) wrote: 'Sadness was visible on people's faces, beginning with the Sultan, shrunk and haggard. There were also many fewer people than usual.'[16]

The Sultan, whose palace was within firing-range of the battleships moored in the Bosphorus, pursued a policy of cooperation with the Allies in the hope of appeasing their wrath and deflecting their support from the Greeks. On 4 March 1919 he chose as Grand Vizier Damad Ferid, husband of his sister Mediha. A rich and cultivated liberal, an enemy of the Young Turks, Damad Ferid, as he himself said, put his trust in God and Great Britain. His English friends described him as the Ottoman equivalent of an English gentleman. On 20 March 1919, in a bid to preserve the Arab provinces and Anatolia for the empire, he asked for a British mandate.[17]

The palace and the Porte relied on Allied goodwill. In the cafés and alleys of the city, however, Young Turks plotted resistance – as Enver had planned in the last days before his departure to Berlin. Their leader in Constantinople was Kara Kemal, the former Minister of Supplies. His underground resistance organization, based on the revolutionary cell system, and mainly recruited from former members of the Committee of Union and Progress, was called Karakol. Headquarters was a tea-house near the bazaar, opposite the Mahmud Pasha mosque. Karakol began to smuggle Ottoman officers and arms out of Allied-controlled Constantinople to Anatolia – the last region where there were undefeated Ottoman armies.[18]

One officer Karakol hoped to send East was the hero of Gallipoli, Mustafa Kemal Pasha. On 13 November, as the Allied ships had steamed into the Bosphorus, he had arrived by train at Haydar Pasha station, back from the Syrian front, and moved into a suite on the first floor of the Pera Palace Hotel. Mustafa Kemal, born in Salonica in 1881, knew Constantinople well. Between 1899 and 1905 he had attended military and staff college there. Shortly before Salonica fell to the Greeks in 1912, he had moved his mother and sister to a house in Beshiktash. He had many friends in the city, among them Selma and Salih Fansa, Arabs from Aleppo, with whom he stayed when the bill at the Pera Palace became too high. He was also a favourite aide-de-camp of the Sultan.

Like most Turks, Mustafa Kemal found the occupation insufferable. When British officers asked him for a drink in the Pera Palace, Kemal is said to have replied: 'We are the hosts here. They are the guests. It is fitting for them to come to my table.' His mother's house in Beshiktash was searched by British patrols. Soon he left the Fansas' house for a modern four-storey terraced house in Shishli.[19]

Kemal had four audiences with the Sultan at Yildiz after the *selamlik* in November and December 1918. Until March he hoped to become Minister of War and resisted zealots urging him to go to Anatolia. The arguments of Karakol, and the realization that he had no hope of a place in the cabinet, finally persuaded him to leave. On 30 April 1919 he obtained an appointment as Inspector-General of troops in northern Anatolia, with extensive authority to pacify the region and ensure observance of the armistice.

Dynastic biology may have played a part in his decision to leave. Kemal's despised rival Enver Pasha had married one princess; Kemal himself, through the Fansas, is reputed to have asked for the hand in marriage of the Sultan's charming and attractive daughter Sabiha Sultan. He was refused for several reasons. Sabiha Sultan and her dashing cousin Omer Faruk Efendi, son of Abdulmecid Efendi, were already in love; Mustafa Kemal had an alarming medical history and was known to be abnormally ambitious, whilst another ambitious imperial son-in-law, Enver Pasha, had done the imperial family no good. However, some believe that it was an offer from the palace which was rejected by Kemal, not the other way around.[20]

Kemal spent his last days in Constantinople meeting officials at the Cercle d'Orient and receiving instructions from Damad Ferid in his house in Nishantash. On 15 May Kemal paid a farewell visit to the Sultan in Yildiz, when the Sultan pronounced the ambiguous words: 'My pasha, my pasha, you may be able to save the nation.' On 16 May, after a farewell dinner with his mother and sister in Shishli, he and his staff of eighteen left for Samsun on the Black Sea from the quay at Galata. In appearance he was the Sultan's servant, leaving to enforce his master's orders in the provinces. In reality, like Ismail Kemal in 1912, and many Arabs in 1919, he was leaving Constantinople to found a new nation.[21]

On 15 May, at the instigation of Britain and France, and transported by their navies, Greek forces had occupied Izmir – a city with a Greek majority surrounded by a province with a Muslim majority. Greeks hung out the blue and white Greek flag and danced for joy in the streets of Constantinople. Muslims shut their shops in mourning. The occupation of Izmir was the blow which galvanized Turkish nationalism into action. The great feminist and writer Halide Edib remembered: 'I suddenly ceased to exist as an individual: I worked, wrote and lived as a unit of that magnificent national madness.' Karakol organized a series of protest meetings in Constantinople and Kadikoy (but not Christian Pera). From one meeting representatives were sent to Yildiz to ask the Sultan to take the side of the people. They were told that he was too ill to see them. The break between the Ottoman dynasty and Turkish nationalism was beginning.

The climax of the protest campaign was a meeting on 6 June in the Atmeydan, before the great mosque of Sultanahmed. Some 200,000 people, by one estimate, were present. Allied planes flew overhead. Muezzin chanted from the minarets. Feeling herself the incarnation of the Turkish nation, Halide Edib spoke before a sea of black flags, red fezzes, white turbans and glistening eyes 'shooting their message and their desire'. Her speech confirms the hold of Constantinople and its monuments on Turkish hearts. Constantinople was seen, not as an alien cosmopolis, but as a stronghold of Islam and the Turkish nation:

Brethren, sons and countrymen! From the tops of the minarets nigh against the heaven, seven hundred years of glory are watching this new tragedy of Ottoman history. I invoke the souls of our great ancestors who had so often passed in procession through this very square. I raise my head before the just wrath of those invincible hearts and say: 'I am an unfortunate daughter of Islam and an equally unfortunate mother of the equally heroic but more ill-fated generation of my own day. I bow to the spirits of our ancestors and declare, in the name of the new Turkish nation presented here, that the dis-armed Turkish nation of today still possesses your invincible hearts; we trust in Allah and in our rights' . . . Now swear and repeat with me: 'The sublime emotion which we cherish in our hearts will last till the proclamation of the rights of the peoples!'

While Constantinople spoke, Anatolia acted. Kemal rapidly took control of Ottoman territory, troops, administration – and, crucially, telegraph wires. He was dismissed by the Sultan on 8 July, but continued his action, using the apparatus of representative democracy. At Sivas in September a congress of delegates drew up the first version of the National Pact. It was still evidence of what Kannengiesser Pasha had called the Turks' 'unshakeable loyalty to their Sultan and Caliph'. It vowed to maintain the integrity and independence of territory with Turkish-speaking majorities, and called Constantinople 'the seat of the Caliphate of Islam, the capital of the sultanate and the headquarters of the Ottoman government'. A French source reported that the entire army supported Kemal and the dynasty. From the summer of 1919 arms and munitions began to leave Constantinople, as nationalist sym-pathizers raided Allied stores in order to supply Kemal's forces. It has been estimated that a third of Kemal's munitions came from the capital.[23]

By late 1919 the streets of Constantinople reflected the success of the nationalists in Anatolia. The run on hats was over. Christians put on the fez again. The Sultan loathed the Young Turks with whom Kemal's nationalists were, widely but wrongly, identified. He was alienated by the congresses and the talk of popular sovereignty with which Kemal fortified his movement. However, at times the Sultan chose to contain and bridle the nationalist movement rather than to confront it. Although the Sultan had dismissed him from the army, Mustafa Kemal continued to affirm his loyalty. On 1 October Damad Ferid was replaced as Grand Vizier by the more nationalist Ali Riza Pasha.

Part of Kemal's entourage remained loyal to the Sultan whilst part of the Sultan's government – particularly officials in the Ministry of War –

were, according to a British intelligence report of 9 January 1920, giving 'every assistance to the national forces'. At the insistence of Kemal's advisers, the last session of the Ottoman parliament was held, not in Ankara as Kemal had wanted, but in Constantinople, in the palace of Munire Sultan beside Dolmabahce. Predictably, the Sultan was too 'ill' to open it in person. On 17 February 1920 parliament adopted the National Pact.[24]

That month the Supreme Allied Council, meeting in Paris, decided, despite the opposition of Curzon and Lloyd George, that Constantinople would not become international or Greek. Religion, the Ottoman dynasty and geography kept it Turkish. In 1919–24 India was swept by the Khilafat movement, an explosion of hostility to Britain and that loyalty to the Ottoman Caliphate which had resurfaced in 1877–8 and 1912–13. Indian Muslims' concern for the future of Constantinople was shared by Gandhi and some Hindus. The All-India Khilafat Conference organized mass meetings in Delhi, Bombay and Karachi and sent a delegation to Constantinople. There was a pro-Khilafat rising in the Muslim province of Kerala.[25]

In contrast to Curzon's aggressive imperialism, both the Viceroy of India in Delhi and the Secretary of State for India in London, echoing Lord Lytton in 1877, warned of 'a last fatal blow' to Indian loyalty, if the Turks were ejected from Constantinople. Moreover the British General Staff believed that the Sultan would be more tractable in Constantinople, 'under our guns', than in an inland capital.[26] In this era of plebiscites, of President Wilson's promise of 'a world made safe for democracy', the population of the Ottoman capital was not consulted.

However Britain did not want Constantinople to pass under the control of the nationalists (always referred to in British sources by the derogatory term 'Kemalist') in the Ottoman parliament. In February 1920 super-dreadnoughts from the Atlantic fleet, and troops from Egypt and Palestine, were despatched to the Straits. On 16 March British forces occupied the ministries, the post office and Galata Tower. British soldiers even marched into the chamber of deputies and began to arrest nationalist deputies. Six Turkish postal workers were killed when the General Post Office was occupied; five Turkish and three Allied soldiers also died. A protest from the speaker of the Ottoman parliament to the 'mother of parliaments' in Westminster, that its 'violation' was 'contrary to all principles of international law', had no effect.

With help from Armenian Dashnaks (who were pursuing their own campaign of revenge against Young Turks and Armenian collaborators) many Ottoman officials and eighty-five deputies were arrested, some in their pyjamas. General Mersinli Cemal Pasha (former Minister of War) was found 'in the arms of a lady not his wife. The lady was in no way perturbed by the irruption of the soldiers, her only preoccupation being to hasten to the mirror to powder her nose.' One hundred and fifty nationalists were sent to Malta for internment. Other nationalists, however, fled to Italian or French battleships in the Bosphorus and thence to Anatolia. Constantinople was a battleground between the Allies as well as between the British and the nationalists. France and Italy, while appearing to cooperate with Britain in Constantinople, secretly supported the nationalists; they were determined to prevent the emergence on the Bosphorus of 'another Egypt' or what one French paper called 'Constantinobraltar'. Neither power favoured a strong British-backed Greece.[27]

For the next two years British power was visible throughout Constantinople: 10,000 British, 8,000 Indian, 8,000 French and 2,000 Italian troops were stationed in the city and the Straits. A British officer, Colonel Shuttleworth, supervised the Ottoman Ministry of War. From the autumn of 1920 General 'Tim' Harington was both General Officer Commanding Allied Forces and President of the Inter-Allied Military Commission of Control. There were also – usually under British presidents – judicial, financial, Kurdistan and Straits commissions, six different boundary commissions and a body called 'the sub-commission of special elements'. Andrew Ryan, Chief Dragoman at the British High Commission, paid 'constant visits to the Grand Vizier', although the Sultan was less accessible. Companies running the telegraphs, tramways and quays of Constantinople appealed to British authorities to set their tariffs. Sherif Ali Haydar, once a committed Young Turk, now entertained British officers at Camlica, and hoped, either through Britain or France, to become King of Iraq or Syria: 'Throughout my career I have been loyal to the Turks but I and my friends are now prepared to be loyal friends to England if she so desires.'[28]

Links between Constantinople and Anatolia appeared to be cut. Karakol was infiltrated by an Indian agent of British intelligence, Mustafa Sagit, and dissolved.* In reality the British occupation, like most British actions in the period 1918–23, strengthened Kemal's position. In a speech of 16 March Kemal expressed the shift from dynastic loyalty to Turkish nationalism: 'The forcible occupation of Istanbul

---

*It is said that the same Indian agent was later sent to Ankara to assassinate Kemal.

today has destroyed the seven-centuries-old existence and sovereignty of the Ottoman Empire. Consequently the Turkish nation is compelled today to defend its rights, its independence and its entire future.' The Sultan, on the other hand, told one of Kemal's supporters, Rauf Bey: 'There is a nation, Rauf Bey: it is a flock of sheep which needs a shepherd. I am that shepherd.'

With British encouragement, the Sultan turned on the nationalists. Damad Ferid returned to power as Grand Vizier on 5 April. On 11 April the 128th Seyhulislam, Abdullah Beyefendi of the famous family of Durrizade, issued a fatwa from Constantinople against Mustafa Kemal. He was a traitor destroying law and order, forming a private army and taxing the people against the will of the Sultan. If his movement could not be suppressed, he should be killed. At the same time Kemal and other leading nationalists including Ismet Bey, Adnan Bey and his wife Halide Edib were condemned to death. These fatwas threatened the future of the nationalists. Since 1911, with a gap in 1913–14, Turkey had been continuously at war. Much of the public was weary of the struggle and despaired of success.[29]

The Sultan backed the fatwa by acts. He sent a British-armed force called the Army of the Caliphate against Ankara. Consisting mainly of Circassians and religious fanatics (since the Sultan's official forces in Constantinople would not have been reliable against the nationalists), it almost captured Eskishehir, but by July 1920 had been defeated. Soon nationalist troops reached the outskirts of Constantinople. Shots were fired from the hills of Beykoz across the Bosphorus, into the garden of the British summer embassy at Yenikoy and, to the fury of the High Commissioner, at HMS *Iron Duke* itself. British troops, battleships and seaplanes counter-attacked in July, assisted by a Greek regiment. The last regimental cavalry charge of the British army, by the 20th Hussars, took place in defence of Constantinople. Finally the nationalists were driven beyond the town of Izmit, seventy kilometres to the east of the city. Constantinople's defences were strengthened by laying a protective wire fence from Izmit to the Black Sea.[30]

In order to give the nationalists a 'knock-out blow', the Allies authorized a large-scale Greek advance in Anatolia and Thrace. On 8 July the Greek army took Bursa. On 26 July King Alexander made a triumphant entry into Edirne. For the next two years, while Greek and Turkish armies fought for Anatolia, with Allied permission Greece used Constantinople as a military and naval base, landing munitions on the quays of Galata and recruiting soldiers in the street. However, the capital's Greeks showed little eagerness to serve. Between March 1921 and March 1922 only 2,850 Constantinople Greeks were recruited. They preferred provocation to action. In December 1921 an ardent Venizelist nationalist called Meletios was elected Patriarch – although, contrary to the law, he was not an Ottoman subject.[31]

On 10 August 1920 Damad Ferid had signed the punitive treaty of Sèvres. By its terms the Straits, while remaining Ottoman territory, were placed under the control of an international commission. Eastern Anatolia was divided between an independent Armenia and autonomous Kurdistan. Greece was awarded Izmir and eastern Thrace. Even the size of the Sultan's bodyguard was regulated by his conquerors. The revival of capitulations was the supreme insult. The Sultan, who called the treaty 'Turkey's death sentence', never ratified it.

The break between Ankara and Constantinople appeared complete. Ankara had agents throughout the city, even in Damad Ferid's house. In cafés and mosques they told people that the Sultan's call to arms against the nationalists was due to British pressure. However, from British accounts it is clear that he was more anti-Kemalist than the British themselves. He threatened to abdicate if the British did not take measures against the 'madhouse' Ankara. Many nationalist leaders such as Rauf, Refet, Kazim Karabekir and Kemal himself had recently served the Sultan as ministers and generals. Nevertheless, in conversation with de Robeck's successor as British High Commissioner, Sir Horace Rumbold, he called the nationalists 'men without any real stake in the country, with which they have no connection of blood or anything else'.

The Ottoman Empire was clearly outdated when the Sultan, forgetting its multinational traditions, complained that there was not a 'real Turk' among the nationalists. Infected by the racial nationalism of the age, although he himself had more Circassian than Turkish blood, he called Kemal

a Macedonian revolutionary of unknown origin. His blood might be anything, Bulgarian, Greek or Serbian. He looked rather like a Serbian! He and his Government were nevertheless powerless before them. The hold was such that there was no means of access to the real Turks even by way of propaganda. The real Turks were loyal to the core but they were intimidated or they were hoodwinked by fantastic misrepresentations like the story of his own captivity.

The Sultan felt in 'a position of complete helplessness and isolation'.[32]

After 1920 the Ottoman government was an impotent rump. The last Ottoman firmans in 1921 and 1922 resemble, in their monochrome simplicity, those of the empire's confident dawn. The government depended on loans from the Ottoman Bank until in January 1921 the Sultan placed the Ministry of Finance, in addition to the Ministry of War, under Allied control. Thereby he hoped, in return for hitherto confiscated Ottoman gold, to resume paying officials' salaries, and stop them deserting to Ankara, where Mustafa Kemal promised high pay and safety from the foreigners. The few people who supported the Sultan's policy were members of the *ulema*, and liberals like Riza Tevfik and Ali Kemal, a British-educated journalist who became Minister of the Interior. They detested the nationalists whom they regarded as remnants of the Committee.[33]

Most Muslims of Constantinople supported the nationalists. Demetra Vaka, a Constantinople Greek, wrote that 'the whole capital breathed, thought and talked of little else than Mustafa Kemal's war against Greece. The Turks spoke of it as if it was the war of all wars.' At one of the mixed tea parties of men and women which were becoming the fashion, she heard a writer say: 'Heart and soul, all are for the movement in Anatolia.' King Constantine had returned to the throne, on the death of his son Alexander in November 1920. Although his pro-German reputation henceforth deprived Greece of Allied support, Greek shops in Pera displayed his portrait with the inscription 'he is coming', and Greeks quoted a proverb about their city: 'A Constantine built it, a Constantine lost it, a Constantine shall regain it.' During Ramadan nights in the city, however, pictures of Mustafa Kemal could be seen in shop windows while mosques displayed illuminated inscriptions: 'Victory comes with patience', or simply 'Patience.' Ankara newspapers hostile to the Sultan and the Allies, in theory forbidden, were read in every club and café.[34]

The Ottoman government itself began to draw near the nationalists in the field of foreign affairs, after the Sultan dismissed Damad Ferid. From 21 October 1920 until 4 November 1922 the Grand Vizier was the 77-year-old Tevfik Pasha, who had been a Minister of Foreign Affairs to Abdulhamid. He corresponded with Kemal and deferred to the nationalist representative during negotiations over revision of the Treaty of Sèvres in London in 1921. Mustafa Kemal himself, in letters and telegrams to Tevfik Pasha, promised maintenance of the sultanate 'when the Khalifat has been saved'. If the Sultan recognized the Grand National Assembly in Ankara and a mission from Ankara replaced his government in Constantinople, Ankara would pay his civil list. In other words Kemal tried to bribe him into becoming a nationalist puppet.[35]

The events of March–July 1920 proved the Sultan to be a British pawn. With the British government sending both Greek troops and the Army of the Caliphate against the nationalists, the Sultan was indirectly ally of the Greeks against his own subjects. Increasing numbers left Constantinople to join the nationalists in Anatolia. Two days after the Allied occupation of parliament, Halide Edib, and her husband Adnan Adivar, with the help of Karakol, went, disguised as a *hoca* and his wife (to elude British police agents), to the small wooden *tekke* of Uzbek dervishes on a hill above Uskudar. The password was 'Jesus has sent us'. They then walked – or in the case of Halide Edib took a carriage – past British check-points, avoiding Greek brigands along the way, until they reached nationalist-controlled territory beyond Izmit.

No two cities could have been more different than Constantinople and Ankara in the 1920s. 'The Mecca of the nationalist movement' was then an impoverished Anatolian town of 20,000. Halide Edib, who became an acting-corporal in the nationalist army, remembered: 'We lived like members of a newly founded religious order in all the exaggerated puritanism of its inception.' While Constantinople contained over 3,000 motor cars, including Rolls-Royces and Mercedes-Benz, the only car in Ankara belonged to Kemal's deputy Ismet Pasha.[36]

Even the heir to the throne tried to leave Constantinople. In June 1919 Abdulmecid Efendi had been reported by British sources to be 'at the head of the nationalist party'. His evening visits to the mosques of the capital alarmed the Sultan. He hated Damad Ferid. On 12 June 1919 he wrote to the Sultan, with unusual prescience, that 'the ministry reduces the whole Ottoman people to utter despair at a time when the Islamic world regards maintenance of the Ottoman Empire as most necessary from the point of view of Islamism.' He feared 'the gravest eventualities' for the imperial house and called the Sultan 'the ruin of the country, the Caliphate and the sultanate'. Out of sympathy for the plight of the people, he fasted once a week. He also corresponded with Mustafa Kemal.[37]

In August 1920, according to British sources, 'several efforts have been made to persuade members of the imperial family to proceed to Angora but with the exception of the heir apparent none of the princes have been willing to go.' During September, to prevent his departure, the Sultan placed him under house arrest. Abdulmecid wrote to one of his old teachers, Canon Whitehouse: *'Je vis dans la terreur du moyen âge. Personne ne rentre et sort de chez moi.'* In early October he was released.[38]

Abdulmecid's son Omer Faruk, a professional soldier educated in Vienna and Berlin, thought of leaving in September 1920. However, like many in Constantinople, he was alarmed by Ankara's close relations with the Soviet government and reputation for irreligion. Again dynastic biology affected Ottoman history. He had married Sabiha Sultan at Yildiz on 29 April – a marriage between cousins without precedent in the history of the dynasty. He may have wanted to stay with her for the birth of their first child; their daughter, Neslishah, was born on 2 February 1921. Only on 27 April 1921, however, driven by what he called, in a letter to the Sultan, an 'irresistible feeling of patriotism' did he land at Inebolu on the Black Sea. He was better received by the people than by Mustafa Kemal. In 1920, when the nationalists were desperate, he might have been welcome. In 1921, when they had begun to defeat the Greeks, Mustafa Kemal refused the prince's services.[39] However this was not the end of the Ottoman dynasty's connection with Turkish nationalism.

While nationalists left Constantinople to join the army, waves of refugees and orphans, Turkish, Kurdish and Armenian, poured into the city. There were so many that they took over military schools, palaces and mosques. A special American-funded charity called Near East Relief fed over 160,000 people a day in Constantinople.[40]

Some horrors, however, were spared the city. In 1919 many died in Cairo and Alexandria during anti-British risings; the Greek occupation of Izmir began with a massacre of Turks; French forces bombarded Damascus in 1920. Constantinople, however, was miraculously free of bloodshed, except in March 1920. Turkish memoirs reveal more injured pride than physical suffering: Turks complained of Greeks' and Armenians' 'intolerable smiles' and 'generally obnoxious' behaviour on ferries and trams. They were accused of such crimes as travelling first-class on second-class tickets, or being given seats on trams by Armenian conductors while Muslims were ejected.[41]

Constantinople was so free of violence that, while nationalists were fighting in Anatolia, Pera had an atmosphere of perpetual carnival – if the poverty and demoralization in its side-streets were ignored. The foreign soldiers and sailors had money to spend. Allied officers crowded three deep around the bar of the Pera Palace Hotel. On 1 December 1918 one newspaper had noted: 'Never in the memory of our *pécheresses*, and they are numerous here, has flirtation been in such vogue as since the arrival of the English. Between six and eight o'clock in the evening, one can see them at work in the salons of the Pera Palace where flirtation is in the air.' For Harold Armstrong, British Acting Military Attaché, 'Life was gay and wicked and delightful. The cafés were full of drinking and dancing. There was none of the clogging drag of home ties.' In the Petit Champ des Morts, wrote Muftizade Zia Bey, son of one of the last Ottoman ministers of foreign affairs, there was 'so much male and female soliciting that no self-respecting man dares any more to venture in the place'. Child prostitution was commonplace.[42]

In 1920 the carnival atmosphere of Pera was reinforced by a peaceful invasion from the North. The Russian revolution provided the third element, after the struggles between the nationalists and the Allies, and the nationalists and the Sultan, in Constantinople's final act as a capital. In November 1920 General Wrangel, the last and most impressive commander of the 'White' forces, was obliged to evacuate the Crimea. The city, which had received so many refugees from different regions, from Spain, Poland and central Asia, now witnessed the arrival of a procession of 126 boats containing 145,693 Russians (and the Russian imperial stud). They came not, as many Russians had once hoped, to hang 'Russia's shield for ever on the gates of Tsarigrad', but as refugees travelling in indescribable squalor. Some were so hungry and thirsty that they lowered their wedding rings on cords, down to boatloads of Greek and Armenian shopkeepers, in return for bread and water.[43]

They slept in the stables of Dolmabahce palace, or prostitutes' vacated rooms in the port hotels of Galata. Aged ladies-in-waiting of the Dowager Empress, heads shaved to eliminate vermin, prayed in front of family icons in a Galata cellar. There were so many Russian soldiers in Constantinople that they seemed to form another army of occupation: at times, driven by poverty and despair, they threatened to seize the city (Russian-officered soldiers in the Cossack Brigade were, a few months later, to help establish Reza Khan, the first Pahlavi, as ruler of Iran). Finally Wrangel's soldiers were housed in French army camps in Lemnos, Catalca and the Dardanelles (in return the French navy acquired the Russian ships). The Russian Council, a multi-party government in exile with its own administration, archives and intelligence service, was established in the Russian embassy on the Grande Rue. Every Sunday after church the embassy courtyard was crowded with Russians exchanging news of their native land, their relations' whereabouts – and where to get the best price for their jewels.[44]

Within a few months, many Russians had established better relations with their old enemies the Turks than with the fellow Christians whom they had once been eager to 'liberate'. Baron Sergei Tornow, a young colonel in the Preobrazhensky Guards, remembered that the Turks treated him and his friends with 'extreme kindness . . . much better than the Greeks'. For Prince Alexander Volkonsky, 'the Greeks were all terribly dishonest. We always had the impression that the Turks were the best there.' The streets of Constantinople were crowded with Russian officers, with the hungry, drawn look of refugees, driving cabs, or selling newspapers, shoe-laces or wooden dolls. The present-day Flower Passage, formerly the Cité de Pera, received its name from the Russian lady flower-sellers who took refuge in it from the attentions of the Allied soldiers on the street outside.[45] A professor of mathematics worked as a cashier in a Russian restaurant. The philosopher Gurdjieff sold caviare.[46] Nikolai Tcharykov, who had been Russian ambassador in 1909–12, returned as a refugee. He lived simply in Bebek, doing his own shopping; his wife gave French and English lessons.

Russians soon dominated the entertainment of the city. 'The Volga Boat-Song' resounded through the music-halls of Pera. The great painter Pavel Tchelitchev designed ballet productions for Boris Kniazeff's Strelna Cabaret and Viktor Zimin's Ballet Company. An American black called Thomas, who had run a jazz-hall in Petrograd before the revolution, opened a successor near the Petit Champ which introduced the Charleston and the fox-trot to Constantinople. Since in Constantinople blacks were called Arabs, as most of them came from Egypt, the music was known as Arab jazz.*

Russians opened restaurants with names like *Le Grand Cercle Moscovite*, *Petrograd Patisserie*, *The Black Rose*. Turkish restaurants could not compete as the Russians offered the irresistible novelty of – waitresses. Some were noblewomen (the waitresses at the Moscovite were known as 'the Duchesses'), whose distinction and elegance won the admiration of the French novelist Paul Morand. Anna Valentinovna told him: 'Look at Constantinople: the poverty is incredible, the extravagance madder than ever; people drink, cheat, tease each other, die or make deals with a cleverness and dishonesty which astonish even Pera.' Ottoman gentlemen were besotted with Russian waitresses who wore white Caucasian jackets, high black boots, thin scarves round their hair and heavy make-up. Turkish novels entitled *Russian Fever* and *Cakeshop Girl* describe men

---

*James Baldwin was called 'Arab' when he lived in Istanbul in the 1960s.

ruined by bars, cocaine and Russian girls. A cartoon in a Constantinople newspaper depicted a Turk asking a Russian woman:

'Parlez-vous français, mademoiselle?
'No, but I know how to say "love" in every language.'

Russians also brought mixed bathing, in the sea, to Constantinople.

If Constantinople inspired Greeks and Turks to extremes of imperial ambition, it led Russians to depths of debauch. Since they needed money to buy visas for western Europe, they were ready for anything. In 1923 a petition from thirty-two wives or widows of beys and pashas to the Governor of Constantinople demanded the immediate expulsion of 'these agents of vice and debauchery who are more dangerous and destructive than syphilis and alcohol'. Russian women had wrought more destruction in two years than Russian armies in centuries:

Today among the young men of 18 to 30 there is hardly one who has not been worn out by the habit of consuming lethal poisons such as morphine, cocaine, ether and alcohol and this is entirely because of the baleful influence of these Russian women. Just in the small district of Beyoglu that lies between the Tunel and Taksim the number of Russian bars, *cafés chantants* and restaurants which ply their reprehensible trade free of all regulation and hygienic control exceeds 25. In these places, each of which is a place of execution for innocence, hundreds of young Turks drag their health, wealth and honour into the whirlpool of calamity every night. Similarly since these evil girls have wormed their way into every social milieu, some Turkish girls have been forced to come into contact with them in public assemblies.

Russian and British matrimonial priorities are revealed in a postscript to a long letter discussing the poor state of Anglo-French relations in Constantinople, sent by Sir Horace Rumbold to Admiral de Robeck on 1 December 1921:

P.S. Little Princess Olga Micheladze is about to marry one Sandford, a nice quiet fellow in the Inter-Allied Police. He has money.[47]

In post-war Constantinople, some Muslim women also began to free themselves. From 1919 they were the first Muslim women of the élite in the world regularly to appear on the street unveiled, although still with headscarves. 'A good many of us are trying to get rid of these obsolete things,' said Mlle Tevfik to a British friend. In a relatively conservative area like Bayezid they might be stoned; elsewhere they were accepted. Muslim women began to work in public as street-sweepers, in shops or in the post office, and to take part in political meetings. Richer women gave mixed parties and dances, went to the Tokatliyan and Pera Palace hotels, even flirted with Allied officers. Nothing, wrote a French visitor, distinguished an elegant Muslim lady from a Christian except lack of a hat. At a *thé dansant* given by the American High Commissioner, four imperial princes and three princesses could be seen 'freely talking to strangers'.[48]

The cosmopolitan unreality of occupied Constantinople, compared by Theotokas to a 'ballet of lunatics', is suggested by these snatches of conversation, recorded by the American writer John Dos Passos:

'*Ah, monsieur, nous avons vécu des journées atroces.*'

'May God give us back the good old days of Abdul Hamid!'

'Collected all the Bolos [Bolsheviks] in town and towed them up into the Black Sea in a leaky scow and left 'em there.'

'Nonsense, the Greeks'll have it – The British – The French – The Bulgarians – The League of Nations – The Turks. – I suggest it be made neutral and presented to Switzerland, that's the only solution.'

'Turkey does not exist. I assure you, sir, it is a mere question of brigandage.'

'Greece is going to fulfill her historic mission.'

'Why do you want to learn Turkish?'

'Kemal! He's finished.'

On the boat to Anatolia, outside Allied-patrolled waters, a different universe. Six Turkish army doctors, off to join the nationalists, came out of hiding.

'You Europeans are all hypocrites . . . If the Allies drive us out of Constantinople, very good. It is a city of misery and decay. We will make Angora our capital . . . The Turks are all in Angora with Mustafa Kemal.[49]

For, like Curzon and Lloyd George, many Turks now considered Constantinople the embodiment of evil; the Sultan's collaboration had added to its aura of treason and corruption. From puritan Ankara the Grand National Assembly criticized the Turks of the capital for mixing with foreigners and adopting their customs. Yakup Kadri, editor of the

Constantinople paper *Ikdam*, who often visited Ankara, brought Turkish nationalism into the Turkish novel. In *Nur Baba* (1921) he denounced the dervish practices at a famous Bektashi lodge in Camlica. In *Kiralik Konak* (Mansion for Rent) (1922), he used the collapse of a *konak* as a symbol of the disintegration of the empire.

In one of the longest hate letters in literature, *Sodom ve Gomore* (1928), the target is not only the enemy occupier but Pera itself. Yakup Kadri combines revolutionary self-righteousness with a Proustian interest in social and sexual ambiguity: his title is a reflection of Proust's *Sodome et Gomorrhe*, published in Paris seven years earlier. The author contrasts the purity of Constantinople, where girls keep their bodies as sacred gifts of God, and patriots treasure newspapers with news of victories in Anatolia, with the horror of Pera, where 'Western civilization has poured all its scum'. He denounces Turks who, like smiling slaves, have admitted the enemy into their homes, and have permitted him to take their sisters, their wives and their mistresses.

The small miseries of the occupation are recorded with venom. The hero Necdet is ordered to take off his fez, supreme symbol of Turkishness, by a drunken British officer in a Russian restaurant. 'Fact' is often written in the margin of the copy in the Istanbul Library near Aya Sofya, for example beside the account of the following incident. A Levantine woman is escorted into a tram by a British officer. With a gesture of his swagger stick, the officer obliges two people to give up their seats. As the woman moves forward to take her seat, she treads on the hand of a legless Ottoman soldier who has crawled in with great difficulty. When the cripple protests, she says 'Silence, dog' and exclaims with fury that such people should not be allowed in. He is forced to descend.

Necdet learns to hate his mistress Leyla, who dances naked in public and has an affair with a British officer; he hates Pera and yearns for Anatolia, and justice. One day the liberators will come and finish with this filth and corruption, but when? Finally, news from Anatolia fills him with 'the intoxication and divine joy of victory'. His last memory of Leyla is the insipid taste of her lipstick in their farewell kiss.[50]

The victory was the final Turkish triumph over the Greeks. As the fighting had grown fiercer, in late July 1922 the Greek army had asked for permission to enter Constantinople. The Allies refused and reinforced their position along the Catalca lines. Thus, whatever the horror of the Allied occupation, it spared Constantinople occupation by Greeks. On 9 September Mustafa Kemal reached Izmir. 'The Paris of the Levant' went up in flames; 200,000 Greeks fled by ship. The commander of the Greek army, Trikoupi, a descendant of the Mavro-cordatos, was captured.

In the streets of Constantinople Turks exchanged glances of triumph and joy. Aya Sofya, symbol of Ottoman victory, was so crowded for prayers that its galleries had to be opened. At news of the Greek victor-ies, the streets of Constantinople had been filled with lorryloads of Greek soldiers, singing patriotic songs and waving blue and white Greek flags. Now cars criss-crossed the city filled with flowers, portraits of Mustafa Kemal and Turks singing songs wishing him a thousand lives (*bin yasha*):

> *Yasha, yasha, bin yasha!*
> *Mustafa Kemal pasha!*

Sherif Ali Haydar wrote in his diary for 9 September: 'The crown prince telephoned and then sent a messenger to say that Smyrna has fallen. I rejoiced and towards evening went in person to congratulate him.' However neither the ministries nor the palace put out the Ottoman flag.[51]

In the next two years events in Constantinople moved at the speed of a newsreel. In early September about 7,600 Allied troops occupying the city and the Straits faced about 50,000 nationalists. The latter were elated with victory and ready for a fight. British forces were reinforced by an aircraft-carrier, troops from Cairo and Palestine (including the 2nd Highland Light Infantry, known as Hell's Last Issue) and, from Britain, Grenadier, Coldstream, Irish and Welsh Guards. One Guards brigade was stationed on each side of the Bosphorus.[52]

A combination of pride and pugnacity, rather than a desire to retain the city, made Lloyd George, Birkenhead and Churchill, Secretary of State for Defence, eager to fight for Constantinople: Lloyd George even proposed to arm 20,000 of its Greek inhabitants. Harington received instructions 'to hold Gallipoli at all costs' and to remove Turkish forces from the British-declared neutral zone around Chanak, on the Asian side of the Dardanelles.

From 23 September Turkish forces crossed the trenches and barbed wire fences into the neutral zone, often walking up to British soldiers, smoking, jeering, watering their horses. On 29 and 30 September the

Cabinet prepared for war. Heroic efforts by British and Turkish army commanders on the spot (Harington refused to deliver an ultimatum), and by Curzon in London, prevented a recourse to arms. Twice Harington expected to hear that operations had started. He knew 'instances of men crying because they felt the limit of endurance had been exceeded. I doubt if troops have ever been called upon to endure such provocation.'

One of the first films of Constantinople, taken in November 1922, shows the banks and waters of the Golden Horn and the Bosphorus thick with boats of every description: battleships, steamboats, sailing-boats, kayiks. Yet the Admiralty sent instructions to destroy all shipping in order to prevent nationalist forces crossing into Europe. As Rumbold pointed out, obedience would have caused an outburst of rage and the cessation of the city's economic life. Like Harington, Rumbold and British naval officers learnt the art of disobedience.

From Constantinople Admiral Brock wrote to the Admiralty, on 26 September, that the Christian population was in a highly nervous condition. Harington ordered the evacuation of British women and children.[53]

The balance of power also helped preserve the peace. The city which had once been 'the world's desire', 'the queen of cities', was beginning to experience the delights of obscurity. The Communist victory in Russia, by diminishing Russian trade and power, lessened Constantinople's political and economic relevance. The reduction of the Ottoman Empire to a nation state, above all the successes of the Turkish army, destroyed the city's double attraction of desirability and vulnerability. The British public, so eager to fight for Constantinople in 1878 and 1915, was sick of war in 1922. The British government could interest neither the Dominions, nor its allies France and Italy, nor the neighbouring states of Serbia, Romania and Bulgaria, in the defence of Constantinople and the Straits. On 3 October a conference at Mudanya on the Sea of Marmara opened between Harington and the Turkish general Ismet Inonu: Halide Edib, whose English was excellent, inter-preted. On 11 October Harington and Ismet Pasha signed an agree-ment by which Turkish forces were allowed into Thrace, and Allied forces remained in Constantinople and the Straits, until signature of a peace treaty.

'The Chanak affair' finished Lloyd George (as Gallipoli had almost finished Churchill). The Conservative Party responded to Bonar Law's plea, 'We cannot alone act as the policeman of the world', and withdrew its confidence. On 20 October Lloyd George resigned as prime minister. He never held office again.[54]

On 19 October Refet Pasha, one of Mustafa Kemal's most important generals, had landed near Beshiktash. Smiling and handsome, looking as if he had arrived from a dance rather than a campaign, he drove through Constantinople acclaimed by a fervent crowd. Sheep were sacrificed and prayers recited along his triumphal route to the mosque of Fatih. There Refet said that Fatih had given the city to the Turks and no Turk would let it be torn from them. Refet was in theory no more than Governor of Thrace, and was accompanied by only 126 gendarmes. Nevertheless the city was so pro-nationalist that he soon, with almost no bloodshed, took control of the Sultan's troops, the police, the municipality, customs and passports. The Allied commissions lost almost all authority.[55]

The nationalist triumph marked Constantinople's loss of the indispensable attribute of an international city: the protection of a powerful state. On 30 October a motion in the Grand National Assembly in Ankara denounced the 'folly', 'ignorance', 'debauch' and 'treachery' of the palace and the Porte over centuries. On 1 November Mustafa Kemal made one of his lethal speeches: 'It was by force that the sons of Osman seized the sovereignty and sultanate of the Turkish nation; they have maintained this usurpation for six centuries. Now the Turkish nation has rebelled and has put a stop to these usurpers and has effectively taken sovereignty and sultanate into its own hands.' That day Refet informed Mehmed VI that he was Caliph, but no longer Sultan. He accepted the change.[56]

The turn of the Sublime Porte was next. On 4 November Refet Pasha confirmed the staff of the *vilayet* and prefecture of Constantinople in office, while ignoring the Sublime Porte. The ministers, although told by Mehmed VI to carry on current business, decided to resign. When Izzet Pasha, Minister of Foreign Affairs, arrived at the Porte in the afternoon, he found four ministries already vacant 'and there was only the rump of a cabinet left. In these circumstances there was nothing to do but to retire with the cabinet.' Officials were told that the nationalist government would see to the payment of their salaries: many had, in any case, already taken the road to Ankara. On 4 November the last Grand Vizier Tevfik Pasha told Sir Horace Rumbold that such a wild and irregularly constituted body as the Grand National Assembly was not competent to decide the future of the sultanate or Caliphate, matters which concerned the whole Muslim world. However the same day he too tried to resign. Since he was no longer Sultan, Mehmed VI denied his competence in the matter. Tevfik Pasha's seal of office is still in his descendants' possession.[57]

The Allied authorities disapproved of what they termed Refet's 're-volution'. 'Billy' Fox-Pitt called the situation 'ticklish'. On 7 November he wrote: 'Things are looking very serious here . . . from a military point of view the situation is very unpleasant as the place is full of Turks and all armed, but we have got the fleet who can make mince meat of Stamboul.' Crowds shouted *A bas les anglais!* outside the British High Commission. British Military Police had to use force to rescue a British intelligence officer and his Turkish agent from Turkish gendarmes. Hitherto 'very friendly', the latter now obeyed the nationalists. Three thousand British sailors paraded through the streets of Pera as a show of force. The Allies were determined to stay, in order to retain a bargaining counter in the forthcoming peace negotiations.[58]

Finally the two sides adopted a system of 'dual control': both Allied and Turkish troops remained in the city. The Turkish government did not 'recognize', but did 'accept' the continued occupation and surveillance. The Allies retained jurisdiction over Allied subjects, Hellenic Greeks (Greeks with passports from the Kingdom of the Hellenes) and Russian refugees, and maintained their own police, intelligence and passport officials in the city. Both sides cooperated to censor the press. Harington described Refet as sometimes 'very correct', sometimes 'impossible'.[59]

Primarily owing to Kemal's statesmanship, Constantinople was spared a blood-bath of collaborators such as France experienced in 1944. However on 7 November the anti-nationalist journalist Ali Kemal was arrested in a barber's shop in Pera, gagged, taken to Izmit by boat (with lights dimmed to evade British sea patrols), interrogated by the Governor and finally stoned to death by a nationalist crowd. Many supporters of the Constantinople government decided to leave; 150 'compromised Turks' camped in the garden of the British embassy and in the embassy itself until they were taken by British boats to Greece. The Seyhulislam left for India; his predecessor, the Durrizade who had delivered the fatwa against Kemal, died in the Hejaz in 1923.[60]

Minorities were even more affected than Ottomans. The Greeks were beginning to pay for their behaviour since 1912. The stock exchange was closed. Nationalist authorities began to apply Turkish law to foreign companies and local Christians. They told Greeks that those who did not consider themselves Ottoman should leave. Soon, despite exhortations from the Patriarch, the boats for Salonica were packed with Greeks, whose abandoned possessions were snapped up at bargain prices. The last meeting of the Syllogos was in 1922. Its building was seized by the Turkish government in 1925, demolished forty years later and is now a car park. Its library and archive belong to the Turkish Historical Society in Ankara. In all about 150,000 Greeks left Constantinople in 1922–4. A harsh light was thrown on Greeks' prospects by Refet's statement to Nevile Henderson in late November, that 'the Greeks if they were not actually expelled would be well advised to leave, as in future in a new Turkey they would be unable to make a living here. The Turks were going to take the commerce into their own hands; he had already started to organize for this purpose.' The National Turkish Commercial Union was founded in 1923.[61]

While Greeks and 'compromised Turks' fled, Mehmed VI at first announced his intention to stay at his post. He was protected by Grenadier Guards, stationed in the barracks built by Abdulhamid beside Yildiz. However, he was the shadow of a monarch. When Sir Horace Rumbold went to Yildiz on 6 November, he was greeted on arrival by one old chamberlain: all others had left. The Sultan, who talked for over three hours without stopping, still thought there could be 'a reaction' if the Allies were prepared to 'call a halt' or to take 'a firm grip'. But, like many protégés, he confused power and the will to exert it. The Allies were indeed strong, but were no more willing to fight for the Ottoman Sultan in 1922, than they had been to fight for other failed protégés, the White Russians, in 1920. Rumbold arranged the despatch of the Sultan's money abroad.[62]

On 10 November the imperial anthem could not be played at the *selamlik* as the band had deserted. Six days later the Sultan sent a letter to Harington (French forces had refused to help):

16 November 1922

Sir,
    Considering my life in danger in Istanbul, I take refuge with the British Government and request my transfer as soon as possible from Istanbul to another place.

                                   Mehmed Vahideddin, Caliph of the Muslims

At 8 a.m. on 17 November, Mehmed VI left by the Orhaniye gate in the palace wall, opposite the barracks occupied by Grenadier Guards. The weather was cold and stormy; it was raining, as it had been for eight days, and few people were out. He was accompanied by his son Ertugrul, in a new London suit, his first chamberlain, his bandmaster and six servants. The Sultan seemed less agitated than his suite. Guards officers drove him away in an ambulance with the cross painted out (so that the British could not be accused of sheltering under the Red Cross), followed by another ambulance for staff and suitcases. Later that day 'Billy' Fox-Pitt, the Guards Brigade transport officer who drove in the second ambulance, wrote his mother a letter whose detail shows his awareness that he was witnessing the end of an empire:

> The road was appalling, it was raining very hard all night and still is, once or twice I thought we were going to upset, after following the Sultan's car for a bit we took a different road arrived at the quay (Tophani) where we were to ship them on to a launch and then on to the 'Malaya' who is taking him to Malta. We arrived first and find the C in C and Gen Anderson M.G.G.S. waiting, we stowed away our old man in the launch and had to wait about 10 minutes for the other ambulance [which had a puncture], it arrived eventually and the old Sultan got out and thanked everybody, shook the Brigadier warmly by the hand. We all bowed and scraped, and he was quickly pushed on board and they went off. The C in C went with him as far as the ship. Everything went very well and I don't think the Kemalists know anything about it . . .
>
> The Sultan wasnt much moved he talked hard the whole time in the car, and said he hoped that we wouldn't think that he was afraid, but he wished to save his honour; I dont quite know how he worked this out!!*

In reality the nationalist government, like the city, was probably relieved by the departure of the Sultan anathematized in the press as traitor, coward and criminal. A Turkish photograph shows the presence, unremarked in British sources, of the Minister of the Civil List, a Turkish officer and a wreath of flowers, as the last Sultan steps off Turkish soil on to a British launch. At 8.45 a.m. HMS *Malaya* sailed to the British naval base at Malta. The Sultan died in San Remo in 1926, near the city of Genoa which, six centuries earlier, had been his dynasty's first Western ally. He was so deep in debt that his creditors seized his coffin, and delayed his burial for two weeks.[63]

By his anti-nationalist policies Mehmed VI had done much to destroy the emotional bond between the dynasty and the nation.

---

*The Sultan may have feared being put on trial if he stayed.

Nevertheless, despite press vilification, the Ottoman dynasty remained so deeply embedded in the patriotism and sense of identity of the Turks that, at this stage, Kemal was not powerful enough to dispense with it. The ideologist of Turkish nationalism, Ziya Gokalp, wrote: 'This respectable family is a blessed dynasty which has served and elevated the Turkish nation for a thousand years and both Islam and the Turkish nation for six centuries.' Kemal decided to make the heir to the throne Caliph. At first, according to British intelligence reports, Abdulmecid was reluctant to accept the title, correctly stating that it was reserved for 'the most powerful monarch in Islam'; he did not want to be 'a mere phantom'. He yielded when Refet promised that the sultanate would eventually be restored, and hinted at 'consequences of a regrettable nature' if he refused. As 'the most moral, learned and pious of this dynasty', Abdulmecid was elected Caliph by the National Assembly on 19 November.[64]

On 29 November, wearing white tie and tails, the new Caliph received the homage of *ulema*, deputies and senior officials, standing in front of (rather than sitting on) the golden throne at Topkapi. To confirm that he was not Sultan, he was not 'girded with the sword of Othman' at Eyup. However, as His Imperial Majesty the Caliph Abdulmecid II he drove to the mosque of Fatih in a state carriage, with Refet beside him. They were escorted by horse guards and followed by a procession of cars and carriages. There was steady hand-clapping from crowds lining the route, many of whom climbed trees and on to roofs in order to obtain a better view. The city seemed to have turned scarlet with Turkish flags. In the mosque, prayers were offered for the preservation of the Turkish people from extinction; for the first time they were said in Turkish, not Arabic. After victory in one holy war, there was a call for another holy war, against ignorance and in favour of commerce and agriculture. On the return journey prayers were offered at the mausoleums of Selim I and Mahmud II.[65]

The new Caliph, who still called himself Servant of the Two Holy Places, continued to attend the different mosques of Constantinople in state every Friday, sometimes arriving by kayik, sometimes riding a white horse called *Konya* presented by Refet. Years later a Turkish officer remembered:

> Mecit would dazzle my eyes when he attended at Bayezit for prayers. I would watch him enthralled, his fine good-looking old face, his bushy white beard, the red fez adding colour to the funereal black of his dress. The band would

play loudly and the soldiers march and the Sultan [*sic*] Mecit would bow from his coach – first to this side he would bow then to that, and the cheers would hoarsely rend the air. The old Sultan would stretch his lips into a wide smile of acknowledgement, putting his hand gracefully to his scarlet fez.

However many were disgusted by the display of splendour and piety. Even in the Ottoman dynasty, Islam was losing its hold. On 15 Ramadan [1 May] 1923, Sherif Ali Haydar was grieved to observe, at the last ceremony of revering the relics of the Prophet, 'a great lack of that reverent attitude which was always such a marked feature at ceremonies of this nature. Few men now seem to have that attitude to their faith that is so essential and their attitude amazed me.' After one *selamlik*, a woman in the crowd asked: 'Of what use was the Caliphate to us during the war? We proclaimed a holy war and what good did that do?'[66]

Indeed, although it added to the surface glitter of the city, the Caliphate was doomed. It was a concession to opinion, not a considered policy. As early as January 1923 Mustafa Kemal told a group of journalists that he planned to abolish it, when they had 'prepared' opinion. On 27 February Rumbold was received in audience by the Caliph in Dolmabahce, having been warned by Adnan Bey, Kemal's representative and Halide Edib's husband, to avoid all political topics. He noted: 'The officials as a whole presented a down at heel appearance which was a marked contrast to that of the court officials in the ex-Sultan's time.' Abdulmecid, 'an intelligent and versatile man deeply interested in politics', was 'a mere puppet whose acts are carefully watched by the national government . . . the shabby ceremonial of which he is the centre cannot fail to impress the observer somewhat painfully.'[67]

After protracted negotiations, the Treaty of Lausanne between Turkey and the Allies was signed on 24 July 1923. Seen at the time as a Turkish triumph, in fact it guaranteed the demilitarization of the Dardanelles (an infringement of sovereignty which the Ottomans had never allowed) and, contrary to Turkish wishes, preserved the Greek community and Oecumenical Patriarchate in Constantinople. Only after the signature of peace did Allied forces in Constantinople consent to return the salutes they had, since 1918, exacted from Turkish troops.

Relations between the Allies and the nationalists in Constantinople had survived the strain of dual control. In March 1923 Fenerbahce, one of the first Turkish football teams, beat a team fielded by the Irish and Grenadier Guards. On 3 June, the King's Birthday, the 1st Guards Brigade trooped the colour on Taksim square. From 24 August to 2

October Allied troops evacuated the city without a hitch. The final departure ceremony took place on 2 October, in the square between the palace and the mosque of Dolmabahce. Generals were received on parade, guards inspected, flags saluted. Relieved by their departure, impressed by their bearing, crowds of Turks cheered the Allies, especially the British guard of honour of 100 guardsmen, all six foot tall. The band of the Coldstream Guards played Turkish nationalist songs, as well as the British national anthem. On 6 October the 1st Infantry Division of the Turkish army entered the city. The foreign post offices and consular courts ceased to function. The British Seamen's Hospital was taken over by the Red Crescent. Soviet diplomats replaced White Russians in the Russian embassy. Wrangel had already left the city with most of his troops for Yugoslavia – although some French officers, in anticipation of the scenes of 1945, had tried to force repatriation to the Soviet Union on White Russian soldiers. Those Christian men who had not already done so provided themselves with fezzes: if they wore European headgear, there was a danger that it would be forcibly removed. A dry regime was briefly imposed to emphasize that Europeans were no longer the masters: the Pera Palace Hotel served wine in teacups.[68]

The Allied occupation of Constantinople had lasted for four years and eleven months – seven months longer than the First World War itself. Constantinople was the only major European capital to suffer enemy occupation between the Napoleonic and the Second World wars. However much it was resented at the time, it spared the city some of the horrors experienced by the unoccupied capitals of its German and Austrian allies. In Berlin there were attempted Communist and right-wing *coups*, civil war and catastrophic inflation. In Vienna the university closed as there was no fuel to heat it; hunger drove people into the country to hunt for food; army officers were attacked in public. Constantinople, however, avoided such extremes: moreover Allied forces had money to spend.[69]

The destruction of the Ottoman Empire, and of inter-communal compromise, were the occupation's principal results. Britain encouraged the Sultan to attack the nationalists, to accept the Treaty of Sèvres and to flee on a British battleship: three events without which the national movement would have taken a different course. The minorities' open alliance with the occupiers instilled in many Turks a determination to be rid of them – as well as a feeling of disgust with Western 'civilization'.

*

The history of Constantinople had been made by individuals such as Catherine II, Mahmud II, Abdulhamid, Enver, Curzon, as well as by the impersonal forces of dynastic power, geography, nationality and religion. No individual, however, had such an impact on the city, since Fatih himself, as Mustafa Kemal. Having removed the Allies, he proceeded to humiliate the city and eliminate the Ottomans. On 13 October the Grand National Assembly approved an amendment to the constitution stating: 'Ankara is the seat of government of the Turkish state.' On 23 October Refet, the only nationalist who had paid court to the Caliph, was deprived of military command of the city. Since Kemal controlled the army and the Grand National Assembly, no action could be taken. On the night of 29/30 October residents of Constantinople were awoken by the sound of 101 guns firing an artillery salute to mark the proclamation of the republic. The city which had been an imperial capital for 1,593 years, longer than any other, was now the second city of a republic.[70]

The demotion of Constantinople revealed that Mustafa Kemal shared the hostility of Yakup Kadri and Tevfik Fikret. In order to 'cleanse' the city of 'the dirt', Kemal said: 'Perhaps the whole Black Sea with its waves will enter the Bosphorus to flood everything . . . The republic decidedly, come what may, will make a man out of Byzantium which by becoming habituated to filth, duplicity, lies and immorality has lost its natural state, its original beauty and its immeasurable value. It will turn it back to its natural state and purity.'

The disenchantment was mutual. Kemal's friend, the journalist Falih Rifki Atay, wrote: 'Istanbul generally was not well disposed towards Ankara.' The Istanbul press subjected the nationalist administration to daily criticism. Many secularists, as well as traditionalists, wanted to maintain the Caliphate, both as a barrier to Kemal's autocracy and a source of international prestige. They said the real difference was between democracy and despotism, not between monarchy and republic. On 11 November *Tanin* wrote that the loss of the Caliphate would be 'totally incompatible with reason, loyalty and national feeling'. The arch-modernizer Lutfi Fikri, president of the Constantinople Bar Association, sent an open letter to the Caliph on 10 November asking for restoration of his temporal authority (he was later jailed by an 'independence tribunal'). Others were too frightened to speak. Idolization of Kemal was intense but not universal. In 1924, when he travelled down the Bosphorus, he did not visit Constantinople – possibly because the police could not guarantee his security.[71]

The city was rapidly losing most of the elements which had made it unique: its strategic importance, the sultanate, the Porte, capital status, and finally the Caliphate. The dynasty was victim of its own multinationalism. In 1918–19, while the existence of Turkey was at stake, the Sultan was hoping to retain the Arab provinces; was sending missions of inter-racial reconciliation, including representatives of the Patriarchate, to Edirne and Bursa, and was hanging the murderers of Armenians. While Mustafa Kemal suppressed Kurdish nationalists in the East, there was a flowering of Kurdish activity in the city, led by clubs such as the Society for the Rise of Kurdistan and the Kurdish Social League and Kurdish newspapers. Kurds like Sayyid Abdulkadir, president of the Council of State, who had the support of the Kurdish hamals of the city, served in the Sultan's government: the head of the Constantinople police, Colonel Halid Bey, was a Kurd. Abdulkadir declared his profound respect for the Caliphate and wanted no more than the autonomy promised by the Treaty of Sèvres, which he considered in Turkey's interests as well as the Kurds'. According to a British intelligence report of 9 January 1920 the Sultan agreed.[72]

The Grand National Assembly governed the Turkish nation; the Ottoman Caliphate was recognized throughout the Islamic world (except Morocco). On 24 November 1923 the Aga Khan and Ameer Ali wrote to the Grand National Assembly from India, expressing concern for the future of the Caliphate – thereby giving Kemal a pretext for denouncing it as a cause of foreign intervention in Turkey's affairs.[73]

In the winter of 1923–4 the Caliph's budget was cut and he was deprived of his state kayik and guard. The last *selamlik* took place on 29 February at the mosque outside Dolmabahce palace, near the spot where Mehmed VI had embarked. On 3 March the Grand National Assembly in Ankara abolished the Caliphate. Dolmabahce was surrounded by troops. Abdulmecid was reading the Koran (or, by some accounts, the essays of Montaigne) late at night when Adnan Bey and the Prefect of Police came to tell him that he had to leave at dawn. His family and servants began to weep. The freedom of life in the West was offered as consolation. The Caliph's beloved daughter Durushehvar, sole survivor today (1995) of this melancholy scene, is said to have remarked in tears: 'I do not want that kind of freedom.'[74]

The abolition of the Caliphate was far from popular. According to the British Acting High Commissioner, there was 'much disquiet in men's minds; the general attitude in Constantinople and so far as I know elsewhere is one of outward indifference or subdued resignation, bred of lassitude and fear of a triumphant minority.'[75] The Caliph took his immediate family (six people), three officials and two servants. For fear of demonstrations, the government obliged the Caliph to leave from outside the city. At 5.30 a.m., having bidden farewell to a small crowd at the palace gate, they were taken in three cars, followed by a lorry of luggage, along the Bosphorus, over Galata bridge, past the Bayezid mosque, out through the Edirne gate, along the old walls to Yedikule and then on to Catalca. The Caliph's secretary Salih Keramet, son of the poet Nigar Hanim, recorded in his diary that the cars frequently got stuck in mud on the road, and the gendarmerie had to put down stones to enable them to drive free. At 11, tired, hungry and sad, the party arrived at Catalca railway station. The Caliph tried to smile when the police and gendarmerie gave him his last salute.

All day they remained at the railway station. The police kept away the loyal and the inquisitive. The station manager tried to make them comfortable in his family's private quarters. He was Jewish and Jews were the only minority to retain the bond of loyalty to the dynasty. When the Caliph expressed his thanks, the station manager replied in words which brought tears to all eyes:

> The Ottoman dynasty is the saviour of Turkish Jews. When our ancestors were driven out of Spain, and looked for a country to take them in, it was the Ottomans who agreed to give us shelter and saved us from extinction. Through the generosity of their government, once again they received freedom of religion and language, protection for their women, their possessions and their lives. Therefore our conscience obliges us to serve you as much as we can in your darkest hour.

At midnight the Orient Express arrived. As the party began to board, watched by the other passengers, the Governor of Istanbul gave the Caliph an envelope containing passports, visas for Switzerland, and £2,000 sterling. While the train sped through the Balkans, past the site in Hungary where the heart of Suleyman the Magnificent is buried, the Caliph lamented: 'My ancestor came with a horse and flags. Now I come as an exile.'[76]

It was the last of the railway journeys which had interred the empires of Europe, taking the Romanovs to death in Siberia, the Hohenzollerns and Habsburgs to exile in the Netherlands and Switzerland respectively. No imperial dynasty had lasted longer than the Ottomans. None left more regrets in its capital.

Epilogue

Constantinople's chief legacy to the world was its role and example as a great international capital, which ignored rigid boundaries, national, cultural, social and religious. There multiple identities were natural; it was a door in the wall between Islam and Christianity. The 'seat of the Caliphate' was part of 'the system of Europe': it was possible in Constantinople to be at once Ottoman and Greek, Muslim and European, and to treat nationality as a job rather than a passion. It was a city where people like Fatih, Sokollu Mehmed Pasha, Busbecq, Ibrahim Muteferrika, Mouradgea d'Ohsson, Mahmud II and the great Ottoman reformers of the nineteenth century could learn about other cultures without being distorted by complexes of superiority or inferiority, orientalism or occidentalism. The only crusades in Constantinople were between Christian sects, rather than between Christianity and Islam.

European powers not only frequently defended the city by diplomacy; they also strengthened its physical defences on five separate occasions – France in 1770 and 1807 and Britain in 1877–8 against Russia; Germany in 1915 against Britain and France; Britain, France and Italy in 1922 against Greece. Until 1918 Constantinople resisted and manipulated European imperialism. If from 1918 to 1923, at the high noon of Western dominance, the city was occupied, this was due to the empire's entry into the war in November 1914 against the wishes of the dynasty, the population and most of the cabinet.

By then each ethnic group in the city had begun to adopt an exclusive modern nationalism. The great Ottoman enterprise had failed. After the departure of the dynasty in 1924, from being the most international city in Europe, Constantinople became one of the most nationalistic. The Ottoman dynasty had been more regretted at the time of its exile in 1924 than other deposed dynasties; however, there was less nostalgia thereafter. In five and a half years as British ambassador during the Second World War, Sir Hugh Knatchbull Hugesson heard not one expression of regret for the empire, a testimony confirmed by all other sources. Unlike Vienna, Constantinople turned its back on the past. Even its name was changed. Constantinople was dropped because of its Ottoman and international associations. From 1926 the post office only accepted Istanbul; it appeared more Turkish and was used by most Turks. Istanbul and Turkey followed Mustafa Kemal, their saviour from destruction, in a fever of patriotism. His successor, President Ismet Inonu, remembered: 'We were on fire.'[1]

Kemal's reforms were effective because he was building on a hundred years of Ottoman modernization. Most of his measures had been discussed since 1908 by the Young Turks and the circle of Ziya Gokalp – or, like the limitation of Islam to the private domain and the unveiling of women, had already been put into practice by the city's élite. In March 1924 the office of Seyhulislam and the *vakifs* were abolished: having lost their hereditary incomes, many *ulema* families turned to commerce. Religious schools were closed; the *sheriat* courts were abolished; the Turkish republic adopted a legal code based on that of Switzerland. A year later the dervish orders were banned, and many of the *tekkes* demolished. Kemal said: 'The Republic of Turkey cannot be the land of *seyhs*, dervishes, disciples and lay brothers. The straightest truest Way is the way of civilization.'

Certain aspects of formal Islam, like pilgrimage to Mecca, were also discouraged. One Friday in 1926, Robert Byron noticed that only 150 Muslims were praying in Aya Sofya. Patriotism had driven the father of the writer Aziz Nesin, despite his devotion to the Ottoman sultanate, to leave his family in Istanbul and fight for the nationalists. After 1924, however, he turned. In secret, for fear of the police, he told his family that Kemal was Jewish, alcoholic and the annihilator of Islam. Harold Armstrong heard a *hoca*'s tirade in the almost deserted mosque at Eyup in 1925: 'Religion was killed by the government, who were *dinsiz*, without any religion; they had taken the religious money, starved the mosque officials and chased away the religious orders; the people wanted to come and pray but were afraid.'[2]

If traditional Muslims felt oppressed, so did Kemal's colleagues. From 1925, under the Law for the Maintenance of Order, the Istanbul press, once so critical, was replaced by Kemalist newspapers. Both the Socialist Party and the Turkish Workers' and Peasants' Socialist Party, were suppressed. Huseyin Hilmi, socialist leader and alleged British agent, had been mysteriously murdered – like several religious leaders – soon after the nationalist take-over of the city. After 1927 socialist May Day demonstrations, which had occurred since 1912, were banned. Internal passports were reintroduced. Kemal's photograph was displayed everywhere, as it still is. Turkey struck one visitor as 'the most insidious of all contemporary dictatorships'.

To challenge Kemal's autocracy, former colleagues planned a new party, or a rebirth of the Committee of Union and Progress. Kemal retaliated with a series of show trials by a supra-legal independence tribunal. Kazim Karabekir and Refet were acquitted. Rauf was briefly imprisoned. Halide Edib and her husband went into exile. Kara Kemal shot himself. Cavid, a former Finance Minister, was hanged.[3]

In exile Halide Edib, while admiring many of Kemal's measures, denounced his 'reign of terror' in her memoirs. Showing how much she had observed as a young girl in her father's office in Yildiz, she also wrote a superb novel of Hamidian Constantinople, *The Clown and his Daughter*, which praises the traditional neighbourhood life, the vivacity of the *tekkes*, the 'honey-gold' voice of a young Koranic singer Rabia in contrast to Western singers who sounded like 'a concert of yells and howls in a lunatic asylum'.

The veil was discouraged, although not explicitly forbidden. Within a few years, so strong was the pressure of the state that it was hard to find veiled women in Istanbul. In 1925 the fez, symbol of the Ottoman Empire and Islam, was outlawed: to wear it remains a criminal offence to this day. Kemal believed that the hat would make Turks 'civilized' in mentality and way of life and enable Turkey to take its 'rightful place in the family of nations'. Overnight Istanbul lost its distinguishing red cones and acquired thousands of black and brown hats. Halide Edib commented: 'The chief result of the "Hat Law" was that it enriched European hat factories at the expense of the already impoverished Turks.'[4]

Kemal had refused many invitations to visit Istanbul: he resented its criticism of his government in 1922–5 as much as its behaviour during the occupation. He finally returned in 1927, greeted by a delirious city. Entering Dolmabahce palace, he proclaimed that henceforth it would be, not the residence of the shadows of god but 'the palace of the nation'. (In reality the palace, where Kemal died in 1938, and lay in state in the throne room, was not opened to the public until 1981.) A year later in the park of Topkapi palace, he unveiled the most revolutionary change of all: the substitution of the Latin for the Ottoman alphabet. The motives were to spread literacy and, again, to align Turkey with western Europe. To a group of officials and their wives he said: 'We must free ourselves from these incomprehensible signs that for centuries have held our minds in an iron vice ... Our nation will show, with its script and with its mind, that its place is with the civilized world.'[5]

In Dolmabahce on 11 August he gave officials a two-hour lesson in the Latin alphabet: their Ottoman education, through which most already knew French, made the change of alphabet relatively easy. It was one of the few reforms of which some members of the élite at first disapproved. Fuad Koprulu, who had briefly been imprisoned by the British in 1920, was then teaching Turkish history and literature at Istanbul University. He wrote: 'Civilization cannot simply be assimilated by a change in alphabet.' The great Turkish Jewish scholar Avram Galante also defended the old alphabet. From visits to the Japanese embassy, he knew that a more complex alphabet had not prevented Japan from being the most successful example of modernization in a non-Western country. However, opposition disappeared, as it always did under Mustafa Kemal. Koprulu later became one of Kemal's circle, paying him more than a hundred visits in Ankara, many to his nocturnal sessions of drink and discussion.[6]

Another change was the expulsion from the Turkish language, after 1932, of what were called the 'linguistic capitulations' of Arabic and Persian words. Turkish was treated as a scientific terminology rather than a living language. Alien and often incomprehensible words derived from old Turkish, French, or the Kemalists' imagination, were substituted for the rich and varied Ottoman vocabulary (used to great effect in Kemal's own early speeches). Thus *mekteb*, the word for 'school', from the Arabic root for 'writing', became *okul* from the French *école*. Turks are cut off from their past. Ottoman literature and documents are incomprehensible: Kemal commissioned translations of Western, but not Ottoman, masterpieces into modern Turkish. The calligraphic inscriptions which are the principal ornament of Istanbul's monuments cannot be read by its inhabitants: the manner of their inscription, however, had usually placed beauty before legibility.

*

The success of Kemal's programme was helped by the élite's loyalty to the state and commitment to reform. There were few émigrés after 1924. The ex-Caliph Abdulmecid lived in Nice and Paris, attending both Friday prayers and classical concerts, wearing a fez made by an Armenian who had also left Istanbul. Like other exiles he believed that the pace of Kemal's reforms was leaving a void in the spirit of the people. 'It is not constitutions which shape souls but souls which shape constitutions,' he said. 'Suddenly to make a clean sweep is blindness.'[7] The last Caliph died in Paris in 1944. His son Omer Faruk Efendi had moved to Cairo. On the main wall of his study hung the framed telegram from Mustafa Kemal, which had ruined his life: 'Send back His Imperial Highness whence he came.'[8] By the end, having divorced Sabiha Sultan and married another cousin, he only wanted to return to die in Turkey. He died in Egypt in 1969.

The other members of the dynasty had been given one week to pack and go into exile. No exceptions were made. Suddenly uprooted from the city which was their whole world, people for whom even a trip on the Bosphorus was a major event scattered to the United States, France and India, as well as former Ottoman lands such as Albania, Lebanon and Egypt. A daughter of Abdulhamid, Ayse Sultan, who lived in France, wrote in her memoirs: 'We were a group of human beings without fatherland, without a home, without shelter. The history of our family in exile was just a sequence of tragic deaths.' Her brother Mehmed Abdulkadir played in an orchestra in Sofia; he was so poor that he was buried in a pauper's grave. Another brother Abdurrahim, a distinguished soldier in the First World War, committed suicide in Paris, leaving barely enough money to pay for his funeral. A sister, Zekiye Sultan, died destitute in a hotel in Pau.[9] Only in 1951 and 1975 respectively were Ottoman princesses and princes allowed to return to Istanbul. The present head of the dynasty occasionally visits Istanbul from his residence in New York.

Istanbul had no royalist movement or quarter like the Faubourg Saint-Germain in nineteenth-century Paris. By one estimate 93 per cent of Ottoman staff officers and 85 per cent of bureaucrats served the republic. The last Grand Vizier Tevfik Pasha, who died at the age of 96 in 1938, was buried with full military honours by the republic. On the site of the family *konak*, near Taksim, a present from Abdulhamid, his grandson erected the Park Hotel, which replaced the Pera Palace as the most fashionable in the city. The last palace eunuchs could be seen sipping coffee in Café Lebon on the Grande Rue de Pera, or walking with a special waddle as they showed visitors around Topkapi palace: it had opened as a museum in 1926.

Most 'compromised Turks' returned to Istanbul after Ataturk's death in 1938. The Caliph's secretary Salih Keramet, for example, taught at Robert College. He spoke so little about the past that many colleagues never knew that he had served the last Caliph. A typical trajectory was that of Edhem Dirvana, grandson of a Grand Vizier of Abdulmecid and descendant of Melek Hanim, author of the amusing but unreliable work *Thirty Years in the Harem*. Born in 1865, educated at Galatasaray and the administrative college, he had worked in Yildiz as a secretary and translator of detective stories for Abdulhamid. Finally, he fled to Europe. He served the Young Turk governments as a provincial governor, and Vahideddin as Minister of Commerce and Posts. In 1918–22, instead of joining Kemal, he preferred to stay in Constantinople in the late eighteenth-century Kibrisli family yali near the Sweet Waters of Asia. He was disgusted that the last Sultan left on a British battleship, but himself briefly left the country in 1923–5, to avoid a possible proscription. However, this product of the Ottoman palace supported every aspect of the Kemalist revolution. Like Salih Keramet, he never prayed or fasted in public; in old age he translated the *Discours de la méthode* of Descartes into Turkish. He died at the age of 96 in 1958, in his yali, which remains in the family to this day.[10]

However, the first years of the republic were, for some groups, an end. Mustafa Kemal was both saviour and destroyer. At the apogee of nationalism after 1920 most international cities were homogenized. Vienna and St Petersburg became provincial, Prague wholly Czech, Trieste Italian, Salonica Greek. Izmir was burnt. Delhi lost its Muslims. Istanbul held out later than most, but it too succumbed.

After 1923 the Turkish republic denied Kurds freedom and identity. Although initially the nationalists favoured Kurdish autonomy, from 1923 to 1991 the language was proscribed and Kurds were known as 'mountain Turks'. Lord Curzon pointed out that, for the first time in history, a Turkish government had decided that Kurds were Turks. During the occupation many Kurds had turned to foreign powers. The Bedir Han family, some of whom had helped Russia during the war, won a reputation for being pro-British and probably received money from the Greek High Commission. British intelligence reported that 'the Kurdish party in Constantinople had been taken over by the Greek authorities owing to the absence of funds at the disposal of the Kurdish leaders'. In 1925 the rebellion of Said Mullah – in favour of the Ottoman Caliphate as well as the Kurdish nation – was crushed.[11]

Thereafter the Turkish government hoped, in the words of the Foreign Minister in 1927, Tevfik Rushdi Bey, that the Kurds, 'inevitably doomed', would suffer the fate of the 'Red Hindus [Indians]'. He told the British High Commissioner in Baghdad that 'it was the intention of the Turkish government to expel the Kurds of Anatolia, just as they have expelled the Greeks and Armenians.' He and Mustafa Kemal talked of 'the defective mentality of the Kurds and of the impossibility of inducing them to accept the realistic and rationalizing policies of modern Turkey'. Thereafter large numbers of troops were deployed in the East; many Kurds were deported west; much of the area slipped out of government control. Istanbul lost its role as a Kurdish centre.[12] The Bedir Han family left for Cairo and Europe. Dr Kamran Bedir Han, born in Constantinople in 1895, died in 1978 in Paris, where he taught Kurdish at the Sorbonne. He had founded and funded the Institut d'Etudes Kurdes, which remains to this day the centre of Kurdish scholarship.[13]

Until 1940 the population of Istanbul remained stable at about 800,000. Cairo, whose population rose from 374,000 in 1882 to 1,312,000 in 1937, replaced it as the largest city in the Middle East and the focus of the Arab world. However much they loved Istanbul, most Arabs returned to their homelands. Like Greeks and Bulgarians in the nineteenth century, they found that the City was not enough. A prominent Syrian intellectual called Sati al-Husri had been head, first of the teachers training college in Constantinople in 1909–12, then of a fashionable mixed sex school at Nishantash called Yeni Mekteb. He had married the daughter of a Minister of Marine, and like many Arabs remained loyal to the Ottoman Empire until 1918. His wife would have preferred to stay in Constantinople. However, he felt that, since the empire had lost its Arab provinces, he had no choice. When he left in 1919, one city newspaper said: 'Syria has been severed from us.'

Through British intervention, another Constantinople Arab, a former deputy in the Ottoman parliament, the Sherif Faisal, had become King of Iraq. In Baghdad, as the new state's director-general of education, Sati al-Husri reorganized Iraqi education. The only links he kept with Istanbul, which he rarely revisited, were his wife (to whom he continued to talk Turkish) and the habit of employing servants. He died in Baghdad in 1969.[14]

Sherif Ali Haydar of the senior branch of the Hashemites also left Istanbul, on 4 March 1926. He wrote:

Of all my former so-called friends, only five came on board to say farewell. I was more pained than surprised because I knew the fickle character of these people but it seemed hard, having spent sixty years of my life in Stamboul . . . When we sailed I could not bear to see the last of my beloved Stamboul but I gazed towards the hills of Scutari and thought of my family at Chumlijah. I prayed also for the souls of my father and mother whose bodies were buried in a distant cemetery on the hillside. I had been unable to visit their graves and say farewell because of my national dress.* Everything is changed and because of this change what has the House of Muhammad not had to endure? May God have mercy on us!

With both his Turkish and his Irish wives, he settled in Beirut where he died in 1935. The house at Camlica was closed, the furniture sold. His sisters returned to Mecca; his brother went to Lahej in the Hadramaut; his son Muhammad and daughter Nimet moved to Baghdad.[15]

The new world of Arab nationalism met the old world of Arab Ottomanism, when a nephew of King Faisal, Abdulilah, Regent of Iraq, visited the city on a British warship with some of his ministers in 1945. Nuri Pasha, the Prime Minister of Iraq, had been a student at the military college in Constantinople but had fought against the Ottomans in the First World War; 'he ran from one side of the ship to the other to see again the places he remembered from his boyhood . . . While the ship passed the old city and the guns began to fire the royal salute, he stood gripping the rail of the deck and I saw the tears in his eyes.' Speaking the Ottoman which they used as a secret court language when they did not want to be understood in their Arab palaces, the Regent and his party called on his grandmother, stranded by history on the banks of the Bosphorus, in a yali in Emirgan: 'Even now in her old age, she had a brightness in her look and a vivacity of mind that would outdo that of many of her contemporaries of equal standing in the surrounding Christian countries.'[16]

However, just as most of the Czech inhabitants of Vienna – who formed up to 20 per cent of the population – stayed there after 1918 and became Austrians, so many Arabs (and Circassians, Albanians and central Asians) stayed in Constantinople and were transformed into Turks: Islam and the city proved stronger than nationalism. Sherif Ali Haydar's eldest son Abdulmecid returned to Turkey in 1951 as Jordanian ambas-

---

*All religious dress had been banned. In this city once so proud of its variety of costume, Arab dress might have been considered provocatively Islamic.

sador (there had been a reconciliation between the two branches of the Hashemites in 1931). His wife Rukiye Sultan combined the conflicting roles of Ottoman princess and Arab ambassadress with dignity and intelligence. She never commented on the new Turkey – although she frequently played the old Ottoman imperial marches on the piano. United by their love of Western music – Rukiye Sultan was said to be the best pianist in the imperial family, while her husband played the violin – the couple, who had no children, retired to a comfortable flat near Dolmabahce palace. Sherif Abdulmecid died in Istanbul in 1967, four years before his wife. Both his brothers, Sherif Muhieddin, a famous musician, and Sherif Faisal, a businessman, also became Turks and lived in Istanbul. They changed their name from Sherif to Targan – Turkish for Sherif – with the introduction of compulsory surnames in 1935. Modern and democratic in spirit, Faisal Targan forgot his Arab roots and became General Motors' representative in Turkey. None of the children of Sherif Ali Haydar inhabited the family house at Camlica. Today (1995) it is a shadow of itself. The different sections (*selamlik*, *haremlik*, library, kitchen) are in a state of decay or collapse. The park is a wilderness, surrounded by apartment blocks and shanty-towns.

The youngest sister, Sherifa Musba, married an Englishman called Fripp, moved to London and wrote a book of memoirs of Ottoman Constantinople called *Arabesque* (1944). The last surviving child of Sherif Ali Haydar is her sister, Sherifa Sfyne, one of the few people who can remember Constantinople before 1914. She married an Egyptian and, now widowed, lives alone in a flat in Alexandria. Like the rest of the family, she continues to receive money from the family *vakif* in Mecca, although the Sherifs lost the Hejaz to the al-Sa'ud in 1925. When asked about the past, she says: 'I forget, my dear, I am old now. I cannot remember all the past. Now I don't see anybody. I am sitting and reading here and doing nothing. People could live together in the old days. These days they are eating their eyes out. He [Kemal] destroyed the country.'[17]

To her regret, Istanbul, like Alexandria, has lost its Greeks. A government which had wanted to expel the Patriarchate itself, and expelled one Patriarch in 1925, did not make Greeks feel secure. From 1934 a law restricting professions such as dentistry, the law and pharmacy to Turkish nationals, caused a further exodus of Greeks with Hellenic nationality. Growing numbers of Istanbul Greeks paraded their sense of cosmopolitan superiority on the streets of Athens. Considering Hellenic Greeks little better than Albanians, and Athens itself primitive and dull, many felt more alienated in Greece than they had done in the Ottoman Empire: some later formed the basis of the Greek Communist Party.[18]

Constantinople was becoming poor and provincial. In 1923 a British officer reported that large numbers of Turks were near starvation: 'Practically all business has ceased in the port, leaving a hundred thousand Kurds and Lazzes out of employment.' Between 1925 and 1935, much against their will, the embassies left for Ankara: the old embassy buildings are now empty palaces, reduced to the status of consulates-general. The fabric of the city was neglected to make funds available for the new capital in Ankara. Travellers found Istanbul 'a dying city', of 'intolerable squalor'.[19]

Lack of money made people leave, as the lure of it had made them come. In 1920 Istanbul had 150,000 'White' Russians; in 1922, 30,000; in 1930, 1,400. Before 1914 the city had welcomed Jewish refugees from Russian pogroms; in 1941 it behaved as callously as other neutral countries. Packed with 769 Jewish refugees from Bulgaria and Romania, the *Struma* moored in the Golden Horn in December 1941. No one was allowed to land – partly at the request of the British Colonial Office, in order to prevent passengers proceeding to British-ruled Palestine, which banned Jewish immigration. On 24 February 1942 the boat was towed by Turkish ships out of the Bosphorus into the Black Sea, outside Turkish waters. There it blew itself up, or was blown up, with the loss of all lives on board.[20]

In 1942, in sinister conjunction with the height of Nazi power in Europe, the *varlik vergisi* or capital tax penalized Armenian, Jewish and Greek firms. In order to help the expansion of Turkish firms, they had to pay respectively 232, 184 and 159 per cent of their capital. Ancient businesses were annihilated overnight: their owners were left with nothing except eyes with which to weep. The printing firm of Fratelli Haim, owned by Italian Jewish brothers, employed Turks, Greeks, Armenians and Jews. It had been used by Avram Galante to publish, at his own expense, his many erudite works celebrating Turco-Jewish friendship down the centuries. As a result of the *varlik vergisi*, the Fratelli Haim had to sell their firm to Sumerbank. Galante, who was then a deputy, did not protest at his publisher's fate.[21] Istanbul lost its role as a magnet of people and ideas. Few refugees from Communist states in the Balkans settled there after 1945. Albanians headed for New York rather than their former capital.

Nevertheless in 1950 Istanbul still contained over 100,000 Greeks. In the early years of NATO, relations with Turks were relatively harmonious. However Refet's warning in 1922, 'that the Greeks if they were not actually expelled would be well advised to leave, as in future in a new Turkey they would be unable to make a living here', was finally fulfilled. The riots of 5–7 September 1955 were the beginning of the end. Troubles between Greeks and Turks in Cyprus, and a newspaper headline proclaiming that there had been a bomb attack on Ataturk's birthplace in Salonica were the pretext. Students, hamals and men from the suburbs smashed and looted Christian shops and houses. An American official wrote: 'I personally witnessed the looting of many shops while the police stood idly by or cheered on [the] mob.' Seventy-one churches and two monasteries were damaged. The next day people woke up to the sight of the former Grande Rue de Pera, by now renamed Istiklal Caddesi (Independence Street), carpeted from side to side in broken glass and bales of cloth. Trams could not run as the tram-lines were blocked. Ian Fleming, in Istanbul to cover an Interpol con-ference held in the Chalet Kiosk in Yildiz, wrote: 'Hatred ran through the streets like lava.'[22] Three factors show that the riots were organized by the government: absence of ministers from Istanbul (where most normally spent the summer); lack of damage to a world-famous target like the patriarchate; and the fact that there was only one death (an old Greek monk, at Balikli). The government used the riots as an excuse to impose martial law and arrest Communists.

The Democrat Party had been in power since 1950. A leading member was Fuad Koprulu, who had left his historical studies to become a deputy for Istanbul, and Foreign Minister. The grand viziers of his family had been famous for their efforts to establish civilized rela-tions with the minorities. Fuad Koprulu tried to blame the riots on Communists, although he later admitted that Adnan Menderes, President of the Republic, was responsible. As increasing numbers of Greeks left Istanbul, Koprulu maintained that their departure was evidence of their desire to expand their businesses abroad.[23]

Menderes was tried and executed in 1960, in part for instigating the riots. However his successors continued his policies. From 1964 to 1970 most remaining Greeks were expelled or encouraged to leave. Still some Greeks continued to live in Istanbul, trapped by old age, optimism, or love of the city. The last Greek layman to live in the Phanar was an official of the Ottoman bank, Theodore Charitonides, a bachelor who lived with his sister. By the end of his life, his clothes and his carpets were in rags: nobody came to their Saturday at-homes. He died in Istanbul in 1972. The last Phanariot by blood, and descendant of the

Mavrocordatos, to live in the city was Alexander Veglery, son of Gregory Veglery Bey, last Prince of Samos, and Anne Karatheodory; he died in Yenikoy in 1985.[24] Mavrocordatos and Mavrogordatos now live in Athens, Edinburgh, London, Paris – anywhere but Istanbul. In Greece and North America Constantinople clubs try to keep the memory of the Greek city alive. Every year a service is held in Athens cathedral on the Sunday nearest 29 May, the date the Conqueror entered the city. Afterwards a few elderly Greeks shout '*Athanatos, athanatos!*' (Immortal! Immortal!) in front of a bronze statue of Constantine XI, the 'Immortal Emperor'.

Of the 2,000 Greeks left in Istanbul today, most are over 65. Their schools and their churches are well maintained, since the Patriarchate still has extensive estates. However, there is almost no one left to attend them. The current Oecumenical Patriarch Bartholomew was enthroned in the Phanar in 1991. But the supply of trained Orthodox priests with the necessary qualification of Turkish citizenship is diminishing. The seminary on Heybeli, one of the Princes' Islands, was closed in 1970. The feeling of some Greeks attached to the Patriarchate, the oldest institution in Europe after the Vatican, resembles that of many Ottoman officials at the end of the empire: 'If we are going to die, let us at least die with dignity.'

The Armenian community has also declined, although not at the same speed. About 50,000 Armenians remain in Istanbul, with thirty-eight churches and twenty-three schools. There are no Dadians, Balians or Duzians in Istanbul today. Of the last Dadians, Anna Dadian went to Egypt in 1922 and married an uncle of the present Secretary-General of the United Nations, Boutros Boutros-Ghali. One Dadian worked on the Istanbul trams, another looked after Ataturk's horses. An Istanbul Armenian echoes Sherifa Sfyne: 'They are leaving, leaving, leaving continually. They are all afraid. People cannot accept to live together side by side.'[25] There are more Christians in the cemeteries than the streets of Istanbul. In the late twentieth century the idea that Greeks and Armenians were once trusted Ottoman officials – often preferred to Muslims – seems as repellent to their descendants as it does to some modern Turks. No peoples have suffered more from the fall of the Ottoman Empire than Greeks and Armenians. No European city has experienced such a transformation in its population as Istanbul.

The Catholic, Levantine world has also evaporated. The Testa family, the first of such families recorded in Pera, was one of the last to leave. The last Testa in Istanbul, Ipolit Bey, lived a life of leisure in a flat off

Istiklal Caddesi, opposite Café Lebon. He had married a member of the wealthy Greek family of Vitalis, but had become Turkish in nationality and sentiment. He died in Istanbul in 1960. His son Frederick also feels Turkish. Nevertheless he left Istanbul for two reasons. He did not want to slip into the condescending Levantine mentality; and he was not wholly accepted in the new world of Turkish nationalism. He had participated in the foundation of the Democrat Party with Celal Bayar and Fuad Koprulu in 1947. Yet he felt he had no future in Turkish public life, despite the many languages he spoke (Turkish, Greek, English, French, German). When his name, the oldest in Istanbul, was mentioned in conversation, because it did not sound Turkish, people asked: 'How can such a name be?' In 1950 he left Istanbul. His first sight of the West was the sign *Bevete Coca-Cola* in the port of Naples. Like many descendants of old Istanbul families, including the Ottomans themselves, he now lives in Paris. He still believes that 'After Istanbul there is nothing', and retails the message of Pera: 'One culture is not sufficient to feed any intellect.' The Turkish embassy is his second home.[26]

The departure of other members of his family from Istanbul to different European states obliged this family of diplomats, for the first time, to serve in armies. One member of the German branch died in the First World War, three in the second. A French Testa died in Mauthausen concentration camp. The Austrian and German branches are now extinct, but those in France and the Netherlands flourish. One Testa returned to Istanbul as French Consul-General in the 1970s – a Frenchman to whom Istanbul was a foreign city.

On 19 May 1971 Angèle Loreley, wife of the owner of the last French-language daily newspaper, *Le Journal d'Orient*, wrote: 'Some of our readers are asking for the articles on diseases and medicine by Dr Izzet de Taranto [member of a famous Sephardic Jewish family]. They are not aware that Dr Izzet de Taranto died in the United States . . . Messieurs Alessandri, Galizzi, Duhani* are also dead. The Baron de Verdor and M. Livio Amédée Missir continue to send their articles when they have something to say.' That year, when it had almost no readers left, *Le Journal d'Orient* closed.[27] The only French words visible on what was once the Grande Rue de Pera are stray inscriptions: *Cité de*

---

*Until his death in 1965, he continued writing light-hearted chronicles of the sunset of the Ottoman capital, ignoring the horrors beneath. He lived like a monk in an apartment off the Grande Rue de Pera: his wife had returned to Paris; his son had committed suicide.

Pera, Passage Oriental, S. Michdjian Architecte. Since they are inscribed in stone, they cannot be removed.

Outside the physical city of Istanbul, survivors from the old international capital were appreciated precisely for their cosmopolitan skills. Four chief ministers of Transjordan (including a son of Abdulhamid's adviser Abu'l-Huda), three prime ministers of Iraq, two presidents of Syria, a prime minister of Albania and the first foreign minister of Libya were among the many national politicians after 1918 who had been educated in Constantinople.[28] In 1919 the Grand Rabbi Haim Nahum had left for Paris – unpopular with Zionists for being pro-Turkish; with the Ottoman government for his support of the Young Turks. In 1924 he was appointed Grand Rabbi of Egypt by King Fuad, a son of the Khedive Ismail who knew Constantinople well. The King often summoned him to Abdine palace to answer questions, in Turkish, about problems of the day. They always began: 'How was it done in the Ottoman Empire?' He died in Cairo in 1960, listening to Turkish radio by the banks of the Nile, having ruined his eyesight by translating into French a collection of Ottoman firmans dealing with Egypt. Nationalism had destroyed his world. [29]

Another legacy of Constantinople was a Queen of Sa'udi Arabia. On a visit there in 1919, the future King Faisal of Sa'udi Arabia met his cousin Iffat al-Thunayan, member of a branch of the al-Sa'ud which had settled in Constantinople in the nineteenth century. After their marriage she brought the freedom of the Ottoman capital to the palaces of Sa'udi Arabia. She was described in 1931 as 'born and educated in Constantinople, strong-minded and determined to make a man of the Amir, who is alleged to be much under her influence and to have agreed to discard his other wives in her favour'. To this day she is the only Sa'udi consort to have received the title of Queen.[30] During her husband's reign, Queen Iffat's young Albanian half-brother, Kemal Adham, born in Constantinople and fluent in Turkish and French, became head of foreign intelligence and the King's most trusted adviser.[31] At present he is wanted by Interpol in connection with the collapse of BCCI.

At the same time as part of its human fabric, Istanbul has lost much of its physical fabric and artistic heritage. The process began in the late nineteenth century. By 1900, in circumstances which have never been elucidated, the 'Houghton' *shahnama*, one of the greatest of all illuminated manuscripts, a present from a sixteenth-century Shah of Persia to the Ottoman Sultan, had left Topkapi palace and entered the collection of Baron Edmond de Rothschild. The sinister dealer-diplomat F. R. Martin, dragoman in the Swedish Legation, who had helped arrange the first great Islamic exhibition at Munich in 1910, suggested that the manuscripts he was studying in Topkapi needed rebinding; he took the old Ottoman bindings for himself. Probably through the corruption of the mosque authorities, museums in Washington, Boston, Lisbon and Berlin contain panels, in some cases entire walls, from other Istanbul mosques. An Iznik panel from the mausoleum of Selim II beside Aya Sofya is now in the Louvre.[32]

Archives have also been lost. In 1931 the Ministry of Finance sold off old papers by the kilogram, for use as waste, to the Bulgarian government. As fragments fell off the lorries taking them to the railway station, the firman of a Sultan or the account book of a princess were found lying in the street. In the end Bulgaria returned its purchase. The remaining archives are so vast, and written in a language known by so few, that Ottoman history remains ill-explored. Once so familiar to the outside world, the Ottoman Empire has been termed 'the forgotten giant'.[33]

The great palaces and almost all the mosques remain. The skyline of domes and minarets is unchanged. However only about fifteen yalis and *konaks* survive. Already in 1921 Abdulmecid had written to Pierre Loti that Constantinople had become almost unrecognizable: 'On the sites of the beautiful yalis which are disappearing horrible factories are being built in reinforced concrete.' Aerial photographs of the period show that Constantinople already had many seven- or eight-storey blocks of flats. Street widening destroyed most remaining old houses in the Phanar in 1926.[34] The great cemetery of Uskudar has been eviscerated by a network of roads. Many other cemeteries, such as the Petit Champ des Morts, have disappeared together with their gravestones. Surviving Ottoman mosques and fountains are marooned in an ocean of concrete – the flats and houses built since 1940.

The 'Sweet Waters' of both Europe and Asia have become cesspits, so thick with filth that litter cannot sink to the bottom, but stays on the surface. The surrounding hills, like those around the Sherifs' *konak* at Camlica, are covered in villas and flats. The Bosphorus is being destroyed by its own beauty; villas and skyscrapers approach closer every year, in order to obtain a better view. It is no longer a 'diamond between two emeralds' but, for part of its length, a sewer between two housing-estates. Two motorway bridges span the Bosphorus, but, in relation to the size of the population, few ferries use the water below. The last kayiks were seen in the 1950s. The motor car rules.

The Istanbul Hilton, where Ian Fleming stayed during the riots in 1955, was the first of the modern blocks which have brutalized the skyline north of the Golden Horn. One of the worst architectural crimes of the last five years has been the construction of a glass and concrete hotel, sprawling insolently in what was once a pine-grove above Dolmabahce palace. Its weight threatens the palace foundations. Another giant hotel obscures the hill of Yildiz.

One reason for the rate of construction in Istanbul is the influx of Anatolians – seen by some as the provinces' revenge for five hundred years of neglect and exploitation. Since the 1940s they have been pouring into the city in search of work. To them Istanbul is an El Dorado of hope and promise. They have caused an economic and demographic explosion without parallel since the reign of Fatih. The city which once lacked large factories now contains almost half Turkey's manufacturing industry. Its inhabitants have incomes of $10,000 dollars per annum, five times the national average. It has become a city of 10,000 villages. Many districts are called 'little Gaziantep' or 'new Kayseri', after towns in eastern Anatolia.

The population of most megalopolises in Europe is stable: since 1945 London has declined from eight to six million. Istanbul, however, like Cairo or Mexico City, is a city whose expansion is out of control. In 1970 the population was three million; in 1985 five and a half; now it is at least ten and a half. Soon it will be, as at the height of the Byzantine and Ottoman empires, the largest city in Europe. Unless there is a relocation of industry to the provinces, or an entrance tax, the city cannot survive. The greatest enemy of Istanbul has proved to be neither Greece, nor Russia, nor the Allies, but its own inhabitants.

People whose families have lived in Istanbul for generations and speak with a traditional Istanbul accent, feel like a hunted minority. Horrified by the consequences of the national state for which they yearned, they make such remarks as: 'We've become aliens in our own city . . . Istanbul now is not Istanbul . . . *C'est devenu l'Anatolie chez nous.*' Some miss the rub of nationalities of the Ottoman city and revive at the sound of Greek spoken in Istanbul by tourists from Athens.

Some aspects of material life are improving. Trees and flowers are being planted throughout the city. However, cars, factories and the continued use of coal for fuel make pollution worse every year. In most districts, air filters are needed in the winter. Two million inhabitants are said to have no running water. Despite public protests, planning restrictions are regularly flouted. In the words of a Turkish proverb, 'He who holds the honey-pot is bound to lick his fingers.' Editorials today denounce corruption in the city with the vigour of Tevfik Fikret's poem *The Fog*, written under Abdulhamid: 'The growing stink engulfs Istanbul. The more people talk, the more we can smell the stink spreading around Istanbul. Plunder and injustice are leading people to turn to the Welfare Party.'[35]

For Istanbul is torn between two identities. On the one hand its role as battleground is symbolized by the rise of the fundamentalist Welfare Party and its victory in the municipal elections in 1993, caused by disgust with other parties as much as love for its programme. It remains unrepresentative of most inhabitants of the city. However, the veil has reappeared; the turban, although illegal, can be seen on the street for the first time in fifty years. *Tekkes* are reopening. The Koran is again recited in the Pavilion of the Holy Mantle in Topkapi palace. The call of the mosque gets louder, both metaphorically and literally, through increased amplification of loudspeakers on minarets. There is a movement to return Aya Sofya (secularized by Ataturk in 1935) to use as a mosque. Already a small section at the rear is used for prayers; and the call to prayer is broadcast from its minarets. In contrast to the melancholy ceremony in Athens, mass rallies, religious services and a reenactment of Fatih's entry on a white horse are now held every year in Istanbul, to celebrate the conquest of the city, and a public hoiliday is observed.

Another challenge facing Istanbul is the number of Kurds in the population, now estimated as 20–30 per cent. Hitherto they have been well integrated. Despite the disparities of wealth, there is less violence than in most other comparable cities. However, the continued war in the East between the Turkish army and Kurdish terrorists, and the policy of mass expulsions there, reminiscent of Kemal's policy in the 1920s, make this harmony unlikely to continue. The Turkish Republic has made impressive material and educational gains, raising literacy from 5 to 80 per cent in seventy years. However, certain human rights (freedom of expression, freedom from torture and imprisonment) are less secure than in some of the last years of the Ottoman Empire. In early 1995 Turkey's most famous writer, Yashar Kemal, was charged under the anti-terror law for expressing views sympathetic to Kurdish separatism.

Despite such tensions, Istanbul is beginning to resume its role as meeting-place. For the first time since the 1920s the city is part of the world economy, with a fully convertible currency. In 1995 the Istanbul Stock Exchange, equipped with the latest technology, opened at Istinye on the Bosphorus. Most Istanbullus accept modern international culture as whole-heartedly as the city's nineteenth-century élite accepted French culture. Only the occasional dome and minaret distinguish parts of modern Istanbul from other European cities. Clothes, music, night-clubs, in most of the city, are the same as in Paris or New York.

The fall of the Soviet Empire has hastened the rebirth of Istanbul as an international city. Manufacturing and selling more blue jeans and leather jackets than carpets and kelims, the Grand Bazaar and the surrounding hans have become the Oxford Street of eastern Europe and central Asia. The Russians are back, not as pilgrims, invaders or refugees, but as traders. At once Muslim and secular, Asian and European, traditional and modern, Istanbul is again, as in its Ottoman past, a crossroads of the world.

Glossary

aga: lit. master or gentleman – term frequently used for the head of an organization or tribe

akce: silver coin, the chief unit of account in the empire

amira: corruption of the Arabic *emir* or prince, generally applied to the wealthiest Armenian notables

avanie: sum arbitrarily levied on Western merchants

ayazma: fountain

Bailo: Venetian representative in Constantinople

berat: diploma bearing the Sultan's *tughra* (q.v.)

bey: gentleman

cariye: female slave, concubine

cavus: messenger, door-keeper, uniformed attendant, often used by the Sultan as an ambassador

celeb: cattle dealer

celebi: educated man, gentleman

dervish: member of a Sufi order, dedicated to reaching a higher plane of spirituality than non-members

devshirme: children levied from the rural Christian population, when needed, for service in the palace, the administration or the army

divan: the council presided over by the Grand Vizier which ruled the empire

donme: 'convert' – term especially used for Jews who converted to Islam in emulation of Shabbetai Sevi in the late seventeenth century

efendi: master, sir

fatwa: a written reply to a question concerning Islamic law

ferace: cloak worn by Muslim women outside the house

firman: an edict of the Sultan, generally bearing his *tughra*

gavur: non-Muslim; thence by implication obstinate, fanatical, cruel

gazi: victorious Muslim general

gozde: 'in the eye' – term used for a harem lady noticed by the Sultan

hadith: recorded tradition of the acts and words of the Prophet which is used to aid interpretation of the Koran

hajj: pilgrimage to the two holy cities of Mecca and Medina, incumbent on every Muslim at least once in their lifetime

hamal: porter

hamam: bath or bath-house

hatt-i humayun or *hatt-i sherif*: a formula written at the top of a *firman* in the Sultan's own hand indicating that he approved of its contents

hoca: teacher

hospodar: term often used for the ruler of Wallachia or Moldavia

hutbe: sermon delivered in a mosque on Friday, preceded by a prayer in which the reigning Sultan was mentioned

ikbal: favourite of the Sultan, with whom he had sexual intercourse

imam: prayer leader

imaret: public kitchen distributing food to the needy

jihad: war for the expansion or defence of Islam, the only form of war, in theory, permissible to Muslims

jirid: javelin-throwing on horseback

Ka'aba: black stone in the middle of the main mosque at Mecca

kadi: a senior judge administering both Islamic law and Ottoman administrative law

kadiasker: the highest posts in the Ottoman legal sysem. The *kadiasker* of Rumeli administered Ottoman law in the European provinces of the empire, the *kadiasker* of Anatolia in the Asian

kadizadeliler: followers of the zealot seyh Kadizade (post-1630)

kaimakam: deputy of the Grand Vizier, especially influential in the administration of the capital

kalfa: senior clerk; foreman in a craft guild

kanun: set of laws and regulations, mostly dealing with administrative or criminal matters, issued by the sultans and designed to complement *sheriat* (q.v.)

Kaptan Pasha: supreme commander of the Ottoman fleets

kayik: boat

kira: title used for female agents, often Jewish, of the Valide Sultan outside the palace

kizilbash: 'red-head': name for Shi'i enemies of the Ottoman state in Anatolia, or Persians, from their red head-gear

konak: mansion

kul: a slave of the Sultan educated to serve the state

kurush: small unit of currency

mahalle: quarter in a town

mahmal: splendidly decorated litter sent every year on horseback from Constantinople and Cairo to Mecca

medrese: colleges in the city which emphasized the study of the Koran, the *hadith* and Islamic law

Mevlevi: a dervish order especially devoted to music and dance

Mevlud: celebration in honour of the Prophet's birthday

millet: a community whose autonomous organization was recognized by the Ottoman government

muezzin: the man who calls to prayer from a minaret

Mufti: the highest religious official whose duties included giving written opinions (*fatwa*: q.v.)

Muharrem: first month of the Muslim year

musavere: consultation; thence, by derivation, consultative assembly

muteferrik: corps of artists and notables' sons attached to the Sultan who often acted as a mounted ceremonial guard

nahil: 'wedding palm' – wire structure decorated with fruit and flowers to symbolize fertility

Nizam-i cedid: 'new decree', term applied to the reforms of Selim III, especially the new military units he established after 1793

oda: room, office, or chamber; term often used for a military unit

orta: middle or centre; often used for a military unit

pasha: title awarded to senior Ottoman dignitaries, derived from *padishah*

peik: a palace guard whose members wore gilded helmets

reis efendi or *reis-ul kuttab*: the chief clerk in the Imperial Divan, who later acquired special responsibility for foreign affairs

sancakbey: governor of a *sancak* or province

selamlik: lit. the male quarters of a residence; also used for the ceremonial parade attached to the Sultan's public Friday prayers

seraskier: commander-in-chief of the Ottoman army for the duration of a campaign; later, the Minister of War

seyh: honorific term generally applied to *ulema* (q.v.) and dervish leaders

seyhulislam: the head of the *ulema* of the city, also known as the Mufti *sheriat*: the holy law of Islam

Shi'i: opponents of Sunni Muslims, who believe that religious and political authority belongs to the descendants of the Prophet's son-in-law Ali

sofa: hall or raised area within it

softa: popular term for students and drop-outs from the *medrese* (q.v.), frequently agents of civil disturbance

solak: a guard of archers with feathered helmets who formed the 60–63rd *odas* of the Janissaries and always accompanied the Sultan to war

sufi: one searching for a higher level of spirituality, through membership of a dervish order

surgun: deportation or forcible resettling of populations in the interests of imperial policy

tandir: brazier used for heating houses

Tanzimat: westernizing reforms imposed in 1839–76

tekke: dervish lodge

temenna: salutation, generally in the form of putting the fingers of the right hand to lips and forehead

tughra: the Sultan's monogram

ulema: graduates of the great *medreses* of the city who became professors, lecturers, theologians or lawyers

usta: master of a trade

vakif: a foundation, generally real estate devoted in perpetuity to religious or charitable purposes

vali: governor of a province

valide: mother of a Sultan

vilayet: province

voivode: title of Slav origin applied to the princes of Wallachia and Moldavia

voynuk: Christian militias maintained in the Balkans by the Ottomans

yali: waterside residence

yashmak: veil or cloak

zeibek: Turkish tribe in the vicinity of Izmir, distinguished by head-dresses, short breeches and slim figures

zikir: recitation of litanies in honour of Allah

Appendix I

Estimated population of Constantinople with percentage proportions
by religious affiliation where available

		Muslim	Orthodox	Armenian	Jewish	Others
1477	100,000	59	23	5	9	4
1557	550,000					
1689	600,000	58	34		8	
1794	426,000					
1885	873,565	44	18	17	5	16
1897	1,059,234	58	22	15.5	4.5	
1914	1,020,000	49	22	25	4	
1920	999,000	56	20	8.5	4	12.5
1927	694,292	65	11	7	7	10
1950	1,035,202	80	10	5	5	
1965	1,541,695	91	3	3	3	
1980	4,741,890	97	1	1	1	
1995	10/12,000,000	99.99	.0001	.005	.002	

'Others' include Catholics (always a small proportion) and foreigners, a large number of whom after 1830 were Greeks with passports from independent Greece.

Appendix II

Population of Constantinople compared to other major cities

	1500	1600	1700	1800	1900	1990
Constantinople	100,000	500,000	600,000	400,000	1,000,000	7,309,190
Cairo	150,000	200,000	200,000	263,000	678,433	8,630,000
London	50,000	200,000	575,000	1,117,000	6,586,000	6,393,000
Paris	200,000	400,000	500,000	547,000	2,714,000	9,318,821
Vienna	30,000	50,000	100,000	247,000	1,666,269	1,539,848

Sources for Appendices I and II: Kemal Karpat, 'The Population and the Social and Economic Transformation of Istanbul', in *Istanbul à la jonction des cultures balkaniques, méditerranéennes, slaves et orientales aux XVIe–XIXe siècles*, Bucharest, 1977, 395–436, and 'Ottoman Population Records and Census of 1881/2–1893', *International Journal of Middle East Studies*, IX, 2, 1978, 237–74; Halil Inalcik, 'Istanbul', in *Encyclopedia of Islam*, 2nd edn.; B. R. Mitchell, *European Historical Statistics 1750–1975*, 2nd rev. edn. 1981; *The Statesman's Yearbook*, 1994–5; Roy Porter, *London: a Social History*, 1994; PRO 371/5190.

Appendix III

Sultans after 1453

Mehmed II	reigned	1444–1481
Bayezid II		1481–1512
Selim I		1512–1520
Suleyman I, the Magnificent		1520–1566
Selim II		1566–1574
Murad III		1574–1595
Mehmed III		1595–1603
Ahmed I		1603–1617
Mustafa I		1617–1618 & 1622–1623
Osman II		1618–1622
Murad IV		1623–1640
Ibrahim		1640–1648
Mehmed IV		1648–1687
Suleyman II		1687–1691
Ahmed II		1691–1695
Mustafa II		1695–1703
Ahmed III		1703–1730
Mahmud I		1730–1754
Osman III		1754–1757
Mustafa III		1757–1774
Abdulhamid I		1774–1788
Selim III		1788–1807
Mustafa IV		1807–1808
Mahmud II		1808–1839
Abdulmecid I		1839–1861
Abdulaziz		1861–1876
Murad V		1876
Abdulhamid II		1876–1909
Mehmed V		1909–1918
Mehmed VI Vahideddin		1918–1922
Caliph Abdulmecid (II)		1922–1924

Key to Appendices IV–VII

SELIM II   Sultan, with dates of reign
Nurbanu   *Valide sultan,* with dates of office
====   Tie of concubinage
==== m.   Tie of concubinage followed by marriage

Sources for genealogies in Appendices IV, V, VI and VII: Yilmaz Oztuna, *Devletler ve Hanedanlar. Turkiye 1074–1990*, cilt 2, Ankara, 1990; Leslie Peirce, *The Imperial Harem*, Oxford, 1993; Milhail Dimitri Sturdza, *Grandes Familles de Grèce, d'Albanie et de Constantinople*, 1983. All genealogies are simplified to include only those individuals mentioned in the text.

Appendix IV

The Ottoman Dynasty 1500–1700

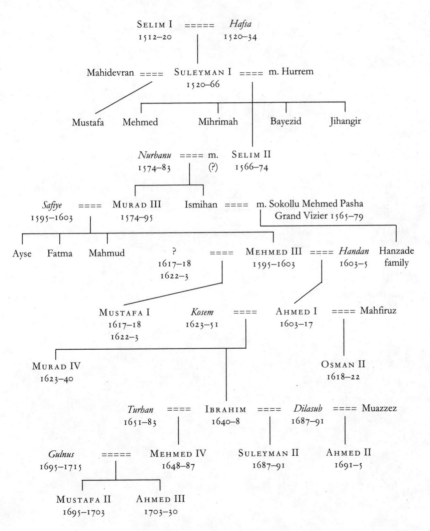

SELIM I ===== *Hafsa*
1512–20   1520–34

Mahidevran ==== SULEYMAN I ==== m. Hurrem
1520–66

Mustafa   Mehmed   Mihrimah   Bayezid   Jihangir

Nurbanu ==== m.   SELIM II
1574–83   (?)   1566–74

Safiye ==== MURAD III   Ismihan ==== m. Sokollu Mehmed Pasha
1595–1603   1574–95   Grand Vizier 1565–79

Ayse   Fatma   Mahmud   ?   ==== MEHMED III ==== *Handan*   Hanzade
1617–18   1595–1603   1603–5   family
1622–3

MUSTAFA I   *Kosem*   ====   AHMED I   ==== Mahfiruz
1617–18   1623–51   1603–17
1622–3

MURAD IV   OSMAN II
1623–40   1618–22

Turhan ====   IBRAHIM   ==== *Dilasub* ==== Muazzez
1651–83   1640–8   1687–91

Gulnus =====   MEHMED IV   SULEYMAN II   AHMED II
1695–1715   1648–87   1687–91   1691–5

MUSTAFA II   AHMED III
1695–1703   1703–30

441

Appendix V

The Last Sultans

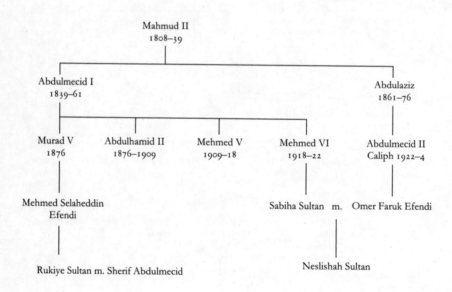

Mahmud II
1808–39

Abdulmecid I
1839–61

Abdulaziz
1861–76

Murad V
1876

Abdulhamid II
1876–1909

Mehmed V
1909–18

Mehmed VI
1918–22

Abdulmecid II
Caliph 1922–4

Mehmed Selaheddin
Efendi

Sabiha Sultan   m.   Omer Faruk Efendi

Rukiye Sultan m. Sherif Abdulmecid

Neslishah Sultan

Appendix VI

Koprulu Grand Viziers
1656–1710

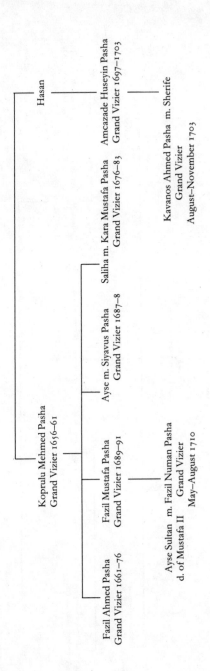

Koprulu Mehmed Pasha
Grand Vizier 1656–61

Hasan

Fazil Ahmed Pasha
Grand Vizier 1661–76

Fazil Mustafa Pasha
Grand Vizier 1689–91

Ayse m. Siyavus Pasha
Grand Vizier 1687–8

Saliha m. Kara Mustafa Pasha
Grand Vizier 1676–83

Amcazade Huseyin Pasha
Grand Vizier 1697–1703

Ayse Sultan m. Fazil Numan Pasha
d. of Mustafa II   Grand Vizier
May–August 1710

Kavanos Ahmed Pasha m. Sherife
Grand Vizier
August–November 1703

Appendix VII

The Mavrocordato and Karatheodory Families

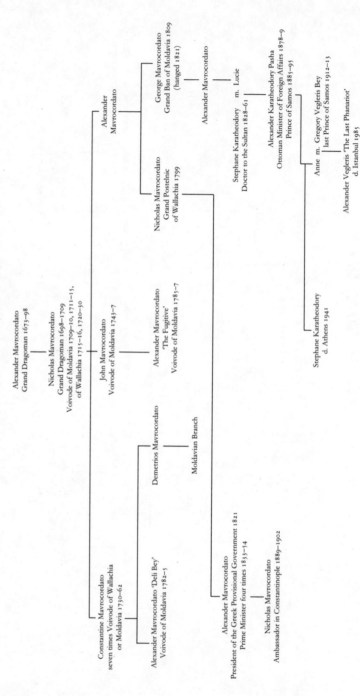

Alexander Mavrocordato
Grand Dragoman 1673–98

Nicholas Mavrocordato
Grand Dragoman 1698–1709
Voivode of Moldavia 1709–10, 1711–15,
of Wallachia 1715–16, 1720–30

Constantine Mavrocordato
seven times Voivode of Wallachia
or Moldavia 1730–62

John Mavrocordato
Voivode of Moldavia 1743–7

Alexander
Mavrocordato

Demetrios Mavrocordato

Moldavian Branch

Alexander Mavrocordato 'Deli Bey'
Voivode of Moldavia 1782–5

Alexander Mavrocordato
'The Fugitive'
Voivode of Moldavia 1781–7

Nicholas Mavrocordato
Grand Postelnic
of Wallachia 1799

George Mavrocordato
Grand Ban of Moldavia 1809
(hanged 1821)

Alexander Mavrocordato

Alexander Mavrocordato
President of the Greek Provisional Government 1821
Prime Minister four times 1833–54

Nicholas Mavrocordato
Ambassador in Constantinople 1889–1902

Stephane Karatheodory
Doctor to the Sultan 1828–61   m.   Lucie

Stephane Karatheodory
d. Athens 1941

Alexander Karatheodory Pasha
Ottoman Minister of Foreign Affairs 1878–9
Prince of Samos 1885–95

Anne   m.   Gregory Vegleris Bey
last Prince of Samos 1912–13

Alexander Vegleris 'The Last Phanariot'
d. Istanbul 1985

444

Appendix VIII

Principal Western artists working in Constantinople

Gentile Bellini 1479–81
Pieter Coecke Van Aelst 1533
Melchior Lorichs 1555–60
Jean-Baptiste Vanmour 1699–1737
Jean-Etienne Liotard 1738–42
Antoine de Favray 1762–71
Louis-François Cassas 1784, 1786
Luigi Mayer *c.* 1785–93
Antoine-Ignace Melling *c.* 1785–1802
Michel-François Préaux 1796–1827
Louis Dupré 1820–4
David Wilkie 1840–1
Amedeo Count Preziosi *c.* 1842–76
Edward Lear 1849
Stanislas Chlebowski 1864–76
Ivan C. Aivazovsky 1845, 1874, 1890
Fausto Zonaro 1893–1910

Notes

1 The Conqueror

1. Nicolò Barbaro, *Diary of the Siege of Constantinople 1453*, tr. J. R. Jones, New York, 1969, 67.

2. Tursun Beg, *History of Mehmed the Conqueror*, ed. Halil Inalcik and Rhoads Murphy, Minneapolis and Chicago, 1978, 37; Steven Runciman, *The Fall of Constantinople 1453*, 1988 edn., 147–8; George Sphrantzes, *The Fall of the Byzantine Empire*, Amherst, 1980, 130; Khoja Sa'd-ud-din, *The Capture of Constantinople*, tr. E. J. W. Gibb, Glasgow, 1879, 36.

3. Philip Sherrard, *Constantinople: Iconography of a Sacred City*, 1965, 16; Robert Liddell, *Byzantium and Istanbul*, 1956, 48; Laurence Kelly, *Istanbul: a Traveller's Companion*, 1987, 151.

4. Dimitri Obolensky, *The Byzantine Commonwealth*, 1974 edn., 375; Franz Babinger, *Mehmed the Conqueror and His Time*, Princeton, 1992 edn., 96.

5. Harry J. Magoulias (ed.), *The Decline and Fall of Byzantium to the Ottoman Turks*, Detroit, 1975, 233; Babinger, 230.

6. J. R. Melville Jones, *The Siege of Constantinople 1453: Seven Contemporary Accounts*, Amsterdam, 1972, 134, letter of 23 June 1453; F. W. Hasluck, *Christianity and Islam under the Sultans*, 2 vols., 1925, II, 737.

7. Julian Raby, 'El Gran Turco: Mehmed the Conqueror as a Patron of the Arts of Christendom', D.Phil. thesis, Oxford, 1980, 188; Babinger, 112.

8. Cornell H. Fleischer, *Bureaucrat and Intellectual in the Ottoman Empire: The Historian Mustafa Ali*, Princeton, 1986, 255–6; George W. Gawrych, 'Tolerant Dimensions of Cultural Pluralism: the Ottoman Empire and the Albanian Community 1800–1912', *International Journal of Middle East Studies*, XV, 1983, 523.

9. Kritovoulos, *History of Mehmed the Conqueror*, Princeton, 1954, 105, 177; Gulru Necipoglu, *Architecture, Ceremonial and Power: the Topkapi Palace in the Fifteenth and Sixteenth Centuries*, Cambridge, Mass., 1991, 250.

10. Babinger, 272; Halil Inalcik, 'The Policy of Mehmed II toward the Greek

Population of Istanbul and the Byzantine Buildings of the City', in *The Ottoman Empire: Conquest, Organisation and Economy*, 1978, 241.

11. Kritovoulos, 140, 148; Babinger, 328.

12. Runciman, *Fall*, 153; Babinger, 195.

13. Charles Schefer (ed.), *Le Voyage de Monsieur Chesneau d'Aramon, ambassadeur pour le Roy au Levant*, 1887, 261 quoting a firman of 7 May 1532; Kritovoulos, 94; Steven Runciman, *The Great Church in Captivity*, 1968, 169, 172–4.

14. A. Papadakis, 'Gennadius II and Mehmed the Conqueror', *Byzantion*, XLII, 1972, 103; Raby, 109.

15. Kritovoulos, 140; Raby, 247; Benjamin Braude, 'Foundation Myths of the Millet System', in Benjamin Braude and Bernard Lewis (eds.), *Christians and Jews in the Ottoman Empire*, 2 vols., 1982, I, 75, 79; Kevork B. Bardakjian, 'The Rise of the Armenian Patriarchate of Constantinople', in ibid., I, 90–1, 94.

16. Halil Inalcik, 'Ottoman Galata 1453–1553', in Edhem Eldem (ed.), *Recherches sur la ville ottomane: le cas du quartier de Galata*, 1991, 18; Jones, 133, letter of 23 June 1453.

17. Inalcik, 'Ottoman Galata', 61; Babinger, 107, 277; Raby, 172; Gertrude Randolph Branletter Richards, *Florentine Merchants in the Age of the Medici*, Harvard, 1932, 147, Giovanni Maringhi to Nicolò Michelozzi 29 October 1501.

18. Fernand Braudel, *Civilisation and Capitalism*, III, 1982–4, 467; Stéphane Yerasimos, 'Galata à travers les récits de voyage (1453–1600)', in Edhem Eldem (ed.), 117; Horatio F. Brown, *Studies in the History of Venice*, 2 vols., 1907, II, 4, 22, 29, 32; Lucette Valensi, *Venise et la Sublime Porte*, 1987, 27–9.

19. Anon., *Letters Historical and Critical from a Gentleman in Constantinople to his Friend in London*, 1730, 8; J. A. Blanqui, *Voyage en Bulgarie pendant l'année 1841*, 1843, 302; Hugo Schuchardt, *Pidgin and Creole Languages*, Cambridge, 1980, 67, 72. Count Pisani, British Dragoman, wrote to his ambassador in 1824 about 'the principal scales': British Museum Additional Manuscripts (hereafter BM Add. MSS) 36301, f. 268v, letter of 14 June 1824.

20. Joseph Hacker, 'The Surgun System and Jewish Society in the Ottoman Empire', in Aron Rodrigue (ed.), *Ottoman and Turkish Jewry: Community and Leadership*, Bloomington, 1992, 5, 9, 17.

21. Stanford J. Shaw, *The Jews of the Ottoman Empire and the Turkish Republic*, 1991, 32; Mark Alan Epstein, *The Ottoman Jewish Communities and their Role in the Fifteenth and Sixteenth Centuries*, Freiburg, 1980, 135; Avigdor Levy, *The Sephardim in the Ottoman Empire*, Princeton, 1992, 47.

22. Babinger, 75, 291.

23. Necipoglu, 57; Cemal Kafadar, 'Yeniceri–Esnaf Relations: Solidarity and Conflict', unpublished Ph.D. thesis, McGill, 1981, 14, 24–6; Apostolos E. Vacalopoulos, *The Greek Nation 1453–1669*, New Brunswick, 1976, 37; A. H. Lybyer, *The Government of the Ottoman Empire in the time of Suleiman the Magnificent*, Cambridge, Mass., 1913, 41.

24. Jones, 33, 128 quoting Leonard of Chios and Zorzi Dolfin; Yerasimos, 158; Nizam al-Mulk, *The Book of Government or Rules for Kings*, 1960, 103–4; Alberto Bobovi, quoted in *Archivum Ottomanicum*, XI, 29–30. By one estimate, of the first 48 grand viziers after 1453, only 12 were Turkish: see J. de Hammer, *Histoire de l'Empire Ottoman*, 16 vols., 1835–40, VIII, 421.

25. Yvelise Bernard, *L'Orient du XVIe siècle à travers les récits de voyageurs français*, 1988, 145: '*la plus frequentée et la plus estendue de toutes . . . d'autant qu'elle est commune aux Janissaires*'; cf. Matei Cazacu, 'Projets et intrigues serbes à la cour de Soliman', Gilles Veinstein (ed.), *Soliman le Magnifique et son temps*, 1992, 512; Babinger, 147. Another pair of brothers, one Muslim, one Orthodox, were the sons of the first Duke of Herzegovina. One succeeded his father in the duchy; another went to Constantinople, became Grand Vizier under the name Ahmad Pasha Hersekzade and married the Sultan's daughter.

26. Michel Lesure, 'Notes et documents sur les relations venéto-ottomanes', *Turcica*, VIII, 129n.; Geoffrey Goodwin, *A History of Otoman Architecture*, 1992 edn., 271–3; Runciman, *Great Church*, 204; J. A. Cuddon, *The Companion Guide to Jugoslavia*, 1986 edn., 323. The bridge is the subject of Ivo Andric's famous novel, *The Bridge at the Drina*. Sokollu Mehmed Pasha also commissioned buildings in Thrace, northern Greece, Anatolia and Medina.

27. Carlier de Pinon, *Voyage en Orient*, 1920, 111, 123; Esther Juhacz (ed.), *Sephardi Jews in the Ottoman Empire*, Jerusalem, 1990, 122; Albert Galante, *Histoire des Juifs d'Istanbul*, Istanbul, 2 vols., 1941–2, I, 112, 115, 122, 127.

28. Nicolas de Nicolay, *Dans l'Empire de Soliman le Magnifique*, 1989, 234, 236; Edmondo de Amicis, *Constantinople*, 1894 edn., 155–6.

29. Babinger, 424.

30. Raby, 231; Necipoglu, 12, 137.

31. Babinger, 472–3; A. Navarian, *Les Sultans poètes (1451–1809)*, 1936, 19.

32. Annemarie Schimmel, *Calligraphy and Islamic Culture*, New York, 1984, 73; E. J. W. Gibb, *A History of Ottoman Poetry*, 6 vols., 1900–9, III, 109, 121.

33. Babinger, 505, 508.

34. Babinger, 432.

35. H. Inalcik, 'Policy of Mehmed II', 244; Babinger, 272; Ashiqpashazade in Khoja Sa'd-ud-din, *The Capture of Constantinople*, tr. E. J. W. Gibb, Glasgow, 1879, 29; Stéphane Yerasimos, *La Fondation de Constantinople et de Sainte-Sophie dans les traditions turques*, 1990, 34, 85, 244.

36. Konstantin Mihailovic, *Memoirs of a Janissary*, Ann Arbor, 1975, 13; Tursun Beg, 33.

37. Nicolas Iorga, *Byzance après Byzance*, 1992 edn., 56–8, 60.

38. C. J. G. Turner, 'The Career of George-Gennadius Scholarius', *Byzantion*, XXXIX, 1969, 445; Vacalopoulos, *Greek Nation*, 121; Magoulias, 202, 208.

39. Donald M. Nicol, *The Immortal Emperor*, 1992, 98–102, 105, 109; Hasluck, II, 721–2; de Amicis, 186.

40. Robert Schwoebel, *The Shadow of the Crescent: the Renaissance Image of the Turk (1453–1517)*, Nieuwkoop, 1967, 153, 161–5.

41. Mihailovic, 145; Babinger, 317.

42. Jones, 134, letter of 23 June 1453; Babinger, 291–2.

2 City of God

1. Halil Inalcik, 'Istanbul: an Islamic City', *Journal of Islamic Studies*, I, 1990, 2; Khoja Sa'd-ud-din, 16, 33.

2. Andres Tietze (ed.), *Mustafa Ali's Counsel for Sultans of 1581*, 2 vols., Vienna,

1979–82, I, 56; Halil Inalcik, *The Middle East and the Balkans under the Ottoman Empire*, Bloomington, 1993, 28; Sir Hamilton A. R. Gibb, 'Lutfi Pasa on the Ottoman Caliphate', 287–95.

3. M. A. Cook (ed.), *A History of the Ottoman Empire to 1730*, Cambridge, 1976, 40; Yerasimos, *Fondation*, 172–3; El-Tangrouti, *Relation d'une ambassade marocaine en Turquie*, ed. Henry de Castries, 1929, 56–7.

4. Metin And, *Istanbul in the Sixteenth Century*, Istanbul, 1994, 90; *Encyclopedia of Islam*, 2nd edn. (henceforward referred to as *EI* 2), art. 'Istanbul' by Halil Inalcik.

5. Raby, 268; Yerasimos, *Fondation*, 147; Babinger, plate Xa; Evliya Celebi, *Narrative of Travels in Europe, Asia and Africa in the Seventeenth Century*, 2 vols., 1834–50, I, 71.

6. El-Tangrouti, 64.

7. Roy Porter, *London: a Social History*, 1994, 13; A. H. Wratislaw (ed.), *Adventures of Baron Wenceslas Wratislaw*, 1867, 32.

8. E. J. W. Gibb, *Ottoman Poetry*, II, 396; Goodwin, *Ottoman Architecture*, 121–31; Theodore Spandouyn Cantacasin, *Petit Traicté de l'origine des turcqz*, ed. Charles Schefer, 1896, 207; Inalcik, 'Islamic City', 10; Robert Mantran, *La Vie quotidienne à Istanbul au siècle de Soliman le Magnifique*, 1990 edn., 158.

9. Lybyer, 42, quoting Lorenzo Bernardo; Henry O. Dwight, *Constantinople and its Problems*, 1901, 79; Gibb, *Ottoman Poetry*, III, 133–51.

10. R. C. Repp, *The Mufti of Istanbul*, 1986, 144, 193; Thomas Naff and Roger Owen, *Studies in Eighteenth-century Islamic History*, Carbonsville, 1977, 19; Abdulkadir Altuna, *Osmanli Seyhulislamlari*, Ankara, 1972, *passim*. A Durrizade was Mufti of Istanbul in 1734–6, 1756–7, 1762–7, 1783–5, 1785–6, 1792–8, 1808–10, 1812–15 and 1920.

11. Faruk Suner, 'Yavuz Selim s'est-il proclamé Calife?', *Turcica*, 1991, XXI–XXIII, 343–54.

12. Suraiya Faroqhi, *Pilgrims and Sultans: the Hajj under the Ottomans*, 1994, 147, 150.

13. Goodwin, *Ottoman Architecture*, 15, 199–203; Aptullah Kuran, *Sinan the Grand Old Man of Ottoman Architecture*, Istanbul, 1987, 29; Evliya Celebi, I, 174.

14. M. Piton de Tournefort, *A Voyage into the Levant: Perform'd by Command of the Late French King*, 2 vols., 1718, II, 59; I. Mouradgea d'Ohsson, *Tableau général de l'Empire Ottoman*, 3 vols., 1787–1820, I, 287; Charles White, *Three Years in Constantinople*, 3 vols., 1845, I, 26.

15. Yerasimos, *Fondation*, 231–2.

16. Howard Crane, 'The Ottoman Sultan's Mosques: Icons of Imperial Legitimacy', in Irene A. Bierman *et al.* (eds.), *The Ottoman City and its Parts*, New Rochelle, 1991 edn., 201, 203.

17. Robert Mantran, *Istanbul dans la seconde moitié du XVIIe siècle*, 1962, 110.

18. Mantran, *Vie quotidienne*, 203; de Amicis, 18–19.

19. Lucy M. J. Garnett, *The Dervishes of Turkey*, 1990 edn., 73–4; Raymond F. Lifchez (ed.), *The Dervish Lodge: Architecture, Art and Sufism in Ottoman Turkey*, Berkeley, 1992, 297–301.

20. Garnett, *Dervishes*, 126.

21. Metin And, *A Pictorial History of Turkish Dancing*, Ankara, 1976, 40; Lifchez, 100; Garnett, *Dervishes*, 93, 119, 131.

22. John Kingsley Birge, *The Bektashi Order of Dervishes*, 1965, 128; Lifchez, 5, 170–1, 191; *Istanbul Ansiklopedisi*, art. 'Halvetilik'.

23. Dr Meryon, *Travels of Lady Hester Stanhope*, 3 vols., 1846, I, 51; Mouradgea d'Ohsson, I, 193; Evliya Celebi, I, 132; Adnan Adivar, *La Science chez les Turcs Ottomans*, 1938, 33.

24. Mouradgea d'Ohsson, II, 82–7; White, I, 230–5; Pierre Ponafidine, *Life in the Muslim East*, 1911, 281.

25. Faroqhi, *Pilgrims and Sultans*, 42, 57; Onnik Jamgocyan, *Les Finances de l'Empire Ottoman et les financiers de Constantinople*, thèse d'état, Paris, I, 1988, 41.

26. Barnette Miller, *Beyond the Sublime Porte*, 1931, 80, 82; Necipoglu, 151.

27. Philippe du Fresne Canaye, *Le Voyage du Levant*, 1986, 221–9; Mouradgea d'Ohsson, I, 205; Thomas Watkins, *Tour through Swisserland... to Constantinople*, 2 vols., 1792, II, 227. In 1828 Charles MacFarlane was impressed by the crowd 'still as death' watching the Sultan's procession: id., *Constantinople in 1828*, 2 vols., 1829, I, 499.

28. White, I, 229.

29. El-Tangrouti, 63; Mouradgea d'Ohsson, I, 305.

30. Stanford J. Shaw, *History of the Ottoman Empire and Modern Turkey*, 2 vols., 1976–8, I, 144; Elizabeth Eisenstein, *The Printing Revolution in Early Modern Europe*, Cambridge, 1993, *passim*; Fatma Muge Gocek, *East Encounters West: France and the Ottoman Empire in the Eighteenth Century*, New York, 1987, 112–13.

31. Yasin Hamid Safadi, *Islamic Calligraphy*, 1987 edn., 29–31; Schimmel, 71–2; Lifchez, 242; Bernard Lewis, *The Muslim Discovery of Europe*, 1982, 232.

32. *The Turkish Legacy*, exhib. cat., Bodleian Library, Oxford, 1988, 26; Runciman, *Great Church*, 273–4.

33. Marios Philippides (ed. and tr.), *The Fall of the Byzantine Empire: a Chronicle by George Sphrantzes*, Amherst, 1980, 123, 131 (chronicle of Makarios Melissenos); Mme B. de Khitrovo, *Itinéraires russes en Orient*, Geneva, 1889, 226; Jones, 108.

34. A. de La Motraye, *Voyages... en Europe, Asie et Afrique*, La Haye, 2 vols., 1727, I, 203.

35. Hammer, IV, 364–5; Jean-Michel Cantacuzène, *Mille Ans dans les Balkans*, 1992, 107.

36. Revd R. Walsh, *A Residence at Constantinople*, 2 vols., 1836, II, 386–8; cf. A. Goodrich-Freer, *Things Seen in Constantinople*, 1926, 112; Khitrovo, 269; Runciman, *Great Church*, 201–2.

37. John Covel, diary entry for 8 November 1674, in J. Theodore Bent (ed.), *Early Voyages and Travels in the Levant*, 1893, 146–8; M. Grelot, *Relation nouvelle d'un voyage de Constantinople*, 1681, 207; Vacalopoulos, *Greek Nation*, 121, 124.

38. La Motraye, II, 364; Runciman, *Great Church*, 324.

39. Runciman, *Great Church*, 331; Vacalopoulos, *Greek Nation*, 176.

40. Macarius, Patriarch of Antioch, *Travels*, 1936, 3, 85; Hammer, XII, 17.

41. Runciman, *Fall*, 189, 201; id., *Great Church*, 184, 190; Mantran, *Istanbul*, 48.

42. Julia Pardoe, *The City of the Sultans*, 2 vols., 1837, I, 443; Runciman, *Great Church*, 189; A. Paliouras (ed.), *The Oecumenical Patriarchate*, Athens, 1989, 65; Pars Tuglaci, *Armenian Churches of Istanbul*, Istanbul, 1991, 77, 121.

43. Wratislaw, 84–96.

44. Antoine Galland, *Journals*, 2 vols., 1881, I, 220, entry for 3 October 1672; cf. Grelot, 282–3; Nikolaos Adjemoglou, *The Ayazmata of the City*, Athens, 1990 (in Greek), 16–17, 167–81.

45. Adjemoglou, 64–5; Walsh, II, 388; Henry Carnoy and Jean Nicolaides, *Folklore de Constantinople*, 2 vols., 1894, I, 65–7.

46. Necipoglu, 231; Lifchez, 193, 133–4.

47. Mouradgea d'Ohsson, I, 286. The antiquarian Richard Pococke 'entered publicly at such of the mosques as I desired to see, and sometimes even on Fridays': Richard Pococke, *A Description of the East and some other Countries*, 2 vols., 1745, II, part 2, 133; Carnoy and Nicolaides, I, 172.

48. Tulay Artan, 'Architecture as a Theatre of Life: Profile of the Eighteenth-century Bosphorus', unpublished Ph.D. thesis, Massachusetts Institute of Technology, 1989, 159; M. A. Ubicini, *Letters on Turkey*, 2 vols., 1856, II, 359.

3 The Palace

1. Necipoglu, 242, 44; Shaw, *History*, I, 130.

2. Necipoglu, 15; Babinger, 418.

3. Necipoglu, 19.

4. Serif Mardin, *The Genesis of Young Ottoman Thought*, Princeton, 1962, 110; Necipoglu, 85, 107.

5. Mustafa Naima, *Annals of the Turkish Empire*, 1842, I, 327; Bernard Lewis, *Islam in History*, 1973, 211.

6. Babinger, 461.

7. B. Miller, *Sublime Porte*, 163; Leslie Peirce, *The Imperial Harem: Women and Sovereignty in the Ottoman Empire*, Oxford, 1993, 243.

8. R. B. Merriman, *Suleyman the Magnificent*, Harvard, 1944, 33.

9. Necipoglu, 36; Kemal H. Karpat (ed.), *The Ottoman State and its Place in World History*, Leiden, 1974, 51; Veinstein, *Soliman le Magnifique*, 166, 169.

10. B. Miller, *Sublime Porte*, 176; Necipoglu, 100; J. M. Rogers (ed.), *The Topkapi Saray Museum: Costumes, Embroideries and Other Textiles*, 1986, 161.

11. Mary Nisbet of Dirleton, Countess of Elgin, *Letters*, 1926, 56, to her mother 27 November 1799; El-Tangrouti, 46, 58; H. F. Brown, I, 20.

12. Lord Charlemont, *Travels in Greece and Turkey 1749*, ed. W. B. Stanford and E. J. Finopoulos, 1984, 168; El-Tangrouti, 61; C. G. and A. W. Fisher, 'Alberto Bobovi's Account of Topkapi Sarayi' (henceforward referred to as Bobovi), in *Archivum Ottomanicum*, XI, 1985, 23, 80; Alexandru Dutu and Paul Cernovodeaunu (eds.), *Dimitrie Cantemir, Historian of South-East European and Oriental Civilisations*, Bucharest, 1973 (henceforward referred to as Cantemir), 171; Necipoglu, 26.

13. Necipoglu, 249, 61–6; Nils Rolamb, 'A Relation of a Journey to Constantinople', in A. C. Churchill (ed.), *A Collection of Voyages*, 5 vols., 1732, V, 683.

14. Bobovi, 55.

15. Esin Atil, *Turkish Art*, 1980, 349; Rogers, *Topkapi: Costumes*, 160.

16. Rogers, *Topkapi: Costumes*, 11, 37 and *passim*; Atil, *Turkish Art*, 350; J. M. Rogers and R. Ward, *Suleyman the Magnificent*, 1988, 166; Babinger, 441.

17. Rogers, *Topkapi: Costume*, 21; J. B. Tavernier, *Nouvelle Relation de l'intérieur du Sérail du Grand Seigneur*, 1675, 112; Norman Itzkowitz and Max Mote, *Mubadele: an Ottoman-Russian Exchange of Ambassadors*, Chicago, 1970, 167.

18. Mouradgea d'Ohsson, II, 142.

19. Necipoglu, 68; Domenico Sestini, *Lettres . . . pendant le cours de ses voyages en Italie, en Sicilie et en Turquie*, 3 vols., 1789, III, 474, letter of 5 December 1778.

20. Esin Atil, *The Age of Sultan Suleyman the Magnificent*, New York, 1987, 62, 113; B. Miller, *Sublime Porte*, 215–21.

21. J. M. Rogers, *The Topkapi Saray Museum: The Treasury*, 1987, 40 and illustrations *passim*.

22. Halil Inalcik and Cemal Kafadar (eds.), *Suleyman the Second and His Time*, Istanbul, 1993, 33, 263–4; Rogers and Ward, 120, 123; Nevber Gursu, *The Art of Turkish Weaving*, Istanbul, 1988, 46; Wratislaw, 58.

23. Janusz Tazbir, 'Les Influences orientales en Pologne au XVIe–XVIIIe siècles', in *La Pologne au XVe Congrès International des Sciences Historiques à Bucarest*, Warsaw, 1980, 214. I am grateful for this reference to André Nieuwaszny.

24. Atil, *Age of Sultan Suleyman*, 31; Rogers and Ward, 187; Gursu, 167; Nurhan Atasoy and Julian Raby, *Iznik: the Pottery of Ottoman Turkey*, 1989, 76–7; Atil, *Turkish Art*, 283.

25. Rogers and Ward, 186; Atasoy and Raby, 14–15, 23; Atil, *Turkish Art*, 163–5, 198, 216; Gursu, 112–13.

26. Aysegul Nadir (ed.), *Imperial Ottoman Fermans*, 1986, *passim*; Rogers and Ward, 56.

27. Raby, 299; Bobovi, 25, 78.

28. *Vers l'Orient*, exhib. cat., Bibliothèque Nationale, 1983, 68; Bobovi, 29–30, 54; Barnette Miller, *The Palace School of Mohammed the Conqueror*, Cambridge, Mass., 1941, 7. The Muteferrik, another unit in the palace, were artists and nobles 'of all nations and all religions'.

29. Necipoglu, 111–16, 149; Bobovi, 37, 49.

30. Carter V. Findlay, *Bureaucratic Reform in the Ottoman Empire: the Sublime Porte 1789–1922*, Princeton, 1980, 37; White, I, 183; Fanny Davis, *The Ottoman Lady: a Social History from 1718 to 1918*, New York, 1986, 193.

31. Bobovi, 45; Carl Max Kortepeter, *The Ottoman Turks: from Nomad Kingdom to World Empire*, Istanbul, 1991, 133; Hammer, VII, 227; Gerald de Gaury, *Rulers of Mecca*, 1951, 129, 155, 161.

32. Celik Gulersoy, *The Caique*, Istanbul, 1991, *passim*; Major-General Sir Grenville Temple, *Travels in Greece and Turkey*, 2 vols., 1836, II, 18; Bobovi, 56, 61; John Sanderson, *Travels in the Levant 1584–1602*, 1931, 89.

33. Hammer, V, 138–45.

34. Evliya Celebi, II, 130, 147; Hammer, VII, 148–63; Jean Palerne, *Pérégrinations*, Lyons, 1606, 459; Peirce, *Imperial Harem*, 193.

35. Hammer, VII, 150–1; Pars Tuglaci, *The Ottoman Palace Women*, Istanbul, 1985, 333–5.

36. Tuglaci, *Palace Women*, 348–50; cf. Sestini, III, 443–9 for a description of a princess's wedding procession on 17 November 1778; F. Davis, 68.

37. Atil, *Turkish Art*, 186–7, 220–1; Tuglaci, *Palace Women*, 336.

38. Tuglaci, *Palace Women*, 341–3; Hammer, XVI, 36; Hans Christian Andersen, *A Poet's Bazaar*, New York, 1988, 120.

39. Tommaso Bertele, *Il palazzo degli ambasciatori di Venezia a Constantinopoli e le sue antiche memorie*, Bologna, 1932–X, 108; du Fresne Canaye, 60; *At the Sublime Porte*, exhib. cat., Hazlitt, Gooden and Fox, 1988, 15.

40. Evliya Celebi, I, 12, 101, 103, 131; Albert Vandal, *Les Voyages du Marquis de Nointel*, 1900, 62–3, despatch of 9 May 1671; C. Snouck Hurgronje, *Mekka in the latter part of the Nineteenth Century*, Leiden–London, 1931, 244n.

4 Harems and Hamams

1. Tuglaci, *Palace Women*, 155; F. Davis, 102.
2. Peirce, *Imperial Harem*, 40–4, 277.
3. Leslie Peirce, 'The Imperial Harem: Gender and Power in the Ottoman Empire 1520–1657', Princeton, 1988 (henceforward referred to as 'Gender and Power'), 98, 100–3.
4. Necipoglu, 163.
5. Gibb, III, 9; Talat Halman, *Suleyman the Magnificent, Poet*, Istanbul, 1989, *passim*; Veinstein, *Soliman*, 99.
6. M. Cagatay Ulucay, *Sultanlarina Ask Mektuplari*, Istanbul, 1950, 1–18 *passim*; Peirce, *Imperial Harem*, 64.
7. Peirce, *Imperial Harem*, 60–4.
8. Babinger, 66, 404–5; A. D. Alderson, *The Structure of the Ottoman Dynasty*, 1956, 26.
9. Sherrard, 54; Rogers and Ward, 9; Merriman, 76–7.
10. Merriman, 121, 122.
11. Bragadin, 1526, quoted in Lybyer, 53n.; Ulucay, 39–40; Geuffroy, quoted in Schefer (ed.), 240n.
12. Halil Inalcik, 'Sultan Suleyman the Man and the Statesman', in Veinstein, *Soliman*, 92–6.
13. Merriman, 185; Necipoglu, 257.
14. Peirce, 'Gender and Power', 157; Merriman, 187.
15. Ogier Ghislain de Busbecq, *Turkish Letters*, Oxford, 1927, 33; Gibb, III, 119, 131; Ulucay, 47.
16. Peirce, 'Gender and Power', 207; Benjamin Arbel, 'A Venetian Sultana?', *Turcica*, XXIV, 1992, 241–59.
17. Necipoglu, 95–6, 171–2.
18. Hammer, VII, 10, 283; Bobovi, 73; James C. Davis (ed. and tr.), *The Pursuit of Power: Venetian Reports on Spain, Turkey, France in the Age of Philip II*, 1970, 2–6.
19. J. M. Rogers (ed.), *The Topkapi Saray Museum. Architecture: the Harem and Other Buildings*, 1988, 27, 32, 34.
20. Peirce, 'Gender and Power', 180; Susan Skilliter, 'The Letters of the Venetian "Sultana" Nur Banu and her Kira to Venice', in *Studia Turcologica ... Alexis Bombacci*, 515–27; Necipoglu, 175; Kuran, 181.
21. Peirce, 'Gender and Power', 351; Tavernier, 257–62.
22. Necipoglu, 175.
23. Mehmed Ipsirli, 'Mustafa Selaniki and His History', *Tarih Enstitusu Dergisi*, IX, 1978, 437; Tietze, I, 60.
24. J. C. Davis, 147–9; Peirce, 'Gender and Power', 186; Spandugino in Lybyer, 144; Hammer, VII, 4.
25. Peirce, 'Gender and Power', 374, 380, 382.
26. White, I, 266; Bobovi, 26; Molly Mackenzie, *Turkish Athens*, 1992, 30–2; Nadir, 113.

27. Tuglaci, *Palace Women*, 84.
28. Mantran, *Vie quotidienne*, 81; Evliya Celebi, II, 11; White, III, 234.
29. Bobovi, 23.
30. Tuglaci, *Palace Women*, 156–9.
31. B. Miller, *Sublime Porte*, 26, 27; Chris Hellier and Franco Venturi, *Splendours of the Bosphorus: Houses and Palaces of Istanbul*, 1993, 215.
32. Peirce, *Imperial Harem*, 104–5, 244–5.
33. Peirce, *Imperial Harem*, 269–70; Hammer, X, 7, 72–5.
34. Hammer, X, 176–8.
35. Peirce, 'Gender and Power', 291, 112, 194–5; Charles Pertusier, *Promenades pittoresques dans Constantinople et sur le Bosphore*, 3 vols., 1815, II, 197.
36. Peirce, 'Gender and Power', 220, 257, 243, 279.
37. Peirce, 'Gender and Power', 273, 280, 286, 337n.; Robert Dankoff (ed.), *The Intimate Life of an Ottoman Statesman*, Albany, 1991, 27.
38. Pars Tuglaci, *Women of Istanbul in Ottoman Times*, Istanbul, 1984, 189–208; Robert Mantran, *Istanbul dans la seconde moitié du XVIIe siècle*, 1962, 504.
39. F. Davis, 132–3.
40. Sevgi Gonul (ed.), *The Sadberk Hanim Museum*, Istanbul, 1988, 172, 176; F. Davis, 69–76; James E. P. Boulden, *An American among the Orientals*, Philadelphia, 1855, 165–9.
41. Ian C. Dengler, 'Turkish Women in the Ottoman Empire', in Nikki Keddie and Lois Beck (eds.), *Women in the Muslin World*, 1978, 235–8; Hammer, XI, 435n.
42. MacFarlane, *Constantinople*, II, 521.
43. Tulay Artan, 'The Palaces of the Sultanas', *Istanbul: Selections*, I, i, Istanbul, 1993, 87–97; Mouradgea d'Ohsson, III, 315; White, I, 325. Until 1914 one reason for officials' reluctance to leave Istanbul was 'the great reluctance of our women to endure the hardships of the deprivations of provincial life': Marmaduke Pickthall, *With the Turk in Wartime*, 1914, 210.
44. Hammer, XVI, 20; Dankoff, 226, 233, 234, 259.
45. Bobovi, 70; Tijen Ozdoganci, 'The Ballad of Adile Sultan', in *Istanbul: the Guide*, May 1993, 55. On the death of Mustafa Reshid Pasha in 1858, his wife learnt for the first time that he had two other harems, each containing two young Circassian slave girls: L. Thouvenel, *Trois Années de la Question d'Orient*, 1897, 223, Comte de Thouvenel to Comte Walewski, 19 January 1858.
46. Cemal Kafadar, 'Women in Seljuk and Ottoman Society up to the Mid-nineteenth Century', in *Women in Anatolia: Nine Thousand Years of the Anatolian Woman*, exhib. cat., Istanbul, 1993, 196–7; F. Davis, 92.
47. Quoted in Alev Lyle Croutier, *Harem: the World behind the Veil*, New York, 1989, 154–5.
48. Peirce, *Imperial Harem*, 269; Kafadar, in *Nine Thousand Years of the Anatolian Woman*, 198, 204; Pertusier, II, 197; Leila Hanoum, *Le Harem impérial et les sultanes au XIXe siècle*, Brussels, 1991 edn., 29; *Don Juan*, V, 158.
49. Marquis de Ferriol, *Correspondance*, Antwerp, 1870, 267. Ferriol, the French ambassador, wrote on 16 February 1708 to M. Blondel de Jouvancourt, of 'les femmes de Constantinople qui me prêtaient de l'argent'; Kafadar, 'Women in Seljuk and Ottoman Times', in *Nine Thousand Years of the Anatolian Woman*, exhib. cat., 219–20.

50. Ulku U. Bates, 'Women as Patrons of Architecture in Turkey', in Keddie and Beck (eds.), 246–7.

51. Peirce, *Imperial Harem*, 209; John Freely, *Stamboul Sketches*, Istanbul, 1974, 110.

52. Fleischer, 53; *Journal of Ottoman Studies*, VII, Istanbul, 1988, 140; Louis Mitler, *Ottoman Turkish Writers*, Washington, 1988, 55, 81; F. Davis, 229–31; Schimmel, 47.

53. De Amicis, 221; Leila Hanoum, 150.

54. Pauline Johnstone, *Turkish Embroidery*, 1985, 9, 84; White, II, 104; Lady Mary Wortley Montagu, *The Turkish Embassy Letters*, ed. Malcolm Jack, 1994, 116, letter of 10 March 1718.

55. Galland, II, 59, diary entry for 20 April 1673; cf. Comte de Guilleragues, *Correspondance*, 2 vols., Geneva, 1976, II, 975, *memoire sur le commerce du Levant* 9 June 1684; Juhacz (ed.), 72–3, 80, 100.

56. Dorothy M. Vaughan, *Europe and the Turk: a Pattern of Alliances*, Liverpool, 1951, 132; Michel Carmona, *Marie de Medicis*, 1981, 126; *National Palaces*, Istanbul, 1992, 138.

5 City of Gold

1. Mantran, *Istanbul*, 25, 74; Grenville Temple, II, 14, 16–17; Pierre Gilles, *The Antiquities of Constantinople*, New York, 1988, 23–5.

2. Andersen, 99; Mantran, *Istanbul*, 72, 95.

3. M. A. Belin, *Histoire de la Latinité de Constantinople*, 2nd edn., 1894, 337, 341; M. du Mont, *Voyages*, 4 vols, La Haye, 1699, II, 374.

4. Necipoglu, 238; Vaughan, 169; Sestini, III, 230–8, letter of 8 May 1778.

5. Mantran, *Istanbul*, 88n., 481, 488, 583; Vacalopoulos, *Greek Nation*, 284–5.

6. Levy, *Sephardim*, 24; Halil Inalcik and Donald Quataert, *An Economic and Social History of the Ottoman Empire*, 1994, 95, 231, 248.

7. Richards, 163, 167, Giovanni Maringhi to Nicolò Michelozzi, 29 March 1502; 'il carico principale di un bailo di Constantinopoli è la difensione delle mercanze della nazione', Navagero, 1553, quoted in Horatio F. Brown, *Studies in the History of Venice*, 2 vols., 1907, I, 25; Paul Masson, *Histoire du commerce français dans le Levant au XVIIIe siècle*, 1911, 612; Susan Skilliter, *William Harborne and the Trade with Turkey 1578–1582*, Oxford, 1977, 50, cf. 115; Alfred C. Wood, *A History of the Levant Company*, 1935, 72.

8. Masson, 429, 454; Braudel, *Civilisation and Capitalism*, II, 471.

9. Mantran, *Istanbul*, 237, 241, 608.

10. M. de Thévenot, *Travels into the Levant*, 3 parts, 1687, I, 18, 62; Lord Charlemont, *Travels in Greece and Turkey 1749*, ed. W. B. Stanford and E. J. Finopoulos, 1984, 209; cf. 'The police of this city is in many respects beyond that of any other', Lord Baltimore, *A Tour to the East in the Years 1763 and 1764*, 1767, 58.

11. Anon., *Letters Historical and Critical*, 30, 38; Mantran, *Vie quotidienne*, 43.

12. Hon. Roger North, *Lives of the Norths*, 3 vols., 1890, II, 48, 53, 71–2, 148; Cemal Kafadar, 'Self and Others: the Diary of a Dervish in Seventeenth-century Istanbul and First Person Narrative in Ottoman Literature', *Studia Islamica*, LXIX, 1989, 121–50; Masson, *Commerce français au XVII siècle*, 468.

13. North, II, 407, III, 58; cf. Naima, I, 138 and Pertusier, II, 108 for other accounts of social relations between Christians and Muslims.

14. Daniel Panzac, 'International and Domestic Maritime Trade in the Ottoman

Empire during the Eighteenth Century', *International Journal of Middle Eastern Studies*, May 1992, 195–201.

15. Hammer, VI, 241; Charles Issawi, *An Economic History of Turkey 1800–1914*, 1980, 27; Mantran, *Vie quotidienne*, 127; Francis Peter Werry, *Personal Memoirs and Letters*, 1861, 90.

16. Mantran, *Istanbul*, 190, 198–9, 446n.; de Amicis, 71.

17. Anthony Greenwood, 'Istanbul's Meat Provisioning: a Study of the Celepjan System', unpublished D.Phil. thesis, Chicago, 1981, 4–5, 9; Naima, I, 37.

18. Greenwood, 13–14, 285, 122; Soraya Faroqhi, *Towns and Townsmen of Ottoman Anatolia*, Cambridge, 1984, 228, 231; Thévenot, I, 61.

19. Daniel Goffman, *Izmir and the Levantine World 1550–1650*, 1990, 34; B. Miller, *Sublime Porte*, 194–5; N. M. Penzer, *The Harem*, 1966 edn., 115, 128, 130.

20. Greenwood, 156, 162; Mantran, *Istanbul*, 181–2; Baltimore, 59.

21. Mantran, *Istanbul*, 351, 353, 380, 390.

22. Babinger, 452.

23. Jean Michel Cantacuzène, *Mille Ans dans les Balkans*, 1992, 102, 105, 121, 125–6; Emile Legrand, *Recueil de poèmes historiques en grec vulgaire*, 1877, 2–3, 8–9.

24. Vacalopoulos, *Greek Nation*, 209, 259, 285; Troian Stoianovic, 'The Conquering Balkan Orthodox Merchant', *Journal of Economic History*, 1960, 272, 302.

25. Greenwood, 54; Mantran, *Istanbul*, 366, 374; id., *Vie quotidienne*, 154.

26. Nicolas Soutzo, *Mémoires*, Vienna, 1896, 10, 24; Rodrigue, 21, 23, 37; Braude and Lewis, I, 105.

27. Richard Fletcher, *Moorish Spain*, 1992, 166–8; Halil Inalcik, 'Ottoman Galata', in Edhem Eldem (ed.), *Recherches sur la ville ottomane*, Istanbul, 1991, 68–70.

28. *Levant Herald*, 19 October 1869; Galante, *Histoire des Juifs*, I, 33.

29. Jak Deleon, *Ancient Districts on the Golden Horn*, Istanbul, 1992, 18 and *passim*; Shaw, *Jews*, 48–9.

30. Shaw, *Jews*, 84–5; Nicolay, 233–4.

31. Cecil Roth, *Dona Gracia Nasi*, Paris, 1990, 96, 115, 143; Epstein, 92–3; Maria Pia Pedani, *In nome del Gran Signore: inviati ottomani a Venezia dalla caduta di Constantinopoli alla guerra di Candia*, Venice, 1994, 154.

32. Cecil Roth, *The House of Nasi: the Duke of Naxos*, Philadephia, 5708/1948, 8–9, 170; Nicolas Iorga, *Byzance après Byzance*, 1992 edn., 50.

33. Roth, *Duke of Naxos*, 41, 43, 46, 95.

34. Galante, *Histoire des Juifs*, I, 188, Suleyman to Charles IX 23 March 1565; Roth, *House of Nasi*, 58, 60; M. de Charrière, *Négociations de la France dans le Levant*, 4 vols., 1848–60, III, 61, despatch of 14 March 1569.

35. Roth, *Duke of Naxos*, 50, 152; Michel Lesure, 'Notes et documents sur les relations venéto-ottomanes 1570–1573: II', *Turcica*, 1972, IV, 148; *Turcica*, 1976, VIII, I, 138.

36. Roth, *Duke of Naxos*, 108, 115, 137, 143.

37. Abraham Galante, *Appendice à l'histoire des Juifs d'Istanbul*, Istanbul, 1941, 163–6; Mantran, *Istanbul*, 605, 61.

38. Levy, *Sephardim in the Ottoman Empire*, 91.

39. Onnik Jamgocyan, 'Les Finances de l'Empire Ottoman et les financiers de Constantinople', unpublished Ph.D. thesis, Paris, I, 1988, 15; H. D. Barsoumian,

'The Armenian Amira Class of Constantinople', unpublished Ph.D. thesis, Columbia, 1980, 87; Walsh, II, 430.

40. Barsoumian, 64, 79, 81.

41. Onnik Jamgocyan, *Une Famille de financiers arméniens au XVIIIe siècle: les Serpos*, Paris, n.d., 368, 371.

42. Barsoumian, 160–2; Zabel Essayan, *Les Jardins de Silihdar*, 1994, 12–14.

43. Mantran, *Istanbul*, 463–4; Celik Gulersoy, *The Story of the Grand Bazaar*, Istanbul, 1990, 21, 55, 56.

44. Halil Inalcik, 'The Hub of the City: the Bedestan of Istanbul', *Studies in Ottoman Social and Economic History*, 1985, IX, *passim*; Gulersoy, *Grand Bazaar*, 29, 37; du Fresne Canaye, 95.

45. Pertusier, II, 177; Gulersoy, *Grand Bazaar*, 32, 50, 53, 70.

46. Hafez Farmayan and Elton L. Daniel (eds.), *A Shiite Pilgrimage to Mecca 1885–6*, 1990, 142–3; Stéphane Lauzanne, *Au chevet de la Turquie*, 1913, 226–7; *Istanbul Ansiklopedisi*, Istanbul, 1994–5, art. 'Buyuk Valide Han'.

47. North, II, 176; Mantran, *Istanbul*, 506–7; id., *Vie quotidienne*, 143; du Fresne Canaye, 94–6; Jean Chesneau, *Le Voyage de Monsieur d'Aramon . . . en Levant*, 1887, 34; Cantemir, 52.

48. Leila Hanoum, 54, 56, 58; Lady Hornby, *Constantinople during the Crimean War*, 1863, 364, letter of July 1860. In a list of 42 prominent slave dealers in the early 1880s, 14 were women: Ehud R. Toledano, *The Ottoman Slave Trade and its Suppression 1840–1890*, Princeton, 1982, 59.

49. Gulersoy, *Grand Bazaar*, 41; Inalcik, *Studies*, VII, 26, 47.

6   Viziers and Dragomans

1. Hammer, VIII, 289, 301, 305n., 310–11; Michael Strachan, *Sir Thomas Roe*, 1989, 145–8; Pierce, *Imperial Harem*, 171.

2. Paul Rycaut, *The Present State of the Ottoman Empire*, 1675, 46; Inalcik and Kafadar, 103.

3. Mantran, *Istanbul*, 102, 293, 303, 307, 321.

4. Findlay, *Bureaucratic Reform*, 55, 87; id., *Ottoman Civil Officialdom*, Princeton, 1992, 22; Charlemont, 168–70; Michel Lesure, *Lepante: la crise de l'Empire Ottoman*, 1972, 17–20; cf. Sir James Porter, an eighteenth-century British ambassador: 'there is no Christian power which can vie with the Porte for care and exactitude in the several offices; business is done with the greatest accuracy, in any important document words are weighed and that signification constantly selected which may most induce to their own advantage – and Papers of the remotest date, if the year of the transaction is but known, may be found at the Porte.'

5. Artan, 'Architecture', 97n.; id., 'The Kadirga Palace shrouded by the Mists of Time', *Turcica*, XXVI, 1994, 80–1, 105; Rifa'at Ali Abou el-Hajj, *The 1703 Rebellion and the Structure of Ottoman Politics*, Istanbul, 1984, 14n.; Nicolas Vatin, 'Les Cimetières mussulmans ottomans: source d'histoire sociale', in Daniel Panzac (ed.), *Les Villes dans l'Empire Ottoman: activité et société*, 1991, 157–8; Yilmaz Oztuna, *Devletler ve Hanedanlar*, II, *Turkiye (1074–1990)*, Ankara, 1990, 834–8; Sir James Porter, *Turkey, its History and People*, 2 vols., 1854, I, 317–18.

6. Mantran, *Istanbul*, 96, 252–3; Sir Thomas Roe, *Negotiations in his Embassy to*

the *Ottoman Porte from the year 1621 to 1628*, 1749, 37, 38; Peirce, 'Gender and Power', 295.

7. Metin Kunt, 'The Koprulu Years 1656–1661, unpublished Ph.D. thesis, Princeton, 1971, 32–4, 41, 141, 148.

8. Dankoff, 204.

9. Hammer, XI, 49–55; Dankoff, 204. The death of the Armenian Patriarch may have been caused by disputes between pro- and anti-papal factions: Leon Arpee, *A History of Armenian Christianity*, New York, 1946, 229.

10. John Covel, in J. Theodore Bent (ed.), *Early Voyages and Travels in the Levant*, 1893, 206, diary entry for 27 May 1675; B. Miller, 117; Bobovi, 57; Peirce, 'Gender and Power', 296n.

11. B. Miller, 116.

12. Hammer, XI, 6, 164; Mantran, *Istanbul*, 374; Madeleine C. Zilfi, 'The Kadizadeliler: Discordant Revivalism in Seventeenth-century Istanbul', *Journal of Near Eastern Studies*, 45, 4, 1986, 251–62; Charles A. Frazee, *Catholics and Sultans*, 1983, 99.

13. Abbé Toderini, *De la Littérature des Turcs*, 3 vols., 1789, I, 57; Bobovi, 57; Abdulhak Adnan, *La Science chez les Turcs Ottomans*, 121–3; Covel, 195, diary entry for 19 May 1676.

14. Levy, *Sephardim*, 84–6; Gershom Scholem, *Sabbatai Sevi: the Mystical Messiah*, 1971, 435, 450, 606, 674–9.

15. Hammer, XI, 260, 366, 379.

16. Abou el-Hajj, 82; Paul Rycaut, *The History of the Turks beginning with the year 1679*, 3 vols., 1687, 6th edn., II, 222.

17. Cantemir, 101, 190; Hammer, VIII, 305n.; Paul Fesch, *Constantinople aux derniers jours d'Abdul Hamid*, 1907, 282 quoting Vakit, 27 October 1876; cf. Findlay, *Ottoman Civil Officialdom*, 62 quoting the Kadi of Istanbul at a council in 1784 to the Grand Vizier: 'We are obedient and subservient outwardly and inwardly to the wishes and commands of our Sovereign who is Commander of the Faithful. It is impossible to obtain from us an explanation of why things have turned out as they have. You are the absolute delegate of our Sovereign. Deign [to tell us] what is the view of the Sovereign in this matter and we shall say we hear and we obey.'

18. Hammer, XII, 238–9, 305; Kenneth M. Setton, *Venice, Austria and the Turks in the Seventeenth Century*, Philadelphia, 1991, 371, 380, Sir William Trumbull to the Earl of Nottingham 6 November 1689, 15 June 1691.

19. Vahid Cabuk, *Koprululer*, 1988, 166, 175, 177; Hammer, XII, 307, 319–22; Cantemir, 102.

20. Cabuk, 178, 182; Lewis V. Thomas, *A Study of Naima*, New York, 1972, 31–2.

21. Rifa'at Ali Abou el-Hajj, 'Ottoman Attitudes towards Peace-Making: the Karlowitz Case', *Der Islam*, 1974, 136; Hammer, XIII, 29–30; visit to Koprulu Yalisi with Feyaz Koprulu, 27 November 1993. Feyaz Koprulu says the divanhane will be restored. But for scaffolding recently erected, this incomparable room, whose condition is an object-lesson in the disadvantages of communal ownership, would have collapsed.

22. Ferriol, 162, Ferriol to Louis XIV, 10 August 1700; A. N. Kurat (ed.) *The Despatches of Sir Robert Sutton Ambassador in Constantinople 1710–1714*, 1953, 17, Sutton to

Sunderland, 7 June 1710; Louis Rousseau, *Les Relations diplomatiques de la France et de la Turquie au XVIIIe siècle*, I, 1908, 298; Cabuk, 195–7; Cantemir, 193.

23. C. Bosscha Erdbrink, *At the Threshold of Felicity: Ottoman-Dutch Relations during the Embassy of Cornelis Calkoen at the Sublime Porte 1726–1744*, Ankara, 1975, 171, Calkoen to States-General 11 April 1733; interview with Orhan Koprulu, 5 November 1991.

24. Setton, 371, Sir William Trumbull to Earl of Nottingham 6 November 1689; Hammer, XII, 322.

25. J. H. Elliott, *Richelieu and Olivares*, 1992 edn., 160.

26. Nestor Camariano, *Alexandre Mavrocordato le Grand Drogman: son activité diplomatique*, Thessaloniki, 1970, passim; A. C. Stourdza, *L'Europe orientale et le rôle historique des Mavrocordato 1660–1830*, 1913, 354; Cantemir, 279; Piton de Tournefort, I, 385–6; Montagu, 126, Lady Mary Wortley Montagu to Lady Birstol 10 April 1718. The present author has met an Armenian lady of advanced age, living near Taksim, who claims to have visited Istanbul proper only three times.

27. N. M. Vaporis, 'A Study of the Zisking MS No. 22 of the Yale University Library', *Greek Orthodox Theological Review*, Fall 1967, XII, 3, 13, 27; G. Chassiotis, *L'Instruction publique chez les Grecs depuis la prise de Constantinople par les Turcs*, 1881, 27.

28. Hammer, XII, 141; Vaporis, 'A Study', 21; Camariano, 34, 68; SOAS Library MSS., Paget Papers, 50 X/4, letters of 23 February, 2 April 1699; Setton, 406.

29. Camariano, 78, 102.

30. E. Miller, 'Alexandre Mavrocordato', *Journal des Savants*, May 1879, 229, Daubert to Torcy 25 July 1698, 264; Galland, I, 237, 18 November 1672; R. W. Seton-Watson, *A History of the Roumanians*, 1934, 93–4n.; Ferriol, 116, Ferriol to Louis XIV 12 May 1700.

31. Hammer, XI, 425; Vaporis, 'A Study', 37; Camariano, 81, Mavrocordato to Patriarch 29 August 1707; Philip P. Argenti, *Chius Vincta*, Cambridge, 1941, clxxv.

32. La Motraye, I, 374; Iorga, *Byzance*, 135, 145; Stourdza, 98; Théodore Blancard, *Les Mavroyenni: histoire d'Orient*, 2 vols., 1909, I, 468; Comte d'Hauterive, *Mémoire sur l'état ancien et actuel de la Moldavie . . . en 1787*, Bucarest, 1902, 339, 346.

33. Cantemir, 158–64; Soutzo, 26–31; Michel Sturdza, *Grandes Familles de Grèce, d'Albanie et de Constantinople*, 1983, 142–3.

34. Camariano, 85; Cantemir, 144–5, 253; A. N. Kurat (ed.), *The Despatches of Sir Robert Sutton, Ambassador in Constantinople 1710–1714*, 1953, 29, Sutton to Earl of Dartmouth 8 December 1710; Cyril Mango, 'The Phanariots and the Byzantine Tradition', in Richard Clogg (ed.), *The Struggle for Greek Independence*, 1973, 44–5.

35. William Wilkinson, *An Account of the Principalities of Wallachia and Moldavia*, 1820, 135; Maréchal Prince de Ligne, *Mémoires*, 5 vols., 1828, I, 211–14, Ligne to Comte de Ségur 1 December 1788; II, 390–2.

36. Stourdza, 98–9; Baron Eudoxiu de Hurmuzaki (ed.), *Documente privitoare la Istoria romanilor*, Bucharest, 1912, XVI, 401, letter of 12 December 1716.

37. C. Mango, 'The Phanariots and the Byzantine Tradition', in Clogg (ed.), *Struggle*, 53; Ariadna Camariano-Cioran, *Les Académies princières de Bucarest et de Jassy et leurs professeurs*, Thessaloniki, 1974, 77; Corneliu Dima Dragan, 'La Bibliophilie des Mavrocordato', in *L'Epoque phanariote*, Thessaloniki, 1974, 209–16.

38. G. P. Henderson, *The Revival of Greek Thought*, Edinburgh, 1971, 23; Stourdza, 134.

39. Jacques Bouchard, 'Nicolas Mavrocordato et l'aube des lumières', *Revue des Etudes du Sud-Est Européen*, XX, 1982, 237–46; id. (ed.), *Les Loisirs de Philothée*, Athens–Montreal, 1989, 79, 101, 119, 149, 151, 181; Sutton, 203, despatch of 3 September 1714; Cantacuzène, 201, 207.

40. Vasile Dragut, 'Le Monastère de Vacaresti: expression des relations artistiques romanou-grecques', in *L'Epoque phanariote*, 295–300; Stourdza, 266–70 and figs. 26–33; Sturdza, 320, 328.

41. N. Iorga, *Histoire des Roumains et de la Romanité orientale*, 9 vols., Bucharest, 1937–44, VII, 20–3; *Fragments tirés des chroniques moldaves et valaques*, 2 vols., Jassy, 1843, II, 16, chronicle of Nicholas Muste.

42. Mihaila Staianova, 'Des Relations entre le Patriarcat oecuménique et la Sublime Porte en Constantinople au courant du XVIIIe siècle', *Balkan Studies*, XXV, 2, 1984, 449–56; Theodore H. Papadopoulos, *Studies and Documents relating to the History of the Greek Church and People under Turkish Domination*, Brussels, 1952, 52; Madame Chénier, *Lettres sur les danses grecques*, 1879 edn., 137, 190–1.

43. Denis Deletant, 'Romanian Society in the Danubian Principalities in the early Nineteenth Century', in Richard Clogg (ed.), *Balkan Society in the Age of Greek Independence*, 1981, 238.

44. Iorga, *Histoire des Roumains*, VII, 9, 154n., 164, 239; Marthe Bibesco, *La Nymphe Europe*, 1960, 306–7, Villeneuve to Maurepas 15 April 1731; Stourdza, 201, 210, 217.

45. Humurzaki, XIX, part I, 224, Raicevich to Kaunitz 30 November 1784; Paschalis M. Kitromilides, *The Enlightenment as Social Criticism: Miosipis Moisiodax and Greek Culture in the Eighteenth Century*, Princeton, 1992, 83, 94; Clogg, *Movement*, 36, 59–60; Richard Clogg, 'The Greek Millet in the Ottoman Empire', in Braude and Lewis (eds.), I, 185, and Braude and Lewis, 'Introduction', in ibid., 16–17.

46. John Cam Hobhouse, *A Journey through Albania and other Provinces of Turkey during the years 1809 and 1810*, 1813, 588–9; cf. A. de Juchereau de Saint Denys, *Révolutions de Constantinople en 1807 et 1808*, 2 vols., 1819, I, 156.

47. Prince Nicholas Ypsilanti, *Mémoires*, n.d., 72.

7 Cushions of Pleasure

1. Tulay Artan, 'Architecture', 9; C. R. Cockerell, *Travels in Southern Europe and the Levant 1810–1817*, 1903, 29.

2. Musbah Haidar, *Arabesque*, 1944, 42; Mouradgea d'Ohsson, II, 177; Du Fresne Canaye, 87; Walter G. Andrews, *Poetry's Voice, Society's Song: Ottoman Lyric Poetry*, Seattle, 1985, 134; Nermin Menemencioglu, *The Penguin Book of Turkish Verse*, 1978, 92.

3. Artan, 'Architecture', 320; White, I, 314; Du Mont, II, 114; Z. Duckett Ferriman, *Turkey and the Turks*, 1911, 300–2.

4. B. Miller, *Sublime Porte*, 151–5; Necipoglu, 200.

5. Thomas Hope, *Anastasius or Memoirs of a Greek*, 2 vols., 1836 edn., II, 124; Thomas Allom and Robert Walsh, *Constantinople and the Scenery of the Seven Churches of Asia Minor*, 2 vols., 1839, I, 25.

6. Allom and Walsh, 25; Boulden, 140–4.

7. Necipoglu, 202; Arthur Barker, 'The Cult of the Tulip in Turkey', *Journal of the Royal Horticultural Society*, LVI, 1931, 234–44; Nurhan Atasoy, 'Les Jardins impériaux sous le règne de Soliman le Magnifique', in Veinstein (ed.), *Soliman*, 239–48; Michiel

Roding and Hans Theunissen, *The Tulip, a Symbol of Two Nations*, Utrecht–Istanbul, 1993, 10, 54.

8. William Wittman, *Travels in Turkey, Asia Minor, Syria and across the Desert to Egypt*, 1803, 14; Dankoff, 107.

9. Artan, 'Architecture', 38, 162–3, 242; Du Mont, II, 113; Hope, I, 53.

10. Un Jeune Russe, *Voyage en Crimée*, 1802, 177, 199; Cockerell, 28–9; Montagu, 141, Lady Mary Wortley Montagu to Abbé Conti 1 April 1718.

11. Skilliter, *William Harborne*, 85; Carlier de Pinon, 111–12; Bobovi, 30; Ferriman, 325.

12. Nubar Gulbenkian, *Pantaraxia*, 1965, 130; Turabi Effendi, *Turkish Cookery*, repr. Rottingdean, 1987, *passim*; James Dallaway, *Constantinople Ancient and Modern*, 1798, 149; Ferriman, 326.

13. Stanley Lane-Poole (ed.), *The People of Turkey: Twenty Years Residence among Bulgarians, Greeks, Albanians, Turks and Armenians by a Consul's Daughter and his Wife*, 2 vols., 1878, II, 39.

14. Lewis, *Muslim Discovery*, 196; Katib Celebi, *The Balance of Truth*, ed. G. L. Lewis, 51, 58; White, II, 127–34.

15. *Istanbul Ansiklopedesi*, art. 'Kahvehaneler'; Allan Ramsay and Francis McCullagh, *Tales from Turkey*, 1914, xxii, xxviii.

16. Hammer, XI, 286, 335; Bernard Lewis, *Istanbul and the Civilization of the Ottoman Empire*, Norman, Oklahoma, 1963, 132–3.

17. White, I, 282.

18. F. Billacois (ed.), *L'Empire du Grand Turc vu par un sujet de Louis XIV*, 1965, 96; Walsh, II, 500; Freely, 93; Ramsay and McCullagh, 57–9.

19. Charlemont, 166–7.

20. Hammer, XVI, 64–5; Baron de Tott, *Memoirs concerning the State of the Turkish Empire and the Crimea*, 4 parts, 1786, I, 140; Mouradgea d'Ohsson, II, 121.

21. Artan, 'Architecture', 207, 410, 411; Gibb, II, 227; Mantran, *Istanbul*, 106; Mitler, 107.

22. Hammer, XV, 143.

23. Talat S. Halman, *Suleyman the Magnificent, Poet*, Istanbul, 1989, 53–4; Evliya Celebi, I, 134; Hammer, VI, 279, VIII, 323; Menemencioglu, 100; Mittler, 151.

24. And, *Istanbul*, 193; Maréchal de Moltke, *Lettres . . . sur l'Orient*, 1877 edn., 36–7, letter of 12 February 1836; Gibb, IV, 68; F. Munir Katircioglu, 'Ottoman Culinary Habits', in Feyzi Halici (ed.), *First International Food Congress Turkey 1986*, Ankara, 1988, 163–5.

25. Murat Bardakgi, *Osmanlida Seks*, 1993, 117.

26. Elias Habesci, *The Present State of the Ottoman Empire*, 1784, 388; Tott, I, 163; Melek Hanim, *Thirty Years in the Harem*, 1872, 245.

27. Bardakgi, 132; Ulucay, *Ask Mektuplari*, 203–5, letter of 11 August 1875.

28. And, *Istanbul*, 211; Alfred C. Wood, 'The British Embassy in Constantinople', *English Historical Review*, XL, 1925, 551; Charlemont, 204–6; Habesci, 175, 393. The sexual use of graveyards continued into this century, as readers of Claude Farrère's *L'Homme qui assassina* will recall.

29. Necipoglu, 210, 216–17; Alderson, Table XXVII; Kritovoulos, 61; Raymond T. Macnuly and Radu R. Florescu, *Dracula, His Life and His Times*, 1989, 150; Babinger, 207.

30. Carlier de Pinon, 119; White, I, 195; And, *Turkish Dancing*, 140–1.

31. Wratislaw, 54 describes Cigala Pasha, originally from the Kingdom of Naples, who 'having once tasted Turkish freedom and pleasures proceeded gradually to worse and worse till now he will have nothing to do with Christianity'; Lady Hornby, 394, on 26 June 1856 meets Slade Pasha who 'infinitely prefers the ease and freedom of an Eastern life to the rigid conventionalisms of London and Paris'; Valensi, 47; Pedani, 42. However in 1577 the government tried to forbid 'quel vitio della natione turchesca': Hammer, VII, 133n.

32. Gibb, III, 55, 123; Menemencioglu, 108–9.

33. Dankoff, 278; Gibb, IV, 56.

34. Gibb, IV, 220–42; Bardakgi, 103–32. Sunbulzade Vehbi, who died in 1809, also alternately praised and criticized, in graphic terms, the sexual advantages of women and boys.

35. De Amicis, 147; Raphaela Lewis, *Everyday Life in the Ottoman Empire*, 124–7; Tott, I, 175.

36. Abou el-Hajj, *The 1703 Rebellion*, 31–3, 86.

37. Necipoglu, 258; Artan, 'Architecture', 36, 38.

38. B. Miller, *Sublime Porte*, 226, 125; Gocek, 77, 79.

39. Gibb, IV, 30; Menemencioglu, 113; Mitler, 106–7; Epiphanius Wilson, *Turkish Literature*, 1901, 181–3; *Anka: Revue d'art et de littérature de Turquie*, VII–VIII, 1989, 44–6.

40. Levy, *Sephardim*, 77; André Philippides, *Hommes et idées du Sud-Est Européen à l'aube de l'âge moderne*, 1980, 243, Daniel de Fonseca to Jean Leclerc 1 March 1724; Montagu, 142, Lady Mary Wortley Montagu to Abbé Conti 19 May 1718.

41. Turhan Baytop, 'The Tulip in Istanbul during the Ottoman Period', in Roding and Theunissen (eds.), 53, 55.

42. Artan, 'Architecture', 166; Gocek, 130; B. Miller, *Sublime Porte*, 125.

43. Artan, 'Architecture', 166, 201, 360, 414; Artun and Beyhan Unsal, *Istanbul la magnifique: propos de table et recettes*, 1991, 77.

44. E. Wilson, 182; Ligne, I, 214, Ligne to Comte de Ségur 1 December 1788.

45. Charlemont, 204–5; Bosscha Erdbrink, 138, Calkoen to States-General 22 March 1739.

46. Niyazi Berkes, *The Development of Secularism in Turkey*, Montreal, 1964, 37–42; Gocek, 113; César de Saussure, *Lettres de Turquie*, ed. Coloman de Thaly, Budapest, 1909, 94, letter of 21 February 1732; B. Miller, *Sublime Porte*, 110.

47. Levy, *Sephardim*, 90; de Saussure, 94, letter of 1 February 1732; Berkes, *Secularism*, 42–5.

48. Robert W. Olson, *The Siege of Mosul and Ottoman-Persian Relations 1718–1743*, Bloomington, 1975, 66, 71, 74–5; Mardin, *Genesis*, 433; Bosscha Erdbrink, 93–5.

49. Olson, 79; Bosscha Erdbrink, 95, despatch of Cornelius Calkoen 13 November 1730; Albert Vandal, *Une Ambassade française en Orient sous Louis XV: la mission de Marquis de Villeneuve 1728–1741*, 1887, 155–6, despatch of Villeneuve 7 October 1730; Gocek, 159.

50. Mary Lucille Shay, *The Ottoman Empire from 1720 to 1734 as revealed in Despatches of Venetian Baili*, Urbana, 1944, 31–3; Olson, 80.

8 Ambassadors and Artists

1. Hammer, VIII, 148.

2. Merriman, 236; Colin Imber, 'The Ottoman Dynastic Myth', *Turcica*, 1987, 22.

3. Naimur Rahman Farooqi, *Mughal-Ottoman Relations*, Delhi, 1989, 23, 29, 88, 195.

4. Lewis, *Muslim Discovery*, 118, 45; Merriman, 133, quoting the chronicle of Kemal Pashazade; Pierre Duparc, *Recueil des instructions données aux ambassadeurs et ministres de France*, 1969, 16, 259, instructions of 22 August 1665, 6 March 1724.

5. Vaughan, 124, 127, 129.

6. M. S. Anderson, *The Rise of Modern Diplomacy*, 1993, 28; Peirce, 'Gender and Power', 120–1.

7. Busbecq, 183; Hammer, VI, 148; Skilliter, *William Harborne*, 63, Joachim Von Sinzendorf to Rudolf II 24 March 1579.

8. Hammer, V, 149, 151n., letter of February 1526, 333, VII, 185; M. S. Anderson, 72.

9. Pedani, 203–8.

10. Jacques Lefort, *Documents grecs dans les Archives de Topkapi Sarayi: contribution à l'histoire de Cem Sultan*, Ankara, 1981, 20; Bobovi, 12; Baron de Dedem de Gelder, *Mémoires*, 1900, 25; Habesci, 268. Fatih boasted that his clandestine network of informers in Italy gave him intimate knowledge of events: Raby, 285.

11. Hammer, IV, 48, 138.

12. Bosscha Erdbrink, 119, 123.

13. Guilleragues, 908–9; Belin, 314; Galland, II, 52, diary entry for 2 April 1673; Vandal, *Une Ambassade française*, 38.

14. Alberto Tenenti, *Piracy and the Decline of Venice 1580–1615*, 1967, 72; *L'Orient des provençaux dans l'histoire*, exhib. cat., Marseilles, 1982, 280.

15. William Hunter, *Travels through France, Turkey and Hungary to Vienna in 1792*, 3rd edn., 2 vols., 1803, I, 323.

16. Wood, *Levant Company*, 238; Hammer, XII, 10. The ostentation of Polish processions continued until the end of the kingdom: see Dedem de Gelder, 37.

17. Marquis de Bonnac, *Mémoire historique sur l'Ambassade de France à Constantinople*, 1894, 12; Gerard Tongas, *Les Relations de la France avec l'Empire Ottoman durant la première moitié du XVIIe siècle*, Toulouse, 1942, 23–31, 37; Hammer, XI, 229–30, 346; G. F. Abbott, *Under the Turk in Constantinople*, 1920, 102, 9 September 1675.

18. Hammer, XI, 255, 259, 282, XII, 8; Covel, in Bent (ed.), 194, diary entry for 19 May 1675; Comte de Saint-Priest, *Mémoires sur l'Ambassade de France en Turquie*, 1877, 231; Vandal, *Voyages*, 216, 232.

19. Guilleragues, I, 192, 436, 473: *mémoire pour servir d'instruction au Sr. de Guilleragues*, 10 June 1679, Guilleragues to Louis XIV 24 May 1680, 12 September, 25 October 1681; Hammer, XII, 56, 167; Piton de Tournefort, II, 27.

20. Bonnac, 43–5; Ferriol, 75–9, Ferriol to Louis XIV 8 January 1700; cf. for other accounts of the same incident, La Motraye, I, 272; Piton de Tournefort I, 397–401.

21. Cantemir, 261; Ferriol, 190, letter of 25 July 1707; William Miller, *Travel and Politics in the Near East*, 1897, 428; Hammer, IX, 113.

22. La Motraye, I, 369; Vandal, *Une Ambassade française*, 40; H. Riondel, *Le Bienheureux Gomidas de Constantinople, prêtre arménien et martyr*, 1929, 137; Hammer, XIII, 41.

23. Archives du Ministère des Affaires Etrangères, Paris (henceforward referred to as AAE), Turquie, 68: *Relation de l'audience que j'aye eue du grand Vizir Ibrahim Pacha Gendre du Grand Seigneur le mardi 10 Octobre dans son palais de Constantinople.*

24. State Archives, Stockholm, Turcica, 100, Bonneval to Hoepken 6 September 1738, 14 May 1741, to G. Bonde 4 September 1736, to Horn 4 August 1735.

25. Hammer, XV, 365–78, Desalleurs to Bonneval 23 December 1746, Castellane to d'Argneson 23 March 1747.

26. State Archives, Stockholm, Turcica, 100, Bonneval to Hoepken 19 December 1735, 21 January 1744.

27. *Revue d'Histoire Diplomatique*, 1987, 234–5; cf. Virginia Aksan, 'Ottoman-French Relations 1739–68', in *Studies in Ottoman Diplomatic History*, ed. Sinan Kuneralp, 5 vols., Istanbul, 1987–90, I, 50, 56; Vassif Efendi, *Précis historique de la guerre des Turcs contre les Russes*, ed. P. A. Caussin de Perceval, 1822, 6–7; Hammer, XVI, 179, 184, 203–5, 228.

28. Onnik Jamgocyan, 'L'Apprivoisonnement de Constantinople, la Révolution française et le déclin du négoce français', *Arab Historical Review for Ottoman Studies*, VII, October 1993, 129–33; Tott, II, 123, 149, 167, 205, 255, III, 149, IV, 255.

29. Berkes, *Development of Secularism*, 54; Itzkowitz and Mote, 161.

30. Hugh Ragsdale (ed.), *Imperial Russian Foreign Policy*, Cambridge, 1993, 82, 99.

31. Masson, 274; Comte de Choiseul-Gouffier, *Voyage pittoresque de la Grèce*, 2 vols., 1782–1809, I, xi; Léonce Pingaud, *Choiseul-Gouffier: La France en Orient sous Louis XVI*, 1887, 179n. Vergennes to Ségur; Duparc, 477, instruction of 2 June 1784.

32. Max Roche, *Education, assistance et culture françaises dans l'Empire Ottoman*, Istanbul, 1989, 17–18.

33. Octave Teissier, *La Chambre de Commerce de Marseille*, Marseilles, 1892, 315, Grand Vizier to Louis XVI 16 January 1791; Pingaud, 85.

34. Stanford J. Shaw, *Between Old and New: the Ottoman Empire under Sultan Selim III 1789–1807*, Harvard, 1971, 17; Archives du Ministère des Affaires Etrangères, Correspondance Politique, Turquie, 176, ff. 72v, 87v, 98, 100, 195v: Choiseul-Gouffier to Montmorin 3, 9, 10, 25 August; cf. A. I. Bagis, *Britain and the Struggle for the Integrity of the Ottoman Empire*, Istanbul, 1984, 42, 45.

35. Pingaud, 253, 255; BM Add. MSS 41567, f. 186: Choiseul-Gouffier to Sublime Porte 24 September 1792.

36. Wanda, *Souvenirs anecdotiques sur la Turquie 1820–1870*, 1884, 174, 175.

37. Colonel Rottiers, *Itinéraire de Tiflis à Constantinople*, Brussels, 1829, 345.

38. Nicolay, 179; Vandal, *Voyages*, 65; id., *Une Ambassade française*, 83n.; Itzkowitz and Mote, 176–7.

39. Un Jeune Russe [H.-C.-R. von Struve], *Voyage en Crimée*, 190; Dedem de Gelder, 23; Wittman, 25.

40. Michel Lesure, 'Notes et documents sur les relations vénéto-ottomanes', *Turcica*, IV, 143, 155.

41. Cantemir, 259; Karl A. Roider jun., *Austria's Eastern Question*, Princeton, 1982, 92–3, 220, Thugut to Kaunitz 21 March 1771. The British ambassador in 1710, Sir Robert Sutton, obtained secret lists of the Ottoman armed forces: Kurat (ed.), 9.

42. J. M. Tancoigne, *Voyage à Smyrne ... suivi d'une notice sur Péra*, 2 vols., 1817, II, 46.

43. Montagu, 122, Lady Mary Wortley Montagu to Lady Mar 16 March 1718.

44. Ausilia Roccatagliata, *Notai genovesi in oltremare: atti rogati a Pera e Mitilene*, I, Genoa, 1982, 140; E. Dalleggio d'Alessio, 'Liste des Podestats de la colonie génoise de Péra', *Revue des Etudes Byzantines*, XXVII, 1969, 152–3; id., 'Une Inscription inédite d'Arab-Djami', *Echos d'Orient*, XXVIII, 1929, 408–11; Belin, 151.

45. Sturdza, 590–6; Antoine Gautier and Marie de Testa, 'Quelques Dynasties de Drogmans', *Revue d'Histoire Diplomatique*, 1991, 89–94; J. F. Labourdette, *Vergennes*, 1990, 48–50; E. L. G. H. de Marcère, *Une Ambassade à Constantinople: la politique orientale et la révolution française*, 2 vols., 1927, I, 42, letter of Testa 28 March 1793.

46. Sturdza, 587; Wood, 'English Embassy', 556.

47. National Library of Scotland (hereafter NLS), Liston MSS, Pisani to Liston *passim* and 24 November, 24 October 1794.

48. Virginia Childs, *Lady Hester Stanhope*, 1990, 67; NLS, Liston MSS, Lady Liston journal 1812, f. 38.

49. Walsh, II, 440; Sir Austen Layard, *Autobiography and Letters*, 2 vols., 1903, II, 140 and n.

50. John Stoye, *Marsigli's Europe*, 1994, 17, 23; Toderini, III, 212; Edward Said, *Orientalism*, 42, 95; *Vers l'Orient*, exhib. cat., Bibliothèque Nationale, 1983, 40.

51. Kemal Beydilli, 'Ignatius Mouradgea d'Ohsson', *Istanbul Universitesi Edebiyat Fakultesi Tarih Dergisi*, XXXIV, 1984, 252, 260; Mouradgea d'Ohsson, III, 312n. Other diplomats and dragomans who wrote accounts of the Ottoman Empire include: Busbecq; Philippe du Fresne Canaye (*Voyage du Levant*, 1573); Sir Thomas Roe; Sir Paul Rycaut; Antoine Galland, translator into French of *One Thousand and One Nights*, who worked in the French embassy in Istanbul from 1671 to 1675, and 1678 to 1683; F. Pétis de La Croix; John P. Brown of the US legation, author of books on dervishes and *Turkish Evening's Entertainment* (1850); and Charles Schefer, First Dragoman of France during the Crimean War, who translated many Ottoman texts and became Directeur de l'Ecole des Langues Orientales Vivantes.

52. Freiherr von Hammer-Purgstall, *Erinnerungen*, Vienna, 1940, 41, 44, 46–7, 133, 134, 137.

53. And, *Istanbul*, 325–6 has identified nineteen such albums.

54. *At the Sublime Porte*, exhib. cat., Hazlitt, Gooden and Fox, 1988; Vandal, *Voyages*, 200–2; Catherine and André Boppe, *Les Peintres du Bosphore au XVIIIe siècle*, 1989, 40–7; *Les Peintures 'turques' de Jean-Baptiste Vanmour 1671–1737*, exhib. cat., Istanbul, 1975. The portrait of Marshal Sébastiani in the Musée de l'Histoire de France in Versailles, with a view of Istanbul in the background, was painted by Winterhalter in 1841 – thirty-three years after Sébastiani had ceased to be French ambassador there.

55. Visit to Biby and interview wth Fredrik von Celsing, 29 August 1994. Other 'embassy pictures' are in the collections of M. de Tugny in France; Prince von Oettingen Wallerstein in Germany; Count von Gudenus in Austria; the Palazzo Mocenigo a San Stae, in Venice; the Villa Valtorta at Dolo, in the Veneto; the Italian Consulate-General in Istanbul; the British Embassy in Ankara; the Musée de l'Histoire de France, Versailles, the Musée des Beaux-Arts, Bordeaux, the Academy of Fine Arts, Cracow and the Rijksmuseum. Four views of Constantinople and eight portraits of its inhabitants belonging to the son of Vergennes were confiscated '*pour la nation*' in 1795 and have since disappeared: see Archives Nationales F 17 1268, no.

226: *Inventaire des objets réservés pour la nation, provenants de Vergennes émigré.* I am grateful for this reference to Mme de Tugny-Vergennes.

56. Gilles, 221, 97, 170; B. Miller, *Sublime Porte*, 24.

57. Strachan, 174; William St Clair, *Lord Elgin and the Marbles*, 1983 edn., 90 and *passim.*

9   The Janissary's Frown

1. Philip Mansel, *Pillars of Monarchy*, 1984, 85, 88.

2. Godfrey Goodwin, *The Janissaries*, 1994, 70, 72; Lybyer, 109; Enis Batur (ed.), *Eccomium to Istanbul*, Istanbul, 1991, 107.

3. Hammer, VI, 263–4, XV, 215–16; BM Add. MSS 36301, f. 263, Pisani to Lord Strangford, 1821.

4. Kafadar, 'Yeniceri–Esnaf Relations', 37, 42, 116.

5. Hammer, VI, 299–302.

6. Kafadar, 'Yeniceri–Esnaf Relations', 47, 81, 86, 24; A. Djevad Bey, *Etat militaire ottoman depuis la fondation de l'Empire jusqu'à nos jours*, Constantinople–Paris, 1882, 76; Galland, II, 137, diary entry for 6 August 1673.

7. Mantran, *Istanbul*, 105; Shaw, *Between Old and New*, 120.

8. Kafadar, 'Yeniceri–Esnaf Relations', 67; Djevad, 43; Hammer, IV, 338. Janissaries also forced the Sultan to return to Istanbul in 1592.

9. Hammer, X, 112, IX, 171, 177, 181; Thomas, *Naima*, 94–5.

10. Bobovi, 42; Hammer, IX, 219, 280.

11. Tott, I, 17–21; Revd E. J. Davis, *Osmanli Proverbs and Quaint Sayings*, 1898, 66; Bosscha Erdbrink, 65; Louis Bonneville de Marsangy, *Le Chevalier de Vergennes: son ambassade à Constantinople*, 2 vols., 1894, I, 266–8 and n., Vergennes to Rouille 30 September 1755.

12. Bonneville de Marsangy, I, 313, Vergennes to Rouille 3 February 1756; cf. Pingaud, 132, Choiseul-Gouffier to Chevalier de Gruyère 2 June 1787.

13. Roy Porter, *London*, 80; Daniel Panzac, *La Peste dans l'Empire Ottoman 1700–1850*, Leuwen, 1985, 117, 283, 341, 59, 41; Alfred C. Wood, *A History of the Levant Company*, 1935, 246; William Turner, *Journal of a Tour of the Levant*, 3 vols., 1820, I, 76; Resad Ekrem Kocu, 'The Records of the Gardener Corps of the Imperial Guards', in Batur (ed.), 108.

14. Panzac, *Peste*, 312; Busbecq, 183; Ali Nami Bey, *Vérité, justice, bonté*, Constantinople, 1918, 63.

15. Hammer, XVI, 46; Mouradgea d'Ohsson, III, 306–9; Paul Wittek, 'Les Archives de Turquie', *Byzantion*, 1938, 697.

16. Findlay, *Reform*, 115; Jamgocyan, *Finances de l'Empire Ottoman*, 110; Pingaud, 228, Choiseul-Gouffier to Noailles 15, 21 May 1789; Shaw, *Between Old and New*, 75–8.

17. Beydilli, 260–8, 289. Mouradgea later persuaded the Empire to recognize the French Republic and served as Swedish minister in Constantinople in 1795–9, when he left on the insistence of the Russian ambassador, who considered him a Jacobn. He died near Paris in 1807.

18. A. F. Miller, *Mustafa Pacha Bairaktar*, Bucharest, 1975, 89, 86; Wilkinson, 219, 234; A. P. Caussin de Perceval (tr.), *Précis historique de la destruction du corps des Janissaires par le Sultan Mahmoud en 1826*, 1833, 14, 223–5, 230–1; Shaw, *Between Old and New*, 92, 135.

19. A. F. Miller, 105–6; Shaw, *Between Old and New*, 182, 194.

20. NLS MSS 5572, Liston to Grenville 25 November 1794; Navarian, 145.

21. Nisbet, 156, Lady Elgin to Mrs Nisbet 11 December 1801; Sturdza, 582; Dedem de Gelder, 32.

22. Cornelis Boschma and Jacques Perot, *Antoine-Ignace Melling (1763–1831), artiste voyageur*, Paris, 1991, 18, 20, 22, 30.

23. Shaw, *Between Old and New*, 358; Edouard Driault, *La Politique orientale de Napoléon*, 1904, 95, 102; H. Deherain, *La Vie de Pierre Ruffin*, 2 vols., 1929–30, II, 84–5, Sébastiani to Talleyrand 3 March 1807.

24. Shaw, *Between Old and New*, 89, 371; Mahmud Raif Efendi, *Tableau des nouveaux règlemens de l'Empire Ottoman*, Constantinople, 1798, 7; Deherain, II, 87, Ruffin to his daughter 10 June 1807.

25. Shaw, *Between Old and New*, 382–92.

26. A. F. Miller, 286, 289.

27. Serge Tatistcheff, *Alexandre Ier et Napoléon*, 1891, 412, Caulaincourt to Napoleon 24 June 1808; Shaw, *History of the Ottoman Empire*, II, 3–5.

28. Hobhouse, 999, 1001; Cyrus Hamlin, *Among the Turks*, 1878, 114; Temple, II, 36.

29. White, III, 269n.; Pars Tuglaci, *The Role of the Balian Family in Ottoman Architecture*, Istanbul, 1990, 17, 21, 26.

30. NLS MSS 5630, Liston to Castlereagh 25 February 1815; 5628, Liston to Castlereagh 24 December 1814.

31. Walsh, I, 342; NLS MSS 5709, ff. 45–6, Lady Liston, Journal 30 October 1812; F. Ismail, 'The Diplomatic Relations of the Ottoman Empire and the Great European Powers from 1800 to 1821', unpublished D.Phil. thesis, London, 1975, 36; P. Coquelle, 'Andreossy, ambassadeur à Constantinople', *Revue d'Histoire Diplomatique*, XX, 1906, 250.

32. W. Turner, I, 69, III, 385, 393; BM Add. MSS 56301, f. 205v, Pisani to Strangford 5 December 1821.

33. Walsh, II, 503–4; Andrew Wheatcroft, *The Ottomans*, 1993, 125.

34. Howard A. Reed, 'The Destruction of the Janissaries by Mahmud II in June 1826', unpublished Ph.D. thesis, Princeton, 1951, 112, 171.

35. MacFarlane, *Constantinople*, II, 380; H. Reed, 200, 203.

36. Caussin de Perceval, 44–6; H. Reed, 284, 295, 213, 238.

37. Stanley Lane-Poole, *The Life of Sir Stratford Canning, Viscount Stratford de Redcliffe*, 2 vols., 1888, I, 422, letter of 22 June 1826.

38. Caussin de Perceval, 103.

39. Caussin de Perceval, 3, 201.

40. White, I, 110; Lane-Poole, *Stratford Canning*, I, 420, Stratford to George Canning 20 June 1826.

41. Allan Cuningham, *Anglo-Ottoman Encounters in the Age of Revolution*, 1993, 293–4; Lane-Poole, *Stratford Canning*, I, 434; Temple, II, 188.

10 Mahmud II

1. G. Frangos, 'The *Philike Etairia*', unpublished Ph.D. thesis, Columbia, 1971, 33, 67, 103, 150, 274; Philip Sherrard, 'Church, State and the Greek War of Independence', in Clogg (ed.), *Movement*, 182, 186, 189.

2. A. Otetéa, 'L'Hétairie d'il y a cent cinquante ans', *Balkan Studies*, VI, 2, 1965, 261.

3. BM Add. MSS 36299, f. 59, Chabert to Strangford 31 March 1821; Walsh, I, 300, 305, 329; Frangos, 203.

4. BM Add. MSS 36301, ff. 10v, 26v, 32, 42, Pisani to Strangford 22 April, 4, 6, 12 May 1821; Walsh, I, 315–16, 336, 349, 361.

5. BM Add. MSS 36301, f. 87, Pisani to Strangford 23 July 1821.

6. BM Add. MSS 36301, f. 85, Pisani to Strangford 5 July 1821.

7. BM Add. MSS 36301, ff. 190, 194v, Pisani to Strangford 13, 18 November 1821.

8. Florin Marinescu, Georgeta Penelea-Filitti, Anna Tabaki (eds.), *Documents gréco-roumains: le Fonds Mourouzi d'Athènes*, Athens–Bucarest, 1991, 47; BM Add. MSS 36301, ff. 5, 59, Pisani to Strangford 16 April, 6 May 1821; Walsh, I, 392; Soutzo, 24.

9. Walsh, I, 389–92; Sturdza, 325; C. M. Woodhouse, 'Kapodistrias and the *Philiki Etairia*', in Clogg (ed.), *Struggle*, 116.

10. Barbara Jelavich, *History of the Balkans: Eighteenth and Nineteenth Centuries*, Cambridge, 1983, 208; *Historic Archive of Alexander Mavrocordato*, Athens, 1963, II, 370, Mavrocordato to M. de Reineck 9/21 July 1823; Edouard Driault and Michel L'Héritier, *Histoire diplomatique de la Grèce de 1821 à nos jours*, 5 vols., 1925–6, I, 218, letter of Mavrocrodato 30 June 1823.

11. Herbert Huscher, 'Alexander Mavrocordato, Friend of the Shelleys', *Bulletin of the Keats–Shelley Memorial Association*, XVI, 1965, 29–37; Frederick L. Jones (ed.), *The Letters of Percy Bysshe Shelley*, 2 vols., Oxford, 1964, II, 617, Shelley to Clare Claremont 2 April 1821.

12. Avigdor Levy, 'The Military Policy of Sultan Mahmud II 1808–1839', unpublished Ph.D. thesis, Harvard, 1968, 244, 248, 371, 378; MacFarlane, *Constantinople*, II, 165.

13. Tuglaci, *Balian*, 41–3, 53–61.

14. MacFarlane, *Constantinople*, I, 499, 501; White, III, 46.

15. Herbert Weinstock, *Donizetti*, 1964, 308–10; MacFarlane, *Constantinople*, I, 517; *National Palaces*, I, 43–4.

16. Colonel Calosso, *Mémoires d'un vieux soldat*, Turin–Nice, 1857, 142, 156–7, 170, 184; Temple, II, 134; MacFarlane, *Constantinople*, II, 174–83.

17. Patricia L. Baker, 'The Fez in Turkey: a Symbol of Modernisation?', *Costume*, 1986, 72–85; Bernard Lewis, *The Emergence of Modern Turkey*, 1960, 100; Pars Tuglaci, *The Role of the Dadian Family in Ottoman Social, Economic and Political Life*, Istanbul, 1993, 187.

18. MacFarlane, *Turkey and its Destiny*, 2 vols., 1850, II, 622–3; Aziz Nesin, *Istanbul Boy*, 3 vols., Austin, Texas, 1977–90, II, 12; Elias Kazan, *A Life*, 1988, 14.

19. Cunningham, *Anglo-Ottoman Encounters*, I, 311; Calosso, 225; Vernon John Puryear, *France and the Levant from the Bourbon Restoration to the Peace of Kutahya*, Berkeley, 1941, 63, despatch of Gordon 26 July 1829, 76.

20. M. S. Anderson, *The Eastern Question*, 1982, 71; R. W. Seton-Watson, *Britain in Europe 1789–1914*, 1937, 137, 177, 195; Allan Cunningham, *Eastern Questions in the Nineteenth Century*, 1993, II, 211.

21. M. S. Anderson, *Eastern Question*, 90–1; Frank E. Bailey, *British Policy and the Turkish Reform Movement*, Harvard, 1932, 132, Canning to Palmerston 7 March 1832; Lane-Poole, *Stratford Canning*, I, 505, Canning to Lady Canning 24 March 1832.

22. Temple, II, 91; Walsh, II 275; John Auldjo, *Journal of a Visit to Constantinople and Some of the Greek Islands in the Spring and Summer of 1833*, 1835, 98; J. W. McCarthy and Constantin Caratheodory, *Relation officielle de la maladie et de la mort du Sultan Mahmoud II*, 1841, 12–13.

23. Cunningham, *Eastern Questions*, II, 40; Walsh, I, 343; Temple, II, 44n.

24. Alderson, Table xliv, n. 3; M. Cagatay Ulucay, *Padishahlarin Kadinlari ve Kizlari*, Ankara, 1992, 107–8. There are no references to her death in the despatches of the French ambassador, the Marquis de Rivière.

25. Lane-Poole, *Stratford Canning*, II, 505, Canning to Lady Canning 24 March 1832.

26. Temple, II, 60, 195, 214; *Istanbul à la jonction des cultures balkaniques, méditer-ranéennes, slaves et orientales aux XVI–XIXe siècles*, Bucarest, 1977, 95, 103.

27. Berkes, *Secularism*, 128; Findlay, *Ottoman Civil Officialdom*, 26.

28. Nathalie Clayer and Alexandre Popovic (eds.), *Presse turque et presse de Turquie*, Istanbul–Paris, 1992, 84; Berkes, *Secularism*, 126–7; Walsh, II, 281–3.

29. Walsh, II, 288; Cunningham, *Anglo-Ottoman Encounters*, 312; BM Add. MSS 36301, f. 52, 114, Pisani to Strangford 24 May, 7 August 1821; Chassiotis, 433.

30. Sturdza, 220; Pardoe, I, 74–82.

31. Barsoumian, 'The Armenian Amira Class', 126, 129, 157.

32. Tuglaci, *Dadian, passim*; Cyrus Hamlin, *My Life and Times*, 1897, 259; Anna Boutros-Ghali and Archag Alboyadjian (eds.), *Les Dadian*, Cairo, 1965, 78–9.

33. Issawi, 160; Allom and Walsh, II, 62.

34. White, I, 126; Berkes, *Secularism*, 113–14.

35. Alexandre Mavroyennis, *Contribution à l'histoire du Proche-Orient*, 2 vols., Istanbul, 1950, II, 125n.; Roderic H. Davison, 'The French Language as a Vehicle for Ottoman Reform in the Nineteenth Century', 126–40; J. J. Sheehan, *German History 1780–1866*, Oxford, 1989, 583.

36. White, I, 151; Panzac, *La Peste*, 476, 482.

37. White, I, 234; Allom and Walsh, I, 69, II, 34; Tuglaci, *Women of Istanbul*, 25–6; Prince de Joinville, *Vieux Souvenirs*, 1970 edn., 130–1.

38. Pardoe, I, 315, 317.

39. Walsh, II, 2; Philip Argenti, *The Massacres of Chios*, 1932, 25, 108, Strangford to Londonderry 25 June 1822, Baron von Militz to Graf von Bernstorff 25 June 1822.

40. Tulay Artan, 'The Palaces of the Sultans', *Istanbul: Selections*, 1992, 94–7; Pardoe, I, 315; Temple, II, 89; Walsh, II, 313, 379.

41. Pardoe, I, 304, 306, 330, 312; White, I, 184n., III, 2; Adolphus Slade, *Turkey and the Crimean War*, 1867, 88.

42. Maréchal de Moltke, *Lettres . . . sur l'Orient*, 1877 edn., 318, letter of 1 September 1839; Maréchal Duc de Raguse, *Voyages*, 5 vols., 1837–8, II, 64; Pardoe, II, 312; cf. MacFarlane, *Constantinople*, I, 53, II, 165, 169.

43. Pardoe, II, 236; Walsh, II, 292; Ubicini, I, 107–8.

44. Pardoe, I, 30; A. Borie, P. Pinon and Stéphane Yerasimos, *L'Occidentalisation d'Istanbul au XIXe siècle*, Ecole d'Architecture, Paris, 1989, 3–4.

45. PRO FO 78/225, 152v, 155, 157v, Ponsonby to Palmerston 19 December 1833; Philip E. Moseley, *Russian Diplomacy and the Opening of the Eastern Question in 1838–1839*, Harvard, 1934, 10, 96, 99.

46. M. S. Anderson, *Eastern Question*, 83; Edouard Driault, *L'Egypte et l'Europe: la crise*

de 1839–1841, 2 vols., Cairo, 1930–1, I, 113, 151, Cochelet to Soult 5 July, 15 July 1839; White, III, 100; McCarthy and Caratheodory, 21–3.

11 City of Marvels

1. Théophile Gautier, *Constantinople*, 228.
2. Edmund Hornby, *An Autobiography*, 1929, 84; Charles de Mouy, *Lettres du Bosphore*, 1879, 179; Mrs Brassey, *Sunshine and Storm in the East, or Cruises to Cyprus and Constantinople*, 1880, 79, diary entry for 28 October 1874.
3. Patricia Herlihy, *Odessa: a History 1794–1914*, 1986, 107; Zeyneb Celik, *The Remaking of Istanbul*, 1989, 84; *Levant Herald*, 2 October 1869; F. Trench Townsend, *A Cruise in Greek Waters*, 1870, 220.
4. Celik, 93; de Amicis, 23–30; Ferriman, 264–6; Samuel S. Cox, *Diversions of a Diplomat in Turkey*, New York, 1887, 183; MacFarlane, *Turkey and its Destiny*, II, 326.
5. De Mouy, 30; F. Marion Crawford, *Constantinople*, 1895, 15; Inalcik and Quataert, 922; Claude Farrère, *L'Homme qui assassina*, 1928, 17.
6. Crawford, 17; Lady Hornby, 63, diary entry for 26 October 1855.
7. Ferriman, 265; Celik, 88–9.
8. Toledano, 53, 146; Melek Hanoum, 46–7. In the 1880s, shopping for the Khedive of Egypt, Dr Comanos Pasha was shown eighty-five slaves in three hours in a private house: Dr Comanos Pasha, *Mémoires*, *c.* 1920, 52.
9. Wanda, 32; Boutros-Ghali and Alboyadjian, 7.
10. Galante, *Histoire des Juifs*, I, 65, 159, 223, II, 133; A. de Lamartine, *Histoire de la Turquie*, 6 vols., 1854, I, 19; S. G. W. Benjamin, *The Turks and the Greeks*, New York, 1867, 76; Sir Henry F. Woods, *Spun-Yarn from the Strands of a Sailor's Life*, 2 vols., 1924, II, 225.
11. Bayram Kodoman, *Les Ambassades de Moustapha Rechid Pacha à Paris*, Ankara, 1992, *passim*; Roderick Davison, *Reform in the Ottoman Empire 1856–1876*, Princeton, 1963, 89; Charles Mismer, *Souvenirs du monde mussulman*, 1892, 110.
12. Davison, 3–4; Lane-Poole, *Stratford Canning*, II, 90–1; Vartan Artinian, *The Armenian Constitutional System in the Ottoman Empire 1839–1863*, Istanbul, 1990, 52; Steven T. Rosenthal, *The Politics of Dependency: Urban Reform in Istanbul*, Westport, 1980, 36, 63.
13. Edouard Driault, *Mohammed Ali et l'Europe: la crise de 1840–41*, 5 vols., Cairo–Rome, 1930–4, III, 40, letter of 17 July 1840; 227, 7 September 1840; I, 193, letter of 27 July 1839; *Levant Herald*, 8 October 1869; Thouvenel, 125, Thouvenel to Benedetti, 1 July 1857.
14. Cunningham, *Eastern Questions*, 135, and Nassau W. Senior, *A Journal kept in Turkey and Greece*, 1859, 35; Tito Lacchini, *I Fossati, architetti del Sultano di Turchia*, Rome, 1943, 88–94.
15. Bailey, 282, 286, memorandum of Baron von Sturmer, March 1841.
16. Rosenthal, 104–5, 107–8, 113, 115, Stratford Canning to Palmerston 31 August 1848.
17. Sir Telford Waugh, *Turkey Yesterday, Today and Tomorrow*, 1930, 25; Davison, 71; Lane-Poole, *Stratford Canning*, II, 334, Lord to Lady Stratford de Redcliffe 24 December 1853; Cunningham, *Anglo-Ottoman Encounters*, 147n.; R. W. Seton-Watson, *Britain in Europe 1789–1914*, Cambridge, 1937, 318, 363; Woods, II, 97.
18. John Shelton Curtiss, *Russia's Crimean War*, Durham, N.C., 1979, 47, 117, 62.

19. Norman Rich, *Why the Crimean War? A Cautionary Tale*, 1985, 35; Curtiss, 93–4.
20. Curtiss, 116; Rich, 39.
21. Rich, 43, 48, 55, 75; Curtiss, 46.
22. Rich, 82–3; Curtiss, 183–4; Lane-Poole, *Stratford Canning*, II, 302, Charles Alison to Lady Stratford 28 September 1853; Seton-Watson, *Britain in Europe*, 312.
23. Slade, *Turkey and the Crimean War*, 187; W. H. Russell, *The British Expedition to the Crimea*, rev. edn. 1858, 52.
24. Rosenthal, 110, 115; Senior, 132, diary entry for 19 October 1857.
25. Hon. and Revd Sydney Godolphin Osborne, *Scutari and its Hospitals*, 1855, 49, 50; Sir Edward Cook, *The Life of Florence Nightingale*, 2 vols., 1914, I, 220.
26. Lady Hornby, 204–213, 8 February 1856.
27. Rich, 193; Rogers, *Topkapi: Costumes*, 161; B. Miller, *Sublime Porte*, 100–2.
28. *National Palaces*, I, Istanbul, 1987, *passim*; Mustafa Cezar, 'The Architectural Decoration of Dolmabahce and Beylerbeyi Palaces', *National Palaces*, II, Istanbul, 1992, 1–20; Gautier, 262; Turhan Baytop, 'The Tulip in Istanbul during the Ottoman Period', in Roding and Theunissen (eds.), 52.
29. Celik Gulersoy, *Dolmabahce Palace and its Environs*, Istanbul, 1990, 54; Lady Hornby, 407–11, letter of 23 July 1856.
30. Felix Ribeyre, *Voyage de Sa Majesté l'Impératrice en Corse et en Orient*, 1870, 153n.; *Levant Herald*, 16 October 1869.
31. *National Palaces*, II, 1992, 137.
32. Braude and Lewis, I, 30; Avigdor Levy, 'The Ottoman *Ulama* and the Military Reforms of Sultan Mahmud II', *Asian and African Studies*, VII, 1971, 18.
33. W. M. Thackeray, *Notes of a Journey from Cornhill to Grand Cairo*, 2nd edn., 1846, 44; W. H. Russell, *A Diary in the East during the Tour of the Prince and Princess of Wales*, 1869, 480–1; Trench Townsend, 217; Woods, II, 224.
34. Thierry Zarcone, *Mystiques, philosophes et franc-maçons en Islam*, 1993, 31, 117, 317.
35. Orhan Kologlu, 'La Formation des Intellectuels', in Clayer and Popovic (eds.), 127; Gibb, V, 20, 22.
36. Hamlin, *My Life and Times*, 477; M. Destrilhes, *Confidences sur la Turquie*, 1855, 67; Layard, II, 47–51; *Catalogue de la Bibliothèque de feu Ahmed Vefyk Pacha*, Constantinople, 1893.
37. Serif Mardin, 'Super Westernisation in Urban Life in the Last Quarter of the Nineteenth Century', in Peter Benedict *et al.* (eds.), *Turkey: Geographical and Social Perspectives*, Leiden, 1974, 406, 417; Layard, II, 86.
38. BM Add. MSS 38979, f. 241, letter of 25 May 1850; 39103, f. 311, 3 August 1862; 38987, f. 49, 15 January 1861; 39024, f. 306; 38985, f. 44, 18 August 1856; Senior, 136, diary entry for 23 October 1857.
39. Jules Blancard, *Etudes sur la Grèce contemporaine*, Montpellier, 1886, 12, 35, 37.
40. H. Exertoglu, 'The Greek Bankers in Constantinople 1856–1881', unpublished Ph.D. thesis, London, 1985, 81, 129, 133.
41. Exertoglu, 141, 147, 159; Rosenthal, 79; Sturdza, 223.
42. Exertoglu, 150, 153, 161, 237–40; Haydar Kazgan, *Galata Bankerleri*, Istanbul, 1991, 133; Sturdza, 152.
43. Charles Brun, 'Les Grecs de Constantinople', *Revue Moderne*, LII, 10 June 1869, 432.

44. C. Th. Dimaras, *Histoire de la littérature néo-hellénique*, Athens, 1965, 312; Thouvenel, 344; Jelavich, *History of the Balkans*, 262.

45. Levy, *Sephardim*, 96; cf. P. Baudin, *Les Israélites de Constantinople*, Constantinople, 1872, repr. 1989: 'On imaginerait difficilement un tableau de misères plus frappant, plus déchirant'; Abraham Galante, *Nouveau Receuil de nouveaux documents concernant l'histoire des Juifs de Turquie*, 1949, 46; Shaw, *Jews*, 160–2.

46. Walsh, II, 436–7; William Miller, *Travel and Politics in the Near East*, 1897, 426; Slade, *Turkey and the Crimean War*, 63n.

47. Duncan M. Perry, *Stefan Stambulov and the Emergence of Modern Bulgaria 1870–1895*, Durham and London, 1993, 6; Mercia MacDermott, *A History of Bulgaria 1393–1885*, 1962, 140, 147–9.

48. Cunningham, *Eastern Questions*, 38–9; PRO FO 78/225, 157v, 172, Ponsonby to Palmerston 19 December 1833; Davison, *Reform*, 59; Braude and Lewis, I, 323.

49. Sturdza, 448, 465; MacDermott, 151–5; B. H. Sumner, 'Ignatyev at Constantinople', *Slavonic Review*, 1933, 571.

50. Hamlin, *My Life and Times*, 439; *Levant Herald*, 1 July 1869; George Washburn, *Fifty Years in Constantinople*, Boston and New York, 1909, 72, 96, 114, 293. Of 435 graduates with honour between 1869 and 1903, 195 were Bulgarian, 144 Armenian and 76 Greeks.

51. Kemal H. Karpat, 'The Population and the Social and Economic Transformation of Istanbul: the Ottoman Microcosm', *International Journal of Middle East Studies*, 1983, 86; M. S. Anderson, *Eastern Question*, 113; Berkes, *Secularism*, 316; Davison, *Reform*, 231.

52. *Correspondance d'Adam Mickiewicz*, ed. Ladislas Mickiewicz, n.d., 363, Adam Mickiewicz to Madame Klustine 25 October 1855; *National Palaces*, I, 88.

53. W. Miller, 429; Gulersoy, *Grand Bazaar*, 35; Rosenthal, 10; Exertoglu, 74.

54. *The Whittalls of Turkey 1809–1973*, n.d., *passim*; A. Gallenga, *Two Years of the Eastern Question*, 2 vols., 1877, I, 260–4.

55. Celik, 62–3; Rosenthal, 39.

56. Rosenthal, 41, 59, 70, 95, 151; White, I, 195, II, 94; Raouf d'Orbey, *Les Amours dangereuses*, Constantinople, 1874, *passim*.

57. Said N-Duhani, *Quand Beyoglu s'appelait Péra*, Istanbul, 1956, 12; Celik, 133–4; Marcelle Tinayre, *Notes d'une voyageuse en Turquie*, 1909, 293.

58. Celik, 136.

59. Celik, 37–8, 158; Rosenthal, 17, 173–4; de Amicis, 20.

60. Walsh, I, 248–51; Celik, 93; Mark Twain, *The Innocents Abroad*, Hartford, Conn., 1869, 372; Mavroyennis Pacha, *Chiens errants de Constantinople, et chiens et chats de bonne maison*, 1900, 8, 14.

61. Albert Smith, *A Month at Constantinople*, 1850, 69, 89; de Amicis, 108.

12   The Road to Tsarigrad

1. P. Oberling, 'The Istanbul Tunnel', *Archivum Ottomanicum*, IV, 1972, 238–40; Celik, 97.

2. Suha Umur, 'Abdulmecit, Opera and the Dolmabahce Palace Theatre', *National Palaces*, I, 50–1; W. H. Russell, *Diary in the East*, 506, 479.

3. Hrant Papazian, *D. Tchouhadjian: vie et œuvres*, Istanbul, 1977, 9, 12; Pars Tuglaci, *Turkish Bands of Past and Present*, Istanbul, 1986, 124–5.

4. Gawrych, 298–300; Davison, 298.

5. Mardin, *Genesis*, 13, 26.

6. *Istanbul Ansiklopedisi*, art. 'Galata Borsasi'; Davison, *Reform*, 247–8; Berkes, *Secularism*, 180, 184; Margaret Stevens Hoell, 'The Ticaret Odasi: Origins, Functions and Activities of the Chamber of Commerce of Istanbul 1885–1899', unpublished MA thesis, Ohio State University, 1973, 1–5, 50.

7. Zarcone, 204, 209, 281; Constantin Svolopoulos, 'L'Initiation de Mourad V à la franc-maçonnerie par Cl. Scalieri; aux origines du mouvement libéral en Turquie', *Balkan Studies*, 1980, XXI, 2, 1964, 451.

8. Artan, 'Architecture', 119; Haidar, 20–2, 33–4, 52–3, 60, 87.

9. Ferriman, 4–5; [Sir Charles Eliot], *Turkey in Europe*, 1900, 142–5.

10. Gérard Groc and I. Caglar, *La Presse française de Turquie de 1795 à nos jours*, Istanbul, 1985, 203, 228.

11. Guity Neshat, *The Origins of Modern Reform in Iran 1870–1880*, Urbana, 1982, 33–7; Mitler, 76; Clayer and Popovic (eds.), 201.

12. Godfrey Hodgson, *A New Grand Tour*, 1995, 165, 199, 214; Robert Pynsent (ed.), *Decadence and Innovation: Austro-Hungarian Life and Art at the End of the Century*, 1989, 54.

13. Ernest Roth, *A Tale of Three Cities*, 1971, 118–19; see e.g. *Levant Herald*, 6 July, 25 October 1869.

14. Artinian, 103; James Etmekjian, *The French Influence on the Western Armenian Renaissance 1843–1915*, New York, 1964, 109.

15. Vartan, 71; Engin Cizgen, *Photography in the Ottoman Empire 1839–1919*, Istanbul, 1987, 96, 98.

16. Butros Ghali, 25, 32; Tuglaci, *Dadian*, 114.

17. Prince Mek-B. Dadian, 'La Société arménienne contemporaine', *Revue des Deux Mondes*, 15 June 1867, 906, 914, 921; Findlay, *Bureaucratic Reform*, 214.

18. Sarkis Atamian, *The Armenian Community*, New York, 1955, 84.

19. Senior, 139, 24 October 1857; Vartan, 87; Etmekjian, 111.

20. G. A. Mavrocordatos, *De la Réforme et de la finance des Romains en Orient*, Athens, 1856, 13; A. Synvet, *Les Grecs de l'Empire Ottoman: étude statistique et ethnique*, 2nd edn., *c.* 1878, 10; Brun, 434.

21. MacDermott, 209; David Kushner, *The Rise of Turkish Nationalism*, 1977, 11, 12.

22. B. H. Sumner, *Russia and the Balkans 1870–1880*, 1937, 110; Barbara Jelavich, *The Ottoman Empire, the Great Powers and the Straits Question 1870–1887*, Bloomington, 1973, 12–13, 152; Sir Henry G. Elliot, *Some Revolutions and other Diplomatic Experiences*, 1927, 205; M. S. Anderson, *Eastern Question*, 166.

23. Count Ignatyev, 'Memoirs', *Slavonic Review*, X, June 1931, 394–7; Michael Boro Petrovich, *The Emergence of Russian Panslavism 1856–1870*, New York, 1956, 263.

24. Roger Owen, *The Middle East in the World Economy 1800–1914*, 1981, 105; Exertoglu, 255; Kazgan, 86, 89.

25. Lewis, *Emergence of Modern Turkey*, 469; Celik Gulersoy, *The Ceragan Palaces*, Istanbul, 1992, 66–76.

26. Henry O. Dwight, *Turkish Life in War Time*, 1881, 1, diary entry for 15 April 1876; Gallenga, I, 140; Davison, 325, 329. For the numbers massacred see Richard Millman, *Britain and the Eastern Question 1875–1878*, Oxford, 1979, 153–4, 162. Many

Bulgarians assumed dead had left their villages in search of work – as they did every summer.

27. Dwight, 7, diary entry for 12 May 1876; Davison, 330.

28. Davison, 332–7; Dwight, 21, diary entry for 31 May 1876; Cléanthe Scalieri, *Appel à la justice des Grandes Puissances*, Athens, 1881, 9; Robert Devereux, 'Suleyman Pasha's "the Feeling of the Revolution"', *Middle Eastern Studies*, XV, 1, 1979, 7–8.

29. Devereux, ibid., 19; Gulersoy, *Ceragan Palaces*, 101–11.

30. Davison, 352–3, 355; Berkes, *Secularism*, 242; Pierre Loti, *Aziyade: Stamboul 1876–1877*, 1892 edn., 64.

31. Davison, 382–3; Robert Devereux, *The First Ottoman Constitutional Period*, Baltimore, 1963, 80–3, 134; Millman, 226.

32. Fesch, 277; Gallenga, II, 307, 310–12.

33. Dwight, 84, 103–6, diary entries for 23 April, 22, 29 June 1876; David MacKenzie, 'Russia's Balkan Policies under Alexander II', in Ragsdale (ed.), 235.

34. Dorothy Anderson, *The Balkan Volunteers*, 1968, 193–4, 196; Dwight, 226–7, 231, diary entries for 25 January, 6 February 1878; MacKenzie in Ragsdale (ed.), 239.

35. Farooqi, 95, 173, 198; Ram Lakhan Shukla, *Britain, India and the Turkish Empire 1853–1882*, New Delhi, 1973, 49, quoting letters of Lord Lytton to Lord Salisbury January–May 1877.

36. D. Anderson, 119–22, 187, 205; Millman,311; Gordon Waterfield, *Layard of Nineveh*, 1963, 396, 505; Robert Blake, *Disraeli*, 1966, 595, 639.

37. Waterfield, 402; Devereux, *First Ottoman Constitutional Period*, 240.

38. Sumner, 361, 366, 375, 391, 397.

39. Dwight, 258–9, diary entry for 27 February 1878; BM Add. MSS 39018, f. 71, Vefyk to Layard January 1878; 39023, f. 258, 39024, f. 306, letters of February 1878; Tuglaci, *Dadian*, 122.

40. Dwight, 66, 137, 263, diary entries for 21 January 1877, 25 July, 8 August, 7 November 1877; Salahi R. Sonyel, *Minorities and the Destruction of the Ottoman Empire*, Ankara, 1993, 262, 282, 284; Devereux, *First Ottoman Constitutional Period*, 224.

41. *La Turquie*, 2 March, 7 April 1878; Sumner, 416–17; Waterfield, 420; A. O. Sarkisian, *History of the Armenian Question to 1885*, Urbana, 1938, 85, 88n.

42. Sturdza, 465.

43. *La Turquie*, 7 April 1878; Exertoglu, 210, 226–7, 283; Elia Institute for the Study of the Greek Diaspora, Athens, MSS: *Mémorandum du Syllogue Grec de Constantinople*, 1878, f. 14.

44. Gulersoy, *Ceragan Palaces*, 131, 135, 141–8.

45. Waterfield, 414, 416; Dwight, 338, diary entry for 18 August 1878; Sumner, 572.

46. Dwight, 418, diary entry for 30 May 1878; W. Miller, 432; BM Add. MSS 48944, Vincent Papers, f. 191, diary of Edgar Vincent 12 November 1880.

13 Yildiz

1. Tuglaci, *Balian*, 546–657, gives a well-illustrated, but at times fantastic, account of Yildiz; Ayse Osmanoglu, *Avec mon Père le Sultan Abdulhamid de son palais à son prison*, 1991, 80–2; Tahsin Pasha, *Yildiz Hatiralari*, 1990 edn., 212.

2. Mrs Max Muller, *Letters from Constantinople*, 1897, 53; Anna Bowman Dodds, *In*

the Palaces of the Sultan, 1904, 75; Woods, II, 230; Prince Nicholas of Greece, *My Fifty Years,* 1929, 201; interview with Mrs Yalter, 13 April 1989.

3. Tahsin Pasha, 30, 61, 66–8.

4. Descriptions of dinner at Yildiz can be found in: Dowager Marchioness of Dufferin and Ava, *My Russian and Turkish Journals,* 1917, 303, diary entry for 17 October 1883; Muller, 88–90; Paul Cambon, *Correspondance,* 3 vols., I, 352, letter of 27 December 1891; Dodds, 93.

5. Tuglaci, *Balian,* 639–46; Lloyd C. Griscom, *Diplomatically Speaking,* 1940, 168; Osmanoglu, 64.

6. Dodds, 91, 104; Dufferin, 303, diary entry for 17 October 1881.

7. Henri de Blowitz, *Une Course à Constantinople,* 1884, 254–5.

8. Dufferin, 221, diary entry of 30 August 1882, cf. Tahsin Pasha, 6–8; BM Add. MSS 39024, f. 296, Longworth to Layard 15 December 1880; Cambon, I, 386, letter of 15 February 1895.

9. Philip Graves, *Briton and Turk,* 1941, 50; Waugh, 99.

10. Tahsin Pasha, 19–22; Blancard, II, 440–3, letter of 19 November 1892; Sturdza, 260; despatch of Layard 30 July 1879, quoted in Sonyel, 258; Theodore Herzl, *Diaries,* 1958, 141, entry for 17 June 1896.

11. Louis Rambert, *Notes et impressions de Turquie,* 1926, 331, diary entry for 22 November 1904; Herzl, 158, entry for 22 June 1896; Graves, 51n.

12. Shukla, 155; Selim Deringil, 'The Invention of Tradition as Public Image in the Late Ottoman Empire, 1808 to 1908', *Comparative Studies in Society and History,* XXXV, 1 January 1993, 15; Serif Mardin, *Religion and Social Change in Modern Turkey,* Albany, New York, 1989, 125–9; Selim Deringil, 'Legitimacy Structures in the Ottoman State: the Reign of Abdulhamid II 1876–1909', *International Journal of Middle East Studies,* XXIII, 1991, 353.

13. Tuglaci, *Balian,* 498; Wilfrid Scawen Blunt, *Gordon at Khartoum,* 1911, 318, diary entry for 24 October 1884.

14. Wilfrid Blunt, *My Diaries,* 2 vols. 1919–20, I, 102, entry for 28 April 1892; Mrs Will Gordon, *A Woman in the Balkans,* 1916, 228–9, 231–2; 'Tercuman', *Grecs et Turcs d'aujourd'hui,* 1898, 16–18.

15. Deringil, 'The Invention of Tradition', 12.

16. Osmanoglu, 54; Herzl, 152, 18 June 1896; Deringil, 'The Invention of Tradition', 10.

17. Blunt, *My Diaries,* I, 102, 28 April 1893.

18. Nikki R. Keddie, *Sayyid Jamal ad-din 'al-Afghani',* Los Angeles, 1972, 371, 375, 381, 385, 406, 408.

19. Engin D. Akarli, 'Abdul Hamid's Attempts to integrate Arabs into the Ottoman System', in David Kushner (ed.), *Palestine in the Late Ottoman Period,* Jerusalem, 1986, 80; Jan Schmidt, *Through the Legation Window 1871–1926,* Istanbul, 1992, 91, 98; Deringil, 'Legitimacy Structures', 351.

20. Charles Didier, *Séjour chez le Grand Schérif de la Mekke,* 1857, 157, 247, 261; George Stitt, *A Prince of Arabia: the Emir Shereef Ali Haidar,* 1948, 37; Senior, 55–7, 6 October 1857; Toledano, 120, 130.

21. Blunt, *Gordon at Khartoum,* 305, 19 October 1884, 331, November 1884; PRO FO 78/3081, Layard to Salisbury 'secret', 9 February 1880; cf. for confirmation of

British-Hashemite links, William Ochsenwald, *Religion, Society and the State in Arabia*, Ohio, 1984, 201–2; Shukla, 170–1.

22. Stitt, 57–9, 93–4, 105.

23. King Abdullah of Jordan, *Memoirs*, 1950, 46, 40; Shirin Devrim, *A Turkish Tapestry: the Shakirs of Istanbul*, 1994, 88.

24. Waugh, 90–1; Cox, *Diversions of a Diplomat*, 152; Rambert, 34, diary entry for 24 October 1896.

25. Said N-Duhani, *Quand Beyoglu s'appelait Péra*, 61.

26. Gulersoy, *The Caique*, 219–26.

27. Gulersoy, *Ceragan Palaces*, 154–62; Alderson, 29n.

28. Celik, 146; Vera Freni and Carla Varnier, *Raimondo d'Aronco: l'opera completa*, Padova, 1983, 123.

29. Halil Halid, *Diary of a Turk*, 1903, 134–5; Blunt, *Gordon at Khartoum*, 304, 18 October 1884; Crawford, 17; Alan Duben and Cem Behar, *Istanbul Households: Marriage, Family and Fertility 1880–1940*, Cambridge, 1991, 210.

30. Duben and Behar, 4, 149, 180–1, 183.

31. Berkes, *Secularism*, 291, 320.

32. Issawi, 275.

33. Donald Quataert, *Social Disintegration and Popular Resistance in the Ottoman Empire 1881–1908*, New York, 1983, 95–6, 98.

34. Louise Nalbandian, *The Armenian Revolutionary Movement*, Berkeley, 1963, 117, 130; Christopher J. Walker, *Armenia: the Survival of a Nation*, 1991 edn., 145–6.

35. Ertugrul Zekai Okte (ed.), *Ottoman Archives. Yildiz Collection. The Armenian Question*, 3 vols., Istanbul, 1989, II, 129, Kamil to General Secretariat 15 July 1879; 157, Sureyya Pasha to Grand Vizier 11 August 1890; 195.

36. Walker, 132; Raymond H. Kevorkian and Paul B. Paboudjian, *Les Arméniens dans l'Empire Ottoman à la veille du génocide*, 1992, 11–12.

37. Hratch Dasnabedian, *History of the Armenian Revolutionary Federation Dashnaktsutiun 1890–1924*, Milan, 1990, 76; Walker, 153–6; Nalbandian, 123–5.

38. Edouard Driault and Michel L'Héritier, *Histoire diplomatique de la Grèce de 1821 à nos jours*, 5 vols., 1925–6, IV, 344, telegram of 12 February 1897; J. K. Hassiotis, 'The Greeks and the Armenian Massacres', *Neo-hellenika*, IV, 1981, 81, 85, despatch of 20 September 1895.

39. *Correspondance respecting the Disturbances at Constantinople in August 1896 presented to both Houses of Parliament by command of Her Majesty*, 1897, 11, Herbert to Lord Salisbury 27 August 1896; 32, letter of Max Muller 31 August 1896; Rambert, 18–19, diary entry for 30 August 1896.

40. Tahsin Pasha, 44; Walker, 165–8; *Correspondance respecting the Disturbances . . .*, 18–20, Herbert to Salisbury 31 August 1896; 22, Calice to Herbert 29 August; J. A. S. Grenville, *Lord Salisbury and Foreign Policy: the Close of the Nineteenth Century*, 1970, 75.

41. *Correspondance respecting the Disturbances . . .*, 15, report by F. A. Barker 26 August 1896; 17, Herbert to Lord Salisbury; Cambon, I, 394, letter of 10 October 1895.

42. Nubar Gulbenkian, *Pantaraxia*, 1966, 10; Stephen Longrigg, *Oil in the Middle East*, 3rd edn., 1968, 31.

43. Tuglaci, *Dadian*, 427, 243, 292.

44. Ibid., 240–1, *mémoire* of 1900; Kevorkian, 15; Boutros Ghali, 109–12; Sarkis Artamian, *The Armenian Community*, New York, 1955, 121–2.

45. Kevorkian, 17, 19; Dasnabedian, 77.

46. Haus-, Hof- und Staatsarchiv, Vienna PA XIV/18, *Mémoire sur le mouvement albanais* by Faik Bey Konitza, January 1899: I am grateful for this reference to Orhan Kologlu; Stefanaq Pollo and Arben Pulo, *Histoire de l'Albanie*, Roanne, 1972, 137, 147, 154, 156; Stavro Skendi, *The Albanian National Awakening 1878–1912*, Princeton, 1967, 169, 317; Stuart E. Mann, *Albanian Literature*, 1955, 38–9, 41–3; J. Swire, *Albania: the Rise of a Kingdom*, 1929, 64.

47. Stephen Constant, *Foxy Ferdinand*, 1979, 180–1; Prince Nicholas of Greece, *My Fifty Years*, 1930, 205.

48. Michel Noe, *Pages d'Orient*, 1895, 174–5; A. J. Pannayotopulos, 'The Great Idea and the Vision of Eastern Federation', *Balkan Studies*, XXI, 2, 1980, 340; cf. Gerasimos Augustinos, *Consciousness and History: Nationalist Critics of Greek Society*, New York, 1977, 128–30.

49. Cambon, I, 428, Paul to Madame Cambon 20 August 1897; Blancard, II, 469.

50. Bertrand Bareilles, *Constantinople*, 1918, 368; Allen Upward, *The East End of Europe*, 1908, 96–7; Mavroyennis, II, 20, diary entry for 25 October/7 November 1907.

51. Keith M. Wilson, 'Constantinople or Cairo?', in id. (ed.), *Imperialism and Nationalism in the Middle East*, 1983, 33, 35; Alan Bodger, 'Russia and the End of the Ottoman Empire', in Marian Kent (ed.), *The Great Powers and the End of the Ottoman Empire*, 1984, 78; Alan Palmer, *The Decline and Fall of the Ottoman Empire*, 1993 edn., 182; J. A. S. Grenville, 50–1, 81.

52. Feryal Irez and Vahide Gezgor, 'The Sale Kosk', in *National Palaces*, II, 114–15; Osmanoglu, 77–8.

53. Sturdza, 590–6; Edouard Fazy, *Les Turcs d'aujourd'hui*, 1898, 160; Donald C. Blaisdell, *European Financial Control in the Ottoman Empire*, New York, 1929, 133, 138, 141; Prince von Bulow, *Memoirs*, I, 1931, 245.

54. Halide Edib, *Memoirs*, 1926, 36n.

55. Woods, II, 271–2; Waugh, 97; Findlay, *Bureaucratic Reform*, 231–2, 243; Gordon, 229.

56. Exortoglu, 299, 301, 310, Owen, 192–4.

57. Rambert, 35, 67, 69, 103, entries for 31 October 1896, 7, 9 October 1899, 23 December 1900; Quataert, *Social Disintegration*, 118.

58. Herzl, 350, 161, entries for 21 May 1901, 22 June 1896; cf. Rambert, 197, entry for 20 December 1902: 'au palais on est tout à coup fort pessimiste sur les affaires de Macédoine.'

59. R. Porter, 257–8; R. J. Olson, 'Cities and Culture', in Theo Barker and Anthony Sutcliffe (eds.), *Megalopolis: the Giant City in History*, 1993, 167; Andrew Lees, *Cities Perceived: Urban Society in European and American Thought 1820–1940*, Manchester, 1985, 6–9.

60. Rambert, 35, entry for 24 October 1896; Mardin, *Religion and Social Change*, 82; *Anka, revue d'art et de littérature de Turquie*, 1989, 48–50; Lewis, *Emergence*, 206.

61. Stitt, 57, 88, 105; cf. Louise Hirszowicz, 'The Sultan and the Khedive 1892–1908', *Middle East Studies*, VIII, 1972, 296, for a similar reaction from the Khedive Abbas Hilmi.

62. Blunt, *Gordon*, 307–8, diary entry for 20 October 1884; Loti, *Les Désenchantées*, 1906 edn., 165; Duben and Behar, 40; PRO FO 800, f. 306v: observations of Arminius Vambery, 1894.

63. Ernest Edmondson Ramsaur jun., *The Young Turks: Prelude to the Revolution of 1908*, Princeton, 1957, 16, 46 and *passim*; Gilles Veinstein (ed.), *Salonique 1850–1918: la ville des Juifs et le réveil des Balkans*, 1992, 108.

14 Young Turks

1. Stitt, 97; Edib. *Memoirs*, 258.

2. Hercule Diamantopoulo, *Le Réveil de la Turquie*, Alexandria, 1908, 59–60; memoirs of Fausto Zonaro, consulted by kind permission of Signora Mafalda Zonaro Meneguzzer.

3. Diamontopulo, 171; C. R. Buxton, *Turkey in Revolution*, 1909, 119, 127; F. R. Bridge, 'The Young Turk Revolution: an Austro-Hungarian Assessment', paper delivered at 'The Young Turk Revolution of 1908', conference held at Manchester University, 23–25 March 1988.

4. Mary A. Poynter, *When Turkey was Turkey*, 1921, 56, diary entry for 1 December 1908; E. F. Knight, *The Awakening of Turkey*, 1909, 300.

5. Poynter, 58, entry for 3 December 1908; Diamantopoulo, 85, 121; Knight, 303; Feroz Ahmad, 'Unionist Relations with the Greek, Armenian and Jewish Communities of the Empire 1908–1914', in Braude and Lewis (eds.), I, 409.

6. Buxton, 199–200; Aubrey Herbert, *Ben Kendim*, 1918, 264; Francis McCullagh, *The Fall of Abdul Hamid*, 1909, 14; Mavroyennis, II, 34, diary entry for 4/17 December 1908.

7. Mavroyennis, II, 34, diary entry for 18/31 December 1908; Ali Cevaat Bey, *Fezleke*, Ankara, 1960, 18, 23; Glen Svenson, 'The Military Rising in Istanbul 1909', *Journal of Contemporary History*, V, 1970, 174.

8. Duhani, *Vieilles Gens*, 144.

9. Feroz Ahmad, *The Young Turks: the Committee of Union and Progress in Turkish Politics 1908–1914*, Oxford, 1969, 25; David Farhi, 'The *Seriat* as a Political Slogan or the Incident of 31 March', *Middle East Studies*, 1971, 7; Svenson, 181; Ahmed Emin, *The Development of Modern Turkey as Measured by its Press*, New York, 1914, 95.

10. Emin, *Development*, 97.

11. Ali Cevaat, 51–2; Farhi, 1–41.

12. Emin, *Development*, 95.

13. Sir W. M. Ramsay, *The Revolution in Constantinople and Turkey*, 1909, 91; Woods, II, 240; McCullagh, 208.

14. Abbott, *Turkey in Transition*, 255; MacCullagh, 244, 249; Osmanoglu, 142–3.

15. McCullagh, 283.

16. W. M. Ramsay, 123–5; *Catalogue des perles, pierreries, bijoux et objets d'art précieux, le tout ayant appartenu a S.M. le Sultan Abdul Hamid II, dont la vente aura lieu à Paris*, November 1911, items 241, 278 and 279.

17. Fesch, 160; A Mavroyennis, II, 41, diary entry for 27/10 May 1909; Gulersoy, *Dolmabahce*, 109.

18. Zafer Toprak, 'Nationalism and Economics in the Young Turk Era 1908–1918', paper delivered at 'The Young Turk Revolution of 1908', conference held at Manchester University, 23–25 March 1988; Issawi, 276.

19. *Guide téléphonique*, Constantinople, 1914, 51, 110; *Moniteur Oriental*, 4 July 1914; Ferriman, 123; Ramsay and McCullagh, xxvii–xxviii.

20. Pierre Loti et Samuel Viaud, *Suprêmes Visions d'Orient*, 1921, 22–3, diary entry for 16 August 1910; Hilary Sumner-Boyd and John Freely, *Strolling through Istanbul*, Istanbul, 1973, 144; A. Goodrich-Freer, *Things Seen in Constantinople*, 1926.

21. Le Corbusier, *Le Voyage d'Orient*, 1966, 69; *Documents on British Foreign Policy*, V, 255, annual report for Turkey for the year 1908; George S. Harris, *The Origins of Communism in Turkey*, Stanford, 1967, 20; Z. A. B. Zeman and W. B. Scharlau, *The Mercant of Revolution*, 1965, 127–8.

22. Mete Tuncay and Erik J. Zurcher, *Socialism and Nationalism in the Ottoman Empire 1876–1923*, 1994, 69, 84–6.

23. Rambert, 279, diary entry for 29 January 1904; Crawford, 17; *Women in Anatolia*, exhib. cat., 201; McCullagh, 7; W. M. Ramsay, 148.

24. Tinayre, 337; Hon. Mrs William Grey, *Journal of a visit to Egypt, Constantinople, the Crimea, Greece etc. in the suite of the Prince and Princess of Wales*, 3rd edn., 1870, 166, diary entry for 9 April 1869.

25. Jacob M. Landau, *Tekinalp: Turkish Patriot 1883–1961*, Istanbul, 1984, 117, 122; Zafer Toprak, 'The Family, Feminism and the State', in Edhem Eldem, *Vie politique*, 447.

26. Tuncay and Zurcher, 25; M. Sukru Hanioglu, *Kendi Mektuplarinda Enver Pasa*, 1989, 188, letter of 23 September.

27. Edib, *Memoirs*, 317–18; Mitler, 186; Robert Olson, *The Emergence of Kurdish Nationalism and the Sheikh Said Rebellion, 1880–1925*, Austin, 1989, 15; Gerard Chaliand (ed.), *A People without a Country: the Kurds and Kurdistan*, 1993 edn., 35, 27, 29.

28. Hassan Saab, *The Arab Federalists of the Ottoman Empire*, Amsterdam, 1958, 226; Sabine Prator, 'The Arab Factor in Young Turk Politics: Aspects from the Istanbul Press', paper delivered at 'The Young Turk Revolution of 1908', conference held at Manchester University, 23–25 March 1988; Abdullah, 70.

29. George Antonius, *The Arab Awakening*, Beirut, 1969, 108, 111, 119; Saab, 234, 238–9.

30. Saab, 236; Zeine M. Zeine, *Arab-Turkish Relations and the Emergence of Arab Nationalism*, Beirut, 1958, 83; Haidar, 30.

31. Haidar, 69, 54; Stitt, 156. For discussion of devolution and separate parliaments in Constantinople in 1913 see Pickthall, 118.

32. C. Ernest Dawn, *From Ottomanism to Arabism: Essays on the Origin of Arab Nationalism*, Urbana, 1973, 6, 12; Abdullah, 45.

33. Kushner, 35, 43, 77.

34. Kushner, 63, 65, 71; Sir Edwin Pears, *Forty Years in Constantinople*, 1917, 271.

35. Odette Keun, *Mesdemoiselles Daisne de Constantinople*, c. 1920, 53n.; Emile Edwards, *Mon Maître chéri*, 1915, 38.

36. Interview with Orhan Koprulu, 30 March 1992; George T. Park, 'The Life and Writings of M. Fuad Koprulu', unpublished Ph.D. thesis, Johns Hopkins University, 1975, 3–5 and n., 7, 9, 14.

37. Lewis, *Emergence*, 343; Park, 20, 28n., 30; Mitler, 187.

38. Lewis, *Emergence*, 231; Emin, *Development*, 109–10; Park, 127, 138n., 140–3, 147.

39. George A. Schreiner, *From Berlin to Baghdad*, New York, 1918, 327, diary entry for 7 August 1915.

40. Landau, *Tekinalp*, 116; Mitler, 187.

41. Berkes, *Secularism*, 373–4; John Reed, *War in Eastern Europe*, 1994 edn., 135; McCullagh, 157.

42. Loti and Viaud, 71, diary entry for 23 August 1910.

43. Ahmad, *Young Turks*, 108; Bilal N. Simsir, *Dis Basinda Ataturk ve Turk Devrimi*, cilt I, Ankara, 1981, 165, 169; Abbas Hilmi Papers, Durham University, 46/248, 67/57, reports of an agent, possibly Damad Ferid, to the Khedive Abbas Hilmi, 10 October 1911, 3 September 1912.

44. William C. Askew, *Europe and Italy's Acquisition of Libya 1911–1912*, Durham, North Carolina, 1942, 206–7, 210–11; Alan Bodger, 'Russia and the Fall of the Ottoman Empire', in Kent, (ed.), 83–4.

45. Tuncay and Zurcher, 47; Lady Grogan, *Life of J. D. Bourchier*, 1921, 136, 139.

46. Constant, 254–61; Andrew Rossos, *Russia and the Balkans: Inter-Balkan Rivalries and Russian Foreign Policy*, Toronto, 1981, 87–90.

47. Lauzanne, 120; Poynter, 90, 95, 101, 115, diary entry for 9, 18 November, 12 December 1912, 26 September 1913; H. Myles, *La Fin de Stamboul*, 2nd edn., 1921, 1, 16.

48. *Moniteur Oriental*, 5 November 1912; Lauzanne, 119, 144, 155, 180; Keun, 43n., 49, 52; Gaston Deschamps, *A Constantinople*, 1913, 178–9.

49. Constant, 259; Poynter, 91, diary entry for 12 November 1912; Lauzanne, 233; *Moniteur Oriental*, 16 November 1912.

50. Poynter, 91–2, diary entry for 17 November 1912; Lauzanne, 227, 230; Harold Nicolson, *Sweet Waters*, 1928 edn., 128; Paul G. Halpern, *The Mediterranean Naval Situation 1908–1914*, Cambridge, Mass., 1971, 104.

51. *Moniteur Oriental*, 29 November, 2 December; Ellis Ashmead-Bartlett, *With the Turks in Thrace*, 1913, 283.

52. Hanioglu 223, 225, letters of 12, 14 January 1913, cf. 54, letter of 7 May 1911.

53. Hanioglu, 230, letter of Enver, 28 January 1913; Joseph Heller, *British Policy towards the Ottoman Empire 1908–1914*, 1983, 78.

54. Poynter, 106, diary entry for 29 March 1913; William I. Shurrock, *French Imperialismi in the Middle East*, Madison, 1976, 168, Mallet to Grey 17 December 1913; Abbas Hilmi Papers, Durham University, 194/62, 66, 72: letters of 4, 11, 18 February 1913 to the Khedive Abbas Hilmi speak of 'la futilité de l'existence de l'empire'; Ahmad, 29.

55. PRO FO 371/9174, f. 68, Memorandum on the Armstrong Vickers' tenure of Turkish Dockyard, by Engineer Captain E. C. Hefford, 1923.

56. D. C. B. Lieven, *Russia and the Origins of the First World War*, 1983, 46, 69; Fritz Fischer, *War of Illusions: German Policies from 1911 to 1914*, 1975, 334; Hans Kannengiesser Pasha, *The Campaign in Gallipoli*, 1927, 47.

57. Sir Andrew Ryan, *The Last of the Dragomans*, 1951, 88–9; *Miniteur Oriental*, 3, 10, 16 July, 28 August 1914.

58. Ahmad, 138–9.

59. Kent, 15; Heller, 98, 134; William Eleroy Curtis, *Turkestan, the Heart of Asia*, 1911, 142; Erik J. Zurcher, *Turkey: a Modern History*, 1993, 117; Dan van der Dat, *The Ship that Changed the World: the Escape of the 'Goeben' to the Dardanelles in 1914*, 1986 edn., 157.

60. Waugh, 150–1; Ryan, 84, 103; A. L. Macfie, *The Straits Question 1909–1934*, Thessaloniki, 1993, 53; Heller, 141, Mallet to Grey 6 September 1914; *Moniteur Oriental*, 10, 11 September.

61. Paul G. Halpern, *The Naval War in the Mediterranean 1914–1918*, 1987, 48; Ulrich Trumpener, *Germany and the Ottoman Empire 1914–1918*, 1968, 33, 36, 40; Heller, 144–5.

62. Ryan, 101; Heller, 150, 156.

63. Halpern, *Naval War*, 77; Van der Dat, 246, 267; Trumpener, 51, 56, 59; Ryan, 105; Heller, 152.

64. Pears, 354; Cdt. Larcher, *La Guerre Turque dans la Guerre Mondiale*, 1926, 39n.; Schreiner, 168, diary entry for 7 April 1915; Osmanoglu, 189, 196.

65. Emile Edwards, *Journal d'un habitant de Constantinople 1914–1915*, 1915, 74, 78, 107; Ahmed Emin, *Turkey in the World War*, New Haven, 1930, 176.

66. Stephane Yerasimos (ed.), *Istanbul 1914–1923: capitale d'un monde illusoire ou l'agonie des vieux empires*, 1992, 17, 171; J. Reed, 131–2; Zeman and Scharlau, 133–4, 136.

67. Martin Gilbert, *Winston Churchill*, 8 vols., 1968–90, III, 189, 411; id., *Churchill: a Life*, 1991, 295, 300; Norman Rose, *Churchill: an Unruly Life*, 1995 edn., 114; Alan Moorehead, *Gallipoli*, 1956, 125–6.

68. Gilbert, *Churchill: a Life*, 303–4; Kannengiesser Pasha, 64, 259, 270; Moorehead, 56, 91, 217, 363.

69. Schreiner, 38, diary entry for 23 February 1915; Walker, 210; Zurcher, *Turkey*, 121.

70. Heath W. Lowry, *The Story behind Ambassador Morgenthau's Story*, Istanbul, 1990, 49; Schreiner, 327, diary entry for 7 August 1915; *Los Angeles Examiner*, 1 August 1926, quoted in Vahakn N. Dadrian, 'The Documentation of the World War I Armenian Massacres in the Proceedings of the Turkish Military Tribunal', *IJMES*, XXIII, 1991, 561, 568.

71. Randall Baker, *King Husain and the Kingdom of Hejaz*, 1979, 115–18, proclamation of 25 Shaaban 1334; Stitt, 163.

72. Emin, *Turkey in the World War*, 173, 176, 236; Berkes, *Secularism*, 417–18; Ernst Jaeckh, *The Rising Crescent*, New York, 1944, 132.

73. Van der Dat, 263; J. Reed, 115; Jaeckh, 137; Schreiner, 63, 277, 6 July 1915.

74. Halpern, *The Naval War*, 559, 560, 568; id. (ed.), *The Royal Navy in the Mediterranean 1915–1918*, 1987, 580; Gwynne Dyer, 'The Turkish Armistice of 1918: 2', *Middle Eastern Studies*, VIII, 3, October 1972, 323–4.

75. Dyer, 324, 330, 333, 337; Halpern, *Naval War*, 568.

15 Death of a Capital

1. PRO WO 161/85, Brigadier-General Sir James E. Edmonds, 'The Occupation of Constantinople 1918–1923', 1944, ff. 10–13 (henceforward referred to as Edmonds); FO 371/6485, f. 33, Note by R. W. Skelton, March 1921.

2. Jean Bernachot, *Les Armées alliées en Orient après l'Armistice de 1918*, 4 vols., 1972–8, II, 12, 17–18, despatch of 22 February 1919.

3. Erik Lance Knudsen, *Great Britain, Constantinople and the Turkish Peace Treaty*, New York, 1987, 22; J. G. Bennett, *Witness*, 1962, 30.

4. General Sir Charles Harington, *Tim Harington Looks Back*, 1940, 137; Nevile Henderson, *Water under the Bridges*, 1945, 105; Fox-Pitt Papers, consulted by kind permission of Sarah Fox-Pitt, W. A. F. L. Fox-Pitt to his father 11 October 1922, 22 May 1923.

5. Edmonds, f. 13; India Office Library Curzon Papers MSS EUR F 112/132: Curzon, 'The Future of Constantinople', 4 January 1919. I am grateful to David Gilmour for this reference.

6. Curzon, 'The Future of Constantinople', 4 January 1919; Knudsen, 29, 53; PRO 371/ 5190, f. 44, for population estimates. In 1914 the population, including suburbs, was estimated at 490,000 Turks, 225,000 Greeks, 155,000 Armenians and 150,000 'other'. Curzon may have obtained his figures from the 1911 *Encyclopedia Britannica*, art. 'Constantinople', by a Greek.

7. Erik Goldstein, 'Holy Wisdom and British Foreign Policy, 1918–1922: the St Sophia Redemption Agitation', *Byzantine and Modern Greek Studies*, XV, 1991, 47; Kent, 70; Myles, 165, article of 9 April 1919.

8. Macfie, 100–1; Mihir Bose, *The Aga Khans*, 1984, 180, Curzon to Montagu.

9. A. E. Montgomery, 'Lloyd George and the Greek Question 1918–22', in A. J. P. Taylor (ed.), *Lloyd George: Twelve Essays*, 1971, 264, quoting memorandum of 29 December 1920; Alexis Alexandris, *The Greek Minority of Istanbul and Greek-Turkish Relations 1918–1974*, Athens, 1983, 53; G. Theotokas, *Leonis, enfant grec de Constantinople*, 1985, 134.

10. PRO FO 371/5190, ff. 31–35, telegram from Patriarchate to Lloyd George, 18 February 1920; ibid., f. 134, committees of 154 associations and organizations to Lloyd George, 7 March 1920.

11. Patriarche Oecuménique, *Mémoire*, Paris, 1919, 8–9.

12. Halide Edib, *The Turkish Ordeal*, 1928, 5; Nesin, II, 57; Harold Armstrong, *Turkey in Travail*, 1925, 97.

13. Edib, *Turkish Ordeal*, 149; Nur Bilge Criss, 'Istanbul during the Allied Occupation 1918–1923', unpublished Ph.D. thesis, George Washington University, 1990, 13.

14. PRO FO 371/5190, f. 76, acting Patriarch to Lloyd George 15 March 1920, and f. 101, *mémoire* of 14 February 1920; ibid., f. 111, petition of 16/9 January 1920.

15. Galante, *Histoire des Juifs*, II, 82; Criss, 35, 71.

16. Nigel Nicolson, *Alex*, 1973, 73; Churchill College, Cambridge, De Robeck Papers 6/1, De Robeck to Curzon 23 August 1920; A. Mavroyennis, II, 86, diary entry for 17/30 June 1919.

17. Knudsen, 115; Ryan, 127; Paul Dumont, *Mustafa Kemal*, Brussels, 1983, 27.

18. Erik J. Zurcher, *The Unionist Factor: the Role of the Committee of Union and Progress in the Turkish National Movement 1905–1926*, Leiden, 1984, 81; Criss, 132, 139, 146.

19. Norman Itzkowitz and Vamik D. Volkan, *The Immortal Ataturk: a Psychobiography*, Chicago, 1984, 114, 116.

20. Yerasimos, *Istanbul*, 115; Alexandre Jevakhoff, *Kemal Ataturk: les chemins de l'Occident*, 1989, 75; Criss, 147.

21. Zurcher, *Unionist Factor*, 82; Itzkowitz and Volkan, 124–5.

22. Anon., *Fusilier Bluff: the Experiences of an Unprofessional Soldier in the Near East 1918–1919*, 1934, 236; Edib, *Turkish Ordeal*, 23, 27–9, 32–33n.

23. Jean Bernachot, *Les Armées alliés en Orient après l'Armistice de 1918*, 4 vols., 1972–8, IV, 118, report of 1 August 1919.

24. Armstrong, 105; PRO 371/4241 memorandum by Ryan, 12 December 1919; 371/4162, summary of intelligence, 9 January 1920.

25. Gai Minault, *The Khilafat Movement*, New York, 1982, 75–6, 83.

26. Knudsen, 143; Macfie, 101, 105, memorandum of British General Staff 6 January 1920; cf. Albert Christiaan Niemeijer, *The Khilafat Movement in India 1919–1924*, The Hague, 1972, 145.

27. Bennett, 32, 34; Knudsen, 169, 171–2; Churchill College, De Robeck Papers 6/1, anon. note 16 March 1920; Criss, 92, 97, 102, 164; PRO FO 371/5162, f. 90, note of 18 March 1920.

28. David Walder, *The Chanak Affair*, 1969, 106; Edmonds, f. 23; Ryan, 128; Stitt, 202.

29. Falih Rifki Atay, *The Ataturk I Knew*, Istanbul, 1982, 138; Lord Kinross, *Ataturk: the Rebirth of a Nation*, Nicosia, 1981 edn., 223.

30. Major-General Sir Edmund Ironside, *High Road to Command*, 1972, 97; Knudsen, 195, 197; Ryan, 145.

31. Criss, 119, 205; Alexandris, 74; Macfie, 138.

32. Criss, 167, 170; *Documents on British Foreign Policy 1919–1938*, First Series (hereafter DBFP), VII, 89, 91, Rumbold to Curzon 23 March 1921.

33. Martin Gilbert, *Sir Horace Rumbold*, 1973, 230–1; Criss, 54, 189; Jevakhoff, 184.

34. Demetra Vaka, *The Unveiled Ladies of Stamboul*, Boston, 1923, 105; Maurice Pernot, *La Question turque*, 1923, 9, 39, 43, 49.

35. DBFP, XVII, 23, 49, Rumbold to Curzon 20 January, 7 February 1921.

36. Edib, *Turkish Ordeal*, 71–3, 84, 89; Kinross, 214, 219; Jevakhoff, 185.

37. PRO FO 371/5170, report by Admiral Calthorpe 17 June 1919, memorandum by Calthorpe 31 July 1919.

38. PRO FO 371/5178, report of 12 August 1920; ibid. 5172, report of 13 October 1920; Whittall Papers, Abdulmecit to Canon Whitehouse, 9 September 1920.

39. PRO FO 371/5172/4131, report of 25 October 1920; *Burke's Royal Families of the World*, 2 vols., 1980, II, 244; PRO FO 371/6469, Rumbold to Curzon 29 April, 5 May 1921; Yerasimos, *Istanbul*, 129; Jevakhoff, 257–8.

40. James L. Barton, *Story of Near East Relief*, New York, 1930, 69, 158, 213.

41. Edib, *Turkish Ordeal*, 7, 9; Muftyzade K. Zia Bey, *Speaking of the Turks*, New York, 1922, 26.

42. *L'Express*, 1 December 1918; Armstrong, 97; Muftyzade, 152, 155; Pernot, 34.

43. Norman Stone and Michael Glenny, *The Other Russia*, 1991 edn., 55; General P. N. Wrangel, *Memoirs*, 1929, 326n.; Véra Dumesnil, *Le Bosphore tant aimé*, Brussels, 1947, 30, 37. General Harington wrote, 'No man in life has impressed me more than General Wrangel': Harington, 222.

44. Paul Morand, *Ouvert la nuit*, 1987 edn., 75; Stone and Glenny, 152–3; Dumesnil, 157; Alexis Wrangel, *General Wrangel, Russia's White Crusader*, 1990, 219, 223–6.

45. Sergei Tornow, 'Unpublished Memoirs', 207, quoted by kind permission of Baroness Elena Tornow; interview with Prince Alexander Volkonsky, Paris, 3 December 1992; John Dos Passos, *Orient Express*, New York, 1926, 12; Jak Deleon, *A Taste of Old Istanbul*, Istanbul, 1989, 44.

46. Stone and Glenny, 231; G. I. Gurdjieff, *Meetings with Remarkable Men*, 1963, 282.

47. Fox-Pitt Papers, W. A. F. L. Fox-Pitt to his mother 15 March 1923: 'Bobs [an English female acquaintance] fairly showed up the duchesses [at the Muscovite restaurant]'; Deleon, 47; Morand, 70; Zafer Toprak, 'Harasolar', *Istanbul*, 76, 78–80; Churchill College, De Robeck Papers 6/18, Rumbold to De Robeck 1 December 1921.

48. Irfan Orga, *Portrait of a Turkish Family*, 1988 edn., 187; Anon., *Fusilier Bluff*, 243; Eliot Granville Mears, *Modern Turkey*, 1924, 145; Myles, 175, article for 27 April 1919, 199, article for December 1920; Muftyzade, 77, 181.

49. Dos Passos, 11, 21–30; Armstrong, 188.

50. Muftyzade, 170; Yakup Kadri, *Sodome et Gomorrhe*, 1928, 16–17, 128, 132, 135.

51. Macfie, 149; Pernot, 8; Louis Francis, *La Neige de Galata*, 1936, 93–4; Alexandris, 104; Stitt, 247.

52. Edmonds, ff. 27–8; Knudsen, 292; Walder, 250–2.

53. Walder, 259, 260, 270–1, 275; Harington, 252, despatch of 20 October 1928 (*sic*); 277, speech of 30 October 1922; David Gilmour, *Curzon*, 1994, 545–6; PRO FO 371/7893, f. 63, Rumbold to Curzon 23 September 1922.

54. Walder, 295, 299, 327; Harington, 211.

55. Nesin, I, 104; PRO FO 371/7907, f. 113, Henderson to Curzon 24 October 1922; 371/9176, f. 84 and 84v.

56. Michael M. Finefrock, 'From Sultan to Republic: Mustafa Kemal Ataturk and the Structure of Turkish Politics 1922–24', unpublished Ph.D. thesis, Princeton, 1976, 65, 78; Kinross, 348.

57. PRO FO 371/7907, ff. 199, 212, 226, Rumbold to Curzon 4, 5 November 1922; 7914, f. 144, Rumbold to Curzon 14 November 1922.

58. Harington, 254, report of 20 October 1923; Fox-Pitt Papers, Fox-Pitt to his father 7 November and his brother Tommy 10 November 1922.

59. Letters in FO 371/7917 describe the situation in November–December 1922. On 28 November Henderson wrote to Curzon of 'dual control here, Turkish civilian and allied military'.

60. Kinross, 346; PRO FO 371/7917, f. 60, Rumbold to Curzon 21 November 1922; Gilbert, *Rumbold*, 279, Lady Rumbold to her mother 6 November 1922; Simsir, I, 79, 109; *Le Journal*, 15, 18 November 1922.

61. PRO FO 371/7917, f. 98, Henderson to Curzon 28 November 1922; Alexandris, 104, 132; DBFP, XVIII, 421n., memorandum of Ryan 26 December 1922.

62. PRO FO 371/7907, f. 226, Rumbold to Curzon 5 November 1922; Gilbert, *Rumbold*, 278–9, Lady Rumbold to her mother 6 November 1922; PRO FO 371/7912/12647, Rumbold to Curzon 7 November 1922.

63. Harington, 130–1; PRO FO 371/7962, f. 150, Henderson to Curzon 17 November, 371/7916/13192, secret eastern summary 24 November; interview with Prince Sami, the Sultan's great-nephew, London, 21 April 1995.

64. Niyazi Berkes (ed.), *Turkish Nationalism and Western Civilisation: Selected Essays of Zia Gokalp*, 1959, 227; Finefrock, 73, 87; PRO FO 371/7917, f. 40, Eastern summary 1 December 1922; 7916, f. 7, Eastern summary 24 November 1922. According to

7917, f. 41, Eastern summary 1 December, public opinion was unfavourable to the abolition of the sultanate but 'public opinion has never counted for much since the institution of so-called parliamentary government in Turkey.'

65. PRO FO 371/7963, f. 142, Henderson to Curzon 28 November 1922; Simsir, I, 151, 164; *Muslim Standard*, 30 November 1922.

66. Finefrock, 106; Orga, 218; Haidar, 258; Stitt, 267.

67. Erik J. Zurcher, *Political Opposition in the Early Turkish Republic: the Progressive Republican Party*, Leiden, 1991, 24; PRO FO 371/9135/2660, Rumbold to Curzon 1 March 1923.

68. Michael Howard and John Sparrow, *The Coldstream Guards 1920–1946*, 1952, 3; Criss, 113; Walder, 349–52; Olga Verkorsky Dunlop, *Register of the Baron Petr Nikolaevich Vrangel Collection in the Hoover Institution Archives*, Stanford, 1991, 72, 103–5; PRO 371/9174, f. 129, 141, Henderson to Curzon 10, 15 October 1923.

69. William M. Johnston, *The Austrian Mind*, 1972, 73.

70. Kent, 193; Lewis, *Emergence*, 255; Finefrock, 230, 249, 262, 273.

71. Itzkowitz and Volkan, 270-3; Atay, 217; Zurcher, *Unionist Factor*, 137; Lewis, *Emergence*, 257; Jevakhoff, 375n.

72. Bernachot, II, 17, 145, despatches of 1 March, 27 April 1919; PRO FO 371/4162, summary of intelligence, 9 January 1920.

73. Lewis, *Emergence*, 258.

74. Simsir, I, 460; *Le Temps*, 6 March 1924; Finefrock, 288, 292, 293; Gulersoy, *Dolmabahce*, 138, 141.

75. PRO FO 371/10217, ff. 30, 155, R. C. Lindsay to Macdonald 5, 24 March 1924.

76. *Istanbul Ansiklopedisi*, art. 'Abdulmecid'; Salih Keramet Nigar, *Halife Ikinci Abdulmecid*, Istanbul, 1964, 7–9.

Epilogue

1. Sir Hugh Knatchbull Hugesson, *Diplomat in Peace and War*, 1949, 138; Kinross, 438.

2. Lewis, *Emergence*, 405; Robert Byron, *Letters Home*, 1991, 65, letter of 29 May 1926; Nesin, I, 68, 124; Harold Armstrong, *Turkey and Syria Reborn*, 1930, 224–5.

3. Harris, 124–6; Harry A. Franck, *The Fringe of the Moslem World*, 1928, 412; Kinross, 402.

4. Franck, 344; Itzkowitz and Volkan, 254; Kinross, 415; Halide Edib, *Turkey Faces West*, New Haven, 1930, 221, 226.

5. *Istanbul Ansiklopedisi*, art. 'Ataturk ve Istanbul'; Kinross, 443.

6. Albert E. Kalderon, *Abraham Galante*, New York, 1983, 50; Park, 38, 61.

7. Simsir, I, 683–5; *Le Journal*, 14 March 1924.

8. Interview with Basri Danishmend, 2 November 1991.

9. Osmanoglu, 236, 240, 245.

10. Landau, 103; Sacheverell Sitwell, *Far from My Home: stories long and short*, 1931, 88; interview with Nigar Alemdar, 1 July 1994; interview with Selim Dirvana, 9 October 1992.

11. Kamal Madhar Ahmad, *Kurdistan during the First World War*, 1994, 92; Olson, *Kurdish Nationalism*, 53, 63, 64, 75; Chris Kutschera, *Le Mouvement National Kurde*, 1979, 31–3.

12. PRO FO 371/12255, f. 63–4, Sir Henry Dobbs to Leo Amery 8 December 1926; f. 86, Sir G. Clerk to Austen Chamberlain 4 January 1927.

13. Kutschera, 42; Chaliand, 40.

14. André Raymond, *Le Caire*, 1993, 317; William L. Cleveland, *The Making of an Arab Nationalist: Ottomanism and Arabism in the Life and Thought of Sati al-Husri*, Cleveland, 1971, 30, 44; interview with Khaldun al-Husri, 28 November 1994.

15. Stitt, 290–1; Haidar, 238.

16. Gerald de Gaury, *Traces of Travel*, 1983, 145–6.

17. Interview with Sherifa Sfyne, Alexandria, 4 January 1993.

18. Alexandris, 162; Theotokas, 168; Thomas Doulis, *Disaster and Fiction: Modern Greek Fiction and the Asia Minor Disaster of 1922*, Berkeley, 1977, 92, 98, 108, 217.

19. PRO FO 371/9174, ff. 153–4, Lieutenant Patterson to director of military operations and intelligence 11 November 1923; Alexandris, 185; Angèle Lorely, 'Esquisses', Istanbul Library; Liddell, 100, 159, 238.

20. Yerasimos, *Istanbul*, 202–3; Nicholas Bethell, *The Palestine Triangle*, 1979, 114–19.

21. Alexandris, 217; interview with Baruh Pinto, 9 November 1993; Kalderon, 59.

22. *Istanbul Ansiklopedisi*, art. 'Alti Yedi Eylul Olaylari'; Alexandris, 257, 262; John Pearson, *The Life of Ian Fleming*, 1966, 271.

23. Feroz Ahmad, *The Turkish Experiment in Democracy 1950–1975*, 1977, 78–9, 89; Alexandris, 265, 271.

24. Interview with Achilles Melas, 1 October 1992; Sturdza, 260, 82.

25. Semih Vaner (ed.), *Istanbul*, 1991, 132; Tuglaci, *Balian*, 290, 427; interview with Istanbul Armenian, 14 July 1992.

26. Interviews with E. F. de Testa, Paris 24, 25 February, 6 May 1994.

27. Clayer and Popovic (eds.), 67.

28. Mary C. Wilson, *King Abdullah, Britain and the Making of Jordan*, Cambridge, 1987, 220.

29. Interviews with Jose Naoum, Paris, 20 April, 20 May 1992.

30. PRO FO 371/16013–16016, Ryan to Simon 21 June 1932. I am grateful for this reference to Alan de Lacy Rush.

31. H. St J. Philby, *Arabian Jubilee*, 257, 250–1; Gerald de Gaury, *Faisal, King of Saudi Arabia*, 1966, 22: I am grateful for these references to Alan Rush. David Holden and Richard Johns, *The House of Saud*, 1981, 203.

32. Godfrey Goodwin, *Sinan and City Planning*, Rome, 1989, 83.

33. Paul Wittek, 'Les Archives de Turquie,' *Byzantion*, 1938, 693.

34. 'Stamboulimies', *Les Carents de l'Exotisme*, XI, Janvier–Juillet 1993, 79, Abdulmecid to Loti 20 May 1921; Ernest Mamboury, *Guide touristique*, 363.

35. *Turkish Daily News*, 26 September 1994.

Bibliography

Primary Sources

Archives du Ministère des Affaires Etrangères, Paris: Correspondance Politique, Turquie, 68, 176: ambassadors' reports, 1724, 1787.

British Library, London, Add. MSS 38979, 38985, 38987, 39018, 39023–4, 39103: Layard Papers, letters of Ahmed Vefyk to Layard; 56301, Pisani to Strangford 1821.

Churchill College, Cambridge, De Robeck Papers, MSS 6/1, 6/18: correspondence of Admiral de Robeck.

Imperial War Museum, London, Fox-Pitt Papers (consulted by kind permission of Sarah Fox-Pitt): letters of W. A. F. L. Fox-Pitt to his parents.

National Library of Scotland, Edinburgh, Department of Manuscripts, Liston Papers, MSS 5572, 5628, 5630: despatches of Liston and Pisani 1794–5, 1815–20; 5709, journal of Lady Liston 1812–13.

Public Record Office, Kew, Middlesex, FO 78/225, 3081: diplomatic despatches 1833, 1880; FO 371/4162, 4241, 5162, 5170, 5172, 5178, 5190, 6469, 7893, 7907, 7912, 7914, 7916, 7917, 7962, 7963, 9174, 12255: papers of the British High Commission in Constantinople, 1918–23; WO 161/85: Sir James E. Edmonds, 'The Occupation of Constantinople 1918–1923'.

School of Oriental and African Studies Library, London, Paget Papers 50 X4: letters of Alexander Mavrocordato 1699.

State Archives, Stockholm, Turcica 22, 24, 100: letters from Comte de Bonneval 1734–45.

Secondary Sources

Unless otherwise stated, all works in English are published in London, all works in French in Paris and all works in Turkish in Istanbul.

Abbott, G. F., *Turkey in Transition*, 1909.

——*Under the Turk in Constantinople*, 1920.

Abdullah of Jordan, King, *Memoirs*, 1950.

Abou el-Hajj, Rifa'at Ali, *The 1703 Rebellion and the Structure of Ottoman Politics*, Istanbul, 1984.
——*Formation of the Modern State: the Ottoman Empire, Sixteenth to Eighteenth Centuries*, Albany, 1991.
Abu-Lughod, Janet, *Cairo: 1000 Years of the City Victorious*, Princeton, 1971.
Abu-Manneh, Butros, 'Sultan Abdul Hamid II and the Sharifs of Mecca 1880–1900', *Asian and African Studies*, 1972, 1–21.
Adivar, Adnan, *La Science chez les Turcs Ottomans*, 1938.
Adjemoglou, Nicolaos, *The Ayazmata of the City*, Athens, 1990 (in Greek).
Adnan, Abdulhak, *La Science chez les Turcs Ottomans*, 1939.
Afetinan, Prof. Dr, *Aperçu général sur l'histoire économique de l'Empire Turc-Ottoman*, 2nd edn., Ankara, 1976.
Ahmad, Feroz, *The Young Turks: the Committee of Union and Progress in Turkish Politics 1908–1914*, Oxford, 1969.
——*The Turkish Experiment in Democracy 1950–1975*, 1977.
Alderson, A. D., *The Structure of the Ottoman Dynasty*, 1956.
Alexandris, Alexis, *The Greek Minority of Istanbul and Greek-Turkish Relations 1918–1974*, Athens, 1983.
Allom, Thomas and the Revd Robert Walsh, *Constantinople and the Scenery of the Seven Churches of Asia Minor*, 2 vols., 1838.
Altuna, Abdulkadir, *Osmanli Seyhulislamlari*, Ankara, 1972.
And, Metin, *Karagoz*, 3rd edn., Istanbul, n.d.
——*A Pictorial History of Turkish Dancing*, Ankara, 1976.
——*Turkish Miniature Painting*, rev. edn., Istanbul, 1982.
——*Istanbul in the Sixteenth Century*, Istanbul, 1994.
Andersen, Hans Christian, *A Poet's Bazaar*, New York, 1988.
Anderson, Dorothy, *The Balkan Volunteers*, 1968.
Anderson, M. S., *The Eastern Question*, 1982.
——*The Rise of Modern Diplomacy*, 1993.
Andrews, Walter G., *Poetry's Voice, Society's Song: Ottoman Lyric Poetry*, Seattle, 1985.
Anon., *Fusilier Bluff: the Experience of an Unprofessional Soldier in the Near East 1918–1919*, 1934.
Anon., *Letters Historical and Critical from a Gentleman in Constantinople to his Friend in London*, 1730.
Antonius, George, *The Arab Awakening*, Beirut, 1969 edn.
Argenti, Philip, *The Massacres of Chios*, 1932.
Armstrong, Harold, *Turkey in Travail*, 1925.
——*Turkey and Syria Reborn*, 1930.
Arnakis, G. Georgiades, 'The Greek Church of Constantinople and the Ottoman Empire', *Journal of Modern History*, 1952, 235–50.
Arpee, Leon, *A History of Armenian Christianity*, New York, 1946.
Artamian, Sarkis, *The Armenian Community*, New York, 1955.
Artan, Tulay, 'Architecture as a Theatre of Life: Profile of the Eighteenth-century Bosphorus', unpublished Ph.D. thesis, Massachussets Institute of Technology, 1989.
Artinian, Vartan, *The Armenian Constitutional System in the Ottoman Empire 1839–1863*, Istanbul, 1990.

Arzik, Imet, *Anthologie de la poésie turque*, 1968.

Ashmead-Bartlett, Ellis, *With the Turks in Thrace*, 1913.

Atamian, Sarkis, *The Armenian Community*, New York, 1955.

Atasoy, Nurhan and Julian Raby, *Iznik: the Pottery of Ottoman Turkey*, 1989.

Atay, Falih Rifki, *The Ataturk I Knew*, Istanbul, 1982.

Atil, Esin (ed.), *Suleymanname: the Illustrated History of Suleyman the Magnificent*, Washington, 1986.

——*The Age of Sultan Suleyman the Magnificent*, New York, 1987.

——*Turkish Art*, New York, 1980.

Auldjo, John, *Journal of a Visit to Constantinople and Some of the Greek Islands in the Spring and Summer of 1833*, 1835.

Avrenche, Henry, *La Mort de Stamboul*, 1930.

Babinger, Franz, *Mehmed the Conqueror and His Time*, Princeton, 1992 edn.

Bailey, Frank E., *British Policy and the Turkish Reform Movement*, Harvard, 1932.

Baker, Patricia, 'The Fez in Turkey: a Symbol of Modernisation?', *Costume*, 1986, 72–85.

Baltimore, Lord, *A Tour to the East in the Years 1763 and 1764*, 1767.

Barbaro, Nicolò, *Diary of the Siege of Constantinople 1453*, tr. J. R. Jones, New York, 1969.

Bardakgi, Murat, *Osmanlida Seks*, 1993.

Bareilles, Bertrand, *Constantinople*, 1918.

Barker, Arthur, 'The Cult of the Tulip in Turkey', *Journal of the Royal Horticultural Society*, LVI, 1931, 234–44.

Barker, Theo and Anthony Sutcliffe (eds.), *Megalopolis: the Giant City in History*, 1993.

Barnett, R. D., *The Sephardi Heritage*, 2 vols., 1971–89.

Baronian, Hagop, *The Perils of Politeness*, New York, 1983.

Barsoumian, Hagop Leon, 'The Armenian Amira Class of Constantinople', unpublished Ph.D. thesis, Columbia, 1980.

Basmadjian, K. J., *Essai sur l'histoire de la littérature ottomane*, Constantinople, 1910.

Batu, Hamit et Jean-Louis Bacqué-Gramont, *L'Empire Ottoman: la République de Turquie et la France*, Istanbul, 1986.

Batur, Enis (ed.), *Encomium to Istanbul*, Istanbul, 1991.

Baudin, P., *Les Israélites de Constantinople*, Istanbul 1872, 1989 edn.

Belin, M. A., *Histoire de la Latinité de Constantinople*, 2nd edn., 1894.

Benbassa, Esther, *Un Grand Rabbin sépharade en politique 1892–1923*, 1991.

Benjamin, S. G. W., *The Turks and the Greeks*, New York, 1867.

Bennett, J. G., *Witness*, 1962.

Bent, J. Theodore (ed.), *Early Voyages and Travels in the Levant*, 1893.

Berk, Nurullah, *Istanbul chez les peintres turcs et étrangers*, Istanbul, 1977.

Berkes, Niyazi, *The Development of Secularism in Turkey*, Montreal, 1964.

——(ed.) *Turkish Nationalism and Western Civilisation: Selected Essays of Zia Gokalp*, 1959.

Bernachot, Jean, *Les Armées alliées en Orient après L'Armistice de 1918*, 4 vols., 1972–8.

Bernard, Yvelise, *L'Orient du XVIe siècle à travers les récits de voyageurs français*, 1988.

Bertele, Tommaso, *Il Palazzo degli ambasciatori di Venezia a Constantinopoli e le sue antiche memorie*, Bologna, 1932–X.

Beydilli, Kemal, 'Ignatius Mouradgea d'Ohsson', *Istanbul Universitesi Edebiyat Fakultesi Tarih Dergisi*, XXXIV, 1984, 248–314.

Bibesco, Marthe, *La Nymphe Europe*, 1960.

Bierman, Irene *et al.* (eds.), *The Ottoman City and its Parts*, New Rochelle, 1991 edn.

Birge, John Kingsley, *The Bektashi Order of Dervishes*, 1965.

Blaisdell, Donald C., *European Financial Control in the Ottoman Empire*, New York, 1929.

Blancard, Théodore, *Les Mavroyenni: histoire d'Orient*, 2 vols., 1909.

Blanqui, J. A., *Voyage en Bulgarie pendant l'année 1841*, 1843.

Blowitz, Henri de, *Une Course à Constantinople*, 1884.

Blunt, Wilfrid Scawen, *Gordon at Khartoum*, 1911.

——*My Diaries*, 2 vols., 1919–20.

Boghossian, Sarkis, *Iconographie arménienne*, 1987.

Bonnac, Marquis de, *Mémoire historique sur l'Ambassade de France à Constantinople*, 1894.

Bonneville de Marsangy, Louis, *Le Chevalier de Vergennes: son ambassade à Constantinople*, 2 vols., 1894.

Boppe, Catherine et André, *Les Peintres du Bosphore au XVIIIe siècle*, 1989.

Boschma, Cornelis and Jacques Perot, *Antoine-Ignace Melling (1763–1831), artiste voyageur*, 1991.

Bosscha Erdbrink, C., *At the Threshold of Felicity: Ottoman-Dutch Relations during the Embassy of Cornelis Calkoen at the Sublime Porte 1726–1744*, Ankara, 1975.

Bouchard, Jacques, 'Nicolas Mavrocordatos et l'époque des tulipes', *Eranisthes*, XVII, Athens, 1981, 120–6.

——'Les Lettres fictives de Nicolas Mavrocordato à la manière de Phalaris: une apologie de l'absolutisme', *Revue des Etudes du Sud-Est Européen*, XIII, 1972, 197–207.

——(ed.), *Les Loisirs de Philothée*, Athens–Montreal, 1989.

Boulden, James E. P., *An American among the Orientals*, Philadelphia, 1855.

Boutros-Ghali, Anna Naguib and Archag Alboyadjian, *Les Dadian*, Cairo, 1965.

Brassey, Mrs, *Sunshine and Storm in the East or Cruises to Cyprus and Constantinople*, 1880.

Braude, Benjamin and Bernard Lewis (eds.), *Christians and Jews in the Ottoman Empire*, 2 vols., 1982.

Brown, Horatio F., *Studies in the History of Venice*, 2 vols., 1907.

Brown, Sarah Graham, *Images of Women: the Portrayal of Women in Photography of the Middle East 1860–1950*, 1988.

Brummett, Palmyra, *Ottoman Seapower and Levantine Diplomacy in the Age of Discovery*, Albany, 1994.

Brun, Charles, 'Les Grecs de Constantinople', *Revue Moderne*, LII, 10 June 1869, 422–39.

Busbecq, Ogier Ghislain de, *Turkish Letters*, Oxford, 1927.

Buxton, C. R., *Turkey in Revolution*, 1909.

Cabuk, Vahid, *Koprululer*, 1988.

Calosso, Colonel, *Mémoires d'un vieux soldat*, Turin–Nice, 1857.

Camariano, Nestor, *Alexandre Mavrocordato le Grand Drogman: son activité diplomatique*, Thessaloniki, 1970.

Camariano-Cioran, Ariadna, *Les Académies princières de Bucarest et de Jassy et leurs professeurs*, Thessaloniki, 1974.

Cambon, Paul, *Correspondance*, 3 vols., 1940–6.

Cantacasin, Theodore Spandouyn, *Petit Traicté de l'origine des turcqz*, ed. Charles Schefer, 1896.

Cantacuzène, Jean Michel, *Mille Ans dans les Balkans*, 1992.

Carayon, Père Auguste, *Relations inédites de la Compagnie de Jésus à Constantinople et dans le Levant*, 1864.

Carlier de Pinon, M., *Voyage en Orient*, 1920.

Carnoy, Henry et Jean Nicolaides, *Folklore de Constantinople*, 2 vols., 1894.

Catalogue de la Bibliothèque de feu Ahmed Vefyk Pacha, Constantinople, 1893.

Catalogue des perles, pierreries, bijoux et objets d'art précieux, le tout ayant appartenu à S.M. le Sultan Abdul Hamid II, dont la vente aura lieu à Paris, November 1911.

Caussin de Perceval, A. P. (tr.), *Précis historique de la destruction du corps des Janissaires par le Sultan Mahmoud en 1826*, 1833.

Celik, Zeyneb, *The Remaking of Istanbul*, Seattle and London, 1989.

Cevaat Bey, Ali, *Fezleke*, Ankara, 1960.

Cezar, Mustafa, *XIX Yuzyil Beyoglusu*, Istanbul, 1991.

Chalcondyle, *L'Histoire de la décadence de l'Empire Grec et de l'établissement de celuy des Turcs*, 2 vols., 1662.

Chaliand, Gerard (ed.), *A People without a Country: the Kurds and Kurdistan*, 1993 edn.

Champonnois, Suzanne, *Le Mythe de Constantinople et l'opinion publique en Russie au XIXe siècle*, Istanbul, 1989.

Charlemont, Lord, *Travels in Greece and Turkey 1749*, ed. W. B. Stanford and E. J. Finopulos, 1984.

Charrière, M. de, *Négociations de la France dans le Levant*, 4 vols., 1848–60.

Chassiotis, G., *L'Instruction publique chez les Grecs depuis la prise de Constantinople par les Turcs*, 1881.

Chénier, Madame, *Lettres sur les danses grecques*, 1879 edn.

Chesneau d'Aramon, Jean, *Le Voyage de Monsieur Chesneau d'Aramon, ambassadeur pour le Roy au Levant*, ed. Charles Schefer, 1887.

Choiseul-Gouffier, Comte de, *Voyage pittoresque de la Grèce*, 2 vols., 1782–1809.

Cizgen, Engin, *Photography in the Ottoman Empire 1839–1919*, Istanbul, 1987.

Clark, E. C., 'The Ottoman Industrial Revolution', *International Journal of Middle East Studies*, V, 1974, 65–76.

Clayer, Nathalie and Alexandre Popovic (eds.), *Presse turque et presse de Turquie*, Istanbul–Paris, 1992.

Cleveland, William I., *The Making of an Arab Nationalist: Ottomanism and Arabism in the Life and Thought of Sati al-Husri*, Cleveland, 1971.

Clogg, Richard (ed.), *Balkan Society in the Age of Greek Independence*, 1981.

——*The Struggle for Greek Independence*, 1973.

——*The Movement for Greek Independence*, 1976.

Cockerell, C. R., *Travels in Southern Europe and the Levant 1810–1817*, 1903.

Constant, Stephen, *Foxy Ferdinand*, 1979.

[Constantinios] *Constantiniade ou Description de Constantinople ancienne et moderne comparée par un philologue et archéologue*, Constantinople, 1846.

Cook, M. A. (ed.), *A History of the Ottoman Empire to 1730*, Cambridge, 1976.

Correspondence respecting the Disturbances at Constantinople in August 1896 presented to both Houses of Parliament by command of Her Majesty, 1897.

Coufopoulos, Demetrius, *A Guide to Constantinople*, 1910.

Cox, Samuel S., *The Isles of the Princes; or, the Pleasures of Prinkipo*, 1887.

——*Diversions of a Diplomat in Turkey*, New York, 1887.

Crawford, F. Marion, *Constantinople*, 1895.

Criss, Nur Bilge, 'Istanbul during the Allied Occupation', unpublished Ph.D. thesis, George Washington University, 1990.

Cunningham, Allan, *Anglo-Ottoman Encounters in the Age of Revolution*, 1993.

——*Eastern Questions in the Nineteenth Century*, 1993.

Curtis, William Eleroy, *Turkestan, the Heart of Asia*, 1911.

Curtiss, John Shelton, *Russia's Crimean War*, Durham, North Carolina, 1979.

Dadian, Prince Mek-B., 'La Société arménienne contemporaine', *Revue des Deux Mondes*, 15 June 1867, 903–28.

Dadrian, Vahakn N., 'The Documentation of the World War I Armenian Massacres in the Proceedings of the Turkish Military Tribunal', *International Journal of Middle East Studies*, XXIII, 1991, 549–76.

Dallaway, James, *Constantinople Ancient and Modern*, 1798.

Dalleggio d'Alessio, E., 'Liste des Podestats de la colonie génoïse de Péra', *Revue des Etudes Byzantines*, XXVII, 1969, 151–7.

Dankoff, Robert (ed.), *The Intimate Life of an Ottoman Statesman: Melek Ahmed Pasha, as Portrayed in Evliya Celebi's Book of Travels*, Albany, 1991.

Dasnabedian, Hratch, *History of the Armenian Revolutionary Federation Dashnaktsutian 1890–1924*, Milan, 1990.

Davis, Revd, E. J., *Osmanli Proverbs and Quaint Sayings*, 1898.

Davis, Fanny, *The Ottoman Lady: a Social History from 1718 to 1918*, New York, 1986.

Davis, James C. (ed. and tr.), *The Pursuit of Power: Venetian Ambassadors' Reports from Spain, Turkey, France in the Age of Philip II*, 1970.

Davison, Roderick H., *Reform in the Ottoman Empire 1856–1876*, Princeton, 1963.

Dawn, C. Ernest, *From Ottomanism to Arabism: Essays on the Origins of Arab Nationalism*, Urbana, 1973.

De Amicis, Edmondo, *Constantinople*, 1894 edn.

Dedem de Gelder, Baron de, *Mémoires*, 1900.

De Gaury, Gerald, *Rulers of Mecca*, 1951.

——*Three Kings in Baghdad*, 1961.

——*Traces of Travel*, 1983.

Deherain, H., *La Vie de Pierre Ruffin*, 2 vols., 1929–30.

Deleon, Jak, *A Taste of Old Istanbul*, Istanbul, 1989.

——*Ancient Districts on the Golden Horn*, Istanbul, 1992.

Deringil, Selim, 'The Invention of Tradition as Public Image in the Late Ottoman Empire, 1808 to 1980', *Comparative Studies in Society and History*, XXXV, 1, January 1993, 1–29.

——'Legitimacy Structures in the Ottoman State: the Reign of Abdulhamid II 1876–1909', *International Journal of Middle East Studies*, XXIII, 1991, 345–59.

Deschamps, Gaston, *A Constantinople*, 1913.

Destrilhes, M., *Confidences sur la Turquie*, 1855.

Devereux, Robert, *The First Ottoman Constitutional Period*, Baltimore, 1963.

——'Suleyman Pasha's "the Feeling of the Revolution"', *Middle Eastern Studies*, XV, 1, 1979, 3–35.

Devrim, Shirin, *A Turkish Tapestry: the Shakirs of Istanbul*, 1994.

Diamandouros, Nikoros P. (ed.), *Hellenism and the First Greek War of Liberation 1821–1830*, Thessaloniki, 1976.

Diamantopoulo, Hercule, *Le Réveil de la Turquie*, Alexandria, 1908.

Dimaras, C. Th., *Histoire de la littérature néo-héllenique*, Athens, 1965.

Djevad Bey, A., *Etat militaire ottoman depuis la fondation de l'Empire jusqu'à nos jours*, Constantinople–Paris, 1882.

Dodds, Anna Bowman, *In the Palaces of the Sultan*, 1904.

Dos Passos, John, *Orient Express*, New York, 1927.

Douglas, Revd J. A., *The Redemption of Saint Sophia*, 1919.

Doulis, Thomas, *Disaster and Fiction: Modern Greek Fiction and the Asia Minor Disaster of 1922*, Berkeley, 1977.

Driault, Edouard, *La Politique orientale de Napoléon*, 1904.

——*L'Egypte et l'Europe: la Crise de 1839–1841*, 2 vols., Cairo, 1930–31.

——and Michel L'Héritier, *Histoire diplomatique de la Grèce de 1821 à nos jours*, 5 vols., 1925–6.

Duben, Alan and Cem Behar, *Istanbul Households: Marriage, Family and Fertility 1880–1940*, Cambridge, 1991.

Dudell, Tim, *Tales from the Orient and Pera: Sketches of Constantinople*, Constantinople, n.d.

Dufferin and Ava, Dowager Marchioness of, *My Russian and Turkish Journals*, 1917.

Du Fresne Canaye, Philippe, *Le Voyage du Levant*, 1986 edn.

Duhani, Said N-, *Vieilles Gens, vieilles demeures*, Istanbul, 1947.

——*Quand Beyoglu s'appelait Péra*, Istanbul, 1956.

Dumesnil, Vera, *Le Bosphore tant aimé*, Brussels, 1947.

Du Mont, M., *Voyages*, 4 vols., La Haye, 1699.

Dumont, Paul, *Mustafa Kemal*, Brussels, 1983.

Duparc, Pierre, *Recueil des instructions données aux ambassadeurs et ministres de France*, 1969.

Durand, Alfred, *Jeune Turquie, Vieille France*, 1909.

Dutu, Alexandru and Paul Cernovodeanu (eds.), *Dimitrie Cantemir, Historian of South-East European and Oriental Civilisations*, Bucharest, 1973.

Dwight, Henry O., *Turkish Life in War Time*, 1881.

——*Constantinople and its Problems*, 1901.

Dyer, Gwynne, 'The Turkish Armistice of 1918: 2', *Middle Eastern Studies*, VIII, 3, October 1972, 313–48.

Edib, Halide, *Memoirs*, 1926.

——*The Turkish Ordeal*, 1928.

——*Turkey Faces West*, New Haven, 1930.

Edwards, Emile, *Mon Maître chéri*, 1915.

——*Journal d'un habitant de Constantinople 1914–1915*, 1915.

Edwards, George Wharton, *Constantinople–Stamboul*, Philadelphia, 1930.

Eldem, Edhem (ed.), *Recherches sur la ville ottomane: le cas du quartier de Galata*, Istanbul, 1991.

——*La Vie politique, économique et socio-culturelle à l'époque jeune-turque*, Istanbul, 1991.

Eldem, Seddad Hakki, *Reminiscences of Istanbul*, Istanbul, 1979.

——*Reminiscences of the Bosphorus*, Istanbul, 1979.

[Eliot, Sir Charles], *Turkey in Europe*, 1900.

Elliot, Sir Henry G., *Some Revolutions and other Diplomatic Experiences*, 1927.

Elliott, J. H., *Richelieu and Olivares*, 1992 edn.

Bibliography

Bibliography

El-Tangrouti, *Relation d'une ambassade marocaine en Turquie*, ed. Henry de Castries, 1929.

Emin, Ahmed, *The Development of Modern Turkey as Measured by its Press*, New York, 1914.

——*Turkey in the World War*, New Haven, 1930.

Encyclopedia of Islam, 2nd edn., Leiden, 1956–.

L'Epoque phanariote, Thessaloniki, 1974 (conference proceedings).

Epstein, Mark Alan, *The Ottoman Jewish Communities and their Role in the Fifteenth and Sixteenth Centuries*, Freiburg, 1980.

Esenbel, Selcuk, 'A *fin de siècle* Japanese Romantic in Istanbul: the Life of Yamada Torajiso and his Toruko Gakan or a Pictorial Look at Turkey', unpublished article, Istanbul, 1994.

Essayan, Zabel, *Les Jardins de Silihdar*, 1994.

Etmekjian, James, *The French Influence on the Western Armenian Renaissance 1843–1915*, New York, 1964.

Exertoglou, H., 'The Greek Bankers in Constantinople 1856–1881', unpublished Ph.D. thesis, London, 1985.

Exhibition catalogues:

Les Peintures 'turques' de Jean-Baptiste Vanmour 1671–1737, Ankara, 1975.

L'Orient des provençaux dans l'histoire, Marseilles, 1982.

Vers l'Orient, Bibliothèque Nationale, 1983.

At the Sublime Porte, Hazlitt, Gooden and Fox, London, 1988.

The Turkish Legacy, Bodleian Library, 1988.

Topkapi en Turkomanie, Museum voor Volkenkunde, Rotterdam, 1989.

Dessins de Liotard, Musée du Louvre, 1992.

C. G. Lowenhielm, Artist and Diplomat in Istanbul 1824–7, Uppsala, 1993.

Women in Anatolia: Nine Thousand Years of the Anatolian Woman, Topkapi Saray Museum, 1993.

Louis-François Cassas 1756–1827, Musée des Beaux-Arts, Tours, 1994.

Evliya Celebi, *Narrative of Travels in Europe, Asia and Africa in the Seventeenth Century*, 2 vols., 1834–50.

Ezgin, Fouad, *Yildiz Saray Tarihcesi*, Istanbul, 1962.

Farmayan, Hafez and Elton L. Daniel (eds.), *A Shiite Pilgrimage to Mecca 1885–6*, 1990.

Farooqi, Naimur Rahman, *Mughal-Ottoman Relations*, Delhi, 1989.

Faroqhi, Suraiya, *Towns and Townsmen of Ottoman Anatolia*, Cambridge, 1984.

——*Pilgrims and Sultans: the Hajj under the Sultans*, 1994.

Farrère, Claude, *L'Homme qui assassina*, 1928.

Fazy, Edouard, *Les Turcs d'aujourd'hui*, 1898.

Ferriman, Z. Duckett, *Turkey and the Turks*, 1911.

Ferriol, Marquis de, *Correspondance*, Antwerp, 1870.

[——(ed.)], *Recueil de cent estampes représentant différentes nations du Levant*, 1914.

Fesch, Paul, *Constantinople aux dernier jours d'Abdul Hamid*, 1907.

Findlay, Carter V., *Bureaucratic Reform in the Ottoman Empire: the Sublime Porte 1789–1922*, Princeton, 1980.

——*Ottoman Civil Officialdom*, Princeton, 1992.

Finefrock, Michael M., 'From Sultan to Republic: Mustafa Kemal Ataturk and the Structure of Turkish Politics 1922–24', unpublished Ph.D. thesis, Princeton, 1976.

Fischer, Fritz, *War of Illusions: German Policies from 1911 to 1914*, 1975.

Fisher, C. G. and A. W. Fisher, 'Topkapi Sarayi in the Mid-Seventeenth Century: Bobovi's Description', *Archivum Ottomanicum*, X, 1985, 5–81.

Fleischer, Cornell H., *Bureaucrat and Intellectual in the Ottoman Empire: the Historian Mustafa Ali*, Princeton, 1986.

Fletcher, Richard, *Moorish Spain*, 1992.

Francis, Louis, *Le Neige de Galata*, 1936.

Franck, Harry A., *The Fringe of the Moslem World*, 1928.

Franco, M., *Essai sur l'histoire des Israélites de l'Empire Ottoman*, 1897.

Frangos, G., 'The *Philike Etairia*', unpublished Ph.D. thesis, Columbia, 1971.

Frazee, Charles A., *Catholics and Sultans*, 1983.

Freely, John, *Stamboul Sketches*, Istanbul, 1974.

Freni, Vera and Carla Varnier, *Raimondo d'Aronco: l'opera completa*, Padova, 1983.

Fuller, John, *Narrative of a Tour through some Parts of the Turkish Empire*, 1829.

Galante, Abraham (all works published in Istanbul):

——*Don Joseph Nasi Duc de Naxos*, 1913.

——*Esther Kyra d'après de nouveaux documents*, 1926.

——*Hommes et choses juifs portugais en Orient*, 1927.

——*Documents officiels turcs concernant les Juifs de Turquie*, 1931.

——*Turcs et Juifs*, 1932.

——*Abdul Hamid II et le Sionisme*, 1933.

——*Nouveaux Documents sur Sabbetai Sevi*, 1935.

——*Médecins juifs au service de Turquie*, 1935.

——*Don Salomon aben Yacche, Duc de Metelen*, 1936.

——*Les Synagogues d'Istanbul*, 1937.

——*Histoire des Juifs d'Istanbul*, 2 vols., 1941–2.

——*Appendice à l'histoire des Juifs d'Istanbul*, 1941.

——*Recueil de nouveaux documents concernant l'histoire des Juifs de Turquie*, 1949.

——*Nouveau Recueil de nouveaux documents inédits concernant l'histoire des Juifs de Turquie*, 1952.

——*Encore un Nouveau Recueil de documents concernant les Juifs de Turquie: études scientifiques*, 1953.

——*Les Juifs d'Istanbul sous le Sultan Mehmed le Conquérant*, 1953.

Galland, Antoine, *Journal*, 2 vols., 1881.

Gallenga, A., *Two Years of the Eastern Question*, 2 vols., 1877.

Garnett, Lucy M. J., *The Dervishes of Turkey*, 1990 edn.

——*The Women of Turkey and their Folk-lore*, 2 vols., 1890.

Gautier, Théophile, *Constantinople*, Istanbul, 1990 edn.

Gawrych, George W., 'Tolerant Dimensions of Cultural Pluralism: the Ottoman Empire and the Albanian Community 1800–1912', *International Journal of Middle East Studies*, XV, 1983, 519–36.

Gerasimos, Augustinos, *Consciousness and History: Nationalist Critics of Greek Society*, New York, 1977.

Germaner, Semra and Zaynep Inankur, *Orientalism and Turkey*, Istanbul, 1989.

Gibb, E. J. W., *A History of Ottoman Poetry*, 6 vols., 1900–9.

Gilbert, Martin, *Sir Horace Rumbold*, 1973.

——*Churchill: a Life*, 1991.

Gilles, Pierre, *The Antiquities of Constantinople*, New York, 1988.
Gilmour, David, *Curzon*, 1994.
Gocek, Fatma Muge, *East Encounters West: France and the Ottoman Empire in the Eighteenth Century*, New York, 1987.
Goffman, Daniel, *Izmir and the Levantine World 1550–1650*, 1990.
Gonul, Sevgi, *The Sadberk Hanim Museum*, Istanbul, 1988.
Goodblatt, Morris, S., *Jewish Life in Turkey in the Sixteenth Century*, New York, 1952.
Goodrich-Freer, A., *Things Seen in Constantinople*, 1926.
Goodwin, Godfrey, *A History of Ottoman Architecture*, 1992 edn.
——*Sinan and City Planning*, Rome, 1989.
——*The Janissaries*, 1994.
Gordon, Mrs Will, *A Woman in the Balkans*, 1916.
Graves, Philip, *Briton and Turk*, 1941.
Greenwood, Anthony, 'Istanbul's Meat Provisioning: a Study of the Celepjan System', unpublished Ph.D. thesis, Chicago, 1981.
Grelot, M., *Relation nouvelle d'un voyage de Constantinople*, 1681.
Grenville, Henry, *Observations sur l'état actuel de l'Empire Ottoman* (1766), Ann Arbor, 1965.
Grenville, J. A. S., *Lord Salisbury and Foreign Policy: the Close of the Nineteenth Century*, 1970.
Groc, Gérard and I. Caglar, *La Presse française de Turquie de 1795 à nos jours*, Istanbul, 1985.
Guilleragues, Comte de, *Correspondance*, 2 vols., Geneva, 1976.
Gulbenkian, Nubar, *Pantaraxia*, 1966.
Gulersoy, Celik (all works published in Istanbul):
——*Hidiver ve Cubuklu Kasri*, 1985.
——*Dolmabahce Palace and its Environs*, 1990.
——*The Story of the Grand Bazaar*, 1990.
——*Taksim: the Story of a Square*, 1991.
——*The Caique*, 1991.
——*The Ceragan Palaces*, 1992.
Gurkan, Dr K. I. *et al.*, *Lectures Delivered on the 511th Anniversary of the Conquest of Istanbul*, Istanbul, 1964.
Gursan-Salzmann, Ayse, *Anyos Muxhos y Buenos: Turkey's Sephardim 1492–1992*, Philadelphia, 1992.
Gursu, Nevber, *The Art of Turkish Weaving*, Istanbul, 1988.
Guys, M., *Voyage littéraire de la Grèce*, 3rd edn., 2 vols., 1783.
Habesci, Elias, *The Present State of the Ottoman Empire*, 1784.
Haidar, Musbah, *Arabesque*, 1944.
Halid, Halil, *Diary of a Turk*, 1903.
Halman, Talat S., *Suleyman the Magnificent, Poet*, Istanbul, 1989.
Halpern, Paul G., *The Mediterranean Naval Situation 1908–1914*, Cambridge, Mass., 1971.
——*The Naval War in the Mediterranean 1914–1918*, 1987.
——(ed.), *The Royal Navy in the Mediterranean 1915–1918*, 1987.
Hamlin, Cyrus, *Among the Turks*, 1878.
——*My Life and Times*, 1897.
Hammer, J. de, *Histoire de l'Empire Ottoman*, 16 vols., 1835–40.

——*Erinnerungen*, Vienna, 1940.

Hanioglu, M. Sukru, *Kendi Mektuplarinda Enver Pasha*, 1989.

Harington, General Sir Charles, *Tim Harington Looks Back*, 1940.

Harris, George S., *The Origins of Communism in Turkey*, Stanford, 1967.

Hasluck, F. W., *Christianity and Islam under the Sultans*, 2 vols., 1925.

Hassiotis, J. K., 'The Greeks and the Armenian Massacres', *Neo-hellenika*, IV, 1981, 69–101.

Hauterive, Comte d', *Mémoire sur l'état ancien et actuel de la Moldavie . . . en 1787*, Bucharest, 1902.

Heller, Joseph, *British Policy towards the Ottoman Empire 1908–1914*, 1983.

Hellier, Chris and Franco Venturi, *Splendours of the Bosphorus: Houses and Palaces of Istanbul*, 1993.

Henderson, Nevile, *Water under the Bridges*, 1945.

Herbert, Aubrey, *Ben Kendim*, 1918.

Herlihy, Patricia, *Odessa: a History 1794–1914*, 1986.

Herzl, Theodore, *Diaries*, 1958.

Hobhouse, John Cam, *A Journey through Albania and other Provinces of Turkey during the years 1809 and 1810*, 1813.

Hope, Thomas, *Anastasius or Memoirs of a Greek*, 2 vols., 1836 edn.

Hornby, Edmund, *An Autobiography*, 1929.

Hornby, Lady, *Constantinople during the Crimean War*, 1863.

Humurzaki, Baron Eudoxiu de (ed.), *Documente privitoare la Istoria romanilor*, vol. XVI, Bucarest, 1912.

Hunter, William, *Travels through France, Turkey and Hungary to Vienna in 1792*, 3rd edn., 2 vols., 1803.

Huscher, Herbert, 'Alexander Mavrocordato, friend of the Shelleys', *Bulletin of the Keats–Shelley Memorial Association*, XVI, 1965, 29–37.

Ignatyev, Count, 'Memoirs', *Slavonic Review*, X, June 1931, 386–407, 627–640; 1932, 341–53, 556–71.

Ihsanoglu, Ekmeleddin, *Istanbul: a glimpse into the Past*, Istanbul, 1987.

Imber, Colin, *The Ottoman Empire 1300–1481*, Istanbul, 1990.

Inalcik, Halil, *The Ottoman Empire: the Classical Age 1300–1600*, 1973.

——*The Ottoman Empire: Conquest, Organisation and Economy*, 1978.

——*Studies in Ottoman Social and Economic History*, 1985.

——*The Middle East and the Balkans under the Ottoman Empire*, Bloomington, 1993.

——and Cemal Kafadar, *Suleyman the Second and His Time*, Istanbul, 1993.

——and Donald Quataert, *An Economic and Social History of the Ottoman Empire*, 1994.

Iorga, Nicolas, *Byzance après Byzance*, 1992 edn.

——*Histoire des Roumains et de la Romanité orientale*, 9 vols., Bucharest, 1937–44.

Ipsirli, Mehmet, 'Mustafa Selaniki's History of the Ottomans', unpublished Ph.D. thesis, Edinburgh, 1976.

Ismail, F., 'The Diplomatic Relations of the Ottoman Empire and the Great European Powers from 1800 to 1821', unpublished D.Phil. thesis, London, 1975.

Issawi, Charles, *An Economic History of Turkey 1800–1914*, Chicago, 1980.

Istanbul à la jonction des cultures balkaniques, méditerranéennes, slaves et orientales aux XVI–XIXe siècles, Bucarest, 1977.

Istanbul Ansiklopedisi, 10 vols., Istanbul, 1993–5.

Istanbul: Selections, Istanbul, 1993– (magazine).

Itzkowitz, Norman and Max Mote, *Mubadele: an Ottoman-Russian Exchange of Ambassadors*, Chicago, 1970.

——and Vamik D. Volkan, *The Immortal Ataturk: a Psychobiography*, Chicago, 1984.

Jaeckh, Ernst, *The Rising Crescent*, New York, 1944.

Jamgocyan, Onnik, 'Les Finances de l'Empire Ottoman et les financiers de Constantinople', thèse d'état, Université de Paris, I, 1988.

——'L'Approvisonnement de Constantinople, la Révolution française et le déclin du négoce français', *Arab Historical Review for Ottoman Studies*, VII, October 1993, 127–42.

Jelavich, Barbara, *The Ottoman Empire, the Great Powers and the Straits Question 1870–1887*, Bloomington, 1973.

——*History of the Balkans: Eighteenth and Nineteenth Centuries*, 1983.

Jevakhoff, Alexandre, *Kemal Ataturk: les chemins de l'Occident*, 1989.

Johnson, Clarence R., *Constantinople Today: the Pathfinder Survey*, New York, 1922.

Johnstone, Pauline, *Turkish Embroidery*, 1985.

Jones, J. R. Melville, *The Siege of Constantinople 1453: Seven Contemporary Accounts*, Amsterdam, 1972.

Juhacz, Esther (ed.), *Sephardi Jews in the Ottoman Empire*, Jerusalem, 1989.

Kadri, Yakup, *Sodome et Gomorrhe*, 1928.

Kafadar, Cemal, 'Yeniceri–Esnaf Relations: Solidarity and Conflict', unpublished Ph.D. thesis, McGill University, 1981.

——'Self and Others: the Diary of a Dervish in Seventeenth-century Istanbul and First Person Narrative in Ottoman Literature', *Studia Islamica*, LXIX, 1989, 121–50.

Kalderon, Albert E., *Abraham Galante*, New York, 1983.

Kaldy-Nagy, G., 'The Holy War in the First Centuries of the Ottoman Empire', *Harvard Ukrainian Studies*, IV, 1980.

Kampman, A. A., *The Swedish Palace in Constantinople*, 1971.

Kannengiesser Pasha, Hans, *The Campaign in Gallipoli*, 1927.

Karahan, Abdulkadir, *Les Poètes classiques à l'epoque de Soliman le Magnifique*, Ankara, 1991.

Karmi, Ilhan, *Jewish Sites of Istanbul: a Guide Book*, Istanbul, 1992.

Karpat, Kemal H., *The Ottoman State and its Place in World History*, Leiden, 1974.

——*Ottoman Population*, Wisconsin, 1985.

Kastoryano, Lidya, *Quand l'Innocence avait un sens*, Istanbul, 1993.

Katib Celebi, *The Balance of Truth*, ed. G. L. Lewis, 1957.

Kayra, Cahit, *Maps of Istanbul*, Istanbul, 1990.

Kazamias, Andrew, *Education and the Quest for Modernity in Turkey*, 1966.

Kazgan, Haydar, *Galata Bankerleri*, Istanbul, 1991.

Keddie, Nikki R., *Sayyid Jamal ad-din 'al-Afghani'*, Los Angeles, 1972.

——and Lois Beck (eds.), *Women in the Muslim World*, 1978.

Kelly, Laurence, *Istanbul: a Traveller's Companion*, 1987.

Kemal Bey, Ismail, *Memoirs*, 1920.

Kent, Marian (ed.), *The Great Powers and the End of the Ottoman Empire*, 1984.

Keun, Odette, *Mesdemoiselles Daisne de Constantinople*, c. 1920.

Kevorkian, Raymond H. and Paul B. Paboudjian, *Les Arméniens dans l'Empire Ottoman à la veille du génocide*, 1992.

Khitrovo, Mme B. de, *Itinéraires russes en Orient*, Geneva, 1889.

Kinross, Lord, *Ataturk: the Rebirth of a Nation*, Nicosia, 1981 edn.

Kitromilides, Paschalis M., *The Enlightenment as Social Criticism: Miosipis Moisiodax and Greek Culture in the Eighteenth Century*, Princeton, 1992.

Kitsikis, Dimitris, *L'Empire Ottoman*, 1985.

Knatchbull-Hugesson, Sir Hugh, *Diplomat in Peace and War*, 1949.

Knight, E. F., *The Awakening of Turkey*, 1909.

Knos, Borje, *L'Histoire de la littérature néo-grecque*, Uppsala, 1962.

Knudsen, Erik Lance, *Great Britain, Constantinople and the Turkish Peace Treaty*, New York, 1987.

Koprulu, M. Fuad, *The Origins of the Ottoman Empire*, ed. Gary Leiser, Albany, 1992.

Kortepeter, Carl Max, *The Ottoman Turks: from Nomad Kingdom to World Empire*, Istanbul, 1991.

Kritovoulos, *History of Mehmed the Conqueror*, Princeton, 1954.

Kuneralp, Sinan (ed.), *Studies in Ottoman Diplomatic History*, 5 vols., Istanbul, 1987–90.

Kunt, Metin, 'The Koprulu Years 1656–1661', unpublished Ph.D. thesis, Princeton, 1971.

Kuran, Aptullah, *Sinan the Grand Old Man of Ottoman Architecture*, Istanbul, 1987.

Kurat, Akdes Nimet (ed.), *The Despatches of Sir Robert Sutton, Ambassador in Constantinople 1710–1714*, 1953.

Kushner, David, *The Rise of Turkish Nationalism*, 1977.

Kutschera, Chris, *Le Mouvement National Kurde*, 1979.

Labourdette, J. F., *Vergennes*, 1990.

La Motraye, A. de, *Voyages . . . en Europe, Asie et Afrique*, 2 vols., La Haye, 1727.

Landau, Jacob M., *Ataturk and the Modernisation of Turkey*, Boulder and Leiden, 1984.

——*Tekinalp: Turkish Patriot 1883–1961*, Istanbul, 1984.

Lane-Poole, Stanley (ed.), *The People of Turkey: Twenty Years Residence among Bulgarians, Greeks, Albanians, Turks and Armenians by a Consul's Daughter and his Wife*, 2 vols., 1878.

——*The Life of Sir Stratford Canning, Viscount Stratford de Redcliffe*, 2 vols., 1888.

Lang, David Marshall, *The Armenians: a People in Exile*, 1988 edn.

Lauzanne, Stéphane, *Au chevet de la Turquie*, 1913.

Layard, Sir Austen, *Autobiography and Letters*, 2 vols., 1903.

Lechevalier, J. B., *Voyage de la Propontide et du Pont Euxin*, 2 vols., 1800.

Lees, Andrew, *Cities Perceived: Urban Society in European and American Thought 1820–1940*, Manchester, 1985.

Lefort, Jacques, *Documents grecs dans les archives de Topkapi Sarayi: contribution à l'histoire de Cem Sultan*, Ankara, 1981.

Legrand, Emile, *Recueil de poèmes historiques en grec vulgaire*, 1877.

Leila Hanoum, *Le Harem impérial et les sultanes au XIXe siècle*, Brussels, 1991.

Lesure, Michel, *Lepante: la crise de l'Empire Ottoman*, 1972.

Levy, Avigdor, 'The Military Policy of Sultan Mahmud II 1808–1839', unpublished Ph.D. thesis, Harvard, 1968.

——'The Ottoman *Ulama* and the Military Reforms of Sultan Mahmud II', *Asian and African Studies*, VII, 1971, 13–39.

——'The Officer Corps in Sultan Mahmud II's New Ottoman Army 1826–1839', *International Journal of Middle East Studies*, II, 1971, 21–39.

——*The Sephardim in the Ottoman Empire*, Princeton, 1992.

Lewis, Bernard, *The Emergence of Modern Turkey*, 1960.

——*Istanbul and the Civilization of the Ottoman Empire*, Norman, Oklahoma, 1963.

——*Islam in History*, 1973.

——*The Muslim Discovery of Europe*, 1982.

——*The Jews of Islam*, 1984.

——*The Political Language of Islam*, Chicago, 1988.

——*Race and Slavery in the Middle East: a Historical Enquiry*, New York, 1990.

Liddell, Robert, *Byzantium and Istanbul*, 1956.

Lieven, D. C. B., *Russia and the Origins of the First World War*, 1983.

Lifchez, Raymond F. (ed.), *The Dervish Lodge: Architecture, Art and Sufism in Ottoman Turkey*, Berkeley, 1992.

Ligne, Maréchal Prince de, *Mémoires*, 5 vols., 1828.

Liskar, Elizabeth (ed.), *Europa und die Kunst der Islam*, Wien, 1985.

Loti, Pierre, *Aziyade: Stamboul 1876–1877*, 1892 edn.

——et Samuel Viaud, *Suprêmes Visions d'Orient*, 1921.

Lowry, Heath W., *The Story behind Ambassador Morgenthau's Story*, Istanbul, 1990.

Lybyer, Albert H., *The Government of the Ottoman Empire in the Time of Suleiman the Magnificent*, Cambridge, Mass., 1913.

Macarius, Patriarch of Antioch, *Travels*, 1936.

MacDermott, Mercia, *A History of Bulgaria 1393–1885*, 1962.

MacFarlane, Charles, *Constantinople in 1828*, 2 vols., 2nd edn. 1829.

——*Turkey and its Destiny*, 2 vols., 1850.

Macfie, A. L., *The Straits Question 1909–1934*, Thessaloniki, 1993.

Mackenzie, Molly, *Turkish Athens*, Reading, 1992.

Magoulias, Harry J. (ed.), *The Decline and Fall of Byzantium to the Ottoman Turks*, Detroit, 1975.

Mamboury, Ernest, *The Tourist's Istanbul*, Istanbul, 1953.

Mamoni, Kyriaki, 'Les Associations pour la propagation de l'instruction grecque à Constantinople (1861–1922)', *Balkan Studies*, 1975, XVI, i, 103–12.

Mango, Cyril, *Studies on Constantinople*, Aldershot, 1993.

Mann, Stuart E., *Albanian Literature*, 1955.

Mansel, Philip, *Sultans in Splendour: the Last Years of the Ottoman World*, 1988.

Mantran, Robert (ed.), *Histoire de l'Empire Ottoman*, 1989.

——*Istanbul dans la seconde moitié du XVIIe siècle*, 1962.

——*La Vie quotidienne à Istanbul au siècle de Soliman le Magnifique*, 1990 edn.

Mardin, Serif, 'Super Westernisation in Urban Life in the Last Quarter of the Nineteenth Century', in Peter Benedict *et al.* (eds.), *Turkey: Geographical and Social Perspectives*, Leiden, 1974, 403–45.

——*The Genesis of Young Ottoman Though*, Princeton, 1962.

——*Religion and Social Change in Modern Turkey: the Case of Bediuzzaman Said Nursi*, Albany, New York, 1989.

Marinescu, Florin, *Etude généalogique sur la famille Morouzi*, Athens, 1987.

——with Georgeta Penelea-Filitti and Anna Tabaki (eds.), *Documents gréco-roumains: le Fonds Morouzi d'Athènes*, Athens–Bucharest, 1991.

Marsigli, Comte de, *L'Etat militaire de l'Empire Ottoman, ses progrès et sa décadence*, La Haye–Amsterdam, 1732.

Masson, Paul, *Histoire du commerce français dans le Levant au XVIIe siècle*, 1896.

——*Histoire du commerce français dans le Levant au XVIIIe siècle*, 1911.

Mavrocordatos, G. A., *De la Réforme et de la finance des Romains en Orient*, Athens, 1856.

Mavroyennis, Alexandre, *Contribution à l'histoire du Proche-Orient*, 2 vols., Istanbul, 1950.

Mavroyennis Pacha, *Chiens errants de Constantinople, et chiens et chats de bonne maison*, 1900.

McCarthy, J. W. and Constantin Caratheodory, *Relation officielle de la maladie et de la mort du Sultan Mahmoud II*, 1841.

McCullagh, Francis, *The Fall of Abdul Hamid*, 1909.

Mears, Eliot Granville, *Modern Turkey*, 1924.

Medlin, William K., *Moscow and East Rome*, Geneva, 1952.

Meienberger, Peter, *Johann Rudolf Schmid zum Schwarzerhorn als Kaiserlicher Resident in Konstantinopel in den Jahren 1629–1643*, Bern, 1973.

Melas, Achilles and Kostas Stamatopulos, *Constantinopolis*, Athens, 1990 (in Greek).

Melek Hanoum, *Thirty Years in the Harem*, 1872.

[Melling, Antoine-Ignace], *Voyage pittoresque de Constantinople et des rives du Bosphore*, 1819.

Menemencioglu, Nermin, *The Penguin Book of Turkish Verse*, 1978.

Meredith-Owens, G. M., *Turkish Miniatures*, 1969.

Merriman, R. B., *Suleyman the Magnificent*, Harvard, 1944.

Meryon, Dr, *Travels of Lady Hester Stanhope*, 3 vols., 1846.

Mihailovic, Konstantin, *Memoirs of a Janissary*, Ann Arbor, 1975.

Miller, A. F., *Mustafa Pacha Bairaktar*, Bucharest, 1975.

Miller, Barnette, *Beyond the Sublime Porte*, New Haven, 1931.

——*The Palace School of Mohammed the Conqueror*, Cambridge, Mass., 1941.

Miller, William, *Travel and Politics in the Near East*, 1897.

Millman, Richard, *Britain and the Eastern Question 1875–1878*, Oxford, 1979.

Minault, Gai, *The Khilafat Movement*, New York, 1982.

Mismer, Charles, *Souvenirs du monde mussulman*, 1892.

Mitler, Louis, *Ottoman Turkish Writers*, Washington, 1988.

Moltke, Maréchal de, *Lettres . . . sur l'Orient*, 1877 edn.

Monconys, M., *Journal des Voyages*, 4 vols., Lyons, 1666.

Moorehead, Alan, *Gallipoli*, 1956.

Morand, Paul, *Ouvert la nuit*, 1987 edn.

Morier, James, *A Journey through Persia, Armenia, Asia Minor, to Constantinople, in the Years 1808 and 1809*, 1812.

Moseley, Philip E., *Russian Diplomacy and the Opening of the Eastern Question 1838–1839*, Harvard, 1934.

Mouradgea d'Ohsson, Ignatius, *Tableau général de l'Empire Ottoman*, 3 vols., 1787–1820.

Mouy, Charles de, *Lettres du Bosphore*, 1879.

Muftyzade, K. Zia Bey, *Speaking of the Turks*, New York, 1922.

Muller, Mrs Max, *Letters from Constantinople*, 1897.

Myles, Henri, *La Fin de Stamboul*, 2nd edn., 1921.

Nadir, Aysegul (ed.), *Imperial Ottoman Fermans*, 1986.

Naff, Thomas and Roger Owen, *Studies in Eighteenth-century Islamic History*, Carbonsville, 1977.

Naima, Mustafa, *Annals of the Turkish Empire*, I, 1842.

Nalbandian, Louise, *The Armenian Revolutionary Movement*, Berkeley, 1963.

Nami Bey, Ali, *Vérité, justice, bonté*, Istanbul, 1918.

National Palaces, Istanbul, 1987, 1992.

Navarian, A., *Les Sultans poètes (1451–1809)*, 1936.

Necipoglu, Gulru, *Architecture, Ceremonial and Power: the Topkapi Palace in the Fifteenth and Sixteenth Centuries*, Cambridge, Mass., 1991.

Nesin, Aziz, *Istanbul Boy*, 3 vols., Austin, Texas, 1977–90.

Neuville, Pierre de, Gilbert Beaupré *et al.*, *Images d'Empire*, Istanbul, 1994.

Nicholas of Greece, Prince, *My Fifty Years*, 1929.

Nicol, Donald M., *The Immortal Emperor: the Life and Legend of Constantine Palaiologos, Last Emperor of the Romans*, Cambridge, 1992.

——*The Last Centuries of Byzantium 1261–1453*, 1993 edn.

Nicolaides, Jean, *Folklore de Constantinople*, 2 vols., 1894.

——*Contes licencieux de Constantinople et de l'Asie Mineure*, 1906.

Nicolay, Nicolas de, *Dans l'Empire de Soliman le Magnifique*, 1989.

Nicolson, Harold, *Sweet Waters*, 1928 edn.

Nicolson, Nigel, *Alex*, 1973.

Nigar, Salih Keramet, *Halife Ikinci Abdulmecid*, 1964.

Nisbet, Mary of Dirleton, Countess of Elgin, *Letters*, 1926.

Noe, Michel, *Pages d'Orient*, 1895.

North, Hon. Roger, *Lives of the Norths*, 3 vols., 1826.

Nubar Pacha, *Mémoires*, ed. Mirrit Boutros-Ghali, Beirut, 1983.

Obolensky, Dimitri, *The Byzantine Commonwealth*, 1974 edn.

Ochsenwald, William, *Religion, Society and the State in Arabia*, Ohio, 1984.

Okday, Sefik, *Der letzte Grossvezir und seine Preussische Sohne*, Gottingen–Zurich, 1991.

Okte, Ertughrul Zekai (ed.), *Ottoman Archives. Yildiz Collection. The Armenian Question*, 3 vols., Istanbul, 1989.

Olson, Robert W., *The Siege of Mosul and Ottoman-Persian Relations 1718–1743*, Bloomington, 1975.

——*The Emergence of Kurdish Nationalism and the Sheikh Said Rebellion, 1880–1925*, Austin, 1989.

Orbey, Raouf d', *Les Amours dangereuses*, Constantinople, 1874.

Orga, Irfan, *Portrait of a Turkish Family*, 1988 edn.

Osborne, Hon. and Revd Sydney Godolphin, *Scutari and its Hospitals*, 1855.

Osmanoglu, Ayse, *Avec Mon Père le Sultan Abdulhamid de son palais à son prison*, 1991.

Ostle, Robin (ed.), *Modern Literature in the Near and Middle East 1850–1970*, 1991.

Owen, Roger, *The Middle East in the World Economy 1800–1914*, 1981.

Ozdamar, Ali, *Beyoglu in the Thirties through the Lens of Selahattin Giz*, Istanbul, 1992.

Oztuna, Yilmaz, *Devletler ve Hanedanlar*, II, *Turkiye (1074–1990)*, Ankara, 1990.

Palerne, Jean, *Pérégrinations*, Lyons, 1606.

Paliouras, A. (ed.), *The Oecumenical Patriarchate*, Athens, 1989.

Palmer, Alan, *The Decline and Fall of the Ottoman Empire*, 1993 edn.

Pannayotopoulos, A. J., 'The Great Idea and the Vision of Eastern Federation', *Balkan Studies*, XXI, 2, 1980, 331–65.

Panzac, Daniel, *La Peste dans l'Empire Ottoman 1700–1850*, Leuwen, 1985.

——'International and Domestic Maritime Trade in the Ottoman Empire during the Eighteenth Century', *International Journal of Middle Eastern Studies*, May 1992, 189–206.

——*Les Villes dans l'Empire Ottoman: activité et société*, 1991.

Papadakis, A., 'Gennadius II and Mehmed the Conqueror', *Byzantion*, XLII, 1972, 88–106.

Papadopoulos, S. A. (ed.), *The Greek Merchant Marine*, Athens, 1972.

Papadopoulos, Theodore H., *Studies and Documents relating to the History of the Greek Church and People under Turkish Domination*, Brussels, 1952.

Pardoe, Julia, *The City of the Sultans and Domestic Manners of the Turks in 1836*, 2 vols., 1837.

Park, George T., 'The Life and Writings of M. Fuad Koprulu', unpublished Ph.D. thesis, Johns Hopkins University, 1975.

Pears, Sir Edwin, *Forty Years in Constantinople*, 1917.

Pedani, Maria Pia, *In nome del Gran Signore: inviati ottomani a Venezia dalla caduta di Constantinopoli alla guerra di Candia*, Venice, 1994.

Peirce, Leslie, 'The Imperial Harem: Gender and Power in the Ottoman Empire 1520–1657', unpublished Ph.D. thesis, Princeton, 1988.

——*The Imperial Harem: Women and Sovereignty in the Ottoman Empire*, Oxford, 1993.

Penzer, N. M., *The Harem*, 1966 edn.

Pernot, Maurice, *La Question turque*, 1923.

Pertusier, J. C., *Promenades pittoresques dans Constantinople et sur le Bosphore*, 3 vols., 1815.

——*La Valachie, la Moldavie et de l'influence politique des Grecs du Fanal*, 1822.

Petrovich, Michael Boro, *The Emergence of Russian Panslavism 1856–1870*, New York, 1956.

Philippides, André, *Hommes et idées du Sud-Est Européen à l'aube de l'âge moderne*, 1980.

Pickthall, Marmaduke, *With the Turk in Wartime*, 1914.

Pingaud, Léonce, *Choiseul-Gouffier: la France en Orient sous Louis XVI*, 1887.

Piton de Tournefort, M., *A Voyage into the Levant: Perform'd by Command of the Late French King*, 2 vols., 1718.

Pococke, Richard, *A Description of the East and some other Countries*, 2 vols., 1745.

Ponafidine, Pierre, *Life in the Muslim East*, 1911.

[Porter, David] *Constantinople and its environs in a series of letters*, 2 vols., New York, 1835.

Porter, Sir James, *Turkey, its History and People*, 2 vols., 1854.

Porter, Roy, *London: a Social History*, 1994.

Poynter, Mary A., *When Turkey was Turkey*, 1921.

Puaux, René, *De Sofia à Tchataldja*, 1913.

Quataert, Donald, *Social Disintegration and Popular Resistance in the Ottoman Empire 1881–1908*, New York, 1983.

——*Ottoman Manufacturing in the Age of the Industrial Revolution*, Cambridge, 1993.

Quella-Villeger, Alain, *Istanbul: le regard de Pierre Loti*, 1992.

Raby, Julian, 'El Gran Turco: Mehmed the Conqueror as a Patron of the Arts of Christendom', unpublished D.Phil. thesis, Oxford, 1980.

Ragsdale, Hugh (ed.), *Imperial Russian Foreign Policy*, 1991.

Rambert, Louis, *Notes et impressions de Turquie*, 1926.

Ramsaur, jun., Ernest Edmondson, *The Young Turks: Prelude to the Revolution of 1908*, Princeton, 1957.

Ramsay, Allan and Francis McCullagh, *Tales from Turkey*, 1914.

Ramsay, Sir W. M., *The Revolution in Constantinople and Turkey*, 1909.

Rankin, Lt-Col. Reginald, *The Inner History of the Balkan War*, 1914.

Raymond, André, *Le Caire*, 1993.

Reed, Howard, 'The Destruction of the Janissaries by Mahmud II in June 1826', unpublished Ph.D. thesis, Princeton, 1951.

Reed, John, *War in Eastern Europe*, 1994 edn.

Repp, R. C., *The Mufti of Istanbul: a Study in the Development of the Ottoman Learned Hierarchy*, 1986.

Revue d'Histoire Diplomatique, 1991, issue on consuls and dragomans.

Rich, Norman, *Why the Crimean War? A Cautionary Tale*, 1985.

Richards, G. R. B., *Florentine Merchants in the Age of the Medici*, Harvard, 1932.

Riondel, H., *Le Bienheureux Gomidas de Constantinople, prêtre arménien et martyr*, 1929.

Roche, Max, *Education, assistance et culture françaises dans l'Empire Ottoman*, Istanbul, 1989.

Roding, Michiel and Hans Theunissen (eds.), *The Tulip, a Symbol of Two Nations*, Utrecht–Istanbul, 1993.

Rodrigue, Aron (ed.), *Ottoman and Turkish Jewry: Community and Leadership*, Bloomington, 1992.

Roe, Sir Thomas, *Negotiations in his Embassy to the Ottoman Porte from the year 1621 to 1628*, 1749.

Rogers, J. M. (ed.), *The Topkapi Saray Museum: Costumes, Embroideries and Other Textiles*, 1986.

——*The Topkapi Saray Museum: the Treasury*, 1987.

——*The Topkapi Saray Museum. Architecture: the Harem and Other Buildings*, 1988.

——and R. M. Ward, *Suleyman the Magnificent*, 1988.

Roider, jun., Karl A., *Austria's Eastern Question*, Princeton, 1982.

Rolamb, Nils, 'A Relation of a Journey to Constantinople', in A. C. Churchill (ed.), *A Collection of Voyages and Travels*, 5 vols., 1732, V, 669–716.

Rose, Norman, *Churchill: an Unruly Life*, 1995 edn.

Rosenthal, Steven T., *The Politics of Dependency: Urban Reform in Istanbul*, Westport, 1980.

Rossos, Andrew, *Russia and the Balkans: Inter-Balkan Rivalries and Russian Foreign Policy*, Toronto, 1981.

Roth, Cecil, *The House of Nasi: the Duke of Naxos*, Philadelphia, 5708/1948.

——*Dona Gracia Nasi*, Paris, 1990.

Rottiers, Colonel, *Itinéraire de Tiflis à Constantinople*, Brussels, 1829.

Runciman, Steven, *The Great Church in Captivity*, 1968.

——*The Fall of Constantinople 1453*, 1988 edn.

Russell, W. H., *The British Expedition to the Crimea*, rev. edn. 1858.

——*A Diary in the East during the Tour of the Prince and Princess of Wales*, 1869.

Ryan, Sir Andrew, *The Last of the Dragomans*, 1951.

Rycaut, Paul, *The Present State of the Ottoman Empire*, 1675.

——*The History of the Turks beginning with the year 1679*, 3 vols., 1687.

Saab, Hassan, *The Arab Federalists of the Ottoman Empire*, Amsterdam, 1958.

Sa'd-ud-din, Khoja, *The Capture of Constantinople*, tr. E. J. W. Gibb, Glasgow, 1879.

Safadi, Yasin Hamadi, *Islamic Calligraphy*, 1987 edn.

Saint Clair, William, *Lord Elgin and the Marbles*, 1983 edn.

Saint-Priest, Comte de, *Mémoires sur l'ambassade de France en Turquie et sur le commerce des Français dans le Levant*, 1877.

Sanderson, John, *Travels in the Levant 1584–1602*, 1931.

Sarkisian, A. O., *History of the Armenian Question to 1885*, Urbana, 1938.

Scalieri, Cléanthe, *Appel à la justice des Grandes Puissances*, Athens, 1881.

Schefer, Charles (ed.), *Le Voyage de Monsieur Chesneau d'Aramon, ambassadeur pour le Roy au Levant*, 1887.

Schimmel, Annemarie, *Calligraphy and Islamic Culture*, New York, 1984.

Schmidt, Jan, *Through the Legation Window 1871–1926*, Istanbul, 1992.

——'Sunbulzade Vehbi's Sevk-Engiz, an Ottoman Pornographic Poem', *Turcica*, XXV, 1993, 9–37.

Scholem, Gershom, *Sabbatai Sevi: the Mystical Messiah*, 1971.

Schreiner, George A., *From Berlin to Baghdad*, New York, 1918.

Schwoebel, Robert, *The Shadow of the Crescent: the Renaissance Image of the Turk (1453–1517)*, Nieuwkoop, 1967.

Senior, Nassau W., *A Journal kept in Turkey and Greece*, 1859.

Sepiha, Haim Vidal, *L'Agonie des Judéo-Espagnols*, 2nd edn., 1979.

Sestini, Domenico, *Lettres . . . pendant le cours de ses voyages en Italie, en Sicilie et en Turquie*, 1789.

Seton-Watson, R. W., *A History of the Roumanians*, 1934.

——*Britain in Europe 1789–1914*, Cambridge, 1937.

Setton, Kenneth M., *Venice, Austria and the Turks in the Seventeenth Century*, Philadephia, 1991.

Shaw, Stanford, J., *Between Old and New: the Ottoman Empire under Sultan Selim III 1789–1807*, Harvard, 1971.

——*A History of the Ottoman Empire and Modern Turkey*, 2 vols., 1976–8.

——*The Jews of the Ottoman Empire and the Turkish Republic*, 1991.

Shay, Mary Lucille, *The Ottoman Empire from 1720 to 1744 as revealed in Despatches of Venetian Baili*, Urbana, 1944.

Sherrard, Philip, *Constantinople: Iconography of a Sacred City*, 1965.

Shmuelevitz, Aryeh, *The Jews of the Ottoman Empire in the late Fifteenth and the Sixteenth Centuries*, Leiden, 1984.

Shukla, Ram Lakhan, *Britain, India and the Turkish Empire 1853–1882*, New Delhi, 1973.

Shurrock, William I., *French Imperialism in the Middle East*, Madison, 1976.

Simsir, Bilal N., *Dis Basinda Ataturk ve Turk Devrimi*, cilt I, Ankara, 1981.

Sitwell, Sacheverell, *Far from my Home: Stories Long and Short*, 1931.

Skendi, Stavro, *The Albanian National Awakening 1878–1912*, Princeton, 1967.

Skilliter, Susan, *Life in Istanbul 1588: Scenes from a Traveller's Picture Book*, Oxford, 1977.

——*William Harborne and the Trade with Turkey 1578–1582*, Oxford, 1977.

Slade, Adolphus, *Turkey, Greece and Malta*, 2 vols., 1837.

——*Turkey and the Crimean War*, 1867.

Smith, Albert, *A Month at Constantinople*, 1850.

Snouck Hurgronje, C., *Mekka in the latter part of the Nineteenth Century*, Leiden–London, 1931.

Sonyel, Salahi R., *Minorities and the Destruction of the Ottoman Empire*, Ankara, 1993.

Soutzo, Prince Nicolas, *Mémoires*, Vienna, 1896.

Sperco, Willy, *Istanbul indiscret*, Istanbul, n.d.

——*L'Orient qui s'éteint*, 1936.

——*Mustafa Kemal Ataturk*, 1958.

Sphrantzes, George, *The Fall of the Byzantine Empire: a Chronicle*, ed. and tr. Marios Philippides, Amherst, 1980.

Stchoukine, Ivan, *La Peinture turque d'après les manuscrits illustrés*, 2 vols., 1966–76.

Stitt, George, *A Prince of Arabia: the Emir Shereef Ali Haidar*, 1948.

Stoianovic, Troian, 'The Conquering Balkan Orthodox Merchant', *Journal of Economic History*, 1960, 234–313.

Stone, Norman and Michael Glenny, *The Other Russia*, 1991 edn.

Stourdza, A. C., *L'Europe orientale et le rôle historique des Mavrocordato 1660–1830*, 1913.

Strachan, Michael, *Sir Thomas Roe*, 1989.

Studia Turcologica Memoriae Alexis Bombacii Dicata, Naples, 1982.

Sturdza, Michel, *Grandes Familles de Grèce, d'Albanie et de Constantinople*, 1983.

Sugar, Peter F., *Southeastern Europe under Ottoman Rule 1354–1804*, Seattle, 1977.

Sumner, B. H., *Russia and the Balkans 1870–1880*, 1937.

Sumner-Boyd, Hilary and John Freely, *Strolling through Istanbul*, 2nd edn., Istanbul, 1973.

Svenson, Glen, 'The Military Rising in Istanbul 1909', *Journal of Contemporary History*, V, 1970, 171–84.

Synvet, A., *Les Grecs de l'Empire Ottoman: étude statistique et ethnique*, Constantinople, 1878.

Tahsin Pasha, *Yildiz Hatiralari*, 1990 edn.

Tavernier, J. B., *Nouvelle Relation de l'intérieur du Sérail du Grand Seigneur*, 1675.

Temple, Bt., Major-General Sir Grenville, *Travels in Greece and Turkey*, 2 vols., 1836.

Tenenti, Alberto, *Piracy and the Decline of Venice 1580–1615*, 1967.

Thalasso, A. et F. Zonaro, *Deri Se'adet ou Stamboul, porte du bonheur*, 1908.

Theotokas, G., *Leonis, enfant grec de Constantinople*, 1985.

Thévenot, M. de, *Travels into the Levant*, 3 parts, 1687.

Thomas, Lewis V., *A Study of Naima*, New York, 1972.

Thouvenel, L., *Trois Années de la Question d'Orient 1856–1859*, 1897.

Thuasne, L., *Gentile Bellini et Sultan Mohammed II*, 1888.

Tietze, Andreas (ed.), *Mustafa Ali's Counsel for Sultans of 1581*, 2 vols., Vienna, 1979–82.

Tinayre, Marcelle, *Notes d'une voyageuse en Turquie*, 1909.

Titley, Norah and Frances Wood, *Oriental Gardens*, 1991.

Toderini, Abbé, *De la Littérature des Turcs*, 3 vols., 1789.

Toledano, Ehud R., *The Ottoman Slave Trade and its Suppression 1840–1890*, Princeton, 1982.

Tongas, Gérard, *Les Relations de la France avec l'Empire Ottoman durant la première moitié du XVIIe siècle*, Toulouse, 1942.

Toros, Taha, *Turco-Polish Relations in History*, Istanbul, 1983.

——*The First Lady Artists of Turkey*, Istanbul, 1988.

Tott, Baron de, *Memoirs concerning the State of the Turkish Empire and the Crimea*, 4 parts, 1786.

Trubetskoy, Professor Prince Eugene Nicolayevich, *Saint Sophia, Russia's Hope and Calling*, 1916.

Trumpener, Ulrich, *Germany and the Ottoman Empire 1914–1918*, 1968.

Tsourkas, Cléobule, *Les Débuts de l'enseignement philosophique et de la libre pensée dans les Balkans: la vie et l'œuvre de Théophile Corydalée (1570–1646)*, Thessaloniki, 1967.

Tuglaci, Pars (all works published in Istanbul):

—— *Women of Istanbul in Ottoman Times*, 1984.

—— *The Ottoman Palace Women*, 1985.

—— *Turkish Bands of Past and Present*, 1986.

—— *The Role of the Balian Family in Ottoman Architecture*, 1990.

—— *Armenian Churches of Istanbul*, 1991.

—— *The Role of the Dadian Family in Ottoman Social, Economic and Political Life*, 1993.

Tuncay, Mete and Erik J. Zurcher, *Socialism and Nationalism in the Ottoman Empire 1876–1923*, 1994.

Turner, C. J. G. 'The Career of George-Gennadius Scholarius', *Byzantion*, XXXIX, 1969, 420–55.

Turner, William, *Journal of a Tour in the Levant*, 3 vols., 1820.

Tursun Beg, *History of Mehmed the Conqueror*, ed. Halil Inalcik and Rhoads Murphy, Minneapolis and Chicago, 178.

Ubicini, M. A., *Letters on Turkey*, 2 vols., 1856.

Ulker, Muammer, *The Art of Turkish Calligraphy from the Beginning up to the Present*, Ankara, 1987.

Ulucay, M. Cagatay, *Sultanlarina Ask Mektuplari*, 1950.

—— *Harem II*, Ankara, 1971.

—— *Padishahlarin Kadinlari ve Kizlari*, 1992.

Un Jeune Russe [H.-C.-R. von Struve], *Voyage en Crimée, suivi de la relation de l'ambassade envoyée de Pétersbourg à Constantinople en 1793*, 1802.

Unsal, Artun and Beyhan, *Istanbul la magnifique: propos de table et recettes*, 1991.

Upward, Allen, *The East End of Europe*, 1908.

Vacalopoulos, Apostolos E., *Origins of the Greek Nation: the Byzantine Period 1204–1461*, New Brunswick, 1970.

—— *The Greek Nation 1453–1669*, New Brunswick, 1976.

Vaka, Demetra, *The Unveiled Ladies of Stamboul*, Boston, 1923.

Valensi, Lucette, *Venise et la Sublime Porte*, 1987.

Vandal, Albert, *Les Voyages du Marquis de Nointel*, 1900.

—— *Une Ambassade française en Orient sous Louis XV: la mission du Marquis de Villeneuve 1728–1741*, 1887.

Van der Dat, Dan, *The Ship that Changed the World: the Escape of the 'Goeben' to the Dardanelles in 1914*, 1986 edn.

Vaner, Semih (ed.), *Istanbul*, 1991.

Varol, Marie-Christine, *Balat, faubourg juif d'Istanbul*, Istanbul, 1989.

Vassif Efendi, *Précis historique de la guerre des Turcs contre les Russes*, ed. P. A. Caussin de Perceval, 1822.

Vaughan, Dorothy M., *Europe and the Turk: a Pattern of Alliances 1350–1700*, Liverpool, 1951.

Veinstein, Gilles (ed.), *Salonique 1850–1918: la ville des Juifs et le réveil des Balkans*, 1992.

—— *Soliman le Magnifique et son temps*, 1992.

Vryonis, Speros, 'The Byzantine Legacy and Ottoman Forms', *Dumbarton Oaks Papers*, XXIII–XXIV, 1969–70, 253–318.

Walder, David, *The Chanak Affair*, 1969.

Walker, Christopher J., *Armenia: the Survival of a Nation*, 1991 edn.

Walsh, Revd R., *A Residence at Constantinople*, 2 vols., 1836.

Wanda, *Souvenirs anecdotiques sur la Turquie 1820–1870*, 1884.

Washburn, George, *Fifty Years in Constantinople*, Boston and New York, 1909.

Waterfield, Gordon, *Layard of Nineveh*, 1963.

Watkins, Thomas, *Tour through Swisserland . . . to Constantinople*, 2 vols., 1792.

Waugh, Sir Telford, *Turkey Yesterday, Today and Tomorrow*, 1930.

White, Charles, *Three Years in Constantinople*, 3 vols., 1845.

Wilkinson, William, *An Account of the Principalities of Wallachia and Moldavia*, 1820.

Wilson, Epiphanius, *Turkish Literature*, 1901.

Wilson, Mary C., *King Abdullah, Britain and the Making of Jordan*, Cambridge, 1987.

Wittek, Paul, 'Notes sur la tughra ottomane', *Byzantion*, XVIII, 1948, 311–34.

Wittman, William, *Travels in Turkey, Asia Minor, Syria and across the Desert to Egypt in the years 1799, 1800 and 1801*, 1803.

Wolff, Sir Henry Drummond, *Rambling Recollections*, 2 vols., 1908.

Wood, Alfred C., 'The English Embassy in Constantinople', *English Historical Review*, XL, 1925, 533–61.

——*A History of the Levant Company*, 1935.

Woods, Sir Henry F., *Spun-Yarn from the Strands of a Sailor's Life*, 2 vols., 1924.

Wortley Montagu, Lady Mary, *The Turkish Embassy Letters*, ed. Malcolm Jack, 1994.

Wrangel, Alexis, *General Wrangel, Russia's White Crusader*, 1990.

Wrangel, General P. N., *Memoirs*, 1929.

Wratislaw, Baron Wenceslas, *Adventures*, ed. A. H. Wratislaw, 1862.

Wright, H. C. Seppings, *Two Years under the Crescent*, 1985 edn.

Yerasimos, Stéphane, *La Fondation de Constantinople et de Sainte-Sophie dans les traditions turques*, 1990.

——(ed.), *Istanbul 1914–1923: capitale d'un monde illusoire ou l'agonie des vieux empires*, 1992.

Yiannias, John, *The Byzantine Tradition after the Fall of Constantinople*, 1991.

Ypsilanti, Prince Nicholas, *Mémoires*, n.d.

Zarcone, Thierry, *Mystiques, philosophes et franc-maçons en Islam*, 1993.

Zeine, M., *Arab-Turkish Relations and the Emergence of Arab Nationalism*, Beirut, 1958.

Zeman, Z. A. B. and W. B. Scharlau, *The Merchant of Revolution*, 1965.

Zurcher, Erik J., *The Unionist Factor: the Role of the Committee of Union and Progress in the Turkish National Movement 1905–1926*, Leiden, 1984.

——*Political Opposition in the Early Turkish Republic: the Progressive Republican Party*, Leiden, 1991.

——*Turkey: a Modern History*, 1993.

Index